Family Travel & Resorts

The Complete Guide

Pamela Lanier

Visit our web site: www.FamilyTravelGuides.com
Email: FamTrav@travelguides.com

A *Lanier* Guide
▲

Other Books by Lanier Publishing

All-Suite Hotel Guide
The Complete Guide to Bed & Breakfasts, Inns & Guesthouses
Bed & Breakfast—Australia's Best
Elegant Small Hotels
Condo Vacations: The Complete Guide
Golf Resorts: The Complete Guide
Cinnamon Mornings & Raspberry Teas
The Back Almanac
Moving Mom & Dad

The information in this book was supplied in large part by the properties themselves and is subject to change without notice. We strongly recommend that you call ahead to verify the information presented here before making final plans or reservations. The author and publisher make no representation that this book is absolutely accurate or complete. Errors and omissions, whether typographical, clerical, or otherwise, may sometimes occur herein.

Distributed to the book trade by:
    Ten Speed Press
    P.O. Box 7123
    Berkeley, CA 94707

Senior editor: Karen Aaronson
Book Design and Production by J.C. Wright and Futura Graphics
Cover Design by Laura Lamar
Contributing editors: Marie Hanson-Hubber, Sarah Morse, Mariposa Valdes, Juan Valdes, Carolyn Strange, Abba Anderson, Mary Flynn, Sally Carpenter
Computer crew: J.C. Wright, Cliff Burdick and Aparna Indharapu

To contact the publishers, please write to:
    Lanier Publishing International, Ltd.
    Drawer D
    Petaluma, CA 94953

Library of Congress Cataloging-in-Publication Data
First printing 1996
ISBN 1-58008-407-9

Printed in Canada on recycled paper.

The text of this book is printed on paper made from a minimum of 50% recycled fiber in compliance with the E.P.A. definition of recycled paper.

Cover photograph courtesy of South Seas Plantation, Captiva, Florida

TABLE OF CONTENTS

Tyler Place Family Resort— Highgate Springs, VT

A Family Resort on Lake Champlain

Four generations of Tylers have owned and operated The Tyler Place in Highgate Springs, Vermont. At the Tyler Place, family fun means creating a balance between kids' fun and private time for parents. There are eight specially designed children's programs for kids from infants to teens. These programs offer sports, playtime, and great meals. Sessions are available in the mornings and evenings, allowing parents time alone and leaving afternoons free for family fun. Recreational opportunities include bicycling, tennis soccer, volleyball, field games and hayrides. Accommodations vary depending on family size and the date of their holiday. Choose from suites, The Inn, or cottages, each offering various amenities from fireplaces to screened-in porches. Family Package rates are available and include all meals, programs and activities. Family Learning Retreats are offered in May, June and September. Guests who first came as children return with their children and grandchildren to have the time of their lives all over again.

*This book is dedicated
to my youngest daughter Clara,
who is eight years old.
Her nickname is "Lightning Bolt."*

*F*AMILY VACATIONING

• •

HOW-TO TIPS FOR FAMILY TRAVEL

INTRODUCTION

Many of us spend a good part of the year dreaming of the next vacation. But it can be intimidating for some, especially parents trying to provide the perfect, affordable vacation that everyone will totally enjoy.

Now, you and your family are ready to get away. What next? Well, start small--how about day trips in your own area? You may be surprised at how easy it can be to travel with small children if you are prepared and organized. We'll give you hints, planning tips and special issues to keep in mind like safety and health issues, as well as advice on food and some great recipes for food that travel well.

Families come in all shapes, sizes and ages. Considerations vary with whether you are new parents with an infant; one grandparent taking a teen on a special trip; a couple with six youngsters of varying ages, temperaments and demands; or a family planning a large-scale reunion. The possible configurations are endless. This guide includes ideas and examples of programs helpful to most family travel situations.

Your vacation should not be a "Let's go some place, it doesn't matter where" event. Figure out what each member of the caravan wants to do. Most families are surprised that they actually do enjoy the same activities. So, canoeing, living history museums, outlet malls, tropical cruising, theme parks and winter or watersports are just some of the topics we delve into in *Family Travel & Resorts—The Complete Guide*. And more and more resort or vacation areas offer a greater variety of activities in a small area.

1

In these wonderful modern times, vacations are accessible to everyone. That's a bold statement—but we'll tell you how to take a day or two and have a vacation right at home, as well as go on exotic voyages to far-away places. And there's no reason you and the kids can't enjoy all of this together. Let the younger set help with the planning. When you go to that "Same-Old-Place" on your next vacation, find out if they have put in place any kid-friendly or teen-friendly programs. These options are hot! Take advantage of them while the two of you slip off for a romantic dinner by the beach.

We are also happy to provide you with a vast array of contacts by location and interest, including state visitor assistance and parks. Or you might want to start by perusing the family resorts listings, all-suite hotel listings, condominiums or all-inclusive resorts.

The most important thing you will get out of your family vacation is shared memories that will last a lifetime. In an age when every family member is busy and time spent in the car rushing from one event to the next is as close as you get to quality time together, a family vacation can be a valuable experience. Take a family vacation before everybody grows up and goes away.

DAY TRIPPING

Sometimes the effort of packing up the brood for an overnight stay is just too much to face, and that can be the perfect time for a day away. We've done a lot of these quick getaways over the years—especially when the kids were small—and have found them to be a lot of fun, and pretty relaxing, especially when the day away is followed by a lazy Sunday!

We often plan these trips around places that we want to see in our area, but never seem to have the time to get to, such as the Indian

Mounds two hours away, or the downtown museum, which takes an hour to get to with traffic.

To get the full benefit of this mini-vacation, you need to treat it as a vacation. Plan ahead. Pack up everything you need the night before for morning reveille. Get an early start while everybody's still in a good mood. Breakfast? Definitely out on the road!

Plan for arriving at your destination mid- to late morning. If the locale is inviting, you might bring a picnic (packed up the night before), or if the dining sounds promising, plan to eat lunch at a local restaurant. Museum restaurants are often fun and in keeping with their subject. Plan for a late afternoon drive home. For dinner, eat out on the way home, or pick up pizza and a movie on the way back in.

Stay in vacation mode on Sunday. That means no work, and no projects. (Renovating the basement is definitely out, and clearing out the rain gutters can wait for another weekend!) Do only what you really want to do, the things you find enjoyable, especially as a family (this could easily entail doing absolutely nothing!). You'll be pleasantly surprised how rested you feel after your mini weekend getaway, and what a good time you and the kids have had together.

THE JOY OF SAME-OLD-PLACE

Sure, it's fun and glamorous to vacation in a new area each time, but it's also cumbersome and requires a great deal of planning, and then there are no guarantees. That's why many families adhere to the joys of "The Same Old Place," be it a family cabin, a rental condo on a favorite beach, or a rustic retreat. Both children and parents are heartened by the ease and familiarity of returning year after year.

With people moving at such a fast pace, and everything in flux, it's reassuring to children to return to a favorite spot, and maybe even see some familiar vacation neighbors. The returning friends come even more into play as children grow older, and as hanging out with their peers becomes an essential part of life.

And this formula works as well for an exotic area as it does for one closer to home. We have friends who have vacationed very happily

each summer at a small rental villa in Jamaica. The cook and house-keeper who attend to the place have become cherished family friends and have added a rich view of another culture to the ease of a same-place vacation.

One thing's for sure, when you don't have to spend time trying to figure out the basics of a new place, it's a lot easier to slip immediately into a relaxation mode.

VACATION AT HOME

Sometimes the thought of planning an itinerary, making plane and hotel reservations, packing up the clan, especially the little ones, makes a vacation sound like drudgery. If you find yourself needing a vacation, but dreading the preparation required, you might consider taking a vacation at home this year.

Home vacations can you give you the break you need, without the stress involved in getting your family from here to there with all the necessary baggage. To make the most of your at-home vacation, follow these few simple ground rules.

1.   Start with a clean house, and then forget about it! Have the house cleaned, or if you absolutely must, clean it yourself before you go "on vacation." And then don't worry about it. Let it get messy!

Nobody will suffer permanent damage if the dirty clothes pile up on the washing machine, and magazines and papers breed like rabbits in the living room. At the end of the vacation, call in the cleaning service again! Remember, you're saving a lot of money by sleeping in your own home!

2. No projects! That means no fix-its, no lawn mowing, no closet cleaning, absolutely no projects! If this is going to be a real vacation, you have to approach it as such, and not spend it futilely trying to accomplish everything on your Super-Person to do list. This week, think of your home as your resort, put your feet up and relax.

3. Lay in a good supply of your family's favorite quick foods, with a special emphasis on picnic fare and quick and easy dinners, such as frozen pizzas, or your own favorite casseroles, made in advance and frozen. Pick up flyers from those new takeout places you've been meaning to try.

4. Plan at least two nights for Mom and Dad to get out without the kids and reserve those baby-sitters in advance. Why not try midweek? Theaters are less crowded, and you'll find food and service is better at most restaurants during the week than on busy weekends.

Plan at least one day just for the two of you, too, to do whatever you like best, or haven't been able to get around to doing in awhile. It might be an afternoon browsing in a bookstore, a movie marathon, fly fishing *a deux*, or just the two of you home alone. Arrange well in advance for the kids to go visiting.

Now, for the all-important itinerary. Your vacation plans should include all the things you love to do best near your home, but don't often take the time to do. Spend a whole day at the park, lolling around the lake, lazily paddling a rental boat. Just go fly a kite!

Pretend you're a tourist, and take in the sights that you always recommend to out-of-town guests, but never get around to seeing yourself. Pick up a stack of brochures at your local visitor's bureau—you're likely to make a few discoveries about your community!

Check out the places you've been driving past for months, or years, but never took the time to stop in. At-home vacations are a good time to explore all your local parks, museums, zoos and wildlife sanctuaries. And now's the perfect time to explore that state park that you usually feel is just a little too far to drive to. Go and make a whole day of it. Or play tourist in a nearby city. And, of course, now you must tour that exotic animal park out on the interstate! And by all means, include a meal out at one of those fun restaurants you've been meaning to try. Let the kids go really wild for a day at the nearest amusement park. Let them ride all the rides, eat everything in sight and stay till closing. After all, it's your vacation.

We hope the foregoing has given you some ideas on vacationing at home. A comfortable, inexpensive alternative to a vacation away, especially when the kids are small or finances tight.

TIPS FOR LAND TRAVEL

Traveling with children can be a wonderful experience. All it takes is a little planning, imagination, and a parent's best friend—patience.

Planning is Half the Fun

Good planning can mean the difference between a relaxing and fun vacation, and a stressful ordeal. What does your family like to do? Sit down together and talk about what you want to see and where you want to go. Contact the local tourist bureaus ahead of time for brochures on local points of interest, and check out a stack of books on your destination, and sites on the route along the way.

The ages and temperament of your children are the first things to consider when planning a trip. Young children need more frequent stops and physical activities than older children and teenagers. Tap into your children's passions and interests along the way—everybody will learn a lot and have more fun in the process. An animal lover will want to go to every zoo and llama ranch in your path and rock collectors brake for gem shops. Build extra time into the itinerary for that all-important, impromptu stop at Max's Snake Farm!

Avoid trying to pack too many activities in—the good old "24 Countries in 12 Days" itinerary. Give yourself plenty of time for flexibility, leave the other 20-plus trips for other trips. When you approach your family trip with a relaxed attitude, and plan it well for your family's needs, you will all have a more enjoyable and memorable vacation together.

Are your traveling by car, bus, boat, plane, train, or all of the above? Camping or hiking, staying in a hotel, resort community, on a cruise-ship, or exchanging homes with another family? No matter how you travel or where you stay, you will need to take along some games, books, toys, and other possibilities for keeping children entertained.

Keeping the Kids Happy = Keeping Them Busy

Infants and smaller children get bored and frustrated in very short order when strapped into a car seat or belt. They can't bend over to retrieve dropped items, they can't twist and look around as much as they'd like, and they're boiling over with childhood energy. As a parent, you can help by bringing along a variety of interesting objects and toys which can keep your infant or toddler entertained for long stretches of time in the car, and by helping to instigate imaginative play when your child needs some inspiration.

Making Tracks Without Making a Mess

To minimize chaos, consider tying small, soft toys onto your child's car seat. (Make sure the string is shorter than six inches so she can't wrap it around her neck.) Toys that don't get lost or drop to the floor will possibly avoid a small crying bout and will definitely save you from twisting your body into impossible configurations to pick them up!

Buy or make a pocketed slipcover to hang over the back of the front seat. This will save space in the car and keep toys, games, and books in one easily accessible place.

TIPS FOR AIRLINE TRAVEL

1. Always arrive at the airport with plenty of time to organize yourself and your children calmly.
2. If possible, have one adult or older child responsible for kids and baggage while another adult checks in.
3. Pre-board if you have small children.
4. Request children's meals in advance, as many airlines now offer these, or other special meal if needed.
5. Ask the flight attendant to serve your children their meals before starting the general meal service so they don't have to wait and you don't have to eat and struggle with the children at the same time.
6. Consider a small meal in the departure lounge before you board if the kids are getting hungry such as yogurt, cheese sticks, etc. Anything to avoid the kids getting hysterical.
7. Try to book a window seat. Sometimes if traveling just one parent and one child, if you book the window seat and aisle seat in three across, you may get lucky and have all three.
8. Always pack as much food and drink as you think you'll need between your home and your final destination.

TRIP PLANNER

This list is extensive and you may not need it all, but hopefully it will jog your memory to bring items you might otherwise have forgotten.

Clothing

Belts	Jackets	Shirts	Suits
Blouses	Jeans	Shoes, walking	Sweaters
Boots	Jewelry	Shoes, dress	Sweatsuit
Bras	Panties	Shorts	Swimsuits
Coats	Pantyhose	Skirts	Ties
Dresses	Rainboots	Slacks	Undershirts
Gloves	Raincoat	Sleepwear	Undershorts
Gowns	Rainhat	Slippers	
Handkerchiefs	Robes	Slips	
Hats	Scarves	Socks	

Beauty & Grooming

Aftershave	Hair Gear	Shower Cap
Bathroom Tissue	Hair Spray	Soap/Soap Dish
Body Creams/ Lotions	Makeup	Spot Remover
Comb	Manicure Items	Sunburn Preventive
Cotton Balls	Moistened Towelettes	Toothbrush/Cover
Dental Floss	Mouthwash	Toothpaste
Deodorant	Nail Polish Remover	Toiletry Kit
Facial Tissues	Perfume/Cologne	Toilet Seat Covers
Hair Brush	Plastic Bottles	Tweezers
Hair Dryer	Razor/Blades/Shaver	
	Shampoo/Rinse	

Personal Medical

Any Prescription
  Medication Taken
  Regularly
Antihistamine
Antiseptic Skin
  Cleanser
Bandaids
Birth Control
Calamine Lotion
Cotton-Tipped
  Swabs

Diarrhea Medicine
Eye Drops
Folding Cup
Foot Powder
Indigestion Remedy
Insect Repellent
Laxative
Motion Sickness
  Remedy
  Spray
Pain Reliever

Rubbing Alcohol
Sanitary Needs
Nasal Sleeping Pills
Thermometer
Extra Pair of Pre-
  scription Glasses
  or a Copy of the
  Prescription
Contact Lens
  Equipment

Miscellaneous

Address Book
Alarm Clock
Book Light
Camera/Film
Cash
Clothesline
Credit Cards
Detergent/Woolite
Diary
Earplugs
Electrical Converter & Adapter Plugs
Expandable Suitcase
Eyeshades
Filmshield
Flashlight
Games/Playing Cards
Gifts
Guidebooks
Immersion Heater or
  Electric Tea Kettle
Inflatable Pillow
International Driver's License
Iron/Steamer
Luggage
Luggage Cart

Luggage Locks
Money Exchange Calculator
Music/Instrument
Passport/Visas
Passport Photos (include extras)
Pens/Pencils
Phrasebook/Dictionary
  /Language Tape
Radio
Reading Material
Safety Pins
Sewing Kit/Scissors
Security wallet
Stamps
Stationary
Student I.D. Card
Sunglasses
Tape Recorder/Tapes
Travel Insurance
Travel Tickets
Traveler's Checks
Umbrella
Watch
Water Bottle

Clothing and Equipment for:

Golf
Horseback Riding
Scuba Diving
Skiing
Tennis
Theme Party Attire

Automobile

Check the Oil _____
Check the Gas _____
Check Battery _____
Check the Tires _____
Emergency Road Kit _____
Extra Set of Keys _____

Air ☞ Bus ☞ Sea

Flight Number _____
Gate Number _____
Time _____ a.m./p.m.
Bus number _____
Cruise Vessel _____
Other _____

Additional

_____
_____
_____
_____
_____
_____

CARRY-ON LIST

I'm a firm believer in traveling as light as possible. But when it comes to carry-on, you want to have all of the little necessities at hand aboard a plane, not stowed in the hold. The following is my list of essentials for myself followed by essentials for children by ages. Please use this as a reminder/checklist and of course add your "can't live withouts."

Kleenex
Wet washcloth in a zip lock bag
Ear plugs
Moisturizing eye drops
Breath mints
Small spray on or splash on
    cologne
Anti-bacterial, individually
    wrapped hand wipes
Makeup kit
Hairbrush
Colorful scarf
Tickets
Passport

Driver's license
Other ID
Reading glasses
Prescription medicine
Moisturizer for face
Hand lotion
Travel itinerary
Pertinent notes regarding hotels,
    rental car, etc.
Paperback book or magazine
Pen and paper
Jacket or change of top appropri-
    ate to destination weather
Socks

Evian mineral water spray   ·
Toothbrush and mini toothpaste
Chapstick or lip gloss

Tampax or pads
Tylenol or other

We usually start out dressed in casual but presentable clothes. Jeans or chinos seem to work well paired with a colorful shirt. We always dress the kids in bright colored clothes to make them easier to spot and pin a whistle on their jacket ages 4 and up so that they can signal if we get separated. We also wear or carry on bulky items such as jackets, training shoes, so we don't have to pack them.

Baby Carry-On

Bunting, the zip up kind which baby slips into. These are great for making a little nest in which the baby can sleep and keeps the baby somewhat confined.

Diapers and wipes
Another wet wash cloth in zip
    lock bag
Small tube diaper cream
Pacifier or teething toy, etc.
Change of clothes
Baby food
Umbrella stroller, narrow ones are
    much easier to fit through the
    aisles
A bag for all this gear which hooks
    on the back of the stroller

Bottle and formula or if not for-
    mula, at least one bottle of
    milk. Some planes carry very
    limited milk supplies.
Dry powdered milk in a baggy
    just in case
Blanket (one or two)
A changing mat or receiving blan-
    ket
Spoon and dish
Bib

Toddler (18 months to 3 years) Carry-On

Bottle if still used or drinking cup
Favorite snack
Doll or stuffed animal
Blanket
A new small toy, wrapped

Favorite small story book
Snack bag, i.e. little boxes of
    raisins, pretzels, animal
    crackers, etc.

Most parents would agree this is the most difficult age for plane travel. Some ideas that have helped include taking a night flight when they'll be asleep anyway. If taking a day flight, try to schedule it during their afternoon nap time and don't let them fall asleep in the car on the way to the airport. Some children become truly hyper in the confines of an airplane. If you've had problems with your child on car trips, you may want to discuss with your doctor a sedative to calm your child on the plane.

Young Children (4 to 8 years) Carry-On

Change of clothes or at least a
    clean top
Favorite stuffed animal or doll
Crayons and coloring book

Story book
Personal stereo with headphones
Etch-a-Sketch™
Small set of Legos™ or Duplos™

Be sure to dress them in something bright, patterned, if possible so it doesn't show stains, and cute. The cuter they look the better your receptions by stewards, et al. This is a great time to bring out the special, new toy for the trip wrapped. With any luck, it may keep your child content for quite some time. We always take a snack bag with goodies that are usually not so available while trying to stay light on the sugar. Some favorites are Cracker Jacks, little cheese cracker packages, gum, apples. This is a great age for a personal cassette player with headphones. A new story tape could be a life saver. And of course bring along some of the old favorites. We usually have our children carry a small backpack on board complete with all the above items and their jacket, etc. This can convert into a very handy daypack for sightseeing.

9 Years and up Carry-On

Journal and pen or pencils
Personal stereo and headset with
    tapes
Game Boy™

Books
School books
Travel guide

By now homework is a fact of life and airplane time can be a great time to knock out some assignments. It's also a great time for older children to peruse the guide book about your destination and organize their ideas on things they would like to do/see. If there is no homework but an outside reading assignment, by all means make sure that book is in the bag.

ARRIVE LOOKING GREAT

There's nothing more harrowing than getting off a long flight and needing to meet with loved ones, friends or business associates and looking as if you just got off a long flight. The following are a few tips that have worked for me and some of my globe-trotting friends.

1. If you set your hair before getting on the plane, finger comb it until it looks presentable but don't comb it all the way out. Save that for your just-before-touchdown fixup.

2. If you have long hair, consider putting it up loosely for the flight and either leaving it up for arrival or brushing it out. Having it up will keep your style from being mussed.

3. Wear lots of moisturizer on your face, neck and hands when you board and periodically mist your face with Evian and add a little light moisturizer and chap stick (about every 2 hours).

4. Drink lots of water and juices and go easy on alcohol, teas, coffee, carbonated beverages, all of which dehydrate you.

5. Wear a dark, comfortable outfit on board to avoid staining and creases. And if possible use that as your arrival outfit with the addition of a bright scarf. Otherwise, carry your arrival outfit on board in a small garment bag such as the ones you get in the department stores with suits.

6. Most importantly, about 45 minutes before arrival, ask one of the flight attendants to sit with your child while you go to the bathroom. Retire there with all of your gear including arrival outfit if necessary and proceed to freshen up your makeup completely. (Some brave friends arrive at the airport wearing only lipstick and do their complete makeup just before touchdown.)

MAKING A HOTEL ROOM A HOME

For those of us who travel a lot, hotels can become pretty tiring. I've picked up a few tricks over time to make a hotel room much more hospitable.

1. Bring along a sarong or other length of fabric to use as both a beach/bath wrap and also to spread over the bed between times to cheer up the room.
2. Hang a scarf around the outside of the lampshade, not over it, to soften the light and create more atmosphere.
3. Carry a small reading light. Few hotels provide adequate ones.
4. Bring a small plug-in tea kettle, a mug, and your favorite hot beverages, like hot chocolate in envelopes, coffee packets, sugar and creamer, tea bags, both herbal and regular, bouillon cubes or other emergency rations.
5. Bring along some of your favorite snacks, chocolate bars, raisins, nuts.
6. Pick up some fruit outside the hotel.
7. Buy yourself some flowers for your room. Room service will almost always be able to supply a suitable vase.
8. Bring your own pillow.
9. Bring a pair of bath slippers and a light weight robe if your accommodation doesn't provide them. Ask first.
10. Have a selection of your favorite magazines including at least one or two local ones to help tune you into the area.

Now, doesn't that feel better?

AIRLINE DISCOUNTERS

The following list is provided to give you a start on comparing air fare prices. Be sure to charge tickets to a credit card.

Magical Holidays
501 Madison Avenue
New York, New York 10022
Phone: (800) 228-2208; (212) 486-9600

Sells cut rate tickets to major African cities only. 11 years in business.

UniTravel Corporation
1177 North Warson Road
St. Louis, Missouri 63132
Phone: (800) 325-2222; (314) 569-0900

Deals with all major routes; trans-Atlantic, trans-Pacific, Australia, Africa, South America and some in the U.S. A large and respected firm which has been in business for 24 years.

Express Apple Vacations
5945 Mission Gorge Road
San Diego, California 92120
Phone: (800) 266-2639

Specialist in flights to Mexico.

Travac Tours and Charters
989 Avenue of the Americas
New York, New York 10018
Phone: (800) 872-8800; (212) 563-3303

Selling trans-Atlantic tickets.

Council Travel
205 East 42nd Street
New York, New York 10017
Phone: (800) 2-COUNCIL; (212) 822-2800

Owned by the nation's semi-official student organization and in business since 1947, a consolidator since 1978, serves persons of all ages using scheduled flights to Europe and some scheduled flights to Martinique in season.

FAMILY TRAVEL AGENTS, TOUR GUIDES & PUBLICATIONS

Here we've listed travel agents, tour guides and publications specializing in family travel.

FamilyHostel
UNH, 6 Garrison Avenue
Durham, New Hampshire 03824
Phone: (800) 733-9753; (602) 862-1147

Educational family trips with a cultural slant.

Grandtravel
6900 Wisconsin Avenue, Suite 706
Chevy Chase, Maryland 20815
Phone: (800) 247-7651; (301) 986-0790

Grandtravel offers two-week tours in Europe for grandparents and grandchildren.

Travel with Your Children
80 Eighth Avenue
New York, New York 10111

Travel with Your Children publishes Family Travel Times, covering worldwide travel news of interest to families. Subscribers also get to take advantage of a phone-in travel advice services.

Traveling with Children
Family Travel Agents & Consultants
2313 Valley Street
Berkeley, California 94702
Phone: (510) 848-0929

Dan & Wendy Hallinan, who have traveled extensively with their three children, operate this unique family-oriented travel agency. "A well-planned trip which allows you all to relax, absorb your new surroundings and enjoy each other as you never have before," their brochure reads. "Travel will improve your children's outlook, their sense of history and their understanding of humanity."

Rascals in Paradise
Family Travel Specialists
650 Fifth Street, Suite 505
San Francisco, California 94107
Phone: (800) U-RASCAL; (415) 978-9800
Fax: (415) 442-0289

Rascals in Paradise started offering family vacation packages in 1987, and today offer a catalog of vacations at the best family resorts nationwide.

MICKEY'S LAND ON A MOUSE'S BUDGET—
Saving Big in Tourist Hot Spots

It's absolutely true that money can melt in the hot Florida or southern California sun as quickly as an ice cream cone. But there are ways, aside from buying package deals, to trim the miscellaneous costs which can really add up! These tips apply specifically to Florida's Disney World experience, but are translatable to similar jaunts.

FOOD   Food is probably the third most expensive part of a trip after transportation and accommodations. Fortunately, it yields easily to our penny-pinching tactics.

Pizza in your room: after a long day at Disney, and before an even longer evening, kick back and order pizza sent in. The on-property hotels have a pizza delivery service, which you should find mention of in your room. Off-site, let your fingers do the walking through the yellow pages to your favorite pizza emporium.

Go grocery shopping: yeah, it's a drag, but the savings are big. On-site there is an extensive but expensive market at The Village Marketplace. If you have a car, a quick trip out of the park will take you to a big supermarket. Stock up on—snack food, high energy ones like granola bars, dried food, nuts, trail mix, are great for days in the park. Save a bundle on breakfast by buying chocolate milk and donuts to eat in your room. (See our article on Food On The Road for more extensive recommendations in this area.)

Most hotels come equipped with mini-fridges. We always immediately unpack each and every item into a bag or box with a note saying that we have not used anything. Stash the box and put your groceries in the refrigerator.

Within the park, dining out is half the fun, but it can really be expensive. Some of our favorite places to dine are: The South Seas Luau at Disney's Polynesian Resort; or, our all-time favorite, The Western Style Comedy and Show at Fort Wilderness. Either of these two make a great big splurge, and makes a high energy evening entertainment. Another favorite is to dine at Epcot at the German Pavilion, where portions are huge! And stay for the outstanding fireworks and lights.

One insider's tip we picked up on our last trip is that anyone can order a child's meal at the restaurants on-site. My teenage daughter and I ordered the children's plate each time we dined, were never questioned about that, and got more food than we could eat. You might also consider splitting meals, as portions are huge. Extra plates were always brought with a smile. Try some of the more expensive restaurants for lunch, when prices are lower.

Pack a picnic lunch from the provisions you bought at the store and enjoy it at a picturesque spot in the shade. Get drinks from the local vendors.

INCIDENTALS & SOUVENIRS Another bottomless pit for your cash! Bring everything you anticipate needing from home, i.e., film, disposable diapers, toiletries, batteries. These are the little things that keep those cash registers ringing.

We have a souvenir rule—If we're staying more than a day at the place, everyone gets to pick any one souvenir that they want, as long as it's within our pre-established price range. And we purchase it at the end of the day. This gives everyone something to look forward to and encourages comparison shopping while discouraging spur-of-the-moment impulse buying. Some of the souvenirs we have enjoyed the most are: Mickey Mouse ears (I made a great Minnie one Halloween), T-shirts (bought big), autograph book (our one exception, bought early) which we carried around, magic wands, and princess hats.

TRAVELING IN DEVELOPING COUNTRIES

Travel in developing countries provides incredible benefits to adventurous families, while at the same time offering considerable challenges. Families get to experience how other people live in cultures and circumstances very different from their own, and to experience wildlife and geographical wonders first-hand. We have found our children to be wonderful goodwill ambassadors who have opened many doors as we've traveled the less developed regions of this planet.

Our first long trip out of country as a family was a real adventure, taking up the challenge of traversing the Pan American Highway from San Francisco to Tierra del Fuego when my husband was doing site research on sabbatical from his engineering firm. Our daughter Mari, then our only child, turned three on the trip, and from the minute we crossed the border into Mexico, she was the center of attention wherever we went. She was soon convinced that her name was "Que Linda" (Spanish for "How pretty"), because that's all she heard. Teenage girls seemed to materialize out of nowhere to fawn over her whenever we got out of the camper. Invitations for our family to join theirs for dinner were often forthcoming.

Mari quietly slept, played with the dolls and other toys, and colored as we drove, springing into vivid life the moment we stopped. Of course, her presence on the trip determined that we visit every zoo, playground, and natural attraction along the road. Around about El Salvador—which has a series of glorious state parks—we began teaching her to swim. By the end of the nine-month trip, she was swimming very well, and just two years later won the junior division regional championship.

We opted to ship the van from Panama to Guayaquil, Ecuador rather than attempt the Darien Gap through Colombia, an impossible path through the jungle, pit vipers and all. We took an inexpensive boat—with accommodations to match!—out to the Galapagos Islands. What a sight! Mari was fascinated by the exotic animals, many of whom allowed her to approach them. From Guayaquil, our trip was all uphill, as in the Andes Mountains. Since gasoline was only 25 cents a gallon in Ecuador, we explored the country thoroughly, settling for a time in Cuenca, a charming historical town noted for its beauty and handicrafts. There we quickly made friends with many families, again through Mari, both Ecuadorians and Europeans living there, and proceeded to have a wonderful time, staying until Christmas. Mari found it hard to eat roast guinea pig, which is one of the national dishes, but otherwise did fine. The altitude in Peru and Bolivia posed quite a challenge for me, but Mari adapted readily. She loved the llamas, the old-fashioned trains and boats which we used as transport, having put our van in storage for a month in Lima. Because the roads are so bad and the extreme temperatures, we opted to take the train then bus up to Cuzco. A long and arduous trip.

A highlight of our trip was Mari's third birthday party in Cuzco, to which we invited all the children of the hotel's staff, and all the tourist children we met for a giddy afternoon of balloons, pin-the-tail-on-the-llama and chocolate cake, specially ordered from the only European-style bakery in town. Heading south from Lima, we stopped at every archeological site along our route, using the "South American Handbook" as our indispensable guide. Mari was fascinated by the adobe ruins near Nazca along the coast of Peru and northern Chile, which seem to be built for people not much bigger than her.

We had our one and only vehicular breakdown in Chile. A local mechanic from the nearby town of Chilan came upon us stalled by the side of the road, and offered to tow us to town. He proceeded to take us home to meet his wife and ten children, all of whom decided our stay for the next three days while parts were obtained would be the focal point for a fiesta, bringing together family and friends from around the area. We were almost sorry to see the van fixed and get back on the road!

Back up over the lower end of the Andes, we made a brief stop in Barriloche and camped for the night at the hot springs there. Mari was entranced with the woods, and the small trees with cinnamon-colored bark that peeled off in sheets. In a rest area a few hours west of Buenos Aires, we encountered two Argentinean families, both of whom urged us to look them up in the capital. We proceeded to do so, and spent three weeks in the city enjoying our new friends. Mari by now was speaking very good children's Spanish, and had a ball with all of the kids.

We headed south for a stop at Peninsula Valdes in Patagonia, sight of the world's largest population of sea lions. And what a sight and smell they were! Mari was beside herself with excitement. We met a family picnicking from a nearby aluminum mining town, who invited us back for dinner, giving us a unique insight into the life of a working family in that part of the world.

We wound up our trip after an excursion down through the wild, desolate and beautiful terrain of Tierra Del Fuego and retraced our steps to end up our trip back with friends in Buenos Aires for a few more days of play, fado music, and Argentinean churrasco (mixed grill). Mari grew up considerably on this trip, and became quite a self-assured young lady, tiny though she was. She developed a gregariousness which is with her still, as is her love for travel and meeting new people. Having those nine months together as a family was an unforgettable experience for us all. Although the trip was overwhelmingly positive, several difficulties arose along the road—as they often do when traveling, especially through emerging countries.

We were all in fine health on this trip, having had numerous shots prior to our departure (including gamma globulin for hepatitis). Mari did develop a 105 degree fever one night in Mexico and was raving. We never did figure out what it was, but we gave her children's pain reliever

to relieve her temperature, and sponged her with cold water all night. The next day she was weak, but the fever was gone, and the day after that she was back to normal.

In Guatemala, Mari and I both picked up pinworms, which are most unpleasant, itchy creatures, but a dose of Vermox cleared them right up. We had occasional mild bouts of diarrhea, and although we carried a prescription diarrhea medicine prescribed by our doctor (Lomotil), we never used it, preferring milder cures. The best thing for mild diarrhea is a bland diet and time. I'm a true believer in crackers and cola, toast, potatoes and white rice. Avoid dairy products. A three-ounce package of flavored jello dissolved in a cup of water tastes good to sweet-toothed kids, and acts as a binder. For medication, start with Pepto Bismol, which is milder than the commonly prescribed diarrhea medicine Lomotil. Be sure to discuss diarrhea medicines with your doctor before you go. Sunburn was a recurring threat, which we fought with hats and sunscreen, and limited time outside during the heat of the day—there is a reason for those afternoon siestas!

Mari got locked in the bathroom aboard the Lake Titicaca steamer (vintage 1905), and the only way to get her out was to dismantle the bathroom stall. That was probably the scariest incident of the entire trip, and one we still talk about!

We did take—and were glad of it—a complete medical kit, and had a thorough conference with our doctor prior to departure. Another issue that came up with Mari was cleanliness in bathrooms. She was potty trained just before we set out on the trip and did very well in our van. The rub came when we were out in restaurants or public places. If the toilet wasn't too bad, I would hold her up over the seat, or put paper on the seat as appropriate. (We've taught all of our children to touch as little as possible in bathrooms while traveling, which definitely includes airplanes!) If the bathroom was just too dreadful, I would take her back to the van, or I admit, find a convenient and discreet bush. Washing hands after using the bathroom is essential, and many restaurants in other parts of the world have a sink in the restaurant where you can wash your hands before eating. I also carried a small soap dish and a few paper towels or Kleenex in my bag.

Food

Street food is always a temptation, and one that I believe in giving into, with a few caveats:

1. All fruits and vegetables must be peeled.
2. The stand and its owner must have a general appearance of cleanliness.
3. No milk products.
4. All hot foods must be freshly prepared in front of me, not previously prepared and left to sit.
5. Plates and silverware must be clean and dry.
6. No shellfish.
7. No raw fish, including ceviche.

Water

Water is one of the main sources of infection. We make it a habit to drink only bottled water that comes to us with a sealed cap. We drink only name-brand soft drinks, sterilized milk that comes in the long-life containers, and hot beverages which we know have been boiled. We do not drink fruit drinks, fresh milk, water in open containers. We carry water purification tablets which we use faithfully when in doubt.

Ice cubes are definitely a no-no.

Safety

Our van was broken into in Peru, during a political rally when the streets were full of police. The thieves got most of our clothes, our camera, and our travelers checks. To add insult to injury, my bag was stolen while we surveyed the broken window and tried to figure out what we'd lost! Someone started kicking the back tire, and my husband got out to see what was going on. While I stuck my head out the window to try to get a glimpse of the action, an arm snaked through and grabbed the bag, which had all of our cash in it (fortunately, not a lot of money). This double whammy left us with only our passports and the numbers of our travelers checks (which we had put in two separate places), along with the address of the local American Express office, to which we retired immediately after reporting the theft to the police. The kindly manager took us home to his beach house for the weekend where his family made up in hospitality for the depredations of their country-men, on Monday our new travelers checks were issued, and our new American Express cards were awaiting us at our next big city stop. That incident, and a minor pick pocketing at the Cuzco train station, were our only run-ins with thieves.

Accommodations

Many of our trips on several continents have been overland in campers, obviating the problem of clean accommodations as camping-oriented trips do. However, as you get into more out-of-the-way places, you may find your family forced to stay in accommodations that simply don't meet your standard of cleanliness.

What to do? First, of course, search out the best hotel you can possibly afford. If that isn't suitable, go to the town hall, or American Express office, or friendly cafe, and inquire about bed and breakfast or guesthouse accommodations. Most families who are sophisticated enough to offer this type of accommodation also have very high standards of cleanliness. But if you're really stuck in a fleabag with no alternative, there are a few things you can do to improve the experience. Check around the room to make sure there's nothing potentially harmful or dangerous to the kids, checking in drawers and under beds. Find the cleaning person, tip her generously, and have her clean the bathroom and mop the floor using a disinfectant solution, under your supervision. If she has no disinfectant solution, you can go to the nearest store or pharmacy and buy some. Diluted bleach will work just fine. Have the cleaning person put three sets of sheets on the bottom of your bed. Don't use their pillow, use your own, if you're traveling with one, or wrap clothing in a T-shirt and use that. Have the cleaning person bring you fresh towels.

Transportation

Book the best class tickets you can afford in developing countries. Bear in mind that first class may not necessarily mean luxurious (on Mexican trains, book first class "especial").

Traveling in developing areas has provided us with experiences which simply can't be matched anywhere else. We've often found that we had to slow our speed of travel to accommodate a less developed infrastructure, and as soon as we did slow down, we started enjoying the trip a lot more. Most importantly, after taking reasonable precautions, don't allow yourself to become preoccupied with the hazards of travel—let go of worry, and enjoy the adventure!

Excellent reading is Maureen Wheeler's *Travel With Children*, Lonely Planet Publications.

TOP TEN TIPS FOR TRAVELERS

The following information is taken from "Department of State Publication 10030," Bureau of Consular Affairs—3/93

1. Make sure you have a signed, valid passport and visas, if required. Also, before you go, fill in the emergency information page of your passport!
2. Read the Consular Information Sheets and any Travel Warnings for the countries you plan to visit. (Look at the end of this listing for where to find Consular Information Sheets).
3. Familiarize yourself with local laws and customs of the countries to which you are traveling. Remember, while in a country, you are subject to its laws!

4. Make 2 photocopies of your passport identification page. This will facilitate replacement if you passport is lost or stolen. Leave one copy at home. Carry the other with you in a separate place from your passport.
5. Leave a copy of your itinerary with family or friends at home so you can be contacted in case of emergency.
6. Notify by phone or register in person with the U.S. embassy or consulate upon arrival.
7. Don't leave luggage unattended in public areas. Don't accept packages from strangers.
8. Don't be a target! Avoid conspicuous clothing and expensive jewelry and don't carry excessive amounts of money or unnecessary credit cards.
9. In order to avoid violating local laws, deal only with authorized agents when you exchange money or purchase art or antiques.
10. If you get into trouble, contact the U.S. Consul!

The Department of State issues Consular Information Sheets for all countries of the world. They describe unusual entry or currency regulations, health conditions, the crime and security situation, political disturbances, areas of instability, and drug penalties.

In general, Consular Information Sheets do not give advice. Instead, they describe conditions so that travelers can make informed decisions about their trips.

However, in some dangerous situations, the Department of State recommends that Americans defer all travel to a country. In these cases, a Travel Warning is issued for the country, in addition to its Consular Information Sheet.

There are many ways to access Consular Information Sheets and Travel Warnings:

❍ You can listen to them 24 hours a day by calling (202) 647-5225 from a touch-tone phone.
❍ From a fax machine, you can dial (202) 647-3000, using the handset as you would a regular telephone. You will hear instructions on how to have them faxed to you.
❍ With a computer and a modem, you can access them through many electronic bulletin boards, including the Consular Affairs Bulletin Board (CABB). Call the CABB on (202) 647-9225, setting your software to N-8-1.

○ You can find them at the 13 regional U.S. passport agencies, or you can learn about them from the airline when you or your travel agent make your international air reservation.

For general travel information, the following pamphlets may be ordered from the Superintendent of Documents, U.S. Government Printing Office, Washington, DC 20402; phone (202) 512-0000. The price of each publication is $1, except where noted.

○ Your Trip Abroad ($1.25)
○ Travel Tips for Older Americans
○ Tips for Americans Residing Abroad

Country specific information can be found in the following publications:

○ Tips for Travelers to Sub-Saharan Africa
○ Tips for Travelers to the Caribbean
○ Tips for Travelers to Central and South America
○ Tips for Travelers to the People's Republic of China
○ Tips for Travelers to Mexico
○ Tips for Travelers to the Middle East and North Africa
○ Tips for Travelers to South Asia
○ Tips for Travelers to Russia

The following publications may be ordered from the Consumer Information Center, Pueblo, Colorado 81009.

○ Foreign Entry Requirements
○ Passports—Applying for Them the Easy Way

EUROPEAN TOURIST OFFICES

Write or call to get information on your European destination of choice. Most tourist offices will send you a sizable package of information to help you plan your trip, free of charge.

Austrian National Tourist Office
P.O. Box 1142
New York, New York 10108
Phone: (212) 944-6880

Belgian Tourist Office
745 Fifth Avenue
New York, New York 10151
Phone: (212) 758-8130

British Tourist Authority
551 Fifth Avenue, 7th Floor
New York, New York 10176
Phone: (212) 396-2266

Danish Tourist Board
655 Third Avenue
New York, New York 10017
Phone: (212) 885-9700

French Government Tourist Office
610 Fifth Avenue
New York, New York 10020
Phone: (212) 838-7800

German National Tourist Office
122 East 42nd Street, 52nd Floor
New York, New York 10168
Phone: (212) 661-0756

Greek National Tourist Org.
Olympic Tower
645 Fifth Avenue, 5th Floor
New York, New York 10022
Phone: (212) 421-5777

Italian Government Travel Office
630 Fifth Avenue, Suite 1565
New York, New York 10111
Phone: (212) 245-4822

Norwegian Tourist Board
655 Third Avenue, 18th Floor
New York, New York 10017
Phone: (212) 885-9700

Netherlands Board of Tourism
355 Lexington Avenue
New York, New York 10017
Phone: (212) 246-1429

Portuguese National Tourist Office
590 Fifth Avenue
New York, New York 10036
Phone: (212) 220-5772

National Tourist Office of Spain
665 Fifth Avenue
New York, New York 10022
Phone: (212) 265-8864

Swiss National Tourist Office
608 Fifth Avenue
New York, New York 10020
(212) 757-5944

Swedish Tourist Board
655 Third Avenue, 18th Floor
New York, New York 10017
Phone: (212) 949-2333;

VACATION SCRAPBOOKS

Just the other night, our 15-year-old son pulled out a scrapbook from one of our family trips. It brought on an avalanche of memories, and we ended up spending the whole evening reliving that trip, talking about the things we saw and did and ate. We even reprised a gin rummy game to see if we could beat the figure on the scorecard we'd saved. Yes, Dad lost. And just for fun, I tried out the hairdo I'd worn five years ago. A scrapbook really brings it all back.

Scrapbooks can become very powerful family mementos. The key is to collect all sorts of stuff on the trip and let every member of the family join in. Sometimes we've actually taken a scrapbook with us, and partially assembled it on the road. Other times we've just stuffed our souvenirs in a manila envelope, or a bag picked up along the way.

We always take lots of action photos which of course, become part of the book—only the best ones though, and no pictures go in that anybody doesn't like. If you doubt your photographic abilities, and you're in an incredible spot, by all means buy a postcard and plan on adding it to the scrapbook. Our rule is we have the photos developed immediately upon our return, and put the scrapbook together on the next free weekend day we have ... but soon.

Some of our scrapbooks include whole essays that the kids were required to write for school, as part of their homework on the road. Others include detailed letters written to family and friends which we asked them to save for us. We find that as we assemble the book, little bits of commentary really help bring it to life, such as World's Best Swimming Hole, or Worst Meal of the Trip (Ugh!). Since we always seem to make up funny songs featuring place names, I usually scribble those lyrics down, along with the name of the tune we used.

To ensure that your memories are truly long-lasting, keep the following pointers in mind when compiling and storing your scrapbook.

1. Store your memorabilia properly. Light, heat and moisture are a photo's worst enemies, so photo albums and scrapbooks should be stored in the house, preferably in a room where the temperature is fairly constant.

2. For all your vacation photos, make sure that your photo lab uses paper that will stand the test of time. According to Henry Wilhelm, author of *The Permanence and Care of Color Photographs*, Fujicolor paper

is the best product in terms of longevity. Wilhelm has done extensive testing in which photos on Fujicolor paper last four times as long as pictures on other brands of photographic paper.

3. Most of the photo albums on the market are not the best way to preserve your vacation memories. The plastics, papers and glues used in many popular products will damage photos irreparably over the years. Experts recommend archival-quality with white or off-white acid-free paper and archival-quality corners. The popular self-stick albums are notorious for discoloring photos, with the exception of 3M's Flashbacks albums, which fared well in tests.

SAFETY ISSUES

PLAYING IT SAFE ON VACATION

With headlines reporting attacks against tourists becoming more and more common, vacationers are on the alert. A recent magazine survey discovered that 85% of their readers said these reports have prompted them to be more cautious while on holiday.

> Don't let a few criminals ruin your vacation. By taking a few precautions and staying alert, you can avoid spending part of your holiday filing a report at an exotic police station.

HAVE A SAFE TRIP AT HOME AND ABROAD

Partially taken from public domain information in "Department of State Publication 10110," Bureau of Consular Affairs.

Millions of U.S. citizens travel abroad each year and use their U.S. passport. When you travel abroad, the odds are in your favor that you will have a safe and incident free trip. Even if you do come into difficulty abroad, the odds are still in your favor that you will not be a victim of crime or violence.

BEFORE YOU GO

What to Bring

Safety begins when you pack. To avoid being a target, dress conservatively. A flashy wardrobe or one that is too casual can mark you as a tourist. As much as possible, avoid the appearance of affluence, i.e., leave the diamond ring and expensive watch at home.

Always try to travel light. If you do, you can move more quickly and will be more likely to have a free hand. You will also be less tired and less likely to set your luggage down, leaving it unattended.

Carry the minimum amount of valuables necessary for your trip and plan a place or places to conceal them. Your passport, cash and credit cards are safest when locked in a hotel safe. When you have to carry them on your person, you may wish to conceal them in several places rather than putting them in one wallet or pouch. Avoid hand bags, fanny packs and outside pockets which are easy targets for thieves. Inside pockets and a sturdy shoulder bag with the strap worn across your chest are somewhat safer. The safest place to carry valuables is probably a pouch or money belt that you wear under your clothing.

If you wear glasses, pack an extra pair. Carry them and any medicines you need in you carry-on luggage.

To avoid problems when passing through customs, keep medicines in their original, labeled containers. Bring a copy of your prescriptions and the generic names for the drugs. If a medication is unusual or contains narcotics, carry a letter from your doctor attesting to your need to take the drug. If you have any doubt about the legality of carrying a certain drug into a country, consult the embassy or consulate of that country first.

Bring travelers checks and one or two major credit cards instead of cash.

Pack an extra set of passport photos along with a photocopy of your passport information page to make replacement of your passport easier in case it is lost or stolen.

Put your name, address and telephone numbers inside and outside of each piece of luggage. Use covered luggage tags to avoid casual observation of your identity or nationality. Last of all, lock your luggage.

What to Leave Behind

Don't bring anything you would hate to lose. Leave at home:

❍ expensive or expensive-looking jewelry
❍ irreplaceable family objects
❍ all unnecessary credit cards
❍ leave a copy of your itinerary with family or friends at home in case they need to contact you in an emergency.

A Few Things to Leave Behind

Make photocopies of your passport identification page, airline tickets, driver's license, and the credit cards that you bring with you. Make two copies. Leave one with family or friends at home; pack the other in a place separate from where you carry your valuables.

Leave a copy of the serial numbers of your travelers checks at home. Carry your copy with you in a separate place and, as you cash the checks, cross them off the list.

What to Learn Before You Go

SECURITY   The Department of State's Consular Information Sheets are available for every country of the world. They describe unusual entry or currency regulations, unusual health conditions, the crime and security situation, political disturbances, areas of instability, and drug penalties. They also provide addresses and emergency telephone numbers for U.S. embassies and consulates. In general, the sheets do not give advice. Instead, they describe conditions so travelers can make informed decisions about their trips.

In some dangerous situations, however, the Department of State recommends that Americans defer travel to a country. In such a case, a Travel Warning is issued for the country in addition to its Consular Information Sheet.

Consular Information Sheets and Travel Warnings are available at the 13 regional passport agencies; at U.S. embassies and consulates abroad; or by sending a self-addressed, stamped envelope to: Overseas Citizens Services, Room 4811, Department of State, Washington, DC 20520-4818. They are also available through airline computer reservations systems when you or your travel agent make your international air reservations.

In addition, you can access Consular Information Sheets and Travel Warnings 24 hours a day from three different electronic systems. To listen to them, call (202) 647-5225 from a touch-tone phone. To receive them by fax, dial (202) 647-3000 from a fax machine and follow the prompts that you will hear on the machine's telephone receiver. To view or download the documents through a computer and modem, dial the Consular Affairs Bulletin Board (CABB) on (202) 647-9225, setting your software to N-8-1. There is no charge to use these systems other than normal long distance charges.

Locales

One of the best things you can do to protect yourself is know where the bad neighborhoods are, and avoid them. Before you leave your hotel, ask which way to turn when you walk out the door, and which direction to avoid.

PRECAUTIONS TO TAKE WHILE TRAVELING

Safety on the Street

Use the same common sense traveling overseas that you would at home. Be especially cautious in, or avoid areas where you are likely to be victimized. These include crowded subways, train stations, elevators, tourist sites, market places, festivals and marginal areas of cities.

- ID your kids. On an index card, write each child's name, your name and hotel address and phone number, as well as the phone number of a close friend or relative back home.
- Always have a recent, clear photo of your child with you. If you do get separated, the authorities will want an up-to-date picture.
- Don't use shortcuts, narrow alleys or poorly-lit streets. Try not to travel alone at night.
- Avoid public demonstrations and other civil disturbances.
- Keep a low profile and avoid loud conversations or arguments. Do not discuss travel plans or other personal matters with strangers.

❍ To avoid scam artists, beware of strangers who approach you, offering bargains or to be your guide.

❍ Beware of pickpockets. They often have an accomplice who will:

- ❏ jostle you
- ❏ ask you for directions or the time
- ❏ point to something spilled on your clothing
- ❏ or distract you by creating a disturbance.

A child or even a woman carrying a baby can be a pickpocket. Beware of groups of vagrant children.

❍ Wear the shoulder strap of your bag across your chest and walk with the bag away from the curb to avoid drive-by purse snatchers.

❍ Try to seem purposeful when you move about.

❍ Even when you are lost, act as if you know where you are going. When possible, ask directions only from individuals in authority.

❍ Know how to use a pay telephone and have the proper change or token on hand.

❍ Learn a few phrases in the local language so you can signal your need for help, the police, or a doctor.

❍ Make note of emergency telephone numbers you may need: police, fire, your hotel, and the nearest U.S. embassy or consulate.

❍ If confronted by superior force, don't fight attackers—give up valuables.

Safety in Your Hotel

❍ Keep your hotel door locked at all times. Meet visitors in the lobby.

❍ Do not leave money and other valuables in your hotel room while you are out. Use the hotel safe.

❍ Let someone know when you expect to return, especially if out late at night.

❍ If you are alone, do not get on an elevator if there is a suspicious-looking person inside.

❍ Read the fire safety instructions in your hotel rooms. Know how to report a fire. Be sure you know where the nearest fire exit and an alternate are. Count the doors between your room and the nearest exit—this could be a life-saver if you have to crawl through a smoke-filled corridor.

❍ Show your children how to call the front desk. While they may know how to dial 911 in case of emergency at home, unless you tell them, they won't know to dial 9 for an outside line, or to dial 0 for the hotel receptionist.

Safety on Public Transport

In countries where there is a pattern of tourists being targeted by criminals on public transport, this information is mentioned in Consular Information Sheets.

TAXIS Only take taxis clearly identified with official markings. Beware of irregular cabs.

TRAINS Well organized, systematic robbery of passengers on trains along popular tourists routes is a serious problem. It is more common at night and especially on overnight trains.

If you see your way blocked by someone and another person is pressing you from behind, move away. this can happen in the corridor of the train or on the platform or station.

Do not accept food or drink from strangers. Criminals have been known to drug passengers by offering them food or drink. Criminals may also spray sleeping gas in train compartments.

Where possible, lock you compartment. If it cannot be locked securely, take turns with your traveling companions sleeping in shifts. If that is not possible, stay awake. If you must sleep unprotected, tie down your luggage, strap your valuables to you and sleep on top of them as much as possible.

Do not be afraid to alert authorities if you feel threatened in any way. Extra police are often assigned to ride trains on routes where crime is a serious problem.

BUSES The same type of criminal activity found on trains can be found on public buses on popular tourist routs. For example, tourists have been drugged and robbed while sleeping on buses or in bus stations. In some countries whole bus loads of passengers have been held up and robbed by gangs of bandits.

Safety When You Drive

When you pick up your car rental, ask which parts of town to stay away from. Staying away from high-crime areas could be the most important safeguard you can take. It's all too easy to inadvertently drive into bad neighborhoods when you're in a strange city, but with a little foresight and a decent map, it's just as easy to avoid them.

Don't look like a tourist. Tuck the Disneyland bags and travel guides discreetly away in the trunk when you're away from your car. It doesn't hurt to leave a local paper in plain sight to further enhance the illusion that you're one of the locals.

Leave nothing in sight. Cars have been broken into for jackets and shopping bags.

Pass up that hot red jeep. Stick to cars that are unobtrusive and blend in. Forget the car wash! A cruise down a dusty road, or through a few mud puddles, will make your rental look lived in!

❍ When you rent a car, don't go for the exotic; choose a type commonly available locally.

Where possible, ask that markings that identify it as a rental car be removed. Make certain it is in good repair. If available, choose a car with universal door locks and power windows, features that give the driver better control of access to the car.

❍ An air conditioner, when available, is also a safety feature, allowing you to drive with windows closed. Thieves can and do snatch purses through open windows of moving cars.

❍ Keep car doors locked at all times. Wear seat belts.

❍ As much as possible, avoid driving at night.

❍ Don't leave valuables in the car. If you must carry things with you, keep them out of sight in the trunk.

❍ Don't park your car on the street overnight. If the hotel or municipality does not have a parking garage or other secure area, select a well-lit area.

❍ Never pick up hitchhikers.

❍ Don't get out of the car if there are suspicious individuals nearby. Drive away.

How to Handle Money Safely

To avoid carrying large amounts of cash, change your travelers checks only as you need currency. Counter sign travelers checks only in front of the person who will cash them.

Do not flash large amounts of money when paying a bill. Make sure your credit card is returned to you after each transaction.

Deal only with authorized agents when you exchange money, buy airline tickets, or purchase souvenirs. Do not change money on the black market.

If your possessions are lost or stolen, report the loss immediately to the local police. Keep a copy of the police report for insurance claims and as an explanation of your plight.

After reporting lost items to the police, report the loss of:

❍ travelers checks to the nearest agent of the issuing company
❍ credit cards to the issuing company
❍ airline tickets to the airline or travel agent
❍ passport to the nearest U.S. embassy or consulate

Assistance Abroad

If you plan to stay more than two weeks in one place, if you are in an area experiencing civil unrest or a natural disaster, or if you  are planning travel to a remote area, it is advisable to register at the Consular Section of the nearest U.S. embassy or consulate. This will make it easier if someone at home needs to locate you urgently or in the unlikely event that you need to be evacuated in an emergency. It will also facilitate the issuance of a new passport should yours become lost of stolen.

Another reason to contact the Consular Section is to obtain updated information on the security situation in a country.

If you are ill or injured, contact the nearest U.S. embassy or consulate for a list of local physicians and medical facilities. If the illness is serious, consular officers can help you find medical assistance from this list and, at your request, will inform you family or friends. If necessary, a consul can assist in the transfer of funds from the United States. Payment of hospital and other medical expenses is your responsibility.

If you become destitute overseas, consular officers can help you get in touch with your family, friends, bank, or employer and inform them how to wire funds to you.

Should you find yourself in legal difficulty, contact a consular officer immediately. Consular officers cannot serve as attorneys, give legal advice, or get you out of jail. What they can do is provide a list of local attorneys who speak English and who may have had experience in representing U.S. citizens. If you are arrested, consular officials will visit you, advise you of your rights under local laws, and ensure that you are held under humane conditions and are treated fairly under local law. A consular officer will also contact your family or friends if you desire. When necessary, consuls can transfer money from home for you and will try to get relief for you, including food and clothing in countries where this is a problem. If you are detained, remember that under international agreements and practice, you have the right to talk to the U.S. consul. If you are denied this right, be persistent; try to have someone get in touch for you.

• •

HEALTH ISSUES

HEALTH & ILLNESS OVERSEAS

A little basic medical knowledge, some well-chosen supplies, and a few precautions can go a long way toward keeping health-related troubles from interfering with your vacation plans. Overseas vacations, too, can introduce a whole new range of potential ailments and health issues.

See our First Aid Kit Checklist for basic guidelines on medications and supplies to take along on vacation, and, of course, contact your personal and family physicians for suggestions regarding your family's specific health needs.

You may wish to ask your doctor to recommend medications to carry along based on your destination. You may want to take Vermox (for worms), Promethazine cream (to prevent infection in skin wounds, including insect bites); diarrhea medicine like Lomotil; anti-malarial tablets; shampoo for head lice; antibiotic tablets; anti-seasickness tablets; or high-altitude medicine.

While an ounce of prevention is always preferable to the cure, if you or one of your family members do suffer an illness or injury overseas, you'll save yourself a lot of hassle by knowing where to turn for treatment. When traveling outside the United States, we've found it very reassuring to be members of the International Association for Medical Assistance to Travelers (IAMAT). For an optional small donation (suggested amount is $25), IAMAT will give you a booklet containing the names of English-speaking physicians and the locations of hospitals worldwide. IAMAT recruits qualified, English-speaking physicians throughout the world. The doctors agree to a set payment schedule for IAMAT members, and the association accepts no fees from doctors, medical institutions or traveling members for this service. IAMAT will also send you information on climate, immunization laws and malaria charts. Participating doctors charge IAMAT members a fixed rate for a call, and have uniformly been excellent in our experience.

U.S. headquarters:
IAMAT
417 Center Street
Lewiston, New York 14092

International headquarters:
IAMAT
40 Regal Road
Guelph, Ontario N1K1B5
Canada

And before you hit the road, *Travelers Medical Resource: A Guide to Health and Safety Worldwide* is an excellent resource by William W. Forgey, Maryland (available for $19.95, ISBN 934-802-629) to dip into.

FIRST AID KIT CHECKLIST

Thermometer
Bandages, band-aids, gauze and cotton wool (for minor injuries)
Adhesive tape
Ace bandage
Tweezers and needle (for splinters)
Insect repellent
Adolph's Meat Tenderizer (mix with water to make a paste for bug bites)
Aloe vera gel (for sunburns and skin irritations)
Hydrogen peroxide
Rubbing alcohol
Eye drops
Lip balm

Pepto Bismol (for upset stomachs, diarrhea)
Dramamine
Children's and adult's decongestant and antihistamine
Acetaminophen (children's and adult's pain reliever)
Calamine lotion (to soothe sunburns, bug bites, poison ivy)
Antibiotic cream
Laxative
Sun block
Syrup of Ipecac (to induce vomiting in case of poisoning)
Prescription medicines, and their prescriptions
Telephone numbers for your doctors back home

SWEET DREAMS FOR ROAD WARRIORS

That first night is always the toughest when you are on the road suffering from jet lag! A survey conducted by Hilton Hotels and the National Sleep Foundation discovered the fact that a night of good, sound sleep is the top concern for business travelers.

The group is now looking for solutions to some of the sleep disorders that hardcore travelers suffer from such as "the first night effect"—the inability to fall asleep the first night away from home ... and the "on-call effect"—the worry that something will awaken you coupled with the fatigue and drowsiness which accompany jet lag.

Exposure to sunlight during the day is probably a better way to minimize or prevent jet lag fatigue says sleep expert Timothy Monk. The light of the sun helps in regulating the body's biorhythms. Further, eating protein in the morning and carbohydrates at night will induce drowsiness. Others claim that taking the hormone melatonin the first 2 or 3 nights on arrival and on return drastically reduces jet lag caused by poor sleep—consult your doctor to see if melatonin is for you.

A free brochure, "Sleep and the Traveler," is available from the National Sleep Foundation, 1522 K Street NW, Suite 500, Washington DC 20005.

A NATURAL STRATEGY FOR BEATING JET LAG

Light—Half an hour outside at the appropriate time of day helps your body to adjust to the new time zone, even if it's overcast. Avoid looking directly at the sun, and if you have to go outside at a time when you are supposed to be avoiding outside light, wear dark sunglasses which filter the harmful rays of the sun.

- ◯ When traveling east 6 time zones or more get midday light, avoid morning light.
- ◯ When traveling east under 6 time zones get morning light.
- ◯ When traveling west 6 time zones or more get midday light, avoid late-afternoon light.
- ◯ When traveling west under 6 time zones get late-afternoon light.

*T*RAVELING TIPS BY AGE GROUP

INFANT

GO BABY GO

Let's begin this discussion with a basic truth. Traveling with your infant is a bit of a hassle and requires more gear and planning than traveling with your older kids. Still, traveling with babies is one of my favorite ways to go, since we both get right-in-the-now, undivided time together. Moreover, infants' charm is negotiable worldwide, making all your travel plans easier and more fun. And, of course, because I can never get enough of my little ones.

Bedding Down

No one sleeps like a baby, and babies generally sleep very well on the road. The rocking, lurching, chugging motions usually knock them right out. Still, having a familiar bed or bed gear reassures infants and small children. For infants, we travel with a small portable crib that can fit under our legs on public transportation, or on our laps. We've also used (and like) little zip-up buntings that keep baby in a cozy, manageable bundle.

By the time baby is six months, it's time to graduate to a portable crib. Our favorites are the Evenflow (easiest to set up and take down) and the Graco, which umbrellas up and fits into a canvas traveling case. The Graco is heavier and takes a bit longer to set up (it's still easy, though) but it's quite a bit larger, making it suitable to do double duty for those outings to grandma's house or as an extra playpen at home. Portable cribs are also very handy for taking to the beach or pool.

A familiar blanket and toy can make all the difference for traveling children. As they get older, they can continue to treasure their favorite blanket. (Our 15-year-old's favorite blanket now resides on a chair in his bedroom where he frequently uses it as a lap warmer while working on his computer!)

Getting Around

We like child-carrying backpacks for traveling with kids up to 3 years old. The Gerry has an inner sling for younger ones that can be dispensed with as they grow. We've even used the Gerry for very small babies, fitting a receiving blanket around baby for stability. We also travel with the lightest umbrella stroller we can find, which we push right onto the plane and store in the overhead compartment. Wheeling the baby or toddler aboard can really save your back on a half-mile long concourse.

Car Seats

We find it much more convenient and cost-effective to take our own car seats with us on vacation. They are also handy for keeping junior in one place in the hotel rooms during feedings and quiet time.

Diapers

I have a hard time justifying disposable diapers at home on ecological grounds, but while on the road, they're just too convenient to resist. We also travel with at least a dozen cloth diapers for when we settle down in a spot. Disposable diapers can be very expensive in developing countries, so we recommend starting out with a good supply from home. Don't forget the rubber pants, and carry a packet of wipes and rash cream in your day bag to make diaper changes easier. We like creams containing Vitamins A and D because they're good for sunburn and other skin irritations as well.

Clothing

Keep it simple and keep it to the minimum, for both you and baby. You can expect to be doing some laundry every few days anyway, so why burden yourself with too many changes of clothes? We usually figure on four changes of clothes, two sets of pajamas, one dress-up outfit and an all purpose jacket, suited to the climate you're traveling in. Add socks, underwear, one pair of shoes and a swimsuit, and you're ready to go. For maximum convenience, take mix-and-match separates in dark and bright colors. In hot climates, all cotton is definitely more comfortable. Be sure to bring a hat that protects baby from the sun. Pack the bags, and then don't worry about it. If you find you're missing some crucial item, you can always pick it up along the way, for a more intimate souvenir. (I treasure my Irish underwear!)

Toys

Take a few small favorites and maybe a favorite book. When those toys have lost their appeal, stop in at a local toy store and buy new playthings along the way. Check them out closely, however, as safety standards vary.

Before you go, here are a few handy phrases to know when traveling with baby.

	"Baby food"	"disposable diapers"
French	_aliments pour bebe_	_couches a jeter_
Spanish	_comida para bebe_	_panales_
Italian	_alimento per bambini_	_pannolini dicarta_
Dutch	_babyvoedsel_	_weggooibare luiers_
Portuguese	_comida para bebe_	_fraldas_

• •

CHILD

ENTERTAINING CHILDREN ON THE ROAD CAN BE FUN & EDUCATIONAL FOR ALL

Leave Your Worries at Home, But Don't Forget the Crayons

Have toys, will travel. Pack a few toys and books in a shoe box or an old lunch box for the child to keep close at hand. An old briefcase makes a handy dual-duty container and writing surface—kids can store their crayons and coloring books and other mess free art materials inside, and use the case for a tabletop to write and draw on. Cookie sheets work well for puzzles and other games requiring a flat, smooth surface. Keep extra toys and activities in the trunk and trade them only when the kids show waning interest in the toys they have.

Don't be bored, play board games! Magnetic or peg board games can be found in many varieties like chess, checkers, or Scrabble. There are many other board games which are suitable for traveling, look them over and find what suits your family best. We love dominoes, which take up little space and can be played many different ways.

OLD MAIDS, GO FISH Cards—they're compact and easy to carry in a pocket, handbag or backpack. And they're incredibly versatile. An only child can keep busy for hours with variations on the game of solitaire, while siblings are virtually unlimited in the games at their disposal. Put a book on card games, pencil-and-paper games, and word games in your glove box.

THE SCRAPBOOK Take an empty scrapbook and build a memory for the whole family! Keep a vacation scrapbook to keep the kids entertained, and to serve as a keepsake. Compiling and organizing post cards, brochures and news clippings in the scrapbook will keep kids involved in the trip, while it teaches them about where they're going, and where they've been along the way. Encourage them to be creative, and write stories and descriptions of their experiences and of the things they see in the scrapbook.

THE NAVIGATOR   Designate a navigator each day. Another way to keep kids interested and involved in the journey, and to teach them map-reading skills at the same time, is to let them help to plan the route. Even the youngest can follow a major highway route with a little help. Older children can track distance driven each day and gas mileage, and mark the family's route with a highlighter on the map as you complete each segment of road. (This can go into the scrapbook later!) Talk about the time it takes to travel certain distances at certain speeds, and let your navigator calculate the ETA of your various destinations.

COUNTING GAMES   Make a list of different states or countries seen on other motorists' license plates. Make it a game with a prize or incentive for the person who spotted the most states at the end of the day.

MOBILE PHONES   Toy telephones are great for the younger kids. If you have an only child, bring along a toy telephone for the parents to use with the child. Some toy phones contain tape recorders, which can be fun for recording messages which your child can play back and 'talk' to.

PUPPETS   Puppets are a great take-along item which can be good for hours of entertainment. They are also an excellent tool for dealing with a child who is having a difficult time. Using the puppet to talk to the child sometimes makes it easier for them to calm down by talking to you via the puppet.

BOOKS   The family that reads together ... Books and stories on tape are an excellent way to keep children entertained. They can bring the family together, or, just as importantly, give Mom and Dad a much-needed break. Reading aloud to each other in the car is a great way for the family to connect and share an experience, and it can facilitate some interesting a nd educational discussions. Pick books related to your trip, your destination or the history of areas you are traveling through or visiting. Skip the dry history lessons, a well-written biography or piece of fiction are better bets. Pick out books which tell stories and involve characters. Younger kids will be much more interested if the protagonist is a child.

STEREO   A hand-held cassette/CD player/ radio with headphones is almost a necessity for the older kids. They can listen to their favorite music or story tapes, or tune into the local radio station, while you get a little 'quiet' time. Extra headphone sets are handy for siblings. Headphones are not recommended for toddlers and very young children because decibel levels—if unmonitored—can damage their hearing. Tape or have a grandparent or auntie tape the books your kids love. Peace—guaranteed!

SING A SONG   Kids love to sing, and face it, sometimes it's easier to join them than listen to them. Children's songbooks often come with accompanying tapes, and tips for parents on playing finger and movement games to accompany the songs. These activities can help release some of that pent up energy in a positive way. Join in with your children and have a great time!

JUST YOUR IMAGINATION   A little imagination goes a long way with kids. Enroute or after you have arrived at your destination, imagination games are probably the best entertainment, and definitely the easiest to pack. Children will utilize anything to become a part of their game. An old soda cap can become a serving bowl, a stick can become a playmate, and a small stone or pebble is suddenly a magic crystal. Let your child lead the way in imagination games. If they have a little trouble getting started sometimes, give them a subtle coax, plant a seed of an idea in their head and let them make it grow. Children can learn a lot about life from role playing games where they interact with a partner. These games can be played anywhere and they stimulate the intellect and the ability to create. Props can be found anywhere for imagination games.

· ·

Keep in mind that what you may view as trash to be disposed of could be a precious plaything to your child. Your children may insist on lugging around (or making you lug around) a bag of miscellaneous scraps of paper, bottle caps, aluminum cans, etc. which they feel are essential to their play or they have become quite attached to. Eventually, they will tire of these 'treasures' and discard them (some may take longer than others to disappear). Treating their desire to keep the items as valid will help foster self-esteem and make the trip go easier as well. A small price to pay for child development and peace of mind.

· ·

GAMES ON THE ROAD

These are road games that our family enjoys. Of course, there are more. (Please contribute your games, we'd love to hear your suggestions.) Some of these games can leave your hotel room in quite a state of disarray, but let's face it: when you're traveling with kids, your room doesn't look like the average business traveler's. The housekeepers at most hotels are poorly paid, and a generous tip will help assuage your guilt. If you are staying several nights in the same place, tip the housekeeper in advance. This gesture may even bring you extra towels and wash cloths!

At the Hotel

1. Ashtray Hide-Away: you guessed it-hide that ashtray while everybody keeps his or her eyes closed. (Hard to play in a non-smoking hotel room!)
2. Waste Basketball: use your brought-along ball and count the number of balls in the basket. Put the basket far away or up high to make the game more difficult.
3. Bubble Time: bring along a bottle of blowing bubbles and let the

kids blow themselves silly in the bathroom. Careful, the floor will be slippery, so put down some towels.

4. Pillow Fight: you know.

In the Car

1. Count the license plates from out-of-state: whoever gets the most (says the name of the state first) wins after a certain time period, i.e., 15 minutes, a half-hour, etc.

2. V-Dub: person who sees the most Volkswagen Beetles and says it first within a certain time period wins.

3. Alphabet: try to get through the whole alphabet by spotting letters on billboards, license plates, road signs, etc.

(Car travel: some great items to have on hand for those rest stops are: a beach ball, Frisbee, jump rope, chalk for hop scotch; all of these encourage movement.)

Restaurant Games

1. Water Snake: scrunch down the paper on a paper-covered straw until it forms a tight accordion shape. Put the paper on the table and, using the straw, put a few drops of water on it. The paper will expand and create a snake.

2. Shuffleboard Pennies: you need several pennies for this game. Two players sit on opposite sides of a table. Place the pennies in the center of the cleared table. The first player hits the penny with their finger to try and get it as close to the opposite edge of the table as possible. Players alternate turns, shooting the pennies form where they last landed. If the penny lands within two inches form the edge = 1 point. If it's slightly over the edge = 5 points. If it falls off the table = lose a point.

3. Guess the Check: this one is always a favorite.

4. Add The Check (a much-loved variation): the kid who finds an error in the check receives an amount equal to it, i.e., for a $1.00 overcharge, they get $1.00, etc.

TOYS FOR THE ROAD

The following list of travel toys is just to give you ideas and jog your memory. Obviously you want to take those toys that are suited to your child's interest or suited to your trip. You can also pick up toys along the way, but be sure to look at them closely for safety's sake.

Stuffed animals
Doll with clothing and bottle
Magic slate
Etch-A-Sketch
Game Boy
Crayons and coloring book
Story books
Personal cassette
   player with head-
   phones and tapes
Pens and paper
Guide/Travel books
Any new toy, wrapped
Journal and pen
Legos or Duplos

Bristle Blocks
Soccer ball
Scissors and tape
Paper dolls
Doll house furniture
Fisher Price Little People
Playing Cards
Small ball
Matchbox cars
Frisbee
Magnetic boards
Magnetic chess, checkers,
   puzzles
Snap beads
Play Dough

TEEN

TRAVELING WITH YOUR TEENS

No doubt about it, once kids pass into those teenage years, coming up with family travel ideas requires more thought, and maybe a change of venue. Perhaps the best place to start when planning a family vacation with older kids is a round table discussion about what everybody would like to do. Sure, it's hard to come up with a consensus, but deciding whether you want to head to the mountains, relax on the beach, venture forth with pack on back, or conquer the museums of DC is essential.

Once you've decided on the type of trip you want, cost factors will obviously come into play. At this point, calling a travel agent looking for transportation deals might be a good idea. Once your kids are out of the 12-and-under, stay-free-with-parents lodging option, you may want to put a little bit different spin on your accommodation thinking. Is the average hotel room really big enough, anyway, to make for a pleasurable stay? Many families have found that switching to accommodations with kitchenette and more than one room makes for a much happier time for everybody. All-suite hotels, condominiums, cabins, and vacation home rentals all fill the bill for more space and truly provide a better value in terms of price/satisfaction. Check out specific locations and various options in Chapter 8—Accommodations Family Style.

STATE PARKS State parks represent a fantastic opportunity for families to vacation on a budget (subsidized by Uncle Sam for a change). The following states offer cabin camping: Alabama, Arkansas, Florida, Georgia, Illinois, Indiana, Iowa, Kentucky, Louisiana, Maryland, Massachusetts, Michigan, Minnesota, Mississippi, Missouri, Nebraska, New Jersey, New York, Ohio, Oklahoma, Pennsylvania, South Carolina, South Dakota, Tennessee, Texas, Virginia, West Virginia. See our National and State Park listings for more information and ideas.

SKI RESORTS Ski resorts offer tremendous value during the summer—their off season. Most offer steep discounts to their on-season prices and have an array of activities to entice all members of your family, and plenty of condo accommodations.

GUEST RANCHES/DUDE RANCHES Long on atmosphere and guest camaraderie, dude ranches could provide you with your best vacation ever. See the references and listings for ranches under the "Various Alternatives" section in Chapter 6—The Great Outdoors.

COLLEGES & UNIVERSITIES Large schools often open their housing during the summer break. Not only are the prices low, but accommodations are most often suite-style and well-suited to families. An especially intriguing prospect in pricey city locations.

ADVENTURE VACATIONS If your family is energetic, a pre-planned adventure vacation might be just the ticket for an unforgettable vacation. Most offer you a chance to experience the great out-of-doors in ways few ever do, while taking all the day-to-day drudgery off your shoulders. Check our "Adventure" section in Chapter 6 for more ideas.

ALL INCLUSIVE RESORTS All inclusive resorts with their many recreation options can be wonderful with teens—make sure the one you choose has a young people's outlook.

Golden Rules for Traveling with Teens

1. Give them some space both physically by selecting accommodations that offer more than just one room, and mentally by not planning a super-tight touring schedule.
2. Get them involved right from the start in planning the trip. Your teen may find reading guide books a new and exciting experience, and calling state and local departments of tourism and chambers of commerce will help them sharpen up their telephone skills.
3. Go where the teens are. Kids like the company of their peers.
4. Night life—Try to pick an area or resort that has something going on in the evening. Avoid super quiet communities where they roll up the sidewalks at 5 p.m., and your loud youngsters will stick out like a sore thumb.
5. Set a budget for incidental spending and stick with it.
6. Allow your young people some free time to pursue their own interests and give everyone a breather from in-your-pocket living. One idea that's worked well for us is occasional dinners apart. We go to that nice quiet restaurant we've been longing to try, and we give them $7 to $10 each to go check out the local pizza, etc., setting a rendezvous time for everybody.
7. If they pack it, they schlep it. If the burden really looks too great, have them try a pre-trip around the block. They may not even make it past the front door.
8. Let them sleep. They have to get up early all year long, so why not allow them the luxury of sleeping in in the mornings—while you have some free time.
9. Make them your trip chronicler/photographer/navigator. They will enjoy the responsibility and hopefully will produce a wonderful album immortalizing your family vacation.
10. Allow them to bring a friend along. This allows them to have fun with a peer and not bug you.
11. Go somewhere they desperately want to visit. This is good for the unmotivated.

12. Teenagers love luxury. Just the prospect of staying in a resort, lolling by the pool, ordering room service, if properly presented, may entice them.

13. Plan a one-on-one trip, i.e., one parent-one child, really good for your relationship, and may allow for a more adventurous trip, such as the one my son took bicycling with his dad in Bali.

14. Schedule a do-your-own-thing day where everyone spends a day pursuing their own interests.

15. Enjoy! The teen years go very fast. Pretty soon they may not want to vacation with you. So minimize the little irritations and maximize the pleasure for everybody.

Teen-Friendly Vacations

There are many, but here are some exceptional opportunities.

○ Huatulco, Mexico—CLUB MED. Huatulco is a great place to discover a less tourist-oriented Mexico. Plus, this site offers Club Med's first-ever TEEN CLUB. There are separate activities for the 12- to 14-year-olds and the 15- to 17-year-olds.

○ Winter Park, Colorado—YMCA of the ROCKIES SNOW MOUNTAIN RANCH. Snow Mountain Ranch is very close to Rocky Mountain National Park, allowing easy access to the Park as well as surrounding country. Choose between camp sites, lodge rooms, or several intermediate styles. Cabins are in high demand, so call well ahead. Obviously more than one can stay in a cabin, but check on limits when booking. For your day-time enjoyment there is horseback riding, rafting, bike rental, hiking, lounging, whatever. There are additional costs for some activities. Call (970) 887-2152 to get a brochure.

○ Washington, D.C.—CLOSE UP. This non-profit organization is devoted to showing high school students a more intense side of Washington. Students room in a hotel along with participants from all over the country. Seminars are active discussions and are conducted by associated professionals on both basic and very current topics. Close Up offers a vehicle to explore and investigate our government, learn how to participate, and provides access rather than an unapproachable bureaucracy. There is also time to get a good look at the capitol. Check with your school counselors about Close Up.

SENIOR

Family members come in all ages. Only recently has the senior level of the family been excluded from the definition. Happily, many vacation providers are re-instituting the concept of the *entire* family participating in a holiday trip. And, with families often segmented, a special holiday may be the only and best way for kids to get to really know and enjoy the company of grandparents. Telling the old family stories while lounging under palm trees or by a mountain stream will do wonders for everyone and brings precious memories alive for new generations.

TRAVELING WITH GRANDKIDS

Thinking of taking the grandkids on the road? Here are some tips for making intergenerational traveling as fun and simple as possible.

1. Keep the trips short, and don't try to do too much. Allow plenty of time to relax and bring plenty of things to keep the kids entertained.

2. Relax and focus on staying flexible. This is supposed to be a pleasure for both you and the grandkid, so don't weigh it down with heavy expectations and rigid schedules. A simple way to tell if you're pushing too hard is to monitor your stress level—if you're starting to worry about sticking to the itinerary, or if you can't enjoy one activity fully because you're thinking about getting to the next one, it's time to drop some "must do's." The wonderful thing about trav-

eling with children is that they have an innate ability to live in the moment, something that we adults can copy and learn from!

3. Keep the kids' interests and age in mind. Go places you know the kids will be excited about, and where they will be surrounded by other children. Either avoid like the plague places that the kids "should" see, or transform them into a fun outing. Why not play frisbee at the historic battlefield?

4. Keep traveling time to a minimum. The grandkids are probably not the best traveling companions for a marathon cross-country road trip. If you are traveling a long distance, be sure to plan for rest stops every hour or so.

5. Ask about baby-sitting services and supervised kids' activities ahead of time, and sign up. We know you love your grandchildren, but child care is a full-time job, and you need a vacation on this trip, too!

Above all, this should be enjoyable for all involved. Don't let a grandparent/grandchild trip turn into an obligation or extended baby-sitting ordeal. When you are comfortable with the itinerary and each other is the time to head off and have fun. Grandparents may well reconnect with their own child within, and grandkids may learn to be more comfortable and respectful around older folks. Families should not only extend, they should embrace.

GRANDPARENT/GRANDKID TRIPS

There are several organizations and companies out there which specifically offer trips for grandparents and grandchildren to enjoy together. Here are a few we know about:

O THE SIERRA CLUB is offering more outings for the senior and junior set, including Just for Grandparents and Grandchildren, at Tahoe Forest in California from late August into September. Ever dreamed about spending more quality time with your grandchildren or sharing your knowledge of the outdoors with them? It can happen on this comfortable outing, based at the Sierra Club's Clair Tappaan Lodge in the Sierras. Swim and hike with the group, or go off on your own adventure. If you think your grandkids are old enough (five and up) to be away from their parents for five days, go for it! Prices are in the $200 and $300 range. Write to the Sierra Club Outing Department, 730 Polk Street, San Francisco, California 94109, or call (415) 923-5630.

○ VISTATOURS currently offers two guided tours specifically for grandparents and grandchildren. The Reno/Tahoe Grandparents tour is a 5-day/4-night visit that covers Squaw Valley, South Lake Tahoe, Carson City, Virginia City, including a visit to the home of Bonanza, and to the Fleischmann Planetarium. The South Dakota Grandparents tour is a 7-day/6-night bus tour covering Mt. Rushmore and Badlands National Park. For more information, call (800) 248-4782.

○ FAMILYHOSTEL offers tours in Europe, Mexico and Australia specifically designed for families—parents, grandparents and school age children. Each program includes activities for children and adults, and for the family to enjoy together. Sponsored by the University of New Hampshire Continuing Education, who also operate, INTERHOSTEL, an international study and travel program for adults over age 50. For a brochure, call (800) 733-9753.

○ Cape Canaveral, Florida—THE BIG RED BOAT. Not many cruises are closer to home, of shorter duration and more economical. The Big Red Boat provides great package deals that the whole family can join in on, including family suites on board, a cruise to The Bahamas and a visit to Walt Disney World. Grandparents and grandkids can spend as little or as much time together as they like between other activities, with or without mom and dad. For more information, write to The Big Red Boat at P.O. Box 573, Cape Canaveral, Florida 32920, or call (800) 327-7113.

○ GRANDTRAVEL has made it their business to offer cross-generational trips. They are into their second decade of this work. Since its inception, Grandtravel has refined its itineraries in consultation with education specialists to enhance school social study programs and to give the separate generations new relationships. Some activities are selected to provide fun for both ages, others to satisfy peer interests. All itineraries give special attention to natural attractions, historical sites and places of current interest. Pre-departure counseling is available from Grandtravel to help grandparents and grandchildren understand each other's needs. Call (800) 247-7651.

Other itineraries cover Washington, D.C., the U.S. southwest, canyons and national parks, Hawaii, Alaska, Ireland, Britain, Holland and Belgium by barge, Italy, Kenya and Australia. Departures are scheduled June through August. How about the covered-wagon ride, cowboy breakfast and rootin', tootin' rodeo that highlight a special journey of Wyoming and South Dakota designed for grandparents with their grandchildren. This 10-day tour starts in Rapid City, South Dakota, and ends in Jackson Hole, Wyoming. Before you commit to this adventure, you might want to start with a New England Sampler. Call (800) 247-7651 or (301) 986-0790.

○ PEARL CRUISES is one of the cruise lines that acknowledges cruising is one of the best ways for the older and younger sets to travel together. This works best with teens rather than younger kids. How about a graduation present of a trip on Pearl's Highlights of Indonesia? Two adults can take an under-21-year-old with them on a 16-day CruiseTour through the Java Sea for $1,000—or $2,000 for a separate cabin (includes some air fare). Along with a regular guest lecturer, a special teen cultural lecturer provides insight for the younger cruiser. For more information, call (305) 774-8600.

*T*RAVELIN' FOOD

TIPS

FEEDING KIDS ON THE ROAD

Adults can go without a meal or prolong their "feeding times," but hungry kids don't make good travel companions! When they want to eat, they want to eat. With a little planning and smart packing, you can keep blood sugar levels on an even keel without breaking the bank. Here are some helpful ideas for feeding your kids from baby to teenager on the road.

Meals on Wheels

A well-packed cooler and picnic basket or box of miscellaneous non-perishable food items in the car will go a long way toward making sure everyone is well-fed on your road trip. Fixings for peanut butter or cheese sandwiches, snack foods and fresh fruit should be stowed in a spot that's easily accessible to an adult or older child. Be sure to give your kids lots of their favorite foods when traveling. Familiar food can help them to feel more at ease on a long trip by giving them a sense of home and stability. Use an empty cardboard six-pack carton to organize your utensils, napkins and condiments. Pack snacks individually in small plastic resealable bags to save time and avoid the dilemma some children feel when presented with too many choices.

Disposable items such as paper plates, bowls, cups, forks, spoons, and wipes can be real time savers. To minimize waste, however, these items can be reused if you take the time to wash them out at rest areas or

in your hotel room before the next leg of the trip. Fill up your reused drink containers with water and ice for the day or bring along a camping canteen. Collapsible drinking cups are handy and don't take up much space.

Find a nice place to stop and have a picnic! Rest areas often have picnic areas, or if you are in the vicinity of a national or state park, take the time to search out a picnic area for a nice break. A relaxed picnic in a park can become a fond family memory of your trip. Bring along a Frisbee to burn off some built-up energy and stretch your travel-weary limbs.

Make water your beverage of choice in the car—kids won't drink more than they need (another way to cut down on potty stops), it's not sticky when it gets spilled and doesn't usually stain. Boxed drinks with straws will make a toddler happy, although you will probably have to set limits on these, or they'll drink one after another. Investing in the 'non-squeezable' plastic holders for individual sized box drinks is a wise thing to do. When you put a box drink into the hand of a child without using a plastic holder, invariably, they will squeeze the box and erupt in tears as their juice squirts all over the place!

Avoid hard items that are difficult to chew and swallow, such as carrots and ice cubes. Also avoid salty foods, and soft drinks, to cut down on potty stops. Foods high in sugar, chocolate, or caffeine can create pandemonium when everyone is confined to a small space for a long period of time. Sticking to healthy foods is the best bet for a peaceful journey—everyone will feel better for it at the end of a long day of traveling!

Breakfast in Bed

Our one indispensable traveling item is a small plasticized duffel bag with a zipper top, which we fill up with dishes, utensils and menu basics. In it we have an aluminum bowl which doubles as a wash pan, salad bowl and more; a small plug-in electric tea kettle, which we change for an international convertible plug-in warmer for travel abroad; a plastic bowl and silverware for each family member; a good quality folding kitchen knife; a peeler; Swiss Army knife with corkscrew and can opener. In the end pocket of the duffel, we carry a handful of bags of sugar; a tiny salt and pepper; condiments in packets from the fast food spots; bouillon cubes; tea bags; and packets of hot chocolate.

With this bag we are equipped for breakfast every day in the comfort of our own room. We usually start the trip with a package of granola, and a packet of dry milk. To this we add local fruit and breads, and fresh milk. Kuchen, croissants, empanadas dulce, whatever local goodies we can find, as well as jams and jellies and cheese. We find these informal family breakfasts not only economical, but fun and a great time saver. With small children, it's much less hassle than corralling everybody into a restaurant.

On a three-month trip to Europe, we saved a small fortune in money and calories by having an expanded salad dinner in our room every other night. We also had fun shopping at the local green grocers for the ingredients and trying new foods. We supplemented the salad with fresh bread, cheeses and cold cuts, often buying enough to pack a picnic lunch for the next day.

An Ounce of Prevention

When traveling in developing countries, a little extra attention to sanitary eating can pay off big in avoiding intestinal problems. Be sure to buy "long-life" or canned milk. Buy refrigerated milk only if it's pasteurized and sold in sealed containers. Be sure to peel all fruit. Eat food that's only been freshly prepared and is served steaming hot. Don't be shy to ask to go into the kitchen and select your dinner by viewing the contents of assorted pots, and pointing to the pots you want. Always wash your hands, and your little one's before eating. And although I don't normally recommend soft drinks, Coca Cola is a well-known folk cure for stomach ailments and is bottled under strict sanitary conditions worldwide.

Baby Food

Babies are the easiest to feed on long trips, and breastfeeding is the most natural way to go. If you've been considering weaning your baby, put it off until after your trip—think of all the bags and bottles and containers you won't have to tote around! Just keep in mind that the same rules for taking care of yourself apply on the road as they do at home. Drink plenty of fluids, eat enough food to satisfy the required calorie intake, and above all, eat healthy food to keep your energy level up.

Nursing etiquette is becoming more and more relaxed, and you needn't skulk away to a dirty public restroom when it's feeding time for baby. However, if you find you are uncomfortable nursing in public for any reason, try to find a private place for yourself and your baby. The baby will pick up on the tension if you aren't comfortable and won't nurse as well. Try to nurse in places which aren't too chaotic or loud, as tumult can also disturb baby.

If your baby is bottle-fed, take along plenty of sterilized water, powdered formula (pre-measured in zip lock baggies or sterilized bottles), a wide mouth thermos with hot water for warm ups and clean ups, and a bottle sterilizer. You may also be able to find a bottle warmer that plugs into the cigarette lighter in your car.

We always travel, until the little one is a year and a half, with a box of instant baby cereal, which can be converted with purified water, and turned into an acceptable meal with the addition of peeled fresh fruit, anywhere, anytime. Instant baby cereal can also be pre-mixed with powdered formula or dry milk and measured into little serving containers or plastic zip lock baggies for an instant meal (just mix with warm water). Children's catalogues and specialty shops carry a selection of feeding dishes, cups, and utensils for kids on the road. The Infafeeder is a useful device that allows you to feed cereal or other mushy foods with the ease of using a baby bottle, and it can be purchased in general merchandise stores.

Don't forget to bring a baby food grinder! Your baby can share appropriate food from your plate in restaurants or at someone else's home. Never serve strained foods or milk as leftovers from previous meals. Warm or room temperature food is a breeding ground for harmful bacteria.

Toddler Tummies

For toddlers, finger foods are a great way to keep their tummies happy. Toddlers function best when they can snack frequently throughout the day. If you are the parent of a toddler, you know they don't always eat when it's time for the big meals. Kids will eat when they are hungry—don't fret if your 3-year-old refuses to eat when you stop in a restaurant. Keep them supplied with a variety of healthy snacking foods and drinks throughout the day, and they will be just fine.

Good on-the-road toddler snacks include cheese chunks and string cheese, bananas, fruit, crackers, bagels or bagel sticks, pretzels (unsalted) and dry cereals (low or no sugar). A can of squirt cheese and crackers is an easy snack to prepare on the go.

Eating Out

A family trip is probably not the best time to try out that famous gourmet restaurant everyone has been telling you about. If you must hit a swanky spot, call first to see if they have any children's items on the menu.

When eating in a restaurant, think about phoning your order in ahead of time, or ordering takeout. If the kids have spent the whole day sitting in the car, they're probably not going to be particularly receptive to sitting in a restaurant for another hour. We wish you happy, healthy, and enjoyable eating experiences in your travels!

PICNICKING ON THE ROAD

I remember waking up as a kid heading on our annual road trip from Tennessee to Florida. While my dad packed the suitcases in the trunk,

Mom prepared her giant food hamper, enough food to last us on our marathon drive (non-stop!) and breakfast when we got there. I think taking a hamper of food with you makes really good sense. Not only is it a big money saver, but you control the quality of what you're eating, and can cut down on the quantities of sugar, salt, food dyes and MSG, all of which make many kids hyper. You may want to carry a basket or simply a box for dry goods, and a small cooler for cold drinks and milk.

A few points to keep in mind:

○ Cool it. To help foods stay cold, fill your cooler with ice and let it stand about an hour before packing.

○ Double-wrapping, first in paper, then in aluminum helps things like sandwiches stay cold. Use plastic containers for things you don't want to squash, and to keep it neat—olives, pickles, custard for the baby, etc.

○ Keep your sandwiches from getting soggy by putting the condiments in the middle of the sandwich, and put meat or cheese directly next to the bread, followed by the tomato, lettuce, then the mustard and mayo sandwiched in between.

One of the joys of picnicking is that you can choose a great spot in which to enjoy your al fresco meal far away from the maddening crowds and the fast food emporium. We always look for state parks, lakes and resort areas, where there are often playgrounds for the kids to enjoy and let off some steam. In the city, search out a park with a kids area, or try the zoo!

· · · · · · · · · · · · · · · · · · · ·

COOKIE JAR

CHOCOLATE CHIP COOKIES

This recipe for chocolate chip cookies is simply the best. And it makes enough to feed a small, hungry army—

2 cups brown sugar   2 cups butter
2 cups white sugar   4 eggs

3 cups oatmeal

1 tablespoon salt

2 tablespoon baking powder

1 tablespoon vanilla

4 cups flour

3 cups chopped nuts

24 oz. chocolate chips

Cream sugar and butter. Add eggs and blend well. Add dry ingredients, vanilla, chips and nuts. Refrigerate overnight. Roll into golf ball size. Place on cookie sheet 2" apart. Press down slightly. Bake at 400 degrees for 6 to 9 minutes.

CHOCOLATE MAPLE NUT BARS

Easy to make and transport and very yummy—

1½ cup unsifted flour

⅔ cup sugar

½ teaspoon salt

¾ cup butter

2 eggs

One 14-oz. can Eagle Brand
   sweetened condensed milk

1 teaspoon Maple flavoring

2 cups chopped nuts

1 cup chocolate chips

Combine flour, sugar and salt. Cut in butter until crumbly. Stir in one beaten egg. Press firmly on bottom of 13" x 9" pan.

Bake at 350 degrees for 25 minutes.

Meanwhile, beat condensed milk, one egg and maple flavoring. Stir in nuts. When it comes out of the oven, sprinkle chocolate chips over the hot crust. Then top with nut mixture. Bake another 25 minutes.

Cool and cut.

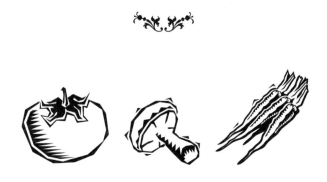

GINGER COOKIES

Ginger tastes good and is good for the digestion. These cookies travel well!

I cup butter	2 teaspoon baking soda
2 cups brown sugar	3 teaspoon ginger
2 eggs	½ teaspoon allspice
¼ cup molasses	¼ teaspoon ground cloves
4½ cups flour	Sugar for rolling (½ to I cup)

Cream together butter and brown sugar. Beat in eggs one at a time. Stir in molasses.

Sift together flour, soda, ginger, allspice, and cloves. Stir into butter mixture. Roll teaspoonsful of dough into balls. Roll in sugar to coat.

Bake at 325 degrees for 12 minutes. Cool on racks.

From Margaret Lukens, Four Seasons Foods

GRANDMOTHER'S OLD FASHIONED SUGAR COOKIES

Cora had 12 kids but always found time to ride her mare—maybe these cookies were what kept the little ones quiet?

½ cup (I stick) butter	¼ teaspoon nutmeg
I cup sugar	¼ teaspoon salt (if using unsalted
3 eggs	butter)
2¼ cup flour	I teaspoon vanilla
2 teaspoons baking powder	

Cream butter and sugar. Add eggs one at a time. Sift baking powder, flour, salt (if using), and nutmeg together and add to creamed mixture a little at a time. Add vanilla. Mix.

Roll out as for cookies. Cut with round biscuit cutter. Bake on greased and floured cookie sheet in preheated 350 degree oven until light brown, 15 to 20 minutes. Be careful not to overbake. If you want to glaze them, sprinkle with ¼ cup sugar before baking.

JILL'S COWBOY COOKIES

This recipe was the favorite of a Humboldt County California country family with little boys. Chewy and filling—

1 cup shortening	1 cup brown sugar
1 cup sugar	2 eggs
1 teaspoon vanilla	2 cups flour
½ teaspoon baking powder	1 teaspoon soda
6 oz. chocolate chips	2 cups oats
1 cup nuts	

Mix it all up and drop on greased cookie sheets. Bake at 350 degrees for 15 minutes or until done.

Makes about 5 dozen.

MEXICAN WEDDING CAKES

These were called Mexican Wedding Cakes in my family. I have since had the same cookies, but called Russian Wedding Cakes, or shaped differently and called Persian Crescent Cookies. They're so popular everyone claims them as their own!

1 cup soft butter	2 cups unbleached white flour
1 cup powdered sugar	1 cup chopped brazilnuts (or
¼ teaspoon salt	pecans)
1 teaspoon vanilla	Powdered sugar

Combine butter, sugar, salt and vanilla. Cream until light and fluffy. Mix in flour and nuts. Form into just under 1" balls and flatten slightly onto ungreased baking sheet.

Bake at 400 degrees for 8 to 10 minutes, or until creamy tan in color. Roll in powdered sugar while still warm.

Makes about 5 dozen rich crisp cookies.

MOM'S MOLASSES COOKIES

Easy (let the kids help) and the cookies travel well—

¾ cup margarine or butter
1 cup granulated sugar
¼ cup molasses
1 egg
2 teaspoons baking soda
2 cups flour, all purpose

½ teaspoon ground cloves
½ teaspoon ground ginger
1 teaspoon cinnamon
½ teaspoon salt
granulated sugar

Melt shortening in pan. Let cool. Add sugar, molasses and egg. Beat well. Sift dry ingredients. Add to wet ingredients. Chill.

Roll dough into balls the size of walnuts. Roll in granulated sugar.

Bake at 375 degrees for 7 to 10 minutes. Makes approximately 50 cookies.

RASPBERRY WALNUT BARS

Perfect for a picnic. These are a little fancy, colorful, and very, very good!

Shortbread Base:
Combine—
   1¼ cup flour

½ cup sugar
½ cup butter

Press into bottom of greased 9" square pan.
   Bake at 350 for 20 minutes.
   Remove and spread with ½ cup raspberry jam.

Next mix the following ingredients and spread over jam:

2 eggs
½ cup packed brown sugar
1 teaspoon vanilla
2 Tablespoons flour

⅛ teaspoon salt
⅛ teaspoon baking soda
1 cup chopped walnuts

Return to oven and bake for 20 to 25 minutes.

Cool and cut into squares.

. . . .

SNACKS

CARROT-ZUCCHINI BREAD

The Longswamp B&B, a rural inn in Mertztown, Pennsylvania was once a stop on the underground railway for slaves escaping from the South. Try out this delicious recipe for Carrot-Zucchini Bread:

2½ cups unsifted all-purpose flour
1 cup unsifted whole wheat flour
1 tablespoon baking powder
1 teaspoon baking soda
½ teaspoon salt
½ cup firmly packed brown sugar
2 eggs

1½ cups buttermilk
2 tablespoons melted butter
Grated rinds of 1 orange and 1 lemon
1 cup coarsely shredded zucchini
1 cup coarsely shredded carrots
Whipped cream cheese
Powdered ginger

Preheat oven to 350 degrees. Butter 9" by 5" by 3" loaf pan.

Mix together flours, baking powder, soda, salt and sugar. Add remaining ingredients. Stir until well blended. Pour into loaf pan and bake for 1¼ hours or until cake is firm. Cool 5 minutes, then unmold onto a rack. Cool before slicing. When cool, top with whipped cream cheese flavored with a touch of powdered ginger. Yields one loaf, which serves 10.

ORANGE DATE BREAD

This recipe comes from Taughannock Farms Inn of Trumansburg which is set among some of central New York State's most spectacular scenery: Taughannock Falls and Gorge and Cayuga Lake.

Rind of 1 orange
1 cup water
½ cup chopped dates
¾ cup sugar 2 tablespoons butter
1 egg, beaten

1 cup (2 sticks) butter
2 cups all-purpose flour
2 teaspoons baking powder
½ teaspoon salt

Preheat oven to 350 degrees. Generously butter an 8" by 4" loaf pan.

Mix together the first 3 ingredients in a saucepan and boil gently. Add sugar and butter, stir until dissolved and remove from heat. When cooled, stir in remaining ingredients.

Put in loaf pan and bake for about 45 minutes or until it tests done. Serve sliced, with cream cheese. Yields one loaf, which serves 8 to 10.

LAUREL'S HONEY CAKE

This one is not too sweet, keeps well, and goes very well with sliced cheese and fruit. I often make one to take on a trip and we enjoy it as a snack for days.

Preheated oven to 350 degrees
Flour a 9" tube pan, well oiled
2 cups honey
1 cup oil
2 cups (1 can) pumpkin
4 eggs, beaten
3 cups flour (half white & half
    wheat is good)

1 Tablespoon baking powder
2 teaspoon soda
2 teaspoon vanilla
1 teaspoon salt
1 cup nuts (optional)
1 cup raisins (we prefer golden)

Mix together dry ingredients. Mix together wet ingredients and combine with dry ingredients. Stir in nuts and raisins and pour into tube pan. Bake at 350 degrees for 1 hour 10 minutes, or until done.

AUNT CARRIE'S HUNGARIAN COFFEE CAKE

This is my most treasured recipe because it always comes out great, it's absolutely scrumptious, and it lasts, if well wrapped, for 4 or 5 days.

1 cup white sugar
1 cup brown sugar

1 cup shortening (butter or
    margarine)

3 cups all-purpose flour
½ cup chopped nuts
1½ teaspoons cinnamon
1 cup buttermilk
2 eggs

1 teaspoon vanilla
½ teaspoon salt
1 teaspoon baking powder
1 teaspoon baking soda

Preheat oven to 350 degrees. Combine the first six ingredients. Take out one level cup and set aside for topping.

To the remaining mixture add the rest of the ingredients from the buttermilk to the baking soda. Mix will be slightly lumpy. Pour into 2" x 8" cake or pie pans (2 or 3).

Cover with the one cup of reserved nut mix and bake at 350 degrees for 20 or 25 minutes. Do not over bake. Will stay fresh for 4 days. Serves 16.

HOME MADE CHEESE CRACKERS

These are a great little goody to make the night before and take with you for car munchies. Cayenne obviously is optional, or put some on half the recipe and package separately.

Saltines
Cayenne
Sharp cheddar

Cover a cookie sheet with saltines, aligning them so that their sides touch. Cover crackers with cheese (grated or thinly sliced, whichever you prefer) and sprinkle with cayenne.

Bake at 350 until cheese bubbles, then turn oven off. Don't open the oven door—just leave them overnight.

. . . .

PICNIC

PICNIC PASTA

Get out the checkered tablecloth. The following recipe presents well and is very tasty!

½ lb. pasta shells, cooked & drained

1 cup turkey ham (or regular ham), cut in strips

One 11-oz. canned mandarin oranges

3 green onions, chopped

½ green pepper, sliced thinly

½ red pepper, sliced thinly

¼ cup sliced black olives

¼ cup crumbled feta cheese

¼ cup toasted walnut pieces

Dressing:

3 Tablespoon B&B Liqueur (optional)

¾ cup mayonnaise

2 Tablespoon fresh pesto

½ teaspoon salt

½ teaspoon tarragon

½ teaspoon fresh ground white pepper

Mix dressing in a bowl with wire whip. Pour over pasta and marinate overnight.

Mix in other ingredients just before serving. Mound on chilled plate with greens at home, or pack in a picnic container and put salad greens in separate container or plastic bag and assemble on site.

Colorful and very tasty.

Babbling Brook Inn
Helen King, Innkeeper
1025 Laurel Street
Santa Cruz, California 95060

OLD-TIME POPCORN BALLS

A good one to make with the kids.

2 cups granulated sugar
1½ cups water
½ teaspoon salt

½ cup light corn syrup
I teaspoon vinegar
I teaspoon vanilla
5 quarts popped corn

Butter sides of saucepan. In it combine sugar, water, salt, syrup, and vinegar. Cook to hard ball stage (250°). Stir in vanilla. Slowly pour over popped corn, stirring just to mix well. Butter hands slightly; shape balls. Makes 15 to 20 balls.

BANANA CHOCOLATE CHIP BREAD

A sure-fire hit, and easier and quicker than chocolate chip cookies. Courtesy of Penny Olson of The Linden Tree in Rockport, Massachusetts.

½ cup margarine
½ cup brown sugar
¼ cup sugar
½ teaspoon vanilla
2 cups flour

I teaspoon baking soda
½ cup chopped nuts
3 ripe bananas, mashed
⅔ cup chocolate chips
2 eggs

Cream together margarine and sugars. Beat in eggs, vanilla, and banana. Add flour and soda. Stir in chips and nuts. Bake in greased loaf pan for 50 minutes in 350-degree oven.

RAY HOUSE LEMON LOAF

Located in the Blue Ridge Mountain town of Asheville, North Carolina, the 3-guestroom Ray House has the atmosphere of an English country home and a library stocked with lots of good books. Try this recipe out for your afternoon snack.

I stick (4 ounces) softened butter
I cup sugar 2 eggs
I½ cups bread or all-purpose flour
I teaspoon baking powder

¼ teaspoon salt
I tablespoon grated lemon rind
½ cup milk
Lemon sauce (see following recipe)

Preheat oven to 350 degrees. Butter and flour a 8½" by 4½" loaf pan.

Cream butter and sugar by hand in a large bowl. Add eggs, one at a time, beating after each addition. Sift flour, baking powder and salt onto a sheet of waxed paper. With fork, stir in lemon rind. Add flour mixture and milk to batter alternately, beginning and ending with the flour mixture.

Pour into loaf pan. Bake for one hour or until cake tester comes out clean. Pour lemon sauce over hot cake. Allow it to cool for 10 minutes, then turn out on rack to cool completely. Yields one loaf. Keeps for one week when well-wrapped and refrigerated.

LEMON SAUCE:
⅓ cup sugar   ¼ cup fresh lemon juice

Stir sugar into lemon juice until it dissolves.

SECRET TOFFEE

An oldie but a goody, fun to take with you and a real conversation starter at potlucks.

½ cup butter
⅔ cup brown sugar
24 unsalted soda crackers

1½ cups semi-sweet chocolate morsels
¾ cups finely chopped walnuts or toasted almonds

Preheat oven to 375 degrees. Line a 13" x 9" baking pan with foil, letting foil extend up the sides. Melt butter in small saucepan; add sugar and let come to a full boil until sugar melts and turns syrupy, about 30 seconds. Pour into the foil-lined pan, tilt to cover bottom evenly. Top with a single layer soda crackers, leaving about ⅛" between crackers.

Bake 10 minutes. Remove from oven and sprinkle chocolate morsels and nuts evenly over top. Return to oven for 1 minute. Spread chocolate-nut mixture with a rubber spatula into an even layer, being careful not to disturb cracker layer. Refrigerate 1 hour until firm. Lift from pan, peel foil and break into chunks. Store in an airtight container in the refrigerator. Yields 1½ pounds.

WACKY CAKE

Quick, easy, and just perfect! Eat it the first or second day.

1½ cups flour
1 cup sugar
½ teaspoon salt
1 teaspoon soda
3 tablespoons cocoa

6 tablespoons vegetable oil (not olive oil)
1 tablespoon apple cider vinegar
1 teaspoon vanilla
1 cup cold water

Preheat oven to 350 degrees. Sift all dry ingredients into an ungreased 9" by 9" cake pan. Make a well in the center and pour the oil, vinegar, vanilla and cold water into it. The combination will start to bubble. Mix well with a fork until smooth. Bake for 25 to 30 minutes. Cool and frost with chocolate frosting.

CHOCOLATE FROSTING:

3 Tablespoons cocoa   2 Tablespoons soft butter
1 cup powdered sugar   2 Tablespoons hot coffee

Sift cocoa and sugar together into bowl. Add butter. Add hot coffee and beat until thick and smooth.

CHAPTER 4

ROAD SCHOLARS

EDUCATING KIDS ON THE ROAD

Like most families, the majority of our travels have taken place during the long summer break and over the Christmas and Easter holidays. Obviously, these pose no challenge to continuing schoolwork, beyond taking along some books about the area to enhance the experience. However, sometimes an opportunity presents itself for a trip during regular school times, and when this happens, the question of continuing the children's education while traveling becomes paramount. Depending upon the duration of the trip, there are several options for schooling your kids on the road.

Work with your child's school to develop what is called in California an "independent study contract." Under an independent study contract, the teacher gives the child the assignments, to be supervised by the parents and completed by the child's return. This is easiest in elementary school, when there is generally only one teacher involved. However, as the student gets into junior high and high school, more advanced preparation is required. Give the school as much advance notice as possible, arrange to have a personal discussion with the teacher, or in the upper grades, the counselor, who will coordinate the independent study. In the upper grades, it helps to not be absent for the semester finals, though this too can be worked around.

On our most recent extended trip, we traveled in Thailand with our children, our daughter a freshman in high school and our son in 5th grade. The freshman had a complete backpack of books to carry and she did very well working independently on her studies, while the 5th grader needed more direction from us. A typical morning, and I do believe mornings are best for study, would begin with 9 o'clock study session. Our daughter would work independently, while with our son we would go through each of his five study topics for 20 to 30 minutes each. Although this doesn't sound like a lot of time, it's actually as much time as most students spend on each topic in a classroom day. We take a break around 10:30 for fifteen minutes of exercise, and then get back at it until 12:30. Every afternoon we would have one to two hours of quiet time for independent reading. Using this schedule, our children completed eight weeks of classwork in five weeks, and upon our return were ahead of their class in every subject. They received complete credit, and it was actually our daughter's best scholastic year. It did require some responsibility on our part (geometry is long ago and far away in my memory!), and some preparation, but it was more than worth it. And when we realized how little our children were actually learning during their long hours at school, we became much more demanding of them in terms of outside reading, preparing study projects just for us, and learning in general.

Private schools perhaps have a longer history of dealing with extended student absences, and most are very accommodating in preparing school work. If you plan to be gone for more than a semester, it probably makes sense to look into an accredited correspondence school. (Correspondence schools that have come highly recommended to us are listed in the resources section.)

Enrolling your child in local schools is another option. Obviously, there may be a language barrier, which is more easily surmountable by some children than others. Most large cities have American schools, or a bilingual English language school. Friends whose daughters attended high school in Mexico for two years at a private Catholic school where they began with only a smattering of Spanish are amazingly poised and confident, and their manners are light years ahead of their all-American peers.

Also, there is Woodstock School in Musoorie, India, which was established in 1854 and continues to provide excellent education for kids 1st through 12th grade. If you are in the region of India and want to do a segment of travel that is unsafe or inappropriate for young travelers, Woodstock School does accept boarding students. They will be safe and in class while you're off climbing, diving, meditating or whatever.

The section "Road Scholars," was written by Virginie Forain, who has traveled the world with her family, and home-schooled her children using correspondence courses. Her eldest daughter is just finishing nursing school at age 21, cum laude, and her younger daughter is a full scholarship student at Stanford University.

ROAD SCHOLARS

How will our children carry on their studies as we travel? It's a common question among adventurous parents. Their children's education is often a factor that prevents parents from undertaking a long trip, or taking a job that takes the kids away from a regular school for long periods of time.

Ironically enough, when one opens one's self to the many opportunities of schooling on the road, it becomes for the children and also for the parents an experience so rich that no one in the family will ever forget. One great advantage of being "on the road" is that one is away from the hundreds of routine chores and tasks of household, office jobs, and regular life. It is in fact one of the best times for real education. By real, I mean something not learned in books. The only condition is that one be ready to accept material as it is presented day by day, event by event, and second by second. Whether we are in a car, on a train, or a bus, what our children see from the windows is constantly changing: different vegetation and crops, factories, cities, architecture, the way people dress, their activities, animals, nature, etc. So much can be noticed, marveled at, recognized, offering countless topics for intense discussion. Depending on the age of the child, a lot of learning can be done from a moving vehicle.

One of the most important items to get before leaving is a study book, preferably hardbound. In France we have found them with one page blank facing a page with lines. They are very good and most convenient, but if they're not available, then blank all the way, as lines will be done as it goes, their size depending on the age of the child and the requirements of the chosen project. Call it a diary, a journal, an art book, a book of reports, essays, stories—either true or fantasy—it will be all at once. The child will love it. He will do his best in it. He will practice a lot of skills because of it.

The toughest problem in my experience is that when one is traveling, there can be very little time to actually sit down with paper and pen. Here is a classic example of a very busy schedule. You arrive in Los Angeles at night. The first day you go to Disneyland, the second to Knott's Berry Farm, and the third to Hollywood studios. The next day you are back on the plane to some other destination. This last Thanksgiving we were with friends at Sea World, the next morning at the Wild Animal Park, and the next day was my birthday. I chose to go out with my husband and to leave my son peacefully at my friend's home to do his school work.

He made a good report of his day at the Wild Animal Park, narrating the train ride and, on the blank page, he drew the train, animals, etc. It was a choice that we had to make. Do we keep in motion or do we let him pause, allowing him time to digest the past outings and reflect on what he saw, and to give him a chance to practice his skills of writing, composing, spelling, punctuation, drawing, presentation, and the completion of a project that will make him very proud? In the afternoon he worked on his Cub Scout project, making a boat for a regatta. One of the oldest sons of our host family helped him to use different tools. He had a great day just being home.

It is not always easy to stop for a full day to accomplish some school work. Often, one has to take it half a day at a time. For example, one can start activities the next day only at 1:00 p.m., and help the child to get up early and find a peaceful spot. In a hotel room, a cousin's house or at friends', it is not always obvious, but kids can be comfortable in the smallest of corners. For these few hours, define the work and be sure it gets done without delay, because the afternoon and evening are all booked. Another option is to come back from the day's outing by 5:00 or 6:00 p.m. and right away hit the books and pens. Plane trips are a great place to study. A child can be comfortable with his little table, and get a lot of work done in transit. If your child is young and needs help with his homework, a plane gets you close with nowhere to go, without phone calls or dirty dishes.

The child "on the road" must always carry his backpack full of school projects with him, not in the hold of the plane or the trunk of the car. It also helps for a child to carry something he really likes to do with his hands, like wood carving, beading, drawing, embroidering, stamp collecting or collage making. My children have done a lot of school work in airports, stations, trains, boats, subways, national parks, beaches, hot springs, and more. We must help the student to understand that it is better for him to use the "traveling time" to perform school work and upon arrival be free to move about. There are times when your child will find it difficult to concentrate, which may be a good time for him to read a good book. You will be grateful that television won't be there to prevent it from happening, so be sure you have taken with you a good supply of these books! Many children who are not great readers will enjoy reading with a parent just because the opportunity is there. You can also buy books along the way—they may become treasured souvenirs!

When my boy was seven, he used to make a game of writing on a notepad all the strange things he could see from the car window. A lot of little projects can be accomplished while traveling, like writing to grandparents or friends along the way. Postcards (big sizes are better), on which you may draw lines, or a beautiful pad of writing paper the child will have chosen himself, or a blank piece of paper on which he can draw and write about what he has seen and experienced will all bring great results.

Another kind of project that young kids love to do is to make little books. Let's say you have been at the zoo. Then, back at what you call home, you may cut one, two or three pages of white paper in half and staple or sew them in the middle, and then let the child draw the animals, write their names and a few facts about them, what they eat, the way they walk or the way they live. If they are very young, let them cut the pictures from the leaflets that you brought back. Have them use tape or glue and crayons to decorate. You can also help them to write a few words under the pictures. The title of the book in itself can be a master project.

Kids can go home after a week, a month or six months of traveling, with a collection of these little books that they will always keep. They may bring back one on medieval castles, one on New York sky towers, one on sea shells, on kangaroos, one on the grand canyons, or one on Disneyland.

If you are visiting a foreign country, it can be a good chance to start on a foreign language. Be sure to bring with you the materials needed, head phones and tapes can be useful. The child will love new ways of expressing himself and of studying with different materials and situations.

When my daughters were nine and six, we decided to go to India, a country that we love dearly. We landed in New Delhi. On the long taxi ride afterwards, the girls were glued to their windows, their eyes bigger than a dozen encyclopedias. I had intentionally chosen the old town so we would not miss the buzz of Indian life. Later we went down in the streets looking for a restaurant. We were amazed by the hundreds of scenes so unfamiliar, so incredible. Our children felt they were walking on another planet. We passed by a stationery store and each one chose a good solid bound notebook to use as a journal. On our second day we were fortunate to join a wedding procession that was parading the streets, elephant, camels, horses, musicians, dancers. How the girls landed on the camels and rode for the next two kilometers is all told in their journals. It is also recorded how they bought bananas, papayas, and peanuts from kids younger than themselves sitting in the street with wide smiles, how the laundry man with a huge turban on his head came in the morning to ask for clothes to be washed, and how he got them clean by beating them on the rocks by the riverside, and how they loved to drink the sugarcane juice that was crushed by a huge machine operated by hand power. They did not miss a thing. They recorded every day as we moved on to different places. Even when we settled down in a large house by the sea, there was still plenty to be told.

We got organized to get back more seriously on a regular schedule. Mornings are usually best because of fresh energy and it is nice for the kids to know that they will be free after lunch. They were able to go deeper in their maths and sciences, but also they studied yoga, Indian dance, Hindi alphabet and language, they found out a lot about the sea and nature, they learned to cook an Indian meal, and make chapatis (bread), cooked directly on an open fire. They sang Indian songs, played drums, did a lot of beading, and learned embroidery with the lady next door. We were employing a tailor who taught the oldest to sew on the sewing machine.

They ran just like the neighbor kids when coconuts fell on the ground, to be the first to get them. They learned to play their games, and rode with their fathers on the buffalo carts. They drew water from the well and carried their baby brother in a cloth on their backs. I could go on and on about what they discovered, what they experienced in such a different society, and how well they blended with the full scene.

What they learned could never have fit in a classroom curriculum. They were enriched and happy. Traveling has no limits.

Seven years later, we returned to India for six months. The girls were teenagers. Their backpacks were much heavier, as we all know the weight of high school books. I had subscribed them to a serious correspondence course for high school students. It was no matter where they were, they could send their tests to their teachers, their questions if any, give a return address and receive corrections and grades. To be honest, it was not always easy to do a lot of school work. Some days so much was going on that they would have been fools to bury themselves in a biology book. If that afternoon, for example, hundreds of people wearing red robes had come to walk barefoot on the sacred fire without being burned, or if it was market day, or if they were invited to a wedding, or if the elephants were out on the street—but they learned to regulate their study time and catch up on the days when the action was slow. We all knew that to experience a different culture and different ways of life would be useful to them for many years after.

Last June my 10-year-old son and I went to Paris for a month. We cruised around the Latin quarter, the Serbonne where ancient homes with inner courtyards paved with cobblestones, and enormous wooden doors with impressive knockers made us reflect on the lives of their previous tenants, nobles, barons, princes … I was eager to show him the Cathedral. the old churches with stained glass windows, sculptures and frescoes, which told us more about history that any book would have done. We even visited the oldest house of Paris, (14th century). We took pleasure in studying the architecture of the many bridges on the Seine River. If we had more time, we would have seen more Impressionists, and back home we still enjoy looking at the books of the French painters.

I lived my first twenty years in Paris. I never had much interest in the historic and artistic value of the city. As soon as I came back with my son, I wanted him to discover and appreciate its beauty. In that process, I realized for myself, how great Paris was. Therefore, I understood that to help a child to learn something, it was best to learn it with him, and to discover it together on the same level and with the same interest. Traveling in places which are often new to everyone, will allow this to happen in a very pleasant way.

My son is now studying the Middle Ages, and drawing castles. It takes me back to ten years ago when, with his sisters we were two weeks in Germany and visited a lot of castles, with their fortresses and dungeons, and had a close view of drawbridges, moats and thick stone walls. He is fascinated with the heraldry and the suits of armor of the knights. He would not mind at all being over there right now. He would be sitting on a stone bench, and with his drawing pad in hand, have a real good look at a castle, and try to understand how it got built, and how people lived in it. We have fantastic books in this country, but there is nothing like climbing to the top of one of the castles and feel how dark it was and how cold people must have been, and estimate the amount of wood they needed for their fires.

Children are grateful for different ways of education. They respond so well to new formulas of learning and they appreciate the change and the challenge. I am never afraid or concerned about their school achievements. When I take my children on long field trips; they learn a tremendous amount.

CORRESPONDENCE SCHOOLS

OAK MEADOW SCHOOL
P.O. Box 740
Putney, Vermont 05346
Phone: (805) 646-4510
Grades K–12

CALVERT SCHOOL
Tuscany Road
Baltimore, Maryland 21210
Phone: (877) 485-8283
Grades K–8

SOURCES FOR EDUCATIONAL BOOKS & TOYS

Adventurers in Learning
Phone: (800) 874-0520

Lakeshore
Phone: (800) 428-4414

Animal Town
Phone: (800) 445-8642

Music for Little People
Phone: (800) 727-2233

Anyone Can Whistle
Phone: (800) 435-8863

Playfair Toys
Phone: (800) 824-7255

Back to Basic Toys
Phone: (800) 356-5360

The Smart Toys Catalog
Phone: (800) 238-8687

Child Craft
Phone: (800) 631-5652

Toys to Grow On
Phone: (800) 542-8338

Gryphon House Early Childhood
   Teachers Books
Phone: (800) 638-0928

Also, send for a Home Education Press catalog, at P.O. Box 1083, Tonasket, Washington 98855

LIVING HISTORY INTRODUCTION

For a new and different family trip that can be fun, educational, and very inexpensive, consider a living history vacation. A living history adventure could take you to a Civil War battle re-enactment at the original site, to America's colonial past at Williamsburg's living museum, or a weekend in costume, round-the-fire storytelling, crafts and jousting with a medieval re-creation group. The variations on this theme are endless. Through family history vacations, parents and youngsters can share in hands-on experiences that interest everybody—grandparents may want to join in the fun as well!

Picking an Historical Holiday

To choose a living history trip, first take a close look at your family's interests. Here are some ideas to get you started:

- Life at a California Mission
- Medieval Europe
- Antique Cars
- Life of the Mountain Men
- Colonial New England
- Civil War

✦ Paddlewheeling on the
  Mississippi River
✦ Barnstorming Aviators
✦ Roman Army Life

✦ The Antebellum South
✦ Traditional Native American
  Life

Start with a very specific interest and see where it leads. For example, if you all enjoy boating and get interested in old sea chanteys, you might end up on a tall ship cruise! If your favorite family hikes always seem to follow old pioneer tracks, where you talk about the pioneers who made the westward trek 150 years ago, you could find yourself building your own equipment and joining a group in Calistoga wagons following the Oregon Trail one summer! If the entire family loves the Civil War era, you might hook up with a group that recreates the battles, clothing and music of that time and find yourself residing on an old plantation for a week! Are your kids fascinated by images of knights in armor, ladies in flowing gowns and veils, and wandering minstrels? If so, the Society for Creative Anachronism awaits you. If Cheyenne blood courses through your veins, you might explore that culture as a family and end up creating authentic tools and explaining Cheyenne customs to curious tourists.

Local Living History

Living history is as close as your own backyard. Many people get involved in living history through an historic site near their home. There is a partial list of living history museums following this section. Most states include local or state history in their elementary school curriculums. When your kids are studying state or local history at school, take the opportunity to visit local historic sites as a family—it will help make history come very much alive for your children, and probably for you as well.

Local libraries are a great resource to consult when researching local history. Don't be intimidated. Ask the librarian for guidance—they're there to help you. You'll find the more research you undertake, the better you will get at it. You may find out more about the history of old buildings in your community or the events that put your local battlefield on the map. Most communities offer some kind of festival honoring its history and heritage. And don't forget to contact your local historical society, which can provide a wealth of information and enthusiastic advice.

And watch for cultural celebrations in your area. You'll probably be surprised at how much each group has contributed to the whole.

Watching Your Ps and Qs

Travel in time is as much a cross-cultural experience as travel to a foreign country. To keep you in good graces with the participants when visiting and/or joining in at an historical re-enactment, festival or site, here are a few basic rules to keep in mind:

Most historical recreationists are happy to share their knowledge and invite you into the experience, but not all events are open to the public—*always ask*. As a visitor, be certain to follow the guidelines presented to you. There may be any number of reasons for various rules—from insurance to land use laws. Please respect their wishes.

Current local laws apply whatever period and style you are re-enacting. Be sure to honor local alcohol use laws, open fire laws, weapons laws, garbage disposal laws, curfew laws, etc. When in doubt—*ask*. Remember, while you are always responsible for your own actions, broken laws can reflect on the host organization, and can cause a great deal of harm. (For instance, under-age drinking violations can close down a group.)

This entire experience is about respect. Respect for all who have come before. Respect for what has brought all of us to here and now. The living historians share their knowledge—show them the respect of listening politely, and thank them for their efforts. Make your children aware that living history participants are not being foolish or strange by dressing and speaking differently. And parents beware! Most kids are born actors and this may bring out the Sarah Bernhardt or Laurence Olivier in each of them.

Most of all, let go of the present, and have a great time learning about the past.

Genealogy

Many people get involved in living history through an interest in family history. When the genealogist in the family discovers roots in a specific locale and circumstance, it's a short stretch to going to that area and learning more about the times and places your forefathers and foremothers experienced. Whether your ancestors were fishermen in Maine, slaves in Georgia, Hopi potters, sod farmers in Nebraska, Hawaiian storytellers, Appalachian musicians or Carolina pirates, miners, canal builders or Texas vaqueros—as a family, you can explore and learn from those roots. Your family heritage may inspire you to visit the countries your ancestors called home.

GETTING BACK TO YOUR ROOTS

Do you ever wish you knew more about your family's history, but don't know where to start? Do you put the idea off, imagining long hours of futility searching through files of dusty documents in the lonely stacks of some dark, cold library? Does the fact that you can never remember the difference between a second cousin and a first cousin once removed scare you off the task? Fear no more. Genealogy, defined as the science of tracing family pedigrees or lineage, is a lot simpler than it may seem at first. With just a few tips on where to look, you can be painlessly on the road to uncovering your roots.

"There's a logical way to go about it, and once you get started, you'll be pointed to other resources," said Charlene Reese, a family history consultant for the Church of Jesus Christ of Latter-Day Saints (more commonly known as the Mormon Church) in Irvine, California. Reese has been researching her family roots for the past year, and recently came upon an ancestral string in one of the church's computerized databases linking her back to royalty in England and France.

I. "The first thing I'd tell you to do, if you're just starting, is to write all your relatives and ask them to tell you everything that they know about the family," Reese said. "Write to everyone, even if it's a distant cousin you've never met," she advised, adding that one of the most valuable resources in her own family research has been a distant cousin she discovered in her search, who shares her interest in genealogy.

And plan on being persistent. I sent out a letter to my extended family two years ago asking for family stories, and every

time I talk to a cousin, they tell me they're planning to write something down, but just haven't gotten around to it. However, the
responses I have gotten have been useful and heartfelt. Think of
your family history as a long-term, evolving process and you won't
be disappointed.

2.   Once you've collected some basic information on names and places
and dates, Reese advises, you're ready to hit the library. Not your
public library, but the genealogical library! The Mormon Church
operates genealogical libraries worldwide, which offer an amazing
collection of computerized genealogical databases, and a library of
books on genealogy. And they are open to the public for free! To
find the library closest to you, turn to your local Yellow Pages section on churches, and look for Jesus Christ of the Latter-Day
Saints. If there's no listing for a genealogical library, call the church
office and ask for their family history consultant. Call the library to
find out when a newcomer should come in—chances are they'll
want to give you an orientation. You'll see a 15-minute video, cough
up a whopping 25 cents for a booklet on the library's resources,
and be taken under the wing of a volunteer
librarian who will get you started.

   Among the resources available is a
computerized Social Security death index,
which will give you data on anybody who
died between 1963 and 1993. They also
carry Vietnamese and Korean War death
records, and an ancestral catalog called the International Genealogical Index contains completely linked pedigrees which you can
search for links to your own family names. (I spent about 45 minutes on the computer scanning through O'Reillys and Scheipers,
however, and didn't find anybody that seemed to be related to me—
it probably takes a bit more persistence than I was up for that
evening!). If you have a family tree in hand, you can also submit that
information for addition to the database with your name and
address attached. Subsequent seekers can then contact you if they
uncover a connection.

   "It's just an incredible resource," says Reese. "The libraries
usually have additional reference materials, to help you figure out
where to write to get more information, and detailed atlases where

you can find the tiniest towns. And the volunteers are there to help you with it all." And there was certainly a friendly sense of camaraderie among the researchers using the library, swapping stories about their most recent discoveries.

3. Once you've got a good start at the genealogical library, you may want to plan a trip to visit one of the six U.S. Census Bureau Archives in the country. The Archives have staff genealogists and librarians on hand to guide your search. "Start with what you know and work your way back," advises JoAnn Williamson, chief of the User Services Branch at the National Archives in Washington, DC. "Start with the 1920 census. It's completely indexed, so if you know what state they were living in, you can get to their records." "Looking in the 1870 census, I found my great grandmother and great grandfather living in a little town," Williamson cites an example from her own search. "I just happened to find, two frames down, her mother and father, and that's how I found out he was from Kentucky."

Passenger arrival lists, Immigration and Naturalization Service and customs records are available to help track your immigrant ancestors. Military service records are another source of information available at the Archives, including pension records which can help you track married children of your Civil War veteran ancestors. "The more information you have, the more successful you will be in finding something," Williamson says.

The national and regional archives conduct a comprehensive program of genealogical workshops for a nominal fee, covering topics including an introduction to genealogy and researching primary documents like census records, passenger lists, and military records. For more information or to register for workshops at the Washington, DC Archives, call the Education Branch at (202) 724-0457.

See the list at the end of this article for phone numbers to call for workshop schedules at the regional archives.

4. Online genealogy forums are another resource to help you in your search.

THE REGIONAL ARCHIVES SYSTEM

New England Region
380 Trapelo Road
Waltham, Massachusetts 02154
Phone: (781) 647-8104
Contains: Connecticut, Maine,
    Massachusetts, Rhode Island,
    Vermont

Northeast Region
201 Varick Street
New York, New York 10014
Phone: (212) 337-1300
Contains: New Jersey, New York,
    Puerto Rico, and the Virgin
    Islands

Mid-Atlantic Region
9th and Market Streets, Room 1350
Philadelphia, Pennsylvania 19107
Phone: (215) 597-3000
Contains: Delaware, Maryland,
    Pennsylvania, Virginia, West
    Virginia

Southeast Region
1557 St. Joseph Avenue
East Point, Georgia 30344
Phone: (404) 763-7477
Contains: Alabama, Florida,
    Georgia, Kentucky, Mississippi,
    North Carolina, South Carolina,
    Tennessee

Great Lakes Region
7358 South Pulaski Road
Chicago, Illinois 60629
Phone: (312) 581-7816
Contains: Illinois, Indiana,
    Michigan, Minnesota, Ohio,
    Wisconsin

Central Plains Region
2312 East Bannister Road
Kansas City, Missouri 64131
Phone: (816) 926-6272
Contains: Iowa, Kansas, Missouri,
    Nebraska

Southwest Region
501 West Felix Street
P.O. Box 6216
Fort Worth, Texas 76115
Phone: (817) 334-5525
Contains: Arkansas, Louisiana, New
    Mexico (most records from fed-
    eral agencies in New Mexico are
    at the Rocky Mountain Region
    Archives), Oklahoma, Texas

Rocky Mountain Region
Building 48
Denver Federal Center
Denver, Colorado 80225
Phone: (303) 236-0817
Contains: Colorado, Montana,
    North Dakota, South Dakota,
    Utah, Wyoming, New Mexico
    (some records in Southwest
    Region Archives)

Pacific Southwest Region
24000 Avila Road
Laguna Niguel, California 92656
Phone: (949) 643-4241
Contains: Arizona, Southern Cali-
    fornia, Clark County/Nevada

Pacific Sierra Region
1000 Commodore Drive
San Bruno, California 94066
Phone: (650) 876-9009
Contains: Northern California,
    Hawaii, Nevada except Clark
    County, the Pacific Trust Territo-
    ries, American Samoa

Pacific Northwest Region
6125 Sand Point Way NE
Seattle, Washington 98115
Phone: (206) 526-6507
Contains: Idaho, Oregon,
    Washington

Alaska Region
654 West Third Avenue
Anchorage, Alaska 99501
Phone: (907) 271-2441
Contains: Alaska

LIVING HISTORY MUSEUMS

There are many living history organizations and sites. This listing will just get you started, and you will probably want to start in your own area, if only to get a feel for how such groups and events operate. The list is alphabetical by state and within each state. You might also like to contact your state parks office. Most of the state-wide offices are listed in Chapter 5. They usually know about interpretive associations in their domain which sponsor public or private living history events. Have fun!

Constitution Hall Village
301 Madison Street
Huntsville, Alabama 35801
Phone: (800) 678-1819

Eklutna Village Historical Park
16515 Centerfield, Suite 201
Eagle River, Alaska 99501
Phone: (907) 696-2828

Native Village of Alaskaland
c/o Fairbanks Native Association
201 First Avenue, 2nd floor
Fairbanks, Alaska 99701
Phone: (907) 452-1648

Pioneer Arizona
3901 West Pioneer Road
Phoenix, Arizona 85027
Phone: (602) 465-1052

Arkansas Territorial Restoration
200 East Third Street
Little Rock, Arkansas 72201
Phone: (501) 324-9351

El Pueblo de Los Angeles Historic Monument
125 Paseo de la Plaza, Suite 400
Los Angeles, California 90012
Phone: (213) 628-3562

La Purisima Mission State Historic Park
2295 Purisima Road
Lompoc, California 93436
Phone: (805) 733-3713

Mission San Juan Capistrano
31882 Camino Capistrano, Suite 107
San Juan Capistrano, California 92675
Phone: (949) 234-1300

Bent's Old Fort National Historic Site
35110 Highway 194 East
La Junta, Colorado 8150
Phone: (719) 383-5010

Mystic Seaport and Maritime Museum
50 Greenmanville Avenue
Mystic, Connecticut 06355
Phone: (860) 572-0711

Delaware Agricultural Museum
866 North DuPont Highway
Dover, Delaware 19901
Phone: (302) 734-1618

Hagley Museum and Library
P.O. Box 3630
Wilmington, Delaware 19807
Phone: (302) 658-2400

**Historic Saint Augustine Spanish
Quarter**
P.O. Box 1987
St. Augustine, Florida 32085
Phone: (904) 825-6830

Agrirama
P.O. Box Q
Tifton, Georgia 31793
Phone: (912) 386-3344

Westville Village
P.O. Box 1850
Lumpkin, Georgia 31815
Phone: (912) 838-6310

**Pioneer Village and Idaho
Historical Museum**
610 North Julia Davis Drive
Boise, Idaho 83702
Phone: (208) 334-2120

**Lincoln's New Salem State Historic
Site**
Rural Route 1, Box 244A
Petersburg, Illinois 62675
Phone: (217) 632-4000

Conner Prairie
13400 Allisonville Road
Fishers, Indiana 46038
Phone: (317) 776-6000

Historic New Harmony
506½ Main Street
P.O. Box 579
New Harmony, Indiana 47631
Phone: (812) 682-4488

Living History Farms
2600 NW 111th Street
Urbandale, Iowa 50322
Phone: (515) 278-2400

Pella's Historical Village
507 Franklin
Pella, Iowa 50219
Phone: (614) 628-4311

Old Cowtown Museum
1871 Sim Park Drive
Wichita, Kansas 67203
Phone: (316) 264-0671

Shaker Village of Pleasant Hill
3501 Lexington Road
Harrodsburg, Kentucky 40330
Phone: (800) 734-5611

Acadian Village
200 Greenleaf Road
Lafayette, Louisiana 70506
Phone: (381) 981-2364

Vermilionville
1600 Surrey Street
P.O. Box 2266
Lafayette, Louisiana 70502
Phone: (800) 992-2968

Norlands Living History Center
290 Norlands Road
Livermore Falls, Maine 04253
Phone: (207) 897-4366

Baltimore City Life Museums
33 S. Front Street
Baltimore, Maryland 21202
Phone: (410) 396-3523

Hancock Shaker Village
P.O. Box 927
Pittsfield, Massachusetts 01202
Phone: (413) 443-0188

Historic Deerfield
P.O. Box 321
Deerfield, Massachusetts 01342
Phone: (413) 774-5581

Old Sturbridge Village
One Old Sturbridge Village Road
Sturbridge, Massachusetts 01566
Phone: (508) 347-3362

Plymouth Plantation
P.O. Box 1620
Plymouth, Massachusetts 02362
Phone: (508) 746-1622

Storrowton Village Museum
1305 Memorial Avenue
West Springfield, Massachusetts
01089
Phone: (413) 787-0136

Historic White Pine Village
1687 South Lakeshore Drive
Ludington, Michigan 49431
Phone: (213) 843-4808

Colonial Michilimackinac
P.O. Box 873
Mackinaw City, Michigan 49701
Phone: (616) 436-5563

Troy Museum and Historic Village
60 West Wattles Road
Troy, Michigan 48098
Phone: (248) 524-3570

Oliver H. Kelley Farm
15788 Kelley Farm Road
Elk River, Minnesota 55330
Phone: (763) 441-6896

Arrow Rock State Historic Site
P.O. Box 1
Arrow Rock, Missouri 65320
Phone: (660) 837-3330

Missouri Town 1855
22807 Woods Chapel Road
Blue Springs, Missouri 64015
Phone: (816) 795-8200

**Stuhr Museum of the Prairie
Pioneer**
3133 West Highway 34
Grand Island, Nebraska 68801
Phone: (308) 381-5316

Canterbury Shaker Village
288 Shaker Road
Canterbury, New Hampshire 03224
Phone: (603) 783-9511

Strawbery Banke
P.O. Box 300
Portsmouth, New Hampshire
03802
Phone: (603) 433-1100

Historic Batsto Village
Wharton State Forest Rural District
9 Batsto
Hammonton, New Jersey 08037
Phone: (609) 561-3262

The Village of Waterloo
525 Village of Waterloo
Stanhope, New Jersey 07874
Phone: (201) 347-0900

El Rancho de Las Golondrinas
Route 14, Box 214
Sante Fe, New Mexico 87505
Phone: (505) 471-2261

Museum Village
Museum Village Road
Monroe, New York 10950
Phone: (914) 782-8247

Old Bethpage Village Restoration
Nassau County Parks & Recreation
Round Swamp Road
Old Bethpage, New York 11804
Phone: (516) 572-8400

Oconaluftee Indian Village
P. O. Box 398
Cherokee, North Carolina 28719
Phone: (704) 497-2111

Old Salem Inc.
Box F, Salem Station
Winston-Salem, North Carolina
 27108
Phone: (919) 721-7300

Hale Farm & Village
P.O. Box 296
Bath, Ohio 44210
Phone: (330) 666-3711

Ohio Village
1982 Velma Avenue
Columbus, Ohio 43211
Phone: (614) 297-2300

Historic Fallsington
4 Yardley Avenue
Fallsington, Pennsylvania 19054
Phone: (215) 295-6567

Middleton Place
Ashley River Road
Charleston, South Carolina 29414
Phone: (843) 556-6020

Museum of Appalachia
P.O. Box 0318
Highway 61
Norris, Tennessee 37828
Phone: (865) 494-7680

Old City Park
1717 Gano Street
Dallas, Texas 72515
Phone: (214) 421-5141

**Ronald V. Jensen Living Historical
 Farm**
4025 South Highway 89-91
Wellsville, Utah 84339
Phone: (801) 245-4064

Shelburne Museum
Route 7, P.O. Box 10
Shelburne, Vermont 05482
Phone: (802) 985-3344

Appomattox Court House
P.O. Box 218
Appomattox, Virginia 24522
Phone: (804) 352-8987

Colonial Willamsburg Foundation
P.O. Box 1776
Willamsburg, Virginia 23187
Phone: (804) 229-1000

Jamestown Settlement
P.O. Drawer JF
Willamsburg, Virginia 23187
Phone: (804) 229-1607

Old World Wisconsin
South 103 West 37890
Highway 67
Eagle, Wisconsin 53119
Phone: (262) 594-6300

Ozaukee County Pioneer Village
P.O. Box 206
Cedarburg, Wisconsin 53012
Phone: (414) 377-4510

CHILDREN'S MUSEUMS IN THE U.S.A.

Most museums have displays and stories that can be interesting to kids of all ages, the problem often is presentation and level of discussion. Children's museums are specifically set up to relate appropriately and effectively to kids—and kids definitely appreciate that. Every child is curious, and that curiosity can turn into a powerful learning tool with the right exposure. And don't kids ask questions! Children's museums have answers!

Happily, more and more children's museums are popping up. This is a recent list that should get you started, and most of the museums know about each other and can point to you a museum or organization in your area.

Tucson Children's Museum
200 South Sixth Avenue
Tucson, Arizona 85701
Phone: (920) 884-7511

Los Angeles Children's Museum
310 North Main Street
Los Angeles, California 90012
Phone: (213) 687-8801

Children's Museum of Denver
2121 Crescent Drive
Denver, Colorado 80211
Phone: (303) 433-7444

Capital Children's Museum
800 3rd Street NE
Washington, D.C. 20002
Phone: (202) 543-8600

Miami Youth Museum
5701 Sunset Drive
Miami, Florida 33143
Phone: (305) 661-2787

Children's Museum of Tampa
7550 North Boulevard
Tampa, Florida 33604
Phone: (813) 935-8441

Chicago Children's Museum
435 East Illinois Street
Chicago, Illinois 60611
Phone: (312) 527-1000

Children's Museum of Indianapolis
3000 North Meridian Street
Indianapolis, Indiana 46208
Phone: (317) 924-5431

Children's Museum of Boston
300 Congress Street
Boston, Massachusetts 02210
Phone: (617) 426-6500

Children's Museum
1217 Bandana Boulevard North
St. Paul, Minnesota 55108
Phone: (612) 644-3818

Magic House
516 South Kirkwood Road
St. Louis, Missouri 63122
Phone: (314) 822-8900

Brooklyn Children's Museum
145 Brooklyn Avenue
Brooklyn, New York 11213
Phone: (718) 735-4400

Children's Museum of Manhattan
212 West 83rd Street
New York, New York 10025
Phone: (212) 721-1234

Discovery Place
301 North Tryon Street
Charlotte, North Carolina 28202
Phone: (704) 372-6261

Adams Corner Rural Village
Cherokee Heritage Center
Tahlequah, Oklahoma 74464
Phone: (918) 456-6007

Children's Museum
3037 Southwest Second Avenue
Portland, Oregon 97201
Phone: (503) 823-2227

Please Touch Museum
210 North 21st Street
Philadelphia, Pennsylvania 19103
Phone: (215) 963-0667

Pittsburgh Children's Museum
One Landmarks Square
Allegheny Center
Pittsburgh, Pennsylvania 15212
Phone: (412) 322-5085

Children's Museum of Houston
3201 Allen Parkway
Houston, Texas 77019
Phone: (713) 522-1138

The Children's Museum
Seattle Center
305 Harrison
Seattle, Washington 98109
Phone: (206) 441-1767

SCIENCE MUSEUMS

Science museums are for adults and for kids. Many have hands-on exhibits and usually have great kits, games and books available. This list is from the Association of Science Technology Centers (1025 Vermont Avenue, NW, Suite 500, Washington, DC 20005. Phone: (202) 783-7200). Museums are listed alphabetically by name within U.S. state or Candaian province. Learning certainly can be fun! And if you need to polish your kids' museum etiquette before a trip, visit a local science museum for some fun, painless practice. And if you just can't get your kids to sit still for a trip to a museum, how about a space museum? These aren't video games—this is the real stuff!

The Imaginarium: A Science Discovery Center
725 West Fifth Avenue
Anchorage, Alaska 99501
Phone: (907) 258-6312

Alabama Museum of Natural History
P.O. Box 870340
Tuscaloosa, Alabama 35487
Phone: (205) 348-7550

Anniston Museum of Natural History
P.O. Box 1587
Anniston, Alabama 36202
Phone: (205) 237-6766

Center for Cultural Arts
P.O. Box 1507
Gadsden, Alabama 35902
Phone: (256) 543-2787

Discovery 2000
1421 22nd Street South
Birmingham, Alabama 35205
Phone: (205) 933-4142

The Exploreum Museum of Discovery
1906 Springhill Avenue
Mobile, Alabama 36607
Phone: (205) 471-5923

Southern Museum of Flight
4343 - 73rd Street North
Birmingham, Alabama 35206
Phone: (205) 833-8226

U.S. Space and Rocket Center
P.O. Box 070015
Huntsville, Alabama 35807
Phone: (256) 837-3400

Arkansas Museum of Science & History
MacArthur Park
Little Rock, Arkansas 72202
Phone: (501) 324-9231

Mid-America Museum
500 Mid-America Boulevard
Hot Springs, Arkansas 71913
Phone: (501) 767-3461

Arizona Museum of Science & Technology
147 East Adams Street
Phoenix, Arizona 85004-2331
Phone: (602) 258-7250

Flandrau Science Center & Planetarium
Planetarium Building 91
University of Arizona
Tucson, Arizona 85721
Phone: (520) 621-4515

Kitt Peak Museum
P.O. Box 26732
Tucson, Arizona 85726-6732
Phone: (520) 322-3426

Bay Area Discovery Museum
557 East Fort Baker
Sausalito, California 94965
Phone: (415) 289-7273

California Academy of Sciences
Golden Gate Park
San Francisco, California 94118
Phone: (415) 221-5100

California Museum of Science and Industry
700 State Drive
Los Angeles, California 90037
Phone: (213) 744-7483

Carter House Natural Science Center
P.O. Box 990185
Redding, California 96099
Phone: (530) 225-4125

Children's Discovery Museum of San Jose
180 Woz Way
San Jose, California 95110
Phone: (408) 298-5437

Discovery Science Center— Launch Pad
201 East Sandpointe, Suite 320
Santa Ana, California 92707
Phone: (714) 540-0404

EXPLORIT! Science Center
P.O. Box 1288
Davis, California 95617
Phone: (916) 756-0191

The Exploratorium
3601 Lyon Street
San Francisco, California 94123
Phone: (415) 563-7337

Fresno Metropolitan Museum
1515 Van Ness Avenue
Fresno, California 93721
Phone: (209) 441-1444

Hall of Health
2065 Kittredge Street, Suite F
Berkeley, California 94704
Phone: (510) 549-1564

Lawrence Hall of Science
University of California, Centennial Drive
Berkeley, California 94720
Phone: (510) 642-4193

Lawrence Livermore National Laboratory
Visitors Center
P.O. Box 808, L-790
Livermore, California 94550
Phone: (925) 422-9797

The Lindsay Museum
1931 First Avenue
Walnut Creek, California 95496
Phone: (925) 935-1978

Monterey Bay Aquarium
886 Cannery Row
Monterey, California 93940
Phone: (408) 648-4802

Museum of History, Technology & Science
101 I Street
Sacramento, California 95814
Phone: (916) 277-6183

Natural History Museum of Los Angeles County
900 Exposition Boulevard
Los Angeles, California 90007
Phone: (213) 744-3543

The Oakland Museum
1000 Oak Street
Oakland, California 94607
Phone: (510) 238-3402

Rancho Santa Ana Botanic Garden
1500 North College Avenue
Claremont, California 91711
Phone: (909) 625-8767

Reuben H. Fleet Space Theater & Science Center
P.O. Box 33303
San Diego, California 92163
Phone: (619) 238-1233

San Francisco Bay Model Visitor Center
2100 Bridgeway
Sausalito, California 94965
Phone: (415) 332-3871

The San Francisco Zoological Society
Education Department
1 Zoo Road
San Francisco, California 94132
Phone: (415) 753-7073

Santa Barbara Botanic Garden
1212 Mission Canyon Road
Santa Barbara, California 93105
Phone: (805) 682-4726

Santa Barbara Museum of Natural History
2559 Puesta del Sol Road
Santa Barbara, California 93105
Phone: (805) 682-4711

The Tech Museum of Innovation
145 West San Carlos Street
San Jose, California 95113
Phone: (408) 279-7150

Children's Museum of Denver
2121 Children's Museum Drive
Denver, Colorado 80211
Phone: (303) 433-7444

Denver Museum of Natural History
2001 Colorado Boulevard
Denver, Colorado 80205
Phone: (303) 322-7009

Discovery Center Science Museum
703 East Prospect Road
Fort Collins, Colorado 80525
Phone: (970) 493-2182

National Center for Atmospheric Research
P.O. Box 3000
Boulder, Colorado 80307
Phone: (303) 497-8600

Discovery Museum
4450 Park Avenue
Bridgeport, Connecticut 06604
Phone: (203) 372-3521

The Maritime Center at Norwalk
10 North Water Street
Norwalk, Connecticut 06854
Phone: (203) 852-0700

Mystic Marinelife Aquarium
55 Coogan Boulevard
Mystic, Connecticut 06355
Phone: (203) 572-5955

Science Center of Connecticut
950 Trout Brook Drive
West Hartford, Connecticut 06119
Phone: (203) 231-2824

Explorers Hall
National Geographic Society
1145 - 17th Street, NW
Washington, D.C. 20036
Phone: (202) 857-7455

National Air and Space Museum
6th and Independence Avenue, SW
Washington, D.C. 20560
Phone: (202) 357-2700

National Museum of American History
14th Street and Constitution Avenue, NW
Washington, D.C. 20560
Phone: (202) 357-2510

National Museum of Natural History
Department of Public Programs
10th Street & Constitution Avenue, NW
Washington, D.C. 20560
Phone: (202) 786-2604

National Zoological Park
Smithsonian Institution
3000 Block of Connecticut Avenue, NW
Washington, D.C. 20008
Phone: (202) 673-4721

Hagley Museum & Library
P.O. Box 3630
Wilmington, Delaware 19807
Phone: (302) 658-2400

The Children's Science Center
P.O. Box 151381
Cape Coral, Florida 33915
Phone: (813) 772-4466

Children's Science Explorium
131 SE Mizner Boulevard, Suite 15
Royal Palm Plaza
Boca Raton, Florida 33432
Phone: (407) 395-8401

Discovery Science Center
50 South Magnolia Avenue
Ocala, Florida 34474
Phone: (904) 620-2555

Fairchild Tropical Garden
10901 Old Cutler Road
Miami, Florida 33156
Phone: (305) 667-1651

Great Explorations, The Hands-On Museum
1120 Fourth Street South
St. Petersburg, Florida 33701
Phone: (813) 821-8992

Gulf Coast World of Science
717 North Tamiami Trail
Sarasota, Florida 34236
Phone: (813) 957-4969

The Imaginarium Hands-On Museum & Aquarium
P.O. Box 2217
Fort Myers, Florida 33902
Phone: (813) 332-6666

Kennedy Space Center
Visitor Center
Kennedy Space Center, Florida
Phone: (407) 452-2121

Miami Museum of Science & Space Transit Planetarium
3280 South Miami Avenue
Miami, Florida 33129
Phone: (305) 854-4247

Museum of Discovery and Science
401 SW Second Street
Ft. Lauderdale, Florida 33312
Phone: (305) 467-6637

Museum of Science & Industry
4801 East Fowler Avenue
Tampa, Florida 33617
Phone: (813) 987-6300

Museum of Science and History of Jacksonville
1025 Museum Circle
Jacksonville, Florida 32207
Phone: (904) 396-7062

Odyssey Science Center
P.O. Box 13355
Tallahassee, Florida 32317
Phone: (850) 576-6520

Orlando Science Center
810 East Rollins Street
Orlando, Florida 32803
Phone: (407) 896-7151

South Florida Science Museum
4801 Dreher Trail North
West Palm Beach, Florida 33405
Phone: (561) 832-1988

Fernbank Science Center
Fernbank Museum of Natural History
156 Heaton Park Drive NE
Atlanta, Georgia 30307
Phone: (404) 378-4311

Georgia Southern University Museum
Rosenwald Building Landrum
Box 8061
Statesboro, Georgia 30460
Phone: (912) 681-5444

The Museum of Arts & Sciences
4182 Forsyth Road
Macon, Georgia 31210
Phone: (912) 477-3232

Savannah Science Museum
4405 Paulsen Street
Savannah, Georgia 31405
Phone: (912) 355-6705

SciTrek – The Science and
  Technology Museum of Atlanta
395 Piedmont Avenue, NE
Atlanta, Georgia 30308
Phone: (404) 577-7351

Astronaut Ellison S. Onizuka
  Space Center
P.O. Box 833
Kailua-Kona, Hawaii 96745
Phone: (808) 329-3441

Bishop Museum
P.O. Box 19000-A
Honolulu, Hawaii 96817
Phone: (808) 847-3511

The Children's Museum
533 - 16th Street
Bettendorf, Iowa 52722
Phone: (319) 344-4106

Grout Museums: Bluedorn Science
  Imaginarium
503 South Street
Waterloo, Iowa 50701
Phone: (319) 234-6357

Science Center of Iowa
4500 Grand Avenue
Des Moines, Iowa 50312
Phone: (515) 274-6868

Science Station
427 First Street, SE
Cedar Rapids, Iowa 52401
Phone: (319) 366-0968

The Discovery Center of Idaho
P.O. Box 192
Boise, Idaho 83701
Phone: (208) 343-9895

The Adler Planetarium
1300 South Lake Shore Drive
Chicago, Illinois 60605
Phone: (312) 922-7827

Chicago Academy of Sciences
2001 North Clark Street
Chicago, Illinois 60614
Phone: (312) 549-0607

Chicago Botanic Garden
P.O. Box 400
Glencoe, Illinois 60022
Phone: (708) 835-8225

Chicago Children's Museum
435 E. Illinois Street, Suite 352
Chicago, Illinois 60611
Phone: (312) 527-1000

Discovery Center Museum
711 North Main Street
Rockford, Illinois 61103
Phone: (815) 963-6769

Fermi National Accelator
  Laboratory
Lederman Science Center
P.O. Box 500, MS 777
Batavia, Illinois 60510
Phone: (708) 840-3092

International Museum of Surgical
  Science
1524 North Lake Shore Drive
Chicago, Illinois 60610
Phone: (312) 642-6502

John R. & Eleanor R. Mitchell
  Foundation
P.O. Box 923
Mt. Vernon, Illinois 62864
Phone: (618) 242-1236

Lakeview Museum of Arts and Sciences
1125 West Lake Avenue
Peoria, Illinois 61614
Phone: (309) 686-7000

Museum of Science and Industry
57th Street and Lake Shore Drive
Chicago, Illinois 60637
Phone: (312) 684-1414

SciTech – Science and Technology Interactive Center
18 West Benton
Aurora, Illinois 60506
Phone: (708) 859-8235

The Science Center
P.O. Box 4041
Carbondale, Illinois 62903
Phone: (618) 529-5431

Children's Museum of Indianapolis
P.O. Box 3000
Indianapolis, Indiana 46206
Phone: (317) 924-5431

Children's Science & Technology Museum of Terre Haute
523 Wabash Avenue
Terre Haute, Indiana 47802
Phone: (812) 235-5548

Evansville Museum of Arts and Science
411 SE Riverside Drive
Evansville, Indiana 47713
Phone: (812) 425-2406

Muncie Children's Museum
P.O. Box 544
Muncie, Indiana 47308
Phone: (317) 286-1660

Children's Museum of Wichita Science Center
209 East William, Suite 500A
Wichita, Kansas 67202
Phone: (316) 267-2281

Kansas Cosmo-sphere & Space Center
Hutchinson, Kansas
Phone: (800) 397-0330

Dane G. Hansen Museum
1001 West Main
P.O. Box 187
Logan, Kansas 67646
Phone: (913) 689-4846

KU Natural History Museum
The University of Kansas
602 Dyche Hall
Lawrence, Kansas 66045
Phone: (786) 864-4540

Louisville Science Center
727 West Main Street
Louisville, Kentucky 40202
Phone: (502) 561-6103

Audubon Institute
P.O. Box 4327
New Orleans, Louisiana 70178
Phone: (504) 861-2537

LSU Museum of Natural Science Louisiana State University
119 Foster Hall
Baton Rouge, Louisiana 70803
Phone: (336) 388-2855

Lafayette Natural History Museum & Planetarium
637 Girard Park Drive
Lafayette, Louisiana 70503
Phone: (318) 268-5544

Louisiana Arts and Science Center
P.O. Box 3373
Baton Rouge, Louisiana 70821
Phone: (225) 344-5272

Louisiana Children's Museum
420 Julia Street
New Orleans, Louisiana 70130
Phone: (504) 586-0725

Sci-Port Discovery Center
101 Milam Street
Shreveport, Louisiana 71101
Phone: (318) 424-3466

Children's Museum
Museum Wharf
300 Congress Street
Boston, Massachusetts 02210
Phone: (617) 426-6500

Computer Museum
300 Congress Street
Boston, Massachusetts 02210
Phone: (617) 426-2800

The Discovery Museums
177 Main Street
Acton, Massachusetts 01720
Phone: (508) 264-4201

Museum of Science
Science Park
Boston, Massachusetts 02114
Phone: (617) 589-0100

National Plastics Center and Museum
P.O. Box 639
Leominster, Massachusetts 01453
Phone: (508) 534-4961

New England Aquarium
Central Wharf
Boston, Massachusetts 02110
Phone: (617) 973-5220

New England Science Center
222 Harrington Way
Worcester, Massachusetts 01604
Phone: (508) 791-9211

Springfield Science Museum
236 State Street
Springfield, Massachusetts 01103
Phone: (413) 733-1194

Woods Hole Oceanographic Institution
Co-Op Building
Woods Hole, Massachusetts 02543
Phone: (508) 457-2000

Maryland Science Center
601 Light Street
Baltimore, Maryland 21230
Phone: (410) 685-2370

National Aquarium in Baltimore
501 East Pratt Street, Pier 3
Baltimore, Maryland 21202
Phone: (410) 576-3821

The Children's Museum of Maine
P.O. Box 4041
Portland, Maine 04101
Phone: (207) 828-1234

Alfred P. Sloan Museum
1221 East Kearsley Street
Flint, Michigan 48503
Phone: (313) 760-1169

Ann Arbor Hands-On Museum
219 East Huron Street
Ann Arbor, Michigan 48104
Phone: (734) 995-5439

Cranbrook Institute of Science
P.O. Box 801
Bloomfield Hills, Michigan 48303
Phone: (313) 645-3230

Detroit Science Center
5020 John R. Street
Detroit, Michigan 48202
Phone: (313) 577-8400

Flint Children's Museum
1602 West Third
Flint, Michigan 48504
Phone: (810) 767-5437

Hall of Ideas
Midland Center for the Arts
1801 West St. Andrews Road
Midland, Michigan 48640
Phone: (517) 631-5930

Henry Ford Museum & Greenfield Village
P.O. Box 1970
Dearborn, Michigan 48121
Phone: (313) 271-1620

Impression 5 Science Museum
200 Museum Drive
Lansing, Michigan 48933
Phone: (517) 485-8116

Kalamazoo Public Museum
315 South Rose Street
Kalamazoo, Michigan 49007
Phone: (616) 345-7092

Kingman Museum of Natural History
175 Limit Street
Battle Creek, Michigan 49017
Phone: (616) 965-5117

Southwestern Michigan College Museum
58900 Cherry Grove Road
Dowagiac, Michigan 49047
Phone: (616) 782-7800

The Bakken: A Library and Museum of Electricity in Life
3537 Zenith Avenue South
Minneapolis, Minnesota 55416
Phone: (612) 927-6508

Headwaters Science Center
P.O. Box 1176
Bemidji, Minnesota 56601
Phone: (218) 751-1110

James Ford Bell Museum of Natural History
University of Minnesota
10 Church Street, SE
Minneapolis, Minnesota 55455
Phone: (612) 624-4112

Minnesota Children's Museum
1217 Bandana Boulevard, North
St. Paul, Minnesota 55108
Phone: (612) 644-5305

Science Museum of Minnesota
30 East 10th Street
St. Paul, Minnesota 55101
Phone: (612) 221-9488

Discovery Center of Springfield
P.O. Box 50162
Springfield, Missouri 65805
Phone: (417) 862-9910

Kansas City Museum
3218 Gladstone Boulevard
Kansas City, Missouri 64123
Phone: (816) 483-8300

The Magic House
St. Louis Children's Museum
516 South Kirkwood Road
St. Louis, Missouri 63122
Phone: (314) 822-8905

Missouri Botanical Garden
P.O. Box 299
St. Louis, Missouri 63166
Phone: (314) 577-5100

Saint Louis Zoo
Forest Park
St. Louis, Missouri 63110
Phone: (314) 781-0900

St. Louis Science Center
5050 Oakland Avenue
St. Louis, Missouri 63110
Phone: (314) 289-4400

Mississippi Museum of Natural Science
111 North Jefferson Street
Jackson, Mississippi 39202
Phone: (601) 354-7303

Museum of the Rockies
Montana State University
Bozeman, Montana 59717
Phone: (406) 994-5283

Edgerton Educational Center
c/o Hamilton Telephone Co.
1001 - 12th Street
Aurora, Nebraska 68818
Phone: (402) 694-5101

Hastings Museum
1330 North Burlington Avenue
P.O. Box 1286
Hastings, Nebraska 68902
Phone: (402) 461-2399

Omaha Children's Museum
500 South 20th Street
Omaha, Nebraska 68102-2508
402) 342-6164

University of Nebraska State Museum
307 Morrill Hall
Lincoln, Nebraska 68588-0332
Phone: (402) 472-3779

Western Heritage Museum
801 South 10th Street
Omaha, Nebraska 68108
Phone: (402) 444-5071

Lied Discovery Children's Museum
833 Las Vegas Boulevard North
Las Vegas, Nevada 89101
Phone: (702) 382-3445

Washoe County Parks and Recreation Department
1502 Washington Street
Reno, Nevada 89503
Phone: (702) 785-5961

Science Enrichment Encounters
324 Commercial Street
Manchester, New Hampshire 03101
Phone: (603) 669-0400

Liberty Science Center
251 Phillip Street
Jersey City, New Jersey 07305
Phone: (201) 451-0006

New Jersey State Aquarium at Camden
1 Riverside Drive
Camden, New Jersey 08103
Phone: (609) 365-3300

The Newark Museum
P.O. Box 540
Newark, New Jersey 07101
Phone: (201) 596-6550

Bradbury Science Museum
Los Alamos National Laboratory
P.O. Box 1633, M/S C330
Los Alamos, New Mexico 87545
Phone: (505) 667-4444

Explora! Science Center
40 First Plaza, Galleria, Suite 68
Albuquerque, New Mexico 87102
Phone: (505) 842-6188

Las Cruces Museum of Natural History
Mesilla Valley Mall
700 Telshor Boulevard
Las Cruces, New Mexico 88001
Phone: (505) 522-3120

New Mexico Museum of Natural History & Science
P.O. Box 7010
Albuquerque, New Mexico 87104
Phone: (505) 841-8837

Space Center
P.O. Box 533
Alamogordo, New Mexico 88310
Phone: (800) 545-4021

American Museum of Natural History
Central Park West at 79th Street
New York, New York 10024
Phone: (212) 769-5000

BNL Science Museum
Brookhaven National Laboratory
Building 184B
Upton, New York 11973
Phone: (516) 282-4049

Brooklyn Botanic Garden
1000 Washington Avenue
Brooklyn, New York 11225
Phone: (718) 941-4044

The Brooklyn Children's Museum
145 Brooklyn Avenue
Brooklyn, New York 11213
Phone: (718) 735-4400

Buffalo Museum of Science & Tifft Nature Preserve
1020 Humboldt Parkway
Buffalo, New York 14211
Phone: (716) 896-5200

DNA Learning Center
1 Bungtown Road
Cold Spring Harbor
New York 11724
Phone: (516) 367-7240

Hudson River Museum of Westchester
511 Warburton Avenue
Yonkers, New York 10701
Phone: (914) 963-4550

Museum of Science & Technology
500 South Franklin
Syracuse, New York 13202
Phone: (315) 425-9068

New York Botanical Garden
200th Street and Southern Blvd.
Bronx, New York 10458
Phone: (212) 220-8700

New York Hall of Science
47-01 111th Street
Flushing Meadows
Corona Park, New York 11368
Phone: (718) 699-0005

New York State Museum
Room 9B52, CEC
Albany, New York 12230
Phone: (518) 474-5877

New York Transit Museum
130 Livingston Street, Room 9001
Brooklyn, New York 11201
Phone: (718) 694-5102

Paleontological Research Institution
1259 Trumansburg Road
Ithaca, New York 14850
Phone: (607) 273-6623

Roberson Museum & Science Center
30 Front Street
Binghamton, New York 13905
Phone: (607) 772-0660

Rochester Museum & Science Center
P.O. Box 1480
Rochester, New York 14603
Phone: (716) 271-4552

Schenectady Museum and Planetarium
Nott Terrace Heights
Schenectady, New York 12308
Phone: (518) 382-7890

Science Discovery Center of Oneonta
State University College, PS-B-11
Oneonta, New York 13820
Phone: (607) 436-2011

Science Museum
Shoreham-Wading River Schools
Route 25A
Shoreham, New York 11786
Phone: (516) 821-8155

Sciencenter
601 First Street
Ithaca, New York 14850
Phone: (607) 272-0600

Staten Island Children's Museum
1000 Richmond Terrace
Staten Island, New York 10301
Phone: (718) 273-2060

Arts & Science Center
1335 Museum Road
Statesville, N. Carolina 28677
Phone: (704) 873-4734

Catawba Science Center
P.O. Box 2431
Hickory, North Carolina 28603
Phone: (704) 322-8169

The Discovery Place
301 North Tryon Street
Charlotte, North Carolina 28202
Phone: (704) 372-6261

Harris Visitors Center
c/o Carolina Power & Light
Route 1, Box 327
New Hill, North Carolina 27562
Phone: (919) 362-3263

Health Adventure
P.O. Box 180
Asheville, North Carolina 28802
Phone: (704) 254-6373

Imagination Station Science Museum
P.O. Box 2127
Wilson, North Carolina 27893
Phone: (252) 291-5113

The Natural Science Center of Greensboro
4301 Lawndale Drive
Greensboro, North Carolina 27408
Phone: (919) 288-3769

North Carolina Museum of Life & Science
P.O. Box 15190
Durham, North Carolina 27704
Phone: (919) 220-5429

North Carolina State Museum of Natural Sciences
P.O. Box 27647
Raleigh, North Carolina 27611
Phone: (919) 733-7450

Rocky Mount Children's Museum
1610 Gay Street
Rocky Mount, North Carolina
27804
Phone: (252) 972-1168

Schiele Museum of Natural History and Planetarium
P.O. Box 953
Gastonia, North Carolina 28054
Phone: (704) 866-6900

SciWorks
The Science Center &
Environmental Park
400 Hanes Mill Road
Winston-Salem, North Carolina
27105
Phone: (336) 767-6730

COSI: Ohio's Center of Science and Industry
280 East Broad Street
Columbus, Ohio 43215
Phone: (614) 228-2674

Cincinnati Museum of Natural History
1301 Western Avenue
Cincinnati, Ohio 45203
Phone: (513) 287-7020

Cleveland Children's Museum
10730 Euclid Avenue
Cleveland, Ohio 44106
Phone: (216) 791-7114

The Dayton Museum of Natural History
2600 DeWeese Parkway
Dayton, Ohio 45414
Phone: (513) 275-7431

The Health Museum
8911 Euclid Avenue
Cleveland, Ohio 44106
Phone: (216) 231-5010

McKinley Museum of History, Science & Industry
800 McKinley Monument Drive,
NW
Canton, Ohio 44708
Phone: (330) 455-7043

Neil Armstrong Air & Space Museum
Wapakoneta, Ohio
Phone: (419) 738-8811

SciMaTec: The University of Toledo
2801 West Bancroft Street
Toledo, Ohio 43606
Phone: (419) 537-3915

Omniplex Science Museum
2100 NE 52nd Street
Oklahoma City, Oklahoma 73111
Phone: (405) 424-5545

The High Desert Museum
59800 South Highway 97
Bend, Oregon 97702
Phone: (503) 382-4754

Oregon Museum of Science and Industry
1945 SE Water Avenue
Portland, Oregon 97214
Phone: (503) 797-4000

WISTEC, Willamette Science & Technology Center
P.O. Box 1518
Eugene, Oregon 97440
Phone: (503) 687-3619

Academy of Natural Sciences
1900 Benjamin Franklin Parkway
Philadelphia, Pennsylvania 19103
Phone: (215) 299-1000

The Carnegie Science Center
One Allegheny Avenue
Pittsburgh, Pennsylvania 15212
Phone: (412) 237-3434

Franklin Institute Science Museum
222 North 20th Street
Philadelphia, Pennsylvania 19103
Phone: (215) 448-1146

Museum of Scientific Discovery
P.O. Box 934
Harrisburg, Pennsylvania 17108
Phone: (717) 233-7969

Philadelphia Zoo
3400 West Girard Avenue
Philadelphia, Pennsylvania 19104
Phone: (215) 243-1100

The Pittsburgh Children's Museum
10 Children's Way
Pittsburgh, Pennsylvania 15212
Phone: (412) 322-5059

Please Touch Museum
210 North 21st Street
Philadelphia, Pennsylvania 19103
Phone: (215) 963-0667

Reading Public Museum and Art Gallery
500 Museum Road
Reading, Pennsylvania 19611
Phone: (610) 371-5838

Roger Williams Park Zoo
1000 Elmwood Avenue
Providence, Rhode Island 02905
Phone: (401) 785-3510

Thames Science Center
77 Long Wharf
Newport, Rhode Island 02840
Phone: (401) 849-6966

Roper Mountain Science Center
504 Roper Mountain Road
Greenville, South Carolina 29615
Phone: (803) 281-1188

South Carolina State Museum
P.O. Box 100107
Columbia, South Carolina 29202
Phone: (803) 737-4921

National Motorcycle Museum
c/o Meade School District 46-1
1230 Douglas
Sturgis, South Dakota 57785
Phone: (605) 347-6544

Siouxland Heritage Museums
200 West Sixth Street
Sioux Falls, South Dakota 57102
Phone: (605) 335-4210

South Dakota Discovery Center & Aquarium
P.O. Box 1054
Pierre, South Dakota 57501
Phone: (605) 224-8295

American Museum of Science & Energy
300 South Tulane Avenue
Oak Ridge, Tennessee 37830
Phone: (615) 576-3200

The Children's Museum of
Memphis
2525 Central Avenue
Memphis, Tennessee 38117
Phone: (901) 458-2678

Cumberland Science Museum
800 Ft. Negley Boulevard
Nashville, Tennessee 37203
Phone: (615) 862-5160

East Tennessee Discovery Center
P.O. Box 6204
Knoxville, Tennessee 37914
Phone: (615) 637-1192

Hands On! Regional Museum
315 East Main Street
Johnson City, Tennessee 37601
Phone: (615) 928-6508

Memphis Pink Palace Museum and
Planetarium
3050 Central Avenue
Memphis, Tennessee 38111
Phone: (901) 320-6369

Austin Children's Museum
1501 West Fifth Street
Austin, Texas 78703
Phone: (512) 472-2499

Children's Museum of Houston
1500 Binz
Houston, Texas 77004
Phone: (713) 522-1138

Dallas Museum of Natural History
P.O. Box 150433
Fair Park Station
Dallas, Texas 75315
Phone: (214) 670-8457

Don Harrington Discovery Center
1200 Streit Drive
Amarillo, Texas 79106
Phone: (806) 355-9547

Fort Worth Museum of Science &
History
1501 Montgomery Street
Fort Worth, Texas 76107
Phone: (817) 732-1631

Houston Museum of Natural
Science
One Hermann Circle Drive
Houston, Texas 77030
Phone: (713) 639-4600

McAllen International Museum
1900 Nolana
McAllen, Texas 78504
Phone: (210) 682-1564

McDonald Observatory
University of Texas
RLM 15.308
Austin, Texas 78712
Phone: (512) 471-5285

Science Land of Denton
P.O. Box 1338
Denton, Texas 76202
Phone: (817) 383-8686

The Science Place
P.O. Box 151469
Dallas, Texas 75315
Phone: (214) 428-7200

Science Spectrum
P.O. Box 93178
Lubbock, Texas 79493
Phone: (806) 745-6200

Space Center Houston
P.O. Box 580653
Houston, Texas 77258
Phone: (800) 972-0369

**Wichita Falls Museum and Art
Center**
2 Eureka Circle
Wichita Falls, Texas 76308
Phone: (817) 692-0923

Witte Museum
3801 Broadway
San Antonio, Texas 78209
Phone: (210) 820-2150

Hansen Planetarium
15 South State Street
Salt Lake City, Utah 84111
Phone: (801) 531-4940

Utah Museum of Natural History
University of Utah
Salt Lake City, Utah 84112
Phone: (801) 581-6927

**Nauticus: The National Maritime
Center Authority**
232 East Main Street
Norfolk, Virginia 23510
Phone: (804) 664-1000

Science Museum of Virginia
2500 West Broad Street
Richmond, Virginia 23220
Phone: (804) 367-1013

**Science Museum of Western
Virginia**
One Market Square
Roanoke, Virginia 24011
Phone: (703) 342-5710

Virginia Air and Space Center
600 Settlers Landing Road
Hampton, Virginia 23669
Phone: (804) 727-0900

Virginia Discovery Museum
P.O. Box 1128
Charlottesville, Virginia 22902
Phone: (804) 977-1025

Virginia Living Museum
524 J. Clyde Morris Boulevard
Newport News, Virginia 23601
Phone: (804) 595-1900

**Virginia Museum of Natural
History**
1001 Douglas Avenue
Martinsville, Virginia 24112
Phone: (703) 666-8600

Montshire Museum of Science
P.O. Box 770, Montshire Road
Norwich, Vermont 05055
Phone: (802) 649-2200

**Hanford Museums of Science &
History**
P.O. Box 1970 A1-60
Richland, Washington 99352
Phone: (509) 376-6374

**Marine Science Society of the
Pacific Northwest**
P.O. Box 2079
Poulsbo, Washington 98370
Phone: (206) 779-5549

Museum of Flight
9404 East Marginal Way South
Seattle, Washington 98108
Phone: (206) 764-5700

Pacific Science Center
200 Second Avenue North
Seattle, Washington 98109
Phone: (206) 443-2001

Discovery World Museum of Science, Economics & Technology
818 West Wisconsin Avenue
Milwaukee, Wisconsin 53233
Phone: (414) 765-9966

Milwaukee Public Museum
800 West Wells Street
Milwaukee, Wisconsin 53233
Phone: (414) 278-2700

Carnegie Hall
105 Church Street
Lewisburg, West Virginia 24901
Phone: (304) 645-7917

Sunrise Museums
746 Myrtle Road
Charleston, West Virginia 25314
Phone: (304) 344-8035

Saskatchewan Science Centre
P.O. Box 5071
Regina, Saskatchewan S4P 3M3
CANADA
Phone: (306) 791-7900

Science World British Columbia
1455 Quebec Street
Vancouver, British Columbia V6A 3Z7
CANADA
Phone: (604) 443-7440

Alberta Science Centre
P.O. Box 2100
Station M
Calgary, Alberta T2P 2M5
CANADA
Phone: (403) 221-3700

Edmonton Space & Science Center
11211 - 142nd Street
Edmonton, Alberta T5M 4A1
CANADA
Phone: (403) 452-9100

Discovery Centre
5201 Duke Street
Halifax, Nova Scotia B3J 1N9
CANADA
Phone: (902) 492-4422

Canadian Museum of Nature
P.O. Box 3443
Station D
Ottawa, Ontario K1P 6P4
CANADA
Phone: (613) 996-9281

National Museum of Science & Technology
P.O. Box 9724
Ottawa Terminal
Ottawa, Ontario K1G 5A3
CANADA
Phone: (613) 991-3044

Ontario Science Centre
770 Don Mills Road
Toronto, Ontario M3C 1T3
CANADA
Phone: (416) 429-4100

Science North
100 Ramsey Lake Road
Sudbury, Ontario P3E 5S9
CANADA
Phone: (705) 522-3701

National Postal Museum
Canadian Museum of Civilization
100 Laurier Street
Hull, Quebec J8X 4H2
CANADA
Phone: (819) 776-8200

Societe des Musees de Sciences
     Naturelles
4777 Pierre-de-Coubertin
Montreal, Quebec H1V 1B3
CANADA
Phone: (514) 868-3051

Denver's new International Airport sports a hands-on science museum for children.

Honolulu International Airport houses the Pacific Aerospace Museum, a $3.5 million facility complete with a diorama, 3-D theater, and a cockpit simulator where visitors can "fly" while waiting for their own takeoff.

REGIONAL DESTINATIONS—U.S.A.

• •

The United States of America is large—spreading across a continent and from the tropics to the tundra. While all of the accommodations listings in other sections of this book are alphabetical by state, here we discuss the country in geographical sections. These sections are arbitrary—other sources may draw different lines.

First, gather information. Unless you know exactly where you want to go, take this opportunity to find about areas you *might* want to go. This is a great exercise for the kids in information gathering. Many states and cities now have sites in the electronic media; there are books in libraries and stores on areas, states and locations; or, you can begin with the state offices whose purpose is to inform you and lure you to visit them. Don't forget travel agencies, AMTRAK, newspapers and magazines, and what friends and acquaintances can tell you about places you may have never even heard of.

Next, expect an onslaught of wonderful and enticing stuff. Keep an eye open for deals, but be sure you want to be in the desert in August when you grab for that super deluxe package. Some travelers really do find the planning as enjoyable as the trip itself.

Finally, if you're driving, take more safety precautions before you leave than you think you will ever need. Having the car break down, not having a copy of your insurance, needing tire chains when you're half up a mountain, not having enough medicine, finding you don't have a spare tire ... most of these problems can be avoided ahead of time. Above all, everyone needs a seat belt, keep extra water and a blanket in the car, and you need to know the laws where you are going. The surprises you meet on the road should all be pleasant ones!

• •

NEW ENGLAND ⪍ CONNECTICUT, MAINE, MASSACHUSETTS, NEW HAMPSHIRE, RHODE ISLAND, VERMONT ⪎

Southern New England doesn't cover a lot of acreage, but it houses quite a bit of the history of the United States of America. The amount of thought, discussion and effort that went into the formation of this nation is often forgotten or taken for granted by today's residents. It was actually a relatively small number of extremely dedicated people that forced the United States into existence. Many reminder landmarks can be visited today. Of course, this is only three states of the original 13 colonies. Each area contributed views, effort and lives.

A great family driving jaunt might be up (or down) the coast of Connecticut, Rhode Island and Massachusetts. A leisurely two days with a couple stops at inns or campgrounds introduces you to the region. You'll certainly recognize the names Cape Cod, Martha's Vineyard and Nantucket along the way. Once the haunts of fisher-folk, now the mon-ied elite make these islands, bays and beach heads their homes.

The major city center is Boston, often compared to its younger sib-ling San Francisco. Cosmopolitan, diverse and with something for every-one—even basketball fans.

New England is home to many fine colleges and universities and if the family wants to go en masse to check out the campuses, plan on turning it into a vacation and get to know these states.

Northern New England is that smallish, wild area in the northeast corner of the United States that is rugged yet refined. It's a concen-trated land of coastlines and mountains, lakes, rivers and forests, wil-derness and tightly-packed villages, rural yet housing fine universities and colleges.

Bordered by the Atlantic Ocean to the East, Canada (New Brun-swick and Quebec) to the East and North, Massachusetts to the South, and New York to the West. Statistics can be a game in this 3-state area, with Maine sporting 3,478 miles of shoreline, while Vermont is only 41 miles wide at its southern border.

Water turns up everywhere. In summer the ocean, lakes and rivers provide great summer water sports and fishing. In winter snow and ice predominates the landscape for more sports opportunities. In fall, it's the freezing water in the leaves that cause the gorgeous colors on the native deciduous forests.

Other popular activities include harness racing (a New England tradition), shopping and historical explorations.

Accommodating vacationers is an art in New England. The American bed & breakfast was perfected in this region where shelter for travelers was a necessity and hospitality a virtue. And this is the region that first developed the American ski resort for the early East Coast winter sporting crowd. So your choices are varied and the quality tends to be quite high.

Connecticut Department of Economic Development
865 Brook Street
Rocky Hill, Connecticut 06067
Phone: (800) 282-6863

Department of Environmental Protection
79 Elm Street
Hartford, Connecticut 06106
Phone: (860) 424-3000

Maine Office of Tourism
59 State Street
Augusta, Maine 04333
Phone: (207) 287-5711

Maine Publicity Bureau
P.O. Box 23000
Hallowell, Maine 04347
Phone: (207) 623-0363

Department of Inland Fisheries & Wildlife
284 State Street
Augusta, Maine 04333
Phone: (207) 287-8000

Massachusetts Department of Commerce & Development
Division of Tourism
100 Cambridge Street
Boston, Massachusetts 02202
Phone: (800) 447-MASS

Department of Environmental Management
251 Causeway Street, Suite 600
Boston, Massachusetts 02114
Phone: (617) 626-1250

New Hampshire Office of Vacation Travel
P.O. Box 856
Concord, New Hampshire 03312
Phone: (800) 258-3608;
(603) 271-2343

Fish & Game Department
2 Hazen Drive
Concord, New Hampshire 03301
Phone: (803) 271-3211

Forest Service
U.S. Department of Agriculture
P.O. Box 2402
Concord, New Hampshire 03302
Phone: (503) 271-1109

Rhode Island Tourism Division
Department of Economic Development
7 Jackson Walkway
Providence, Rhode Island 02903
Phone: (800) 556-2484;
   (401) 277-2601

Department of Environmental Management
83 Park Street
Providence, Rhode Island 02903
Phone: (401) 222-6822

Forest Division Headquarters
1037 Hartford Pike
North Scituate, Rhode Island 02857
Phone: (401) 647-3367;
   (800) 280-CAMP

Vermont Travel Division
6 Baldwin Street
Montpelier, Vermont 05602
Phone: (800) VERMONT

Fish & Wildlife Division
Agency of Natural Resources
103 South Main Street
Waterbury, Vermont 05676

Green Mountain National Forest
231 North Main Street
Rutland, Vermont 05701
Phone: (802) 747-6700

Department of Forests, Parks & Recreation
103 South Main Street
Waterbury, Vermont 05676
Phone: (802) 241-3670

• • • • • • • • • • • • • • • • • • •

EASTERN SEABOARD 🦅 DELAWARE, MARYLAND, NEW JERSEY, NEW YORK, NORTH CAROLINA, VIRGINIA, WASHINGTON D.C. 🦅

The hub of the East Coast is New York City, and whatever you've heard about the Big Apple is true, and more as well. This gigantic city has long, deep roots and has been a focus of entry and activity for the U.S.A. for quite a while. It's surprising how many of the symbols of the United States are in this metropolis: the Statue of Liberty, the Empire State Building, U.N. Headquarters, the Metropolitan Museum, Times Square, the Brooklyn Bridge, Carnegie Hall, Yankee Stadium, Central Park, Harlem, Broadway! ... and the list goes on.

   New York City is an adventure—it can be gaudy and loud, intensely intellectual or artistic, politically exuberant or historically exciting. Perhaps this is where you will see your first Van Gogh, visit an 18th-century African-American graveyard, watch a Baryshnikov ballet, or stand where your grandparents entered at Ellis Island. Or, perhaps you will visit Wall Street, 5th Avenue, be a part of the Letterman audience—who knows?

Well, you should know. It is worth the effort to write ahead
and confirm any plans. Most main libraries
have phone books from all the major cities in
the country, so do some browsing and confirm your plans so you can make the most of
your trip. Also, the major New York newspapers are usually
available at large stands.

Get ready for some excitement! The Big Apple is a trip! (Let's see—
Greenwich Village, the Museum of Modern Art, Rockefeller Center,
Lincoln Center, Staten Island, the New York Stock Exchange, Coney
Island, the Bowery, Grand Central Station, Chinatown. . . .)

The Empire State seems to be large in every way—whether huge
populations in New York City, endless waterways including the Hudson,
Lake Ontario, Thousand Islands, canals and several substantial lakes, an
amazing array of cultures, and large holiday playgrounds interspersed
with farmland and parks.

When exploring New York State, you might choose to stay in the
eastern portion of the state and go to the Adirondacks or Catskills
either in Summer to cool down or in Winter to heat up the slopes. The
central state is dominated by a series of large lakes for some serious, or
not so serious, watersports. The western part of the state houses Buffalo
and Niagara Falls and is a major thoroughfare to Canada. Up-state New
York is justly known for its natural beauty and can be a wonderful place
for a family gathering.

New Jersey often seems overshadowed by its bigger-than-life neighbor, New York, but the Garden State has much to offer visitors. New
Yorkers themselves may opt to take a short trip out of town to a completely different world in New Jersey. One favorite getaway area is Cape
May on the southern tip of New Jersey on the northern peninsula lead-
ing to Delaware Bay. Another destination for fun is Atlantic City with its
glitz, glamour and gambling tables. There is also a great deal for history
buffs to explore, especially relating to the Revolutionary War period.

Next on your voyage south are Delaware and Maryland. These
states share a peninsula and a visitor to either should make it a double-
header. Bounded by the Delaware and Chesapeake Bays, this land has a
rich history and is known for its seagoing culture. Bays, inlets, peninsulas
and islands dot the coast. Again there are many opportunities to find
historical spots. The War of 1812 is prominent in Maryland's history,
including providing the inspiration for the writing of The Star-Spangled

Banner. The capital of Maryland, Annapolis, still houses the U.S. Naval Academy and produces the cream of the crop of our seagoing officers. From lighthouses to the Allegheny Mountains, Maryland touches on many east coast cultures and traditions.

Our nation's capital, Washington in the District of Columbia, is worth at least one visit. Whether your family's greatest interests are political, historical, scientific, artistic or social, D.C. can keep you interested and enlightened. Originally a swampy area some found a poor choice for the seat of government, Washington now opens its doors to all citizens. And those doors are remarkable. Consider your choices: the Houses of Congress, the White House, the Smithsonian Institution, the National Gallery of Art, the Wall of the Vietnam Veterans Memorial, the Kennedy Center for the Performing Arts, the Library of Congress, the National Museums of—you name it. Plan your time very carefully. The Smithsonian alone can take weeks! While much history is evident in Washington, history is being made all around you. The chance to witness Congress in session is a memory that will stick.

The last states we're including in this section are North Carolina and Virginia. These states have a great deal in common. What can you say about Virginia? It can easily fall into a variety of categories—Colonial, Confederate, Old World, cosmopolitan, it is mountain, piedmont or seaside. The Alexandria area to the north is almost a working part of Washington D.C. To the east are the Allegheny, Shenandoah, Blue Ridge and Appalachian Mountains with all the scenery, playgrounds and culture they imply. The Piedmont area evokes images of the Old South with wide vistas and plantation lands, and here and there a fine old residence sits patiently. The memories of such cities as Richmond, Greensboro, Fredericksburg, Raleigh, Petersburg, Williamsburg and Charlottesville carry the weight of battles, revolution and mighty tales.

The coastal area of Virginia, the Tidewater, is another experience again, and the area runs south through North Carolina. Ocean breezes, broad expanses of sand and deltas, bays and sounds and peninsulas, long, private islands, and wide, slow rivers provide just the right ambiance for a relaxed vacation on the shore. Whatever the family is looking for just might be found on the coast of Virginia and North Carolina.

Delaware Tourism Office
99 Kings Highway
P.O. Box 1401
Dover, Delaware 19903
Phone: (800) 441-8846;
 (302) 739-4271

Department of Parks & Recreation
89 Kings Highway
P.O. Box 1401
Dover, Delaware 19903
Phone: (302) 739-4702

Department of Fish & Wildlife
89 Kings Highway
P.O. Box 1401
Dover, Delaware 19903
Phone: (302) 739-4431

**Washington D.C. Convention &
 Visitors Association**
1575 Eye Street NW, Suite 250
Washington, District of Columbia
 20005
Phone: (202) 789-1600

National Parks Service
1100 Ohio Drive SW
Washington, District of Columbia
 20242
Phone: (202) 208-6843

Smithsonian Institution
Washington, District of Columbia
 20560
Phone: (202) 357-2700

Maryland Office of Tourism
217 East Redwood Street
Baltimore, Maryland 21202
Phone: (800) MDISFUN

**Maryland State Forest & Parks
 Services**
580 Taylor Avenue
Annapolis, Maryland 21401
Phone: (410) 974-3771

**Maryland Tidewater
 Administration**
580 Taylor Avenue
Annapolis, Maryland 21401
Phone: (410) 974-3365

Maryland Wildlife Administration
580 Taylor Avenue
Annapolis, Maryland 21401
Phone: (410) 974-3195

**New Jersey Division of Travel &
 Tourism**
P.O. Box 820
Trenton, New Jersey 08625
Phone: (800) VISIT-NJ;
 (609) 777-0885

State Park Service
Parks & Forestry Division
501 East State Street, CN 404
Trenton, New Jersey 08625
Phone: (609) 984-0370;
 (800) 852-7899

**Department of Fish, Game &
 Wildlife**
501 East State Street, CN 400
Trenton, New Jersey 08625
Phone: (609) 292-9410

New York State Dept. of Commerce
Division of Tourism Development
30 South Pearl Street
Albany, New York 12245
Phone: (800) STATE-NY;
 (518) 474-4116

**New York Convention and Visitors
 Bureau**
2 Columbus Circle
New York, New York 10019
Phone: (212) 397-8222

New York State Office of Parks, Recreation and Historic Preservation
Agency Building 1
Empire State Plaza
Albany, New York 12238
Phone: (518) 474-3521

State Division of Fish & Wildlife
50 Wolf Road
Albany, New York 12233
Phone: (518) 457-3521

Forest Supervisor
Finger Lakes National Forest
P.O. Box W
Montour Falls, New York 14865
Phone: (800) 280-CAMP

North Carolina Travel & Tourism Division
Department of Commerce
430 North Wilmington Street
Raleigh, North Carolina 27020
Phone: (919) 733-7561

North Carolina Parks & Recreation
1615 Mail Service Center
Raleigh, North Carolina 27699
Phone: (919) 733-7275;
   (919) 733-4181

State Wildlife Resources
512 North Salisbury Street
Raleigh, North Carolina 27604

U.S. Forest Service
P.O. Box 2750
Asheville, North Carolina 28802
Phone: (828) 257-4200;
   (800) 280-CAMP

Virginia Division of Tourism
901 E. Byrd Street
Richmond, Virginia 23219
Phone: (800) 321-3244

Department of Fish & Game
4010 West Broad Street
Richmond, Virginia 23230
Phone: (804) 367-1000

• • • • • • • • • • • • • • • • •

SOUTHEAST ~ ALABAMA, FLORIDA, GEORGIA, LOUISIANA, MISSISSIPPI, SOUTH CAROLINA ~

The South is large and varied, but basically it all faces the water and is fairly warm and often sunny and humid. From the mighty Mississippi to the west to the huge Florida peninsula, the south offers gracious hospitality, diverse and colorful cultures, an historical heritage that often seems present, and the beauty of a temperate-to-tropical zone. Once considered a slow mover, the New South is proving to be a dynamic forward force for the country and tackling all problems with imagination and verve.

But fear not, the Old South is still there for the visiting. A slow afternoon on a porch by the River, a walk in the bayou, a cajun cookout in a small town, plantation tours and tales of pirates, gamblers, ghosts and great deeds are available with a little looking.

Many people, when they want to go to an exotic spot within the continental U.S.A., think of Louisiana. This land on the delta of North America's greatest river is a polyglot of cultures surrounded by beautiful and dramatic wild areas.

Louisiana is a point where cultures have met, melded and interacted for centuries. The French, Spanish, Caribbean, African, British and Native Americans have expressed themselves and contributed, and everyone seems to have a reason to celebrate, especially in New Orleans. This influx and blending is happily experienced in the food and music— Cajun, Creole, zydeco, jazz, high French and traditional Southern. . . . And sometimes it seems like food and music are either interchangeable or necessary companions.

History surrounds you in most areas of Louisiana, whether it's the old French pirates, the Confederacy, Mississippi riverboat life, or the freedom riders of this century. It is a fascinating and very visual state in which to explore your roots or interests.

Mardi Gras draws huge numbers to New Orleans for the Shrove Tuesday pre-Lenten festivities, as does the Jazz Fest in May. Be certain to carefully make your plans, and be certain such a trip is appropriate for all members of the family. The excess and craziness is legendary—which may or may not be what you are looking for. Whether Mardi Gras is the right time for you to visit or not, you will definitely find much to keep you occupied, curious, well-fed and entertained.

Miami is definitely the capital of southern Florida, and some say of South and Central America—the gateway to the Everglades, gateway to the Keys, gateway to the Caribbean, and queen of the Gold Coast. Sunbathing along the southeastern shores, old Miami is on the mainland, while several causeways lead over to the string of islands that make up Miami Beach.

Miami and its environs are meant to be enjoyed daytime or evening, with a distinctive international flair at all times. The hub of Miami's Hispanic communities is Little Havana, a great place for some dining adventures. Water sports, of course, are available all along the coast.

Hialeah is on the western edge of Miami for those interested in taking in the races.

The southern Florida peninsula is a natural wonder store house for the U.S., with the Everglades, Biscayne Park, Big Cypress—a seemingly immense area, but in fact all that remains of our subtropical region. There are many nature-oriented spots to visit, enjoy, and learn from. (See our article in this section)

In the middle of Florida, Orlando is the local city for Walt Disney World and the Epcot Center. While in the area, don't miss Universal Studios, the Orlando Toy Train Station & Museum or Sea World of Florida, always a fun day.

This is Alligator Country, so don't forget to get out and interact with the Florida wildlife, and expect to hear a little Cajun music while you all settle down for some great seafood and Caribbean cuisine.

But there's more to Florida than fun and games. Historical monuments, military establishments, art and science museums and cultural centers are available for exploration. And water sports is serious business in this tropical paradise. But, as always when near the ocean—keep an eye on the weather and be careful. Now go have fun!

Georgia's history is full of twists and surprises. For instance, it joined the United States twice—once at the birth of the nation, and then again in 1870. The first real gold rush in the U.S.A. took place in Georgia in 1828. And Georgia's past and present live in the state capital—Atlanta.

Atlanta lies in the north central part of the state on the Chattahoochee River. The city has long been focused around Peachtree Street. And while there are abundant historical sights—Atlanta is unquestionably the focus of the New South, with innovative architecture and businesses scattered throughout.

But when you and your family do visit Atlanta, don't forget to check out the natural beauty and historical sites of north Georgia. Go up to Lake Lanier or down to Pine Mountain for starters.

Alabama Bureau of Tourism & Travel
401 Adams Avenue
Montgomery, Alabama 36103
Phone: (334) 242-4169;
  (800) ALABAMA

Florida Division of Tourism
Visitor Inquiry Section
P.O. Box 1100
Tallahassee, Florida 32302
Phone: (888) 735-2872

Greater Miami Convention & Visitors Bureau
701 Brickell Avenue, Suite 2700
Miami, Florida 33131
Phone: (305) 539-3000

Orlando Tourist Information Center
7208 Sand Lake Road, Suite 300
Orlando, Florida 32819
Phone: (407) 363-5871

Greater Orlando Chamber of Commerce
P.O. Box 1234
Orlando, Florida 32802
Phone: (407) 425-1234

Florida Division of Tourism
Office of Visitor Inquiry
126 West Van Buren Street
Tallahassee, Florida 32399
Phone: (850) 487-1462

National Forest Information
325 John Knox Road, Suite F-100
Tallahassee, Florida 32303
Phone: (850) 942-9300;
  (800) 280-CAMP

Game & Freshwater Fish Commission
620 South Meridian Street
Tallahassee, Florida 32399
Phone: (850) 488-4676

Department of National Resources
Saltwater Fishing
License, Titles & Permits
3900 Commonwealth Boulevard
Tallahassee, Florida 32399
Phone: (850) 488-7326

Department of Natural Resources
Division of Recreation & Parks
3900 Commonwealth Boulevard
Mail Station 535
Tallahassee, Florida 32399
Phone: (850) 488-9872

Georgia Department of Industry, Trade & Tourism
285 Peachtree Center Avenue NE, Suite 1000
Atlanta, Georgia 30303
Phone: (404) 656-3590;
  (800) VISIT-GA

Department of Natural Resources
Communications Office
205 Butler Street SE, Suite 1258
Atlanta, Georgia 30334
Phone: (404) 656-3530

Wildlife Resources
Department of Natural Resources
2070 U.S. Highway 278 SE
Social Circle, Georgia 30025
Phone: (706) 557-3024;
  (706) 557-3022

U.S. Forest Service
1720 Peachtree Road NW
Atlanta, Georgia 30367
Phone: (404) 248-9142;
  (800) 280-CAMP

Louisiana Office of Tourism
P.O. Box 9429
Baton Rouge, Louisiana 70804
Phone: (225) 342-8119;
  (800) 334-8626

Louisiana State Parks
P.O. Box 44426
Baton Rouge, Louisiana 70804
Phone: (504) 342-8111

Kisatchie National Forest
2500 Shreveport Highway
Pineville, Louisiana 71360
Phone: (318) 473-7160

Louisiana Wildlife & Fisheries
P.O. Box 98000
Baton Rouge, Louisiana 70898
Phone: (504) 765-2800

**Mississippi Department of
Economic Development**
Division of Tourism
P.O. Box 2849
Jackson, Mississippi 39205
Phone: (601) 359-3297;
(800) 647-2825

**Department of Wildlife, Fisheries
& Parks**
P.O. Box 451
Jackson, Mississippi 39205
Phone: (601) 432-2400

U.S. Forest Service
100 West Capitol Street
Jackson, Mississippi 39269
Phone: (601) 965-4391;
(800) 280-CAMP

**South Carolina Department of
Parks, Recreation & Tourism**
1205 Pendleton Street, Suite 106
Columbia, South Carolina 29201
Phone: (803) 734-1700

Department of Fish & Game
P.O. Box 167
Columbia, South Carolina 29202
Phone: (803) 734-3886

U.S. Forest Service
1000 Assembly Street
Columbia, South Carolina 29201
Phone: (803) 734-3888

• • • • • • • • • • • • • • • • • • • •

BLUEGRASS COUNTRY ⪻ TENNESSEE, KENTUCKY, WEST VIRGINIA ⪼

Kentucky, Tennessee and West Virginia bridge several worlds, from the Appalachia Mountains to the east to the Mississippi River on the west. In between are the major cities of Knoxville, Louisville, Nashville, Charleston, Chattanooga and Memphis. Each has a unique flavor and good reasons for a visit.

Many defining periods in U.S. history are reflected in Bluegrass and Appalachian country—this was Cherokee country and the beginning of the Trail of Tears; the Appalachian and Smoky Mountains evoke the early settlers and pioneer days; Kentucky and Tennessee were major players in the Civil War and the site of far too many battlefields; the Tennessee Valley Authority epitomizes the country's struggles to recover from the Great Depression; Nashville and the Grand Ole Opry are the heart of 20th- and soon 21th-century American country music; Memphis encompasses Mississippi lifestyles with riverboats and muddy-water blues; while the Ohio River bordering northern Kentucky was probably the strongest section of the Mason-Dixon Line and sported its own river life. Another sort of river life you'll find in the region is whitewater rafting. Small companies are tucked here and there, so if this is a type of adventure you want to try out, check with the tourist departments.

Slow down when you're driving with the kids through a quiet wooded area and come upon a marked historical site—you may have happened upon a cabin of Daniel Boone's or a link in the Underground Railroad.

Translating all this into a family vacation is more fun than challenge. There's great outdoor sporting in the mountains, as well as on the many rivers and lakes. Cultural and music events await you in the country and the cities. Civil War buffs may choose to start their explorations in Chattanooga, where General Sherman began his own march. When you go to Nashville, you will want to include Nashville and at least do a little "star-gazing."

And how can you go to Bluegrass Country and not enjoy a little horse racing—or *the* horse race—the Kentucky Derby at Churchill Downs in Louisville. But even if you don't make it to a big race, the vast expanses of bluegrass fields with young foals frolicking is a fine sight, and the power of the yearlings and two-year-olds running their own races across meadows could turn anyone into a racing aficionado.

But wherever you go in Bluegrass Country you are likely to be struck by the natural beauty and be tempted to just kick back for a while to enjoy a refreshing pause. Which isn't a bad choice for a vacation.

Kentucky Department of Travel Development
500 Mero Street, 22nd Floor
Frankfort, Kentucky 40601
Phone: (800) 225-8747;
  (502) 564-4930

State Parks Department
500 Mero Street, Suite 1000
Frankfort, Kentucky 40601
Phone: (800) 255-PARK

Department of Fish & Wildlife Resources
1 Game Farm Road
Frankfort, Kentucky 40601
Phone: (502) 564-4336

U.S. Forest Service
Daniel Boone National Forest
100 Vaught Road
Winchester, Kentucky 40391
Phone: (606) 745-3100;
  (800) 280-CAMP

**Department of Tourist
Development**
P.O. Box 23170
Nashville, Tennessee 37202
Phone: (615) 741-2158

**Department of Environment &
Conservation**
401 Church Street, 7th Floor
Nashville, Tennessee 37243
Phone: (615) 532-0001;
    (800) 421-6683

Wildlife Resources
Ellington Agriculture Center
P.O. Box 40747
Nashville, Tennessee 37204
Phone: (615) 781-6500

U.S. Forest Service
Cherokee National Forest
2800 North Ocoee Street
Cleveland, Tennessee 37320
Phone: (423) 476-9700;
    (800) 280-CAMP

**West Virginia State Travel
Development**
1900 East Kanawha Boulevard
Building 6, Room B-564
Charleston, West Virginia 25305
Phone: (304) 348-2766;
    (800) 225-5982

**State Division of Natural
Resources**
State Capitol Complex
Charleston, West Virginia 25305
Phone: (304) 558-2771

West Virginia State Parks
200 Sycamore Street
Elkins, West Virginia 26241
Phone: (304) 636-1800;
    (800) 280-CAMP

• • • • • • • • • • • • • • • • • • •

MIDWEST ⌖ ARKANSAS, IOWA, KANSAS, MISSOURI, NEBRASKA, NORTH DAKOTA, SOUTH DAKOTA ⌖

You and your family do not have to go to the Caribbean or California, the Rockies or Disney World to have a fun-filled vacation complete with sports, theme parks, history and natural beauty. The Midwest offers all of this, and it's no more than half way across the country for anyone—right?

The Bread Basket of America is good, solid land. Much of this area was prairie and supported herds of buffalo until the last century. Those who crossed the country in the push westward often headed out from St. Louis and met their first tests in these open prairie lands. Now farms, industry, towns and recreation areas fill the landscape.

Arkansas blends great national parks, a vast array of watersports activities on its many lakes and rivers, and cultural centers and museums enough to interest just about anybody. There are forts and historical reminders of the westward expansion as well as the Civil War. Be sure to check out Eureka Springs, the Ozark Folk Festival, the theme park Dogpatch (anyone remember Li'l Abner?), Hot Springs and the state capitol, Little Rock. The country is beautiful and the people friendly.

Iowa is one of those unassuming places which quietly goes about its business providing for everyone else and taking its pleasure in simple things. One of the peoples who contributed to this lifestyle is the Amana community. These communities now open their doors to those who are curious or wish to reconnect with their roots. Take the time to stop and see what life is like without call-waiting, in-line skates and 50 cable channels.

Settled fairly late and still predominantly agricultural, Iowa provides watersports on its various rivers and hiking and camping in its various parks. Easy to get to from such metropolitan areas as Chicago and St. Louis, Iowa can be the ideal getaway without having to go too far. Fishermen especially enjoy the many waterways available, while shoppers are quite happy with the many outlets and malls.

Kansas to many of us is where Auntie Em and Dorothy lives. Somehow this state ends up starring in songs: We know there are pretty little women in Kansas City, and of course the Atchison, Topeka and the Santa Fe passes through. The Wichita lineman will be on the job as you drive by, and check to see if you're as corny as Kansas in August.

But in reality Kansas is a mainly farming state with a strong railroad tradition and famous for cattle ranches and cattle drives. Favorite sons and daughters of Kansas include Carrie Nation and President Dwight D. Eisenhower. Like Iowa, Kansas recreation centers around water sports and hiking, with the added excitement of greyhound racing.

Missouri, like Arkansas, is bordered to the east by the Mississippi River, which has been a major influence throughout the state's history. Altogether, in Missouri you will find plains, prairie, the Ozark Mountains and Mississippi River flatlands. For many years Missouri, and especially St. Louis, was the gateway to the west, the jumping-off point for early travelers going off to start new lives in Oregon or California, Colorado or New Mexico. This was the end of the comforts of civilization—the door to the wilderness.

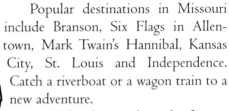

Popular destinations in Missouri include Branson, Six Flags in Allentown, Mark Twain's Hannibal, Kansas City, St. Louis and Independence. Catch a riverboat or a wagon train to a new adventure.

Nebraska was the path of many peoples as they wandered west. It bridges the Great Prairie from the Missouri River to the Rocky Mountain foothills. Early settlers found it ideal for planting, and it still is corn country. But this was also good hunting, fishing and trapping country. Nebraska seems pretty tame these days, but when Buffalo Bill Cody was growing up here, life was rough-and-tumble. Sod houses were a standard and some still exist for you to examine. You develop a new respect for those who settled and worked the plains when you see the homes they built and lived in. So take your time and check out the history between fishing, hunting and shopping jaunts.

The Dakotas can be daunting with their very wide open spaces and silence. If a city confines you most of the year and you just want to drive straight into nowhere, this might be the place to do it. But there are also very special destinations in the Dakotas, including the Badlands,

Arkansas Department of Parks & Tourism
1 Capitol Mall
Little Rock, Arkansas 72201
Phone: (501) 682-7777;
(800) NATURAL

Game & Fish Commission
2 Natural Resource Drive
Little Rock, Arkansas 72205
Phone: (501) 223-6300

Iowa Tourism Office
200 East Grand Avenue
Des Moines, Iowa 50309
Phone: (515) 242-4705

Department of Natural Resources
East 9th Street at Grand Avenue
Des Moines, Iowa 50319
Phone: (515) 281-5918

Kansas Department of Commerce
Travel & Tourism
700 SW Harrison St., Suite 1300
Topeka, Kansas 66603
Phone: (800) 252-6727;
(785) 296-7091

Department of Wildlife & Parks
900 Jackson St., Suite 502
Topeka, Kansas 66612
Phone: (316) 672-5911

Missouri Division of Tourism
Truman Office Bldg, Box 1055
Jefferson City, Missouri 65102
Phone: (573) 751-4133

Department of Natural Resources
P.O. Box 176
Jefferson City, Missouri 65102
Phone: (800) 334-6946

Conservation/Fishing & Hunting
P.O. Box 180
Jefferson City, Missouri 65102
Phone: (314) 751-4115

National Forests
401 Fairgrounds Road
Rolla, Missouri 65401
Phone: (573) 364-4261

Nebraska Department of Economic Development
Division of Travel & Tourism
P.O. Box 94666
Lincoln, Nebraska 68509
Phone: (402) 471-3111;
   (800) 426-6505

Department of Game & Parks
P.O. Box 30370
Lincoln, Nebraska 68503
Phone: (402) 471-0641

North Dakota Tourism Promotion
604 East Boulevard
Bismark, North Dakota 58505
Phone: (800) HELLO-ND

North Dakota Parks & Recreation
1835 Bismarck Expressway
Bismarck, North Dakota 58505
Phone: (701) 328-5357

Department of Game & Fish
100 North Bismarck Expressway
Bismarck, North Dakota 58501
Phone: (701) 221-6300

South Dakota State Department of Tourism
Capitol Lake Plaza
711 Wells Avenue
Pierre, South Dakota 57501
Phone: (605) 773-3301;
   (800) 952-2217

Department of Game, Fish & Parks
523 East Capitol
Pierre, South Dakota 57501
Phone: (605) 773-3485

Black Hills National Forest
Rural Route 2, Box 200
Custer, South Dakota 57730
Phone: (605) 343-8755;
   (800) 280-CAMP

• • • • • • • • • • • • • • • • • • •

GREAT LAKES/NORTH CENTRAL ⤜ ILLINOIS, INDIANA, MICHIGAN, MINNESOTA, OHIO, PENNSYLVANIA, WISCONSIN ⤝

Dominated by the Great Lakes, the north central portion of the U.S. covers many miles and many lifestyles. From Pennsylvania to the east to Minnesota to the west, the land is highly seasonal, rolling hills and expansive valleys with water seemingly everywhere.

Pennsylvania, the Keystone State, has always held a prominent position in the history of the United States. One of the original colonies and the site of the formation of the new rebel nation, here is where you will find numerous reminders of earlier times. When you get to Philadelphia, be sure to visit Independence National Historic Park and take the time to explore. Some people somewhere in the world is struggling for their freedom and setting up a new nation—this is where the struggle centered that produced our system. Pennsylvania also hosted the battle of Gettysburg, another decisive moment for this country.

Heavily populated to the east and west, Pennsylvania also contains mountain ranges, lakes, farmlands and wild areas. From the Poconos to Lake Erie, there are many choices for relaxed vacations or outdoor adventure. You might also like to include a visit to Amish country and maybe a sweet side-trip to Hershey.

Stretching out to the west from Pennsylvania, with the Ohio River as a southern border and the Great Lakes to the north, are Ohio, Indiana and Illinois. These lush fertile valleys, watersheds and open land have been the backbone of America's growth and stability. Once heavily forested, these three states now feed and house many residential and industrial centers. Recreation often revolves around watersports, hunting and fishing, auto racing and golf. Most parts of Illinois, Indiana and Ohio are extremely accessible and lodging is rarely a problem. This is great car-trip territory. Just be ready for the wind in the Windy City and treat the Great Lakes like the wild open water they truly are.

While various states touch on the Great Lakes, Michigan and Wisconsin are dominated by the Lakes, each in its own way. Michigan is truly the automotive hub of the nation, with cars, trucks and tires rolling out hourly. Being on the great traffic lanes of the Lakes definitely contributed to the growth and success of Detroit. Now many people also come for the music of Motown, the connections with Canada and the wildlife preserves. Oh, and don't miss Kalamazoo!

Wisconsin is probably best known for lumber and dairy production, the beers of Milwaukee and the football of Green Bay. For a large part of the country, Wisconsin is a somewhat nearby destination with summer and winter recreation for all—not too tame and not too wild. Special effort is made in this state in the area of parks and interpretive centers, which makes for an ideal trip to encompass both outdoor fun and education. This is also where you may choose to begin your family's trek from the headwaters of the Mississippi down to the Gulf.

Farthest north and west in this group is Minnesota. With its expanses of forest, cold winters and heavily Swedish and Norwegian population, Minnesota can seem like a bit of Scandinavia on the wrong continent. Hard-working farmers and foresters have slowly developed a very stable economy without sacrificing the beauty of the landscape. But that doesn't mean there wasn't an air of excitement. It was this life that inspired the stories of Paul Bunyon and his blue ox. And the community traditions continue to be lovingly remembered and parodied as Lake Wobegone by favorite son Garrison Keiller.

Illinois Office of Tourism
310 S. Michigan Ave., Suite 108
Chicago, Illinois 60616
Phone: (800) 2CONNECT

Department of Conservation & Fisheries
524 South Second Street
Springfield, Illinois 62706
Phone: (217) 782-7454

Indiana Department of Commerce
Tourism Development Division
1 North Capitol, Suite 700
Indianapolis, Indiana 46204
Phone: (317) 232-8860;
  (800) 289-6646

Department of Natural Resources
402 W. Washington Street, Rm 298
Indianapolis, Indiana 46204
Phone: (317) 232-4220

Hoosier National Forest
811 Constitution Avenue
Bedford, Indiana 47421
Phone: (812) 275-5987;
  (800) 280-CAMP

Michigan Department of Commerce
Travel Bureau
P.O. Box 30004
Lansing, Michigan 48909
Phone: (517) 373-1820

Department of Natural Resources
P.O. Box 30028
Lansing, Michigan 48909
Phone: (517) 373-1220

Minnesota Tourist Information
121 E. 7th Place
500 Metro Square
St. Paul, Minnesota 55101
Phone: (651) 296-2755

Department of Natural Resources
500 Lafayette Road
P.O. Box 40
St. Paul, Minnesota 55146
Phone: (651) 296-6157

U.S. Forest Service
1992 Folwell Avenue
St. Paul, Minnesota 55108
Phone: (651) 649-5243;
  (800) 280-CAMP

Ohio Office of Travel & Tourism
600 West Springs Street
Columbus, Ohio 43215
Phone: (800) BUCKEYE

Ohio State Parks & Recreation
1952 Belcher Drive
Columbus, Ohio 43224
Phone: (614) 265-6561

Department of Wildlife
1840 Belcher Drive
Columbus, Ohio 43224
Phone: (614) 265-6300

Pennsylvania Dept. of Community and Economic Development
400 North Street, 4th Floor
Harrisburg, Pennsylvania 17120
Phone: (717) 787-5453

State Fish & Boat Commission
P.O. Box 67000
Harrisburg, Pennsylvania 17110
Phone: (717) 787-4250

Allegheny National Forest
P.O. Box 847
Warren, Pennsylvania 16365
Phone: (814) 723-5150;
(800) 280-CAMP

Wisconsin State Division of Tourism
P.O. Box 7976
Madison, Wisconsin 53707
Phone: (800) 432-TRIP

Department of Natural Resources
101 S. Webster Street
Madison, Wisconsin 53707
Phone: (608) 266-2621

U.S. Forest Service
310 West Wisconsin Avenue,
Suite 500
Milwaukee, Wisconsin 53203
Phone: (312) 353-4242;
(800) 280-CAMP

• • • • • • • • • • • • • • • • • • • •

MOUNTAIN STATES ᐟ COLORADO, IDAHO, MONTANA, UTAH, WYOMING ᐟ

Perched atop the Continental Divide and sloping down east and west toward the Atlantic and the Pacific Oceans, Colorado is dominated by the Rocky Mountains. Additionally, high plateau covers the western section and the eastern section begins the Great Plains.

Historically, much of the area that is now Colorado was long peopled by agriculturally-based Native Americans whose cliff dwellings can be admired today. Following the arrival of Europeans, the discovery of first gold and then silver dramatically opened the state to settlers, hunters, and scalawags. The health advantages of clean, clear mountain air and water drew thousands of early settlers for "the cure." Colorado became a state in 1876.

Colorado has natural wonders galore for anyone interested in snow sports, water sports, outdoor adventure and ranches. There is also an abundance of more domestic sporting available, such as golf and tennis. Cultural past-times and the arts abound in some of the most beautiful scenery the lower-48 has to offer.

Idaho incorporates all of the beauty and excitement of high mountains. Still sparsely settled, the pioneer spirit is still alive among those living in town or country. There is white water and snow-capped peaks for the adventurous, abundant wildlife for the photographer and hunter, and peace and quiet in most corners.

If your family wants a taste of the old wild west but doesn't really want to rough it, try taking U.S. Highway 30 between Yellowstone and Boise, following the route through the Snake River Plain. We do recommend, however, that you don't take this trip in winter.

But if you *are* looking for adventure, this is a super spot for a wild water ride, skiing, backpacking, trekking and horse packing. You might like to incorporate this adventure with a thorough visit to neighboring Yellowstone National Park.

And that Yellowstone Park trip took you to Wyoming, a remarkable and striking state to please both the cowboy and the mountain man in everyone. Cheyenne sits in the flat cattle country that slopes down to the Missouri River, while Jackson Hole sits high in the Rocky Mountains. Probably one of the best-known views of the Rockies is the Maroon Bells in Grand Teton National Park. Make it a point to visit Jackson Hole!

When you are in the Rocky Mountains, monitor the behavior and health of each member of the family. Acute Mountain Sickness (AMS) is a real thing which occur when you go above an 8,000-foot elevation. While this can be painful, it is easily avoided and recovery can be quick if handled correctly.

If Wyoming wasn't extreme enough for you, head north for Montana. Big Sky Country deserves its name. Like Wyoming, there are plains, mountains, and long stretches of empty road. But Montana is being discovered; golfers and skiers, canoers and horse packers are all finding this rugged state just to their liking. Chances are you won't hit heavy traffic, but you will surely hear the coyotes, and maybe a few ghosts left over from the Little Bighorn. Whenever you go to Montana, be prepared for the cold. Summer days get very warm, but the evening temperature can dip quickly at this elevation and latitude.

Colorado Department of Tourism
1625 Broadway, Suite 1700
Denver, Colorado 80202
Phone: (800) 433-2656

Colorado Parks & Outdoor Recreation
1313 Sherman Street, Room 618
Denver, Colorado 80203
Phone: (303) 866-3437

Colorado Division of Wildlife
6060 Broadway
Denver, Colorado 80216
Phone: (303) 297-1192

U.S. Forest Service
11177 West Eighth Avenue
Lakewood, Colorado 80225
Phone: (303) 275-5350;
(800) 280-CAMP

Colorado Ski Country
1560 Broadway, Suite 1440
Denver, Colorado 80202
Phone: (303) 837-0793

Idaho Travel Council
Hall of Mirrors, 2nd Floor
700 West State Street
Boise, Idaho 83720
Phone: (208) 334-2470;
(800) 842-5858

State Parks & Recreation
P.O. Box 83720
Boise, Idaho 83720
Phone: (208) 334-4199

Idaho Fish & Game
600 South Walnut Street
P.O. Box 25
Boise, Idaho 83707
Phone: (208) 334-3700

Montana Promotion Division
1424 Ninth Avenue
Helena, Montana 59620
Phone: (406) 444-2654;
(800) 847-4868

Department of Fish, Wildlife & Parks
1420 East Sixth Avenue
Helena, Montana 59620
Phone: (406) 444-2535

U.S. Forest Service
Federal Building
P.O. Box 7669
Missoula, Montana 59807
Phone: (406) 329-3750;
(800) 280-CAMP

Utah State Travel Council
300 North State Street
Salt Lake City, Utah 84114
Phone: (801) 538-1030

National Forests
324—25th Street
Ogden, Utah 84401
Phone: (801) 625-5182;
(800) 280-CAMP

Wyoming State Travel Commission
I-25 and College Drive
Cheyenne, Wyoming 82002
Phone: (307) 777-7777;
(800) 225-5996

**Wyoming State Museums &
  Historic Sites**
Barrett Building
2301 Central
Cheyenne, Wyoming 82002
Phone: (307) 777-7014

Department of Fish & Game
5400 Bishop Boulevard
Cheyenne, Wyoming 82002
Phone: (307) 777-4600

Wyoming Recreation Commission
Herschler Building, 2 West
122 West 25th Street
Cheyenne, Wyoming 82002
Phone: (307) 777-7695

• • • • • • • • • • • • • • • • • • • •

SOUTHWEST ⋙ ARIZONA, NEVADA, NEW MEXICO, OKLAHOMA, TEXAS ⋘

The American southwest lures many looking for sunshine or moonlight, quiet or excitement, history or the future, new beginnings or retirement. The focus tends to be outdoor life and riches. How you wish to experience this life and wealth is up to you. The southwest has seen oil strikes, silver strikes, Las Vegas jackpots and successful cattle ranches larger than some states. Nature provides a Grand Canyon, a painted desert, wonderful rock formations, amazing plant and animal life, and opportunities for hiking, spelunking, off-roading, ballooning, rock climbing, and horseback riding 'til the cows come home—because you'll have to bring them in.

Texas is the epitome of the southwest for many. Texas covers over a quarter million square miles, encompassing lush semi-tropical areas along the Gulf of Mexico to very flat, dry and arid land up in the north and west. Rivers have always been important in Texas life, and the northern, eastern and southern borders are largely defined by rivers, the Rio Grande, of course, being the best known.

Aside from the obvious pleasures of vacationing on the Gulf of Mexico, southern Texas offers such unique spots as the Alamo in San Antonio, Space Center Houston, numerous nature preserves, Fiesta Texas in San Antonio, the Astrodome in Houston, and many more finds in a state that proudly displays its past while welcoming the future.

Northern Texas is the country America thinks of as the true home of the cowboys and the get-rich-quick oil strikes. And at one time that was true. A tour that will introduce the family to the land of cattle raising and cattle drives would include Amarillo, Lubbock and Abilene.

The oil boom side of things is best explored in Dallas. Dallas is a diverse and exciting city with parks and entertainment throughout. Lakes and rivers provide water sports, and of course professional sports are well represented.

Texas' neighboring oil-rich state is Oklahoma. Many families have become quite wealthy off these rigs, including Native American families originally from the South who were forced into Oklahoma via the Trail of Tears.

Oklahoma is the home of the Dust Bowl and Will Rogers and cattle drives. Quite arid in the western panhandle, eastern Oklahoma has rivers and lakes enough for anyone looking for water sports and hiking terrain.

Anyone who has seen a New Mexico license plate knows it is "The Land of Enchantment," and only a short visit will prove that true. An average-sized average-shaped state on our Mexican border, New Mexico is full of unique surprises.

New Mexico's flavor is a blend of cultures and eras. Native American, Spanish, Mexican, American and European cultures mix in almost every aspect of life. And all is overshadowed and shaped by the landscape. With near-desert conditions to the south, there are snow skiing areas to the north. The landscape has drawn large numbers of artists to centers like Albuquerque and Taos, most notable perhaps being Georgia O'Keefe. The ancient indigenous peoples' heritage draws many to the state for archaeological exploration and visits to the cliff dwellings and Anasazi ruins, the pueblos and current Native American culture and arts, the awareness and study of traditional spiritual practices, and the current struggles of Indian nations such as those in the Four Corners region.

For the family looking for something different and exciting, New Mexico can be an ideal choice. Outdoor sports opportunities include traditional camping, hiking, climbing, riding and off-road driving, plus air sports and water sports. Keep an eye out for rodeos and horse racing events as well. And don't forget to take a trip down into Carlsbad Caverns, a cool, magical world hidden beneath the hot dry sun. If shopping and artistic exploration is preferred—no problem—Santa Fe and Albuquerque are well noted for these more refined pleasures, as well as fabulous restaurants and museums.

Arizona draws a variety of folks looking for warm dry air, a stay at a dude ranch or a baseball spring camp, the Grand Canyon and maybe a little winter golf. This is also a good spot to try out your equipment and your stamina if you're headed down to Baja California for an adventurous journey.

Another major aspect of Arizona is the Indian reservations. These are sovereign nations and private residences of the people who live on them. Contact a tribe before you go, or check in local towns if you want to meet and talk with any given group. Don't just head onto the land to hike, sightsee or knock on doors. There are numerous culture centers, museums and universities where you can learn more about the indigenous people of an area. And, be warned, once you fall in love with the southwest, you will want to meet the people who have been part of it for so long.

Nevada puts yet another spin on wide-open vistas and desert-like conditions. From Las Vegas in the south to Reno in the northwest to the Salt Flats stretching outward to the east, Nevada provides opportunities for you to accept and turn into an adventure.

Las Vegas was one man's dream that has become a booming city with a very stable and loyal population. Aside from the tempting casinos and nightclubs, many folks go to Las Vegas to shop, or to use as a homebase while visiting more remote areas of the southwest.

In the Lake Tahoe/Reno area there is a lively nightlife with casinos, including shows and theater. The history of the area is exciting and somehow familiar——including tales of the Donner Party and the truly difficult journey over the Sierra Nevadas, and the Ponderosa country of the Bonanza series, which often featured old Virginia City and Carson City (the Nevada state capital).

Reno has a reputation all its own. It is a fine university town, has casinos and quite a night life. And in August Reno draws car buffs from all corners for its Hot August Nights. Whatever you go for, you'll enjoy the scenery and find the locals very friendly.

REMEMBER—PERSONS MUST BE AT LEAST 21 YEARS OF AGE TO GAMBLE IN CASINOS IN NEVADA.

Arizona Office of Tourism
2702 N. 3rd St., Suite 4015
Phoenix, Arizona 85004
Phone: (800) 842-8257

Arizona State Parks
1300 West Washington Street,
Suite 415
Phoenix, Arizona 85007
Phone: (602) 542-4174

State Fish & Game
2221 West Greenway Road
Phoenix, Arizona 85023
Phone: (602) 942-3000

Nevada Commission on Tourism
401 North Carson Street
Carson City, Nevada 89701
Phone: (800) NEVADA-8

Nevada Division of State Parks
South Curry Street
Carson City, Nevada 89703
Phone: (775) 687-4384

Nevada Department of Wildlife
1100 Valley Road
Reno, Nevada 89612
Phone: (775) 688-1500

New Mexico Department of Tourism
Lamy Building, Room 106
491 Old Santa Fe Trail
Santa Fe, New Mexico 87503
Phone: (800) 733-6396

State Parks & Recreation
P.O. Box 1147
Santa Fe, New Mexico 87504
Phone: (888) NMPARKS

Department of Game & Fish
Villagra Building
State Capitol
Santa Fe, New Mexico 87503
Phone: (800) 863-9310

National Forests—Southwestern Region
517 Gold Avenue, S.W.
Albuquerque, New Mexico 87102
Phone: (505) 842-3292;
(800) 280-CAMP

Oklahoma Tourism & Recreation Department
500 Will Rogers Boulevard
P.O. Box 6078
Oklahoma City, Oklahoma 73146
Phone: (800) 652-6552;
(405) 521-2406

Department of Wildlife Conservation
1801 North Lincoln Boulevard
Oklahoma City, Oklahoma 73105
Fax: (405) 521-6535

Texas Tourist Development
P.O. Box 5064
Austin, Texas 78711
Phone: (800) 888-8839;
(512) 462-9191

Tourism Division
Texas Department of Commerce
Box 12728
Austin, Texas 78711
Phone: (512) 936-0101

Travel & Information
State Department of Highways
P.O. Box 5000
Austin, Texas 78763
Phone: (800) 452-9292

U.S. Forest Service
701 North First Street
Lufkin, Texas 75901
Phone: (936) 639-8501;
   (800) 280-CAMP

Parks & Wildlife
4200 Smith School Road
Austin, Texas 78744
Phone: (512) 389-4800

• •

PACIFIC STATES ≪ CALIFORNIA, OREGON, WASHINGTON ≫

California is one large state that covers a number of types of destinations for your family to choose from. We'll start at the south and head north, and then go out-of-state north into Oregon and Washington.

San Diego was the first town to grow in California following the arrival of Europeans, and its mission—Mission Basilica San Diego de Alcala—was the first in the string of 21 missions up the Camino Real. As the territory and then state grew, the hub of activity moved northward out of San Diego. But for the last 100 years San Diego has been putting itself back on the map.

The weather and ocean are beautiful and mild in the San Diego area, often with the Summer morning fogs so common in San Francisco and other coastal towns. And San Diego does revolve around the water, despite increased growth inland. The Coronado, Mission Bay, and Balboa Park are among the most lovely areas.

San Diego is best known for two things—the San Diego Zoo and Wildlife Park and the military establishments. While both are well worth a visit, don't leave out Sea World, Old Town, the Mission, Point Loma, Del Mar, the water sports and ocean fishing available. There is excellent shopping downtown, and San Diego continues to provide great convention and meeting facilities.

Heading north, we come to the Los Angeles area, which everyone knows is the home of Hollywood and Disneyland. Fantasyland fits right in in Southern California. But not only is Disneyland available for you to enjoy (again and again)—there is also Knott's Berry Farm and Universal Studios. To be more exact, and to get you pointed in the right direction, Disneyland is in Anaheim, Knott's Berry Farm is in Buena Park, and Universal Studios is in Universal City. But Hollywood is still in Hollywood, unless it's on location elsewhere. Many studios open their doors to guests, so check with your favorite film studio or one located near your lodgings.

There is so much packed into this area. Some folks come just for Disneyland—which is always fun—but at least be aware of all the rest the Los Angeles area has to offer. There is a museum honoring each of numerous cultures and human endeavors, there are libraries and gardens and zoos tucked here and there. Many colleges and universities are in the area for the family to check out for future college students. Science, especially marine science, looms large on the southern California coast. History pops up in odd places in a city that, the more carefully you look, the less plastic it becomes. Cultures come together here and people try out their dreams under the sun. And while the sun does seem to be shining most of the time, right along the coast it is usually mild all year long.

Bridging from southern to northern California, you have your choice of following the coastal route, or giving the Central Valley a try. The Valley is very large and very special. Basically, the San Joaquin River flows up from the south and the Sacramento from the north, meeting in the Delta and dumping into San Francisco Bay. When Europeans first arrived, the Central Valley was mostly marshland— lush and teaming with game. Now, this is a long drive through agricultural lands and growing towns, or you might want to include Palm Springs or Death Valley.

The coastal route is at least as long a drive and includes some great scenery. Parts of Highway I are not comfortable for those afraid of heights or who tend to carsickness. Favorite stops along the way are San Luis Obispo, San Simeon (reservations required at Hearst Castle), Monterey (and that great aquarium), Carmel, Santa Cruz, and maybe a fair and festival like Gilroy's Garlic Festival or Watsonville's Artichoke Festival.

Even those who don't know much about San Francisco and the Bay Area have an opinion about it. There is so much history, such a multiplicity of peoples and things, that everyone seems to be touched somehow by happenings in and near San Francisco—whether it's Silicon Valley, sports teams, universities, social upheaval and re-evaluation, seismic and wildlife activities including wayward whales, immigration events. . . .

Perhaps the most interesting aspect of the San Francisco Bay is the gathering of cultures. You can immerse yourself in several Asian cultural areas (Chinatown in San Francisco, Oakland and San Jose; Japan Town in San Francisco; Southeast Asian communities), Hispanic areas (the Mission in San Francisco, Mexican, Central American and Filipino areas throughout the Bay Area); European (North Beach's Italian community, the Russian community out in the Avenues); Native American enclaves quietly maintained here and there (remember when the Indians reclaimed Alcatraz?); and African American communities of long standing in San Francisco and Oakland. Oakland was the end of the pullman lines in the first half of the 20th century, and many black railroad employees who had seen just about every part of the U.S. and who had been saving for years chose to settle and raise families or retire in Oakland. A very proud and elite community has grown from those settlers. Also, San Francisco became the seat of the Russian Royalists in exile, providing the basis for a Russian community which now welcomes a new generation of Russians out exploring the world.

For natural wonders, expect diversity in opportunities and in weather. Water sports are not as popular as in warmer, more southern climes, but whale watching and ocean fishing trips are available, there are yacht harbors and marinas here and there, and the San Francisco Maritime Museum is fascinating. Angel Island is a great getaway by ferry from Tiburon in Marin with bike and hiking trails. The Golden Gate National Recreational Area encompasses large chunks of land along the ocean, including Fort Mason and the Golden Gate Bridge. Extreme effort by many individuals is working toward a natural hiking trail that will completely encircle the Bay Area. The trail down the East Bay is complete, and other portions are in place, but the final trail will be awesome and definitely will not be possible in one day's march. There are resorts, spas, tennis clubs, golf courses, skating rinks, race tracks, etc., to meet anyone's desires.

The entire San Francisco Bay Area loves to party. Opening Day on the Bay, Mardi Gras, St. Patrick's Day, Cinco de Mayo, Chinese New Years, and the list goes on and on. And the Bay Area has been a favorite home for many musicians and artists, from the conservative to the avant garde. Rarely will you see such diversity of peoples and architecture— OK, rarely on the West Coast.

Whether you are looking for a quiet foggy day in the Japanese Tea Garden in Golden Gate Park, a fast and furious day of shopping Down-

town, a day at the races at Golden Gate Fields, museum hopping at the De Young, the Mexican, the Asian, the California Museum of History, the Cartoon Art, the Performing Arts, the Oakland Museum, or the Exploratorium, bicycling down the Peninsula, enjoying the grand old hotel-now-spa Claremont in the Oakland hills, re-visiting the Old Fillmore Theater and the Haight-Ashbury, hitting the theater district (don't forget Beach Blanket Babylon!), or roundtripping on the various ferries on the Bay, watching the seals and windsurfers, circling Alcatraz and flying a kite off the stern—it's worth a trip.

Several hours east of San Francisco is Lake Tahoe. Lake Tahoe perches atop the Sierra Nevada Mountains in the elbow angle between California and Nevada. At over 6,000 feet elevation, the weather is alpine. Long known for its pure, deep, blue waters, this jewel is surrounded by mountain peaks, smaller lakes, meadows, and the long slow decline to the Nevada salt flats to the east and the Sacramento Valley to the west.

Tahoe is not a cosmopolitan metropolis, but it does abound with natural beauties and nature explorations, water sports, snow sports and hiking in excess. Needless to say, this is a small sampling of what the Golden State has to offer.

But there is a lot more to the Pacific states. North of California is Oregon, renown for its beautiful coastline, its green, fertile valleys, and its rugged mountain ranges. Two main arteries north-south are Highway 101 which runs right along the Pacific Ocean and is beautiful if slow (be sure and stop in Tillamook for some great cheese), and Highway 5 which runs up through Ashland, Eugene, Salem and on to Portland. Ashland is the home of a great Shakespeare festival that runs all summer long, Eugene is a very pleasant and welcoming university town, Salem is the capital of the state and Portland is a lovely city that just gets better and better. Portland is also a major port on the Columbia River which borders Oregon and Washington. There are great outdoor opportunities on the Columbia, as well as several parks on either side of the river.

Oregon's interior has destinations that you will want to fit into your itinerary. Crater Lake is a geological wonder with a beauty all its own;

the Cascade Mountains and Siskiyou National Forest provide miles and miles of wilderness; and the eastern side of the state offers more mountains, high plains and open country.

Washington state is no slouch in the area of great scenery and outdoor recreation either. From the forested Olympic Peninsula to the enormous inland waterways and lakes of the Straits and Sound to the many lakes and mountains farther inland, Washington is a wonderland for hiking, packing, watersports, hunting and fishing. And in just about all of these locales you will find evidence of the Native American cultures that have maintained continuous residence—this is the land of totem poles and huge war canoes.

Seattle, Tacoma and the cities of Puget Sound are very cosmopolitan and have many sights. These are also the jumping-off points for those visiting the islands of the Sound, and Seattle is a great spot to board ship for Vancouver Island or an Alaskan cruise. Just be sure to take along your wet weather gear when you visit the Washington coastal areas. The Olympic Peninsula is one of the few remaining cool-weather rainforests, and that takes a lot of moisture.

Disneyland
1313 Harbor Boulevard
Anaheim, California
Phone: (714) 781-4560

Los Angeles City Recreation & Parks Department
200 North Main Street
Los Angeles, California 90012
Phone: (213) 485-5555
California Office of Tourism

Department of Commerce
801 K Street, Suite 1600
Sacramento, California 95814
Phone: (800) 862-2543

California Department of Fish & Game
1416 Ninth Street
Sacramento, California 95814
Phone: (916) 653-7664

California State Park System
Department of Parks & Recreation
P.O. Box 942896
Sacramento, California 94296
Phone: (916) 653-6995

San Diego International Visitors Information Center
11 Horton Plaza
San Diego, California 92101
Phone: (619) 236-1212

National Park Service
Fort Mason, Building 201
San Francisco, California 94111
Phone: (415) 556-0560

San Francisco Visitor Information Center
201 3rd St., Suite 900
San Francisco, California 94103
Phone: (415) 391-2000

California Office of Tourism
Department of Commerce
P.O. Box 9278
Van Nuys, California 91409
Phone: (916) 322-2881;
    (800) 862-2543

Oregon Tourism Commission
755 Summer Street NE
Salem, Oregon 97310
Phone: (503) 986-0000;
    (800) 547-7842

Oregon Department of Parks &
    Recreation
1115 Commerical Street, NE
Salem, Oregon 97301
Phone: (503) 378-6305;
    (800) 551-6949

Department of Fish & Wildlife
2502 SW First Street
P.O. Box 59
Portland, Oregon 97207
Phone: (503) 872-5268

U.S. Forest Service
333 SW 1st Avenue
Portland, Oregon 97208
Phone: (503) 808-2971;
    (800) 280-CAMP

Washington State Travel
    Development Division
101 Genl. Administration, AX-13
Olympia, Washington 98504
Phone: (800) 544-1800

• •

HAWAII & ALASKA

H A W A I I

We've watched Hawaii from afar in movies, on TV, on travel posters and every vacation book in print. It seems everyone goes to Hawaii as often as possible. And why not? It's paradise!

Hawaii is the southernmost of the 50 United States, and is an archipelago of 125 islands. There are 8 main islands. Looking at a map, they read (from southeast to northwest) Hawaii, Kahoolawe, Maui, Lanai, Molokai, Oahu, Kauai and Niihau. The territory reaches from sea level as far as the eye can see to a height of over 13,000 feet at Mauna Kea on the Big Island— Hawaii. If you're at all interested in the birth of an island, the first chapter of James Michener's "Hawaii" is a must read. Read it aloud to your kids (or have them read it aloud to you) so they can get a feel for the tremendous time and change involved.

Most of the islands have national or state parks and each has some unique feature—a glowing lava flow, the best curls for surfing in the U.S., super snowskiing, pineapple and other plantations, superb beaches, whale and dolphin areas, and the list goes on.

The history of the islands is comparatively short, humans having been a late addition to the chain. The Polynesians only arrived about 1000 to 1400 years ago, with Europeans and Asians arriving on the Sandwich Islands in the late 18th century. There are cultural centers and historical museums dotted around, including, of course, Pearl Harbor.

There are so many ways to enjoy the Hawaiian Islands. You can laze in the shade on a quiet beach, take advantage of the water sports, the night life, the shopping, the many natural parks, or rely on the resort areas to entertain you. When you are browsing the various resorts, notice how many provide special children's programs. For pure romance or for family frolics, its hard to beat Paradise.

ALASKA

The 49th state to enter the United States of America (in 1959), Alaska has always been full of surprises, treasures and magnificence. Chances are that will never change. Originally the bridge between Asia and the Americas, this was the original highway by which animals, plants and humans entered vast new lands. In more recent years, Seward's Folly has provided a gold rush in the 1880s and an oil rush that began in 1968 and resulted in the Alaska Pipeline. The human pipeline in Alaska tends to be the Alcan Highway.

Alaskan geography is widely varied, from sand dunes above the arctic circle, to dense, incredibly lush forests, backed by 1000-foot-high sheer cliffs in Tracy Arm. Three mountain systems delineate Alaska's land mass: the Coast Range, the Alaska/Aleutian Range, and the Brooks range. There are 19 mountains higher than 14,000 feet, topping out with Mt. McKinley at 20,320 feet. So how about some major climbing or photo expeditions?

The tidal shoreline of Alaska is almost 45,000 square miles; one reason there are so many cruise ships plying the Inland Passage. Alaska has three million lakes which are over two acres in size each, which makes this a fishing paradise, if you can stand the mosquitos. All of this water also provides a necessary ingredient for an abundance of animal life.

If you plan on driving, find out all you possibly can about the route, where you're staying and what may be going on weather-wise. The Alaska-Canadian Highway is very, very long and an adventure in itself. Be prepared!

The isolated position of Alaska and its proximity to Siberia provides for some especially interesting vacation opportunities: The native cultures of Alaska are very much alive and there are many cultural centers and events that welcome visitors. Reminders of Imperial Russia's occupation of Alaska can be found in such spots as Seldovia and Sitka.

By the way, Alaska has no snakes, but it does have ice worms (really!).

Alaska State Division of Tourism
P.O. Box 110810
Juneau, Alaska 99811
Phone: (907) 465-2010

Alaska Marine Highway System
P.O. Box 102344
Anchorage, Alaska 99510
Phone: (800) 642-0066

Alaska Railroad Corporation
P.O. Box 7-2111
Anchorage, Alaska 99510
Phone: (907) 265-2300

State of Alaska Division of Parks and Outdoor Recreation
550 W. 7th Avenue, Suite 1260
Anchorage, Alaska 99508
Phone: (907) 269-8400

U.S. Department of the Interior
U.S. Fish and Wildlife Service
605 West 4th Avenue, Suite 105
Anchorage, Alaska 99501
Phone: (907) 271-2737

Alaska Department of Fish and Game
P.O. Box 25526
Anchorage, Alaska 99802
Phone: (907) 465-4100

Hawaii Visitors Bureau
Waikiki Business Plaza
2270 Kalakaua Avenue
Honolulu, Hawaii 96815
Phone: (808) 923-1811

Division of State Parks
Department of Land & Natural Resources
1151 Punchbowl Street
Honolulu, Hawaii 96813
Phone: (808) 548-0300

Fishing & Hunting Regulations
Department of Land & Natural Resources
1151 Punchbowl Street
Honolulu, Hawaii 96813
Phone: (808) 587-0166

THE GREAT OUTDOORS

• •

SPORTS

BACKPACKING WITH KIDS

To some people, the wilderness is a home away from home. This belief includes backpacking and taking part in nature. Backpacking is an inexpensive and fun way for families and friends to escape from cars and city life. Backpacking takes little time to plan and can be a great all-day adventure. Your body may be sore after trekking through the woods, but your soul and mind will be at peace. Children love taking part in nature with all the different sights and sounds and smells they are extremely curious about. Parents can relish spending a relaxing time with their kids knowing the children will sleep well that night. And years later, parents and children can laugh and reflect on all the wonderful times they had in the woods.

While staying in a hotel or cabin for a night can be quite costly, backpacking for a day then making a campsite can be fairly cheap. Although backpacking takes a little work, it's time well spent. Children will love being a part of planning the trip and helping their parents along the way. You should first find out what areas are best to backpack and if camping (if you choose to do so) is permitted.

Pack as lightly as possible. Don't over-burden yourself with too many clothes. You'll probably start out wearing shorts and a t-shirt, so bring along a pair of pants, sweater, light jacket, a pair of underwear, and a pair of socks and shoes. Nothing too bulky or heavy. Cotton or linen are the best fabrics to wear in the heat. Don't forget a swimsuit if you'll be near water.

Try to backpack fairly close to home. Sitting in a car too long will bore you and the kids. And you want to start out early in the day to ensure plenty of time to travel, rest, and play.

Make sure to bring the kids' favorite foods. They will need some comforts from home and you want them to fully enjoy themselves on the trip. Pack a lot of food that doesn't require refrigeration and is light-weight like bread and trail mix. On the trip, it's best to eat small portions at frequent intervals to avoid stomach aches. And unless you want to treat the water you'll use for cooking and drinking, bring a couple jugs of bottled water.

Pack a few toys and try to think about some stories to tell on the walk. Also, don't forget the sun lotion, hat and sunglasses. A small medical kit will also be helpful.

If you're planning on camping over, bring light-weight camping gear. A tarp can be placed over a tent in case of rain and to provide shade. And camp close to a lake so you and the children can take a swim after a long day of walking.

Wear comfortable hiking boots which fit over the ankle. Make sure to double-knot the laces to avoid tripping. If the shoes aren't water-resistant, bring a pair of rain boots with good bottom grips. If you have a problem with corns or blisters pack some Band-aids.

Along the walk, take numerous breaks to rest and eat. Don't push yourself too hard and don't force young children to walk many miles in a day. In fact, it's best to backpack when children are very young and can travel on your back or when they're older and are beyond the stage of needing a nap during the day. However, backpacking is a fun thing for anyone at any age.

· ·

Backpacking Tips to Keep in Mind

1. Find out what areas are the best to backpack and camp.
2. Pack light; a few extra clothes are all you'll need.
3. Don't travel too far from home and start out early in the day.
4. Pack kids' favorite foods; bring food that isn't heavy and doesn't require refrigeration.
5. Bottled water or water treatment tablets will work for cooking and drinking.
6. Pack toys, maps and the essentials like sun lotion, sunglasses, and a medical kit.

7. Bring a tarp to put over the tent and other light-weight camping gear.
8. Camp near a lake so you can take a swim and wash out some clothes.
9. Wear hiking boots which fit over your ankle; bring rain boots just in case, and extra socks.
10. Give yourself plenty of time to take in the view and rest when you need it. Don't forget the camera!

• •

BICYCLING WITH KIDS

You get to know a place better on a bicycle than you do whizzing past it in a car and kids love riding bicycles. Why not take advantage of that affinity when making your vacation plans? Bicycling is something the whole family can participate in. Children that are too young to ride on their own can come along in a child seat or trailer. Older kids relish the independence of covering the countryside under their own power. And everybody gets plenty of fresh air and exercise. Can you see yourself gliding along winding back roads, stopping for chats with a local farmer, or for a picnic with a view? A bicycling trip may be the solution for your next vacation.

You can plan to make a series of day trips from a central base, or an extended tour for the more ambitious families (with careful planning, you can carry camping gear along). And bicycles can be rented just about anywhere, so you might consider a day or two of bicycling at whatever vacation destination you've picked for your next trip. And don't forget to check the Adventure Travel section for bicycle trips designed with families in mind! The advantage of a planned tour, of course, is that you don't have to worry about equipment, accommodations or meals—it's all taken care of for you.

Whether you're taking a planned tour, or striking out on your own, we've put together some hints to make your touring go smoothly.

• •

Tips for Bicycling with Kids

1. Take it easy! This is a vacation, not the Tour de France. Don't set a rigid itinerary for your trip—nothing is worse

than stressing about getting to the next stop along the road when you're supposed to be enjoying the great outdoors. Get an early start, but park the bikes early, too, to give the kids time to play, and yourself some time to relax. Let the kids set the pace on the road—remember, they're working harder than you are, and if you're toting a little one in a child seat or trailer, you'll appreciate the leisurely approach they take. Plan on taking frequent short breaks, and don't be afraid to take time for distractions and mini-adventures along the way—they're the stuff memories are made of!

2. Safety first! Make sure that you have good bicycles, helmets and child seats for the little ones. Ride with one parent in front and one in back. Always bicycle with the flow of traffic and be sure your kids know about hand signals and traffic laws (like obeying traffic lights and stop signs).

3. Pack a small bag for each child to carry on the handlebars, with favorite toys and a notebook. You might give each child one of those disposable cameras to chronicle their favorite sights along the road.

4. Pack snacks and plenty of liquids. Everybody should have their own water bottle attached to the bike, to cut down on drink breaks.

5. Juice boxes are a nice treat.

6. Think layers. The early morning chill may progress to intense heat with a bit of exertion under the midday sun. Make sure everybody is dressed comfortably, and bring along extra sweaters and jackets in case the weather changes.

Enjoy the ride!

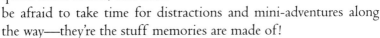

GOLF WITH KIDS

If you've decided that a golfing vacation with the younger set is what you want, you should consider a few things. First off, be honest, do you want to play a lot of golf and hope the kids will get the bug, or have you tested the waters and determined that this is what everyone wants? You could always go to a wonderful golf mecca such as Palm Springs, Myrtle Beach or Scottsdale and stay in a hotel or motel and take lessons at one of the good golf schools. Or you could spend the bucks to go to a fantastic resort, take advantage of a good golf package, and send the kids to the driving range. Golf resorts generally cater to adults and serious golfers take a dim view of kids on the course—plus the fact that you'll be forking over hefty green fees for that kid. We think a good way is to rent a condo in a golf community, take lessons, and be able to practice whenever the urge hits. Golf communities abound in the Carolinas, Arizona, Hawaii and even New England. After you've had your lessons, you can use the practice greens, chipping areas, and you have all the recreational amenities.

Could be you want to sign the kids up for golf camp. Try the Leadbetter schools—they cater to kids and adults and are in places we all want to go, such as Palm Springs, Orlando, Atlanta, and Naples and Bradenton, Florida. Their number is (800) 424-DLGA. Another reputable teaching program for younger people is a place in Massachusetts called Winchendon, and their number is (800) 824-7336. And there's the "Coaches" program with schools in various places. Call them at (800) 929-1108. Prices vary—everyone charges what the traffic will bear, so check around, and if you're willing to go to Arizona in July, you'll probably find some fantastic deals. Ask the sales people for a referral list in your area, then call those people and see what they thought. Any good school will give you names of previous students. Also, ask among your friends, and where you play golf, people are eager usually to share a good experience.

・ ・

Tips for Junior Golfers

1. Get a copy of the United States Golf Association's Official Rules of Play booklet. Read it and carry it in your bag. Older players will be in awe, and you'll learn the basics of the game plus the elements of etiquette on the course.
2. Understand and abide by the dress code of golf. This is the time to leave tank tops, baggy clothes and gorilla suits in the closet.

3. When you're playing golf, *PLAY*. Don't practice, and don't hold up the group behind you—the foursome waiting for you might have the guy who was going to give a new golfer his old set of Big Berthas, but when you dawdled he muttered "Forget that tortoise."

4. Don't get sucked into expensive equipment. A beginner can use garage sale clubs, and when your handicap starts to come down and your Dad is ashamed to be seen with you, maybe he'll surprise you.

5. Never play in a thunderstorm—head for the clubhouse and watch the storm on TV.

6. Walk whenever possible—it's good exercise, carts cost too much, and you should save using them 'till the day your age matches your total score for 18 holes.

7. Be courteous to the people in the pro shop; they could be your new best friends.

8. Learn to control your temper on the golf course. Just because you shanked a drive into the parking lot and heard shattering glass doesn't mean you can explode to the point that old ladies sneer and report you to the marshal.

9. Be adventuresome. Frequently when you want to play, the starter will pair you with a stranger, and this can be a learning experience. Don't act disgusted that you have to play with a stranger—he might be annoyed that he has to play with you.

10. Above all, enjoy the game, the camaraderie, and the chance to meet a new challenge in a gorgeous setting.

. . . .

HIKING

When people think about spending time away from home, they tend to think about spending money. However, hiking is a great, inexpensive way to exercise and spend time with the family. Hiking, when done safely, can relax a person when they needed relaxation most. It is also a way to learn about nature and sometimes the history of the area. In some parks, markers are available for hikers to read about outcroppings and other geographic formations. Hiking is a way for kids to expend some of the vast amount of energy they have and get away from the confines of school and home.

Before starting out, get a map of the area you will be hiking in order to plan a safe route. The map will keep you from getting completely lost and will allow for you to think about what trails to take, about how long the hiking will last, best places to rest, etc. Parents need to be concerned about the length of trails since kids will get too tired if the trip is long and difficult. Choose trails without large rocks on the ground where you could trip and avoid trails with steep embankments when you have small children.

Watch the weather forecasts; rain will certainly dampen your perfectly planned trip. Even if sunny weather is predicted, bring along a rain coat just in case. A cap and thin gloves will be comforting in cooler weather. A sweater and light jacket can be tied around the waist and an extra pair of socks and shoes should be taken.

Bring a compass, flashlight, map, matches, and a Swiss army knife. Getting lost isn't any fun and can be dangerous; the light, matches, and knife will probably not be used but are helpful around dusk when the sun goes down and the temperature decreases. If fires are permitted in the area, make sure to surround the fire with rocks and put out the fire completely when you're ready to move on.

Snack foods should be in large supply. Children will need frequent snacks along the way and lots to drink. Don't overeat before you begin, though. You don't want to cramp up or become sick on the walk. Take along food that is light, compact, and won't melt or go bad in warm weather. Peanut butter sandwiches are good for the energy you'll need to keep going. Trail mix is also good. Bottled water is best to drink since soda will dehydrate you. Put all the food in air-tight bags.

Your feet are the most important body part when hiking. Make sure your shoes are comfortable and have good grips on the bottom. Invest in a pair that are durable and water-proof and break them in at home. Double knot your shoes to avoid tripping and wear thick cushioning socks (and bring at least one extra pair). When you get home, soak and massage your feet since they will probably be a little sore.

Sunglasses with good UV protection are important, along with sunscreen and lip block and a hat. You may be shaded by trees for part of your walk, but don't be fooled; the sun's rays are still quite strong and a bad burn can be avoided with lotion.

Favorite toys should be brought along, as well as diapers (if necessary) and a thin roll of toilet paper for rest stops. Also, you don't want to be stuck on a trail without a medical kit and medication such as an asthma inhaler. You might want to carry a cellular phone in case of an emergency. A camera is a must to capture the wilderness and great fun.

Hiking Tips to Keep in Mind

1. Get a map of the trails you'll be hiking in order to plan for a safe and fun trip.
2. Watch weather forecasts to avoid rain and cold, but bring rain gear and warm clothes as a precaution.
3. Bring along articles such as a compass, flashlight, map, matches, and Swiss army knife to stay on the right track and light your way if necessary.
4. Food should be plentiful, light-weight, and high-energy.
5. Wear shoes with good grips, plenty of foot space, and that are water-resistant.
6. Soak and massage your feet at the end of the day.
7. Sunglasses, sunblock, lip block and a hat are essential to avoid hurting your eyes and skin.
8. Toys for the kids, diapers, and toilet paper are also necessary.
9. Don't forget a medical kit and medication like an asthma inhaler.
10. A camera will capture the beautiful sights.

SAILING & CANOEING

Sailing the seas can be peaceful, beautiful, romantic, and a great way for families to work and play together. Even for the novice, learning to sail a small boat can be done in a matter of hours. Classes are available from charter services, and your local recreation facilities can also be helpful in teaching you the finer points of boating. If you would rather do more sight-seeing than steering, hiring an experienced boater is the ticket. Boating is certainly an easy way to travel with all the comforts of home in a compact space. Children will love the experience of helping with the rowing and steering, as well as the accessibility to water for swimming and fishing.

First you have to decide what type of boat you want and whether you want to hire someone to get, and keep, the boat moving. Buying a boat is not cheap, but renting a boat for a day or two can be relatively inexpensive. Just call around for the best time to go and area to travel.

Familiarize yourself with the area you are sailing. Watch the weather forecast to avoid storms or heavy rains. Don't try a long or difficult trip if you are a novice.

Safety is critical. Everyone needs a life-preserver. Small children may wear a buoy float which fits around the chest. Harnesses may be helpful for walking children under the age of three. Safety nets are important in avoiding falls.

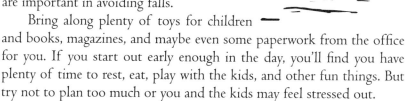

Bring along plenty of toys for children and books, magazines, and maybe even some paperwork from the office for you. If you start out early enough in the day, you'll find you have plenty of time to rest, eat, play with the kids, and other fun things. But try not to plan too much or you and the kids may feel stressed out.

Make sure you stock up on a lot of food. Since stores are not easy to get at once you're on the water, over-estimate how much food to bring. Non-refrigerated food is best such as breads, peanuts, crackers, etc. Stock a cooler with bottled water. Soda is not a good idea to bring along since it will dehydrate you.

Sunscreen, hats and lip block are a must. Buy the water-resistant lotion to avoid having to reapply if you take a swim.

Make use of the water and take a short swim every so often. It will cool you off and relax your muscles. If you want to see more than what's above the water, bring along a snorkel, goggles, and flippers. An under-water camera is great for capturing sealife.

If you're prone to seasickness, Dramamine can calm your nervous stomach. If you prefer to avoid medication, try a wristband called Sea-Band which can be ordered through most boat catalogs. Keeping your stomach full helps to avoid sickness. If children are kept busy, they often don't suffer from stomach mal de mer.

Canoeing is a great way to see the outdoors at a slow pace. Although space is limited, a canoe can easily accomodate three adults or two adults and two children, along with a cooler, fishing poles, bait box, etc. Life preservers should be worn at all times since light canoes can tip easily.

Sailing Tips to Keep in Mind

1. Decide the best boat to fit your economic, time, and spacial needs.
2. Don't be afraid to ask for help if you're inexperienced; take along a knowledgeable companion for added protection.
3. Know the area and weather forecast before going out.
4. Have the proper life preservers available for every person.
5. Make sure the boat has safety nets for children.
6. Bring along plenty of toys and books.
7. Too much food is better than not enough at sea.
8. Bring all necessary medications and sunscreen to ensure a pleasant day.
9. Don't forget any underwater devices you want.
10. Buy or rent a heavy canoe to avoid easy tipping.

FAMILY CRUISE ROUND-UP

Most of the major cruise lines offer supervised activities for children, similar to the camp-like programs offered by large resorts. (More active families should see the adventure travel listings for information on rafting trips!)

When you're picking a cruise line for your family, be sure and ask specifically for a cruise that offers the kid's programs, and check to make sure that it covers your child's age group. Some cruise lines offer children's programs only during the holidays, or offer programs for very small children only in the mornings, for example. Also ask about babysitting services and how much they cost. You'll find descriptions of some of the children's programs offered by major cruise lines, as well as an alternative vacation for floating families. Following are examples of a few cruise line offerings.

Princess Cruises

Four of the line's vessels feature special youth centers, while other ships offer a special children's program when 15 or more children are on board. Youth centers are open from 9am to midnight every day.

Board game tournaments, coloring contests, arts and crafts, bingo, scavenger hunt, ice cream, pizza parties, and storytelling. Showings of kids' movies such as The Wizard of Oz, Bambi and Cinderella happen every night. Counselors supervise individual swimming, pool games and snorkeling lessons. For teenagers, there's exercise classes, arts and crafts, Italian lessons and video games, and a different PG or PG-13 movie every night. Babysitting and nursery services are not available, minimum age is 24 months, and meals are not provided in the youth centers. The fare for children traveling as 3rd and 4th berth passengers is about half of the minimum rate. For more information, contact a travel agent.

Premier Cruise Lines

First Mates, for 2- to 4-year-olds, offers a club house with stories, singalongs and treasure hunts, toys and games. Kids Call for 5- to 7-year-olds offers ice cream parties, a kiddie pool and magic show, a tour of the ship's bridge by the Captain, and starring roles in the ship's current theatrical production; Starcruisers, 8- to 10-year-olds, have their own junior pool; the 11- to 13-year-old Navigators enjoy sports activities; and 14- to 17-year-old Teen Cruisers get to know each other at their own dances and karaoke parties. And if you're a single parent looking to get away with the kids, Premier Cruise Lines can help you plan your great escape. Single parents sail at 125% of the regular fare, and kids 17 and under cruise for the lower 3rd, 4th and 5th guest rate. Ask your travel agent for more information.

Norwegian Cruise Line

Norwegian Cruise Line's Kid's Crew program offers activities for youths ages 3 to 17, including games, parties, scavenger hunts on the line's private island in the Bahamas, and autograph-signing parties with professional athletes. Youngsters can pick their meals from their own kids menu, including the Space Mouse Special, King Kong Burger and Jaws Dawgs, and Universal Studio characters such as Woody the Woodpecker, Rocky and Bullwinkle put in personal appearances. The program is offered year round for ages 6 to 17 aboard all vessels, with programs for ages 3 to 5 available during the summer months and holidays (though restricted to sea days and mornings). For more information and reservations, call a travel agent or call (800) 327-7030.

Carnival Cruise Line

Carnival Cruise Line's Camp Carnival provides morning-to-night activities for kids in four age groups: 2 to 4, 5 to 8, 9 to 13 and 14 to 17 years old. The program operates from 9:30 a.m. to 9:30 p.m. most days, after which babysitting services are available, for a nominal charge, at slumber parties in the children's playrooms. Carnival's Fun Ships include a 15-foot-high, 114-foot-long water flume slide. Carnivals nine ships sail to the Bahamas, Caribbean and Mexican Riviera on three-, four- and seven-day cruises, and the line also offers Carnival Cruise and Disney Vacations. Call a travel agent for more information.

The Barge Lady

As an alternative to the giant cruise ship, families can try floating the canals of France and Britain in barges. The Barge Lady offers a personalized brokering service for European barges, matching customers "to that perfect barge—perfect in terms of price, amenities, special interests, number and composition of group, specific area desired and previous travel history." Ellen Sack, who operates the service, says that the barge trips are less expensive than the large lines, and cater to a variety of interests. "The informal La Belle Aventure is an especially good choice for families with small children. Facilities aboard include both a child-sized bicycle and a tandem bicycle, and the sightseeing program can be customized to include everyone's interests." For more information, and to request a copy of The Barge Lady's current offerings, call (800) 880-0071.

American Hawaii Cruises

American Hawaii Cruises offers children's programs seasonally, or anytime 12 or more children are on board a ship. Both of the company's ships offer a youth recreation center and full-time recreation coordinators who organize shipboard activities for kids age 5 to 16 including pool games, talent shows, arts and crafts, hula lessons and ukulele classes. Freshwater swimming pools and a movie theater are also onboard. American Hawaii Cruises sail from Honolulu with shore excursions including raft adventures off the coast of Kauai, snorkeling and sailing near Kona, a trip to Volcanoes National Park on the Big Island, bicycling down the 10,000-foot Haleakala Volcano on Maui and seasonal whale watching trips. For information, call (800) 513-5022.

SKIING WITH KIDS

Like the rest of the tourism industry, ski areas have developed a focus on services for families and children to keep up with the changing demographics of their customers. They offer classes for children of all ages, and nursery and child-care facilities for the youngest members of the family. Most ski resorts offer half-day and full-day skiing programs for children ages 4 to 12, which usually include instruction, lift tickets, rental equipment, food and supervision. And you might consider eschewing the slopes for the cross-country trails, which can be a less costly alternative and provide a relaxing, wilderness experience with your family. Here are tips on making your family ski vacation go smoothly.

Staying Warm is Your First Priority!

The most important thing you can do in planning a ski trip is to be sure that everybody is dressed for the weather. While it may be a fashion show on the slopes, everybody will be happier if you make staying warm your first priority. A cold skier is an unhappy skier, and hypothermia is scary and avoidable.

Insulated bib overalls, a turtleneck, good water-resistant ski gloves and a wool hat are a good bet for children. (Turtlenecks or neck cuffs are better than scarfs, which could get caught in lift machinery, and are just another thing to deal with anyway.) Remember that beginning skiers fall down a lot, and pay attention to your child's complaints about being cold, or just being miserable. Remember that leaving the slopes for a warming hot chocolate at the lodge is no great loss—why are you there, anyway? (I hope the answer is to spend time with your kids!) Bring an extra pair of gloves for the kids to change into mid-day. If you're just up for the day, pack dry clothes to change into for the drive home.

Other Skiing Tips

1. Pack some high-energy snacks, and a thermos of hot chocolate. Dried fruit and peanuts, even a pastry left over from breakfast are great for a break in the snow, and provide an energy boost between meals.

2. Avoid the crowds—plan your ski trips for midweek when the slopes are less crowded.

3. Try cross-country skiing—you may never go back to the slopes! Travel literature usually focuses on downhill skiing, but downhill skiing is not everybody's cup of tea, and indeed, looks a little absurd to cross-country enthusiasts. Why spend most of your day standing in noisy, crowded lift lines, when you could be gliding gracefully across silent, empty fields? If your child is scared of the slopes, they might enjoy 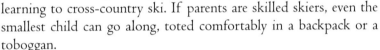 learning to cross-country ski. If parents are skilled skiers, even the smallest child can go along, toted comfortably in a backpack or a toboggan.

4. Rent equipment at the ski area for the first year or two. Kids grow and equipment needs change as skill levels improve.

5. Don't burden your child with expectations about their abilities—you're in this for the fun, remember? Encourage them and congratulate them for whatever progress they make, and for the simple fact that they're putting in the effort.

6. Plan several trips when the kids are first learning and the learning curve is steep. Don't make them wait till next winter to ski just when they're getting the hang of it.

7. Use plenty of sunblock. Winter sunlight reflecting off the snow at high altitudes is intense. Protect their eyes from the sun, with a hat with a wide brim or visor, kid-size ski goggles or sunglasses attached with Croakies.

BEGINNER'S SKI SLOPES

Sunday River Ski Resort
P.O. Box 450
Bethel, Maine 04217
Phone: (800) 543-2SKI;
   (207) 824-3000

Suicide Six in Woodstock
(not scary, just sounds that way ...)
Woodstock Inn
14 The Green
Woodstock, Vermont 05091
Phone: (800) 448-7900;
   (802) 457-1100

Ski Windham
(3 hours from New York City)
Windham, New York 12496
Phone: (518) 734-4300;
   (800) 729-SKI-W

Arrowhead Mountain
(in Vail area)
Drawer A
Edwards, Colorado 81632
Phone: (800) 622-3131;
   (926) 926-3029

Ski Sunlight
(between Vail and Aspen)
10901 Road 117
Glenwood Springs, Colorado 81601
Phone: (800) 445-7931;
   (970) 945-7491

Telluride Ski and Summer Resort
(5-star beginner hill)
P.O. Box 11155
Telluride, Colorado 81435
and **The Peaks at Telluride**
Phone: (800) 789-2220

Ski Santa Fe
1210 Luisa Street
Santa Fe, New Mexico 87501
Phone: (505) 982-4429.

Coeur d'Alene Resort
(In Coeur d'Alene packages include
   free skiing at Silver Mountain)
Silver Mountain
610 Bunker Avenue
Kellogg, Idaho 83837
Phone: (208) 783-1111

Northstar Ski Resort
(Near Lake Tahoe)
P.O. Box 129
Truckee, California 96160
Phone: (800) GO-NORTH;
   (916) 562-1010

Cross-Country Skiing

Although winter can be an uneasy time of cold, sickness, and "cabin fever," there are many alternatives to change your attitude from depression to relaxation. All it takes is a pair of skis, boots, poles, and some fluffy snow to make the lows drift away. Not only is cross-country skiing a relaxing mode of exercise, it is also healthy, invigorating, and a beautiful way to travel. The cost is quite inexpensive compared to downhill skiing, and it offers more time to spend with your skiing companions, breathe in the clean air, and view the majestic scenery.

Go to your local sporting goods store and ask plenty of questions about the proper skis, boots, and poles which will fit your size, level, etc. You want the boots especially to be comfortable. Walk around the store for a while with the boots on and keep in mind you will be wearing thick socks so choose a larger size. Children's feet grow fast, so always buy a larger size for them.

A talk and perhaps an appointment with your physician may be necessary before you plan a cross-country skiing excursion. You certainly don't want to over-exert yourself in the woods if you have a heart or any other type of medical problem which could prompt an emergency. An exercise program may be designed by your doctor a few months before the first snowfall so your body will be better equipped to handle the vigors of skiing.

Once you've decided on a place to ski, check out the area before you actually put on your gear. If you're going on a ski vacation miles from home, call park stations and get the best advice for the safest area to ski. If it's your first time, hire an instructor to ski with you. They can keep you and your family on the right track.

Make sure you dress for the weather. It may be fairly warm when you begin skiing, but after a few hours the temperature will surely drop. Wear plenty of layers: thermal underwear; long-sleeved shirt (preferably a turtle-neck); a thick sweater; pants; wool socks, cap, and gloves. Make sure your coat does not extend too far down from your waist, as it will hinder your leg movements. You may need to shed layers as your body warms from exertion.

Sunglasses and sunblock with plenty of protection are necessary. And a tube of lip block is also helpful.

If you have a cellular phone which will still work well in the cold, bring it along. You can tuck it into a zippered pocket. If an emergency arises, the phone will be a blessing.

Bring along some snacks. Have some trail mix, sandwiches, crackers, and a small container of bottled water handy in a backpack. Try not to eat too much before you begin skiing or you may experience some cramping. Just take regular breaks and nibble here and there.

Don't push yourself or your children too much. Ski slowly in the beginning and gradually build up some speed. Take rest stops and check out the view. You could bring a compact set of binoculars to get a better look at the wildlife surrounding you.

Plan for a hot bubble bath after skiing. And, if possible, sit in a warm hot tub and have everyone give each other a massage. Your muscles will thank you!

Tips for Cross-Country Skiing

1. Talk to your physician about cross-country skiing as a form of exercise and how it works with your health.
2. Get the proper gear for the family's skiing needs.
3. Make sure you are somewhat familiar with the area you'll be skiing.
4. Hire an instructor if necessary to help you with the trails or take a lesson first time out.
5. Wear warm, comfortable, and free-moving clothing in layers you can remove.
6. Bring protection like sunglasses, sunblock, hat and lip block.
7. Bring along a cellular phone in case of an emergency.
8. Snacks will help give you and your children energy to keep you from getting tired too quickly.
9. Carry a backpack to store food, water, and other essentials.
10. Don't over-work your muscles; keep a slow pace if you're inexperienced.

WATERSPORTS

Rather than spelling the end of sporting holidays, travelling with your children can actually mark a new beginning, opening up new sports and new ways of doing things.

Snorkeling

Snorkeling is an activity very well suited to family involvement. Some of the best snorkeling takes place in very shallow water. (In just 3 feet of water off the island of Cozumel we counted 10 varieties of tropical fish!) Best advice is to start slowly, wear plenty of sun block and keep safety uppermost in your mind. One problem that may arise is finding gear to fit children. Many resorts simply don't have it to rent. A better idea, if you love to snorkel, is to buy the gear before you leave home. Check your local diving store for the brands Body Glove Junior and Voit.

For special diving packages, Rascals in Paradise offers several diving and snorkeling oriented vacations around the world, (800) 872-7225.

Surfing

Who hasn't listened to the Beach Boys and dreamed of shooting the curl? For older kids, a vacation at a surf camp could be incredibly appealing. And almost anyone can learn how—all you need know is how to swim and have a good sense of balance. If "hanging 10" sounds like fun, check out these programs:

Richard Schmidt Surf Camp
Santa Cruz, California
Phone: (831) 423-0928

Summer Fun Surf Camp
San Clemente, California
Phone: (949) 361-9526

Surf Sessions
Fenwick Island, Delaware
Phone: (302) 539-2126

Margo Oberg's Surfing School
Kaui, Hawaii
Phone: (808) 742-8019

Fishing

Long renowned as a prime whiler away of time and a good opportunity to talk and bond, fishing continues to be more popular than ever; you can go about your fishing from a very low-tech or high-tech viewpoint, and find togetherness along the way. You, too, can develop famous family fish tales about the ones you caught and ate as well as those that got away. Small children may enjoy using a net attached to a stick in shallow water to see what they come up with. Catches of tiny animals may be observed and released. Digging for clams and collecting mussels are other easy and gratifying pursuits.

. . . .

Fishing Tips to Keep in Mind

1. Pay attention to the tide and make sure you don't get caught on isolated rocks with the tide coming inn.
2. In most places you need a fishing permit for both fishing and clamming. Some states make exceptions if only children are fishing. Check it out, fines are steep.
3. Be very careful with fish hooks, which can easily become imbedded in human skin and may necessitate a visit to a hospital for removal.
4. Spear fishing should only be attempted by older children accompanied by experienced spear fishers.

5. Sea sickness—come prepared if your gang is susceptible.
6. Sunburn is a real threat as light reflected off the water intensifies the sun's burning rays. Be sure to wear sunscreen, sun block on sensitive areas, and a broad brimmed hat. Long sleeves will protect your arms.
7. Don't forget the lemons, oil, etc. you'll need to cook up your catch.

PARKS & CAMPING

Park: "A plot of ground used as a public place for recreation."

Many people gauge a town, a city, a country, by the quantity and quality of parks available. And ideas about what a park should be change with the times. A century ago, parks were places to stroll and socialize; a place to go to listen to musical performances and political speakers before radio, TV and movies.

Today, parks come in all sizes and to many purposes. The **town park** with its gardens, benches and playground can make city life more pleasant, and can be the perfect spot for the kids to let off steam while the family stays at a city hotel on a vacation.

The **community park** is often a *fairground* and may well be your destination for a specific gathering—collectors show, fair, or event. Originally this was probably that field near town where the traveling circus would set up; traveling preachers would put up a tent here for revival meetings; barnstorming pilots would use the open land as a landing strip for selling rides. When you get to a new area, be sure and check the schedule at the local fairgrounds.

Communities set aside land for specific purposes—historic parks, memorial parks, playing fields, amusement parks, public gardens, zoological gardens, RV parks, etc. These can be refreshing stops when on car trips, and can provide stretching room when you are on a heavy schedule of planes, meetings and rooms. They can also be quick and painless learning experiences about an area and its history.

Humans generally love to have a good time, and the entrepreneurs of the world haven't missed this cue—*theme parks* are essentially non-stop fairs. And theme parks aren't all that new—Coney Island has been bustling a long time. But what theme parks have to offer today is remarkable. You can be sure that if you are headed for a theme park like a Disney or Six Flags there will be ample support services nearby. But you will probably also be dealing with crowds and high prices—so be prepared. Humans get pretty serious about having fun.

Then there are the nature parks. Long ago special natural areas were set aside and preserved as holy. Later, wooded parks were marked off and protected by royalty as private hunting preserves. In the United States, we can thank President Theodore Roosevelt for making an issue of preserving areas of great natural beauty for their own right. He combined a love of the outdoors with the power of a president and began the National Parks program. Happily, there is now an array of national, state and local parks which showcases the beauty to be found in every corner of the country.

RULE ONE—Follow The Rules! Every park posts its rules, including hours, restrictions and what is available for the public. These rules protect the park, the visitors, and the community that supports it. Please respect the park and the others who have come to enjoy the park or who work in the park.

Visiting the national parks can be more than a family vacation, it can be a job hunting trip for the teens. Many young people every year go to work for park services. It can be a great first job! It's usually physical, often outdoors, invariably educational, environmentally positive, is good experience in dealing with the public, plus you earn some money.

Parks are also becoming repositories for endangered species, means to protect culturally important locations, and study arenas for ecosystems. We need these areas to remember what the earth is like when not under the heavy hand of man. We need sanctuaries for the variety and wonder of this earth. And we happily have many parks where we can visit the earth. Please honor the parks and all they represent.

U.S. NATIONAL PARKS

Get out your maps! Here are the U.S. National Parks—just location, mailing address and phone number. So, once you know the direction you're headed, get in touch with the parks in that area.

ALASKA

Lake Clark National Park & Preserve
4230 University Drive Suite 311
Anchorage, Alaska 99508
Phone: (907) 781-2218

Yukon-Charley Rivers National Preserve
P.O. Box 167
Eagle, Alaska 99738
Phone: (907) 547-2233

Gates of the Arctic
P.O. Box 26030
Bettles, Alaska 99726
Phone: (907) 661-3520

Wrangell-St. Elias National Park & Preserve
P.O. Box 439
Copper Center, Alaska 99573
Phone: (907) 822-5234

Glacier Bay National Park & Preserve
P.O. Box 140
Gustavus, Alaska 99826
Phone: (907) 697-2230

Alagnak Wild River
c/o Katmai National Park and Preserve
P.O. Box 7
King Salmon, Alaska 99611
Phone: (907) 246-3305

Aniakchak National Monument & Preserve
P.O. Box 7
King Salmon, Alaska 99613
Phone: (907) 246-3305

Cape Krusenstern National Monument
P.O. Box 1029
Kotzebue, Alaska 99752
Phone: (907) 442-3890

Noatak National Preserve
P.O. Box 1029
Kotzebue, Alaska 99752
Phone: (907) 442-3760

Denali National Park & Preserve
P.O. Box 9
Denali Park, Alaska 99755
Phone: (907) 683-2294

Bering Land Bridge National Preserve
P.O. Box 220
Nome, Alaska 99762
Phone: (907) 443-2522

Kenai Fjords National Park
P.O. Box 1727
Seward, Alaska 99664
Phone: (907) 224-3175

Sitka National Historical Park
106 Metlakatla Street
Sitka, Alaska 99835
Phone: (907) 747-6281

Klondike Gold Rush National Historical Park
P.O. Box 517
Skagway, Alaska 99840
Phone: (907) 983-9224

ALABAMA

Russell Cave National Monument
Route 1, Box 175
Bridgeport, Alabama 35740
Phone: (256) 495-2672

Horseshoe Bend National Military Park
11288 Horseshoe Bend Road
Daviston, Alabama 36256
Phone: (205) 234-7111

Little River Canyon National Preserve
P.O. Box 45
2141 East Gault Avenue North
Fort Payne, Alabama 35967
Phone: (256) 845-9605

Tuskegee Institute National Historic Site
125 National Forest Road 949
Tuskegee, Alabama 36083
Phone: (334) 727-2652

ARKANSAS

Fort Smith National Historic Site
P.O. Box 1406
Fort Smith, Arkansas 72902
Phone: (501) 783-3961

Arkansas Post National Memorial
1741 Old Post Road
Gillett, Arkansas 72055
Phone: (870) 548-2207

Buffalo National River
402 N. Walnut, Suite 136
Harrison, Arkansas 72601
Phone: (870) 439-2502

Hot Springs National Park
P.O. Box 1860
Hot Springs, Arkansas 71902
Phone: (501) 623-3383

Pea Ridge National Military Park
P.O. Box 700
Pea Ridge, Arkansas 72751
Phone: (501) 451-8122

ARIZONA

Organ Pipe Cactus National Monument
Route 1, Box 100
Ajo, Arizona 85321
Phone: (520) 387-6849

Fort Bowie National Historic Site
P.O. Box 158
Bowie, Arizona 85605
Phone: (520) 847-2500

Montezuma Castle National Monument
P.O. Box 219
Camp Verde, Arizona 86322
Phone: (520) 567-3322

Tuzigoot National Monument
P.O. Box 219
Camp Verde, Arizona 86322
Phone: (520) 634-5564

Canyon De Chelly National
Monument
P.O. Box 588
Chinle, Arizona 86503
Phone: (520) 674-5500

Casa Grande Ruins National
Monument
1100 Ruins Drive
Coolidge, Arizona 85228
Phone: (520) 723-3172

Sunset Crater Volcano National
Monument
Route 3, Box 149
Flagstaff, Arizona 86002
Phone: (520) 526-0502

Walnut Canyon National
Monument
Walnut Canyon Road #3
Flagstaff, Arizona 86004
Phone: (520) 526-3367

Wupatki National Monument
H.C. 33, Box 444A
Flagstaff, Arizona 86004
Phone: (520) 679-2365

Hubbell Trading Post National
Historic Site
P.O. Box 150
Ganado, Arizona 86505
Phone: (520) 755-3475

Grand Canyon National Park
P.O. Box 129
Grand Canyon, Arizona 86023
Phone: (520) 638-7888

Coronado National Memorial
4101 East Montezuma Canyon Rd.
Hereford, Arizona 85615
Phone: (520) 366-5515

Pipe Spring National Monument
HC 65 Box 5
Fredonia, Arizona 86022
Phone: (520) 643-7105

Glen Canyon National Recreation
Area
P.O. Box 1507
Page, Arizona 86040
Phone: (520) 645-6404

Rainbow Bridge National
Monument
c/o Glen Canyon Recreation Area
P.O. Box 1507
Page, Arizona 86040
Phone: (520) 608-6200

Petrified Forest National Park
P.O. Box 2217
Petrified Forest National Park,
Arizona 86028
Phone: (520) 524-6228

Tonto National Monument
HC02 Box 4602
Roosevelt, Arizona 85545
Phone: (520) 467-2241

Navajo National Monument
H.C. 71, Box 3
Tonalea, Arizona 86044
Phone: (520) 672-2700

Saguaro National Monument
3693 South Old Spanish Trail
Tucson, Arizona 85730
Phone: (520) 733-5758

Tumacacori National Historical
Park
P.O. Box 67
Tumacacori, Arizona 85640
Phone: (520) 398-2341

Chiricahua National Monument
c/o Dos Cabezas Route
Box 6500
Wilcox, Arizona 85643
Phone: (520) 824-3560

CALIFORNIA

Santa Monica Mountains National Recreational Area
401 West Hillcrest Drive
Thousand Oaks, California 91360
Phone: (805) 370-2301

Redwood National Park
1111 Second Street
Crescent City, California 95531
Phone: (707) 464-6101

Eugene O'Neill National Historic Site
P.O. Box 280
1000 Kuss Road
Danville, California 94526
Phone: (925) 838-0249

Death Valley National Monument
P.O. Box 579
Death Valley, California 92328
Phone: (760) 786-2331

Manzanar National Historic Site
c/o Death Valley National Park
P.O. Box 426
Independence, California 93526
Phone: (760) 878-0062

John Muir National Historic Site
4202 Alhambra Avenue
Martinez, California 94553
Phone: (925) 228-8860

Muir Woods National Monument
Mill Valley, California 94941
Phone: (415) 388-2595

Lassen Volcanic National Park
P.O. Box 100
Mineral, California 96063
Phone: (530) 595-4444

Pinnacles National Monument
5000 Hwy 146
Paicines, California 95043
Phone: (831) 389-4485

Point Reyes National Seashore
Point Reyes, California 94956
Phone: (415) 663-1092

Cabrillo National Monument
1800 Cabrillo Memorial Drive
San Diego, California 92106
Phone: (619) 557-5450

Fort Point National Historic Site
P.O. Box 29333, Presidio
San Francisco, California 94129
Phone: (415) 556-1693

Golden Gate National Recreation Area
Fort Mason, Building 201
San Francisco, California 94123
Phone: (415) 556-0560

San Francisco Maritime National Historical Park
Fort Mason, Building E
San Francisco, California 94123
Phone: (415) 556-3002

Devils Postpile National Monument
P.O. Box 501
Mammoth Lakes, California 93546
Phone: (760) 934-2289

Kings Canyon National Park
47050 Generals Highway
Three Rivers, California 93271
Phone: (559) 565-3341

Sequoia National Park
47050 Generals Highway
Three Rivers, California 93271
Phone: (559) 565-3341

Lava Beds National Monument
P.O. Box 867
Tulelake, California 96134
Phone: (530) 667-2282

Joshua Tree National Historic Site
74485 National Monument Drive
Twentynine Palms, California 92277
Phone: (760) 367-5500

Channel Islands National Park
1901 Spinnaker Drive
Ventura, California 93001
Phone: (805) 658-5730

Whiskeytown-Shasta-Trinity
National Recreation Area
P.O. Box 188
Whiskeytown, California 96095
Phone: (530) 246-1125

Yosemite National Park
P.O. Box 577
Yosemite National Park, California 95389
Phone: (209) 372-0200

COLORADO

Hovenweep National Monument
McElmo Route
Cortez, Colorado 81321
Phone: (970) 562-4282

Dinosaur National Monument
4545 E. Highway 40
Dinosaur, Colorado 81610
Phone: (970) 374-2215

Rocky Mountain National Park
1000 Highway 36
Estes Park, Colorado 80517
Phone: (970) 586-1206

Florissant Fossil Beds National
Monument
P.O. Box 185
Florissant, Colorado 80816
Phone: (719) 748-3253

Colorado National Monument
Fruita, Colorado 81521
Phone: (970) 858-3617

Curecanti National Recreation Area
102 Elk Creek
Gunnison, Colorado 81230
Phone: (970) 641-2337

Bent's Old Fort National Historic
Site
35110 Highway 194 East
La Junta, Colorado 81050
Phone: (719) 383-5010

Yucca House National Monument
c/o Mesa Verde National Park, P.O.
Box 8, Colorado 81321
Phone: (970) 529-4465

Black Canyon of the Gunnison
National Monument
102 Elk Creek
Gunnison, Colorado 81230
Phone: (970) 641-2337

Great Sand Dunes National
Monument
11500 Highway 150
Mosca, Colorado 81146
Phone: (719) 378-2312

Mesa Verde National Park
P.O. Box 8
Park, Colorado 81330
Phone: (970) 529-4465

CONNECTICUT

Weir Farm National Historic Site
735 Nod Hill Road

Wilton, Connecticut 06897
Phone: (203) 834-1896

DISTRICT OF COLUMBIA

Constitution Gardens
c/o National Capital Parks
900 Ohio Drive, SW
Washington D.C. 20242
Phone: (202) 426-6841

Ford's Theater National Historic Site
c/o National Capital Parks
900 Ohio Drive, SW
Washington D.C. 20242
Phone: (202) 426-6924

Frederick Douglass National Historic Site
1411 W Street, SE
Washington D.C. 20020
Phone: (202) 426-5961

John F. Kennedy Center for the Performing Arts
2700 F Street, NW
Washington D.C. 20566
Phone: (800) 444-1324

Lincoln Memorial
c/o National Capital Parks
900 Ohio Drive, SW
Washington D.C. 20242
Phone: (202) 426-6841

Mary Mcleod Bethune Council House
1318 Vermont Avenue, NW
Washington D.C. 20005
Phone: (202) 673-2402

National Capital Parks
900 Ohio Drive
Washington D.C. 20242
Phone: (202) 485-9880

National Mall
c/o National Capital Region
900 Ohio Drive, SW
Washington D.C. 20024
Phone: (202) 485-9880

Pennsylvania Avenue National Historic Site
900 Ohio Drive, SW
Washington D.C. 20024
Phone: (202) 485-9880

Rock Creek Park
3545 Williamsburg Lane, NW
Washington D.C. 20008
Phone: (202) 426-6828

Vietnam Veterans Memorial
c/o National Capital Parks
900 Ohio Drive, SW
Washington D.C. 20224
Phone: (202) 426-6841

Washington Monument
c/o National Capital Parks
900 Ohio Drive, SW
Washington D.C. 20242
Phone: (202) 426-6841

The White House
c/o National Capital Region
1100 Ohio Drive, SW
Washington D.C. 20242
Phone: (202) 208-1631

Fort Washington Park
13551 Fort Washington Road
Washington D.C. 20744
Phone: (301) 736-4600

Piscataway Park
13551 Fort Washington Road
Washington D.C. 20744
Phone: (301) 763-4600

Thomas Jefferson Memorial
c/o National Capital Parks
900 Ohio Drive, SW
Washington D.C. 20024
Phone: (202) 426-6841

F L O R I D A

Biscayne National Park
9700 SW 328 Street
Bomestead, Florida 33033
Phone: (305) 230-7275

De Soto National Memorial
P.O. Box 15390
Brandenton, Florida 34280
Phone: (941) 792-0458

Gulf Islands National Seashore
1801 Gulf Breeze Parkway
Gulf Breeze, Florida 32561
Phone: (850) 934-2600

Dry Tortugas National Park
P.O. Box 6208
Key West, Florida 33041
Phone: (305) 242-7700

Everglades National Park
40001 State Road 9336
Homestead, Florida 33034
Phone: (305) 242-7700

Fort Caroline National Memorial
12713 Fort Caroline Rd.
Jacksonville, Florida 32225
Phone: (904) 641-7155

**Timucuan Ecological & Historic
Preserve**
12713 Ft. Caroline Road
Jacksonville, Florida 32225
Phone: (904) 641-7155

Big Cypress National Preserve
HCR 61, Box 110
Ochopee, Florida 33141
Phone: (941) 695-2000

**Castillo De San Marcos National
Monument**
1 South Castillo Drive
St. Augustine, Florida 32084
Phone: (904) 829-6506

**Fort Matanzas National
Monument**
8635 AIA South
St. Augustine, Florida 32080
Phone: (904) 471-0116

Canaveral National Seashore
308 Julia Street
Titusville, Florida 32796
Phone: (321) 267-1110

GEORGIA

**Andersonville National
Historic Site**
496 Cemetery Road
Andersonville, Georgia 31711
Phone: (229) 924-0343

**Martin Luther King, Jr., National
Historic Site**
450 Auburn Avenue, NE
Atlanta, Georgia 30312
Phone: (404) 331-3920

**Chattahoochee River National
Recreation Area**
1978 Island Ford Parkway
Dunwoody, Georgia 30350
Phone: (770) 399-8070

**Chickamauga & Chattanooga
National Military Park**
P.O. Box 2128
Fort Ogelthorpe, Georgia 30742
Phone: (706) 866-9241

**Kennesaw Mountain National
Battlefield Park**
900 Kennesaw Mountain Drive
Kennesaw, Georgia 30152
Phone: (770) 427-4686

Ocmulgee National Monument
1207 Emery Hwy
Macon, Georgia 31217
Phone: (912) 752-8257

**Jimmy Carter National
Historic Site**
P.O. Box 392
300 North Bond Street
Plains, Georgia 31780
Phone: (229) 824-4104

Fort Pulaski National Monument
P.O. Box 30757
Savannah, Georgia 31410
Phone: (912) 786-5787

**Cumberland Island National
Seashore**
P.O. Box 806
St. Marys, Georgia 31558
Phone: (912) 882-4336

**Fort Frederica National
Monument**
Route 9, Box 286-C
St. Simons Island, Georgia 31522
Phone: (912) 638-3639

GUAM

**War in the Pacific National
Historical Park**
115 Haloda Building, Marine Drive
Asan, Guam 96922
Phone: (671) 472-7240

HAWAII

Hawaii Volcanoes National Park
P.O. Box 52, Hawaii 96718
Phone: (808) 985-6000

**Pu'uhonua O Honaunau National
Historical Park**
P.O. Box 129
Honaunau, Hawaii 96726
Phone: (808) 328-2326

U.S.S. Arizona Memorial
1 Arizona Memorial Place
Honolulu, Hawaii 96818
Phone: (808) 422-2771

Kaloko-Honokohau National
   Historical Park
73-4786 Kanalani Street, Suite 14
Kailua Kona, Hawaii 96740
Phone: (808) 329-6881

Kalaupapa National Historical Park
P.O. Box 2222
Kalaupapa, Hawaii 96742
Phone: (808) 567-6802

Puukohola Heiau National
   Historic Site
P.O. Box 44340
Kawaihae, Hawaii 96743
Phone: (808) 882-7218

Haleakala National Park
P.O. Box 369
Makawao, Hawaii 96768
Phone: (808) 572-4400

I O W A

Effigy Mounds National
   Monument
151 Highway 76
Harpers Ferry, Iowa 52146
Phone: (319) 873-3491

Herbert Hoover National
   Historic Site
P.O. Box 607
West Branch, Iowa 52358
Phone: (319) 643-2541

I D A H O

Craters of the Moon National
   Monument
P.O. Box 29
Arco, Idaho 83213
Phone: (208) 527-3257

Nez Perce National Historical Park
Route 1, Box 100, Highway 95
   South
Spalding, Idaho 83540
Phone: (208) 843-2261

City of Rocks National Reserve
P.O. Box 169
Almo, Idaho 83301
Phone: (208) 824-5519

Hagerman Fossil Beds National
   Monument
P.O. Box 570, 221 North State
   Street
Hagerman, Idaho 83332
Phone: (208) 837-4793

I L L I N O I S

Lincoln Home National
   Historic Site
413 South Eighth Street
Springfield, Illinois 62701
Phone: (217) 492-4241

INDIANA

Lincoln Boyhood National Memorial
P.O. Box 1816
Lincoln City, Indiana 47552
Phone: (812) 937-4541

Indiana Dunes National Lakeshore
1100 North Mineral Springs Road
Porter, Indiana 46304
Phone: (219) 926-7561

George Rogers Clark National Historical Park
401 South Second Street
Vincennes, Indiana 47591
Phone: (812) 882-1776

KANSAS

Fort Scott National Historic Site
P.O. Box 918
Fort Scott, Kansas 66701
Phone: (620) 223-0310

Fort Larned National Historic Site
Route 3
Larned, Kansas 67550
Phone: (316) 285-6911

KENTUCKY

Abraham Lincoln Birthplace National Historic Site
2995 Lincoln Farm Road
Hodgenville, Kentucky 42748
Phone: (207) 358-3137

Mammoth Cave National Park
P.O. Box 7
Mammoth Cave, Kentucky 42259
Phone: (270) 758-2251

Cumberland Gap National Historical Park
P.O. Box 1848
Middlesboro, Kentucky 40965
Phone: (606) 248-2817

LOUISIANA

Poverty Point National Monument
c/o State Commemorative Area
P.O. Box 248
Epps, Louisiana 71237
Phone: (318) 926-5492

Jean Lafitte National Historical Park & Preserve
365 Canal Street, Suite 2400
New Orleans, Louisiana 70130
Phone: (504) 589-3882

MAINE

Acadia National Scenic Trail
P.O. Box 177
Bar Harbor, Maine 04609
Phone: (207) 288-3338

Saint Croix Island International Historic Site
c/o Acadia National Park
P.O. Box 177
Bar Harbor, Maine 04609
Phone: (207) 288-3338

Keweenaw National Historical Park
P.O. Box 471
Calumet, Michigan 49913
Phone: (906) 337-3168

Sleeping Bear Dunes National Lakeshore
P.O. Box 277
9922 Front Street
Empire, Michigan 49630
Phone: (213) 326-5134

Isle Royale National Park
800 East Lakeshore Drive
Houghton, Michigan 49931
Phone: (906) 482-0984

Pictured Rocks National Lakeshore
P.O. Box 40
Munsing, Michigan 49862
Phone: (906) 387-3700

MARYLAND

Fort McHenry National Monument & Historic Shrine
End of East Fort Avenue
Baltimore, Maryland 21230
Phone: (410) 962-4290

Assateague Island National Seashore
7206 National Seashore Lane
Berlin, Maryland 21811
Phone: (410) 641-1441

Monocacy National Battlefield
4801 Urbana Pike
Frederick, Maryland 21704
Phone: (301) 662-3515

Clara Barton National Historic Site
5801 Oxford Road
Glen Echo, Maryland 20812
Phone: (301) 492-6245

Greenbelt Park
6565 Greenbelt Road
Greenbelt, Maryland 20770
Phone: (301) 344-3948

Thomas Stone National Historic Site
6655 Rosehill Road
Port Tobacco, Maryland 20677
Phone: (301) 934-6027

Antietam National Battlefield
P.O. Box 158
Sharpsburg, Maryland 21782
Phone: (301) 432-5124

Chesapeake & Ohio Canal National Historical Park
P.O. Box 4
Sharpsburg, Maryland 21782
Phone: (301) 739-4200

Catoctin Mountain Park
6602 Foxville Road
Thrumont, Maryland 21788
Phone: (301) 663-9388

Hampton National Historic Site
535 Hampton Lane
Towson, Maryland 21286
Phone: (410) 823-1309

MASSACHUSETTS

Boston African American National Historic Site
14 Beacon Street, Suite 506
Boston, Massachusetts 02108
Phone: (617) 742-5415

Boston National Historical Park
Charlestown Navy Yard
Boston, Massachusetts 02129
Phone: (617) 242-5601

Marxh-Billings National Historical Park
c/o North Atlantic Region
15 State Street
Boston, Massachusetts 02109
Phone: (617) 223-5200

Frederick Law Olmsted National Historic Site
99 Warren Street
Brookline, Massachusetts 02445
Phone: (617) 566-1689

John Fitzgerald Kennedy National Historic Site
83 Beals Street
Brookline, Massachusetts 02446
Phone: (617) 566-7937

Longfellow National Historic Site
105 Brattle Street
Cambridge, Massachusetts 02138
Phone: (617) 876-4491

Minute Man National Historical Park
174 Liberty Street
Concord, Massachusetts 01742
Phone: (978) 369-6993

Lowell National Historical Park
67 Kirk Street
Lowell, Massachusetts 01852
Phone: (978) 970-5000

Adams National Historic Site
P.O. Box 531
135 Adams Street
Quincy, Massachusetts 02169
Phone: (617) 773-1175

Salem Maritime National Historic Site
c/o Custom House
174 Derby Street
Salem, Massachusetts 01970
Phone: (978) 740-1650

Saugus Iron Works National Historic Site
244 Central Street
Saugus, Massachusetts 01906
Phone: (781) 233-0050

Cape Cod National Seashore
99 Marconi Station Site Road
South Wellfleet, Massachusetts 02667
Phone: (508) 255-3421

Springfield Armory National Historic Site
1 Armory Square
Springfield, Massachusetts 01105
Phone: (413) 734-8551

MINNESOTA

Grand Portage National Monument
P.O. Box 668, 315 So. Broadway
Grand Marais, Minnesota 55604
Phone: (218) 387-2788

Voyageurs National Park
3131 Highway 53 South
International Falls, Minnesota 56649
Phone: (218) 286-5258

Pipestone National Monument
36 Reservation Avenue
Pipestone, Minnesota 56164
Phone: (507) 825-5464

Mississippi National River & Recreation Area
111 East Kellogg Blvd.
St. Paul, Minnesota 55101
Phone: (651) 290-4160

MISSOURI

George Washington Carver National Monument
5646 Carver Road
Diamond, Missouri 64840
Phone: (417) 325-4151

Harry S. Truman National Historic Site
223 North Main Street
Independence, Missouri 64050
Phone: (816) 254-9929

Wilson's Creek National Battlefield
6424 West Farm Rd. 182
Republic, Missouri 65738
Phone: (417) 732-2662

Jefferson National Expansion Memorial
11 North Fourth Street
St. Louis, Missouri 63102
Phone: (314) 655-1700

Ulysses S. Grant National Historic Site
7400 Grant Street
St. Louis, Missouri 63123
Phone: (314) 842-3298

Ozark National Scenic Riverways
P.O. Box 490
Van Buren, Missouri 63965
Phone: (573) 323-4236

MISSISSIPPI

Natchez National Historical Park
640 South Canal Street Box E
Natchez, Mississippi 39120
Phone: (601) 446-5790

Gulf Islands National Seashore
3500 Park Road
Ocean Springs, Mississippi 39564
Phone: (850) 934-2600

Brices Cross Roads National Battlefield Site
2680 Natchez Trace Parkway
Tupelo, Mississippi 38804
Phone: (800) 305-7417

Natchez Trace National Scenic Trail
2680 Natchez Trace Parkway
Tupelo, Mississippi 38804
Phone: (800) 305-7417

Natchez Trace Parkway
2680 Natchez Trace Parkway
Tupelo, Mississippi 38804
Phone: (800) 305-7417

Tupelo National Battlefield
2680 Natchez Trace Parkway
Tupelo, Mississippi 38804
Phone: (800) 305-7417

Vicksburg National Military Park
3201 Clay Street
Vicksburg, Mississippi 39183
Phone: (601) 636-0583

MONTANA

Little Bighorn Battlefield National Monument
P.O. Box 39
Crow Agency, Montana 59022
Phone: (406) 638-2621

Grant-Kohrs Ranch National Historic Site
P.O. Box 790
Deer Lodge, Montana 59722
Phone: (406) 846-3388

Bighorn Canyon National Recreation Area
P.O. Box 7458
Fort Smith, Montana 59035
Phone: (406) 666-2412

Glacier National Park
West Glacier, Montana 59936
Phone: (406) 888-7800

Big Hole National Battlefield
P.O. Box 237
Wisdom, Montana 59761
Phone: (406) 689-3155

NEBRASKA

Homestead National Monument of America
8523 W. State Highway 4
Beatrice, Nebraska 68310
Phone: (402) 223-3514

Agate Fossil Beds National Monument
301 River Road
Gering, Nebraska 69346
Phone: (308) 668-2211

Scotts Bluff National Monument
P.O. Box 27
Gering, Nebraska 69341
Phone: (308) 436-4340

Missouri National Recreational River
P.O. Box 591
O'Neill, Nebraska 68763
Phone: (402) 336-3970

Niobrara National Scenic Riverway
P.O. Box 591
O'Neill, Nebraska 68763
Phone: (402) 336-3970

Brown v. Board of Education
  National Historic Site
424 South Kansas Avenue, Suite 220
1709 Jackson Street
Omaha, Nebraska 68102
Phone: (785) 354-4273

NEW HAMPSHIRE

Saint-Gaudens National Historic
  Site
Rural Route 3, Box 73
Cornish, New Hampshire 03745
Phone: (603) 675-2175

NEW JERSEY

Edison National Historic Site
Main Street and Lakeside Avenue

West Orange, New Jersey 07052
Phone: (973) 736-0550

NEW MEXICO

Petroglyph National Monument
6001 Unser Blvd NW
Albuquerque, New Mexico 87120
Phone: (505) 899-0205

Aztec Ruins National Monument
84 County Road 2900
Aztec, New Mexico 87410
Phone: (505) 334-6174

Chaco Culture National Historical
  Park
P.O. Box 220
Nageezi, New Mexico 87037
Phone: (505) 786-7014

Capulin Volcano National
  Monument
P.O. Box 40
Capulin, New Mexico 88414
Phone: (505) 278-2201

Carlsbad Caverns National Park
3225 National Parks Highway
Carlsbad, New Mexico 88220
Phone: (505) 785-2232

El Malpais National Monument
123 E. Roosevelt Avenue
Grants, New Mexico 87020
Phone: (505) 783-4774

White Sands National Monument
P.O. Box 1086
Holloman AFB, New Mexico
  88330
Phone: (505) 479-6124

Bandelier National Monument
Hcr, Box 1, Suite 15
Los Alamos, New Mexico 87544
Phone: (505) 672-0343

Salinas Pueblo Missions National Monument
P.O. Box 517
Mountainair, New Mexico 87036
Phone: (505) 847-2585

Pecos National Historical Park
P.O. Drawer 418
Pecos, New Mexico 87522
Phone: (505) 757-6414

El Morro National Monument
Route 2, Box 43
Ramah, New Mexico 87321
Phone: (505) 783-4226

Zuni-Cibola National Historical Park
c/o Southwestern Region
P.O. Box 728
Santa Fe, New Mexico 87504
Phone: (505) 988-6012

Gila Cliff Dwellings National Monument
HC 68 Box 100
Silver City, New Mexico 88061
Phone: (505) 536-9344

Fort Union National Monument
P.O. Box 127
Watrous, New Mexico 87753
Phone: (505) 425-8025

NEVADA

Great Basin National Park
Highway 488
Baker, Nevada 89311
Phone: (702) 234-7331

Lake Mead National Recreation Area
601 Nevada Highway
Boulder City, Nevada 89005
Phone: (702) 293-8907

NEW YORK

Gateway National Recreation Area
Floyd Bennett Field Building 69
Brooklyn, New York 11234
Phone: (718) 338-3799

Theodore Roosevelt Inaugural National Historic Site
641 Delaware Avenue
Buffalo, New York 14202
Phone: (716) 884-0095

Eleanor Roosevelt National Historic Site
4097 Albany Post Road
Hyde Park, New York 12538
Phone: (845) 229-9115

Home of Franklin D. Roosevelt National Historic Site
4097 Albany Post Road
Hyde Park, New York 12538
Phone: (845) 229-9115

Vanderbilt Mansion National Historic Site
4097 Albany Post Road
Hyde Park, New York 12538
Phone: (845) 229-9115

Martin Van Buren National Historic Site
1013 Old Post Road
Kinderhook, New York 12106
Phone: (518) 758-9689

Saint Paul's Church National Historic Site
897 South Columbus Avenue
Mount Vernon, New York 10550
Phone: (914) 667-4116

Castle Clinton National Monument
26 Wall Street
New York, New York 10005
Phone: (212) 344-7220

Federal Hall National Memorial
26 Wall Street
New York, New York 10005
Phone: (212) 825-6888

General Grant National Memorial
122nd Street and Riverside Drive
New York, New York 10003
Phone: (212) 666-1640

Hamilton Grange National Memorial
287 Convent Avenue
New York, New York 10005
Phone: (212) 283-5154

Statue of Liberty National Monument
Liberty Island
New York, New York 10004
Phone: (212) 363-3200

Theodore Roosevelt Birthplace National Historic Site
28 East 20th Street
New York, New York 10003
Phone: (212) 260-1616

Sagamore Hill National Historic Site
20 Sagamore Hill Road
Oyster Bay, New York 11771
Phone: (516) 922-4788

Fire Island National Seashore
120 Laurel Street
Patchogue, New York 11772
Phone: (631) 289-4810

Fort Stanwix National Monument
112 East Park Street
Rome, New York 13440
Phone: (315) 336-2090

Women's Rights National Historical Park
136 Fall Street
Seneca Falls, New York 13148
Phone: (315) 568-2991

Saratoga National Historic Park
648 Route 32
Stillwater, New York 12170
Phone: (518) 664-9821

NORTH CAROLINA

Blue Ridge Parkway
199 Hemphill Knob Road
Asheville, North Carolina 28801
Phone: (828) 298-0398

Moores Creek National Battlefield
40 Patriots Hall Drive
Currie, North Carolina 28435
Phone: (910) 283-5591

**Carl Sandburg Home National
 Historic Site**
1928 Little River Road
Flat Rock, North Carolina 28731
Phone: (828) 693-4178

**Guilford Courthouse National
 Military Park**
2332 New Garden Road
Greensboro, North Carolina 27410
Phone: (336) 288-1776

Cape Lookout National Seashore
131 Charles Street
Harkers Island, North Carolina
 28531
Phone: (919) 728-2250

**Kings Mountain National
 Military Park**
2625 Park Road
Blacksburg, South Carolina 29702
Phone: (864) 936-7921

Cape Hatteras National Seashore
1401 National Park Drive
Manteo, North Carolina 27954
Phone: (252) 473-2111

Fort Raleigh National Historic Site
c/o Cape Hatteras Seashore
Route 1, Box 675
Manteo, North Carolina 27954
Phone: (252) 473-5772

**Wright Brothers National
 Memorial**
c/o Cape Hatteras Seashore
Route 1, Box 675
Manteo, North Carolina 27954
Phone: (252) 441-7430

NORTH DAKOTA

Theodore Roosevelt National Park
P.O. Box 7
Medora, North Dakota 58645
Phone: (701) 623-4466

**Knife River Indian Villages
 National Historic Site**
P.O. Box 9
Stanton, North Dakota 58571
Phone: (701) 745-3300

**Fort Union Trading Post National
 Historic Site**
15550 Highway 1804
Williston, North Dakota 58801
Phone: (701) 572-9083

OHIO

**Cuyahoga Valley National
Recreation Area**
15610 Vaughn Road
Brecksville, Ohio 44141-3018
Phone: (216) 524-1497

**Hopewell Culture National
Historical Park**
16062 State Route 104
Chillicothe, Ohio 45601-8694
Phone: (740) 774-1125

**William Howard Taft National
Historic Site**
2038 Auburn Avenue
Cincinnati, Ohio 45219
Phone: (513) 684-3262

**Dayton Aviation Heritage National
Historical Park**
P.O. Box 9280
Wright Brothers Station
Dayton, Ohio 45409
Phone: (937) 225-7705

James A. Garfield Historical Site
8095 Mentor Avenue
Mentor, Ohio 44060
Phone: (440) 255-8722

**Perry's Victory & International
Peace Memorial**
P.O. Box 549
93 Delaware Avenue
Put-in-Bay, Ohio 43456-0549
Phone: (419) 285-2184

OKLAHOMA

**Chickasaw National Recreation
Area**
P.O. Box 201
Sulphur, Oklahoma 73086
Phone: (580) 622-3165

OREGON

Fort Clatsop National Memorial
92343 Forth Clatsop Road
Astoria, Oregon 97103
Phone: (503) 861-1620

Oregon Caves National Monument
19000 Caves Highway
Cave Junction, Oregon 97523
Phone: (541) 592-2100

Crater Lake National Park
P.O. Box 7
Crater Lake, Oregon 97604
Phone: (541) 594-2211

**John Day Fossil Beds National
Monument**
HCR 82, Box 126
Kimberly, Oregon 97848
Phone: (541) 987-2333

PENNSYLVANIA

Delaware National Scenic River
c/o Delaware Water Gap National
  Recreation Area
Bushkill, Pennsylvania 18324
Phone: (570) 588-2451

**Delaware Water Gap National
  Recreation Area**
1 River Road
Bushkill, Pennsylvania 18324
Phone: (570) 588-2451

**Allegheny Portage Railroad
  National Historic Site**
110 Federal Park Road
Gallitzin, Pennsylvania 16641
Phone: (814) 886-6150

**Johnstown Flood National
  Memorial**
733 Lake Road
South Fork, Pennsylvania 15956
Phone: (814) 495-4643

**Hopewell Furnace National
  Historic Site**
2 Mark Bird Lane
Elverson, Pennsylvania 19520
Phone: (610) 582-8773

Fort Necessity National Battlefield
1 Washington Parkway
Farmingtown, Pennsylvania 15437
Phone: (724) 329-5805

Eisenhower National Historic Site
97 Taneytown Road
Gettysburg, Pennsylvania 17325
Phone: (717) 338-9114

Gettysburg National Military Park
97 Taneytown Road
Gettysburg, Pennsylvania 17325
Phone: (717) 334-1124

**Great Egg Harbor Scenic &
  Recreational River**
c/o Mid-Atlantic National Park
  Service
143 South Third Street
Philadelphia, Pennsylvania 19106
Phone: (215) 597-1582

**Edgar Allan Poe National Historic
  Site**
532 North Seventh Street
Philadelphia, Pennsylvania 19123
Phone: (215) 597-8780

**Independence National Historical
  Park**
313 Walnut Street
Philadelphia, Pennsylvania 19106
Phone: (215) 597-8974

**Thaddeus Kosciuszko National
  Memorial**
301 Pine Street
Philadelphia, Pennsylvania 19106
Phone: (215) 597-9618

**Friendship Hill National
  Historical Site**
223 New Geneva Road
Point Marion, Pennsylvania 15474
Phone: (724) 725-9190

Steamtown National Historic Site
150 South Washington Avenue
Scranton, Pennsylvania 18503
Phone: (570) 340-5200

**Valley Forge National Historical
  Park**
P.O. Box 953
Valley Forge, Pennsylvania 19482
Phone: (610) 783-1077

PUERTO RICO

San Juan National Historic Site
Fort San Cristobal
Norzagaray Street
San Juan, Puerto Rico 00901

Phone: (787) 729-6960

RHODE ISLAND

Roger Williams National Memorial
282 North Main Street
Providence, Rhode Island 02903
Phone: (401) 521-7266

SOUTH CAROLINA

Cowpens National Battlefield
P.O. Box 308
Chesnee, South Carolina 29323
Phone: (864) 461-2828

Ninety-Six National Historic Site
P.O. Box 496
Ninety-Six, South Carolina 29666
Phone: (864) 543-4068

Charles Pinckney National Historic Site
1214 Middle Street
Sullivans Island, South Carolina 29482
Phone: (843) 881-5516

Fort Sumter National Monument
1214 Middle Street
Sullivans Island, South Carolina 29482
Phone: (843) 883-3123

SOUTH DAKOTA

Jewel Cave National Monument
Rural Route 1, Box 60AA
Custer, South Dakota 57730
Phone: (605) 673-2288

Wild Cave National Park
Rural Route 1, Box 190
Hot Springs, South Dakota 57747
Phone: (605) 745-4600

Badlands National Park
P.O. Box 6
Interior, South Dakota 57750
Phone: (605) 433-5361

Mount Rushmore National Memorial
P.O. Box 268
Keystone, South Dakota 57751
Phone: (605) 574-3171

TENNESSEE

Big South Fork National River & Recreation Area
4564 Leatherwood Road
Oneida, Tennessee 37841
Phone: (931) 879-3625

Fort Donelson National Battlefield
P.O. Box 434
Dover, Tennessee 37058
Phone: (931) 232-5706

Great Smoky Mountains National Park
107 Park Headquarters Road
Gatlinburg, Tennessee 37738
Phone: (865) 436-1200

Andrew Johnson National Historic Site
P.O. Box 1088
Greeneville, Tennessee 37744
Phone: (423) 638-3551

Stones River National Battlefield
3501 Old Nashville Highway
Murfreesboro, Tennessee 37129
Phone: (615) 893-9501

Shiloh National Military Park
1055 Pittsburg Landing Road
Shiloh, Tennessee 38376
Phone: (901) 689-5696

Obed Wild and Scenic River
P.O. Box 429
Wartburg, Tennessee 37887
Phone: (423) 346-6294

TEXAS

Big Thicket National Preserve
3785 Milam
Beaumont, Texas 77701
Phone: (409) 246-2337

Big Bend National Park
P.O. Box 129
Big Bend National Park, Texas 79834
Phone: (915) 477-2251

Rio Grande Wild & Scenic River
c/o Big Bend National Park
P.O. Box 129
Big Bend National Park, Texas 79834
Phone: (915) 477-2251

Palo Alto Battlefield National Historic Site
1623 Central Blvd., RM213
Brownsville, Texas 78520
Phone: (956) 541-2785

Padre Island National Seashore
P.O. Box 181300
Corpus Christi, Texas 78480
Phone: (361) 949-8068

Amistad National Recreational Area
HCR3 Box 55 Highway 90 West
Del Rio, Texas 78840
Phone: (830) 775-7491

Chamizal National Memorial
800 South Sam Marcial
El Paso, Texas 79905
Phone: (915) 534-7273

Fort Davis National Historic Site
P.O. Box 1456
Fort Davis, Texas 79734
Phone: (915) 426-3224

Alibates Flint Quarries National
   Monument
c/o Lake Meredith Recreation Area
P.O. Box 1460
Fritch, Texas 79036
Phone: (806) 857-3151

Lake Meredith Recreation Area
P.O. Box 1460
Fritch, Texas 79036
Phone: (806) 857-3151

Lyndon B. Johnson National
   Historical Park
P.O. Box 329
Johnson City, Texas 78636
Phone: (830) 868-7128

Guadalupe Mountains National
   Park
H.C. 60, Box 400
Salt Flat, Texas 79847
Phone: (915) 828-3251

San Antonio Missions National
   Historical Park
2202 Roosevelt Avenue
San Antonio, Texas 78210
Phone: (210) 932-1001

UTAH

Timpanogos Cave National
   Monument
Rural Route 3, Box 200
American Fork, Utah 84003
Phone: (801) 756-5238

Golden Spike National Historic
   Site
P.O. Box 897
Brigham City, Utah 84302
Phone: (435) 471-2209

Bryce Canyon National Park
P.O. Box 170001
Bryce Canyon, Utah 84717
Phone: (435) 834-5322

Cedar Breaks National Monument
2390 West Highway 56, Suite 11
Cedar City, Utah 84720
Phone: (435) 586-9451

Natural Bridges National
   Monument
HC 60, Box 1
Lake Powell, Utah 84533
Phone: (435) 692-1234

Arches National Park
P.O. Box 907
Moab, Utah 84532
Phone: (435) 719-2319

Canyonlands National Park
2282 S. West Resource Blvd.
Moab, Utah 84532
Phone: (435) 719-2313

Zion National Park
SR 9
Springdale, Utah 84767
Phone: (435) 772-3256

Capitol Reef National Park
HC 70, Box 15
Torrey, Utah 84775
Phone: (435) 425-3791

VIRGINIA

Appomattox Court House National Historical Park
P.O. Box 218
Appomattox, Virginia 24522
Phone: (804) 352-8987

Fredericksburg & Spotsylvania County Memorial
120 Chatham Lane
Fredericksburg, Virginia 22405
Phone: (540) 371-0802

Booker T. Washington Monument
12130 Booker T. Washington Hwy.
Hardy, Virginia 24101
Phone: (540) 721-2094

Shenandoah National Park
3655 U.S. Highway 211 East
Luray, Virginia 22835
Phone: (540) 999-3500

Manassas National Battlefield Park
12521 Lee Highway
Manassas, Virginia 22109
Phone: (703) 361-1339

Lyndon Baines Johnson Memorial Grove On Potomac
c/o Washington Memorial Parkway
McLean, Virginia 22101
Phone: (703) 289-2553

Theodore Roosevelt Island
c/o George Washington Memorial Parkway
Turkey Run
McLean, Virginia 22101
Phone: (703) 289-2500

Arlington House, The Robert E. Lee Memorial
c/o George Washington Memorial Parkway
Turkey Run
McLean, Virginia 22101
Phone: (703) 557-0613

George Washington Memorial Parkway
Turkey Run Park
McLean, Virginia 22101
Phone: (703) 289-2500

Petersburg National Battlefield
1539 Hickory Hill Road
Route 36 East
Petersburg, Virginia 23803
Phone: (804) 732-3531

Maggie L. Walker National Historical Site
3215 East Broad Street
Richmond, Virginia 23223
Phone: (804) 771-2017

Richmond National Battlefield Park
3215 East Broad Street
Richmond, Virginia 23223
Phone: (804) 226-1981

Prince William Forest Park
18100 Park Headquarters Road
Triangle, Virginia 22172
Phone: (703) 221-7181

Wolf Trap Farm Park For The Performing Arts
1551 Trap Road
Vienna, Virginia 22182
Phone: (703) 255-1800

George Washington Birthplace
National Monument
1732 Popes Creek Road
Washington's Birthplace, Virginia
22443
Phone: (804) 224-1732

Colonial National Historical Park
P.O. Box 210
Yorktown, Virginia 23690
Phone: (757) 898-3400

VIRGIN ISLANDS

Buck Island National Monument
2100 Church Street, Suite 100
Danish Customs House, Kings
Wharf, St. Croix, U.S. Virgin
Islands 00820
Phone: (340) 773-1460

Salt River Bay National Historic
Park & Ecological Reserve
Christiansted National Historic Site
Christiansted, St. Croix, U.S. Virgin
Islands 00820
Phone: (340) 773-1460

Christiansted Historical Site
2100 Church Street, Suite 100
Danish Customs House,
Christiansted, St. Croix, U.S.
Virgin Islands 00820
Phone: (340) 773-1460

Virgin Islands National Park
P.O. Box 710
St. John, U.S. Virgin Islands 00831
Phone: (340) 776-6201

WASHINGTON

Mount Ranier National Park
Tahoma Woods, Star Route
Ashford, Washington 98304
Phone: (360) 569-2211

Olympic National Park
600 East Park Avenue
Port Angeles, Washington 98362
Phone: (360) 452-0330

Coulee Dam National Recreation
Area
1008 Crest Drive
Coulee Dam, Washington 99116
Phone: (509) 633-9441

Lake Chelan National Recreation
Area
2105 Highway 20
Sedro Woolley, Washington 98284
Phone: (206) 856-5700

Ebey's Landing National Historical
Reserve
P.O. Box 774
Coupeville, Washington 98239
Phone: (360) 678-6084

North Cascades National Park
2105 Highway 20
Sedro Woolley, Washington 98284
Phone: (360) 856-5700

San Juan Island National Historical
Park
P.O. Box 429
Friday Harbor, Washington 98250
Phone: (360) 378-2902

Ross Lake National Recreation Area
2105 Highway 20
Sedro Woolley, Washington 98284
Phone: (360) 856-5700

Fort Vancouver National Historic Site
612 East Reserve Street
Vancouver, Washington 98661
Phone: (800) 832-3599

Whitman Mission National Historic Site
328 Whitman Mission Road
Walla Walla, Washington 99362
Phone: (509) 522-6360

WISCONSIN

Apostle Islands National Lakeshore
Route 1, Box 4
Bayfield, Wisconsin 54814
Phone: (715) 779-3397

Saint Croix National Scenic Riverway
P.O. Box 708
Saint Croix Falls, Wisconsin 54024
Phone: (715) 483-3284

WEST VIRGINIA

Bluestone National Scenic River
c/o New River George National River
P.O. Box 246
Glen Jean, West Virginia 25846
Phone: (304) 465-0508

Gauley River National Recreation Area
c/o New River George National River
P.O. Box 246
Glen Jean, West Virginia 25846
Phone: (304) 465-0508

New River George National River
P.O. Box 246
Glen Jean, West Virginia 25846
Phone: (304) 465-0508

Appalachian National Scenic Trail
c/o Harpers Ferry Center
Harpers Ferry, West Virginia 25425
Phone: (304) 535-6278

Harpers Ferry National Historical Park
P.O. Box 65
Harpers Ferry, West Virginia 25425
Phone: (304) 535-6298

WYOMING

Devils Tower National Monument
P.O. Box 10
Devils Tower, Wyoming 82714
Phone: (307) 467-5283

Fort Laramie National Historic Site
HC 72, Box 389
Fort Laramie, Wyoming 82212
Phone: (307) 837-2221

Fossil Butte National Monument
P.O. Box 592
Kemmerer, Wyoming 83101
Phone: (307) 877-4455

Grand Teton National Park
P.O. Drawer 170
Moose, Wyoming 83012
Phone: (307) 739-3300

John D. Rockefeller, Jr. Memorial Parkway
c/o Teton National Park
P.O. Drawer 170
Moose, Wyoming 83012
Phone: (307) 733-2880

Yellowstone National Park
P.O. Box 168
Yellowstone National Park, Wyoming 82190
Phone: (307) 344-7381

THEME PARKS ACROSS THE U.S.A.

ALABAMA

Point Mallard Park
1800 Point Mallard Drive, S.E.
Decatur, Alabama 35501
Phone: (256) 350-3000
Days open: All year long!
🔲 *Point Mallard gives you 750 acres of family fun with activities ranging from golf to swimming and tennis to ice-skating.*

Water World
P.O. Box 2128
Dothan, Alabama 36302
Phone: (205) 793-0297

ARKANSAS

Dogpatch Usa
P.O. Box 20
Dogpatch, Arkansas 72648
Phone: (501) 743-1111

Wild River Country
6801 Crystal Hill Road
North Little Rock, Arkansas 72115
Phone: (501) 753-8600

ARIZONA

Island of Big Surf
1500 North McClintock Road
Tempe, Arizona 85281
Phone: (602) 947-7873

CALIFORNIA

Disneyland
P.O. Box 3232
Anaheim, California 92803
Phone: (714) 999-4565
🔲 *Need we say more!*

Knott's Berry Farm
8039 Beach Boulevard
Buena Park, California 90620
Phone: (714) 220-5200
Days open: every day of the year except Christmas!
🔲 *Knott's Berry Farm started as a small berry stand. Now it's America's biggest independently owned theme park.*

Skandia Family Center
4300 Central Palace
Fairfield, California 94585
Phone: (707) 864-8558
Days open: Every day of the year!
🔲 *Scandia is a 9-acre family fun center with arcades, mini-golf, and more.*

Wild Rivers Water Park
8770 Irvine Center Drive
Laguna Hills, California 92653
Phone: (949) 768-9453

Oakwood Lake Resort
874 East Woodward
Manteca, California 95336
Phone: (209) 239-2500
Days open: Campground, all year.
 Slide Park, weekends in May and
 September, daily in June, July and
 August.
▧ *Enjoy full hook-up camping sites, great water slides, a pool, a lake, and even bungee jumping!*

Children's Fairyland
1520 Lakeside Drive
Oakland, California 94612
Phone: (510) 452-2259
▧ *Come enjoy the wonders of fairy tales and the magic of childhood.*

Oasis Waterpark
1500 Gene Autry Trail
Palm Springs, California 92264
Phone: (619) 325-7873
Days open: Daily from mid-March
 through Labor Day, weekends
 from Labor Day to Halloween.
▧ *Oasis Waterpark is more a water resort. Enjoy all the fun of a waterpark with a great surrounding and a european health spa.*

Sea World of San Diego
1720 South Shores Road
Mission Bay
San Diego, California 92109
Phone: (619) 222-6363
Days open: Year round!
▧ *WOW! Sea World not only allows you to see the wonders of a life we don't normally get to see but also helps preserve it.*

Raging Waters
111 Raging Waters Drive
San Dimas, California 91773
Phone: (714) 592-6453
Days open: Weekends late April to
 early June and after Labor Day
 until Halloween. Daily early June
 into September.
▧ *44-acres of slippin' and slidin'... 5-million gallons of splishin' and splashin'... surf and sand ... sun and fun!*

Great America
P.O. Box 1776
Santa Clara, California 95052
Phone: (408) 988-1800

Santa Cruz Beach Boardwalk
400 Beach Street
Santa Cruz, California 95060
Phone: (831) 426-7433
Days open: Weekends of all months
 except June, July and August, when
 it is open every day. Only open on
 the 31st in December.
▧ *Open for about 88 years, Santa Cruz Beach Boardwalk has combined fun, sun and much more!*

Pixie Woods
Louis Park
Stockton, California 95202
Phone: (209) 466-9890

Universal Studios Hollywood
100 Universal City Plaza
Universal City, California 91608
Phone: (818) 508-9600
Days open: Year Round except
 Thanksgiving and Christmas!
▧ *This is the world's #1 motion picture and television attraction. Explore behind the scenes of the world's biggest and busiest motion picture and television studio.*

Six Flags Magic Mountain
P.O. Box 5500
Valencia, California 91355
Phone: (805) 255-4111
Days open: Early April until early
   October

▦ *At Six Flags Magic Mountain journey
through ten lushly landscaped themed lands
to experience some of the world's best rides.*

Marine World Africa Usa
Marine World Parkway
Vallejo, California 94950
Phone: (707) 644-4000
Days open: Every day of the
   summer, and Wednesday-Sunday
   all year long.

▦ *See animals of land, sea and air performing in shows, roaming in their habitats
and strolling with their trainers through the
park.*

Sengme Oaks Water Park
Box 158
Valley Center, California 92082
Phone: (619) 742-1921

Windsor Waterworks & Slides
8225 Conde Lane
Windsor, California 95492
Phone: (707) 838-7360
Days open: May through Sepember

▦ *For safe, clean, fun for the entire family
there is only one place to be. . . . Windsor
waterworks and slides.*

COLORADO

Elitch Gardens
4620 West 38th Avenue

Denver, Colorado 80212
Phone: (303) 455-4771

FLORIDA

**Weeki Wachee Spring & Buccaneer
   Bay**
P.O. Box 97
Brooksville, Florida 34605
Phone: (904) 596-2062

▦ *Water Mania, A 38-acre water park,
offers a variety of water thrill rides and
dry-land activities. Water Mania has been
in operation since 1986.*

Water Mania
60073 West Highway 192
Kissimmee, Florida 34746
Phone: (407) 396-2626

Walt Disney World
P.O. Box 10,000
Lake Buena Vista, Florida 32830
Phone: (407) 824-4321

▦ *Does "Once upon a time is here" tell
you anything about Walt Disney World?
This 43-square-mile theme park is one of a
kind. Walt Disney World consists of seven
individual theme parks.*

Marineland, Inc.
9507 Ocean Shore Boulevard
Marineland, Florida 32086
Phone: (904) 471-1111
Days open: All year long!
⊚ *See the wonders of the under water world at Marineland.*

**Jungle Larry's Zoological Park
Caribbean Garden**
1590 Goodlette Road
Naples, Florida 33940
Phone: (813) 262-4053

Sea World of Florida
7007 Sea World Drive
Orlando, Florida 32821
Phone: (407) 351-3600
Days open: Every day of the year!
⊚ *Sea World gives you a chance to get close up to marine life such as the killer whale Shamu, Manatees, Penguins, Dolphins and more.*

Universal Studios Florida
1000 Universal Studios Plaza
Orlando, Florida 32819
Phone: (407) 363-8000
Days open: Every day of the year!
⊚ *Universal Studios Florida, the #1 movie studio and theme park in the world! Go back stage and see how things work in the movies and ride a few thrillers while your there.*

Wet 'n Wild
6200 International Drive
Orlando, Florida 32819
Phone: (407) 351-3200
Days open: Every day of the year!
⊚ *Acres of slides, chutes, flumes, floats and plunges make Wet'n Wild the perfect place to get wet, go wild and soak up the warm Florida sunshine.*

Miracle Strip Amusement Park
P.O. Box 2000
Panama City, Florida 32402
Phone: (850) 234-5810
⊚ *Miracle Strip is a pay-per-ride amusement park but of course you can pay one price for all the rides. It has a variety of rides and has a sister water park named Shipwreck Island.*

Shipwreck Island
P.O. Box 2000
Panama City, Florida 32402
Phone: (850) 234-0368
Days open: Saturady in mid-April and May; Daily from early June through Labor day weekend.
⊚ *This is a themed water park centering around the "Great Shipwreck."*

Silver Springs & Wild Waters
P.O. Box 370
Silver Springs, Florida 32688
Phone: (904) 236-2121

Adventure Island
P.O. Box 9158
Tampa, Florida 33674
Phone: (813) 971-7978
Days open: Daily from late March to Labor Day. Weekends from Labor Day to Halloween.
⊚ *Tampa Bay's largest water park. Adventure Island is right next door to Busch Gardens.*

**Busch Gardens, The Dark
Continent**
P.O. Box 9158
Tampa, Florida 33624
Phone: (813) 971-8282
Days open: All year
⊚ *Mixing thrills with nature is Busch Gardens Tampa Bay. Having personally been there I strongly advise visitors and locals in the Tampa Bay area to visit.*

Lion Country Safari
P.O. Box 16066
West Palm Beach, Florida 33416
Phone: (407) 793-1084
Days open: Open Daily year
round—rain or shine.

▓ *Drive through 500 acres of wildlife preserve while occasionally being stopped by animals crossing the road! This park offers a close look at exotic animals.*

GEORGIA

Six Flags Over Georgia
P.O. Box 43187
Atlanta, Georgia 30378
Phone: (404) 739-3440

▓ *Six Flags is a thrill seekers paradise. With five hard-core coasters and many more gut-wrenching rides thrill seekers will feel right at home.*

White Water
250 North Cobb Parkway
Marietta, Georgia 30062
Phone: (404) 424-9283
Days open: Weekends in May, daily
from Memorial day to late
summer.

▓ *Thrills and spills abound amid acres of trees, flowers, waterfalls, rivers, and rides and slides suited to every water personality.*

HAWAII

Waimea Falls Park
59-864 Kamehameha Highway
Haleiwa, Hawaii 96712
Phone: (808) 638-8511
Days open: Year round!

▓ *Zoom to the top of a ridge, Cruise downhill on a trail, Paddle down a stream and Explore Hawaii's natural and cultural history. These are just some of the things to do there.*

Sea Life Park Hawaii
Makapuu Point
Waimanalo, Hawaii 96795
Phone: (808) 259-7933
Days open: Year Round!

▓ *The excitement of Hawaii's undersea world comes to life at Sea Life Park Hawaii. A dazzling array of the islands most colorful and talented creatures awaits you.*

IOWA

Adventureland Park
P.O. Box 3355
Des Miones, Iowa 50316
Phone: (515) 266-2121

▓ *A classic amusement park with plenty of rides. Adventureland Park also features an Inn and a campground for Rv's.*

IDAHO

Wild Waters
1850 Century Way
Boise, Idaho 83709
Phone: (208) 322-1844

Wild Waters
2119 North Government Way
Coeur d'Alene, Idaho 83814
Phone: (208) 667-6491

ILLINOIS

The Three Worlds of Santa's Village
Routes 25 and 72
Dundee, Illinois 60118
Phone: (708) 426-5560

🔲 *Santa's Village is a large village made up of 3 parts which all offer their share of fun activities. Racing Rapids is an action water park with lots of fun attractions.*

Six Flags Great America
542 North Route 21
Gurnee, Illinois 60031
Phone: (708) 249-1776

INDIANA

Holiday World
P.O. Box 179
Santa Claus, Indiana 47579
Phone: (800) 284-1466

🔲 *Holiday World is our nations first theme park with actual rides from when it first opened. Enjoy over 60 rides, shows, and attractions as well as Splashing' Safari, a water park.*

LOUISIANA

Water Town USA
P.O. Box 29009
Shreveport, LA 71149
Phone: (318) 938-5475

MICHIGAN

Deer Forest
P.O. Box 817
Coloma, Michigan 49038
Phone: (800) 752-3337

Boblo Island
4401 West Jefferson Avenue
Detroit, Michigan 48209
Phone: (313) 843-8800

Deer Acres Fantasy Park
2346 M-13
Pinconning, Michigan 48650
Phone: (517) 879-2849
Days open: Daily from mid-May to
Labor Day, weekends from Labor
Day until October.

*See all your favorite Mother Goose
characters and live animals.*

MINNESOTA

Valleyfair! Family Amusement Park
1 Valleyfair Drive
Shakopee, Minnesota 55379
Phone: (612) 445-7600

MISSOURI

Silver Dollar City
Branson, Missouri 65616
Phone: (417) 338-2611

Six Flags Over Mid-America
P.O. Box 60, Allenton
Six Flags Road
Eureka, Missouri 63025
Phone: (314) 938-4800
Days open: Daily from mid-May to
Labor Day, weekends from Labor
Day through October.

*Thrill seekers get ready for Six Flags
Over Mid-America. With plenty of coasters,
rides, and more you are sure to have a good
time.*

Worlds of Fun
4545 Worlds of Fun Avenue
Kansas City, Missouri 64161
Phone: (816) 454-4545

*Join in the fun from mild to wild rides
... foot-stomping toe-tapping shows ...
sumptuous and savory taste treats...and then
visit Oceans of Fun for a splashing' good
time in a tropical paradise.*

MONTANA

Big Sky Waterslide
P.O. Box 2311
Junction of Highways 2 & 206
Colombia Falls, Montana 59912
Phone: (406) 892-2139

NORTH CAROLINA

Tweetsie Railroad
Highway 321
P.O. Box 388
Blowing Rock, North Carolina
   28605
Phone: (828) 264-9061

Carowinds
P.O. Box 410289
Charlotte, North Carolina 28241
Phone: (800) 822-4428
Days open: Weekends late March
   through early June and late August
   through early October. Daily early
   June through late August.

   This 92-acre theme park brings movie magic to life with world-class rides, exciting shows, unique shops and delicious restaurants.

Santa's Land
Route 1, Box 134 A
Cherokee, North Carolina 28719
Phone: (704) 497-9191
Days open: End of April through the
   end of October

   Santa's Land fun park and zoo offers family fun with a Christmas theme. Santa's Land is a great place for family fun all day long for one low admission price.

Ghost Town in the Sky
P.O. Box 369
Maggie Valley, North Carolina
   28751
Phone: (704) 926-1140
Days open: Daily from early May
   through October

   Ghost Town in the Sky is set in the majestic mountains of North Carolina.

NEW HAMPSHIRE

Attitash Alpine Slide & Waterslides
U.S. Route 302
Bartlett, New Hampshire 03812
Phone: (603) 374-2368

Story Land
P.O. Box 1176
Glen, New Hampshire 03838
Phone: (603) 383-4293

   This park, as the title suggests, is based on story books.

Santa's Village
Route 2
Jefferson, New Hampshire 03583
Phone: (603) 586-4445

   Santa's Village brings the joy and magic of childhood and that of Christmas into one park!

Clark's Trading Post
Box 1, Route 3
Lincoln, New Hampshire 03251
Phone: (603) 745-8913
Days open: Daily in July and August,
   weekends from Labor Day until
   mid-October

   Enjoy bear shows, train rides and much more at this theme park which was opened in 1928.

Whale's Tale Water Park
P.O. Box 67
Lincoln, New Hampshire 03251
Phone: (603) 745-8810

Canobie Lake Park
P.O. Box 190
Salem, New Hampshire 03079
Phone: (603) 893-3506
Days open: Weekends from mid-
    April to mid-May, daily from
    Memorial day to Labor day

▧ *Built in 1902 Canobie Lake ranks as one of the most beautiful amusement parks in the country. It combines the leisurely charm of yesterday with the thrills and excitement today.*

NEW JERSEY

Six Flags Great Adventure
P.O. Box 120
Jackson, New Jersey 08527
Phone: (201) 928-2000

▧ *Six Flags Great Adventure is reportedly the largest seasonal theme park in the nation and the home of the worlds tallest and fastest steel roller coaster in the world.*

NEVADA

Ponderosa Ranch
P.O. Box 18 A. P.

Incline Village, Nevada 89450
Phone: (702) 831-0691

NEW YORK

Darien Lake Theme Park & Camping Resort
Darien Center, New York 10486
Phone: (716) 599-4641

▧ *One of the largest theme parks in the NY, Darien Lake offers 2,000 sites suitable for RVs and tents.*

The Great Escape
P.O. Box 511
Lake George, New York 12845
Phone: (518) 792-6568

▧ *One of the oldest theme parks in the U.S., The Great Escape is NY's most popular vacation spots as well as NY's largest theme park.*

Midway Park
Route 430, Box E
Maple Springs, New York 14756
Phone: (716) 386-3165

▧ *Coming up on their 98th season, Midway Park is one of the oldest continually operating amusement facilities in the nation. Midway says that their park is a great place for families with pre-teens.*

Splish Splash
P.O. Box 1090
Riverhead, New York 11901
Phone: (516) 727-3600
Days open: Memorial Day to Labor
    Day except mid-June

▧ *"Long Island's Water Park" Splish Splash has plenty of slides, slips, twists and turns for a great day of fun.*

**Seabreeze Amusement & Raging
   Rivers Water Park**
4600 Culver Road
Rochester, New York 14622
Phone: (716) 323-1900

Days open: Weekends from early
   May to mid-June, daily from mid-
   June to Labor day
◈ *This park combines old looks with new
thrill rides as well as a water park.*

O H I O

Geauga Lake
1060 North Aurora Road
Aurora, Ohio 44202
Phone: (800) 843-9283
Days open: Weekends during most
   of the year, daily from Memorial
   Day to Labor Day
◈ *Swim, play, ride, slide, eat, scream,
twist and turn all at Geauga Lake*

Sea World of ohio
1100 Sea World Drive
Aurora, Ohio 44202 Phone:
   (800) 637-4268
Days open: Daily from Memorial
   Day to Labor Day, plus weekends
   in September
◈ *Set on a scenic glacial lake, Sea World of
Ohio is a great chance for visitors to experi-
ence the underwater life.*

Kings Island
Kings Island, Ohio 45034
Phone: (513) 398-5600

The Beach Waterpark
2590 Waterpark Drive
Manson, Ohio 45040
Phone: (513) 398-7946

Cedar Point
P.O. Box 5006
Sandusky, Ohio 44871
Phone: (419) 626-0830
Days open: Daily mid-May 13 to
   Labor Day, plus some weekends in
   September
◈ *To say the least, Cedar Point has won
the #1 rating of amusement parks in the
U.S. from "Inside Track" an amusement
park magazine 3 times running.*

O K L A H O M A

Frontier City
11601 North East Expressway
Oklahoma City, Oklahoma 73131
Phone: (405) 478-2412

Big Splash Water Park
P.O. Box 14156
Tulsa, Oklahoma 74159
Phone: (918) 749-7385
◈ *Body Surf, Ride water slides, have fun,
soak sun ... what else would you want to
do?*

OREGON

Wildlife Safari
P.O. Box 1600
Winston, Oregon 97496
Phone: (503) 679-6761
Days open: Year round!

▦ *The only one of its kind in Oregon, Wildlife Safari lets you drive through exotic animals' natural habitats.*

PENNSYLVANIA

Dorney Park & Wildwater Kingdom
3830 Dorney Park Road
Allentown, Pennsylvania 18104
Phone: (215) 395-3724

Conneaut Lake Park
Rural District 4, Box 283
Conneaut Lake, Pennsylvania 16316
Phone: (800) 828-9619

Dutch Wonderland
2249 Route 30
East Lancaster, Pennsylvania 17602
Phone: (717) 291-1888
Days open: Daily from Memorial Day through Labor Day.

▦ *Stroll through botanical gardens and see high diving shows, as well as rides, stores and much more.*

Knoebels Amusement Park
P.O. Box 317
Route 487
Elysberg, Pennsylvania 17824
Phone: (717) 672-2572
Days open: Weekends in April, May and Sept. Daily from Memorial Day to Labor Day.

▦ *In a recent poll taken from INSIDE TRACK Knoebels was voted the 2nd best park in the world, the 3rd best with friendliness, the 5th best bumper cars, the 5th best roller coaster and the best pizza.*

Hersheypark
100 West Hersheypark Drive
Hershey, Pennsylvania 17033
Phone: (800) 437-7439

▦ *"The sweetest place on earth!" claims Hersheypark. Remember the Hershey Kiss or the Hershey Milk Chocolate Bar? Enjoy Great food, fun and rides all at Hersheypark.*

Sesame Place
100 Sesame Road
P.O. Box 579
Langhorne, Pennsylvania 19047
Phone: (215) 757-1100

Idlewild Park
Route 30 East
Legionnaire, Pennsylvania 15658
Phone: (412) 238-3666

Shawnee Place Play & Water Park
P.O. Box 93
Shawnee on Delaware, Pennsylvania 18356
Phone: (717) 421-7213
Days open: Daily from Memorial weekend through Labor day. Weekends in Fall.

▦ *Jump, swing, climb, glide, slide and splash—all at Shawnee Place.*

Kennywood Park
4800 Kennywood Boulevard
West Mifflin, Pennsylvania 15122
Phone: (412) 461-1500

TENNESSEE

Ober Gatlingburg
1001 Parkway
Gatlingburg, Tennessee 37738
Phone: (615) 436-5423
Days open: Year round except for 2
   weeks in March.
▓ *Enjoy a combination of a scenic sur-*
rounding, fun rides, and friendly people.

Libertyland
940 Early Maxwell Boulevard
Memphis, Tennessee 38104
Phone: (800) 552-7275
▓ *Libertyland is a historical, educational*
and recreational amusement park that offers
fun for the entire family.

Opryland
2802 Opryland Drive
Nashville, Tennessee 37214
Phone: (615) 889-6600

Dollywood
700 Dollywood Lane
Pigeon Forge, Tennessee 37863
Phone: (615) 428-9400
▓ *Enjoy live music shows, unique attrac-*
tions, fun rides and craft showcases in a
flowery '50s atmosphere.

TEXAS

Wonderland Park
P.O. Box 2325
Amarillo, Texas 79105
Phone: (806) 383-4712
Days open: Early April to mid-
   September
▓ *Built in 1953, Wonderland park still*
has rides in operation from that time.

Six Flags Over Texas
P.O. Box 191
Arlington, Texas 76010
Phone: (817) 640-8900

Wet 'n Wild
12715 LBJ Freeway
Garland, Texas 75041
Phone: (214) 271-5637

Schlitterbahn
305 West Austin
New Braunfels, Texas 78105
Phone: (512) 625-2531

Sea World of Texas
10500 Sea World Drive
San Antonio, Texas 78251
Phone: (800) 422-7989

Splashtown USA
P.O. Box 2929
Spring, Texas 77383
Phone: (713) 350-4848

UTAH

**Lagoon Amusement Park &
Pioneer Village**
P.O. Box N
Farmington, Utah 84025
Phone: (801) 451-0101
Days open: Weekends April, May
and September, plus the first
weekend in October. Daily from
Memorial Day through August.

*From our exhilarating thrill-rides and
top-notch musical entertainment, to Pioneer
Village and Lagoon A Beach, Lagoon really
does have something for everyone.*

VIRGINIA

Kings Dominion
Doswell, Virginia 23047
Phone: (804) 876-5000

Ocean Breeze Fun Park
849 General Booth Boulevard
Virginia Beach, Virginia 23451
Phone: (800) 678-9453

Busch Gardens, The Old Country
7901 Pocahontas Trail
Williamsburg, Virginia 23185
Phone: (804) 253-3350
Days open: Early April through
October

*Busch Gardens Williamsberg is a Euro-
pean-themed park nestled on 350 acres of
Virginia Woodlands. Thirty-plus thrilling
rides, delicious foods, entertainment, shops
and exhibits are featured in nine settings.*

Water Country USA
P.O. Box 3088
Williamsberg, Virginia 23187
Phone: (804) 229-1500

WASHINGTON

Wild 'n Wet Water Park
4874 Birch Way at LLynden Road
Blain, Washington 98230
Phone: (206) 371-7500
Days open: Weekends from mid-
May 20 to mid-June, daily from
mid-June to Labor Day

*Splash it up! Thrill it up! Fun it up!
Soak it up! Lounge it up!*

Splash-Down
East 12727 Piper Road
Spokane, Washington 99207
Phone: (509) 924-3079

WISCONSIN

Dells Crossroads Fun Park
Highway 12
P.O. Box 328
Wisconsin Dells, Wisconsin 53969
Phone: (608) 254-2535

Family Land
Highway 12
Wisconsin Dells, Wisconsin 53969
Phone: (608) 254-8560

WEST VIRGINIA

Camden Park
P.O. Box 9245

Huntington, West Virginia 25704
Phone: (304) 429-4321

CAMPING

Whether you have a tent or a camper, camping is a wonderful way for families to work together and enjoy each other away from the stresses of work and school. You need to plan ahead and be prepared, but all the work will be worth it. You might not have electricity during the trip, but if you bring the essentials and think simply, you will not be bothered by not having some modern conveniences. And years later you and your family will remember fondly all the time you spent around a campfire laughing, singing, and telling stories.

Depending on your budget and the amount of people going camping, you have to decide what style and size of tent or camper to buy or rent. Dome-style tents can easily be set up and have few pieces. Although a camper is more expensive, they attach easily to the hitch of a car and have pull-out beds, a stove, refrigerator, sink, dining table and drawers for dishes, etc. They can sleep six and you don't have to worry about leaks in a rain storm.

If you have a tent, spray it with rain-resistant spray and buy a tarp to put over the top for shade. Make sure the tent is large enough for everyone to sleep comfortably and for the baggage. Foam pieces or air mattresses work well to sleep comfortably and are more compact than extra blankets.

Don't pack too much. Two sets of clothes are enough for a four-day trip. Bring one warm sweater, a light jacket, a couple shirts, shorts, pants,

extra underwear, socks, and two pairs of shoes. If you plan on hiking, bring a pair of hiking boots that fit over your ankles for ankle support. Bring a large basin so you can wash clothes and small children. A clothes line and ten clothes pins will also be needed.

If you have a tent you'll need a couple of coolers packed with ice for perishables. Try to bring mostly non-refrigerated food like bread and nuts. Don't allow the children to eat large quantities at one sitting since they'll want to do a lot of exploring and swimming. Small meals will keep up their energy and eliminate stomach aches.

Plan a menu before you go and have the kids help choose the foods they want. This way you'll save time at the campsite deciding what to make and you can plan how much food will be enough. Keep the meals simple like hamburgers and hot dogs. If you want to avoid bringing a lot of utensils and food, you can always eat out one night at a close-by restaurant.

Bring toys and books and games for the kids. Create a play area for them near the tent or camper. Pack a frisbee, soccer ball, and baseball equipment so the whole family can play.

Include the children in helping set up the campsite, doing the dishes and laundry, and making a fire. They will feel important for working beside the adults and will gain confidence from their accomplishments. Even if they create a mess that requires more work for the adults, remember they learn not only by watching but also by doing.

Don't set up a rigid schedule where every minute of each day is planned. Let the children have plenty of time to play and rest. Avoid boredom by taking walks, swimming, flower hunting or bring along a boat or canoe and fishing poles. Just because you spent time planning the campsite and setting it up doesn't mean you have to spend every second there. Just remember to have a good time, relax, and avoid television!

Camping Tips to Keep in Mind

1. Decide if a tent or camper is best for your economic and spatial needs.
2. Buy rain-resistant spray for a tent if your's doesn't have a rain fly and a tarp; foam pieces and air mattresses work great for comfortably sleeping.
3. Bring appropriate clothing and pack light; bring along a large basin for washing clothes and small children; don't forget the clothes line and clothes pins.
4. Pack a first aid kit.
5. Don't serve children large portions of food during the day since they'll want to swim and hike.
6. Plan a menu before you go; keep the meals simple.
7. Bring lots of toys and create a play area for the children.
8. Things like a frisbee, soccer ball, and baseball equipment can be used for the entire family.
9. Have the children help out setting up the campsite, doing dishes and laundry, and making a fire so you're not doing all the work.
10. Don't set up a rigid schedule; plan enough outings to keep everyone happy but not stressed.

FAMILY CAMPS

Family camps have always been popular and are becoming more so. Like a resort minus some of the amenities, family camps offer a wide range of activites and usually a dining hall where meals are taken.

The camps are usually found in areas rich in beauty and are well equiped for family fun. As most family camps provide meals and activities, planning and packing maybe kept to a minimum, maximizing you vacation time. Family camps can be one of the most economical vacations and one of the most relaxing for everybody as there are many activities typically offered. Some families coordinate their vacation times to go to family camps with other family friends or relatives doubling the fun.

Many traditional children's summer camps are offering family camping on designated weeks or weekends. Be sure to check. This type of vacatio offers a great opportunity to spend time togehter as a family with very few hassles to deal with all in a beautiful setting. The following is a partial list of family camps around the country. There are many, many others. If you would like to visit an area with no camp mentioned here, contact the state tourist board, they'll be able to help you.

Lair of the Golden Bear
Lair Reservations
Alumni House
Berkeley, California 94720
Phone: (888) CAL-ALUM

Camp Concord
Phone: (925) 671-3273;
   (530) 541-1203

San Jose Family Camp
11401 Cherry Lake Road
Groveland, California 95321
Phone: (209) 962-7277

Tuolumne Family Camp
31585 Hardin Flat Road
Groveland, California 95321
Phone: (209) 962-7234

Montecito-Sequoia Lodge
1485 Redwood Drive
Los Altos, California 94024
Phone: (800) 227-9900

Feather River Camp—Oakland
P.O. Box 3229
Quincy, California 95971
Phone: (530) 283-2290

Camp Sacramento
Phone: (916) 277-6098

Camp Mather
San Francisco Parks & Recreation
Phone: (415) 831-2715

San Jose Family Camp
San Jose Department of Recreation,
   Parks & Community Services
4 North 2nd Street, Suite 600
San Jose, California 95113
Phone: (408) 277-4661

Family Vacation Center
UCSB Alumni Association
Santa Barbara, California 93106
Phone: (805) 893-3123

Emandal Farm
16500 Hearst Post Office Road
Willits, California 95490
Phone: (800) 262-9597

Skylake Yosemite Camp
37976 Road 222, #25G
Wishon, California 93669
Phone: (559) 642-3720

The Trails End Ranch Family Camp
P.O. Box 1170
Estes Park, Colorado 80517
Phone: (970) 586-4244

Shaw-Waw-Nas-See 4-H Camp
Northern Illinois 4-H Camp
   Association
6641 North 64000 West Road
Manteno, Illinois 60950
Phone: (815) 933-3011

Attean Lake Lodge
Jackman, Maine 04945
Phone: (207) 668-3792 (summer);
  (207) 668-7726 (winter)

Alden Camps
3 Alden Camps Cove
Oakland, Maine 04963
Phone: (207) 465-7703

Migis Lodge
P.O. Box 40
South Casco, Maine 04077
Phone: (207) 655-4524

**Al-Gon-Quian Fun & Fitness
  Family Camp**
Ann Arbor Y
350 Fifth Avenue
Ann Arbor, Michigan 48104
Phone: (734) 663-0536

YMCA Storer Camps
7260 South Stoney Lake Road
Jackson, Michigan 49201
Phone: (800) 536-8607;
  (517) 536-8607

Camp Ojiketa Family Camp
27500 Kirby
Chicago City, Minnesota 55117
Phone: (651) 257-0600

**Camp Lincoln/Camp Lake Hubert
  Family Camp**
10179 Crosstown Circle
Eden Prairie, Minnesota 55436
Phone: (800) 242-1909;
  (612) 922-2545

Camp Merrowvista
147 Canaan Road
Ossipee, New Hampshire 03864
Phone: (603) 539-6607

Purity Spring Resort
HC 63, Box 40, Route 153
East Madison, New Hampshire
  03849
Phone: (603) 367-8896;
  (800) 373-3754

Rockywold—Deephaven Camps
P.O. Box B
Holderness, New Hampshire 03245
Phone: (603) 968-3313

Lock Lyme Lodge
Route 10
Lyme, New Hampshire 03768
Phone: (603) 795-2141

Twin Lake Village
21 Twin Lake Villa Road
New London, New Hampshire
  03257
Phone: (603) 526-6460

Hemlock Hall
P.O. Box 110
Blue Mountain Lake, New York
  12812
Phone: (518) 352-7706 (summer);
  (518) 359-9065 (winter)

Weona Family Camp
280 Cayuga Road
Buffalo, New York 14225
Phone: (716) 565-6008

Canoe Island Lodge
P.O. Box 144
Diamond Point, New York 12824
Phone: (518) 668-5592

**Dorothy P. Flint Nassau County
  4-H Camp**
1425 Old Country Road, Building J
Plainview, New York 11803
Phone: (516) 454-0900

Timberlock
P.O. Box 1052
Sabael, New York 12864
Phone: (518) 648-5494;
   (802) 453-2540 (Winter)

Camp Chingachgook
Capital District YMCA
1872 Pilot Knob Road
Kattskill Bay, New York 12844
Phone: (518) 656-9462

Seafarer Family Camp
2744 Seafarer Road
Arapahoe, North Carolina 28510
Phone: (252) 249-1212

**Camp Christopher Family Camp –
CYO Family Camp**
812 Biruta Street
Akron, Ohio 44307
Phone: (800) 296-2267;
   (330) 376-2267

**Cleveland Area YMCA Family
   Camps**
Camps Division
8558 Crackel Road
Chagrin Falls, Ohio 44022
Phone: (440) 543-8184

**Great Smoky Mountains Institute
   at Tremont**
9275 Tremont Road
Townsend, Tennessee 37882
Phone: (865) 448-6709

**Quimby Country Lodge &
   Cottages**
Averill, Vermont 05901
Phone: (802) 822-5533

The Tyler Place
Highgate Springs, Vermont 05460
Phone: (802) 868-4000;
   (802) 868-4291

Camp Friendship
P.O. Box 145
Palmyra, Virginia 22963
Phone: (800) 873-3223;
   (804) 589-8950

RV TRAVEL

If you plan a camping trip, but want to avoid the hassle of tents and want to have attached mobility unlike campers, then an RV is your style. An RV, unlike a hotel, is like your second home. Your home on wheels. Since space is tight, don't plan for overly-long trips; you'll go crazy if you drive too much and the kids will get bored and agitated. Campgrounds are numerous around the nation and many don't require a reservation. Just bear in mind that RVs are not cheap, but they are practical in the respect that you don't have to pack up to move on! RVs may be bought used, often at quite low prices or be rented.

Before you buy or rent an RV make sure you know how everything works and that everything is in working order. Consult with the salesperson on the best models, how much gas is necessary, maintenance required, etc. Since some campgrounds won't accept RVs over 30 ft. long, buy one that is smaller. Actually, pop-top vans fitted out as campers are quite comfortable and adaptive to your at-home life.

Buy every map and travel book you'll need and plan the route before you start. You don't want to waste any time on the trip asking for directions or becoming frustrated about finding a place to stop. Allow the kids to help in deciding the best places to visit and camp. They can help with navigating on the road too.

Although space is tight, there is room to keep books and games. Bring some flat bins which will fit under seats or beds for extra storage.

Since you have more space to store food in an RV than a tent, remember to bring plenty of snacks. The long periods of time you'll spend in the RV will make you hungry, so eat small portions of food at several intervals. But don't bring too many sweets; rain may be a big issue so you don't want hyper kids in a confined area.

Pack light, but be prepared for cool weather and rain. A few changes of clothes will be sufficient. Make sure you pack the appropriate clothing for any activities you will participate in such as a swimming suit, hiking boots, or more formal attire for a night out on the town.

Necessities like a flashlight, medical kit, and repair kit will be needed. A flat tire or some other car problem is certainly a possibility so be prepared.

Young children will get bored with the small quarters unless you plan many outings along the way. Shopping trips and stops at a zoo or museum will keep their interest up. Older children are easier to have along since they can handle the monotony a bit better and don't need space for things like a changing area, high chair, toys, etc. A portable tape player with headset and appropriate kids' tapes is a blessing.

RV Tips to Keep in Mind

1. Make sure you know how everything works in the RV; buy or rent a style smaller than 30 feet long. Actually, a pop-top van is big enough for a family of four.
2. Plan the route ahead of time and let your kids help with the planning.
3. Bring every map and travel book you'll need; have the kids help with the navigating.
4. Bring flat bins that will provide extra storage space for books and games.
5. Treats should be in large supply, but keep the sugar to a minimum.
6. Pack light; don't forget a swimming suit, hiking boots, etc.
7. Flashlights, medical kits, and a repair kit are necessary.
8. Plan small outings along the way such as to a historical sight or museum.
9. Consider breaking up the trip every few days with a stay in a hotel or motel (with a pool!)
10. Accomplish long or boring hauls at night after the kids are asleep.

ADVENTURE

Welcome to Adventure!

One of the hottest areas in travel these days is Adventure.

People are in better shape physically. Now they want to get out in the world, flex new-found vitality, and participate. For many, sitting on a tour bus, taking a cruise, or day trips from some hotel like any other hotel just doesn't fit the bill any more.

Outdoor adventure vacations appeal to an increasing number of travelers. River rafting, photo safaris, wilderness hikes, mountain climbing, skin diving, jungle boating, spelunking, archaeological and anthropological expeditions, spiritual quests, ballooning...the possibilities are seemingly endless. More available and less expensive means of travel and increasing international cooperation has opened most continents to visitors.

This is more than college-age kids heading off with backpacks for youth hostels and pensions. Families, seniors and women have joined the ranks of adventure travel. Growing realization of the tremendous importance of the environment, especially among the young, has opened the entire area of eco-travel—a style of meeting the world that will continue to expand, and often includes a touch of excitement.

Of course, no need to ask the kids whether they would rather climb a mountain in Tibet or visit a museum in Paris (not that Paris isn't an adventure). There are mountains and rivers, peoples and animals to meet that will satisfy any kid's dreams. Why shouldn't the entire family share the kids' dreams and go on that adventure?

This is not as easy as packing a case and heading for the airport, where planes and taxis will take you from point to point on your itinerary, porters and doormen keeping you dry and unburdened along the way. Expect to do research, pack serious first aid items, maybe you'll have to learn at least part of a totally new language, check on health issues, do you need a visa? What shots will you need? You will participate at every step of the way.

You will not forget these trips! Camel rides, helicopter hiking, schussing the Andes, helping gather data on Galapagos—these sort of trips more than fill a couple weeks, they are shared experiences of great potential power that will probably test you and will definitely open new vistas.

ADVENTURE TRAVEL COMPANIES

A brief listing—

New adventure travel companies are successfully providing tours every year. And many companies are obscure, esoteric, or we simply haven't heard of them. The listings below should be a good start for browsing, finding out what sort of trip tickles your fancy, and the entries do provide contact information. We have only given one sample trip along with a description. Describing one trip does not do justice to any of these fine companies. For complete catalogs of any group's trips, please contact that company. Information is provided. Let your imagination soar!

All Adventure Travel

5589 Arapahoe Road, Suite 208
Boulder, Colorado 80303
Phone: (800) 537-4025

All Adventure Travel sifts through eighty tour catalogs, and picks the best adventure tour operators worldwide to list in their catalogs. Contact them for a copy of the catalog, or for detailed itineraries on any of their trips. Below are some trips from the 1995 offerings specifically scheduled for families.

Sample Trip Banff & Jasper National Parks, 6 days, bicycling/camping. Along the western edge of Alberta winds one of the finest bicycling roads in the world—the spectacular Icefields Parkway. The vistas are magnificent as you cycle the gradual hills and wide-shouldered roads that make this the easiest trip in the Rockies—you will cycle between the mountain ranges, not over them. The Canadian Rockies are perfect for camping. All our camp sites are set near lakes or rivers and hiking trails. Our final night is spent at the Sunwapta Falls Resort.

Family Trips Two in July and four in August. Tour includes bike rental, van transfer.

A.W.E.! American Wilderness Experience, Inc.

P.O. Box 1486
Boulder, Colorado 80306
Phone: (303) 444-2622

Celebrating a quarter century, the American Wilderness Experience catalog presents a dazzling array of possibilities. Gleaned from numerous tour companies, there should be something for everyone in this line-up. It will also give you an idea of the vast number and variety of tour operators and outfitters. These people understand "the human need for the quiet solitude and beauty of the wilds. Wilderness is not merely a nicety, it's a necessity." This catalog includes

Sample Trip Teton Country Covered Wagon Adventure—Jackson, Wyoming. 4- and 6-day trips

The creak of the wagons, the smell of leather, sagebrush and woodsmoke, breathtaking mountain panoramas around every bend ... if you didn't know better, you'd swear that you were back in the days of America's hearty western pioneers. If only they had it so good! Our modern day wagons have been cushioned with rubber tires and foam padded seats. Seasoned trail chefs serve savory family-style meals with a well-provisioned chuckwagon as cowboy crooners sing old favorites to the crackle of the campfire.

Seldom used logging roads provide the ideal system of trails as we wind our way through the Teton National Forest. In the distance the Grand Tetons, Gros Ventre and Wind River Ranges come into view. Help drive the wagon team or hop in the saddle for a sensational side ride. Anyone, from the youngest to the oldest, will enjoy reliving this slice of American history!

Outfitter Wagons West

Trips depart from early June through August.

English Adventures

803 Front Range Road
Littleton, Colorado 80120
Phone: (800) 253-3485

The Englishman Alan English and his American wife Judy began this Colorado-based company in 1990. They offer one-week and two-week tours. English Adventures specializes in the English Lake District, England's first National Park and premier walking area. It is a region of stunning natural beauty of mountains, lakes and villages that has inspired artists and writers for centuries. The tours cleverly balance moderate walks in magnificent countryside with daily visits to castles, ancient ruins, stately homes, quaint villages, excellent restaurants, and friendly pubs.

Sample Trip On the two week tours, one day is spent in the nearby Yorkshire Dales of James Herriot, and another day visiting the impressive 2,000 year-old Roman wall built by the Emperor Hadrian right across England to defend against the marauding Picts from Scotland. Guests are accommodated in charming apartments in the grand Victorian mansion in the lovely lakeside town of Windermere in the Lake District. Each tour of only 12 guests is escorted by one or two experienced guides, and a private bus provides drop off and pick-up before, during and after the walks.

Finnway, Inc.
228 East 45th Street
New York, New York 10017
Phone: (800) 526-4927; (212) 818-1198

Tour Specialists to Finland, Scandinavia, Russia and the Baltics. Below is a description of the "Northern Lights" tour. FinnWay also operates a week-long "Wilderness Safari" in Lapland.

Sample Trip Northern Lights—An 8-day tour based mainly at the town of Levi in Finnish Lapland, features such options as an icebreaker cruise on the frozen Baltic and husky and snowmobile safaris over Lapland's snowy fells and tundra.

A choice of 3 Levi hotels for a 5-night stay in Lapland and a night in Helsinki at the Inter-Continental Hotel, breakfast daily, 5 lunches and dinners, traditional Lapp activities and 2 days free for options. After a short flight from Helsinki to Lapland, start with a welcoming reception and dinner in Levi and continue on to visit a reindeer farm for a reindeer-drawn sleigh ride and lunch in a Lapp cabin.

Also on the itinerary are an evening snowmobile safari with a picnic dinner in a Lapp hut; a tour of Lapland's oldest ski resort, followed by a sauna and Lapp dinner; and a farewell dinner and ceremonial initiation into the Lapp community at the Tuikku (Twinkle) restaurant, with a panoramic view of the surrounding countryside.

Optional icebreaker cruise aboard the Sampo, which can crush its way through 11½ foot thick ice and ride over banks of ice that are often as much as 28 feet deep. Passengers can stroll on the ice as the ship pauses in the middle of the ocean(!) or, wearing "survival suits," take a dip amid broken ice in the area (!!).

Well-trained Siberian huskies pull sleds on the husky safari. Snowmobile safaris are available as a half-day option, or for a full day with an overnight stay in a log cabin and a traditional Lapp dinner of reindeer meat cooked over a campfire.

Other options include downhill or cross-country skiing in either or both of 2 winter sports centers, Levi and Yllas; a visit to Santa's home and workshop at Rovaniemi, on the Arctic Circle; and a day at the Levi-tunturi Spa, which has Finnish and Turkish saunas, a swimming pool with waterfalls, other spa facilities and a sports center with squash courts, golf simulators and children's playhouse.

The tour can be extended with additional nights in Helsinki, weekends in St. Petersburg or Tallinn, or a 2-night, round-trip Baltic cruise to Stockholm.

Round-trip Finnair flights from New York are included in the price of "Northern Lights."

❋

Gunflint Northwoods Outfitters
143 South Gunflint Lake
Grand Marais, Minnesota 55604
Phone: (218) 388-2294; (800) 328-3325

In Northern Minnesota the famed Boundary Waters Canoe Area Wilderness and the Quetico Provincial Park of Ontario comprise the largest waterways wilderness in the world. This vast area with its thousands of lakes is dedicated to the paddling canoer. We travel and explore this country as temporary visitors, leaving only our footprints. Each visit to this area is a wilderness adventure. You encounter a never ending variety of clearwater lakes and enjoy nature as it happens—from a feeding moose to a calling loon. Our unique trips set the standards for adventure in the Boundary Waters country, from our care for the environment, to the thorough planning of your trip, and the commitment to excellence we offer based on our 68 years of outfitting at Gunflint.

Sample Trip Family Guided Canoe Trip
New adventures for the kids are a priority on this trip, but everyone has fun. From exploring new lakes to watching beaver feeding; from helping set up camp to sitting around the evening campfire listening to the sounds of the forest. A comfortable travel pace gets you well into the paddle zone of the wilderness. You stop at 3 different camp sites during your 4 night-5 day trip in the wilderness.

❋

Hostelling International—
American Youth Hostels (HI-AYH)

Department 860
733 15th Street NW , Suite 840
Washington, D.C. 20002
Phone: (202) 783-6161; (800) 444-6111
E-mail: dkalter@attmail.com

HI-AYH is a not-for-profit corporation which promotes international understanding through its network of hostels for travelers and its educational travel programs. HI-AYH is the U.S. affiliate of the International Youth Hostel Federation (IYHF) which encompasses more than 5,000 hostels in over 70 countries—the largest network of accommodations in the world.

Hostelling International and the Blue Triangle are the new trademark and seal of approval of the IYHF, assuring quality budget accommodations and travel programs for travelers of all ages.

The HI-AYH Discovery Tours trip catalog is available free of charge. Nearly 30 hiking, cycling, backpacking and canoeing trips in the USA, Canada, Europe and Israel are listed in detail.

Discovery Tours feature small friendly groups, trained leaders, flexible itineraries and tours for different age groups, from teens to 50+. Hiking and cycling tours are rated for all levels of experience, from beginner to expert. They are a bargain, ranging from about $450 for a 10-day cycling trip in New York's Finger Lakes Area to a 15-day hiking trip in western Ireland for only about $960. Prices include lodging, group-prepared meals, leadership costs and a group activities budget.

Overnight accommodations are in hostels which feature dormitory-style lodgings with separate quarters for males and females, self-service kitchens and common rooms for relaxing and socializing.

You might spend the night in a lighthouse on the California coast or a Swiss chalet. Some Discovery Tours include camping and HI-AYH provides the tents, cooking utensils and stoves.

Sample Trip Cross-Country Peace Tour—a 91-day odyssey across the USA.

Stopping approximately seven times to provide community service to organizations striving for peace—a little different than your average bicycle trip.

Mountain Travel Sobek

6420 Fairmont Avenue
El Cerrito, California 94530
Phone: (800) 227-2384

Mountain Travel Sobek is one of the pioneers in the adventure travel industry. They started organizing exciting trips around the world in the late 1960s, including sailing through the Galapagos Islands, African safaris, and kayaking among the glaciers. Currently over 80 trips are offered.

Sample Trip: Sailing the Turquoise Coast—14 days easy boat travel along the Turkish coast.

Island-hopping his way throughout the Mediterranean, Odysseus left his mark not only on literature, but on the world's concept of adventure travel. At the heart of his journey was the sailing ship, and this adventurous odyssey makes full use of its charms.

Aboard a comfortable 65-foot gulet (motor-sailer-yacht), we skim the waters of southwestern Turkey's Turquoise Coast, so named for the attractive colors of its sea and well-known for its awe-inspiring archaeological sites. Anchoring in quiet bays and coves, we go ashore to explore hidden beaches and hike to ancient Greek, Roman, and Lycian ruins. We also hike to the haunting Greek ghost town of Kayakoyu, explore one of the Mediterranean's best beaches at Dalyan, and experience the spectacular Lycian antiquities near Antalya.

Our gulet grants us leisured freedom, a chance to see places rich in history that can't be seen—or sometimes even reached—by any other means. Daily sailing time ranges from two to five hours, with ample time to hike, swim, walk along quaint waterfront streets and indulge in delightful fruit and vegetables fresh from local farms. A knowledgeable guide accompanies us on all our endeavors and we are well taken care of by the friendly crew and on-board chef. Group size is limited to 12, just enough for good companionship! Trips are scheduled from May into September. Prices range with the season, beginning at about $2,300 per person.

National Wildlife Federation

11100 Wildlife Center Drive
Reston, Virginia 20190
Phone: (800) 822-9919; (703) 438-6000

The National Wildlife Federation offers educational conservation "summits" at the gateway to Rocky Mountain National Park in Colorado, on Hawaii's Big Island and in the Blue Ridge Mountains of western North Carolina. Parents plan their own daily schedules, and kids attend daily programs for preschoolers, youth and teens including nature walks, field trips and classes led by expert naturalists, folk dancing. Accommodations are extra.

OARS

P.O. Box 67
Angels Camp, California 95222
Phone: (800) 346-6277

OARS has been operating rafting trips for 20 years, and give each trip a "minimum age rating." These age limits are based on a number of factors, including how well most kids can handle the duration of the trip, their ability to feel comfortable in water and the difficulty of the logistics.

Sample Trip San Juan River, Utah—4 nights, 5 days Minimum age is 5 years. Rating is Class II

The red-rock country of the American Southwest is the ideal outdoor vacationland for the young family, or for a three-generation wilderness reunion. The San Juan, a tributary of the Colorado that flows out of the mountains of New Mexico, is marked along its course with ancient sites of the vanished Anasazi Indians. While the youn'uns explore the rock paintings and search for Indian ruins, parents and grandparents can paddle the mild rapids in one-person or tandem inflatable kayaks. And everyone can enjoy the spectacular sunsets and starry nights around the campfire on this extraordinary river journey into the timeless past.

Pocono Environmental Education Center

Rural Route 2, Box 1010
Dingmans Ferry, Pennsylvania 18328
Phone: (510) 828-2319

The Pocono Environmental Education Center offers affordable year-round family camps and weekends with nature study and outdoor recreation activities designed for adults and children alike. The center is located in the National Park Service's Delaware Water Gap National Recreation Area. Each family stays in a rustic single-room cabin which includes a full bathroom with modern plumbing and electricity. Nature study workshops are scheduled throughout the year.

❧

R.O.W. (River Odysseys West)

P.O. Box 579-PR
Coeur d'Alene, Idaho 83816
Phone: (800) 451-6034

Peter Grubb is founder and president of River Odysseys West, an Idaho-based rafting company that specializes in family trips on North America's most highly-touted river ... the wildly scenic Salmon—Idaho's "River of No Return." (R.O.W. offers trips on more Idaho rivers than any other rafting company, as well as treks and yacht cruises as far afield as Ecuador, Turkey, Nepal and France.)

The company's 5-day "Family Focus" trips, for families with kids aged 5–12, are offered in the Summer through Salmon River Canyons. "ParenTeen Fun" adventures for families with teenagers 13-18, are being offered in the Summer as well. Costs begin at about $850 per adult, and $725 per child. (Three and four day trips are also available by request.)

The trips, led by guides with degrees in environmental education, provide a perfect classroom for children to learn about geography, Indian and pioneer history and nature through hikes, games and simply floating through some of America's most remote wilderness. All guides are trained in river rescue, CPR and first aid. To ensure guests' welfare, R.O.W. maintains the best guide-to-guest ratio in the industry!

❧

Sierra Club Family Trips

Sierra Club Outing Department
85 2nd Street, Second Floor
San Francisco, California 94105
Phone: (415) 977-5500

A Sierra Club family trip creates a cooperative atmosphere that allows children to experience the fun of outdoor living with other children. Everyone shares camp chores, outdoor skills, and knowledge about area plants, animals, and ecology. The wilderness offers many enjoyable opportunities—nature study, hiking, swimming, fishing.

On some trips you drive to your campsite and take daily hikes; on others, pack animals transport food and equipment from trailhead to camp; while on some you stay in lodges or cabins. Difficulty levels and age restrictions vary. General good health is necessary, and some physical conditioning is advisable.

The Sierra Club welcomes single parents, grandparents, or aunts and uncles, in addition to two-parent families. Children 12 years of age and older are required to have their own Sierra Club memberships.

Sample Trip Acadia Toddler Tromp—Acadia Park, Maine

With activities planned to accommodate family demands, this outing is designed for families with children aged 2 to 14. Grandparents and single-parent families are also welcome. Opportunities include hiking, cycling, exploring the carriage roads, canoeing, boat trips to islands, the Oceanarium, Otter Cliffs, beaches, lighthouses, lobster, and blueberries. Campsites are located near Acadia National Park.

The Tromp is usually scheduled for August.

Wildland Adventures

3516 NE 155th Street
Seattle, Washington 98155
Phone: (800) 345-4453

In 1986, Wildland Adventures was founded on the ideal of offering the most authentic, enlightening and personal travel experiences in the world's exotic natural environments and native cultures. Destinations vary from Nepal to Africa to Costa Rica, and includes an entire category of trips to the Andes. Trips are generally scheduled and filled on demand, although a few are scheduled. Because of this dual focus, in this instance two sample trips are given.

Sample Trip Nepal Annapurna Family Trek—16 days

Offers families the opportunity to explore the Annapurna massif without ascending to a high altitude. Special attention is paid to the needs of young trekkers. Parents and children explore the villages and schools of central Nepal and discover the warmth and hospitality of the Nepalese people. The families of our Nepali staff co-lead these trips. Smaller children can be carried by a porter in a specially converted woven basket when they get tired! We also offer private departures. The trip includes 8 days of camping and trekking.

Sample Trip Amazon Rain Forest Expeditions

The protected Amazon wildlands of the Manu Biosphere Reserve, Tambopata-Candamo Reserve and Alto Madidi National Park (proposed) are one of the most untouched natural regions on earth where you will find the highest diversities and densities of rare rain forest mammals, birds, and reptiles anywhere. Sites visited on these scientifically-planned itineraries offer the highest probabilities on earth of viewing jaguar, ocelot, tapir, giant otter, monkeys, black caiman, tayra and agoutis. There are 13 species of monkeys and more than 1,000 bird species, including the highest concentration in the world of blue, gold and scarlet macaws, as well as many colorful parrots, toucans and shorebirds. Manu Camping Expedition: Grade, II-III; Total days, 11; Monthly departures May–October.

꘎

Wilderness Southeast

428 Bull Street
Savannah, Georgia 31401
Phone: (912) 897-5108

For 23 years Wilderness Southeast has been offering trips that "gently stretch both mind and muscles." They take people to fascinating places, off the beaten track, where they find that "Nature is not an adversary to conquer but a storehouse of fascinating knowledge to absorb." They are non-profit, environmental educators who practice low-impact camping, recycling and conservation. They also offer special programs for teens!

Sample Trip Pritchards Island—5-day Sea Turtle Watch

Almost every night in June and July, huge loggerhead sea turtles struggle laboriously onto the hardpacked sand to dig their nests and deposit a clutch of eggs. The ancient loggerheads are now protected by the Endangered Species Act. On deserted beaches from South Carolina to Florida, teams of sea turtle researchers patrol at night searching for signs of these reptiles in order to collect data on their nesting patterns and protect the precious contents of the nests.

Participants in Sea Turtle Watch observe the ritual themselves and to become part of a team of volunteers helping with the research and conservation effort of the University of South Carolina at Beaufort. For half the night, you'll patrol 2½ miles of beach. Mornings are for sleeping late, but there is also time each day to comb the beach and explore the lush interior forest, sea marshes and canoe the saltwater tidal creeks. We will stay in the comfortable, air-conditioned Research House. Six people share a room with bunk beds and full bath. Experience is not needed, but you do need enthusiasm and a willingness to assist professional researchers with their demanding work. Minimum age recommended is 12; must be accompanied. Suggested group size is 14.

Wilderness Voyageurs
P.O. Box 97
Ohiopyle, Pennsylvania 15470
Phone: (800) 272-4141

The East Coast's original outfitter, Wilderness Voyageurs pioneered rafting on the Lower Yough in 1964. The headwaters of the Yough (pronounced "yock") are on Backbone Mountain in West Virginia and Maryland. From there the Yough flows 132 miles to its confluence with the Monongahela. Whatever your age, from 4 to 104, these folks can help you experience the fun and excitement of white water rafting. Most of these are day trips, the price is VERY reasonable, and it's close to home for many. This might be the ideal first 'practice' adventure for the family. Ask about the Guided Middle Yough trip. And is someone in the family not that interested in being on the water? They also rent mountain and speed bikes, offer guided fishing trips and teach rock climbing.

Sample Trip Lower Youghiogheny Overnighter
Class II-IV; minimum age 12; Trip length 15 miles. No prior experience necessary.

Day one is on the Lower Yough. When your trip reaches Bruner Run, the customary takeout, we will switch from rafts into duckies or canoes and continue downstream to our riverside camp. Day two will find us getting a midmorning start and a relaxing day floating through Class I and II rapids. Bring your fishing pole or a good book, today is at your pace. Hearty meals, a crackling campfire, quiet time with family or friends in a primitive setting awaits you. Sit back, relax, and let the staff pamper you.

⁕⋇⋇⁕

As mentioned above, this is only a beginning. There are many, many adventure travel providers, from the dedicated local group to such large entities as Earth Watch. Take a chance on the world, and on yourselves, and go have an adventure.

VARIOUS ALTERNATIVES

FAMILY REUNION

Family reunions are becoming increasingly important as people look to the basic family unit for satisfaction. Also, more and more families are searching for their "roots" as each culture and social strata learns to honor itself. And the human family is again very mobile. The old connections to land and tight community are stretched and often broken. The extended birth family is a source of great comfort and provides a sense of belonging.

But with improved communication and transportation, families are in closer contact with more far-flung members of the clan. Suddenly a reunion means at least 50 people from thousands of miles apart. The main family doesn't live in the same village as in days of old. The large multi-generation farm or house is long gone. Grandma and Grandpa sure can't put everybody up for a week.

And today every member of the family has his or her own interests and is used to multiple activities in a day. Not many families will be happy sitting around talking for several days in a row. The kids have their interests, curiosity draws many into surrounding areas they may never see again, and many people need a great deal of physical activity or sports to enjoy a vacation.

Where to go? What are some ideal locations for a family reunion? That's what this section is all about. And we invite input from families who have found great spots.

Locations and ideas in the *Family Travel – The Complete Guide* that are recommended for family reunion vacation generally provide at least the following:

- ○ Sufficient accommodations to meet the needs of a good-sized family.
- ○ Low to medium costs for accommodations.
- ○ Child-supporting facilities such as babysitting and planned children's activities.
- ○ The facility specifically welcomes family reunion groups.
- ○ Check out our listings for Condos, All-Suite Hotel companies, parks, ranches and regional destinations.

Where a family decides to go relies on a number of factors. Many families want to go back to the land they consider the family home. Many families want to go off together where they won't be interrupted or bother anyone else. Many families want to experience an exciting trip together like a cruise or festival. What works for you?

Call Up The *Entire* Family And Take A Trip!

PLANNING A FAMILY REUNION VACATION

The first phase of planning is definitely up to you. Only you know the guest list and where everyone in your clan will be able to enjoy some time together. Of course, the affordability range should exclude as few as possible.

An indispensable assistance in planning, and good reading even when you are not in the midst of planning a reunion, is *Reunions* magazine. *Reunions* comes out 5 times a year. Call them at (414) 263-4567.

NEXT—where you can turn for some additional assistance in your family reunion vacation planning:

TOURISM BUREAUS & CHAMBERS OF COMMERCE   Every area has at least one. Start with the State (or Province) and then narrow down to

the county, major cities and towns. There are also regional bureaus and chambers, as well as visitors bureaus for parks and often for specific areas like wine countries, resort areas, etc. Use the 800-number toll-free directory for some of these numbers.

HOTEL & RESORT CHAINS   Chains can be very advantageous in a number of ways. For one, you know what to expect at a Best Western wherever it is. Many people are uncomfortable traveling and are only going to go because of the comfort of the family surrounding them. If they know they're going to a Holiday Inn, many worries may be relieved. Also, chains often offer group discounts, tickets to nearby attractions, etc. And remember, "chain" can mean Hilton as well as Howard Johnson's, just as restaurant chains range from Taco Bell to the Hard Rock Cafe. Here are a couple of numbers to get you started: Holiday Inn (800) 633-8464, and Best Western (800) 334-7234.

ALL-INCLUSIVE RESORTS   These folks have already done all of the work for you. They have put together great locations, provide all the normal needs of a family, and sponsor a seemingly endless variety of activities. The one everyone knows is Club Med—which isn't just for young singles any more. They have special family vacation spots in numerous hot spots, and special deals for groups.

Call 800-4-LE-CLUB. There are other all-inclusives, and this is a term recognized in the travel industry. Browsing the travel magazines should bring a number to light, as will talking with your travel agent.

CRUISES   Here's one way to keep everyone under one roof (so to speak) but still have room to move. And most cruise ships have various activities—from bridge to walking races to libraries to gyms to shore excursions to lectures to ?—which should satisfy just about everyone. Most cruise companies also offer babysitting and children's activities along with the entertainment, dancing and special parties. And it does feel right to talk about and remember family members while sitting comfortably gazing out over a sparkling sea. This is another area where group bookings can be helpful, providing discounts or even a free passage or two. With a large group, it is very important to plan ahead and reserve well in advance if you want to be in the same area of the ship or need special accommodations. Be certain to confirm any assistance available from the cruise line for air transport to and from the ship. And do discuss special dietary requirements. Ocean going hotels are used to dealing with quite a variety of dining needs and should be able to meet everyone's special needs. Also, check regarding any handicaps that must be dealt with. Most ships are fully accessible, but some older ones may be very difficult, with narrow passages and high sills. If medical care is an issue, the line *must* know all of the details.

REUNITING ABROAD   A variety of accommodation types are available outside the U.S. which might work perfectly for you and your family. The Caribbean and Mexico are dotted with beachside villas and resorts well versed in hosting family gatherings. You may find your own mini-village complete with domestic help at weekly rates. When researching this, watch for offerings of villas. Are you ready to visit your ancestral land or lands en masse? Don't rule it out until you have explored the possibilities. You'll be strangers who aren't quite strangers. And this will be an experience the kids will *not* forget. Again, remember to always check out any group rate or discount.

So—There are a few suggestions to chew on. Each family is unique and once some ideas are tossed out, there will probably either be an unimaginable mix of ideas, or an obvious and mutually agreeable direction to take. You want your reunion memories to be good. So take the time to plan a great trip.

LAST TIP   If you have an idea where you all want to go geographically, but aren't sure where to stay or what to do while you're there, consider subscribing to a publication from the area. Not only will you have a feel for who lives there and what's going on by the time you arrive, but you may find little-known gems through reviews and special offers.

Have Fun! And take plenty of film for the cameras!

FARMS & RANCHES

Not many of us have the old family farm available for a visit. But there are farms which welcome the family to come out, stay a while and reconnect with the land on a farm. You will notice in our listings below that there is often mention of "Children limited." These are usually age limits that the farm has found optimal for both the farm and the guests. Please talk to the farm managers about your own family. And be certain your children understand the importance of following the rules, especially around the animals and the farm equipment. Lastly, be prepared to develop a big appetite!

De Haven Valley Farm
39247 North Highway 1
Westport, California 95488
Phone: (707) 961-1660
Farm managers: Kathleen and Jim
   Tobin
Season: All year
Price: $85 (double occupancy rate),
   Breakfast included
Type of breakfast offered: Full
   breakfast

Other foods available: Restaurant,
   lunch
Credit cards accepted: Mastercard,
   Visa
Restrictions: Children limited,
   Smoking not allowed, Pets not
   allowed.
Services: 4-course dinner Wednesday
   through Saturday, sherry or tea,
   sitting room, library, hot tubs.

1885 farmhouse and cottages on 20 acres of hills, meadows and streams, by beach. Horses, donkeys, sheep, more. Explore Mendocino, tide pools, redwood forest.

Howard Creek Ranch

P.O. Box 121
Westport, California 95488
Phone: (707) 964-6725
Farm managers: Charles and Sally Grigg
Season: All year
Price: $55 (double occupancy rate), Breakfast included
Type of breakfast offered: Full ranch breakfast

Other foods available: Complimentary tea
Restrictions: Children limited, Smoking limited, Pets limited, Limited handicap access.
Languages spoken: German, Italian, Dutch
Services: Piano, hot tub, cabins, sauna, massage by reservation, horses, a working ranch.

Historic farmhouse filled with collectibles, antiques and memorabilia, unique health spa with privacy and dramatic views adjoining a wide beach. Award-winning flower garden.

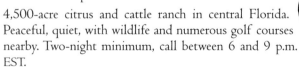

Kelsall's Ute Creek Ranch

2192 County Road 334
Ignacio, Colorado 81137
Phone: (303) 563-4464
Season: All year
Price: $55 (double occupancy rate), Breakfast included
Type of breakfast offered: Full breakfast

Other foods available: Cooking facilities
Credit cards accepted: Mastercard, Visa
Restrictions: Children welcome, Smoking allowed, Pets not allowed, Handicap no access.
Services: Sitting room.

Working cattle ranch. Let us introduce you to the West! Complimentary breakfast. Open year-around. Close to two ski areas.

Double M Ranch B&B

Route 1, Box 292 Zolfo Springs, Florida 33890
Phone: (813) 735-0266
Farm managers: Mary Jane & Charles Matheny
Season: All year
Price: $55 (double occupancy rate), Breakfast included
Type of breakfast offered: Continental plus

Restrictions: Smoking not allowed, Pets not allowed, Handicap no access.
Services: Pool table, sitting room, ranch tour, nearby golf, canoeing, fishing, and riding.

4,500-acre citrus and cattle ranch in central Florida. Peaceful, quiet, with wildlife and numerous golf courses nearby. Two-night minimum, call between 6 and 9 p.m. EST.

Wingscorton Farm Inn

Olde Kings Highway 6A
East Sandwich, Massachusetts
02537
Phone: (508) 888-0534
Season: All year
Price: $75 (double occupancy rate),
Breakfast included
Type of breakfast offered: Full
breakfast

Other foods available: Picnic basket
lunch
Credit cards accepted: American
Express, Mastercard, Visa
Restrictions: Children welcome,
Smoking allowed, Pets allowed,
Handicap access. Services: Dinner,
complimentary library, bicycles,
private ocean beach.

A special retreat for couples seeking a private, intimate getaway. Eclectic mix of antiquity and modern conveniences in a setting of a working New England farm. Private beach.

Wood Farm

40 Worcester Road
Townsend, Massachusetts 01469
Phone: (508) 597-5019
Farm managers: Debra Jones, Jim
Mayrand
Season: All year
Price: $45 (double occupancy rate),
Breakfast included

Type of breakfast offered: Full
breakfast
Restrictions: Children limited,
Smoking not allowed, Pets
limited, Handicap no access.
Languages spoken: French, Spanish
Services: Sitting room, gardens,
bicycles, box stalls for horses.

Restored 1716 Cape in antique country; country breakfast at working sheep farm; warm conversation by the hearth. Wooded trails and waterfall. Special theme weekends.

The Crane House

6051 – 124th Avenue
Fennville, Michigan 49408
Phone: (616) 561-6931
Farm manager: Nancy Crane
McFarland
Season: All year
Price: $65 (double occupancy rate),
Breakfast included
Type of breakfast offered: Full
breakfast

Other foods available: Restaurant
Credit cards accepted: Visa,
Mastercard, American Express,
Discover
Restrictions: Children limited,
Smoking not allowed, Pets not
allowed, Handicap access.
Services: Sitting room, close to
beaches, watersports.

"Elegantly primitive" 1870 family farmhouse on working 300-acre fruit farm. Minutes from Saugatuck, Holland, and South Haven. Featured in Country Living magazine.

Ellis River House

P.O. Box 656, Route 16
Jackson, New Hampshire 03846
Phones: (603) 383-9339;
  (800) 233-8309
Farm managers: Barry & Barbara
  Lubao
Season: All year
Price: $69 (double occupancy rate),
  Breakfast included
Type of breakfast offered: Full
  country breakfast

Other foods available: Tea, coffee,
  cookies
Most credit cards accepted.
Restrictions: Children welcome,
  Smoking allowed.
Languages spoken: Polish
Services: Sitting room, atrium, air-
  conditioning, cable TV, VCR,
  fishing, whirlpool spas, sauna

Turn-of-the-century house with balconies overlooking Ellis River. Honey-
moon cottage. Homemade breads. Cross-country skiing, outdoor heated pool.

Sonka's Sheep Station Inn

901 NW Chadwick Lane
Myrtle Creek, Oregon 97457
Phone: (503) 863-5168
Farm managers: Louis and Evelyn
  Sonka
Season: All year
Price: $50 (double occupancy rate),
  Breakfast included

Type of breakfast offered: Full
  breakfast
Other foods available:
  Complimentary tea, cookies
Restrictions: Children welcome,
  Smoking not allowed, Pets not
  allowed, Handicap no access.
Services: Sitting room, bicycles

Working sheep ranch; house furnished in sheep country motif and antiques.
Quiet setting along river. Guests may partake of ranch activities as hosts and
guests agree.

Spring Creek Llama Ranch

14700 NE Spring Creek Lane
Newberg, Oregon 97132
Phone: (503) 538-5717
Fax: (503) 538-5717
Farm managers: Dave and Melinda
  Van Bossuyt
Season: All year
Price: $55 (double occupancy rate),
  Breakfast included

Type of breakfast offered: Full
  breakfast
Other foods available: Snacks
Restrictions: Children welcome,
  Smoking not allowed, Pets not
  allowed, Handicap no access.
Languages spoken: Spanish
Services: Library, Llama farm
  experience.

Spacious and contemporary. Comfortable rooms. Completely secluded in a
picturesque and peaceful setting of forest and pasture. Trails, friendly llamas.

Weatherbury Farm

1061 Sugar Camp Run Road
Avella, Pennsylvania 15312 Phone:
   (412) 587-3763
Farm managers: Dale, Marcy and
   Nigel Tudor
Season: All year
Price: $60 (double occupancy rate),
   Breakfast included
Type of breakfast offered: Full
   breakfast

Other foods available: Snacks
Credit cards accepted: Visa,
   Mastercard
Restrictions: Children welcome,
   Smoking limited, Pets not
   allowed, Handicap no access.
Languages spoken: German
Services: Sitting room, library,
   bicycles, swimming pool.

1860s farmhouse on working farm. Meadows and gardens. Spectacular views.
Perfect getaway from everyday pressures. Bountiful farm breakfast. Convenient
to Pittsburgh.

Winding Glen Farm Home

107 Noble Road
Christiana, Pennsylvania 17509
Phone: (215) 593-5535
Farm managers: Minnie and Robert
   Metzler
Season: All year
Price: $45 (double occupancy rate),
   Breakfast included

Type of breakfast offered: Full
   breakfast
Restrictions: Children welcome,
   Smoking limited, Pets not
   allowed, Limited handicap access.
Services: Sitting room, piano, slide
   shows.

Working dairy farm situated in beautiful valley. Stores and quilt shops nearby.
Handcrafted furniture made on premises.

Barley Sheaf Farm

P.O. Box 10, Route 202
Holicong, Pennsylvania 18928
Phone: (215) 794-5104
Farm managers: Don and Ann Mills
Season: Except Christmas, weekdays
   to mid-February
Price: $95 (double occupancy rate),
   Breakfast included
Type of breakfast offered: Full farm
   breakfast

Restrictions: Children limited,
   Smoking allowed, Pets not
   allowed, Handicap access
Languages spoken: French
Services: Swimming pool, sitting
   room
30-acre working farm—raise sheep.
   Rooms all furnished in antiques.
   Good antiquing and historic
   sights in area.

Meadow Spring Farm B&B

223 East Street Road
Kennett Square, Pennsylvania 19348
Phone: (610) 444-3903
Farm managers: Anne Hicks and
  Debbie Aselrod
Season: All year
Price: $65 (double occupancy rate),
  Breakfast included
Type of breakfast offered: Full
  country breakfast

Other foods available: Dinner upon
  request
Credit cards accepted: American
  Express
Restrictions: Children welcome,
  Smoking allowed, Pets not
  allowed, Handicap no access.
Services: Complimentary wine, tea,
  snacks, hot tubs, game room, pool,
  pond for fishing

1836 farmhouse on working farm with sheep, pigs & cows; filled with antiques, dolls & teddy bears. Full country breakfast served on porch, spacious dining room or by the pool.

Cedar Hill Farm

305 Longenecker Road
Mount Joy, Pennsylvania 17552
Phone: (717) 653-4655
Farm managers: Russel and Gladys
  Swarr
Season: All year
Price: $65 (double occupancy rate),
  Breakfast included

Type of breakfast offered:
  Continental plus
Most credit cards accepted.
Restrictions: Children limited,
  Smoking not allowed, Pets not
  allowed, Handicap no access.
Services: Central air-conditioning,
  porch, private balcony, roam this
  working farm.

Host born in this 1817 Fieldstone farmhouse (but not in 1817). Quiet area overlooks stream. Near Lancaster's Amish country & Hershey. Near farmers' markets & quaint villages.

The Whitehall Inn

Rural District 2, Box 250
New Hope, Pennsylvania 18938
Phone: (215) 598-7945
Farm managers: Mike and Suella
  Wass
Season: All year
Price: $130 (double occupancy rate),
  Breakfast included
Type of breakfast offered: Full
  candlelight breakfast
Other foods available: High tea,
  complimentary sherry
Most credit cards accepted.

Restrictions: Smoking not allowed,
  Pets not allowed, Handicap no
  access.
Services: Pool & rose garden, library,
  sun room, piano & pump organ

Experience the four-course candlelit breakfast using European china and crystal and heirloom sterling silver. Formal tea; fireplaces; working dressage horse farm.

⁕ ❧ ⁕

Kaltenbach's B&B Inn

Rural District 6, Box 106A
Wellsboro, Pennsylvania 16901
Phones: (717) 724-4954;
  (800) 722-4954
Farm manager: Lee Kaltenbach
Season: All year
Price: $60 (double occupancy rate),
  Breakfast included
Type of breakfast offered: Full
  breakfast

Other foods available: Afternoon tea,
  snacks, wine
Credit cards accepted: Visa,
  Mastercard
Restrictions: Children welcome,
  Smoking not allowed, Pets not
  allowed, Handicap access.
Languages spoken: Spanish
Services: Lunch and dinner by
  reservation, sitting room, library,
  tennis court, hot tubs.

Famous for all-you-can-eat country-style breakfast—homemade jellies, jams, blueberry muffins, farm-raised pork, ham, bacon, sausage. Golf, skiing, hunting, fishing nearby.

⁕ ❧ ⁕

Lenape Springs Farm

P.O. Box 176
West Chester, Pennsylvania 19366
Phone: (215) 793-2266
Farm manager: Bob and Sharon
  Currie
Season: All year
Price: $65 (double occupancy rate),
  Breakfast included
Type of breakfast offered: Full
  breakfast

Other foods available: Tea, coffee,
  sodas in the evening.
Credit cards accepted: Visa,
  Mastercard
Restrictions: Children welcome,
  Smoking limited, Pets not
  allowed, Handicap no access.
Services: Rooms overlook gardens,
  creek, hot tub.

Lenape Springs Farm is a secluded 32-acre farm conveniently located to all Brandywine Valley tourist attractions. The old stone farm house dates back to 1847.

⁕ ❧ ⁕

Ponda-Rowland B&B Inn

Rural Route 1, Box 349
Wilkes-Barre, Pennsylvania 18612
Phones: (717) 639-3245;
   (800) 854-3286
Fax: (717) 639-5531
Farm managers: Jeanette and Cliff
   Rowland
Season: All year
Price: $65 (double occupancy rate),
   Breakfast included

Type of breakfast offered: Full
   candlelight breakfast
Other foods available: Picnics Most
   credit cards accepted
Restrictions: Children welcome,
   Smoking not allowed, Pets not
   allowed.
Services: Satellite TV, fireplaces,
   wildlife sanctuary, walking, hiking.

130-acre farm in the Endless Mountains. Beautiful mountain and forest scenery. Farm includes 30-acre wildlife refuge, canoeing and swimming.

Skoglund Farm

Route 1, Box 45
Canova, South Dakota 57321
Phone: (605) 247-3445
Farm managers: Alden and Delores
   Skoglund
Season: All year
Price: $30 (double occupancy rate)
Type of breakfast offered: Full
   breakfast

Other foods available: Dinner
   included
Restrictions: Children welcome,
   Smoking limited, Pets allowed,
   Handicap no access.
Languages spoken: Swedish
Services: Sitting room, piano,
   bicycles.

Enjoy overnight on the South Dakota prairie. Return to your childhood—animals, country walking, home-cooked meals. Children 5 & under are free.

Roghair Herefords B&B

Hcr 74 Box 16
Okaton, South Dakota 57562
Phone: (605) 669-2529
Farm managers: Mel and Clarice
   Roghair
Season: All year
Price: $45 (double occupancy rate),
   Breakfast included

Type of breakfast offered: Full
   breakfast
Other foods available: Bedtime snack
Restrictions: Children welcome,
   Smoking not allowed, Pets
   allowed, Handicap no access.

In central South Dakota 7 miles from I-90. We raise wheat, cattle & kids. Stop by and visit the farm.

Lakeside Farm B&B
Rural Route 2, Box 52
Webster, South Dakota 57274
Phone: (605) 486-4430
Farm managers: Glenn and Joy
   Hagen
Season: All year
Price: $40 (double occupancy rate),
   Breakfast included
Type of breakfast offered: Full
   breakfast

Other foods available: Other meals
   possible
Restrictions: Children welcome,
   Smoking not allowed, Pets not
   allowed, Handicap no access.
Services: Complimentary coffee, tea,
   snack, sitting room, bicycles,
   piano.

Sample country life. A family-owned and operated dairy farm. Northeastern South Dakota lakes area. Fresh air, open spaces. Fresh milk, homemade cinnamon rolls. Complimentary treats.

Parish Patch Farm & Inn
625 Cortner Road
Normandy, Tennessee 37360
Phones: (615) 857-3017;
   (800) 876-3017
Farm managers: David and Claudia
   Hazelwood
Season: All year
Price: $62 (double occupancy rate),
   Breakfast included
Type of breakfast offered: Full
   breakfast

Other foods available: Dinner, lunch,
   snacks
Credit cards accepted: Mastercard,
   Visa
Restrictions: Children welcome,
   Smoking allowed, Pets allowed,
   Handicap no access.
Services: Restaurant, bar service,
   sitting room, library, bicycles,
   canoe, fish.

A working cattle farm secluded in smoky, blue hills along Duck River. Restaurant in 1848 grist mill.

New Canaan Farm
P.O. Box 1173-I
Elkhart, Texas 75839
Phone: (214) 764-2106
Season: All year
Price: $55 (double occupancy rate),
   Breakfast included
Type of breakfast offered: Full
   breakfast

Other foods available: Lunch ($5
   extra) & dinner ($10 extra)
Restrictions: Children welcome.
Services: Afternoon tea, snacks,
   sitting room, library, no alcohol
   allowed.

Earth sheltered two-story farmhouse with vegetable garden on the roof. Overlooking rolling meadows, forests and streams. Horses, cattle and other ranch animals.

Berkson Farms

Rural Route 1, Box 850
Enosburg Falls, Vermont 05450
Phone: (802) 933-2522
Farm managers: Susan and Terry
  Spoonire
Season: All year
Price: $55 (double occupancy rate),
  Breakfast included Type of
  breakfast offered: Full breakfast

Other foods available: Lunch, dinner
Restrictions: Children welcome,
  Smoking not allowed, Pets
  allowed, Handicap no access.
Services: Sitting room, bicycles,
  working dairy farm, farm animals.

Homey 150-year-old farmhouse on working dairy farm. Relax on 600 acres
surrounded by animals, nature and warm hospitality.

Echo Ledge Farm Inn

P.O. Box 77, Route 2
St. Johnsbury, Vermont 05838
Phone: (802) 748-4750
Fax: (802) 748-1640
Farm managers: Dorothy and Fred
  Herman
Season: All year
Price: $45 (double occupancy rate),
  Breakfast included

Type of breakfast offered: Full
  breakfast
Other foods available: Tea, coffee,
  cookies
Credit cards accepted: Mastercard,
  Visa
Restrictions: Children welcome,
  Smoking limited, Pets not
  allowed, Handicap no access.
Services: Sitting room, color TV.

Come spend the night in the real Vermont at a farm settled in 1793. Recommended by National Geographic Traveler. Freshly papered or stenciled walls,
hardwood floors.

Knoll Farm Country Inn

RFD 1, Box 179
Waitsfield, Vermont 05673
Phones: (802) 496-3939;
  (802) 496-3527
Farm manager: Ann Day
Season: Except April & November
Price: $75 (double occupancy rate),
  Breakfast included
Type of breakfast offered: Full
  breakfast

Other foods available: Dinner, lunch,
  teas
Restrictions: Children welcome,
  Smoking not allowed, Pets not
  allowed, Handicap no access.
Languages spoken: some Spanish
Services: Sitting room, library,
  swimming pond, hiking, farm
  animals, 150 acres.

Unique combination of inn and farm; pond, spectacular views; peaceful, away
from highway; delicious family-style farm-grown meals; 150 acres of nature.

Caledonia Farm—1812

47 Dearing Road
Flint Hill, Virginia 22627
Phones: (540) 675-3693;
(800) 262-1812
Farm managers: Phil Irwin
Season: All year
Price: $80–140 (double occupancy rate), Breakfast included
Type of breakfast offered: Full breakfast

Other foods available:
Complimentary wine
Most credit cards accepted.
Restrictions: Children limited, Smoking not allowed, Handicap access.
Languages spoken: German, Danish
Services: Bikes, lawn games, VCR, evening fun hayrides, 68 miles to D.C.

Beautifully restored 1812 stone farm home adjacent to Shenandoah National Park and Blue Ridge Mountains. Virginia Landmark, on National Register. AAA rates 3 diamonds.

Oak Spring Farm & Vineyard

5895 Borden Grant Trail
Raphine, Virginia 24472
Phone: (800) 841-8813
Farm managers: Jim and Pat Tichenor
Season: All year
Price: $85–155 (double occupancy rate), Breakfast included
Type of breakfast offered: Full
Other foods available:
Complimentary refreshments

Credit cards accepted: Most credit cards accepted
Restrictions: Children limited, Smoking not allowed, Pets not allowed, Handicap no access
Languages spoken: some French & German
Services: Sitting room, hiking trails, animals, near swimming, skiing

Oak Spring Farm is a working farm and vineyard. The old plantation house (c. 1826) is filled with antiques and views. This is a special place where guests will feel relaxed.

West Shore Farm B&B

2781 West Shore Drive
Lummi Island, Washington 98262
Phone: (206) 758-2600
Farm managers: Polly and Carl
 Hanson
Season: All year
Price: $90 (double occupancy rate),
 Breakfast included
Type of breakfast offered: Full
 breakfast, snacks

Other foods available: Lunch, dinner,
 afternoon tea
Credit cards accepted: Visa,
 Mastercard
Restrictions: Children welcome,
 Smoking not allowed, Pets not
 allowed, Handicap access.
Services: Complimentary wine,
 sitting room, library, bikes, sauna,
 live music by arrangement.

Island seaside organic farm. Memorable view: islands, sunsets, Canadian mountains. Quiet beach, eagles, seals. Octagonal owner-built home. Restorative comfort.

Just-N-Trails B&B/Farm

Route 1, Box 274
Sparta, Wisconsin 54656
Phones: (608) 269-4522;
 (800) 488-4521
Farm managers: Donna and Don
 Justin
Season: All year
Price: $55 (double occupancy rate),
 Breakfast included
Type of breakfast offered: Full
 breakfast

Other foods available: Lemonade,
 apple cider
Credit cards accepted: Mastercard,
 Visa
Restrictions: Children welcome,
 Smoking not allowed, Pets not
 allowed, Handicap no access.
Services: Specialize in recreation,
 relaxation & romance, log cabin
 available.

Roam on a 200-acre dairy farm, daydream by a pond. Ride on nearby Elroy-Sparta bike trail, cross-country ski or hike our 20 km. of trails. Relax in the charming country home.

Kananaskis Guest Ranch

P.O. Box 964 Banff, Alberta T0L
 0C0
CANADA
Phone: (403) 762-3737
Fax: (403) 762-3953
Farm managers: The Brewster Family
Season: May—October 15
Price: $90 (double occupancy rate),
 Breakfast included
Type of breakfast offered: Full
 breakfast

Other foods available: Licensed
 dining room, lounge
Credit cards accepted: Mastercard,
 Visa
Restrictions: Children welcome,
 Smoking allowed, Pets not
 allowed, Handicap access.
Services: Seminar facility, golf,
 whirlpool, horses, Western
 barbecues

Turn-of-the-century guest ranch; private cabins & chalet units; antique furniture. Operated by 5th-generation Brewsters. 45 miles west of Calgary, 30 miles east of Banff.

Anola's B&B

P.O. Box 340
Claresholm, Alberta T0L 0T0
CANADA
Phone: (403) 625-4389
Fax: (403) 625-2277
Farm managers: Anola and Gordon Laing
Season: All year
Price: $50 (double occupancy rate), Breakfast included

Type of breakfast offered: Full breakfast
Other foods available: Evening tea & muffins
Restrictions: Children limited, Smoking not allowed, Pets not allowed, Handicap access
Services: Complimentary wine with cottage, library, bikes, hot tub, museum, grain farm

Relax in the country cottage guest house. Antique furnishings and Franklin stove. Visit Granddad's museum. Close to Head-Smashed-Inn Buffalo Jump.

Swallow Hill Farm B&B

4910 William Head Road
Victoria, British Columbia V9B 5T7
CANADA
Phone: (604) 474-4042
Farm managers: Gini & Peter Walsh
Season: All year
Price: $65 (double occupancy rate), Breakfast included
Type of breakfast offered: Full farm breakfast

Other foods available: Complimentary tea and coffee
Credit cards accepted: Mastercard, Visa, American Express
Restrictions: Children limited, Smoking not allowed, Pets not allowed, Handicap no access.
Services: Sitting room, bicycles, books & games for guests, many activity brochures.

Mountain and sea views. Delicious homebaked breakfasts. Friendly conversation. Guest rooms with antiques. Central to S. Vancouver Island.

Reid Farms Tourist Home

Rural Route I
Centreville, New Brunswick E0J
   1H0 CANADA
Phone: (506) 276-4787
Farm managers: Ken and Shirley
   Reid
Season: All year
Price: $45 (double occupancy rate),
   Breakfast included

Type of breakfast offered: Full
   breakfast
Other foods available: Lunch, tea,
   dinner
Restrictions: Children welcome,
   Smoking not allowed, Pets not
   allowed, Limited handicap access.
Services: Sitting room, bicycles, log cabin
   near lake, fishing, skiing, golfing.

Enjoy a rural atmosphere and old-fashioned hospitality down on the farm. We have a lake stocked with trout. Also log cabin in the woods with 5 miles of cross-country trails.

Roduner Farm

Rural Route I
Cardinal, Ontario K0E 1E0
CANADA
Phones: (613) 657-4830
Farm managers: Walter and
   Margareta Roduner
Season: All year
Price: $40 (double occupancy rate),
   Breakfast included

Type of breakfast offered: Full
   breakfast
Other foods available: Afternoon tea
Restrictions: Smoking allowed, Pets
   allowed, Handicap no access.
Languages spoken: German, some
   French
Services: Snacks, swimming pool
   nearby.

Enjoy Swiss hospitality and hearty breakfasts on our bustling dairy farm just north of Transcanada 401 (exit 730). One-hour drive from Ottawa. Discount for seniors.

Happy Trails!

Down on the Ranch

If your kids love horses or are enthralled by Westerns, a ranch vacation may be for you. But even if they show no inclination to wear cowboy boots and yodel around the campfire, if blue jeans and flannel shorts are your kind of dress code, a week on a ranch may surprise you. Today's ranch resorts offer a variety of activities for all ages, including hiking, tennis, golf, fishing, swimming, white-water rafting, or just lazing by the pool with a good book. While rates may seem high, remember when you're shopping around that they generally include all your meals and activities. Some resorts offer special children's programs including overnight camp-outs and arts and crafts projects, and can help you arrange for a babysitter. So if evenings spent watching for shooting stars and listening for owls and coyotes around a blazing camp fire are tempting, the following guide to ranch resorts in the U.S. and Canada should help in your search for the perfect ranch.

These listings are provided by the Dude Rancher's Association and the British Columbia Guest Ranch Association. The Dude Rancher's Association publishes an annual magazine called "The Dude Rancher," which lists and describes their 110 member ranches, located in 12 Western states and two Canadian provinces. The magazine is available from:

The Dude Rancher's Association P.O. Box 471 LaPorte, Colorado 80535 Phone: (303) 223-8440 Fax: (303) 223-0201

The British Columbia Guest Ranch Association can be reached at: P.O. Box 2560 Williams Lake, British Columbia V2G 4P2 Canada Phone: (604) 398-7755 Fax: (604) 398-7738

You may also wish to read Eugene Kilgore's definitive and extensive guide, *Ranch Vacations.* John Muir Publications.

The Origins of Dude Ranching and the Dude Ranchers' Association

By the end of the 1800s most of the American West had been explored and the stories of its natural wonders had spread throughout the eastern portion of the country and Europe. Lured by the promise of awesome beauty, a spirit of romance and adventure, and the honest simplicity of the western way of life, many easterners sought, in the West, a respite from the crowded, noisy squalor of fast-paced cities. With the ease of travel provided by the transcontinental rail systems, the stream of visitors soon became a torrent. The West was ill-prepared to receive this onslaught. Those limited accommodations that did exist in the frontier towns hardly measured up to the standards of the new visitors.

The dude ranch industry soon evolved to, in part, meet the need for safe, comfortable accommodations from which the easterner could experience the wonders of the West. The original dude ranches of the late 1800s and early 1900s were established by rugged individualists who frequently had started as cattle and horse ranchers. These early ranchers were besieged with requests for summer accommodations from relatives, friends, and friends of friends, for nowhere else could they find adequate food, shelter, and hosts that would help them enjoy the natural wonders.

As was typical of the times, the ranchers offered the hospitality of their homes and ranches to all who asked.

Most of these early visitors came to stay for extended periods, weeks or months, and all were seen as guests in the rancher's home. Each ranch developed its own special flavor, reflecting the personality of its owner. It quickly became apparent that it was not only the natural beauty of the area that was attracting the returning visitors, but also the sharing of the picturesque, charming, and peculiar western ranch experience and the ranchers' love of their way of life. The shared experiences quickly formed lasting bonds between ranchers and guests and between the guests themselves. This was an experience far different from the impersonal, often isolated, lot of guests in hotels.

In order not to feel they were a burden, the visitors began offering to pay for their room and board. Who first accepted payment for their hospitality is unclear. What is know is that independently many ranches in the Montana-Wyoming area began accepting paying visitors as a part of their normal operation. Soon other enterprising individuals, often early guests on other ranches, began developing lodges and ranches in breathtaking locations for the specific purpose of receiving guests.

Dude ranching did not begin at a defined time. It evolved slowly from several divergent sources in different locales. The first organizational gathering of these independent-minded pioneers occurred in Bozeman, Montana in September of 1926 at the urging of the Northern Pacific Railroad. The railroad, looking for an additional source of revenue and a means to combat the new method of travel, the automobile, saw the dude ranches of the area as natural partners in the burgeoning tourism industry of the west. This meeting of ranchers from the Yellowstone area lead to the formation of The Dude Ranchers' Association.

The Association's original membership of 35 ranches from the Yellowstone area has now grown to over 110 member ranches in 12 western states and two Canadian provinces. In spite of this growth, the Association today remains dedicated to preserving the beauty, natural resources, and the original western ranch experiences that attracted the first visitors. Within this context, the Association has produced industry standards, a common means for promoting dude ranch vacations, and a single source for the exchange of ideas and information.

True to its roots, The Dude Ranchers' Association is still a diverse group, composed of cattle ranches who accept paying guests and mountain top lodges that offer a ranch atmosphere. All preserve the open warmth and hospitality of the first ranches and allow for the original western ranch experience by requiring an extended stay. The formation of lasting bonds and memories still brings families back to ranches generation after generation. This is truly a living testimony to the timelessness of the values and standards of the original dude ranchers. Today, as it did over a century ago, the western dude ranch experience offers relief for both the body and spirit of those seeking refuge from the pressures and routine of modern life.

The Horseshoe Ranch on Bloody Basin
HCR 34 – Box 5005
Mayer, Arizona 86333
Phones: (520) 632-8813
Fax: (520) 632-8813
Capacity: 20, Season: Year-round, Altitude: 5000 feet

Circle Z Ranch
P.O. Box 194
Patagonia, Arizona 85624
Phones: (520) 394-2525;
   (888) 854-2525
Jerry and Nancy Holmes, Managers.
Capacity: 40, Season: November to mid-May, Altitude: 4000 feet

Grapevine Canyon Ranch
P.O. Box 302
Pearce, Arizona 85625
Phones: (520) 826-3185;
   (800) 245-9202
Fax: (520) 826-3636
Capacity: 30, Season: Year-round, Altitude: 5000 feet

Elkhorn Ranch
HCI, Box 97
Tuscon, Arizona 85736
Phones: (520) 822-1040
Capacity: 32, Season: November 15 to May 1, Altitude: 3600 feet

Lazy K Bar Ranch
8401 North Scenic Drive
Tuscon, Arizona 85743
Phones: (520) 744-3050;
   (800) 321-7018
Fax: (520) 744-7628
Capacity: 50, Season: Year-round, Altitude: 2300 feet

White Stallion Ranch
9251 West Twin Peaks Road
Tuscon, Arizona 85743
Phones: (520) 297-0252;
   (888) 977-2624
Fax: (520) 744-2786
Capacity: 50, Season: October 1 to April 30, Altitude: 2300 feet

Flying E Ranch
2801 W. Wickenburg Way
Wickenburg, Arizona 85390
Phone: (520) 684-2690;
   (888) 684-2650
Fax: (520) 684-5304
Vi Wellik, Owner/Manager for over 33 years
Capacity: 34, Season: November to May, Altitude: 2500 feet

Kay El Bar Ranch
P.O. Box 2480 Wickenburg, Arizona 85358
Phones: (520) 684-7593;
   (800) 684-7583
Capacity: 20, Season: October 15 to May 1, Altitude: 2100 feet

Scott Valley Ranch
P.O. Box 1447
Mountain Home, Arkansas 72653
Phone: (870) 425-5136;
    (888) 855-7747
Fax: (501) 424-5800
Your hosts: Tom and Kathleen
    Cooper
Capacity: 65+, Season: March-
    Thanksgiving, Altitude: 1200 feet

Hunewill Circle "H" Ranch
P.O. Box 368
Bridgeport, California 93517
Phones: (760) 932-7710 summer;
    (775) 465-2201 winter
Capacity: 40, Season: May 1 to
    September 20, Altitude: 6500 feet

Coffee Creek Ranch
HC 2 Box 4940, Department DRA
Trinity Center, California 96091
Phones: (530) 266-3343;
    (800) 624-4480
Fax: (530) 266-3597
Capacity: 50, Season: Year-round,
    Altitude: 3100 feet

Lazy H Guest Ranch
P.O. Box 248
Allenspark, Colorado 80510
Phones: (800) 578-3598
Capacity: 50, Season: Year-round,
    Altitude: 8300 feet

Rainbow Trout Ranch
P.O. Box 458
Antonito, Colorado 81120
Phones: (719) 376-2240;
    (800) 633-3397
Fax: (719) 376-5659
Your hosts: Lisa Robinson, Doug
    and Linda Van Berkum and
    Family.
Capacity: 60, Season: Late May to
    mid-September, Altitude: 9000
    feet

Sky Corral Guest Ranch
8233 Old Flowers Road
Bellvue, Colorado 80512
Phone: (970) 484-1362
Fax: (970) 484-1362
Capacity: 30, Season: Year-round,
    Altitude: 8200 feet

Elk Mountain Ranch
P.O. Box 910
Buena Vista, Colorado 81211
Phone: (800) 432-8812
Capacity: 30, Season: May to
    September, Altitude: 9600 feet

The Home Ranch
P.O. Box 822
Clark, Colorado 80428
Phone: (970) 879-1780
Your hosts, Ken and Cile, Harmony
    and Jasmine, Jones.
Capacity: 40, Season: Summer and
    Winter, Altitude: 7200 feet

Colorado Trails Ranch
12161 Country Road 240-R.
Durango, Colorado 81301
Phone: (800) 323-3833
Fax: (970) 385-7372
Your hosts, Dick and Ginny Elder.
Capacity: 60, Season: early June to
    mid-September, Altitude: 7500
    feet

Lake Mancos Ranch
P.O. Box 206 ID
Durango, Colorado 81302
Phones: (800) 325-9462
Capacity: 55, Season: early June to
    early October, Altitude: 8000 feet

Wilderness Trails Ranch
1776 Country Road, 302
Durango, Colorado 81301
Phone: (970) 247-0722;
    (800) 527-2624
Capacity: 48, Season: late May to
    early October, Altitude: 7800 feet

Aspen Lodge Ranch Resort
6120 Highway 7
Estes Park, Colorado 80517
Phones: (970) 586-8133;
    (800) 322-6867 Capacity: 150,
    Season: April to October,
    Altitude: 9100 feet

Wind River Ranch
Box 3410
Estes Park, Colorado 80517
Phones: (970) 586-4212;
    (800) 523-4212
Your hosts, Rob and Jere Irvin.
Capacity: 56, Season: June to
    September, Altitude: 9200 feet

C Lazy U Ranch
P.O. Box 379 D
Granby, Colorado 80446
Phone: (970) 887-3344
Capacity: 115, Season: late May to
    mid-October and mid-December
    to late March, Altitude: 8200 feet

Drowsy Water Ranch
P.O. Box 147D
Granby, Colorado 80446
Phones: (970) 725-3456;
    (800) 845-2292
Ken and Randy Sue Fosha, owners
    and hosts.
Capacity: 60, Season: early June to
    mid-September, Altitude: 8200
    feet

Tumbling River Ranch
Box 30
Grant, Colorado 80448
Phone: (800) 654-8770
Owned and operated by Jim and
    Mary Dale Gordon.
Capacity: 55, Season: May to
    October 1, Altitude: 9200 feet

Waunita Hot Springs Ranch
8007 Country Road, 887
    Department B
Gunnison, Colorado 81230
Phone: (970) 641-1266
Your hosts, the Pringle Family.
Capacity: 50, Season: June to
    September, Altitude: 8946 feet

White Pine Ranch
7500 Country Road 887
Gunnison, Colorado 81230
Phone: (970) 641-6410;
    (888) 700-7463
Capacity: 14, Season: Year-round,
    Altitude: 9000 feet

7W Guest Ranch
3412 Country Road 151
Gypsum, Colorado 81637
Phones: (970) 524-9328;
    (800) 524-1286
Capacity: 18, Season: Year-round,
    Altitude: 9000 feet

Latigo Ranch
Box 237
Kremmling, Colorado 80459
Phones: (970) 724-9008;
    (800) 227-9655
Capacity: 35, Season: All year,
    Altitude: 9000 feet

Tarryall River Ranch
27001.5 County Road 77
Lake George, Colorado 80827
Phones: (719) 748-1214;
    (800) 408-8407
Your hosts, Jimmy and Jeannine
    Lahrman.
Capacity: 30, Season: late May to
    late September, Altitude: 8600
    feet

Echo Canyon Ranch
P.O. Box 328
La Veta, Colorado 81055
Phones: (719) 742-5524;
(800) 341-6603
Capacity: 44, Season: Year-round,
Altitude: 8400 feet

Cherokee Park Ranch
P.O. Box 97
Livermore, Colorado 80536
Phones: (970) 493-6522;
(800) 628-0949
Capacity: 40, Season: mid-May–
September, Altitude: 7200 feet

Sylvan Dale Guest Ranch
2939 North Country Road 31D
Loveland, Colorado 80538
Phone: (970) 667-3915;
(877) 667-3999
Capacity: 60, Season: Year-round,
Altitude: 5325 feet

Peaceful Valley Lodge
Star Route, Box 2811
Lyons, Colorado 80540
Phones: (303) 747-2881;
(800) 955-6343
Fax: (303) 747-2167
Capacity: 100, Season: June 17–
Sep 31, Full winter resort season,
Altitude: 8500 feet

The Fryingpan River Ranch
32042 Fryingpan Road
Meredith, Colorado 81642
Phone: (970) 927-3570
Fax: (970) 927-9273
Capacity: 35, Season: early June to
October, Altitude: 8800 feet

Deer Valley Ranch
Box W
Nathrop, Colorado 81236
Phones: (719) 395-2353;
(800) 284-1708
Capacity: 130, Season: Year-round,
Altitude: 8400 feet

Whistling Acres Guest Ranch
4397 O 50 Drive
Paonia, Colorado 81428
Phones: (970) 527-4560;
(800) 346-1420
Capacity: 21, Season: Year-round,
Altitude: 6200 feet

Aspen Canyon Ranch
13206 Country Road #3
Parshall, Colorado 80468
Phones: (970) 725-3600;
(800) 321-1357
Fax: (970) 725-0044
Capacity: 35, Season: mid-May to
mid-November and mid-
December to mid-March,
Altitude: 8400 feet

Bar Lazy J Guest Ranch
P.O. Box N
Parshall, Colorado 80468
Phone: (970) 725-3437;
(800) 396-6279
Capacity: 42, Season: Memorial Day
through Labor Day, Altitude:
7500 feet

Powderhorn Guest Ranch
Powderhorn, Colorado 81243
Phone: (800) 786-1220
Capacity: 30, Season: early June to
mid-September, Altitude: 8500
feet

The Don K Ranch
2677 South Siloam Road
Pueblo, Colorado 81005
Phones: (719) 784-6600;
(800) 874-0307
Fax: (719) 784-6600
Capacity: 40, Season: mid-May to
early October, Altitude: 6500 feet

Sundance Trail Guest Ranch
17931 Red Feather Lakes Road
Red Feather Lakes, Colorado 80545
Phones: (970) 224-1222;
    (800) 367-4930
Capacity: 16, Season: early June to
    mid-October, Altitude: 8000 feet

Coulter Lake Guest Ranch
80 Country Road 273 KRW
Rifle, Colorado 81650
Phones: (970) 625-1473;
    (800) 858-3046
Fax: (970) 224-1222
Capacity: 25–30, Season: Year-
    round, Altitude: 8100 feet

Lost Valley Ranch
29555 Goose Creek Road, Box KRW
Sedalia, Colorado 80135
Phone: (303) 647-2311
Fax: (303) 647-2315
Capacity: 95, Season: mid-March
    thru Nov., Altitude: 7500 feet

North Fork Ranch
Box B
55395 Highway 285
Shawnee, Colorado 80475
Phone: (800) 843-7895
Capacity: 40–45, Season: Memorial
    Day through Labor Day, Altitude:
    8100 feet

Focus Ranch
Slater, Colorado 81653
Phone: (970) 583-2410
Capacity: 30, Season: Year-round,
    Altitude: 7000 feet

Vista Verde Ranch
Box 465
Steamboat Springs, Colorado 80477
Phones: (970) 879-3858;
    (800) 526-7433
Capacity: 36, Season: June to
    September, Altitude: 7800 feet

Skyline Guest Ranch
P.O. Box 67
7214 Highway 145
Telluride, Colorado 81435
Phone: (970) 728-6728;
    (888) 754-1126
Capacity: 35, Season: early June to
    Labor Day, Altitude: 9600 feet

The Pines Ranch
P.O. Box 311
Westcliffe, Colorado 81252
Phones: (719) 783-9261;
    (800) 446-9462
Capacity: 40, Season: mid-May
    through October, Altitude: 8700
    feet

Wapiti Meadow
HC 72
Cascade, Idaho 83611
Phones: (208) 633-3217
Fax: (208) 633-3219
Capacity: 12, Season: May through
    October and December through
    March, Altitude: 5086 feet

Hidden Creek Ranch
7600 East Blue Lake Road
Harrison, Idaho 83833
Phones: (208) 689-3209;
    (800) 446-3833
Fax: (208) 689-9115
Iris Behr and John Muir, owners.
Capacity: 48, Season: Year-round,
    Altitude: 2400 feet

Twin Peaks Ranch
P.O. Box 774
Salmon, Idaho 83467
Phones: (208) 894-2290;
    (800) 659-4899
Capacity: 55, Season: June–
    December, Altitude: 5200 feet

Teton Ridge Ranch
200 Valley View Road
Tetonia, Idaho 83452
Phone: (208) 456-2650
Fax: (208) 456-2218
Capacity: 12, Season: January–
March and mid-May–October,
Altitude: 6700 feet

Moose Creek Ranch
P.O. Box 350 Victor, Idaho 83455
Phones: (208) 787-2784;
(800) 676-0075
Fax: (208) 787-2284
Your hosts, Kelly and Rocky.
Capacity: 35, Season: June through
September, Altitude: 6500 feet

JJJ Wilderness Ranch
P.O. Box 310
Agusta, Montana 59410
Phone: (406) 562-3653
Fax: (406) 562-3826
Your hosts, Max and Ann or Ernie
and The Barker Family.
Capacity: 20, Season: June to mid-
September, Altitude: 5200 feet

Klick's K Bar L Ranch
"Beyond All Roads"
Augusta, Montana 59410
Phones: (406) 467-2771;
(406) 562-3589
Capacity: 30, Season: June 1 to mid-
September, Altitude: 5000 feet

Lazy K Bar Ranch
P.O. Box 550
Big Timber, Montana 59011
Phone: (406) 537-4404
Your host, Paul L. Van Cleve, IV.
Capacity: 35,
Season: late
June through
Labor Day,
Altitude:
8900 feet

Sweet Grass Ranch
HC 87, Box 2161
Big Timber, Montana 59011
Phones: (406) 537-4477;
(406) 537-4477 (fax also)
Your hosts, The Carroccia Family.
Capacity: 20, Season: mid-June to
Labor Day, Altitude: 6100 feet

Averill's Flathead Lake Ranch
Box 248
Bigfork, Montana 59911
Phone: (406) 837-4391
Fax: (406) 837-6977
Capacity: 90, Season: May 1 through
September, Altitude: 3000 feet

Mountain Sky Guest Ranch
P.O. Box 1128
Bozeman, Montana 59771
Phones: (406) 587-1244;
(800) 548-3392
Capacity: 75–80, Season: End of
May to October, Altitude: 5600
feet

CB Cattle & Guest Ranch
P.O. Box 146
Cameron, Montana 59720
Phones: (406) 682-4608;
(760) 723-1932
Your host, Sandy Vander Lans.
Winter address is 4321 Orange
Hill, Fallbrook, California 92028,
(619) 723-1932.
Capacity: 14, Season: mid-June to
early Sept., Altitude: 6000 feet

Lost Fork Ranch
11-12 Highway 287
Cameron, Montana 59720
Phone: (406) 682-7690
Your hosts, Merrit and Barbara
Pride.
Capacity: 30, Season: mid-May to
mid-October, Altitude: 6300 feet

Pine Butte Guest Ranch
HC 58, Box 34C
Choteau, Montana 59422
Phone: (406) 466-2158
Capacity: 25, Season: May through
   September, Altitude: 5180 feet

Seven Lazy P Guest Ranch
P.O. Box 178
Choteau, Montana 59422
Phone: (406) 466-2044
Your hosts, Chuck and Sharon
   Blixrud.
Capacity: 20, Season: May through
   September, Altitude: 5280 feet

G Bar M Ranch
P.O. Box 29
Clyde Park, Montana 59018
Phone: (406) 686-4423
Your hosts, the Leffingwells.
Capacity: 15, Season: May to Sept.,
   Altitude: 5280 feet

Diamond J Ranch
Box 577
Ennis, Montana 59729
Phone: (406) 682-4867;
   (877) 929-4867
Your hosts, Mr. and Mrs. Peter
   Combs
Capacity: 20–25, Season: June
   through September, Altitude:
   5800 feet

Laughing Water Ranch
P.O. Box 157 KRW
Fortine, Montana 59918
Phone: (406) 882-4680;
   (800) 847-5095
Fax: (406) 882-4680
Your host: Ted Mikita.
Capacity: 32, Season: May through
   September, Altitude: 3200 feet

Covered Wagon Ranch
34035 W. Gallatin Road
Gallatin Gateway, Montana 59730
Phone: (406) 995-4237
Your host, Will King.
Capacity: 24, Season: mid-May
   through October and February 1
   to mid-April, Altitude: 6680 feet

Elkhorn Ranch
33133 Gallatin Road
Gallatin Gateway, Montana 59730
Phone: (406) 995-4291
Your host, Linda G. Miller.
Capacity: 45, Season: mid-June
   through September, Altitude:
   6800 feet

Nine Quarter Circle Ranch
5000 Taylor Fork Road
Gallatin Gateway, Montana 59730
Phone: (406) 995-4276
Your hosts, The Kelsey Family.
Capacity: 70, Season: mid-June to
   mid-September, Altitude: 7000
   feet

63 Ranch
Box 979 KRW
Livingston, Montana 59047
Phone: (406) 222-0570
Your hosts, Bud, Sandra, or Jeff
   Cahill.
Capacity: 30, Season: mid-June to
   mid-September, Altitude: 5600
   feet

Hargrave Cattle & Guest Ranch
Thompson River Valley
300 Thompson River Road
Marion, Montana 59925
Phone: (406) 858-2284
Fax: (406) 858-2444
Hosts/Owners Leo and Ellen.
Capacity: 20, Season: Year-round,
   Altitude: 3400 feet

Aller's Boulder River Ranch
2815 Main Boulder Road
McLeod, Montana 59052
Phone: (406) 932-5926
Your hosts, Steve and Jeane Aller.
Capacity: 30, Season: June through
  September, Altitude: 5050 feet

Hawley Mountain Guest Ranch
Box 4
McLeod, Montana 59052
Phone: (406) 932-5791
Capacity: 20, Season: June–Sept. and
  hunting season in mid-Oct.,
  Altitude: 6400 feet

X Bar A Ranch
McLeod, Montana 59052
Phone: (406) 932-6109
Your hosts, Jean and Pat
Capacity: 30, Season: mid-May –
  September, Altitude: 5000 feet

Beartooth Ranch & JLX
HC 54, Box 350
Nye, Montana 59061
Phones: (406) 328-6194;
  (406) 328-6205
Your hosts, Jim and Ellen Langston.
Capacity: 30, Season: June 1 to
  Labor Day, Altitude: 5058 feet

Circle Bar Guest Ranch
HRC 81, Box 61
Utica, Montana 59452
Phone: (406) 423-5454
Fax: (406) 423-5686
Your host, Sara Stevenson. Capacity:
  35, Season: April–November,
  Altitude: 5000 feet

Spur Cross Ranch
P.O. Box 38
Golconda, Nevada 59414
Phone: (800) 651-4567
Richard Hubbard will be your
  personal host and guide.
Capacity: 12, Season: Year-round

Hartley Guest Ranch
HCR 73, Box 55
Roy, New Mexico 87743
Phones: (505) 673-2244;
  (800) OUR DUDE
Fax: (505) 673-2216
Your hosts, Doris and Ray Hartley.
Capacity: 12, Season: April–Sept.,
  Altitude: 4800–6000 feet

Bar M Ranch
58840 Bar M Lane
Adams, Oregon 97810
Phone: (541) 566-3381
Your hosts, the Baker family.
Capacity: 30, Season: April through
  October, Altitude: 2200 feet

Rock Springs Guest Ranch
64201 Tyler Road
Bend, Oregon 97701
Phones: (541) 382-1957;
  (800) 225-3833
Fax: (541) 382-7774
Capacity: 50, Season: mid-June
  through August, Conferences
  Spring, Fall and Winter, Altitude:
  3500 feet

Triple R Ranch
Box 124
Keystone, South Dakota 57751
Phone: (605) 666-4605;
  (888) 777-2624
Your hosts, Jack and Cherylee Bradt.
Capacity: 15, Season: mid-May to
  mid-Sept., Altitude: 5280 feet

Silver Spur Guest Ranch
P.O. Box 1657
Bandera, Texas 78003
Phones: (830) 796-3037;
  (830) 460-3639
Fax: (830) 796-7170
Your host, Tom Winchell.
Capacity: 20, Season: Year-round,
  Altitude: 2500 feet

Paradise Guest Ranch
Box 790
Buffalo, Wyoming 82834
Phone: (307) 684-7876
Fax: (307) 684-9054
Your host, Leah Anderson.
Capacity: 70–75, Season: mid-May
   to mid-Sept., Altitude: 7500 feet

Blackwater Creek Ranch
1516 North Fork Highway
Cody, Wyoming 82414
Phone: (307) 587-5201;
   (888) 243-1607
Your hosts, the Carlton Family.
Capacity: 40, Season: May to
   September, Altitude: 7000 feet

Castle Rock Ranch
412 Country Road 6NS/Box DR
Cody, Wyoming 82414
Phones: (307) 587-2076;
   (800) 356-9965
Capacity: 32, Season: mid-June
   through August, Altitude: 5100
   feet

Double Diamond X Ranch
3453 Southfork Road
Cody, Wyoming 82414
Phones: (307) 527-6276;
   (800) 833-7262
Fax: (307) 587-2708
Capacity: 38, Season: Year-round,
   Altitude: 6700 feet

Rimrock Ranch
2728 Northfork Route
Cody, Wyoming 82414
Phone: (307) 587-3970;
   (800) 208-7468
Fax: (307) 527-5014
Your hosts, The Fales.
Capacity: 32, Season: May to Sept.,
   Altitude: 6200 feet

Seven D Ranch
P.O. Box 100
Cody, Wyoming 82414
Phone: (307) 587-3997
Your host, David D. Dominick.
Capacity: 30, Season: June through
   mid–September, Altitude: 6800
   feet

Squaw Creek Ranch
4059 Crandall Road
Cody, Wyoming 82414
Phones: (307) 587-6178;
   (800) 532-7281
Fax: (307) 587-5249
Rich and Wanda Smith, Managers.
Capacity: 20, Season: Year-round,
   Altitude: 6500 feet

David Ranch
P.O. Box 5
Daniel, Wyoming 83115
Phone: (307) 859-8228
Capacity: 10, Season: late May to
   October, Altitude: 8000 feet

Absaroka Ranch
P.O. Box 929
Dubois, Wyoming 82513
Phone: (307) 455-2275
Your hosts, Budd and Emi Betts.
Capacity: 18, Season: mid-June to
   mid-September, Altitude: 8000
   feet

Bitterroot Ranch
P.O. Box 807
Dubois, Wyoming 82513
Phones: (307) 455-3363;
   (800) 545-0019
Fax: (307) 455-2354
Your hosts, Bayard and Mel Fox.
Capacity: 32, Season: late May to
   September, Altitude: 7500 feet

Brooks Lake Lodge
458 Brooks Lake Road
Dubois, Wyoming 82513
Phone: (307) 455-2121
Fax: (307) 455-2221
Capacity: 26, Season: July 1 through
mid-September, Altitude: 9100
feet

Lazy L & B Ranch
1072 East Fork Road
Dubois, Wyoming 82513
Phones: (307) 455-2839;
(800) 453-9488
Fax: (307) 455-2634
Capacity: 35, Season: late May
through September, Altitude:
7200 feet

T Cross Ranch
Box 638 KRW
Dubois, Wyoming 82513
Phones: (307) 455-2206;
(307) 733-2225
Fax: (307) 455-2720
Your hosts, Ken and Garey Neal.
Capacity: 20, Season: June through
October, Altitude: 7800 feet

**Flitner Ranch/Hideout
Adventures**
P.O. Box 206
Shell, Wyoming 82441
Phones: (307) 765-2080;
(800) 354-8637
Fax: (307) 765-2681
Your Host, Kathryn Flitner.
Capacity: 24, Season: May through
October, Altitude: 4,200-10,000
feet

Darwin Ranch
P.O. Box 10430
Jackson, Wyoming 83002
Phone: (307) 733-5588
Capacity: 20, Season: Year-round,
Altitude: 8200 feet

Spotted Horse Ranch
12355 S. Highway 191
Jackson Hole, Wyoming 83001
Phones: (307) 733-2097;
(800) 528-2084
Fax: (307) 733-3712
Capacity: 35, Season: June through
September, Altitude: 6200 feet

Old Glendevey Ranch Ltd.
Glendevey Colorado Route
3219 County Road 190
Jelm, Wyoming 82063
Phones: (970) 435-5701;
(970) 490-1444
Your hosts, Garth and Olivia
Peterson.
Capacity: 18, Season: early June –
mid-Nov., Altitude: 8500 feet

Rawah Ranch
Glendevey, Colorado Route
11447 County Road 103
Jelm, Wyoming 82063
Phones: (970) 435-5715;
(800) 820-3152
Fax: (970) 435-5705
Your hosts, Pete and Ardy Kunz.
Capacity: 32, Season: early June –
September, Altitude: 8400 feet

Red Rock Ranch
P.O. Box 38
Kelly, Wyoming 83011
Phone: (307) 733-6288
Fax: (307) 733-6287
Capacity: 30, Season: June to mid-
October, Altitude: 7200 feet

Schively Ranch
1062 Road 15
Lovell, Wyoming 82431
Phones: (307) 548-6688;
(406) 259-8866
Fax: (307) 548-2322
Capacity: 18, Season: April through
October, Altitude: 6000 feet

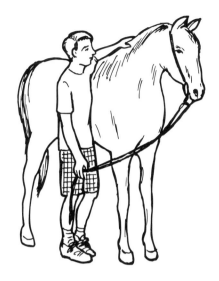

Gros Ventre River Ranch
P.O. Box 151
Moose, Wyoming 83012
Phone: (307) 733-4138
Fax: (307) 733-4272
Capacity: 35, Season: May through
    October and December through
    March, Altitude: 7100 feet

Moose Head Ranch
P.O. Box 214
Moose, Wyoming 83012
Phone: (307) 733-3141
Your host, Louise Mettler
Capacity: 40, Season: mid-June
    through August, Altitude: 6800
    feet

Triangle X Ranch
2 Triangle X Ranch Road
Moose, Wyoming 83012
Phone: (307) 733-2183
Fax: (307) 733-8685
Capacity: 70, Season: May 1 through
    October, Altitude: 6700 feet

Turpin Meadow Ranch
P.O. Box 10
Moran, Wyoming 83013
Phones: (307) 543-2496;
    (800) 743-2496
Fax: (307) 543-2850
Capacity: 45, Season: Year-round,
    Altitude: 6900 feet

Heart Six Ranch
P.O. Box 70
Moran, Wyoming 83013
Phones: (307) 543-2477;
    (888) 543-2477
Fax: (307) 543-0918
Capacity: 35, Season: June 1 to mid-
    October, Altitude: 7500 feet

Flying A Ranch
771 Flying A Ranch Road
Pinedale, Wyoming 82941
Phones: (307) 367-2385;
    (800) 678-6543
Fax: (307) 367-2385
Capacity: 12, Season: mid-June to
    October, Altitude: 8200 feet

Brush Creek Guest Ranch
Star Route, Box Ten
Saratoga, Wyoming 82331
Phones: (307) 327-5241;
 (800) 726-2499
Capacity: 25, Season: Year-round,
 Altitude: 7500 feet

Kadesh Ranch
1940 Highway 14
Shell, Wyoming 82441
Phones: (307) 765-2791;
 (800) 845-3320
Your hosts, Chuck and Gail Lander.
Capacity: 24, Season: late May to
 October, Altitude: 4200 feet

Spear-O-Wigwam Ranch
P.O. Box 1081
Sheridan, Wyoming 82801
Phones: (307) 674-4496;
 (888) 818-3833;
 (307) 655-3217;
Fax: (307) 655-3951
Jim and Barbara Niner, Managers.
Capacity: 30, Season: mid-June to
 mid-September, Altitude: 8300
 feet

R Lazy S Ranch
Jackson Hole, Wyoming
Box 308
Teton Village, Wyoming 83025
Phone: (307) 733-2655
Your host, Claire C. McConaughy.
Capacity: 45, Season: mid-June to
 October, Altitude: 6200 feet

Two Bars Seven Ranch
P.O. Box 67
Tie Siding, Wyoming 82084
Phone: (307) 742-6072
Fax: (307) 265-9046
Capacity: 22, Season: May through
 November, Altitude: 7700 feet

Crossed Sabres Ranch
Box KRW
Wapiti, Wyoming 82450
Phone: (307) 587-3750
Your hosts, Buck & Kerry Norris.
Capacity: 45, Season: Late May to
 October, Altitude: 7000 feet

Trail Creek Ranch
Box 10
Wilson, Wyoming 83014
Phone: (307) 733-2610
Fax: (307) 733-0208
Your host, Elizabeth Woolsey.
Capacity: 25, Season: mid-June to
 mid-September, Altitude: 6280
 feet

Eaton's Ranch
Wolf, Wyoming 82844
Phones: (307) 655-9285;
 (800) 210-1049
Fax: (307) 655-9269
Capacity: 120, Season: June 1 to
 October 1, Altitude: 4500 feet

Homeplace Ranch
Site 2, Box 6, Rural Route 1
Priddis, Alberta T0L 1W0
CANADA
Phone: (403) 931-3245
Fax: (403) 931-3245
Capacity: 14, Season: Year-round,
 Altitude: 4700 feet

The Hills Guest Ranch
Box 26
108 Mile Ranch, British Columbia
 V0K 2Z0
CANADA
Phone: (250) 791-5225
Fax: (250) 791-6384

Sundance Guest Ranch
P.O. Box 489
Ashcroft, British Columbia V
  0K 1A0
CANADA
Phones: (250) 453-2422;
  (250) 453-2554
Fax: (250) 453-9356
Season: Year-round

Wells Gray Ranch
Rural Route 1, Box 1766
Clearwater, British Columbia
  V0E 1N0
CANADA
Phones: (250) 674-2792;
  (250) 674-2774
Fax: (250) 674-2197

Big Bar
Box 27, Jesmond
Clinton, British Columbia V0K 1K0
CANADA
Phone: (250) 459-2333

Cariboo Rose Guest Ranch
P.O. Box 160
Clinton, British Columbia V0K 1K0
CANADA
Phone: (604) 395-6315
Capacity: 6

Circle H Mountain Lodge
P.O. Box 7, Jesmond
Clinton, British Columbia V0K 1K0
CANADA
Phones: (250) 459-2565;
  (250) 850-1873
Fax: (250) 459-2565
Capacity: 18, Altitude: 7000 feet

Three Bars Cattle & Guest Ranch
9500 Wycliffe Perry Cr. Rd.
Cranbrook, British Columbia
  V1C 7C7
CANADA
Phone: (250) 426-5230
Fax: (250) 426-8240
Capacity: 40, Season: Year-round,
  Altitude: 3500 feet

Top of the World Guest Ranch
P.O. Box 29
Fort Steele, British Columbia
  V0B 1N0
CANADA
Phone: (888) 996-6306
Fax: (250) 426-6377
Capacity: 30

Wild Rose Ranch
Box 181
Kimberly, British Columbia
  V1A 2Y6
CANADA
Phone: (250) 422-3403;
  (800) 324-6188
Fax: (250) 422-3149
Capacity: 10

Elkin Creek Guest Ranch
4462 Marion Road
North Vancouver, British Columbia
  V7K 2V2
CANADA
Phone: (604) 984-4666;
  (800) 984-4666
Fax: (604) 984-4686

Apex Mountain Guest Ranch
P.O. Box 426
Penticton, British Columbia V2A
    6K6
CANADA
Phone: (250) 492-2454
Fax: (250) 490-8537
Season: Year-round, Altitude: 3000
    feet

Chilcotin Holidays
Gun Creek Road
Goldbridge, British Columbia
    V0K 1P0
CANADA
Phone: (250) 238-2274
Fax: (250) 238-2274

TS'YL-OS Park Lodge &
    Adventures
P.O. Box 2560
Williams Lake, British Columbia
    V2G 4P2
CANADA
Phones: (250) 398-7755;
    (800) 487-9567
Fax: (250) 398-7487

Smart Shopping

SHOPPING ON THE ROAD

Even when the goal is to buy the tickets and accommodations and not deal with money while on vacation, shopping usually becomes a necessity. Who doesn't leave something vital at home? And, of course, most people do make the effort to plan ahead carefully. For most travelers in the U.S., this is no problem, with familiar store names just about everywhere. But there are exceptions and special considerations—

I Came to Shop

One couple I knew would leave on a trip with just one small overnight bag. Part of the purpose of the trip was to shop, so they built a wardrobe along the way and came home with luggage full. And each new piece of clothing or bauble had a story and memory attached. While this may sound very jet-setty, a family might consider something similar and combine shopping for school with a vacation. Instead of dreading the return home followed by shopping for school, everyone can have fun shopping in new places and the only problem coming home will be to find space for all the new goodies.

Shopping Packages

Many fine hotels in cosmopolitan areas are learning just how much their clientele enjoys shopping and they are putting together shopping packages. Such a package may include two nights' lodging, a meal or two, discounts at certain stores, and maybe even a limo ride. Hotels in cities like Boston, San Francisco, Seattle and Chicago are beginning to include these shopping packages, and are finding them especially attractive to couples on business trips and the like. And, what a special trip to take a teenager on—truly a rite of passage into adulthood!

How Much is That in Dollars?

Shopping in foreign countries can be difficult enough, but then comes the exchange rate and making change. Keep posted on the exchange rates you will be dealing with ahead of time. Why not set the kids on this task? They'll learn how to read the daily rates in the paper, become familiar with the terms and rates, and might even be moved to go to a coin collector's shop. Many banks sell travelers' cheques in foreign currency and some even sell the foreign currency itself. You will probably get a better rate at home than abroad, and if you're really planning ahead you can watch the exchange rates and buy the cheques or currency when the rates are in your favor.

Don't find out whether you're dealing with lire or francs after you get off the plane. It's surprising how quickly you get used to a new currency, as long as you haven't wasted most of your cash the first day. And, take your time! There are those folks everywhere who will try and hurry your money decisions or demand payment quickly in order to take advantage—be sure exactly how much you are paying and exactly what for before you hand over the money. Holiday times are notorious for quick-change moves. Don't find you paid triple the price when you're three blocks away.

After you really get into the swing of things shopping abroad, it's time to stop and remember two things: luggage weight and going through customs. Unless you're flying first class or are taking a cruise ship, there are per person weight limits for overseas luggage. That great deal may not be such a great deal if you have to pay by the pound to get it home. Personally, I enjoy sending purchases home by mail as I buy them. Yes, the postage is an added expense, but each purchase will go through customs individually, most reputable shops will pack and ship for you directly, you don't have to lug the extra weight, you won't break or lose your new purchases before they even get home, and after you've settled in at home, all these great gifts will start arriving. And, if the purchases are gifts for other, you know they'll love the surprise of receiving a special package from abroad. And if you show the value in the foreign currency, it won't be an obvious price tag. Finally, you'll thank yourself when the luggage coming home is actually lighter than when you left, having used up some things along the way and shipped others home. Some people actually mail their dirty clothes home as they go, which might make sense if you're going from the arctic to the tropics!

INTRODUCTION TO OUTLET SHOPPING

Outlet shopping has increasingly become something around which to plan trips and vacations. There are currently approximately 300 outlet centers in America with over 6,500 factory direct stores (and growing). In these stores you can find first quality merchandise at fantastic prices! A well planned outlet shopping trip could become a very special addition to your next family vacation.

Outlet complexes are built to attract designers such as Liz Claiborne, Osh-Kosh, Calvin Klein, Bass Shoes, Ellen Tracy, Carole Little, Mondi, Harve Benard and Adrienne Vittadini and they aren't just selling clothing anymore! In outlet stores you can also purchase furnishings, home appliances, and miscellaneous items by top designers, manufacturers, and suppliers such as West Point Pepperell, Brown Jordan, Alessi, Anichini, Vicente Wolf, The Nature Company, and Annieglass just to name a few.

The outlet store of the '90s boasts an attractive and inviting environment employing attentive salespersons and providing dressing rooms. Some even have restaurants, lounge areas and entertainment so that you can take a break from a busy day of shopping. Outlet stores accept most out of state checks and credit cards and generally have a liberal return policy as they realize that the majority of their customers have travelled some distance just to shop there.

HISTORY OF OUTLETS

The outlet concept dates back 100 years beginning in the late 1800s. Manufacturers used to display irregular merchandise on tables in great piles for their employees to purchase at a great savings from what they would have spent retail. The word spread and soon manufacturers realized that they could open their stores to the public and reap an even greater harvest on their excess goods by selling them at incredibly low prices.

For about 75 years outlets continued to be a successfully run business venture although they weren't common knowledge. In 1970, Vanity Fair opened up VF Factory Outlet in Reading, Pennsylvania, only this time it was done a little differently. VF decided to take a chance on putting several different name brand outlet stores in one complex housed in an old factory. Others followed suit and soon outlet centers began springing up all over the country. Most modern outlet centers are built from the ground up unlike their predecessors, but the mission of the outlet to provide great value without compromising quality and selection remains the same. Randy Marks, editor of Outletbound estimated that by the end of 1993, more than 9,000 outlet stores would be online around the country, doubling the number that existed in 1989.

In the 1980s the motto was "Shop 'til you drop"—in the 1990s we are looking for ways to save money while not sacrificing our tastes. The outlet store is a great place to follow that credo.

HINTS FOR SUCCESSFUL OUTLET SHOPPING TRIPS

Make a List—Check it Twice!

When outlet shopping, it is important to remember that with the wide variety of merchandise and shops it is easy to become confused and lose sight of what you came for. Make a list before you go of the items you would like to find and the stores which you expect to find them in. Take down the sizes of friends and relatives who you would like to purchase clothing for beforehand. Sometimes it may be inconvenient to return items although returns are widely accepted.

Planning is the Key ...

A little time on the telephone can save you hours in the stores and help you plan your trip. You can find out about upcoming sales and price reductions, the hours the stores are open, and labels and sizes they carry. Keep in mind that a visit to an outlet center is a big event which will take

all day. Pace yourself and make it a point to take time to enjoy being there by not planning too many stops in too little time.

Take along maps to help you find the place, brochures you may have collected from the stores or center and pick up a center directory when you get there (if you haven't already procured one) to make the most efficient use of your time. And don't forget to jot down the section of the parking lot you parked in (just in case …)!

Start by visiting the stores you came to shop at first and save the exploring for later. Shop with a friend to help with buying decisions. Remember to set up a time and meeting place should you become separated. Stick to a schedule of sorts by choosing a time and place for lunch where you and your shopping companion can relax, regather, and rejuvenate for the afternoon round!

What you wear is important! No, not necessarily to make a fashion statement—although it's always nice to be dressed in a manner which you feel good about—but, for comfort and ease of shopping. Wear comfortable shoes and clothing which is easy to remove and lightweight.

Making the Purchase …

When you begin your day at the outlet center, it is likely you will find many more items you wish to purchase than you can manage to carry (or afford). Check labels and price tags for descriptions of items such as:

❍ Irregular—small imperfection exists in the garment
❍ Seconds—signal that a major flaw exists
❍ Past season—usually a great bargain

❍ Sample—has been on display, offered in limited sizes and cuts, check carefully

❍ Open Stock—usually means you can purchase pieces separately at a later date (i.e., dinnerware/crystal)

❍ Discontinued—close-out items manufacturers no longer plan to carry, buy extras if purchasing sets of items.

Generally, most of the items for sale will be first quality merchandise from the current season.

Happy Bargain Hunting!

"OUTLET BOUND'S" RANDY MARKS

When looking for the best advice on outlet shopping and the various outlets in the country, your best bet is Randy Marks. Marks operates the Outlet Marketing Group, Inc. in Connecticut (P.O. Box 1255, Orange, Connecticut 06477) and has put out a wonderful book: *Guide To The Nation's Best Outlets: Outlet Bound*. To date, this guide is being updated yearly and the staff at Outlet Bound is up on what is going on. The large, 200-plus page book currently sells for $6.95 and with your good shopping skills can be worth many times more. To order the book, call (800) 336-8853. You'll get insider tips and news, as well as comprehensive lists of which manufacturers are represented at which outlet sites. Marks' crew will also provide Smart Shopper Coupons and can help you get in touch with specific manufacturers. For the serious outlet shopper, Outlet Bound is a must!

*A*CCOMMODATIONS FAMILY STYLE

• •

RECOMMENDED FAMILY RESORTS

The following resorts were specially chosen for their family oriented atmosphere and special kid programs. Be sure to call ahead to get exact rates (ask for packages, "special" rates, seasonal programs—then ask "Is that your best rate?" Just asking questions will often turn up a lower rate—persist!) and confirm availability of the services and amenities your family requires. Rates for a double room are expressed to give you a general idea of a given lodging's prices and are subject to change. Children under 18 in parents' room are often free—inquire.

Inexpensive	=	less than $100
Moderate	=	$100 – $200
Luxury	=	over $200

Shadow Mountain Resort & Club

PALM DESERT, CA

Shadow Mountain, the "gem of the desert," has a quiet, unpretentious charm that invites guests to return time after time.

Shadow Mountain, the home of the acclaimed Desert Tennis Academy, is a paradise for golfers and tennis players alike. Enjoy virtually unlimited tennis on 16 championship courts. Daily clinics focus on perfecting one particular skill in an easy half-hour clinic, or challenge you in a 2- to 5-hour intense program. Tee times can be arranged from the Resort at more than 80 renowned golf courses.

Shadow Mountain offers Kidz Kamp for children 5–12 years of age for four hours on Saturdays and Sundays during high season. The Coyote Club is available on Saturday nights to entertain children, so that their parents may spend an evening together. Friendly basketball or volleyball games can be played on the spectacular courts at the Resort. Close by, high-flying fun abounds on hot air balloon rides; or you might spend a soaking wet afternoon at the Oasis Water Park.

Address: 45750 Sun Luis Rey, Palm Desert, CA 92260

Ph: 619-346-6123, 800-472-3713

Fax: 619-346-6518

E-mail: res@shadow-mountain.com

Web: http://www.shadow-mountain.com

Accommodates: 134

Rates: 91-520-US$

Dates Open: open year round

Services: Package rates for families—call for details. Restaurant with children's menu, Children free in room with parents. 4 swimming pools, 5 spas, fitness center, basketball

Baby-sitting: yes

Activities: 16 tennis courts, 18-holes of golf

Attractions: Aerial Tram, The Living Desert

Kids' Programs: Kidz Kamp & Coyote Club

The Alisal Guest Ranch & Resort

SOLVANG, CA

Tucked away in a quiet corner of the picturesque Santa Ynez Valley is the Alisal Guest Ranch & Resort. At the heart of the splendor is a horse lover's paradise, where wranglers and spirited horses guide guests on one-of-a-kind journeys. Morning rides to the Adobe camp are complete with breakfast around a campfire. All-day lunch rides introduce guests to remote areas of the ranch.

Activities for kids of all ages include Ping-Pong, dodge ball, relay races, and scavenger hunts, not to mention the pool table, heated swimming pool, and spa. And don't forget the horseback riding lessons for older children, petting zoo, and arts and crafts. Children may participate in tennis, fishing, and golf lessons offered by the ranch. The teen program includes mountain bike excursions, hikes on scenic trails, movie nights, and a special evening at the Lake where teens will enjoy volleyball games, boat races, and other activities. In the evenings, families enjoy bingo, sing-alongs, talent shows, and line dancing.

The cottages of The Alisal are warm and inviting, offering splendid views of the garden. Families will enjoy the variety of accommodations ranging from studio rooms to two-room suites. The Alisal offers its Round-Up Vacation Package during select times of the year, enabling families to enjoy unlimited golf, horseback riding, tennis, and fishing: a wonderful opportunity to experience all the Alisal has to offer.

The combination of fresh air, mild climate, and scenic beauty provide the perfect opportunity for quality leisure time as a family.

Address: 1054 Alisal Rd, Solvang, CA 93463
Ph: 805-688-6411
800-4-ALISAL
Fax: 805-688-2510
E-mail: sales@alisal.com
Web: www.alisal.com
Accommodates: 73
Rates: 385-475 US$
2 night minumum
Dates Open: year round
Services: Babysitting, Compl. newspaper, Free parking, Children's menu, Special Round-Up Vacation Packages, Children's menu at restaurants, Evening activities during summer and holidays, Petting zoo
Baby-sitting: $8.00 hour
Attractions: Quaint Danish town of Solvang, Miniature horse farms, Over 60 wineries, Missions
Kids' Programs: Programs for children of all ages

The Lost Whale

TRINIDAD, CA

The Lost Whale Inn was built 12 years ago with families in mind. The inn is situated on four spectacular ocean front acres and has a private beach with tide pools.

A huge elaborate playground in the corner of the fenced-in property is especially enticing to children. The inn also offers a quiet and secluded outdoor hot tub, sleeping lofts for kids, as well as games and toys. Families are heartily welcome, and everyone eats together.

Host to over 3,000 children, the inn is close to parks, woods, and a resident pygmy goat farm located at the farmhouse. This two-bedroom accommodation is down the street on three acres of gardens, which include a pond, orchard, fire pit, and deck. The farmhouse is perfect for families and contains a kitchen, TV/VCR and fireplace. The inn is also host to a spectacular three-bedroom ocean view home for families with children over 7 years old.

Address: 3452 Patrick's Point Dr., Trinidad, CA 95570

Ph: 707-677-3425
800-677-7859

Fax: 707-677-0284

E-mail: lmiller@ lostwhaleinn.com

Web: http://www. lostwhaleinn.com

Accommodates: 8

Rates: 132-250 US$

Dates Open: open year round

Services: Farmhouse available, Sitting room, Breathtaking views, Private baths, Room rate includes gourmet breakfast and afternoon tea

Attractions: Redwood National Park, Trinidad Village, Private beach with tidepools, Pygmy goat farm, Several beaches nearby, Hiking, Horseback riding, Fishing, Boating, Lagoon, Gardens, Playground, Greenhouse and deck

The Colony Beach & Tennis Resort
LONGBOAT KEY, FL

Perhaps the greatest escape for families who enjoy tennis, The Colony Beach & Tennis Resort offers 21 tennis courts with free court time and game matching, and caters to players of all ages, with daily clinics for kids, juniors, and adults of all levels.

"Kinder Kamp" and "Kidding Around" are complimentary children's camps for ages 3–6 and 7–12. Supervised indoor and outdoor activities are offered, such as beach games, nature walks, arts and crafts, and off-property day trips. "Family Fare" is a program requiring parent and child participation in such events as Sundae Social, Sand Sculpting, and Fishing. For a small fee, programs are also available in the evenings.

Children always stay free with their parents, and adults may choose from a variety of vacation packages catering to each guest's need for family fun, relaxation, tennis, or golf. The spacious apartment-sized suites with full kitchens and either one or two bedrooms are ideal for families. Besides tennis amenities, a swimming pool, spa, and fitness center are available.

Address: 1620 Gulf of Mexico Dr, Longboat Key, FL 34228
Ph: 941-351-6464, 800-4-COLONY
Fax: 813-383-7549
E-mail: colonyfl@ ix.netcom.com
Web: colonybeachresort.com
Accommodates: 234
Rates: 195-625-US$
Dates Open: 1/5–12/17
Services: Full fitness center, Dining Room, Bistro, Patio dining with kid's menu and evening entertainment, Business facilities, swimming pool, tennis, golf nearby
Baby-sitting: yes, $8/ per hour
Activities: Spa, Sailing, Game room
Attractions: Mote Marine Aquarium

The Lodge on Little St. Simon's Island

LITTLE ST. SIMON'S ISLAND, GA

Virtually untouched for centuries, Little St. Simons Island is a privately owned, 10,000-acre barrier island along the coast of Georgia. Accessible only by boat, the Lodge permits only 30 guests at a time, so the natural surroundings are intimately enjoyed.

Seven miles of shell-strewn, breathtaking beaches invite swimming, fishing, and relaxing walks. In addition, year-round activities include bicycling, canoeing, kayaking, horseback riding, and naturalist tours. During the summer, special "Summer Fun for Families" programs combine learning and adventure, encouraging, children and adults to discover this exquisite coastal wilderness. Among the activities are old-fashioned scavenger hunts along the coast, beach seining and salt marsh adventures, and evening stargazing.

At the Lodge on Little St. Simons Island, guests experience the best of Southern hospitality. All meals are served family style in the main dining room of the Hunting Lodge, where the perfect meal begins with oysters for hors d'oeuvres, the celebrated crispy fried flounder for an entrée, and is deliciously ended with homemade ice cream or sorbet.

Two, three, and four-bedroom houses, as well as exclusive full-island rentals are ideal for family gatherings and reunions. Guests can delight in spectacular views of marshes, rivers, and maritime forests, and all guestrooms have access to a shared common area with fireplace. Children of all ages are welcome May through September; children 8 years and over are welcome October through April. The Lodge at Little St. Simons, winner of the Condé Nast 2000 Reader's Choice Award for "Best Small Hotel in North America," is the ideal haven to experience nature at its best.

Address: PO Box 21078, Little St. Simons Island, GA 31522-0578

Ph: 912-638-7472
888-733-5774

Fax: 912-634-1811

E-mail: lssi@mindspring.com

Web: http://www.littlestsimonsisland.com

Accommodates: 15

Rates: 375-550 US$

Dates Open: open year round

Services: Private baths, Porches, Fireplaces, Summer Fun For Families Programs, Naturalist programs, High chairs, cribs and cots available

Attractions: 7 mile beach for swimming, shelling, and strolling, Pool, Eco-adventures, Pristine environment

Kids' Programs: Summer Fun For Families - May through September

The Cloister

SEA ISLAND, GA

The personality of The Cloister is unmistakable, where guests develop sports skills, explore nature, and pursue quality family time while relaxing and basking in the sun's rays.

Parents appreciate the daily playtime, provided without charge for children ages 3 to 12, that is available throughout the summer. Jeep train tours, dance parties, sand sculpture contests, and beach games are just a few of the many pleasures children will enjoy. For teens, tennis mixers, volleyball games, and weekly evening get-togethers are perfect for youthful fun.

For families, the fun begins with horseback riding on the beach, Lawn Olympics, or a treasure hunt. The golf course and tennis courts let families enjoy friendly competition. Speckled trout abound in the spring and fall, and in the summer, tarpon teem in the inlets. The Cloister evening activities include Bingo, theme parties, and dancing.

The Cloister rates are all-inclusive, and children stay free when lodging with their parents; during the summer Family Festival, children's meals are also free. Delicious meals are served at each of the resort's restaurants, where guests may dine in style or opt for more casual fare.

On lush and sunny Sea Island off the coast of Georgia, guests will experience more than a vacation and never want to leave this island paradise.

Address: Sea Island Road, Sea Island, GA 31522

Ph: 912-638-3611, 800-SEA ISLAND

Fax: 912-638-5823

Web: seaisland.com

Accommodates: 262

Rates: 311-814-US$

Dates Open: open year round

Services: Valet, barber shop, beauty shop, hair salon, garage and parking, car hire, babysitting, card/game area, laundry, room service. Children stay free with parents.

Baby-sitting: yes

Activities: Kayaking, biking, shooting school

Attractions: Strolling & shopping on Sea Island

Kids' Programs: Playtime at the Beach Club

Napili Kai Beach Club

LAHAINA, HI

For more than thirty years, Napili Kai Beach Resort has welcomed guests to its ten lavish, tropically landscaped acres on one of the best swimming and snorkeling bays anywhere. A low-rise resort with 163 accommodations, it has maintained its "Plantation" style.

Recreational facilities offered at the Napili Kai Beach Resort include two 18-hole putting greens and shuffleboard courts. Authentic Hawaiian activities, such as lei making and hula lessons, embody the true spirit of the land. You can snorkel in the reefs, soak in the heated whirlpool, or simply soak up the sun's magnificent rays on this island paradise.

The children's Keiki Club is offered seasonally for kids 6 through 12 years of age. For a few hours each day, children will delight in crafts and Hawaiian activities. Unexpectedly spying a whale is one of the most thrilling experiences for guests at the Napili Kai, whose bay has near-perfect conditions for the seasonal sightings.

Dining is an experience all its own at the Sea House Restaurant, where guests enjoy Hawaiian food, entertainment, and the magnificent ocean view.

Address: 5900 Honoapiilani Road, Maui, Lahaina, HI 96761

Ph: 808-669-6271
800-367-5030

Fax: 808-669-0086

E-mail: stay@napilikai.com

Web: http://www.napilikai.com

Accommodates: 163

Rates: 185-635 US$

Dates Open: open year round

Services: Special packages - room & car available in studios and suites, Children's menu, Live Hawaiian music 7:00 p.m.-9:00 p.m., Compl. a.m. coffee and p.m. tea, Daily maid service, Iron/ironing board, Hairdryers, Free parking, Dry Cleaning service, Laundry room

Baby-sitting: $10-$12/ hour

Attractions: Maui Ocean Center, Haleakala, Iao Valley, Lahaina Towne, Helicopter tours, Whale watching, Theater

Kids' Programs: Seasonal Keiki Club

Schweitzer Mountain Resort

SANDPOINT, ID

At Schwietzer we invite folks to come up and "ski the view". Down below the mountain is deep, blue 40-mile long Lake Pend Oreille. Staying on the mountain at the Green Gables Lodge you have sweeping vistas, heated pool, 3 hot tubs, and affordable dining at Jean's NW Bar & Grill. In the summer, experience mountain biking, hiking and tubing. Golf packages available. What's more, the off-season summer rates are a bargain.

Address: 10000 Schweitzer Mountian Road, Sandpoint, ID 83864

Ph: 208-263-9555, 800-831-8810

Fax: 208-263-0775

E-mail: caroline@schweitzer.com

Web: schweitzer.com

Accommodates: 82

Rates: 50-415-US$

Dates Open: 11/25-3/27,6/12-9/27

Services: Children free in parent's room, Kid's playroom, Jean's Northwest Bar & Grill, Evening entertainment, swimming pool, skiing, horseback riding, game room, hiking

Attractions: Lake cruises on Pend O'Reille

Kids' Programs: Funatics—special ski program

Chatham Bars Inn

CHATHAM, MA

Chatham Bars Inn is one of the last of America's grand oceanfront resorts and a renowned Cape Cod landmark, offering from one to eight bedrooms, dotting the surrounding landscape.

Activity lovers of all ages can putt or volley, splash or stroll on a corner of Cape Cod that weathers the seasons and seasons even the shortest of getaways. Awaiting you is a secluded private beach, tennis courts, adjacent golf, heated pool, fitness center, deep sea fishing, and picnics via launch to the Outer Bar.

Families are favored with yet another: the complimentary Beach Buddies and Wash-A-Shores children's programs that allow adults and our younger guests to savor Summer apart ... and together. Offered daily from the end of June through Labor Day, the children's programs meet mornings (9:30–11:30am), afternoons (2–4pm) and evenings (5:30–9pm). Dinners are an additional nominal fee. Beach Buddies is for children 4–8 years old. Wash-A-Shores is for children aged 9–12.

Address: Shore Road, Chatham, MA 02633

Ph: 508-945-0096, 800-527-4884

Fax: 508-945-5491

E-mail: salesbi@ chathambarsinn.com

Web: chathambarsinn.com

Accommodates: 203

Rates: 105-1100-US$ depending on season

Dates Open: open year around

Services: Kids free in parent's room, Restaurant with children's menu, swimming pool, croquet, golf, fitness center, tennis, private beach and boat launch

Baby-sitting: yes/$8 per hour

Activities: Ferry boats to Nantucket & Martha's Vnyd

Attractions: Whale watching, boat tours, bike trails

Kids' Programs: Beach Buddies & Wash-A-Shore

Oakland House

BROOKSVILLE, ME

Idyllic location, spectacular views. Casually elegant seaside inn and family-sized cottages are sprinkled along a half-mile of shorefront or nestled in the trees. Fine dining, fine wines, hearty breakfasts, beaches, dock, boat cruises, lobster picnics. A warm tradition in Down East Hospitality for more than 100 years. Some year round.

Address: 435 Herrick Road, Brooksville, ME 04617

Ph: 207-359-8521 800-359-RELAX

Fax: 207-359-9865

E-mail: jim@oakland-house.com

Web: http://www.oakland-house.com

Accommodates: 25

Rates: 415/week to 4,040/week depending on season

Dates Open: open year round

Services: Family-sized cottages, Restaurant w/kid's menu, High chairs/cribs, Life jackets

Attractions: Holbrook Island Sanctuary (nature preserve), Lumberjack Show, Blue Hill Fair, Mailboat trip to Isle Au Haut, Oceanarium in Bar Harbor, Wooden Boat School, Haystack Mountain School of Crafts, Sandy Lake, Ocean beaches

Inn by the Sea

CAPE ELIZABETH, ME

Inn by the Sea is Portland's premiere family vacation destination. The Inn is designed to blend every contemporary amenity with the understated elegance of classic resort architecture.

Created as a year-round luxury resort for families, the 43 condo-style accommodations offer a choice of one- and two-bedroom suites, each with full kitchen, living and dining area, one or 1½ baths, private patios and porches. All have a minimum of two TV's, I VCR and three telephones, microwave, coffee maker and fully equipped kitchens. Pets are welcome, too.

Recreational opportunities include tennis, bicycling, swimming, shuffleboard, croquet, volleyball, badminton, and one of the finest sandy beaches on the Maine coast. Just steps from the Inn's acres of green lawns is the guest-only entrance to Crescent Beach State Park, a place of rolling highlands, sweeping vistas, and the secrets of the salt marsh. Golf at one of the area's golf courses just 15 minutes from the Inn. Nearby, you'll find horseback riding, amusement parks, kayaking, museums, a petting zoo and much more.

Address: 40 Bowery Beach Road, Cape Elizabeth, ME 04107

Ph: 207-799-3134, 800-888-4287

Fax: 207-799-4779

E-mail: innmaine@aol.com

Web: innbythesea.com

Accommodates: 43

Rates: 150-499-US$

Dates Open: open year round

Services: All suites have kitchens, full baths, dining area, sitting area, 2 TVs, 3 phones, a balcony or porch. 2 Meeting rooms accommodate up to 60 people. Pets are welcome.

Baby-sitting: yes

Activities: all beach activities, bikes

Attractions: 7 golf courses nearby, Sunset cruises

Attean Lake Lodge

JACKMAN, ME

Attean Lake Lodge is located on Birch Island in Attean Lake near Jackman, Maine. Guests park their cars on the shore of the five-mile-long lake and take a five minute boat ride to the private island, where memories of hectic work schedules and school days soon fade away. The Holden family has operated the lodge since 1900, and because the summertime resort is the lake's one and only establishment, guests can enjoy the forty islands and countless beaches without intrusion.

Fifteen lakefront cottages with private porches are nestled amid spruce, birch, and towering pine trees. Accommodating from 2–6 guests, each cottage has a full bath, Franklin fireplace, kerosene lamps and living room.

The main lodge has a large fireplace, which guests gather around in the evenings, a library and "kids room" stocked with good books and board games, and a public telephone that is available twenty-four hours a day. Meals are served in the lodge at your own private table. The lodge prides itself on serving delicious home-cooked food, and vegetarian dishes are available.

Guests enjoy the many miles of hiking trails that lead to remote ponds and mountaintops. Boats, canoes, sailboats and kayaks are also available.

Address: PO Box 457, Jackman, ME 04945
Ph: 207-668-3792 summer 207-668-7726 winter
Fax: 207-668-4016
E-mail: info@atteanlodge.com
Web: http://www.atteanlodge.com
Accommodates: 15
Rates: 260 US$
Dates Open: May–Sept.
Services: Kid's playroom, Beach toys, Office offers fishing tackle, licenses, t-shirts, sourvenir items. Fishing & sightseeing guides available, Boat rental, Daily maid service, Woodburning fireplace, Private porch, Lake/mountain views, Full bath, Special touches
Baby-sitting: yes, $5.00/hour
Attractions: Quebec City (2 hours away), White water rafting, Hiking trails, Beaches, Bay, Islands, Sally Mountain, Wildlife, Fall foilage

Sans Souci Euro Inn
NEW BUFFALO, MI

Just a few miles inland from the shores of Lake Michigan, amid 50 acres of rolling hills and ravines, lies the Sans Souci Euro Inn. Here, families will enjoy a relaxing vacation in the harmonious landscape of meadows, wildwoods, and spectacular trees.

The Inn has been owned by the same family since 1963 and has developed into a stunning lakefront property, offering serene privacy where guests can retreat from the hustle of everyday life. The buildings have been refurbished since 1988 and accommodations range from beautiful suites to cozy cottages. The Kingfisher Suite emulates the elegance and simplicity of nature's most beautiful flower. The Green Heron Suite is an enchanted cavern of solitude complemented by a view of Lake Sans Souci and a warm fireplace. The cottages of Lake Sans Souci will delight guests with a spectacular view of the Lake where the early morning sunshine will glisten upon the water. Cottages are complete with a fireplace and fully equipped kitchen. The Inn also offers houses for couples wishing to relax as they work while enjoying modern-day comfort. Full breakfast is served any time of day for the guests' convenience.

The Sans Souci Euro Inn is located near two spring-fed lakes constructed in natural ravines, offering families the pleasure of enjoying the water while relaxing in the trees and evergreens. Family packages are available at the Inn, creating an ideal family vacation at a lovingly landscaped resort.

The Sans Souci Euro Inn provides a ranch-style sanctuary where guests can get away from it all.

Address: 19265 S. Lakeside Rd., New Buffalo, MI 49117

Ph: 616-756-3141,

Fax: 616-756-5511

E-mail: sans-souci@worldnet.att.net

Web: sans-souci.com

Accommodates: 9

Rates: 110-195-US$ per couple

Dates Open: open year around

Services: Family packages and special weekly rates. Suites include breakfast served at any chosen time. Cottages and houses complete with fireplace and fully equipped kitchens.

Activities: fishing, boating, swimming, hiking

Attractions: Wildlife sanctuary

Nantahala Village
BRYSON CITY, NC

Unique mountain resort and meeting center on 200 acres in the heart of the Great Smoky Mountains. New lodge features 11 rooms, superb restaurant, 6 meeting spaces, fitness room, and comfortable public spaces/decks with views. Fifty other rooms, cottages, log cabins, and homes. Swimming pool, game room, tennis, volleyball, whitewater rafting, and horseback riding, all on the property.

Address: 9400 Highway 19 West, Bryson City, NC 28713

Ph: 828-488-2826
800-438-1507

Fax: 828-488-9634

E-mail: nvinfo@nvnc.com

Web: http://www.nvnc.com

Accommodates: 61

Rates: 100-130 US$

Dates Open: open year round

Services: Kids under 12 free in parent's room, Restaurant with children's menu, Playground, Telephones, TVs, Jacuzzi, Woodburning fireplace, Small porch, Air conditioning, 7th night free

Attractions: Cherokee reservation nearby—museum, authentic village. Great Smokey Mountains Railroad Scenic Excursion Train, Fontana Dam, Joyce Kilmer Nat'l Forest, Gem mines, Great Smokey Mt. Nat'l Park—trails, waterfalls, Blue Ridge and Cherohala Parkways

The Mount Washington Hotel & Resort
BRETTON WOODS, NH

This grand resort in the heart of New Hampshire's majestic White Mountains is the perfect place for an unforgettable family getaway. Located in an ideal setting for either winter or summer activities, guests will experience endless opportunities for recreation. Golf, tennis, swimming, skiing, plus sleigh and carriage rides are just a few of the diversions waiting to be enjoyed.

The Mount Washington offers a unique summer program geared just for kids that parents are sure to love. The "King of the Mountain Kids' Kamp" is available for guests age 5–12 for half-day, full-day, and evening programs. Each week features a different fun-filled theme, so kids won't run out of things to do. Whether it's cooking with the Chef, wacky water games, or adventure activities, this camp is sure to please your kids.

In the winter months, the popular Hobbit Ski & Snowboard School will keep kids aged 3–12 entertained at the Bretton Woods Ski Area, located just across the street. The program includes equipment rentals, lessons, lift tickets, lunch and unimaginable fun and games. Well known for its family-oriented atmosphere, Bretton Woods is the ideal mountain for beginning and intermediate skiers.

A variety of accommodations are available to fit any family's needs. The Mount Washington hotel offers the specially designed Family Chambers, with two guestrooms connected by a private bath. Also available are the contemporary Bretton Woods Motor Inn, the charming Bretton Arms Country Inn, and the private 1- to 5-bedroom Townhouses at Bretton Woods.

Address: Route 302, Bretton Woods, NH 03575

Ph: 603-278-1000, 800-258-0330

Fax: 603-278-8838

Web: mtwashington.com

Accommodates: 335

Rates: 210-1195-US$

Dates Open: open year around

Services: Shops, Masseuse, Game room, Specially designed "Family Chambers" include 2 guest rooms adjoined by private bath, Restaurants with children's menu, Evening activities for kids

Baby-sitting: yes, $5 per hour

Activities: Carriage & sleigh rides, Theme weeks

Attractions: Mt. Washington Cog Railway

Kids' Programs: King of the Mountain Camp

Purity Springs Resort

EAST MADISON, NH

For over 100 years, Purity Springs Resort has offered fantastic family fun throughout the year. Nestled in the Mt. Washington Valley near the White Mountains National Forest, the resort is located on 1,000 acres of land overlooking its own private lake. Three full meals and all activities are included with accommodations.

Choose your style of accommodations from the ten different lodges. Each is ideally suited for couples, families and groups of various sizes. Most rooms feature air conditioning, phone, two beds, and private bath. The luxury rooms have wet bar, refrigerator and microwave. Each lodge has at least one common room with TV and fireplace.

During the winter, guests can ski day and night at Purity's own King Pine Ski Area. Children ages 4 to 7 enjoy the Knee-Hi Ski School, whose weekend program increases children's skills through three ability levels.

During fair weather, golfing, tennis, water sports, and regular cookouts dominate the land activities, while boating, swimming, and water skiing are favorites on the pristine lake. Complimentary childcare is available to guests using the Fitness Room. Weekly canoe trips, mountain hikes, five golf courses, and nearby Story Land round out the area's recreational offerings. (A nominal fee applies to off-site activities.)

Address: Route 153 (HC 63 Box 40), East Madison, NH 03849
Ph: 603-367-8896, 800-FREE SKI
Fax: 603-367-8664
E-mail: info@ purityspring.com
Web: purityspring.com
Accommodates: 75
Rates: 26-174-US$
Dates Open: open year round
Services: Library, VCR's, Game room, Laundry, Winter nightly entertainment, Major credit cards, Restaurant, Fireplaces and TVs in common areas, Full conference facilities, Skiing, Spa
Baby-sitting: yes
Activities: Summer—hiking, canoe trips, waterskiing
Attractions: 5 golf courses, Storyland, Waterslides
Kids' Programs: Kid's Club

Franconia Inn
FRANCONIA, NH

Since 1886, Franconia Inn has been welcoming guests. White clapboard and green shutters; 3 stories, 29 rooms and 3 suites, library, dining room, Rathskeller Lounge, 2 spacious verandas with spectacular mountain views. We are located in the Easton Valley, on the north side of Franconia Notch.

The Franconia Inn is a full service inn, with extensive outdoor activities, which include tennis, fishing, horseback riding, soaring, hiking, biking, cross-country skiing, alpine skiing, ice skating, and snowshoeing.

Address: 1300 Easton Road, Franconia, NH 03580

Ph: 603-823-5542, 800-473-5299

Fax: 603-823-8078

E-mail: info@ franconiainn.com

Web: http://www. franconiainn.com

Accommodates: 32

Rates: 91-245 US$

Dates Open: Closed April through mid-May

Services: Special package rates on Family Suites, Children's menu, Weekend evening entertainment, Game room, Children's bikes and toys, Family movies, Swimming pool, Croquet, Spa

Activities: Airfield with glider airplanes, Tennis, Jacuzzi, Horseback riding, Gliding, Sleigh rides, Badminton

Attractions: Franconia Notch State Park w/airtel tram, Cannon Mountain, Robert Frost Museum

Luxury Mountain Getaways
WHITE MOUNTAINS, NH

New Hampshire's White Mountains Most Requested Award-Winning Resorts ... Nordic Village and Highlands, The Chateaus at Highland Ridge, Nestlenook Inn and Victorian Village. Choose among the resort's variety of deluxe accommodations ranging from Suites, Penthouses, Townhouses, Villas and luxurious Chateaus, to the timeless elegance of an 18th Century Victorian Inn and Estate located on 65 beautiful acres. You will experience the ultimate for your family vacation with fireplaces, 2-person Jacuzzi spas, fully equipped kitchens, and magnificent views of the White Mountains.

As a guest, you will enjoy our indoor and outdoor heated pools (open year round), steam rooms and therapy spas. The young at heart will enjoy our playground, tennis courts, and basketball and volleyball courts. Seasonally, there is nightly entertainment at our Nordic Falls. For the outdoors person, we offer a variety of activities including mountain bikes, hiking trails and rowboats. Bring your rod and reel, as there are numerous fly-fishing opportunities on the Ellis River, which surrounds our Nestlenook property.

Our magical wonderland comes alive in the winter. There is ice-skating on Emerald Lake, snowshoeing, cross country skiing, old-fashioned Austrian sleigh rides, and nightly bonfires.

Address: Rt. 16, Jackson, NH 03846
Ph: 603-383-9101
800-472-5207
Fax: 603-383-9823
Web: http://www.luxury-mountaingetaways.com
Accommodates: 224
Rates: 79-575 US$
Dates Open: open year round
Services: Kid's playyard, Woodburning stoves, Daily housekeeping by arrangement, Compl. firewood, Jacuzzis, A/C, Fireplaces, Fully equipped kitchen, Views
Attractions: Storyland Amusement Park, Santa's Village, Conway Scenic Railroad, Emerald Lake, Ellis River, Entertainment Pavillion, Sleigh rides, Storyland, Shopping
Kids' Programs: Supervised children's programs

Rocking Horse Ranch
HIGHLAND, NY

The only New York ranch-resort to be honored with a Mobil Guide rating and AAA 3-Diamonds. A great combination of dude ranch, casual hospitality and year 'round resort comforts. Voted "Favorite in the USA" by readers of Family Circle Magazine.

Vacation packages include modern accommodations, outstanding meals, horseback riding, water skiing, paddle boats, water slides, ball sports, and dozens of other facilities. In winter, ski or tube down their beginner's slope, ice skate or take a sleigh ride. There's an alphabet of activities for each season. And it's all—even the equipment and instruction—included in your room rate.

The whole family will find lots to do together—or apart. The resort's outstanding children's program provides that option. Kids love the independence of visiting the barn with the friendly wranglers, stopping at the archery range, playing with the llama in the petting zoo, or swimming in the heated indoor/outdoor pools. You'll rest easy knowing that there is safe supervision for all activities. And for late nights out, enjoy a show or dance band in one of the lounges. It's the most fun your family will ever have!

Address: 600 Route 44-55, Highland, NY 12528

Ph: 845-691-2927, 800-647-2624

Fax: 845-691-6434

E-mail: ranchrhr@ aol.com

Web: http://www. rhranch.com

Accommodates: 120

Rates: 85-150 US$

Dates Open: open year around

Services: Children's nursery, Kid's playroom, High chairs/cribs/cots, Indiv. climate control, Private bath, Direct dial phone, Daily maid service, TV

Baby-sitting: yes, $7/per hour

Activities: Playground, Petting zoo, Pony rides, Hayrides, Volleyball, Softball, Basketball, Sleigh rides, Water skiing and more!

Attractions: Hyde Park – home of Franklin Roosevelt, West Point, Hugenot Street – oldest street in America with original houses circa 1600

Kids' Programs: Complete Day Camp Program

Woodloch Pines

HAWLEY, PA

Since 1958, Woodloch Pines has been welcoming guests with fabulous food, superb accommodations, a seemingly endless array of activities, and genuine, warm hospitality.

The activities are limitless, and Woodloch has created an excellent program just for kids. Children will play a variety of games within their own age group, from soccer and bowling, to mini-golf and a peanut hunt. Families will enjoy Family Double Dare, Family Bowling, and an awesome treasure hunt. For an evening of fun, karaoke, line dancing, and movies are wonderful ways to wrap up an exciting day.

Woodloch Pines offers numerous action-filled packages. Guests can choose from a weekend, midweek, or mini-midweek special. Each package includes various activities, depending on the season. Families can enjoy Easter arts and crafts, horseracing get-togethers, or horse-drawn sleigh rides. Accommodations vary depending on the chosen package, but all packages include full use of the resort's facilities and feature delicious meals (for which they are famous).

Address: RD 1, Box 280, Hawley, PA 18428
Ph: 717-685-7121, 800-572-6658
Fax: 717-685–1205
E-mail: woodmark@woodloch.com
Web: woodloch.com
Accommodates: 185
Rates: 156-1185-US$ 2 days all inclusive
Dates Open: Closed Christmas wk
Services: 4 Restaurants on property w/children's menu, Excellent corporate facilities, Bumper cars, go carts, waterslide, snowtubing.
Baby-sitting: yes $5/per hour
Activities: Daily activities for kids of all ages
Attractions: Whitewater rafting, paintball, skiing
Kids' Programs: Children's program

Kiwah Island Resorts

HOT SPRINGS, VA

Kiawah Island Resorts consists of the 150-room oceanfront Kiawah Island Inn, the Villas of Kiawah Island Resorts (which includes nearly 600 villas and luxury homes) and a future $110 million luxury oceanfront hotel and spa, scheduled for completion in the spring of 2003. Both the Inn and the Villas carry AAA's Four-Diamond rating.

Thoughtfully developed on a barrier island off coastal South Carolina, Kiawah Island Resorts lies along 10 miles of pristine beach bordered by the Atlantic Ocean. It includes five championship golf courses, two award-winning tennis complexes, and a variety of restaurants and lounges. In 1991, The Ocean Course at Kiawah Island Resorts hosted the infamous "War by the Shore" Ryder Cup matches.

Kiawah Island Resorts is located near historic Charleston, SC, which is widely regarded as the most beautiful and historic city in America. Since its founding in 1670, Charleston has played a pivotal role in the course of American history. It is also host to internationally acclaimed events, including Spoleto Festival USA and the Southeastern Wildlife Exposition. With the newly opened South Carolina Aquarium and IMAX Theater, Charleston is a perfect family destination.

Address: 12 Kiawah Beach Dr, Kiawah Island, SC 29455

Ph: 843-768-2121
800-654-2924

Fax: 843-768-9339

E-mail: reservations@ kiawahresort.com

Web: http://www. kiawahresort.com

Accommodates: 150/Inn, 600/Villas

Rates: 79-759 US$

Dates Open: open year round

Services: Barber/beauty services, Children stay free, Cribs available, Dry cleaning/laundry service, Guest laundry facilities, Medical services, Free parking, Safe deposit box, Self-parking, Transp. to airport/city, Express Check-Out, Elevator, Cable TV, Fridge

Baby-sitting: yes

Attractions: Historic Charleston (21 miles away), Cobblestone streets, Antique shops, Boutiques, Arts & crafts, Tours, Charleston Aquarium, IMAX theatre

Kids' Programs: Camp Kiawah during summer and holidays, 8:30 a.m.-5:00 p.m.

The Tides

IRVINGTON, VA

Perched on the shores of Carter's Creek, just off the majestic Chesapeake Bay and Rappahannock River, lies the "grande dame of the Chesapeake Bay"—The Tides. Whether you're looking for family fun on the water, a golf weekend with friends, or a tranquil vacation full of scenic walks and exploration, The Tides is the place to be. They offer an impressive array of golf options, including the Golden Eagle, the Inn's own golf course, which is rated one of the top ten courses in Virginia. If tennis is your game, there are eight fine courts that are complimentary with your stay. Boasting two marinas on the bay, The Tides offers boating, sailing and cruising opportunities galore. There are two pools available for guest use. One is fresh water and the other is salt water. Both fresh- and saltwater fishing are abundant.

As a guest at The Inn, your breakfast and dinner are included Modified American Plan accommodations rate. Guests at The Lodge follow the European plan, which offers complete dining flexibility. There are 6 dining areas for your mood and convenience. The 127-foot yacht "Miss Ann" is available for lunch, cocktail, and dinner cruises.

Just for kids 4–12, the "Crab Net Kids" day camp program includes swimming, boating, fishing, crabbing, playing games and eating together under the supervision of resort counselors. This summer program, complimentary to Inn guests, is available to Lodge guests for an additional fee.

The Inn and The Lodge combine casual elegance with traditional Virginia charm, making The Tides the ultimate vacation destination on the Chesapeake Bay.

Address: 480 King Carter Drive, Irvington, VA 22480

Ph: 804-438-5000, 800-24 TIDES

Fax: 804-438-5222

Web: the-tides.com

Accommodates: 194

Rates: 120-755-US$

Dates Open: March 20-November 24

Services: Room service, shops, Tides Inn Main Dining Room, Evening Entertainment, 3 Swimming pools, Fitness center, Daily yacht cruises, boat rentals, complimentary bikes, Meeting rooms

Baby-sitting: yes

Activities: 7 Tennis courts, 45 holes of golf

Attractions: Colonial Williamsburg, Jamestown

Kids' Programs: Every day—Memorial-Labor Day

The Tyler Place

HIGHGATE SPRINGS, VT

Four generations of Tylers have owned and operated this family resort on 165 acres of woods, meadows, and private lakeshore since 1933. At the Tyler Place, family fun means creating a balance between kids' fun and private time for parents.

Tyler Place has nine specially designed children's programs for kids from infants to teens. The programs offer sports, playtime, and great meals. Sessions run in the mornings and evenings, allowing parents time alone and leaving afternoons free for family fun. A fleet of over 250 bikes is available for a family ride, or you may enjoy tennis, soccer, or volleyball. As if that isn't enough, various activities, including field games and hayrides, are also scheduled for afternoons.

Accommodations at The Tyler Place vary depending on family size and date of holiday. Families can choose from suites, The Inn, or cottages, each offering various amenities from fireplaces to screened-in porches. Family Package rates are available and include family suites and cottages (with separate kids' rooms), all meals, programs, and activities. Family Retreats are also offered in May, early June, and September. All of the standard family sports and traditions are available, in addition to activities centered around learning about the local area. These vary depending on the time of year, but guests can expect to learn about rural Vermont folklore, farm life, gardening and outdoor skills.

Guests who first came as children return with their children and grandchildren to have the time of their lives all over again.

Address: PO Box 1, Old Dock Road, Highgate Springs, VT 05460

Ph: 802-868-4000

Fax: 802-868-5621

E-mail: tyler@together.net

Web: http://www. tylerplace.com

Accommodates: 60

Rates: 70-251 US$

Dates Open: May–September

Services: Some fireplaces in the suites, cottages, and farm house. Suites have separate kids' rooms. All meals, sports programs and activities included in price.

Baby-sitting: $3.50–6.50/ hour

Attractions: Wildlife Refuge, French Quebec, Montreal

Kids' Programs: Yes for all ages

The Golden Eagle Resort

S T O W E ,   V T

The Golden Eagle Resort's park-like 80 acres is laid out in a walking village design, and they are located a mere ½ mile from Stowe, one of the best year-round recreational areas in the Northeast.

Guests find gracious rooms, suites and specialty housekeeping apartments for added privacy, each tastefully decorated with casual charm and comfortable attention to detail. Children 12 and younger stay free, when sharing a room with adults, making family travel a vacation value. The resort restaurants (Colonial Café and Partridge Inn) welcome children, and menus are available for those smaller appetites.

The warmer months feature a time to explore nature and enjoy the resort amenities. In addition, many adult children travel with their parents, continuing the multi-generation guest profile at the Golden Eagle. Resort facilities include indoor and outdoor swimming pools, walking trails through their own nature preserve, tennis, a children's playground, fishing in the stocked resort trout ponds, and lawn games. In winter, the ponds are carved by ice skaters during weekly skating parties and a horse-drawn sleigh travels around the property. Seasonal supervised children's programs are popular. Opposite the resort is the award-winning Stowe Recreation Path for walking, biking, and in-line skating. Also available are canoeing trips sponsored by a local outfitter. There are craft fairs and local theater companies. Other area attractions designed for family participation include Ben & Jerry's Ice Cream Factory, Green Mountain Chocolate Company, Cold Hollow Cider Mill and the Vermont Teddy Bear Factory, each producing a unique Vermont-made product.

The family friendly, affordable Golden Eagle Resort makes family fun a four-season commitment.

Address: The Mountain Road, PO Box 1090, Stowe, VT 05672

Ph: 802-253-4811
800-626-1010

Fax: 802-253-2561

E-mail: info@ stoweagle.com

Web: http://www. stoweagleresort.com

Accommodates: 89

Rates: 89-229 US$

Dates Open: open year around

Services: Cribs, Playyard, Children stay free with parents, Kid's menu, Breakfast included, Playroom, Ind. heat/air conditioning, Color TV, Refrigerators, Coffee makers, Private balcony/patio

Baby-sitting: Babysitting by appointment

Attractions: Ben & Jerry's Ice Cream Factory, Stowe Recreation Path, Biking, Rollerblading, Stowe Mountain Resort, Special events

Kids' Programs: Children's programs

Meadowbrook Resort

WISCONSIN DELLS, WI

Meadowbrook Resort, located on 12 scenic and secluded acres of north woods scenery, features modern log accommodations in a variety of styles and sizes, and is just a pleasant walk to downtown Wisconsin Dells.

Choose from standard or deluxe suites, log cabins with 1, 2, or 3 separate bedrooms (most with full kitchens), whirlpools, and fireplaces. All of the units have picnic tables and BBQ grills nearby, and daily housekeeping is provided in all rooms.

Activities include an indoor and outdoor water activity play land with waterslides, swimming pools, whirlpool, game room, hiking, fishing, a boat launch to the Wisconsin River, wildlife and bird watching. Gather round and relax by the nightly campfires. The spacious grounds, complemented by a small, private lake with covered bridge and waterfront gazebo, are perfect for family reunions, outdoor weddings, scout activities, youth groups or company outings and retreats. They also have meeting rooms for indoor gatherings and are host to over 100 family reunions each year!

In 2001, the resort is adding 36 deluxe suites with a choice of 6 room styles, a new north woods themed indoor water activity pool, a large outdoor pool, 2 meeting rooms, and an expanded game room.

Address: 1533 River Rd., Wisconsin Dells, WI 53965

Ph: 608-253-3201
877-993-3557

Web: http://www. meadowbrookresort.com

Accommodates: 66

Rates: 59-169 US$

Services: Kid's playroom and playyard, Wall to wall carpeting, Full bathrooms with modular tub and shower, Indv. heat/air conditioning, Color/cable TV, Daily housekeeping, Full-size refrigerator, Coffee maker, Microwave, Toaster, Crockery

Attractions: World famous scenery, America's largest waterparks, Tommy Bartlett Thrill Show, Circus World Museum, World's largest go-kart amusement park, Amphibious Duck Tours, Ho-Chunk Gambling Casino, and much, much more!

ADDITIONAL FAMILY RESORTS

▓ *Arizona*

──────────────── LITCHFIELD PARK ────────────────

The Wigwam Resort
300 Wigwam Blvd., 85340
Ph: 800-327-0396
602-935-3811   Fax: 602-856-1081
Number of Rooms: 331
Web site: http://www.wigwamresort.com

At The Wigwam, activities abound for every visitor. The facilities include two swimming pools, water volleyball, water slide, Jacuzzi & poolside cabana, basketball and volleyball courts, tennis courts, horseback riding, and a children's activities program. For day trips there are hot air balloon rides, an Apache Trail tour, desert jeep tours, desert botanical gardens, the Grand Canyon, Wildlife World Zoo, museums, shopping, and golf courses.

──────────────── PHOENIX ────────────────

Arizona Biltmore
24th Street & Missouri, 85016
Ph: 602-955-6600
800-950-0086   Fax: 602-954-2548
Number of Rooms: 730
Web site: http://www.arizonabiltmore.com

Rate Code: Inexpensive-Luxury
Services: Valet, beauty shop, garage and parking, card or game area, laundry, room service, free daily newspaper.

The Kids Kabana follows a 64-year tradition of children's activities by offering arts and crafts, bike rides, games, movies, sports, storytime, and snacks. The Biltmore Nanny Pool offers baby-sitting services.

──────────────── PHOENIX ────────────────

Pointe Hilton at Squaw Peak
7672 North 16th Street, 85020
Ph: 602-997-2626
800-974-9784 Fax: 602-997-2391
Number of Rooms: 576
Web site: http://www.pointehilton.com/squa/default.stm

Rate Code: Inexpensive-Moderate
Services: Fitness center, massage, car rental. All children receive free benefits of Vacation Station after check-in.

Children's program from 9 a.m. to 5 p.m., for ages 4 to 12. The sessions are offered year round. The programs offer desert survival skills, geology lessons, panning for gold, nature walks, Hohokam pottery workshops, and identifying edible wild plants.

──────────────── SCOTTSDALE ────────────────

Marriott's Camelback Resort
5402 E Lincoln Dr, 85253
Ph: 602-948-1700 800-242-2635
Fax: 602-951-8469
Number of Rooms: 423

Rate Code: Inexpensive-Luxury
Services: In-room dining, full service spa
salon, taxi service, baby-sitting,
concierge, facilities for the disabled,
doctor on 24-hour call.

Guests can rest, relax and revitalize with a variety of recreation. Championship golf, tennis courts, 3 pools and a health spa are just a few highlights. And for kids, there's fun at Hopalong College. The program offers a great assortment of fun, educational festivities sure to make youngsters feel at home. Teen programs are also available.

──────────────── SCOTTSDALE ────────────────

The Phoenician
6000 E Camelback Rd, 85251
Ph: 602-941-8200
800-888-8234
Fax: 602-947-4311
Number of Rooms: 580

Rate Code: Moderate-Luxury
Services: 24-hour room service, Lanai
decks, mini bar, wall safe, meeting and
dining facilities, children's pools and a
165 foot water slide.

In addition to the resort's exceptional recreational facilities, they offer something for everyone—adults, teens and children. For teens, there is water volleyball and a resort scavenger hunt. Children's activities include relay races, painting and storytelling. For the entire family, there are family walks and cookouts, a medicine wheel ceremony and musical entertainment.

──────────────── TUCSON ────────────────

Loews Ventana Canyon Resort
7000 N Resort Dr, 85715
Ph: 520-299-2020
800-234-5117
Fax: 510-644-2651
Number of Rooms: 400

Rate Code: Moderate-Luxury
Services: Valet, beauty shop, parking,
babysitting, laundry, room service

The Coyote Kids Club offers a supervised program which includes sports, duck feeding, sun visor art, pinatas, hula hoop contests, and much more. Friday and Saturday are nights at the movies with pizza, popcorn and games.

──────────────── TUCSON ────────────────

Westin La Paloma
3800 E Sunrise Dr, 85718
Ph: 520-742-6000
800-742-6000
Fax: 520-577-5886
Number of Rooms: 487

Rate Code: Luxury
Services: Valet, beauty shop, garage and
parking, car hire, babysitting, card/game
area, laundry, room service, boutiques

Our Children's Lounge has supervised fun for tots (6 months to 5 years) including storytelling, games, cartoons, and an outdoor play yard. Kactus Kids is a day camp environment for 6- to 12-year-olds and offers swimming, games, movies, crafts and lots, lots more.

▩ California

―――――――――― **ANAHEIM** ――――――――――

Anaheim Hilton & Towers
777 Convention Way, 92802
Ph: 714-750-4321
800-932-3322
Fax: 714-740-4737
Number of Rooms: 1600

Rate Code: Moderate
Services: Complimentary Disneyland shuttle, Gift Shop, Full health club, Beauty and barber salon, Car rental

Vacation Station is for ages 5–12, and is a complimentary program. Supervised arts and crafts, children's theatre, and sports are just a few of the many things offered to entertain the kids. The program is from 10 a.m. to 4 p.m.

―――――――――― **CARLSBAD** ――――――――――

La Costa Hotel & Spa
Costa Del Mar Rd, 92009
Ph: 619-438-9111
800-544-5000
Fax: 619-438-3758
Number of Rooms: 487

Rate Code: Luxury
Services: Valet, beauty shop, car hire, house doctor, babysitting, laundry, card/game area, room service

Camp La Costa has very imaginative activities such as kite flying, walks to a nearby fire station, learning about the world, arts and crafts, golf, and lots, lots more. The night program on Friday and Saturday evenings offers dinner, with scavenger hunt, a story hour, or a pinata.

―――――――――― **CITY OF INDUSTRY** ――――――――――

Industry Hills Sheraton
1 Industry Hills Pkwy, 91744
Ph: 818-810-HILL
800-524-4557
Fax: 818-964-9535
Number of Rooms: 294

Rate Code: Moderate
Services: Two golf courses, tennis courts, olympic size swimming pool, equestrian trails, health spa, in-house laundry.

There are many more services in addition to the outstanding golf and tennis facilities. Dine in their award winning restaurants, browse through the golf library and museum, or visit the equestrian facility.

―――――――――― **CORONADO** ――――――――――

Loews Coronado Bay Resort
4000 Coronado Bay, 92118
Ph: 619-424-4000
800-235-6397
Fax: 619-424-4400
Number of Rooms: 440

Rate Code: Moderate-Luxury
Services: Five bayside tennis courts, full service Fitness Center with saunas and steam rooms, laundry/valet service, on-site comprehensive business center.

The Resort offers its younger guests entertaining and ecuational activities with the "Commodore Kids Club." A variety of half-day, full-day and evening activities include face painting, nature walks, sandcaslte building and G-rated movies. For parents, baby-proofing kits are provided which include faucet guard, outlet covers, toilet lid lock and other safety items. Located on a private 15-acre peninsula off the historic community of Coronado.

DANA POINT

Dana Point Resort
25135 Park Lantern, 92629
Ph: 800-243-1166
800-533-9748
Fax: 714-661-3688
Number of Rooms: 350

Rate Code: Inexpensive-Moderate
Services: Terraces, Robes, Twice-daily
maid service

The kid's program "Camp Cowabunga" is for those 5–12 in age. The program is offered all summer and on weekends year round. The program is fully supervised and offers a large variety of activities. Evening sessions are also also offered, with dinner included and movies or video games, crafts or an evening hike to the park's amphitheater and marshmallow roast.

HUNTINGTON BEACH

Waterfront Hilton Beach Resort
21100 Pacific Coast Hwy, 92648
Ph: 714-960-7873
800-822-3322
Fax: 714-960-2642
Number of Rooms: 300

Rate Code: Moderate-Luxury
Services: Minibars, Private balconies.
Health and fitness center, Golf shop,
Laundry, Valet

The Dolphin Youth Club is for ages 5 to 12, and is a complimentary program. The program is offered summers and weekends during the rest of the year. There are many different activities including arts and crafts, beach excursions, poolside games and much more.

KELSEYVILLE

Konocti Harbor Resort & Spa
8727 Sode Bay Rd, 95451
Ph: 707-279-4281
800-862-4930
Fax: 707-279-9205
Number of Rooms: 240

Rate Code: Inexpensive
Services: Full health spa, Massages

A great kid's program runs from 10 in the morning to 10 at night with an hour break for dinner. Miniature golf, arts and crafts, swimming and tennis, and movies are just some of the fare offered.

KINGS CANYON NAT'L PARK

Montecito-Sequoia Lodge
Box 858, Grant Grove, 93633
Ph: 209-565-3388
800-843-8677
Fax: 209-565-3223

Rate Code: Inexpensive-Moderate

A year round facility with uses as different as the seasons. The facility is family-oriented, especially during summer, with special programs for ages 2 through 7 and counselor-led activities for ages 8 thru adult, such as a play yard for parents with kids under 2. Baby-sitting is offered during certain hours. Three buffet meals are offered daily, and for an additional charge water skiing and horseback riding are available.

─────── **LAGUNA BEACH** ───────

Inn at Laguna
211 N Coast Hwy, 92651
Ph: 714-497-9722
800-544-4479
Number of Rooms: 70

Rate Code: Inexpensive
Services: Swimming pool, spa, valet
parking, sun terrace, panoramic views,
T.V. and VCR, honor bar.

Dramatically perched on an oceanfront cliff, the Inn offers, within walking distance, numerous unique shops, galleries and restaurants located in the village.

─────── **LAKE SAN MARCOS** ───────

Lake San Marcos Resort
1025 La Bonita Dr, 92069
Ph: 619-744-0120
Fax: 619-744-0748
Number of Rooms: 142

Rate Code: Inexpensive-Luxury

Conveniently secluded on its own lake, the resort is only 8 miles away from the Carlsbad beaches. Take a leisurely ride on the lake in a party boat that holds up to 8 people, or relax by one of 4 pools. The resort offers picnic grounds, three restaurants, and a championship golf course.

─────── **LOS ANGELES** ───────

Renaissance Los Angeles Hotel
9620 Airport Blvd, 90045
Ph: 310-337-2800
Fax: 310-216-6681

Rate Code: Inexpensive

While at the hotel, families can enjoy the entertainment, shopping and restaurants of Santa Monica, Marina del Rey, Venice, Manhattan Beach and Hermosa Beach; all within 10 miles of the hotel.

─────── **MONTEREY** ───────

Hotel Pacific
300 Pacific St, 93940
Ph: 800-554-5542   408-373-5700
Fax: 408-373-6921
Number of Rooms: 105

These adobe-style guest rooms are arranged in clusters around 2 courtyard areas both with spas. Each room has separate sitting and sleeping areas, fireplace, feather bed with down comforter, individual patio or balcony, and complimentary tea social every afternoon.

─────── **MONTEREY** ───────

Monterey Bay Inn
242 Cannery Row, 93940
Ph: 800-424-6242   408-373-6242
Fax: 408-373-7603
Number of Rooms: 47

The Monterey Bay Inn stretches out over the ocean offering spectacular ocean views, where guests may see sea otters playing in the bay. Each room has a king-sized bed and an oversized double sofa sleeper, refrigerator, remote-control TV, a game table, and desk. A continental breakfast is delivered to the room each morning. The inn is convenient to all the popular shops, sights, and water sports of Monterey Bay.

──────── OLYMPIC VALLEY ────────

Resort at Squaw Creek
400 Squaw Creek Rd, 96146
Ph: 916-583-6300
800-583-6300
Fax: 916-581-6632
Number of Rooms: 405

Rate Code: Inexpensive-Luxury

This year round luxury resort offers activities for the entire family. For children 3–12 there is The Mountain Buddies program which incorporates living, learning and leisure activities. For teens, there are programs that vary daily and include ski boot volleyball, campfire parties, hip hop aerobics, ice skating and climbing wall competition to name a few.

──────── OXNARD ────────

Casa Sirena Marina Resort
3605 Peninsula R, 93035
Ph: 805-985-6311
800-228-6026
Fax: 805-985-4329
Number of Rooms: 275

Rate Code: Inexpensive-Moderate
Services: Each room equipped with refrigerator, microwave, cable TV, VCR. Video rental library in lobby, heated pool and spa, tennis, sauna, excercise room, massage.

Located 60 minutes north of Los Angeles and 25 minutes south of Santa Barbara. Nearby attractions include Fisherman's Wharf with restaurants and shopping, Maritime Museum, miles of clean beaches, boating and sport fishing from Channel Islands Harbor. Children under 12 are free in same room.

──────── OXNARD ────────

Mandalay Beach Resort
2101 Mandalay Beach Rd, 93035
Ph: 805-984-2500
Fax: 805-984-8339
Number of Rooms: 249

Rate Code: Luxury
Services: Complimentary breakfast each morning, nearby golf courses and shopping, the largest swimming pool in California, tennis courts, 2 large whirlpools.

Families love the casual atmosphere of this resort. Tennis, beachcombing, swimming, movies, biking and a host of other activities await you. The customized Mandalay cooler is filled with games and snacks for the kids and a complimentary beverage for mom and dad. The Lifestyles Family Coupon Book offers fabulous discounts on activities, food and area attractions.

──────── RANCHO MIRAGE ────────

Ritz Carlton, Rancho Mirage
68-900 Frank Sinatra Dr, 92270
Ph: 619-321-8282
800-241-3333
Fax: 619-321-8282
Number of Rooms: 240

Rate Code: Luxury
Services: Valet Parking, Valet, Car Rental, Secretarial, Boutiques

The children's program is "Ritz-Kids." A supervised summer program is offered for children 5 and over. The activites are often fitness-oriented, but also offer beach scavenger hunts and movie matinees. Parents may also register their children in "Kid's Night Out," which features a children's menu for dinner, with movies and activities included.

─────────── **RANCHO SANTA FE** ───────────

Rancho Valencia Resort
5921 Valencia Circle, 92067
Ph: 619-756-1123
800-548-3664
Fax: 619-756-0165
Number of Rooms: 43

Rate Code: Luxury
Services: In-room wet bar and refrigerator, daily housekeeping service, bathrobes, orange juice, newspaper and rosebud delivered to each room daily. Valet parking.

The residential style Spanish-Mediterranean accommodations offer all the comfort and extra touches that make you really feel at home. Rancho Valencia is an exclusive romantic getaway, a perfect hideaway for honeymooners, a private corporate retreat and a sports paradise.

─────────── **SAN DIEGO** ───────────

Rancho Bernardo Inn
17550 Bernardo Oaks Dr, 92128
Ph: 800-854-1065
800-542-6096
Number of Rooms: 287

Rate Code: Moderate
Services: Car rental, Reading and game rooms, Boutiques, Sports shops

The kid's camp is run by an expert in the outdoor and recreation fields, and runs from 9 in the morning until 9 at night. The sessions are designed to please those from 4 to 17. Different age groups have activities planned for their interest levels such as: crafts, scavenger hunts, and much more. The camps are free of charge, and are offered during August, and over Christmas and Easter holidays.

─────────── **SAN FRANCISCO** ───────────

The Westin St. Francis
335 Powell Street, 94102
Ph: 415-397-7000
Fax: 415-403-6850

Rate Code: Moderate-Luxury
Services: Babysitting service, room service, laundry/valet, hairstyling, fitness center, concierge, car rental, business center, airport transportation.

Located in the heart of San Francisco on Union Square, the St. Francis is surrounded by the city's finest shops, theaters and restaurants. And of course, the cable cars stop right at our front door. The Westin Kits Club is a comprehensive program geared to families travelling with kids 12 and under. No charge for children 18 years and under if occupying same room with parents.

─────────── **SANTA MONICA** ───────────

Loews Santa Monica Beach Hotel
1700 Ocean Avenue, 90401
Ph: 310-458-6700
800-235-6397
Fax: 310-458-0020
Number of Rooms: 350

Rate Code: Luxury
Services: Full health & fitness facilities, spa, 24-hour room service, business centers, concierge, mini-bar, twice-daily maid service.

"Splash Club" makes full use of the beachfront with sandcastle building contests and relay races. There are also treasure hunts in the pool, sandcastle building contests, and relay races. Kits also make t-shirts, puppets and kites.

—————— SOUTH LAKE TAHOE ——————

Camp Richardson's Resort & Marina
P.O. Box 9028, 96158
Ph: 530-541-1801
800-544-1801   Fax: 530-541-2793

Rate Code: Luxury

—————————— TRUCKEE ——————————

Northstar-at-Tahoe
P.O. Box 129, 96160
Ph: 530-562-1010
800-533-6787   Fax: 530-587-0221
Number of Rooms: 144

Rate Code: Inexpensive-Luxury
Services: Free shuttle buses, Sundries,
Newsstand, Deli, Concierge, Saunas

Northstar offers something for everyone, year round. Summer activities include swimming, free outdoor Sunday concerts, moutain biking, golf courses, tennis and horseback riding. Winter activites include skiing, snowshoeing, sleigh rides, snowmobiling and more. The Minor's Camp Child Care Center is an all-day licensed child care with organized activities, field trips and lunch.

—————————— WILLITS ——————————

Emandal
16500 Hearst Rd., 95490
Ph: 707-459-5439   800-262-9597
Fax: 707-459-1808
Number of Rooms: 22

Rate Code: Moderate
Services: Cold spring water in cabin,
Electricity, Hammocks, 3 meals daily
included in price

Each summer during August and September, Emandal, located along the Eel River in Willits, California, is open to families who want to enjoy the outdoors in a farm environment. The first part of the summer is devoted to the Children's Camp, where enhancing a young person's self-esteem is the primary goal.

▓ *Colorado*

—————————— ALMONT ——————————

Harmel's Ranch Resort
P.O. Box 399, 81210
Ph: 800-235-3402

Rate Code: Inexpensive-Moderate

Several flexible vacation packages available. The resort offers horseback riding, river rafting, mountain biking, fishing floats, chuck wagon cookouts, square dancing, children's program every afternoon, bingo, hayrides, trap fun events. From the youngest buckaroo to the most weathered cowboy, Harmel's has a mount and program for your horseback riding pleasure.

—————————— ASPEN ——————————

Crestahaus Lodge
1301 E Cooper Ave, 81611
Ph: 970-925-7081
Number of Rooms: 30

Rate Code: Inexpensive-Luxury
Services: Cross country ski trails,
Snowmobile tours, Outdoor saunas, Bike
trails, Horseback ridinng, Kayaking,
Rafting.

Discover a winter or summer wonderland at Crestahaus Lodge. Experience sunny warm days and cool, comfortable evenings, strolling the lively downtown mall area. Or spend your day on miles of scenic cross-country ski trails.

―――――――――――― **BAYFIELD** ――――――――――――

Wit's End Guest Ranch & Resort
254 County Rd 500 (Vallecito Lk),
   81122
Ph: 303-884-4113
Number of Rooms: 15

Rate Code: Luxury

Great way to enjoy the outdoors. Offerings include horseback riding, hayrides, campfire cookouts (with a supervised overnight cookout for kids), wilderness trail hikes, mountaintop motor tours, river and lake fishing, tennis, motor boat rides, swimming and hot tubs, and a children's program (for kids 4 and older) plus a children's activity center. Additional activities available for an extra charge.

―――――――――――― **BRECKENRIDGE** ――――――――――――

The Village at Breckenridge
P.O. Box 8329, 80424
Ph: 303-453-3159
800-332-0424
Fax: 303-453-1878
Number of Rooms: 306

Rate Code: Inexpensive-Moderate
Services: Indoor/outdoor heated pool, health club, medical clinic, guest services, underground, heated parking, outdoor education center.

Located only 90 minutes from Denver. There are year round activities to be enjoyed in Breckenridge. In the summer, play golf on the Jack Nicklaus deisgned course, horseback ride, or go rafting. In the winter, enjoy world-class skiing, ice skate on Maggie Pond, snowmobile, and much more.

―――――――――――― **CEDAREDGE** ――――――――――――

Alexander Lk & Thunder Mtn Lodges
P.O. Box 900, 81413
Ph: 303-856-6700
Fax: 970-856-7215

Rate Code: Inexpensive

In the winter there is snowmobiling, cross country skiing, downhill skiing, and ice fishing. In the summer there is horseback riding, fishing, biking and hiking with the beautiful scenery of Western Colorado. At any time of the year, the lodge offers a wonderful relaxed atmosphere everyone will enjoy.

―――――――――――― **COLORADO SPRINGS** ――――――――――――

The Broadmoor
1 Lake Circle, 80901
Ph: 719-577-5777
800-634-7711
Fax: 719-577-5779
Number of Rooms: 700

Rate Code: Inexpensive-Moderate
Services: Valet, barber shop, beauty shop, garage and parking, car hire, international currency exchange, house doctor, babysitting, laundry, card/game area, room service.

Morning to evening children's program called the Bee Bunch for ages 5 through 12. The Toddler Bee Bunch is designed for ages 3 through 4. There are zoo trips, games, paddle boating, scavenger hunts, and for the older children golf and tennis clinics. There are also evening activities offered.

―――――――――――― CORTEZ ――――――――――――

Kelly Place
14663 Road G, 81321
Ph: 303-565-3125   800-745-4885
Fax: 303-565-1232
Number of Rooms: 8

Rate Code: Luxury
Services: An outdoor educational facility with a relaxed, southwestern style. Services include classes, expiditions, tours and excursions.

Dedicated to providing a unique educational experience for the entire family. Activities include archaeology, botany, basketry, horseback riding, covered wagon trips, pioneer era activities, artist workshops and retreats. Family excursions include all lodging and meals and choice of three one-half day activities.

―――――――――――― DURANGO ――――――――――――

Tamarron
P.O. Box 3131, 81302
Ph: 303-259-2000   800-678-1000
Fax: 303-259-0745
Number of Rooms: 400

Rate Code: Inexpensive-Moderate
Services: Spa and health club, shops, unisex hair salon, free movies, complimentary breakfast.

The children's programs offers a full day (or evening) of activities: Hiking, exploring, games, arts and crafts. Kampfire Kids is an evening spent singing around a campfire, & roasting marshmallows.

―――――――――――― DURANGO ――――――――――――

Wilderness Trails Ranch
1766 County Rd 302, 81301
Ph: 970-247-0722
800-527-2624

Rate Code: Moderate-Luxury
Services: The Trading Post (the ranch store), Guest Laundry, and The Watering Hole (a great place to hang out).

Wilderness Trails Ranch is a very special place and offers a very special vacation. Our family and our staff are dedicated to making this your finest vacation ever. Families definitely love the Ranch. The kids and teens have special programs to see that they have a busy, fun-filled week.

―――――――――――― EDWARDS ――――――――――――

The Seasons — Arrowhead at Vail
0600 Sawatach Dr,
P.O. Box 1370, 81632
Ph: 970-926-8300   800-846-0233
Fax: 970-926-2390
Number of Rooms: 30

Rate Code: Inexpensive-Luxury

An excellent option for extended families sharing space for a Colorado ski or summer vacation. The Lodge is located on a private golf course designed by Jack Nicklaus. Situated within a gated residential community only 1.5 mi 12 miles from Vail, privacy and security are highlighted. The Lodge staff is glad to help visitors make their visit memorable.

―――――――――――― ESTES PARK ――――――――――――

Aspen Lodge at Estes Park
HC, 6120 Hwy 7, 80517
Ph: 800-332-6867   970-586-8133

A magnificent 3000-acre ranch resort celebrating Colorado's largest log lodge and cozy cabins with fantastic food and recreation and incredible views. Activities offered include horseback riding, hot tub, sauna, hayrides, BBQ racquetball, hikes, van tours, sleigh rides, and a great children's program.

─────────────── **ESTES PARK** ───────────────

Wind River Guest Ranch
P.O. Box 3410AC, 80517
Ph: 970-586-4212   800-523-4212

Rate Code: Moderate

A unique guest ranch combining rustic and antique Western charm with modern comforts — a great place for busy families to relax and get away from it all, near base of Longs Peak. Activities, instructional riding, children's programs and hayride. Rates include meals, activities, and lodging.

─────────────── **GRANBY** ───────────────

Drowsy Water Ranch
P.O. Box 147, 80446
Ph: 303-725-3456
800-845-2292

Rate Code: Luxury
Services: Horseback riding, swimming, horseshoes, steak frys, trout fishing, square dancing, Jeep trips, campfires, pack trips, movies, children's programs and more.

Drowsy Water Ranch is a genuine, western ranch on 640 acres in Colorado's beautiful Rocky Mountains, 1½ miles from the nearest paved highway. The children's programs are designed for age groups of 5 years and under and 6 years through teens.

─────────────── **GRAND LAKE** ───────────────

Grand Lake Lodge
P.O. Box 569, 80447
Ph: 970-759-5848
Number of Rooms: 55

Rate Code: Moderate-Luxury
Services: Private cabins, kitchenette, barbeque area, outdoor pool, a full service resort.

The Grand Lake Lodge was established in 1921 and has been owned by the Ted James Family since 1953. Our relaxed atmosphere and friendly service will ensure a pleasant visit for your group. Since we are surrounded by Rocky Mountain National Park, there are many activities to choose from—hiking, backpacking, fishing, boating, golf, tennis, horseback riding and more.

─────────────── **SHAWNEE** ───────────────

North Fork Guest Ranch
Box B, 80475
Ph: 303-838-9873   800-843-7895
Fax: 303-838-1549
Number of Rooms: 22

Rate Code: Moderate-Luxury
Services: Activities and meals included in one price, Private baths, Fireplace, Kids' playyard, Evening activities, High chairs/cots/cribs available

An all-inclusive family oriented ranch invites you for a week of western fun and hospitality. Ride in meadows filled with wildflowers at 8,000 ft. to a mountaintop for lunch. Days are action packed: whitewater rafting, fly-fishing, swimming, hiking, square dancing and more. Peaceful river setting, kids program, home-cooked meals. Lasting memories!

─────────────── **STEAMBOAT SPRINGS** ───────────────

Vista Verde Guest Ranch
P.O. Box 465, 80477
Ph: 303-879-3858
800-526-RIDE

Rate Code: Moderate-Luxury
Services: Adventures include: Cattle Drives, Hiking in the Rockies, Fly Fishing, Pack Trips, Golf, & much more.

The Vista Verde is a dude and guest ranch and by definition provides an inclusive package price for all meals, accommodations and activities. The experiences and settings are authentically western. We can tailor a vacation to suit individual needs with or without children.

VAIL

The Lodge at Vail
174 East Gore Creek Dr, 81657
Ph: 303-476-5011
800-331-LODG
Fax: 303-476-7425

Rate Code: Luxury
Services: Mountain balloon adventures, whitewater rafting, jeep tours, mountain biking, western adventures, fly-fishing, athletic training, salon treatments.

Whatever your pleasure, from a relaxing retreat for the whole family to an invigorating adventure for two, experience the natural alternative at The Lodge.

WINTER PARK

Snow Mountain Ranch
P.O. Box 169, 80482
Ph: 303-887-2152
Number of Rooms: 40

Rate Code: Inexpensive-Moderate
Services: Crafts center

A youth day camp will give your child 6 hours of unforgettable memories each day. Nature walks, games arts and crafts, and so much more. Your child is sure to enjoy his/her visit as much as you will.

🔲 *Florida*

AMELIA ISLAND

Ritz Carlton, Amelia Island
4750 Amelia Island Pkwy, 32034
Ph: 904-277-1100   800-241-3333
Fax: 904-277-1145
Number of Rooms: 449

Rate Code: Moderate
Services: Valet Parking, Valet, Car Rental, Secretarial, Boutiques

The children's program is "Ritz-Kids." A supervised summer program is offered for children 5 and over. The activites our often fitness oriented, but also offer beach scavenger hunts and movie matinees. Parents may also register their children in "Kid's Night Out," which features a children's menu for dinner, with movies and activities included.

BLUEWATER BAY

Niceville
1950 Bluewater Bay Blvd, 32578
Ph: 904-897-3613
800-874-2128
Fax: 904-897-2424

Rate Code: Inexpensive-Moderate

Recently rated one of America's top-ten family vacation resorts, supervised activities for children 3 through 12 are offered on a daily basis during the summer season. Evening programs are offered frequently for a small fee. Best bet for families is a Family Summer Fun Package.

BOCA RATON

Boca Raton Resort & Club
501 East Camino Real, 33432
Ph: 407-395-3000
800-327-0101
Fax: 407-391-3183

Rate Code: Moderate-Luxury

The resort's unique array of amenities, recreation and services provides the perfect backdrop to make any vacation memorable. Activities include golf, tennis, watersports, bicycling, racquetball and fitness centers. For kids, there are 4 choices of age-appropriate programs. Activities range from "I Wish I Were a Fish," to "Junior Olympics," to "Night Volleyball."

CAPTIVA ISLAND

South Seas Plantation
P.O. Box 194, 33924
Ph: 813-472-5111
800-237-3102
Fax: 813-472-7541
Number of Rooms: 500

Rate Code: Luxury
Services: Trolleys

Captiva Kids Club offers a creative program of activities for children ages 3-11 including arts & crafts and a close up look at Captiva Island wildlife. Activities include either lunch or dinner. Teenagers in Paradise—volleyball tournaments, pool parties, moonlight movies, specialized activities, sports, and more. The whole family can learn about local flora and fauna from a series of complimentary nature programs.

CLEARWATER

Belleview Mido Resort Hotel
25 Belleview Blvd, Box 2317, 34617
Ph: 813-442-6171   800-237-8947
Fax: 813-443-6361
Number of Rooms: 292

Rate Code: Moderate
Services: Golf course, pools, spa and fitness club, babysitting service, car and boat rentals, jogging course, free parking.

Everything you need is here. But should you wish to venture out, we are conveniently located near area attractions including Busch Gardens, Disney World, Sea World and Epcot Center.

DUCK KEY

Hawk's Cay Resort and Marina
Mile Marker 61, 33050
Ph: 305-743-7000   800-432-2242
Fax: 305-289-0651
Number of Rooms: 176

Rate Code: Moderate-Luxury
Services: Boutiques and speciality shops, most rooms have Ocean or Gulf views, each room has a mini-refrigerator, private balcony and separate dressing area.

Hawk's Cay is a 60-acre private island unlike any other. Our West Indies-style resort offers a quartet of dining experiences, tropical surrounding and attentive care. Our children's programs run year round on weekends and holidays. Activities include snorkeling, educating kids about dolphins through our on-site dolphin facility, fishing (catch & release program), water aerobics, and lagoon olympics.

FORT MYERS BEACH

Best Western Pink Shell Beach Rsrt
275 Estero Boulevard, 33931
Ph: 813-463-6181
800-237-5786
Fax: 813-463-1229
Number of Rooms: 208

Rate Code: Inexpensive-Luxury
Services: 3 heated pools, children's wading pool, shuffleboard, tennis, on-site rentals of bikes, boats, and waverunners, guest laundry rooms, outdoor bbq grills, lighted fishing pier.

A trained recreation staff offers a daily "camp" for kids of all ages, with varying activities such as water games, environmental learning games, beach crafts and pool bingo. The camp allows parents to drop their children off in the morning and enjoy time alone, or kids can pick out single activities to attend and spend the rest of the day with their family.

FT. LAUDERDALE

Bonaventure Spa & Fitness Resort
250 Racquet Club Road, 33326
Ph: 305-389-3300   800-327-8090
Fax: 305-348-0563
Number of Rooms: 500

Rate Code: Luxury
Services: Laundry and valet, secretarial, children's activities, shopping transportation, facilities for the handicapped.

This luxury resort is a combination hotel, health fitness spa and convention facility. Enjoy fine dining, go dancing or explore the intriguing possibilities of downtown. The BonAventurers is a discovery program for kids of all ages. Activities include face painting, mask making, creating stationary, cooking, hula hoop competition and more.

FT. MYERS

Sanibel Harbour Resort & Spa
17260 Harbour Point Dr, 33908
Ph: 941-466-4000
Fax: 941-466-6050
Number of Rooms: 340

Rate Code: Moderate-Luxury
Services: European spa and fitness facility, whirlpools, aerobics studio, indoor pool, 13 tennis courts, exercise facility.

The resort responds to families by catering activities just for them. The Kids Klub, with counselor-supervised activities, allow parents time to relax and enjoy the resort's amenities while their children participate in activities and excursions designed just for them. Or together, families can venture into downtown Ft. Myers to experience some of the many family attractions.

HOWEY-IN-THE-HILLS

Mission Inn Golf & Tennis
10400 County Road 48, 34737
Ph: 904-324-3101
800-874-9053
Fax: 904-324-2350
Number of Rooms: 187

Rate Code: Moderate-Luxury
Services: Valet, Garage and parking, Car hire, Babysitting, Card or other game area, Laundry, Room service

The mission Inn offers a full program of children's activities.

—— HUTCHINSON ISLAND ——

Indian River Plantation
385 NE Plantation Rd, 33996
Ph: 407-225-3700
800-444-3389
Fax: 407-225-3948
Number of Rooms: 326

Rate Code: Inexpensive-Luxury
Services: Cable TV, VCR, Radio, Hair
dryer, Wet-bar & refrigerator, Room
Service, Laundry

For children 3–12 there is the "Pineapple Bunch Children's Camp" which offers arts and crafts, beach and nature walks, excursions, swimming, field games, and bike hikes. For teenagers there is a game room, movie nights, parties, snorkeling, and golf and tennis instruction.

—— ISLAMORADA ——

Cheeca Lodge
Overseas Highway,
P.O. Box 527, 33036
Ph: 305-664-4651   800-327-2888
Fax: 305-664-2893
Number of Rooms: 203

Rate Code: Moderate-Luxury
Services: VCR's in-room, day and night
skin and scuba diving trips,

"Camp Cheeca" is a unique children's program centering on environmental awareness. The program is designed for 6-12 year olds and centers on the Florida Keys' natural habitats. Field trips are always an exciting part of the events with trips to the Dolphin Research Center, the coral reef state park, and other locations of interest.

—— KEY BISCAYNE ——

Sonesta Beach Hotel
350 Ocean Drive, 33149
Ph: 305-361-2021
800-SONESTA
Fax: 305-361-3096
Number of Rooms: 300

Rate Code: Moderate-Luxury
Services: Laundry and dry cleaning, mail
and postage facilities, concierge, social
director, business/meeting facilities.

We offer many services and facilities for families with children including bicycle rentals, jewelry classes, the sports court and baby-sitting. The "Just Us Kids" program is a year-round educational and entertaining program supervised by experienced couselors. The hotel concierge will be happy to assist the entire family with area tours and excursions.

—— KEY LARGO ——

Sheraton Key Largo Resort
97000 S Overseas Hwy MM97, 33037
Ph: 305-852-5553
800-826-1006
Fax: 305-852-5198
Number of Rooms: 200

Rate Code: Luxury

The resort has one of the Keys' largest private beaches. Available are jet skiing, parasailing, Hobie-catting, sailing, "snuba" (a combination of snorkeling and scuba-diving), sport fishing, glass bottom boat tours, and nature. The resort has a family pool, several restaurants, and the Keys Kids Club, a fully supervised children's recreation program for youngsters ages 5 thru 12 that offers fun and educational games and events.

KISSIMMEE

Holiday Inn Hotel & Suites
5678 I Bronson Memorial Hwy, 34746
Ph: 407-396-4488
800-HOLIDAY
Fax: 407-396-8915
Number of Rooms: 670

Rate Code: Inexpensive
Services: Free shuttle to all 3 Walt
Disney World theme parks, 2 swimming
pools, 2 whirlpool spas, 24-hour
security and welcome center, 2
playgrounds, heated kiddie pool.

When you stay with us at Holiday Inn Main Gate East, a world of fantasy is just minutes away. We're three miles from the Magic of Walt Disney World Resort, ten minutes from Sea World, and fifteen minutes from Universal Studios.

LAKE BUENA VISTA

Disney Institute
P.O. Box 10095, 32821
Ph: 407-827-7049
800-496-6337
Fax: 407-827-7454
Number of Rooms: 457

Rate Code: Luxury
Services: A broadcast-quality
performance center, outdoor
amphitheater, state-of-the-art-cinema,
closed-circuit TV and radio station,
sports and fitness center, full-service spa.

The first Disney resort planned exclusively for adults and families with older children. Guests will create their own schedule of activities, explore new interests, sharpen old skills and develop hidden talents. Some programs include Disney character drawing, rock climbing, riding the radio waves, culinary technique, the starving student, Disney architecture, sunrise nature walks, and much, much more.

LAKE BUENA VISTA

Holiday Inn SunSpree Resort
13351 S R 535,
P.O. Box 22184, 32830
Ph: 407-239-4500
800-HOLIDAY
Fax: 407-239-7713
Number of Rooms: 507

Rate Code: Inexpensive-Moderate
Services: All rooms include a
refrigerator, microwave and coffee/tea
maker. Heated pool, kiddie pool and
playground, fitness ceneter.

The SunSpree Resort is designed to offer family-friendly accommodations at mid-market value prices. The Service Desk will help families coordinate daily events and activities. Children from 2-12 can participate in Camp Holiday, a year-round, fully supervised, state-licensed child care and activity program.

MARATHON

Marathon Key Beach Club
4560 Overseas Highway, 33050
Ph: 305-743-6522

Rate Code: Moderate
Services: Each condo is equipped with
linens, dinnerware, cookware, utensils,
microwave, dishwasher, full size
appliances, and washer and dryer.

On our grounds are 2 tennis courts, swimming pool and a hot tub spa. We offer bar-b-que grills, picnic tables, board games, tennis rackets, puzzles, snorkel gear, volleyball, horseshoes and bicycles. The marina offers a put in/out boat ramp free of charge. Boat dockage, boat rental and other water equipment is available for a fee.

─────────────── **MIAMI** ───────────────

Turnberry Isle Country Club
19735 Turnberry Way, 33180
Ph: 305-932-6200
800-327-7028
Fax: 305-933-6560
Number of Rooms: 340

Rate Code: Moderate-Luxury
Services: Valet, barber shop, beauty shop, garage and parking, car hire, international currency exchange, house doctor, babysitting, card/game area, laundry, room service.

Turnberry Isle offers a Children's Program over the Christmas Holidays and summer vacation season.

─────────────── **MIAMI BEACH** ───────────────

Fontainebleau Hilton Resort
4441 Collins Avenue, 33140
Ph: 505-538-2000
800-932-3322
Fax: 305-534-7821
Number of Rooms: 1206

Rate Code: Luxury
Services: Health spa with professional supervised exercise, 28 shops, multi-lingual hosts, business center, water taxi, many area attractions, Resort Activities Program.

The Resort Activities Coordinators plan year round events geared to kids, teens, singles, adults and families. They provide recreational activities the entire family can enjoy. Whether the family wishes to play together or apart, our program offers a wide variety of entertaining options. In addition to activities located at the resort, we also offer supervised field trips for kids to local area attractions.

─────────────── **NAPLES** ───────────────

Naples Beach Hotel & Golf Club
851 Gulf Shore Blvd S, 33940
Ph: 813-261-2222   800-237-7600

Rate Code: Moderate-Luxury

─────────────── **NAVARRE BEACH** ───────────────

Holiday Inn — The Tropics
8375 Gulf Blvd, 32566
Ph: 904-939-2321
800-HOLIDAY
Number of Rooms: 250

You get the peace of mind that comes with knowing the kids have plenty to do. From the game room to the Tropics Pizzeria to the "Beach Brigade"—a special, complimentary program of fun activities just for the youngsters—guests enjoy their stay. You get to indulge in the whirlpool, relax on the sun deck by the swimming pool, get busy on the tennis courts, or enjoy one of the world's most beautiful beaches.

─────────────── **NICEVILLE** ───────────────

Bluewater Bay
1950 Bluewater Blvd, 32578
Ph: 904-897-3613
800-874-2128

Rate Code: Inexpensive-Moderate

Recently rated one of America's top ten family vacation resorts. Supervised activities for children 3–12 are offered on a daily basis during the summer season. Evening programs are offered frequently for a small fee. Best bet for families is a Family Fun Package.

―――――――――――――――― **ORLANDO**―――――――――――――――

Hyatt Regency Grand Cypress
1 Grand Cypress Blvd, 32819
Ph: 407-239-1234   800-228-9000
Fax: 407-239-3891
Number of Rooms: 750

Rate Code: Moderate-Luxury

Camp Hyatt children's program is open all year from 7 a.m. to 11 p.m. for 3 to 12 year-olds. An outdoor playground with sand toys, swings and climbers is offered along with indoor fun such as a real toy kitchen, marionette stage with puppets, arts and crafts, and plenty more.

―――――――――――――――― **PALM BEACH** ―――――――――――――――

The Breakers
One South County Rd, 33480
Ph: 407-655-6611   800-833-3141
Fax: 407-659-8403
Number of Rooms: 528

Rate Code: Moderate-Luxury
Services: Valet, Barber shop, Beauty shop, Car hire, International currency exchange, Nurse, Babysitting, Card/ Game area, Room service, Library

The Parrot Pack is for ages 3-5, from 9-11 a.m., arts & crafts, story telling and nature walks are only a small part of the program. The Coconut Crew is for the 6-12 group, from 9 a.m. to 3 p.m. Lunch is included and there are field trips, outdoor games, crafts and more. Summer sports camps are also a yearly feature.

―――――――――――――――― **SANIBEL ISLAND** ―――――――――――――――

Sanibel Island Beach Resort
3287 West Gulf Drive, 33957
Ph: 813-472-1700   800-645-6559
Fax: 813-472-5032
Number of Rooms: 13

Services: Large heated pool, Tennis court, 357 feet of white beach, BBQ grills and picnic tables.

Guests need only to step from their rooms to reach the warm tropical waters of the Gulf of Mexico. And for those who want to do a little exploring, bicycles for both children and adults are available.

―――――――――――――――― **SANIBEL ISLAND** ―――――――――――――――

Sundial Beach Resort
1451 Middle Gulf Drive, 33957
Ph: 813-472-4151
800-237-4184
Fax: 813-472-1809
Number of Rooms: 265

Rate Code: Moderate-Luxury
Services: 5 Swimming pools, Whirlpool spa, Fitness room, Tennis, Shuffleboard, Video game room, Bike, Catamaran, Kayak, and Canoe rentals, Environmental Coastal Observervation Center.

Quietly nestled among thirty-three lush tropical acres on sunny Sanibel Island, the Sundial Beach Resort offers picturesque views of the blue Gulf waters, and a beautiful expanse of shell-covered beach.

STEINHATCHEE

Steinhatchee Landing
P.O. Box 789, 32359
Ph: 904-498-3513
Fax: 904-498-2346
Number of Rooms: 20

Rate Code: Moderate-Luxury
Services: Fireplaces, spas and whirlpool
baths in some cottages. Private decks
with river views. Many outdoor
activities.

This gulf coast resort is reminiscent of a 19th century fishing village. Catering to the nature lover, there are many outdoor activities including hiking, canoeing, and scuba diving. There are more than 100 major springs in the area, many suitable for scub diving.

TARPON SPRINGS

Innisbrook Hilton Resort
P.O. Drawer 1088, 34688
Ph: 813-942-2000
800-456-2000
Fax: 813-942-5578
Number of Rooms: 1000

Rate Code: Moderate-Luxury
Services: Golf, fine dining, tennis,
swimming, fishing,

Family packages included the Preferred Golf Package which allows kids under 18 to play on the course with their parents. The Relax Under The Sun Package allows children under 17 to stay free and enjoy the same recreational privileges as Mom and Dad. The Zoo Crew is a year round supervised children's program for children ages 4-12. Activities include excursions, games, arts and crafts. For teenagers there are dances and pool parties.

▦ Georgia

JEKYLL ISLAND

Jekyll Island Club Hotel
371 Riverview Drive, 31527
Ph: 912-635-2600
800-333-3333
Fax: 912-635-2818
Number of Rooms: 134

Rate Code: Moderate
Services: Sightseeing and recreational
activities are available every day, multi-
lingual staff, guest laundry, concierge.

Club Juniors for ages 5–12 is offered June through August on weekdays. Activities include bicycle safaris, crabbing, kite flying, mini-golf, handcrafts, and trips to Summer Waves Water Park and much, much more.

LAKE LANIER ISLANDS

Renaissance PineIsle Resort
9000 Holiday Road, 30518
Ph: 770-945-8921
800-468-3571
Fax: 770-945-0351
Number of Rooms: 250

Rate Code: Moderate
Services: Valet, Library, Parking, Car
hire, Complimentary shoeshine, House
doctor, Babysitting, Card or other game
area, Laundry, Room service, 45 minutes
to downtown Atlanta

An unbeatable white sand beach for unlimited castle-building and a special "Kids Knew" program ensure that children will have the time of their lives. 45 minutes north of downtown Atlanta.

PINE MOUNTAIN

Callaway
U.S. Highway 27, 31822
Ph: 706-663-2281
800-282-8181 Fax: 706-663-5080
Number of Rooms: 800

Rate Code: Inexpensive-Luxury
Services: Butterfly center, Horticultural center, Country store, Conference Center

Our Summer Family Adventure program is available in the summer and covers from ages 1 to 18. The programs are professionally supervised and offer a wide and imaginative variety of activities. There is also a game room with ping-pong, electronic games, and a disc jockey for a weekly dance. There are also twice weekly movies.

STONE MOUNTAIN

Comfort Inn Stone Mountain
5355 Stone Mountain Highway, 30087
Ph: 770-465-1888
Fax: 770-465-3424
Number of Rooms: 69

Rate Code: Inexpensive–Moderate
Services: Cribs, Children under 12 free, Cable TV, Movie channels, Hair dryer, Alarm clock/radio, Coffee/tea service, Data ports, Safe, Iron/ironing board, Microwave, Refrigerator, Free continental breakfast, Free parking, Laundry service, Rollaways, Safe deposit

Come! Discover Stone Mountain Park. Enjoy fourteen attractions and the world's largest granite monolith. Experience the wonder of the Yellow River Game Ranch, Georgia's premier animal attraction. Visit the Village of Stone Mountain and browse the unique shops, restaurants, and museums. New! Comfort Inn at Stone Mountain, the closest to the park.

▦ Hawaii

HONOLULU

Sheraton Moana Surfrider
2365 Kalakaua Avenue, 96815
Ph: 808-931-8425   808-931-8409
Fax: 808-922-9567
Number of Rooms: 793

Rate Code: Moderate-Luxury
Services: Fitness center, Freshwater pool, Valet parking, Limousine service, Children's play area.

The Victorian elegance of the "First Lady of Waikiki" has been completely and lovingly restored, from her grand porte cochere to her Palladian windows and her sweeping Banyan Veranda overlooking the Pacific. Enjoy a seasonal beach BBQ or a Shiatsu massage.

HONOLULU, OAHU

Hilton Hawaiian Village
2005 Kalia Road, 96815
Ph: 808-949-4321   800-445-8667
Fax: 808-947-7898
Number of Rooms: 2543

Rate Code: Moderate-Luxury
Services: Shops, 1-acre super pool

A year round kid's program that is free! The program is for children 3–12 years old. They offer a children's olympics, bird shows, a cruise, treasure hunts, storytelling, games and many excursions to local spots of interest. Lunch and snacks are all part of the offering.

HONOLULU, OAHU

Kahala Hilton
5000 Kahala Avenue, 96816
Ph: 808-734-2211   800-367-2525
Fax: 808-737-2478
Number of Rooms: 369

Rate Code: Moderate-Luxury
Services: 24-hour room service,
Secretarial & courier services, Health
club, Conference Center, baby-sitting

"Kamp Kahala" is a day camp for 6 to 12 years of age, during the summer and holiday vacation weeks. There are excursions, Hawaiian games, mask making, sand castle building, sand painting, and much more.

KAILUA-KONA, HAWAII

Kona Village Resort
P.O. Box 1299, 96745
Ph: 808-325-5555
800-367-5290
Fax: 808-325-5124
Number of Rooms: 125

Rate Code: Luxury
Services: Thatched hales (cottages) in 9
architectural styles representing the
major island cultures of ancient
Polynesia. No room telephones, radios
or televisions.

A secluded paradise offering something for every member of the family. Area attractions include parks, museums and of course, beaches. Take a helicopter tour, dive in the unspoiled waters off the Big Island, play tennis or fish. Kids will learn about Hawaii's culture, crafts and games in the children's program "Keikis in Paradise."

KAPALIA, MAUI

Ritz Carlton, Kapalua
1 Ritz Carlton Drive, 96761
Ph: 808-669-6200
800-262-8400
Fax: 808-669-3908
Number of Rooms: 550

Rate Code: Luxury
Services: 24-hour room service, baby-
sitting, transportation to/from airport,
full service beauty salon, executive
business services, safe deposit boxes.

This ocean-front hotel is located on 37 acres of historic land. Recreational facilities include 3 championship golf courses, 10 tennis courts, a 3-tiered cascading swimming pool and a secluded beach. The Ritz Kids program gives children a fun, action-packed day while parents relax and enjoy the resort. The full and half day programs are distincly Hawaiian. Kids hunt for shells, build sandcastles, learn the hula and make jewelry with shells.

KAPOLEI

Ihilani Resort & Spa
92-1001 'Olani Street, 96707
Ph: 808-679-0079
800-626-4446
Fax: 808-679-0080
Number of Rooms: 387

Rate Code: Luxury
Services: Lagoon, Spa, Golf course,
Tennis, Mini-bars, Air-conditioning.

We offer travelers a comprehensive list of vacation plans to enjoy all year. Children will be treated like their parents, with freedom, fun and all the amenities. The Keiki Beachcomber Club is an extensive, thoughtful and dynamic supervised children's program designed to please young guests between the ages of 4 and 12.

──────────── KIHEI, MAUI ────────────

Maui Prince Hotel
5400 Makena Alanui, 96753
Ph: 808-874-1111
800-321-6284
Number of Rooms: 310

Rate Code: Luxury
Services: Valet, garage and parking, car
hire, international currency exchange,
house doctor, babysitting, laundry,
robes, newspaper, room service

The Prince Kids Club is for kids ages 4-12, and is open from 9 a.m.-12 noon. Activities include hula lessons, bamboo pole fishing, sand castle building, nature walks, kite flying and much more. The Saturday night movies are an additional treat.

──────────── KOHALA COAST ────────────

Ritz-Carlton Mauna Lani
1 North Kaniku Drive, 96743
Ph: 808-885-2000
800-241-3333
Fax: 808-885-1064
Number of Rooms: 541

Rate Code: Luxury
Services: Valet Parking, Valet, Car
Rental, Secretarial, Boutiques

The children's program is "Ritz-Kids." A supervised summer program is offered for children 4-12. The activites are often fitness-oriented, but also offer beach scavenger hunts and movie matinees. Parents may also register their children in "Kid's Night Out", which features a children's menu for dinner, with movies and activities included. Ask about The Great Hawaiian Vacation Package.

──────────── KOHALA COAST ────────────

The Royal Waikoloan
69-275 Waikaloa Beach Dr
Kamuela, 96743
Ph: 800-688-7444
303-369-7777
Fax: 800-622-4852

Rate Code: Moderate-Luxury

Hawaii's only all-inclusive resort, the Fantasy Vacation package includes meals, luau and Polynesian show, unlimited beverages, botanical tour, ancient petroglyph tour, lei making and Hawaiian crafts, daily cultural series, entertainment, use of fitness center, tennis lessons, and more, plus catamaran and snorkel sails, and a variety of beach and water activities and equipment. Tips and taxes included.

──────────── LAHAINA, MAUI ────────────

Hyatt Regency Maui
200 Nohea Kai Drive, 96761
Ph: 808-661-1234   800-233-1234
Fax: 808-667-4498
Number of Rooms: 815

Rate Code: Luxury
Services: Concierge, in-room safe,
church services, recreational activities,
game room and library, water sports,
health club.

Recreational activities include aqua volleyball and water excercise classes in the half-acre swimming pool with a 150 foot waterslide. Guests can snorkel, sail, golf, bike or work out in the health club. Camp Hyatt is a daily supervised activity program for children ages 3–12. Rock Hyatt offers social, sports and off-property excursions for teens ages 13–17.

─────────────── **LANA'I CITY** ───────────────

The Lodge at Koele
P.O. Box 774, 96763
Ph: 808-565-7300   800-223-7637
Fax: 808-565-4561
Number of Rooms: 102

Rate Code: Luxury
Services: Library, music room, Hawaiian
artifact room, tea room, tennis,
swimming pool, croquet, lawn bowling,
hiking, horseback riding.

The Lodge at Koele combines the charm and refined atmosphere of a traditional English country manor, with the special allure and breath-taking natural beauty of Lana'i, Hawaii's best kept secret.

─────────────── **LANA'I CITY** ───────────────

The Manele Bay Hotel
P.O. Box 774, 96763
Ph: 808-565-7300   800-223-7637
Fax: 808-565-4561
Number of Rooms: 250

Rate Code: Luxury
Services: Jeep trips, deep sea fishing,
sailing, whale watching, cycling, cruises
to other islands, scuba diving.

Luxuriant, multi-level gardens with waterfalls and ponds, and an infinite variety of exotic plants and flowers, offer a colorful diversion and a romantic, private setting.

─────────────── **MAUI** ───────────────

Kea Lani Hotel Suites & Villas
4100 Wailea Alanui, Wailea, 96753
Ph: 808-875-4100 Fax: 808-875-2247
Number of Rooms: 440

Rate Code: Luxury

Keiki Lani, the resort's children's program, offers sports, nature hikes, storytelling, kite flying and crafts. Daily activities are supervised by an accredited staff for children ages 5 and up. One time enrollment fee of $10 per child which includes a Keiki Lani logo T-shirt.

─────────────── **THE BIG ISLAND, HAWAII** ───────────────

Mauna Kea Beach Hotel
One Mauna Kea Beach Dr, 96743
Ph: 808-882-7222   800-882-6060
Fax: 808-882-7657
Number of Rooms: 310

Rate Code: Luxury
Services: Private lanai, Refrigerator,
Conference Center, Fresh flower lei

The children's program operates from mid-June to the end of summer and Christmas and Easter holidays. The program is free and is for ages 6 through 11. The morning is generally the time for the most active events, with movies and crafts in the afternoon. There is also an evening program which includes dinner.

─────────────── **THE BIG ISLAND, HAWAII** ───────────────

Mauna Lani Bay Hotel
One Mauna Lani Drive, 96743
Ph: 808-885-6622   800-327-8585
Fax: 808-885-1484
Number of Rooms: 350

Rate Code: Luxury
Services: Health Spa, Sauna, Massage,
Conference rooms, shops, Medical clinic

The children's activities, Camp Mauna Lani Bay, is for ages 5–12, and is free. The camp is run daily in the summer, and during Christmas and Easter. Hawaiian arts and crafts, water sports and fishing are just a few of the offerings. The hours are 9 a.m. to 3 p.m. and 5 to 11 p.m..

WAIKIKI

Sheraton Hotels In Waikiki
Ph: 800-782-9488

Rate Code: Moderate-Luxury

The "Keiki Aloha Children's Program" is open to young guests ages 5 thru 12 staying at any of the Sheraton Hotels in Waikiki and is free of charge. Offered year-round, the program includes a special children's activity cente TV area and library. Activities include movies, dances, Hawaiian story-telling, board games, water/beach sports, kite flying, shell collecting, arts and crafts, and excursions to popular attractions.

WAILEA, MAUI

Four Seasons Resort Wailea
3900 Wailea Alanui, 96753
Ph: 808-874-8000   800-334-6284
Fax: 808-874-6449
Number of Rooms: 380

Rate Code: Luxury
Services: Full health club Twice daily maid service, Overnight shoe shine, Orchid lei greeting, Conference rooms

Kids For All Seasons is truly offered in all seasons! The program is free and runs from 9 in the morning to 5 in the afternoon, for ages 5–12. Hula dancing, Hawaiian craft making, and Hawaiian songs are only a few of the activities offered.

WAILEA, MAUI

Stouffer Wailea Beach Resort
3550 Wailea Alanui, 96753
Ph: 808-879-4900
800-992-4532
Fax: 808-874-5370
Number of Rooms: 347

Rate Code: Luxury
Services: Newspaper, morning coffee, complimentary shuttle, comlimentary fitness center, room service, parking, boutique, beauty salon, babysitting, laundry.

Camp Wailea is a supervised children's program offered year round at a nominal fee.

WAIMEA

Waimea Plantation Cottages
P.O. Box 367, 96796
Ph: 808-338-1625
800-9-WAIMEA
Fax: 808-338-1619
Number of Rooms: 48

Rate Code: Moderate-Luxury
Services: Adult and kiddie pool, two-acre grass courtyards, tennis courts, baby-sitting services. Cottage amenities include full kitchens, stereos, cable tv, large tubs and showers.

A welcome retreat for travellers looking for a unique vacation experience that is reminiscent of Hawaii in the early 1900s.

▦ *Idaho*

─────────────── MCCALL ───────────────

Bear Creek Lodge
MM I 49 Highway 55, 83654
Ph: 208-634-3551

Rate Code: Moderate-Luxury
Services: There are a variety of activities depending on the season. We will assist you in making reservations for such activities as skiing, river rafting, fishing trips and more.

Bear Creek Lodge is the newest and most unique lodging accommodations in the McCall area. There are 65 acres of beautiful meadows, views of the surrounding snow-capped mountains and of course, Bear Creek meandering through the meadows.

─────────────── PRIEST LAKE ───────────────

Hill's Resort, Inc.
HCR5 Box 162A, 83856
Ph: 208-443-2551 Fax: 208-443-2363

Nestled in the majestic wilderness of North Idaho on Priest Lake, Hill's Resort has been providing unique quality retreats and family vacations since 1946. Its facilities have been recognized nationally, and "Better Homes & Gardens" magazine has called it an outstanding family resort. Cross-country skiing is its main winter focus, with fishing, lake activities, and hiking and biking enjoyable the rest of the year.

▦ *Illinois*

─────────────── GALENA ───────────────

Eagle Ridge Inn & Resort
P.O. Box 777, 61036
Ph: 800-323-8421   800-892-2269
Fax: 815-777-0445
Number of Rooms: 280

Rate Code: Moderate
Services: Childrens program, game room.

The youth program is offered for ages 3 to 12, and has full- and half-day programs. There is also a Kids Night Klub with a fully equiped playroom, movies, crafts and even sleeping mats. The teens also have group games such as volleyball, boating and horseback riding on site, and Alpine slider outings, movies and bowling.

▦ *Maine*

─────────────── OGUNQUIT ───────────────

Pink Blossoms Family Resort
66 Shore Rd, P.O. Box 763, 03907
Ph: 207-646-7397

Rate Code: Inexpensive-Luxury

Here families can relax in comfort within easy strolling distance of Maine's most beautiful beach, visiting galleries, shops, fine restaurants, the harbor of Perkins Cove, the famous Ogunquit Playhouse, or fine golf courses. The units are luxurious, the grounds designed to create a relaxing atmosphere. Picnics and BBQs, swimming and garden walks are some of the activities available to guests.

─────────── ROCKPORT ───────────

Samoset Resort
P.O. Box 78, 04856
Ph: 207-594-2511
800-341-1650
Number of Rooms: 150

Rate Code: Inexpensive-Moderate
Services: Valet, Garage and Parking,
Card or other game area, Room service

Children need a vacation, too, and they'll be happy campers Monday to Saturday at Samo-camp.

▦ **Massachusetts**

─────────── BOSTON ───────────

Boston Park Plaza Hotel
64 Arlington St, 02116
Ph: 617-426-2000
800-899-2076
Fax: 617-654-1999

Rate Code: Moderate
Services: Four restaurants, Fitness
Facilities, Gift shops, Pharmacy, Men's
bootery, Jewelry shop, Airline offices,
Car Rental, 24-hour room service, Cable
TV, Lounge.

One of the country's finest family-owned hotels, we make family travel affordable and fun with our popular Cub Club, one of Boston's best family values. Located in the heart of downtown Boston.

─────────── BOSTON ───────────

Le Meridien
250 Franklin St, 02110
Ph: 617-451-1900
800-543-4300
Fax: 617-423-2844
Number of Rooms: 326

Rate Code: Moderate-Luxury
Services: Indoor swimming pool,
whirlpool, sauna, health club amenities,
24-hour room service, florist, express
ironing.

Families are encouraged to spend the weekend at Le Meridien and take advantage of our special amenities just for children. A unique package provides an adjoining room for kids. Milk and cookies are offered in rooms upon check in, and a number of games for all ages are available at the Concierge.

─────────── NEW SEABURY ───────────

New Seabury
P.O. Box. 549, 02649
Ph: 508-477-9111
800-999-9033
Fax: 508-477-9790
Number of Rooms: 291

Rate Code: Inexpensive-Moderate
Services: Boutiques, Some private pools

The children's activities are divided into three different age groups: Ages 4-5 years old are called "Summersalts", and offer half and full days with swimming instruction and arts and crafts. Ages 6-13 are called "Adventurers", and meet from 9 to 3 on weekdays, the activities have a theme week with a t-shirt at the end. "Teen Challenge" gives sailing, golf, karate, and tennis lessons. The fees are quite reasonable.

—————————— **WEST DENNIS** ——————————

Lighthouse Inn
02670
Ph: 508-398-2244
Number of Rooms: 61

Rate Code: Moderate-Luxury
Services: Recreation room

Lighthouse Inn has a full morning program for children, and also offers evening interntainment. The program is designed for ages 3 to 9, and offers the children a fully varied and exciting vacation experience.

▦ Michigan

—————————— **ACME** ——————————

Grand Traverse Resort
P.O. Box 404, 49610
Ph: 616-938-2100
800-253-7350
Fax: 616-938-2399
Number of Rooms: 750

Rate Code: Inexpensive-Luxury
Services: Barber shop, beauty shop, parking, car hire, international currency exchange, babysitting, card/game area, room service.

During summer the children's program is offered every Saturday from 10 a.m. to 6 p.m. Half-day programs also available. During the fall and winter the program is offered Tuesday thru Saturday. Activities such as Tie Dye T-shirts, Jewelry and Friendship Bracelet making, Super Swim, and Sat. Night Carnival are a few of the choices. Fees vary depending on the program chosen.

—————————— **WALLOON LAKE** ——————————

Springbrook Hills
P.O. Box 19, 49796
Ph: 616-535-2227

This resort offers a several programs suitable for families: snowmobile and skiing packages in the winter, canoeing, fishing and golfing packages in the spring/summer/fall, and their speciality — mushroom outings in the spri Billed as a family resort, Springbrook Hills has evening campfire activities, a complete playground, and a heated pool with lifeguard on duty daily.

▦ Minnesota

—————————— **ALEXANDRIA** ——————————

Arrowwood — A Radisson Resort
2100 Arrowwod Ln,
P.O. Box 639, 56308
Ph: 612-762-1124   800-333-3333
Fax: 612-762-0133

An award-winning resort, the facility offers Camp Arrowwood for kids ages 4-12 with adult-supervised activities that include horse-drawn wagon rides, nature walks, arts & crafts, fishing, swimming, and horseback riding. For the family there are beach bonfires, sunset cruises on Lake Darling, a rodeo, and a family beach cookout in addition to numerous other sporting and outdoor activities.

―――――――――――――― NISSWA ――――――――――――――

Grand View Lodge Golf & Tennis
S 134 Nokomis, 56468
Ph: 800-345-9625
Number of Rooms: 98

Rate Code: Inexpensive-Moderate
Services: Guided walk, babysitting, TV room

Their is no charge for the kid's programs. It is offered for 3 to 13 year olds, and has a camp-style program. An evening session offers beach dinners and movies. Some activities for the older kids are trips to the water slides, earth ball games, golf and tennis lessons, and sporting events. There are also pool tables and video games in the game room.

▦ Missouri

―――――――――――― LAKE OF THE OZARKS ――――――――――――

Lodge of the Four Seasons
P.O. Box 215E, 65049
Ph: 314-365-3001   800-843-5253
Number of Rooms: 350

Rate Code: Inexpensive-Moderate
Services: Full health and fitness center, Full service beauty salon, Massage

Baby-sitting is provided, and a host of children's activities are geared for the younger set, such as cookouts, nature walks, and arts and crafts hours.

▦ Montana

―――――――――――――――― UTICA――――――――――――――――

Circle Bar Guest Ranch
HCR 81, PO Box 61, 59452
Ph: 406-423-5454   888-570-0227
Fax: 406-423-5686
Number of Rooms: 15

Rate Code: Luxury
Services: 3 meals daily, Bath/shower, Compl. laundry soap, Library, Use of own horse for the week

The Circle Bar Guest Ranch is located in the heart of "Big Sky Country" and is surrounded by a national forest and a state elk preserve. It is a full-service working ranch with horseback riding, trout fishing behind your cabin, and all the amenities of a first-class ranch. Pack trips are available.

▦ Nevada

―――――――――――――――― LAS VEGAS ――――――――――――――――

Hard Rock Hotel Las Vegas
4455 Paradise Rd, 98109
Ph: 702-693-5000 800-HRD-ROCK
Fax: 702-693-5010
Number of Rooms: 340

Rate Code: Inexpensive-Luxury
Services: 24-hour room service, European-style concierge, baby-sitting, Beach Club, Athletic Club.

Built on the site adjacent to the ever-popular Hard Rock Cafe, the hotel features a state-of-the-art concert facility, unique sand-bottom lagoon pool and sand beach, music-inspired gambling chips and slot machines which will raise money to save the rainforest. It also houses the largest collection of memorabilia from the worlds of music, entertainment and sports.

Harrah's at Lake Tahoe
P.O. Box 10, 89504
Ph: 800-648-3773
Number of Rooms: 540

Rate Code: Moderate-Luxury

Kids will love the all-new indoor playground where they can enjoy two levels of slides, ball pools, climbing areas, games of skill and the latest, coolest and most rad video and pinball games ever. The new Family Fun Center is a safe, well-lit, non-smoking and alcohol-free environment.

▓ *New Hampshire*

—————————————— DIXVILLE NOTCH ——————————————

The Balsams
03576
Ph: 603-255-3400   800-255-0800
Fax: 603-255-4221
Number of Rooms: 232

Rate Code: Moderate-Luxury
Services: Two golf courses, tennis courts, heated pool, hiking trails, ice skating rink, snowboarding, snowshoeing.

A staff naturalist directs a daily program of walks, hikes, picnic tours, discussions and other presentations focused on the natural wonders found at The Balsams. The professionally staffed children's program called Camp Wind Whistle provides activities for kids.

—————————————— FRANCESTOWN ——————————————

Tory Pines Resort
Box 655, Route 47, 03043
Ph: 603-588-2000 Fax: 603-588-2275
Number of Rooms: 44

Rate Code: Inexpensive-Luxury
Services: 18 hole golf course, Golf School, Cable TV, Air-conditioning.

Located just 90 minutes from Boston, our Resort is situated on 780 acres of designated forest preserve and game sanctuary in the heart of the Monadnock Region. The panoramic views of the Crotched Mountain are breathtaking. Nearby, there is exceptional summer theater and concerts to enjoy, as well as unique shops.

—————————————— HOLDERNESS ——————————————

Rockywold-Deephaven Camps
P.O. Box B, 03245
Ph: 603-968-3313
Number of Rooms: 60

Rate Code: Moderate
Services: Library-sitting rooms

A supervised children's program that's split into two groups: ages 3–5, and 6–13. The older children go on picnics, hiking, and field trips. And often enjoy watching movies.

—————————————— LYME ——————————————

Loch Lyme Lodge
70 Orford Rd., 03768
Ph: 800-423-2141   603-795-2141

Rate Code: Inexpensive-Luxury

Billed as a rustic vacation spot, Loch Lyme offers no phones, no TV, no hot tubs, but plenty of fresh air, clean water, stars in a clear sky at night, and 125 acres of fields and woodlands with ample play opportunities. Activities include swimming, fishing, and boating at the lake and numerous outdoor games and play areas on the grounds.

---------------------------- **WATERVILLE VALLEY** ----------------------------

Waterville Valley Resort
PO Box 540, Town Square, 03215
Ph: 603-236-8311
800-468-2553
Fax: 603-236-4344
Number of Rooms: 425

Rate Code: Inexpensive-Moderate
Services: Children's menu, Evening entertainment, Kid's playroom, Kid's playyard, Childcare in winter for children 6 months to 4 years

Enjoy year-round recreation in a spectacular White Mountain setting. Waterville Valley, New Hampshire's premier ski and snowboard resort, includes a top ranked snow sports school, Nordic skiing, and snowshoeing. A value packed summer lodging package includes golf, tennis, boating, mountain biking, and Summer Recreation Camps for children ages 4—16. Indoor ice skating, hiking, and a town recreation department rounds out family activities.

▥ New Jersey

---------------------------- **EAST BRUNSWICK** ----------------------------

Brunswick Hilton & Towers
3 Tower Center Blvd, 08816
Ph: 908-828-2000   800-HILTONS
Fax: 908-828-6958

Rate Code: Inexpensive
Services: Fitness center, indoor pool, continental breakfast.

The Brunswick Hilton is ideally located near many major summer attractions including the university towns of New Brunswick and Princeton, the Jersey Shore, Liberty Science Center, the Statue of Liberty, Ellis Island, and Six Flags Great Adventure.

---------------------------- **LONG BRANCH** ----------------------------

Ocean Place Hilton Resort
One Ocean Boulevard, 07740
Ph: 908-571-4000   800-932-3322
Fax: 908-571-3314
Number of Rooms: 255

Rate Code: Moderate-Luxury
Services: Full service spa, Conference rooms, Massage

Kids Camp Fun has treasure walks, movies and popcorn, games and races, sand castle building, story time and more. The hours are from 9:30 a.m. to 8 p.m. and is for ages 4—12. There is a fee.

▥ New Mexico

---------------------------- **ANGEL FIRE** ----------------------------

The Legends Hotel at Angel Fire
P.O. Drawer B, 87710
Ph: 505-377-6401
800-633-7463
Number of Rooms: 157

Rate Code: Moderate
Services: Spa with indoor swimming pool, hot tub and exercise equipment, apres ski lounge, gift shop and game room, fine art gallery.

At Angel Fire you're surrounded by a friendly family atmosphere and warm Southwestern hospitality. Ski programs include Family Renunion where family members learn how to ski together. Family Practice is for families of experienced skiers. Programs at The Children's Ski Center are perfect for kids ages 3—12.

▨ New York

──────── AT BOLTON LANDING ────────

The Sagamore
On Lake George, 12814
Ph: 518-644-9400
800-358-3585
Fax: 518-644-2851
Number of Rooms: 350

Rate Code: Inexpensive-Luxury
Services: Concierge, shoeshine, valet parking, games room, laundry, hair salon, upervised children's program, complimentary island transportation, room service.

Our children's program, "Sagamore Teepee Club" is run by childcare professionals and staffed by teachers and college students majoring in elementary education. A child is guided in developing an interest in the arts, discovering nature, and learning new athletic abilities.

──────── COOPERSTOWN ────────

The Otesaga Hotel
P.O. Box 311, 13326
Ph: 607-547-9931
800-348-6222
Fax: 607-547-9675
Number of Rooms: 138

Rate Code: Moderate-Luxury
Services: Golf, tennis, pool or lake swimming, sailing, canoeing, power boating, deep sea fishing, sports facility, aerobics, basketball, bowling, technical climbing.

The surrounding landscape of The Otesaga Hotel offers magical landscape, history and a variety of recreation to our guests. Visit The Farmers Museum, The National Baseball Hall of Fame and The Fenimore House.

──────── LAKE PLACID ────────

Holiday Inn Sunspree Resort
1 Olympic Drive, 12946
Ph: 518-523-2556
800-874-1980
Fax: 518-523-9410
Number of Rooms: 209

Rate Code: Inexpensive-Moderate
Services: Complete health club, indoor pool, sauna, tennis courts, professional putting green. Guest rooms include microwaves, refrigerators and coffee makers.

Home of the 1932 and 1980 Olympic Winter Games, the town of Lake Placid offers a world of recreation and events for visitors to the area. Skiing, hiking, skating, mountain biking, golf, fishing, are just a few of the activities that have made this region of the Adirondacks an "all season" destination. Ask about the Gold Medal Pass which includes lodging, unlimited skiing and skating, a bobsled ride and much more.

──────── NEW PALTZ ────────

Mohonk Mountain House
Lake Mohonk, 12561
Ph: 914-255-1000   800-772-6646
Fax: 914-256-2161
Number of Rooms: 275

Rate Code: Inexpensive-Luxury
Services: Laundry room

The children's activities center around nature and outdoor events. The program for 2- to 4-year-olds is the only exception, with most of the activities indoors, with an occasional outing. Children from 5 to 12 are separated into three different groups. And the program is from 9:30-12:30 and again from 2 to 5. Evening entertainments are also available. There are no teen programs or for the under two-year-olds.

─────────────── NEW YORK ───────────────

Le Parker Meridien
118 West 57th St, 10019
Ph: 212-245-5000
800-543-4300
Fax: 212-307-1776
Number of Rooms: 700

Rate Code: Luxury
Services: Renowned fitness center,
Racquetball, Squash, Indoor pool,
Sundeck, Complimentary shoe shine,

Each aspect of Le Parker Meridien reflects its grand European heritage. Le Parker has an exquisite view of Central Park, New York's most beautiful attraction.

─────────────── SILVER BAY ───────────────

Silver Bay Association
12874
Ph: 518-543-8833
Number of Rooms: 265

Rate Code: Moderate
Services: Crafts workshop for pottery,
weaving, jewelry-making,
leatherworking, stained glass,
photography, and silkscreening

The kid's program is open Monday through Friday. Programs are designed around age groupings and children from infants to high schoolers all have activities designed to satisfy their interests.

▩ North Carolina

─────────────── ASHEVILLE ───────────────

Grove Park Inn & Country Club
290 Macon Avenue, 28804
Ph: 704-252-2711   800-438-5800
Fax: 704-253-7053
Number of Rooms: 510

Rate Code: Inexpensive-Moderate
Services: In-room safe, Meeting rooms,
Full health center

The children's day programs start in late May and continue through Labor Day, and are held every Saturday year-round. The programs are fully supervised and offered in two groups: ages 3 to 5, and 6 to 11. The fee for the program includes meals. Sessions are from 9:30 in the morning until 4:30 in the afternoon. Fridays and Saturdays also have evening sessions, which include pizza parties, night swimming, campfires, and face painting.

─────────────── ATLANTIC BEACH ───────────────

Sheraton Atlantic Beach Resort
Salter Path Rd, P.O. Box 3040, 28512
Ph: 800-624-8875   252-240-1155
Fax: 252-240-1452

Atlantic Beach is surrounded by attractions such as golf, fishing, and boating. Historical buffs and shoppers alike will marvel over the quaint town of Beaufort, Fort Macon, and the North Carolina Aquarium. The family will love nature walks and amusement parks. A premiere oceanfront resort, it is located on 1,200 feet of white sandy beaches.

FONTANA DAM

Fontana Dam and Village Resort
State 28, 28733
Ph: 704-498-2211   800-849-2258
Fax: 704-498-2209
Number of Rooms: 300

Rate Code: Inexpensive

Their are activities such as horseback riding, craft classes, badminton and archery designed for the small children in your group.

▥ Oregon

BEND

Rock Springs Guest Ranch
64201 Tyler Rd, 97701
Ph: 800-225-3833   541-382-1957
Fax: 541-382-7774

Rate Code: Moderate

The property offers terrain varying from rimrocks and high desert plateaus to lush meadows and creeks, plus numerous lakes for fishing and other activities. Horseback riding is available for all levels of ability. The day camp includes such activities as riding, outdoor games, nature walks, swimming, sports, arts & crafts, overnight camp-out, folklore and storytelling, and playgrounds and playhouse.

DIAMOND LAKE

Diamond Lake Resort
97731
Ph: 503-793-3333   800-733-7593
Number of Rooms: 93

Rate Code: Inexpensive-Moderate
Services: Snowboarding, Cross country skiing, Ice skating.

Open 365 days a year, we are Oregon's finest multiple use resort. Diamond Lake is nestled in the heart of the Umpqua National Forest at the feet of three volcanoes. There are year round activities to enjoy from fishing, camping, hiking and skiing.

SUNRIVER

Sunriver Lodge and Resort
Highway 97, 97707
Ph: 503-593-1221   800-547-3922
Number of Rooms: 300

Rate Code: Inexpensive-Moderate
Services: Apres-ski parties, Ice skating, Hot tubs, Warren Miller ski movies, Indor mini-golf

"Kid's Klub" is geared for ages 6-12, and is a half day program with canoeing, swimming, field trips, games, and arts and crafts. There is also a licensed day-care center for those ages 3 months to 10 years.

⬚ Pennsylvania

──────────────── CLARKS SUMMITT ────────────────

The Inn at Nichols Village
1101 Northern Blvd, 18411
Ph: 800-642-2215 717-587-1135
Fax: 717-586-7140
Number of Rooms: 134

Rate Code: Moderate

The Inn at Nichols Village is an attraction unto itself. Our facilities are woven into a soothing network of exquisitely landscaped grounds, gardens and waterfalls. A wealth of year-round recreational opportunities and cultural treasures surrounds the Inn.

──────────────── HERSHEY ────────────────

Hotel Hershey
P.O. Box 400, Hotel Rd, 17033
Ph: 717-533-2171
800-533-3131
Fax: 717-534-8887
Number of Rooms: 241

Rate Code: Luxury
Services: Room service, laundry service, gift shop and newsstand, business services available upon request.

We look forward to offering you a sparkling lineup of entertainment, more than 50 thrilling rides and attractions, a selection of food that is sure to appeal to the most discriminating taste buds, an assortment of quality merchandise, and a variety of state-of-the-art video and midway games.

──────────────── SKYTOP ────────────────

Skytop Lodge
One Skytop, 18357
Ph: 717-595-7401
800-345-7759
Fax: 717-595-9618
Number of Rooms: 166

Rate Code: Luxury
Services: Library, Glassed-in sun porch, sitting and game rooms

"Camp in the Clouds," is our free children's program, available everyday but Sunday in July and August. The playroom is a boathouse on the lakeshore. Group instructions in various sports, arts and crafts, storytelling, or excursions offer a varied and exciting program. The program is designed for ages 3 through 12. There is also a game room with many board games for everyone.

⬚ South Carolina

──────────────── CHARLESTON ────────────────

Wild Dunes Resort
P.O. Box 20575, 29413
Ph: 843-886-2260
800-845-8880
Fax: 843-886-2916

Rate Code: Inexpensive-Luxury
Services: Golf course, tennis courts, fitness center, meeting facilities.

Wil Dunes is noted for its natural beauty and beach, family oriented activities, organized children's progam, and its award-winning golf and tennis. Family recreation programs are complimentary.

──────────── HILTON HEAD ISLAND ────────────

Crystal Sands Resort
130 Shipyard Dr, 29928
Ph: 843-842-2400
800-465-4329
Fax: 843-842-9975
Number of Rooms: 340

Rate Code: Inexpensive-Luxury
Services: Coffee maker, Hair dryer,
Health club

A children's program called Camp Castaways is offered in the summer, for ages 3–12. A modified program is offered during the rest of the year. There is also a teen program.

──────────── HILTON HEAD ISLAND ────────────

Hilton Head Island Hilton
23 Ocean Lane, P.O. Box 6165, 29938
Ph: 843-842-8000   800-932-3322
Number of Rooms: 324

Rate Code: Inexpensive-Moderate
Services: Health Club, Conference
rooms

Vacation Station is for ages 4-11, offers dolphin excursions, scavenger hunts, nature hikes, miniature golf and plenty more to keep the kids happy and busy.

──────────── HILTON HEAD ISLAND ────────────

Westin Resort Hilton Head
Two Grasslawn Ave, 29928
Ph: 843-681-4000   800-228-3000
Fax: 843-681-1087
Number of Rooms: 410

Rate Code: Moderate
Services: Valet, barber & beauty shops,
parking, car hire, babysitting, laundry,
art gallery, room service, complete beach
service, newsstand.

The children's program, "Camp Wackatoo" is for 4-12 year-olds and is a learning based recreational program. Activities include special theme days, beach olympics, giant artistic creations, safety swimmers, earthlings, cooking with kids.

──────────── JOHNS ISLAND ────────────

Kiawah Island Inn
12 Kiawah Beach Dr, 29455
Ph: 843-768-2121   800-654-2924
Fax: 843-768-9339
Number of Rooms: 450

Rate Code: Moderate

A children's program is offered during the summer for ages 3 through 12. The hours are 9 a.m. to 4:30 p.m., Monday through Friday. There is a small fee to enroll your children. There are also many activities especially planned for the teens in your party, such as theme parties and volleyball.

──────────── MYRTLE BEACH ────────────

Myrtle Beach Hilton
10000 Beach Club Dr, 29572
Ph: 843-449-5000
800-HILTONS
Fax: 843-449-2161
Number of Rooms: 392

Rate Code: Inexpensive-Luxury
Services: Golf, tennis, pool,
entertainment.

Myrtle Beach and its fantastic Grand Strand offer more dining, shopping, entertainment and amusements than any other place. For the little ones, our social director has planned a full schedule of exciting activities that is sure to please children of all ages.

⊞ *Tennessee*

─────────────── NASHVILLE ───────────────

Loews Vanderbilt Plaza Hotel
2100 West End Ave, 37203
Ph: 615-320-1700
800-235-6397
Number of Rooms: 338

Rate Code: Moderate
Services: Full health & fitness facilities, spa, 24-hour room service, business centers, concierge

Through the hotel's "Kidstuff" program, children can choose from a range of activities such as a "behind-the-scenes" tour or excursions to nearby sightseeing attractions.

⊞ *Texas*

─────────────── HOUSTON ───────────────

Houston Marriott Astrodome
2100 South Braeqood, 77030
Ph: 713-797-9000
800-228-9290
Fax: 713-799-8362
Number of Rooms: 339

Rate Code: Inexpensive

Includes kids activities, and a Kids Eat Free for those twelve and under.

─────────────── SAN ANTONIO ───────────────

Hyatt Regency Hill Country
9800 Resort Dr, 78251
Ph: 219-647-1234   800-228-1234
Fax: 210-681-9681
Number of Rooms: 500

Rate Code: Moderate-Luxury
Services: Full health club, Conference rooms

Camp Hyatt, for ages 3 through 12, is offered daily in the summer, also on weekends during holiday periods. Rock Hyatt is for teens 13-17 has offers sports, excursions and social events, as well as a Rock Zone meeting place.

⊞ *Utah*

─────────────── ST. GEORGE ───────────────

St. George Hilton Inn
1450 South Hilton Dr, 84770
Ph: 435-628-0463
800-662-2525
Fax: 435-628-1501
Number of Rooms: 100

Rate Code: Inexpensive
Services: Gift shop, newstand, pay-per-view movies, 3 lighted tennis courts, complimentary airport shuttle, tropical courtyard, outdoor pool & spa, voice mail and data ports.

The St. George Hilton Inn can accommodate all your needs, whether you're planning a meeting or going to one of the area's various year-round recreational facilities. Nestled in a relaxing southwestern atmosphere with spectacular rooms and personalied Hilton service. Children receive a package upon check-in which includes games, kids magazines, toys, and information on things to do in town.

⊠ *Vermont*

──────────────── AVERILL ────────────────

Quimby Country Lodge
05901
Ph: 802-822-5533
Number of Rooms: 20

Rate Code: Moderate
Services: Library, Recreation building

For ages 5-15 will have lots of fun here, always a different adventure to look forward to. Some events include magic shows, from-jumping contests and peanut hunts, to name just a few. One night there's a campfire with all the usual campfire stories and fun.

──────────────── BOLTON VALLEY ────────────────

Bolton Valley Resort
05477
Ph: 802-434-2131
800-451-3220
Fax: 802-434-4547
Number of Rooms: 276

Rate Code: Inexpensive-Moderate
Services: Exercise room, Tanning room,
Game room, Gift shop

Our day care nursery takes children from 3 months to 5 years. There are plenty of different activities for these little ones, and the ages are grouped with others of like interests. Camp Bear Paw is for ages 6-12. Indoor and outdoor activities are offered, depending on the weather. Hikes, fishing trips, arts and crafts are must some of the popular options.

──────────────── CHITTENDEN ────────────────

Mountain Top Inn and Resort
195 Mountain Top Rd
Ph: 802-483-2311
800-445-2100
Fax: 802-483-6373

Rate Code: Moderate-Luxury
Services: Dining Room, Sitting Room,
Conference Room, Den and Porch

Eleven miles from Killington, amidst the Green Mountains of Vermont, adjacent to the Green Mountain National Forest overlooking a pristine recreational lake. Pets welcome in cottages. Limited stalls available for boarding guest horses. Handicapped accessible. Endless activities for kids and adults.

──────────────── SMUGGLERS' NOTCH ────────────────

Smuggler's Notch
Route 108, 05464
Ph: 802-644-8851
800-451-8752
Fax: 802-644-2713
Number of Rooms: 560

Rate Code: Inexpensive-Moderate
Services: A complete Mountain Village
with convenient restaurants, lounges,
entertainment, sport shop, courtside
pool with sauna, waterslide, toddler's
pool, child care.

With family fun guaranteed and flexibility built in the programming, the outdoor action in a mountain setting means exceptional value for families. Adult activities include guided hikes and walks, massage clinic, swimming, garden tours and horseback riding. Children's programs include Little Rascals, Discovery Dynamos, Mountain Explorers and Adventure Rangers.

WOODSTOCK

The Woodstock Inn & Resort
14 The Green, 05091
Ph: 802-457-1100
800-448-7900
Fax: 802-457-3824
Number of Rooms: 136

Rate Code: Moderate-Luxury
Services: Valet service, complimentary morning coffee & afternoon tea, some rooms have refrigerators and fireplaces, concierge, room service, indoor/outdoor pools, tennis, massage room.

For over 200 years, there's been an Inn on Woodstock's village green. If you're here to ski, the Suicide Six combines a family atmosphere with great terrain for all ability levels. The diverse facilities offer something for everyone making the Resort a favorite for vacationing families.

Virginia

VIRGINIA BEACH

The Founders Inn
5641 Indian River Rd, 23464
Ph: 804-366-5785   800-926-4466
Fax: 804-424-5511

Rate Code: Moderate

At the Founders Inn, children's programs have been known to inspire saintly behavior and convert many a parent to enthusiastic believers in the hotel's well-conceived and professionally implemented programs for youngsters. The hotel uses its unique setting on a small lake for nature walks, feeding ducks and other outdoor activities.

Washington

PORT LUDLOW

Resort at Port Ludlow
9483 Oak Bay Rd, 98365
Ph: 360-437-2222 Fax: 360-437-2482
Number of Rooms: 180

Rate Code: Inexpensive-Moderate
Services: Car rental

During the summer months there are supervised children's activities for 5 year-olds and up. The program is more activity based than a camp style with things like treasure hunts, aqua scout races, and various other games. Equipment for softball, football, basketball, volleyball badminton, croquet, Frisbee, lawn darts, lawn bowling, and various other games is also available.

West Virginia

WHEELING

Oglebay Resort, Wilson Lodge
Oglebay, 26003
Ph: 304-243-4000   800-624-6988
Fax: 304-243-4070
Number of Rooms: 210

Rate Code: Inexpensive-Moderate

Day camps are held for children at the Children's Center. The camps are for kids 4–12 years old. A special favorite is zoo camp, with access to the animals. There is always something to do, including arts and crafts, movies and science playshops.

─────────────── **WHITE SULPHUR SPRINGS** ───────────────

The Greenbrier
24986
Ph: 304-536-1110
800-624-6070
Number of Rooms: 650

Rate Code: Moderate-Luxury
Services: Indoor and outdoor tennis
courts, indoor and outdoor pools,
parcourse fitness trails, bowling, skeet
shooting, fishing, golf, Spa, shops.

The perfect environment for a truly enjoyable vacation. Surrounded by the panoramic beauty of the Allegheny Mountains, you'll enjoy breathtaking scenery. There are age appropriate programs for kids from 3–12. Some activities include field trips, scavenger hunts, nature walks, tennis and golf lessons, swimming, bowling and much more.

▩ **Wisconsin**

─────────────── **ELKHART LAKE** ───────────────

Barefoot Bay
P.O. Box 0, 53020
Ph: 920-540-9300   800-345-7784
Number of Rooms: 150

Rate Code: Moderate

The children's program is complimentary and runs a full 13 hours! The kids are divided into age groups, and activities are geared differently for each group. Swimming at the beach, nature walks, stories, games arts and crafts, and field games are the mainstays of the program.

─────────────── **WISCONSIN DELLS** ───────────────

Yogi Bear's Camp-Resort
S1915 Ishnala Rd., 53965-0510
Ph: 608-254-2568
800-462-9644 ext.FTR
Fax: 608-254-8071
Number of Rooms: 385

Rate Code: Inexpensive–Moderate
Services: Special packages, 20 week-long
theme special events, Amenities available
—refrigerators, microwaves, grills, air
conditioning/heat, TV

Stay in Cindy's Cabins, Yogi's Bungalows, Deluxe Trailers or campsites, ranging from Economy to Red Carpet "Camp-Suites" with Yogi Bear and friends at the Most Award Winning Family Camp-Resort in the Nation! Celebrate Jellystone Park's 30th anniversary with daily parades, character appearances and autograph signings with over 30 weeklong special events.

▩ **British Columbia**

─────────────── **WILLIAMS LAKE** ───────────────

Ts'yl-os Park Lodge
Chilko Lake,
c/o P.O. Box 2560, V2G 4P2
Ph: 604-398-7755   800-4-TSYLOS
Fax: 604-398-7487
Number of Rooms: 16

Rate Code: Luxury

We cater to people who enjoy the outdoors combined with comfortable accommodations. The main log lodge with its stone fireplace, beautiful view, and large front porch with Jacuzzi provides a very personal ambiance. The many outdoor activities include fly fishing, horseback riding, and canoeing. Or spend a lazy day in the Jacuzzi with a good book.

▣ Prince Edward Island

——— PRINCE EDWARD ISLAND ———

Rodd Hotels & Resorts
P.O. Box 432,
Charlotte Town, C1A 7K7
Ph: 800-565-RODD

Rate Code: Inexpensive-Luxury

The setting for the novels about Anne of Green Gables, Prince Edward Island provides a chance to relax yet offers plenty to do. The largest hotel chain on the Island, Rodd Hotels & Resorts offers a choice of hotels and inns across the Island. For families visiting during July and August kids eat free at participating resorts.

▣ Province of Quebec

——— BEAUPRE ———

Chateau Mont-Sainte-Anne
500, boulevard Beau-PreF, G0A 1E0
Ph: 418-827-5211
800-463-4467
Fax: 418-827-5072
Number of Rooms: 240

Rate Code: Luxury
Services: Shrine of Sainte-Anne-de-Beaupre, Mont Sainte-Anne Park, National Wildlife Park, Grand Canyon and Rapids of Saint-Anne, Montmorency Fall at Beauport-Boischatel.

Located at the base of Mont Sainte-Anne, our hotel is in one of the most magnificent parks of the province. Parc du Mont Sainte-Anne offers an exciting variety of activities, from downhill skiing to horseback riding, and more. A year-round host to gatherings and those seeking real country atmosphere.

——— BROMONT ———

Le Chateau Bromont Hotel-Spa
90, rue Stanstead, J0E 1L0
Ph: 514-534-3433
800-304-3433
Fax: 514-534-0514
Number of Rooms: 147

Rate Code: Inexpensive
Services: Pool, Squash, Raquetball, Sauna, Games room, Water Slides, Skating Rink, Snowmobiling, Tennis, Mountain biking, Health Centre, Sleigh rides.

For an almost endless choice of things to do year-round, this is the place! The ski hill descends to a golf course which offers excellent cross-country skiing in winter. In the heart of an attractive regional recreation center, Chateau Bromont Hotel-Spa features a European-style spa, panoramic views, and the authentic flavor of rustic Quebec hospitality.

CARLETON-SUR-MER

Hotel Motel Baie Bleue
482, boulevard Perron,
Box 150F, G0C 1J0
Ph: 418-364-3355
800-463-9099
Fax: 418-364-6165
Number of Rooms: 95

Rate Code: Moderate
Services: Museums, MicMac
Interpretation Centre, New Richmond
Loyalist Village, Quebec Acadian
Museum, St-Elzear Cavern, Paspebiac
Historical Site.

Let yourself be lulled by the poetry of the sea, the majesty of the mountain, spacious comfortable rooms and our expecially courteous staff. Our "La Seingneurie" dining room with a sea view is a favorite rendezvous for discerning gourmets. Visitors to Carleton can choose from a wide variety of sports and leisure activities. Children age 6 and under are free.

LA BALEINE, ILE-AUX-COUDRES

Hotel-Motel La Rouche Pleaureuse
22, rue Principale, G0A 2A0
Ph: 418-438-2734 800-463-6855
Fax: 418-622-8346
Number of Rooms: 6

Rate Code: Inexpensive-Moderate
Services: Game room, Mountain biking,
Whale-watching, Cruises, Bike rentals

Named for its location at the famous crying rock on Ile-aux-Coudres, the hotel-motel is famous for its rustic decor and warm, inviting atmosphere, as well as dining and dancing. Home of the truly relaxing vacation, there are enough things to do in the area to attract you to this charming part of Quebec.

LAC-ETCHEMIN

Le Manoir Lac Etchemin
187, 3e avenue, G0R 1S0
Ph: 418-652-2101
800-463-8489
Fax: 418-625-5424
Number of Rooms: 44

Rate Code: Moderate-Luxury
Services: Lake beach, Canoe, Rowboats,
Cruises, Mountain biking, Playground,
Exercise center, Tennis, Fishing, Tanning
salon, Mini-putt, Sleigh rides,
Babysitting, Tobogganing, Seadoos

Le Manoir Lac Etchemin is beautifully situated on the shore of Lake Etchemin, at one hour from Quebec City. The warm hospitality, the four seasons activities and an excellent cuisine are appreciated by many persons each year. The Manoir Lac Etchemin is ideal for memorable holiday or business stays. National Tourism award.

SAINTE-ADELE

Hotel Le Chantecler
1474, chemin Chantecler,
Box 1048, J0R 1L0
Ph: 514-229-3555
800-363-2420
Fax: 514-229-5593
Number of Rooms: 300

Rate Code: Inexpensive
Services: Village of Seraphin Museum,
Santa Claus Village, Bistro a Champlain
(visit a wine cellar).

The year-round resort with something for everyone, Le Chantecler presides over a magnificent piece of the Laurentian mountains. Here, it practices renowned Quebec hospitality in a country atmosphere that offers excellent cuisine, well-appointed facilities, and all only 45 minutes from Montreal! Children 4-12 have free entry to Chantecler Youth Club.

▣ Caribbean

─────────────────────── ARUBA ───────────────────────

Aruba Sonesta Suites & Casino
L G Smith Blvd 9, Oranjestad
Ph: 297-8-36000
Fax: 297-8-34389
Number of Rooms: 250

Rate Code: Luxury
Services: Valet services, baby-sitting, auto rental, shopping, meeting facilities, daily happy hour, daily guest activities program, fitness center.

A vacation should be a chance for every family member to relax and have fun, doing things they enjoy. The "Just Us Kids" program offers activities for children 5–12. Activities include rock hunting tour, field trips, swimming and games, mini-golf night, and more.

─────────────────────── BAHAMAS ───────────────────────

Atlantis Paradise Island
P.O. Box N4-777,
Nassau
Ph: 242-363-2202
Fax: 242-363-3703
Number of Rooms: 1150

Rate Code: Moderate–Luxury
Services: World's largest outdoor, open-water aquarium, swimming pools, waterfalls, water rides.

The Atlantis Family Plan is loaded with amenities including free offers for children and the opportunity for youngsters to frolic in a new "Camp Paradise" program. Activities include swimming and searching for buried treasure, story telling, nature walks, talent shows and ice cream eating contests.

─────────────────────── BERMUDA ───────────────────────

Sonesta Beach Resort Bermuda
P.O. Box HM 1070,
Hamilton 5, HMEX
Ph: 809-238-8122
Fax: 809-238-8463
Number of Rooms: 400

Rate Code: Luxury
Services: Concierge, laundry, safe deposit box, wake-up service, resorts shops, meeting facilities.

The whole family will love the Sonesta Beach Resort. Just outside the door you will find everything to make your family vacation the best ever. Complimentary "Just Us Kids" program offers supervised activities for children ages 5 to 12.

─────────────────────── JAMAICA ───────────────────────

Sonrise Beach Retreat
Robins Bay P.A., St. Mary
Ph: 876-776-7676
Fax: 876-999-7169

Rate Code: Inexpensive–Moderate
Services: Private baths available, Kitchenette available, Safe for valuables, Ceiling fans, Private terrace available

A unique and affordable Eco-Tourism experience awaits visitors at Sonrise Private Beach Retreat. Activities include horseback riding, boat and fishing trips, Hidden Jungle Waterfalls, the River Water Therapy Experience, Greencastle Estate Farm and the Blue Mountain Downhill Bicycle Tour. On weekends, experience Jamaica's rich culture during Family Fun Days.

─────────────── **JAMAICA** ───────────────

Franklin D. Resort
PO Box 201
Ph: 876-973-4591
800-654-1FDR
Fax: 876-973-3071

Rate Code: Luxury
Services: All-inclusive, Vacation Nanny
assigned to each family, 3 meals daily,
Satellite TV, Convertable sofas, Private
bath, Terrace, Fully equipped kitchen,
Special kiddies dinner, Compl. cribs,
high chairs, cots

The Franklyn D. Resort in Runaway Bay is Jamaica's only all-suite, all-inclusive beachfront family resort. A vacation Nanny is assigned to each family between 9 a.m. to 5 p.m. Kids will enjoy the Mini Club with its variety of activities including arts and crafts and the computer learning center. Kids under 16 free of charge.

─────────────── **JAMAICA** ───────────────

FDR Pebbles
PO Box 1933, Falmouth, Trelawny
Ph: 876-617-2500
800-654-1FDR
Fax: 876-617-2512

Rate Code: Luxury
Services: Balconies/terrace, Air
conditioning, Satellite TV, Convertable
sofas, Private baths, Fully equipped
kitchen, All inclusive, Children stay free
with parents, Kiddies dinner

Located in Trelawny, the all-inclusive FDR Pebbles offers families an exciting soft adventure holiday. The comprehensive teen program incorporates hiking, swimming, bonfire parties and camping. The Mini-Club, for younger children, includes arts and crafts, tennis, shell hunts, walks along the beach and more! Vacation nannies are assigned to families with smaller children. Kids under 16 free of charge.

─────────────── **PUERTO RICO** ───────────────

El Conquistador Resort
Las Croabas,
800-468-5228

Rate Code: Luxury
Services: Snorkeling, Scuba diving,
Volleyball, Hiking, Kayaking, Fitness
Center, 6 swimming pools, Casino,
Retail Shops.

El Conquistador Resort & Country Club is spread over 500 acres in the quaint fishing village of Las Croabas, Puerto Rico. It is the perfect place for a warm-weather family getaway offering plenty of entertaining diversions for both generations in a picture-perfect Caribbean setting. Ask about family packages.

─────────────── **ST. CROIX, VI** ───────────────

The Buccaneer Hotel
Estate Shoys, Christiansted, 00824
Ph: 340-773-2100
800-223-3881
Fax: 340-778-8215
Number of Rooms: 138

Rate Code: Moderate–Luxury
Services: Full breakfast, Children free in
summer (same room as parents), Kids
Camp, Welcome cocktail, Twice daily
maid service, Terrace/balcony/patio,
Refrigerator, Safe, Telephone, Hair
dryer, A/C, Cable TV, Cribs & coffee
makers available upon advance request

The historic Buccaneer boasts 138 exquisite accommodations in a country club atmosphere on 340 tropical acres. Three lovely beaches, a championship golf course, a renowned tennis center, and a variety of water sports create a luxury playground for all ages. Family owned and operated since 1947, The Buccaneer offers the finest family options in the Virgin Islands.

―――――――――――――― ST. LUCIA ――――――――――――――

Windjammer Landing
P.O. Box 1504, Castries,
Ph: 809-452-0913
800-743-9609
Fax: 809-452-9454
Number of Rooms: 114

Rate Code: Moderate
Services: All villas feature terraces and
sun-decks, refrigerator and coffee maker.
Two bi-level pools connected by a
waterfall, private beach, golf, snorkeling.

Windjammer Landing gives you a whole playground full of sports and recreation—scuba lessons, tennis, fishing charters and other island adventures. There are plenty of supervised activities and wading pools to keep the kids busy. Baby-sitting and nanny services keep them safe and secure when you want to have time alone.

―――――――――――――― ST. THOMAS, VI ――――――――――――――

Sapphire Beach Resort & Marina
Box 8088, 00802
Ph: 809-775-6100   800-524-2090
Fax: 809-775-4024

Rate Code: Luxury
Services: All suites have fully equipped
kitchens and daily maid service. Private
baby-sitting can be arranged.

There is no charge for children ages 12 and under and they eat free at the Seagrape restaurant. The Teen Scene program is for kids age 13-17. The KidsKlub for ages 3—12 includes swimming, building sand castles, lizard walks, crafts and lunch. All programs are free with the exception of some Teen Scene activities.

▦ Mexico

―――――――――――――― CANCUN ――――――――――――――

Melia Turquesa in Cancun
Ph: 800-33-MELIA
Number of Rooms: 444

For parents who have always wanted to share with their children the magic of a Mexican island vacation, the Melia Turquesa in Cancun has made the dream an affordable reality. Two kids under the age of 12 can share their paren "Caribbean Adventure" package, which includes a 50% discount for kids on all food and beverage consumed in the company of their parents. Located on Cancun Island, the wonders of Mexico are nearby.

―――――――――――――― SAN DIEGO CA ――――――――――――――

Rosarito Beach Hotel & Spa
P.O. Box 430145, 92143
Ph: 800-343-8582
011-52-661-20144
Fax: 011-52-661-21176

Rate Code: Inexpensive-Luxury

U.S. address shown is for reservations. Two children up to 12 years old are allowed with parents at no extra charge and receive 3 free meals a day. Rooms, suites, apartments, two-bedroom suites, and a presidential suite are available. Playground all year and summer supervised activities for children. Friday and Saturday nights there is a "Fiesta Mexicana" floor show of folkloric dancers and a sumptuous Mexican buffet.

• •
MORE FAMILY RESORTS

The following resorts are also notable for their family friendly atmosphere and, in some cases, children's programs. Call to inquire.

Alabama

Holiday Inn Anniston/Oxford, US Hwy 431 & AL 21S, PO Box 3308, 36203 Ph: 205-831-3410	Anniston/ Oxford
Residence Inn by Marriott, 3 Greenhill Parkway @ US Hwy 280, 35242 Ph: 205-991-8686	Birmingham
Tutwiler Hotel, 2021 Park Place North, 35203 Ph: 205-322-2100	Birmingham
Hampton Inn Dothan, 3071 Ross Clark Circle, 36301 Ph: 334-671-3700	Dothan
Holiday Inn Dothan, 3053 Ross Clark Circle, 36301 Ph: 334-794-6601	Dothan
The Guest House, 63 S. Church St., 36532 Ph: 334-928-6226 334-928-0720	Fairhope
Holiday Inn Express Gadsden, 801 Cleveland Ave., 35954 Ph: 256-538-7861	Gadsden
Ramada Inn, 610 W. Beach Blvd., 36542 Ph: 256-948-8141	Gulf Shore
Brooks Motel, 3800 Governors Dr., Ph: 256-539-6562	Huntsville
Hampton Inn Huntsville, 4815 University Dr., 35816 Ph: 256-830-9400 800-HAMPTON	Huntsville
Holiday Inn - Research Park, 5903 University Dr., 35816 Ph: 256-830-0600 800-HOLIDAY	Huntsville
Huntsville Hilton, 401 Williams Ave., 35801 Ph: 256-533-1400 800-HILTONS	Huntsville
Huntsville Marriott, 5 tranquility Base, 35805 Ph: 256-830-2222 800-228-9290	Huntsville
Parkway Motel, 2101 S. Memorial Pkwy, 35810 Ph: 256-536-8511	Huntsville
Howard Johnson Park Square Inn, 8721 Hwy 20 W., PO Box 520, 35758 Ph: 205-772-8855	Madison
Adam's Mark, 64 S. Water St., 36602 Ph: 205-438-4000	Mobile
Clarion Hotel Mobile, 3101 Airport Blvd., 36606 Ph: 800-476-6400	Mobile
Perdido Beach Resort, 27200 Perdido Beach Blvd., 36561 Ph: 205-981-9811 800-634-8001	Orange Beach
Twin Pines Resort, 1200 Twin Pines Rd., 35147 Ph: 205-672-7575	Sterrett
Sheraton Capstone Inn, 320 Bryant Dr., 35401 Ph: 205-752-3200	Tuscaloosa

Alaska

Anchorage Hotel, 330 E St., 99501 Ph: 907-272-4553 800-544-0988	Anchorage
Kennicott Glacier Lodge, PO Box 103940, 99510 Ph: 907-258-2350	Anchorage
Voyager Hotel, 501 K St., 99501 Ph: 907-277-9501 800-247-9070	Anchorage
Glacier Bay Lodge, PO Box 199, 99826 Ph: 907-697-2226 800-451-5952	Bartlett Cove
Denali Princess Lodge, PO Box 110, 99755 Ph: 907-683-2282 800-835-8907	Denali National Park
Denali Riverview Inn, PO Box 48, 99755 Ph: 907-683-2663 206-384-1078 Winter	Denali National Park
Glacier Bay Country Inn, PO Box 5, 99826 Ph: 907-697-2288 801-673-8480 Winter	Gustavas
A Puffin's B&B, PO Box 3, 99826 Ph: 907-697-2260	Gustavus
Gustavus Inn at Glacier Bay, PO Box 60, 99826 Ph: 907-697-2254 800-649-5220	Gustavus

Whalesong Lodge, PO Box 5, 99826 Ph: 907-697-2288 801-673-8480 Winter	Gustavus
Captain's Choice Motel, 2nd & Dalton, PO Box 392, 99827 Ph: 907-766-3111 800-247-7153	Haines
Eagle's Nest Motel, 1183 Haines Hwy, PO Box 250, 99827 Ph: 907-766-2891	Haines
Ft. Steward Condos, PO Box 75, 99827 Ph: 907-766-2425	Haines
Ft. Steward Lodge, PO Box 307, 99827 Ph: 907-766-2009	Haines
Summer Inn B&B, 117 Second Ave., PO Box 1198, 99827 Ph: 907-262-6631	Haines
Thunderbird Motel, 216 Dalton St., PO Box 589, 99827 Ph: 907-766-2131 800-327-2556	Haines
Kachemak Bay Wilderness Lodge, Bhina Poot Bay, PO Box 956 K, 99603 Ph: 907-235-8910	Homer
Baranof A Westmark Hotel, 127 N. Franklin St., 99801 Ph: 907-586-2660 800-544-0970	Juneau
Blueberry Lodge B&B, 9436 N. Douglas Hwy, 99801 Ph: 907-463-5886	Juneau
Cashen Quarters B&B, 315 Gold St. J93, 99801 Ph: 907-586-9863	Juneau
Jan's View B&B, PO Box 32254, 99803 Ph: 907-463-5897	Juneau
Prospector Hotel, 275 Wittier St., 99801 Ph: 907-586-3737 800-331-2711	Juneau
Westmark Juneau, 51 W. Egan Dr., 99801 Ph: 907-586-6900 800-544-0970	Juneau
Best Western Landing, 3434 Tongass Ave., 99901 Ph: 907-225-5166 800-428-8304	Ketchikan
Cedar Lodge, 1471 Tongass Ave., PO Box 8331, 99901 Ph: 907-225-1900	Ketchikan
Great Alaska Cedar Works B&B, 1527 Pond Reef Rd., 99901 Ph: 907-247-8287	Ketchikan
Ingersoll Hotel, 303 Mission St., 99901 Ph: 907-225-2124 800-478-2124	Ketchikan
Salmon Falls Resort, Mile 17 N Tongass Hwy, PO Box 5700, 99901 Ph: 907-225-2752 800-247-9059	Ketchikan
Super 8 Motel, 2151 Sea Level Dr., 99901 Ph: 907-226-9088	Ketchikan
Waterfall Resort Alaska, PO Box 6440, 99901 Ph: 907-225-9461 800-544-5125	Ketchikan
Westmark Cape Fox Lodge, 800 Venetia Way, 99901 Ph: 907-225-8001 800-544-0970	Ketchikan
Annahootz B&B, PO Nox 2870, 99835 Ph: 907-747-6498	Sitka
Creek's Edge Guest House, PO Box 2941, 99835 Ph: 907-747-6484	Sitka
Helga's B&B, 2827 Halibut Point Rd., PO Box 1885, 99835 Ph: 907-747-5497	Sitka
Potlatch Motel, 713 Katlian St., PO Box 58, 99835 Ph: 907-747-8611	Sitka
Westmark Shee Atika, 330 Seward St., 99835 Ph: 907-747-6241	Sitka
Gold Rush Lodge, PO Box 514 SE, 99840 Ph: 907-983-2831	Skagway
Skagway Inn B&B, 7th & Broadway, 99840 Ph: 907-983-2289	Skagway

Arizona

Copper Queen Hotel, PO Box Drawer CQ, 85603 Ph: 520-432-2216 800-247-5829	Bisbee
The Bisbee Inn, 45 OK St., PO Box 1855, 85603 Ph: 520-432-5131	Bisbee
The Boulders, PO Box 2090, 85377 Ph: 520-488-9009 800-553-1717	Carefree
Price Canyon Ranch, PO Box 1065, 85608 Ph: 520-558-2383	Douglas
Sprucedale Ranch, PO Box 880 K, Ph: 520-333-4984	Eagar
Inn at Four Ten B&B, 410 N. Leroux St., 86001 Ph: 520-774-0088	Flagstaff
Bright Angel Lodge, Grand Canyon National Park Lodges, PO Box 699, 85203 Ph: 520-638-2474	Grand Canyon
East & West Yavapai Lodge, Grand Canyon National Park Lodges, PO Box 699, 85203 Ph: 520-638-2474	Grand Canyon
El Tovar, Grand Canyon National Park Lodges, PO Box 699, 86023 Ph: 520-638-2474	Grand Canyon
Kachina, Grand Canyon National Park Lodges, PO Box 699, 86023 Ph: 520-638-2474	Grand Canyon

Maswik Lodge, Grand Canyon National Park Lodges, PO Box 699, 86023 Ph: 520-638-2474	Grand Canyon
Thunderbird, Grand Canyon National Park Lodges, PO Box 699, 86023 Ph: 520-638-2474	Grand Canyon
Comfort Inn, 2602 E. Navajo Blvd., 86025 Ph: 520-524-6131	Holbrook
Saguaro Lake Ranch Resort, 13020 Bush Hwy, 85215 Ph: 602-984-2194	Mesa
The Triangle L Ranch, PO Box 900, 85623 Ph: 520-896-2804 520-896-9070	Oracle
Circle Z Ranch, PO Box 194-BP, 85624 Ph: 520-287-2091	Patagonia
Ritz-Carlton, Phoenix, 2401 E. Camelback Rd., 85016 Ph: 602-468-0700 800-241-3333	Phoenix
San Carlos Hotel, 202 N. Central Ave., 85004 Ph: 602-253-4121 800-528-5446	Phoenix
Rancho de la Osa, PO Box 1, 85633 Ph: 520-823-4257	Sasabe
Holiday Inn SunSpree Resort, 7601 E. Indian Bend Rd., 85250 Ph: 602-991-2400 800-852-5205	Scottsdale
Red Lion's La Posada, 4949 E. Lincoln Dr., 85253 Ph: 602-952-0420 800-547-8010	Scottsdale
Wyndham Paradise Valley Resort, 5401 N. Scottsdale Rd., 85253 Ph: 602-947-5400 800-822-4200	Scottsdale
Canyon Villa, 125 Canyon Circle Dr., PO Box 204, 86336 Ph: 520-284-1226 800-453-1166	Sedona
Casa Sedona, 55 Hozoni Dr., 86336 Ph: 520-282-2938 800-525-3756	Sedona
Junipine Resort Condo Hotel, 8351 N. Hwy. 89A, 86336 Ph: 520-282-3375 800-742-7463	Sedona
L'Auberge de Sedona, 301 L.Auberge Lane, 86339 Ph: 520-282-7131 800-282-6777	Sedona
Casa Tierra, 11155 West Cale Pima, 85743 Ph: 520-578-3058	Tucson
La Posada del Valle, 1640 N. Campbell, 85719 Ph: 520-795-3840	Tucson
Suncatcher, 105 N. Avenida Javalina, 85748 Ph: 520-885-0883 800-835-8012	Tucson
Westward Look Resort, 245 E. Ina Roa, 85704 Ph: 520-297-1151 800-722-2500	Tucson
White Stallion Ranch, 9251 W. Twin Peaks Rd., 85743 Ph: 520-297-0252 800-782-5546	Tucson
Flying E Ranch, 2801 W. Wickenburg Way, 85358 Ph: 520-684-2690	Wickenburg

Arkansas

Dairy Hollow House, 515 Spring St., 72632 Ph: 501-253-7444 800-562-8650	Eureka Springs
Red Bud Valley Resort, Off Hwy 62 E, Rt 1, Box 500, 72632 Ph: 501-253-9028	Eureka Springs
The Tweedy House, 16 Washington, 72632 Ph: 800-346-1735	Eureka Springs
Beland Manor, 1320 S. Albert Pike, 72903 Ph: 501-782-3300	Fort Smith
Anderson House Inn, 201 E. Main St., PO Box 630, 72543 Ph: 800-264-5279	Heber Springs
Oak Tree Inn, Vinegar Hill & Hwy 110 W , 72543 Ph: 501-362-7731	Heber Springs
Edwardian Inn & Allin House, 317 S. Biscoe, 72342 Ph: 501-338-9155 501-572-9105	Helena
Arlington Resort Hotel & Spa, 239 Central Ave., 71901 Ph: 501-623-7771 800-643-1502	Hot Springs
DeGray Lake Resort, St. Rt. 7, Ph: 501-865-2851 800-737-8355	Hot Springs
Downtowner Motor Inn, 135 Central Ave., 71901 Ph: 501-624-5521	Hot Springs
Happy Hollow Motel, 231 Fountain St., 71901 Ph: 501-321-2230	Hot Springs
Hot Springs Inn, 1871 E. Grand Ave., 71901 Ph: 501-624-4436	Hot Springs
Lake Hamilton Resort, 2803 Albert Pike, 71913 Ph: 501-767-5511	Hot Springs
Quality Inn, 1125 E. Grand Ave., 71901 Ph: 501-624-3321	Hot Springs
Sunbay, 4810 Central Ave., 71913 Ph: 501-525-4691 800-468-0055	Hot Springs

Vintage Comfort B&B Inn, 303 Quapaw Ave., Ph: 501-623-3258	Hot Springs
Wildwood 1884, 808 Park Ave., Ph: 501-624-4267	Hot Springs
Gaston's White River Resort, 1 River Road, Rt 1, Box 176, 72642 Ph: 501-431-5202 501-431-5216	Lakeview
Country School Inn, Hwy 84 & 396, PO Box 6, 71952 Ph: 501-356-3091	Langley
Capital Hotel, 111 W. Markham, 72201 Ph: 501-374-7474 800-766-ROOM	Little Rock
Queen Wilhelmina Lodge, Queen Wilhelmina State Park, HC-07, Rt 7, Box 53A, 71953 Ph: 501-394-2863 800-264-2477	Mena
Tanyard Springs Resort, Rt 3, Box 335, 72110 Ph: 501-727-5200 800-533-1450	Morrilton
Inn at Mountain View, 307 Washington St., PO Box 812, 72560 Ph: 800-535-1301	Mountain View
Ozark Folk Center, Spur 382 off Hwy 5, PO Box 500, 72560 Ph: 800-264-3655	Mountain View
The Commercial Hotel, Courthouse Square, PO Box 72, 72560 Ph: 501-269-4383	Mountain View
Wildflower B&B, Peabody & Washington Sts., PO Box 72, 72560 Ph: 800-362-2632	Mountain View
Margland B&B Inn, PO Box 7111, 71611 Ph: 501-536-6000	Pine Bluff
Buffalo Outdoor Center, PO Box 1, 72670 Ph: 800-221-5514	Ponca

California

Pavilion Lodge, 513 Crescent Ave., 90704 Ph: 310-510-1788 800-4-AVALON	Avalon
Hotel Durant, 2600 Durant Ave., 94704 Ph: 510-845-8981	Berkeley
Beverly Hilton, 9876 Wilshire Blvd., 90210 Ph: 310-274-777 800-HILTONS	Beverly Hills
Big Sur Lodge, California 1, PO Box 190, 93920 Ph: 408-667-3100	Big Sur
Sea Horse Guest Ranch, 2660 California 1, 94923 Ph: 707-875-2721	Bodega Bay
Hunewill Circle H Guest Ranch, PO Box 368, 93517 Ph: 619-932-7710 702-465-2201 Winter	Bridgeport
Rankin Ranch, PO Box 36-PD, 93518 Ph: 805-867-2511	Caliente
Capitola Venetian Court, 1500 Wharf Rd., 95010 Ph: 408-476-6471 800-332-2780	Capitola
Marriott's Tenaya Lodge at Yosemite, 1122 Hwy 41, 93623 Ph: 209-683-6555 800-635-5807	Fish Camp
Circle Bar B B&B, 1800 Refugio Rd., 93117 Ph: 805-968-1113	Goleta
Sorensen's Resort, 14255 Hwy 99, 96120 Ph: 916-694-2203 800-423-9949	Hope Valley
Colonial Inn, 910 Prospect St., 92037 Ph: 619-454-2181 800-832-5525	La Jolla
Lake Arrowhead Resort, 27984 Hwy 189, PO Box 1699, 92352 Ph: 909-336-1511	Lake Arrowhead
The Inn at Schoolhouse Creek, 7051 N. Hwy. 1, 95456 Ph: 707-937-5525	Little River
Hotel Del Capri, 10587 Wilshire Blvd., 90024 Ph: 310-474-3511	Los Angeles
1849 Condominiums, 826 Lakeview Blvd., PO Box 835, 93546 Ph: 760-934-7525 800-421-1849	Mammoth Lks
Alpenhof Lodge, Minaret Rd., PO Box 1158, 93546 Ph: 760-934-6330	Mammoth Lks
Convict Lake Resort, Rt 1, Box 204, 93546 Ph: 619-934-3800	Mammoth Lks
Mammoth Mountain Inn, Minaret Rd., PO Box 353, 93546 Ph: 760-934-2581 800-228-4947	Mammoth Lks
Snow Goose Inn, 57 Forest Trail, PO Box 387, 93546 Ph: 760-934-2660 800-TRI-RENT	Mammoth Lks
Snowcreek Resort, PO Box 1647, 93546 Ph: 760-934-3333 800-544-6007	Mammoth Lks
Tamarack Lodge Resort, Twin Lakes Rd., PO Box 69, 93546 Ph: 760-934-2442	Mammoth Lks
Marina Del Ray Hotel, 13534 Bali Way, 90292 Ph: 310-301-1000 800-882-4000	Marina Del Ray
Point Montara Lighthouse Hostel, 16th St. @ State Hwy 1, PO Box 737, 94037 Ph: 415-728-7177	Montara

Best Western Monterey Beach Hotel, 2600 Sand Dunes Dr., 93940 Ph: 408-394-3321 800-242-8627	Monterey
Holiday Inn Resort Monterey, 1000 Aguajito Rd., 93940 Ph: 408-373-6141	Monterey
Monterey Marriott, 350 Calle Principal, 93940 Ph: 408-649-4234 800-325-3535	Monterey
Monterey Plaza, 400 Cannery Row, 93940 Ph: 408-646-1700 800-631-1339	Monterey
Marriott's Desert Springs Resort, 74855 Country Club Dr., 92260 Ph: 760-341-2211 800-228-9290	Palm Desert
Shadow Mountain Resort & Racquet, 45-750 San Luis Rey, 92260 Ph: 760-346-6123	Palm Desert
Oasis Villa Hotel, 4190 E. Palm Canyon, 92264 Ph: 760-328-1499 800-247-4664	Palm Springs
Palm Springs Hilton, 400 E. Tahquitz Way, 92262 Ph: 760-320-6868 800-541-3129	Palm Springs
Quality Inn, 1269 E. Palm Canyon Dr., 92264 Ph: 760-323-2775 800-472-4339	Palm Springs
Pigeon Point Lighthouse Hostel, 210 Pigeon Point Rd., 94060 Ph: 650-879-0633	Pescadero
Pinecrest Lake Resort, PO Box 1216, 95364 Ph: 209-965-3411	Pinecrest
Point Reyes Hostel, Box 247, 94956 Ph: 415-663-8811	Point Reyes Station
Marriott's Rancho Las Palmas Resort, 41000 Bob Hope Dr., 92270 Ph: 760-568-2727 800-458-8786	Rancho Mirage
Westin Mission Hills Resort, Dinah Shore & Bob Hope Dr, 92270 Ph: 619-328-5955	Rancho Mirage
Spanish Springs Ranch, Hwy 395, PO Box 70, 96123 Ph: 916-234-2050 800-560-1900	Ravendale
Drakesbad Guest Ranch, 2150 N. Main St., Ste. 5, 96080 Ph: 530-529-1512	Red Bluff
Lakeview Marina Resort, PO Box 2272, 96099 Ph: 530-223-3003	Redding
Red Lion Hotel, 1830 Hilltop Dr., 96002 Ph: 530-221-8700	Redding
Residence Inn by Marriott, 1530 Howe Ave., 95825 Ph: 916-920-9111	Sacramento
Bahia Resort hotel, 998 W. Mission Bay Dr., 92109 Ph: 619-488-0551 800-288-0770	San Diego
Catamaran Resort Hotel, 3999 Mission Blvd., 92109 Ph: 619-488-1081 800-288-0770	San Diego
Dana Inn and Marina, 1710 W. Mission Bay Dr., 92109 Ph: 619-222-6440 800-445-3339	San Diego
Embassy Suites Hotel, 4550 La Jolla Village Dr., 92122 Ph: 619-453-0400 800-EMBASSY	San Diego
The Beach Cottages, 4255 Ocean Blvd., 92109 Ph: 619-483-7440	San Diego
The Glorietta Bay Inn, 1630 Glorietta Blvd., Coronado Island, 92118 Ph: 619-435-3101 800-283-9383	San Diego
Campton Place Hotel, 340 Stockton Street, 94108 Ph: 415-781-5555 800-426-3135	San Francisco
Coventry Motor Inn, 1901 Lombard St., 94123 Ph: 415-567-1200	San Francisco
Four Seasons Clift Hotel, 495 Geary St., 94102 Ph: 415-775-4700 800-332-3442	San Francisco
Galleria Park Hotel, 191 Sutter St., 94104 Ph: 415-781-3060 800-792-9639	San Francisco
Grand Hyatt San Francisco, 345 Stockton St., 94108 Ph: 415-398-1234 800-228-9000	San Francisco
Hyatt at Fisherman's Wharf, 555 N. Point St., 94133 Ph: 415-563-1234 800-233-1234	San Francisco
Hyde Park Suites, 2655 Hyde St., 94109 Ph: 415-771-0200 800-227-3608	San Francisco
Quality Hotel, 2775 Van Ness Ave., 94109 Ph: 415-928-5000 800-228-5151	San Francisco
Ramada Hotel at Fisherman's Wharf, 590 Bay St., 94133 Ph: 415-885-4700 800-2-RAMADA	San Francisco

San Francisco Hilton & Towers, One Hilton Square, 94102 Ph: 415-771-1400 800-HILTONS	San Francisco
San Francisco Hyatt Fisherman's Wharf, 555 North Point St., 94133 Ph: 415-563-1234	San Francisco
Sheraton at Fisherman's Wharf, 2500 Mason St., 94133 Ph: 415-362-5500 800-325-3535	San Francisco
The Savoy, 580 Geary St., 94102 Ph: 415-441-2700 800-227-4223	San Francisco
Tuscan Inn at Fisherman's Wharf, 425 North Point St., 94133 Ph: 415-561-1100 800-648-4626	San Francisco
White Swan Inn, 845 Bush St., 94108 Ph: 415-775-1755	San Francisco
Wonder Valley, 6450 Elwood, 93657 Ph: 209-787-2551	Sanger
Harbor View Inn, 28 W Cabrillo Blvd., 93101 Ph: 805-963-0780	Santa Barbara
Miramar Resort Hotel, PO Box 429, 93102 Ph: 805-969-2203 800-322-6983	Santa Barbara
Seawat Gitek, 176 W. Cliff Drive., 95060 Ph: 408-426-4330 800-662-3838	Santa Cruz
Miramar Sheraton Hotel, 101 Wilshire Blvd., 90401 Ph: 310-394-3731 800-325-3535	Santa Monica
Camp Richardson's Resort & Marina, PO Box 9028, 96158 Ph: 530-541-1801 800-544-1801	South Lake Tahoe
Lakeland Village Beach & Ski Resort, 3535 Lake Tahoe Blvd., 96150 Ph: 530-544-1685	South Lake Tahoe
Lazy S Lodge, PO Box 7676, 95731 Ph: 530-541-0230 800-822-5922	South Lake Tahoe
Tahoe Chalet Inn, 3860 Lake Tahoe Blvd, 96150 Ph: 530-544-3311 800-821-2656	South Lake Tahoe
Timber Cove Lodge, 3411 Lake Tahoe Blvd., 95705 Ph: 530-541-6722 800-528-1234	South Lake Tahoe
Villa Vista Resort, 6750 N. Lake Blvd, 95732 Ph: 916-546-3333	Tahoe Vista
Lost Whale B&B Inn, 3452 Patrick's Point Dr., 95570 Ph: 800-677-7859	Trinidad
Bonanza King Resrot, Rt 2, Box 4890, 96091 Ph: 916-266-3305	Trinity Center
Trinity Alps Resort, 1750 Trinity Alps Rd., 96091 Ph: 916-286-2205	Trinity Center
Sheraton Universal, 333 Universal Terrace Parkway, 91608 Ph: 818-980-1212 800-325-3535	Universal City
Howard Creek Ranch, 40501 N. Hwy 1, PO Box 121, 95488 Ph: 707-964-6725	Westport
Emandal, 16500 Hearst Rd., 95490 Ph: 707-459-5439	Willits
Ahwahnee Hotel, Ahwahnee Dr., 95389 Ph: 209-252-4848	Yosemite National Park
Curry Village, California 41 & 140, 95389 Ph: 209-252-4848	Yosemite National Park
Wawona Hotel, PO Box 2005, 95389 Ph: 209-252-4848	Yosemite National Park
Yosemite Lodge, California 41 & 140, 95389 Ph: 209-252-4848	Yosemite National Park

Colorado

Little Red Ski Haus, 118 E. Cooper, 81611 Ph: 303-925-3333	Aspen
Beaver Creek Lodge, 26 Avondale Rd, 81620 Ph: 303-845-9800 800-732-6777	Avon
Hyatt Regency, Beaver Creek, Beaver Creek Resort, PO Box 1959, 81620 Ph: 303-949-1234 800-233-1234	Avon
Sky Corral Ranch, 8233 Old Flowers Rd., Dept. K, 80512 Ph: 303-484-1362	Bellvue
Breckenridge Hilton Resort, 550 Village Rd., PO Box 8059, 80424 Ph: 303-453-4500	Breckenridge
Elk Mountain Ranch, PO Box 910K, 81211 Ph: 719-539-4430 800-432-8812	Buena Vista
The Home Ranch, Box 822K, 80428 Ph: 303-879-1780	Clark
4UR Ranch, PO Box 340K, 81130 Ph: 719-658-2202	Creede

Comfort Inn Downtown, 401 17th St., 80202 Ph: 303-296-0400 800-4-CHOICE	Denver
Embassy Suites Hotel Downtown, 1881 Curtis, 80202 Ph: 303-297-8888 800-733-3366	Denver
Hyatt Regency Denver, 1750 Welton St., 80202 Ph: 303-295-1234 800-233-1234	Denver
Residence Inn by Marriott Downtown, 2777 Zuni St., 80211 Ph: 303-458-5318	Denver
Westin Hotel Tabor Center, 1692 Laurence St., 80202 Ph: 303-752-9100 800-228-3000	Denver
Colorado Trails Ranch, 12161 County Rd. 240, 81301 Ph: 970-247-5055 800-323-3833	Durango
Tall Timber, SSR Box 90 K, 81301 Ph: 303-259-4813	Durango
Lodge at Cordillera, PO Box 1110, 81632 Ph: 303-926-2200 800-877-3529	Edwards
Lane Guest Ranch, PO Box 1766K, 80517 Ph: 303-747-2493	Estes Park
Longs Peak Inn Guest Ranch, Longs Peak Route, Box K, 80517 Ph: 303-586-2110 800-262-2034	Estes Park
Tumbling River Ranch, PO Box 30K, 80448 Ph: 303-838-5981 800-654-8770	Grant
Lookout Lodge, 6975 Howard Ave., 80819 Ph: 719-684-2303	Green Mountain Falls
Waunita Hot Sprngs Ranch, 8007 County Rd. 887, 81230 Ph: 303-641-1266	Gunnison
7W Guest Ranch, 3412 Country Rd. 151K, 81637 Ph: 303-524-9328	Gypsum
Sweetwater Guest Ranch, 2650 Sweetwater Lake Rd., Drawer K, 81637 Ph: 303-524-7949 303-758-9177 Winter	Gypsum
Keystone Resort, Box 38, 80435 Ph: 303-468-2316 800-222-0188	Keystone
Latigo Ranch, PO Box 237K, 80459 Ph: 303-724-0990 800-227-9655	Kremmling
Cherokee Park Ranch, PO Box 97K, 80536 Ph: 303-493-6522 800-628-0949	Livermore
Sylvan Dale Ranch, 2939 N. County Rd. 31D, Dept K, 80537 Ph: 970-667-3915	Loveland
Peaceful Valley Lodge, 475 Peaceful Valley Rd., 80540 Ph: 303-747-2881	Lyons
Lake Mancos Ranch, 42688 CR-N, Dept. K, 81328 Ph: 303-533-7900	Mancos
Diamond J Guest Ranch, 26604 Frying Pan Rd., Drawer K, 81642 Ph: 303-927-3222	Meredith
Deer Valley Ranch, Drawer K, 81236 Ph: 719-395-2353	Nathrop
Davidson's Country Inn, PO Box 87, 81147 Ph: 303-264-5863	Pagosa Springs
Aspen Canyon Ranch, 13206 Country Rd., 80468 Ph: 303-725-3518	Parshall
Bar Lazy J, PO Box NK, 80468 Ph: 303-725-3437	Parshall
Powderhorn Guest Ranch, County Hwy 27, Drawer K, 81243 Ph: 303-641-0220	Powderhorn
Don K Ranch, 2677 S. Siloam Rd., Dept K 81005 Ph: 719-784-6600 719-549-0481	Pueblo
San Juan Guest Ranch, 2882 Hwy 23, Dept. K, 81432 Ph: 303-626-5360 800-331-3015	Ridgway
Coulter Lake Guest Ranch, PO Box 906 K, 81650 Ph: 303-625-1473	Rifle
Lost Valley Ranch, Route 2, Box K, 80135 Ph: 303-647-2311 303-647-2495	Sedalia
Stonebridge Inn, 300 Carriage Way, 81615 Ph: 303-923-2420 800-922-7242	Snowmass
Pokolodi Lodge, 25 Daly Lane, P.O. Box 5640, 81615 Ph: 303-932-4310 800-666-4556	Snowmass Village
The Ice House, 310 S. Fir, 81435 Ph: 970-728-6300 800-544-3436	Telluride
The Peaks At Telluride, PO Box 2702, 81435 Ph: 303-728-6800	Telluride
The Pines Ranch, PO Box 311 K, 81252 Ph: 719-783-9261	Westcliffe
Iron Horse Resort Retreat, PO Box 1286, 80482 Ph: 970-726-8851 800-621-8190	Winter Park

Connecticut

Jared Cone House, 25 Hebron Rd., 06043 Ph: 203-643-8538 203-649-5678	Bolton
The Inn at Chester, 318 W. Main St., 06412 Ph: 860-526-9541 800-949-STAY	Chester
Bishop Gate Inn, Goodspeed Landing, 06423 Ph: 860-873-1677	East Haddam
Homestead Inn, 420 Field Point Rd., 06830 Ph: 203-869-7500	Greenwich
Goodwin Hotel, 1 Haynes St., 06103 Ph: 860-246-7500 800-922-5006	Hartford
Copper Beech Inn, Main St., 06442 Ph: 860-767-0330	Ivoryton
Madison Beach Hotel, 94 W. Wharf Rd., 06443 Ph: 860-245-1404	Madison
Sunrise Resort, P.O. Box 415, 06469 Ph: 203-873-8681 800-225-9033	Moodus
Comfort Inn of Mystic, 132 Greenmanville, 06355 Ph: 860-572-8531 800-228-5150	Mystic
Days Inn, 55 Whitehall Ave., 06355 Ph: 860-572-0574 800-325-2525	Mystic
Steamboat Inn, 73 Steamboat Wharf, 05355 Ph: 860-536-8300 800-364-6100	Mystic
Taber Inn & Townhouses, 29 Williams Ave., Rt 1, 06355 Ph: 860-536-4904	Mystic
Homestead Inn, 5 Elm St., 06776 Ph: 860-354-4080	New Milford
Inn on Lake Waramaug, North Shore Rd., 06777 Ph: 203-868-0563	New Preston
Randall's Ordinary, PO Box 243, 06359 Ph: 203-599-4540	North Stonington
Red Brook Inn, PO Box 237, 06372 Ph: 203-572-0349	Old Mystic
Saybrook Point Inn & Spa, 2 Bridge St., 06475 Ph: 860-395-2000 800-243-0212	Old Saybrook
Fellshaw Tavern, Five Mile River Rd., 06260 Ph: 860-928-3467	Putnam
Stonehenge Inn, Rt. 7, PO Box 667, 06877 Ph: 203-438-6511	Ridgefield
Under Mountain Inn, 483 Undermountain Rd., 06068 Ph: 860-435-0242	Salisbury
Yesterday's Yankee, Rt 44 East, 06068 Ph: 203-435-9539 203-435-9539	Salisbury
Inn at National Hall, 2 Post Rd. West, 06880 Ph: 203-221-1351 800-628-4255	Westport

Delaware

Sea Colony, Drawer L, 19930 Ph: 800-732-2656	Bethany Beach
Darley Manor Inn B&B, 3701 Philadelphia Pike, 19703 Ph: 302-792-2127	Claymont
Wilmington Hilton, 639 Naamans Rd., 19703 Ph: 302-792-2700	Claymont
Best Western - Gold Leaf Hotel, 1400 Hwy 1, 19971 Ph: 302-226-1100	Dewey Beach
Surfside Plaza, McKinley St. & Oceanfront, 19971 Ph: 800-826-1575	Dewey Beach
The Bay Resort, Bellevue Street On the Bay, 19971 Ph: 302-227-6400	Dewey Beach
The Surf Club, 1 Read St., 19971 Ph: 302-227-7059	Dewey Beach
Savannah Inn B&B, 330 Savannah Rd., 19958 Ph: 302-645-5592	Lewes
The Beacon Motel, 514 E. Savannah Rd., 19958 Ph: 302-645-4888 800-735-4888	Lewes
The Inn at Canal Square, 122 Market St., 19958 Ph: 302-645-8499	Lewes
David Finney Inn, 216 Delaware St., 19720 Ph: 302-322-6367	New Castle
Janvier-Black House, 12 The Strand, 19720 Ph: 302-328-1339	New Castle
Ross House, 129 E. Second St., 19720 Ph: 302-322-7787	New Castle
The Jefferson House, 5 The Strand, 19720 Ph: 302-322-8944	New Castle
The Terry House, 130 Delaware St., 19720 Ph: 302-322-2505	New Castle
William Penn Guest House, 286 Delaware St., 19720 Ph: 302-328-7736	New Castle
Christiana Hilton Inn, 100 Continental Dr., 19713 Ph: 302-454-1500	Newark
Admiral Hotel, 2 Baltimore Ave., 19971 Ph: 302-227-2103	Rehoboth Bch
Atlantic Oceanside Suites, 2802 Highway 1, 19971 Ph: 302-227-3430	Rehoboth Bch
Boardwalk Plaza Hotel, 2 Olive Ave. at the Boardwalk, 19971 Ph: 302-337-7169 800-33-BEACH	Rehoboth Bch
Brighton Suites Hotel, 34 Wilmington Ave., 19971 Ph: 800-227-5788	Rehoboth Bch

One Virginia Avenue, One Virigina Ave., 19971 Ph: 302-227-9533 — Rehoboth Bch
Comfort Inn, 225 Dual Highway, N, 19973 Ph: 302-629-8385 — Seaford
Best Western Brandywine Valley Inn, 1807 Concord Pike, 19803
  Ph: 302-656-9436 — Wilmington
Holiday Inn North, 4000 Concord Pike, 19803 Ph: 302-478-2222 — Wilmington
Hotel Dupont, 11th & Market Sts., 19801 Ph: 302-594-3100 — Wilmington
Radisson Hotel Wilmington, 4727 Concord Pike, 19803 Ph: 302-478-6000 — Wilmington
Sheraton Suites Wilmington, 422 Delaware Ave., 19801 Ph: 302-654-8300 — Wilmington

District of Columbia

Channel Inn, 650 Water St., SW , 20024 Ph: 800-368-5668 202-554-2400 — Washington
Embassy Suites Hotel, 1250 22nd St., 20037 Ph: 800-362-2779
  202-857-3388 — Washington
Four Seasons Hotel, 2800 Pennsylvania Ave., NW , 20007 Ph: 202-342-0444 — Washington
Hay Adams Hotel, 1 Lafayette Square, NW , 20006 Ph: 202-638-6600 — Washington
Holiday Inn Capitol, 550 C Street, SW , 20024 Ph: 202-479-4000 — Washington
Hotel Washington, 515 15th St., NW , 20004 Ph: 202-638-5900 — Washington
J. W. Marriott Hotel, 1331 Pennsylvania Ave., NW , 20004 Ph: 202-393-2000 — Washington
Loew's L'Enfant Plaza Hotel, 480 L'Enfant Plaza, SW , 20024
  Ph: 202-484-1000 — Washington
Omni Shoreham Hotel, 2500 Calvert St., NW , Ph: 202-234-0700 — Washington
Park Hyatt Hotel, 1201 24th, NW , 20037 Ph: 202-789-1234 — Washington
Renaissance Washington D.C., 999 9th St., NW , 20001 Ph: 202-898-9000 — Washington
Ritz-Carlton Hotel, 2100 Massachusetts Ave., NW , 20008 Ph: 202-293-2100 — Washington
Savoy Suites Hotel, 2505 Wisconsin Ave., NW , Ph: 202-337-9700 — Washington
The Williard Inter-Continental, 1401 Pennsylvania Ave., NW , 20004
  Ph: 202-628-9100 — Washington

Florida

Amelia Surf & Racquet Club, 900 Amelia Pkwy S, 32034 Ph: 904-261-0511
  800-323-2001 — Amelia Island
Palm Island Resort, 7092 Placida Rd., 33946 Ph: 941-697-4800
  800-824-5412 — Cape Haze
'Tween Waters Inn, PO Box 249, 33924 Ph: 941-472-5161 800-223-5865 — Captiva Island
Safety Harbour Club, PO Box 476, 33924 Ph: 941-472-9223 — Captiva Island
Ocean Landings Resort, 900 N. Atlantic Ave., 32931 Ph: 407-783-9430 — Cocoa Beach
Destin Beach Club, 1150 Hwy. 98 East, 32541 Ph: 904-837-3985 — Destin
Sandestin Resort, 5500 US Highway 98 E, 32541 Ph: 904-267-8000
  800-277-0800 — Destin
Doubletree Guest Suites Waterfront, 2670 E. Sunrise Blvd., 33304
  Ph: 954-565-3800 800-424-2900 — Fort Lauderdale
Howard Johnson Oceans Edge Resort, 700 N. Atlantic Blvd, 33304
  Ph: 954-563-2451 — Fort Lauderdale
Logo Mar Resort, 1700 S. Ocean Lane, 33316 Ph: 954-523-6511
  800-255-5246 — Fort Lauderdale
Marriott's Harbor Beach Resort, 3030 Holiday Dr., 33316 Ph: 954-525-4000
  800-222-6543 — Fort Lauderdale
Sheraton Yankee Beach Resort, 321 North Atlantic Blvd, 33304
  Ph: 305-467-1111 800-958-5551 — Fort Lauderdale
Grenelefe Resort, 3200 State Rd., 33884 Ph: 813-422-7511 800-237-9549 — Grenelefe
Chesapeake Resort, Mile Marker 83.5 - US 1 Oceanside, PO Box 909, 33036
  Ph: 305-664-4662 — Islamorada
Pelican Cove Resort, 84457 Overseas Highway, PO Box 633, 33036
  Ph: 305-664-4435 800-445-4690 — Islamorada

Banyan Resort, 323 White Head St., 33040 Ph: 305-296-7786 800-225-0639	Key West
Hyatt Key West, 601 Front St., 33040 Ph: 305-296-9900 800-233-1234	Key West
Key West Hilton Resort & Marina, 245 Front St., 33040 Ph: 305-294-4000	Key West
Marriott's Beach Resort, 1435 Simonton St., 33040 Ph: 305-296-5000 800-874-4118	Key West
Marriott's Casa Marina, 1500 Reynolds St., 33040 Ph: 305-296-3535 800-228-9290	Key West
Pier House Resort, 1 Duval St., 33040 Ph: 305-296-4600 800-327-8340	Key West
Sheraton Suites Hotel, 2001 S. Roosevelt Blvd, 33040 Ph: 305-292-9800 800-325-3535	Key West
Southernmost Motel, 1319 Duval St., 33040 Ph: 305-296-6577 800-354-4455	Key West
Traveler's Palm, 815 Catherine, 33040 Ph: 305-294-9560 800-294-9560	Key West
Hyatt Orlando, 6375 US Rt 192 West, 32741 Ph: 407-396-1234 800-233-1234	Kissimmee
Lago Vista Vacation Resort, 180 Royal Palm Dr., 32743 Ph: 407-348-5246	Kissimmee
Buena Vista Palace, PO Box 22206, 32830 Ph: 800-327-2990	Lake Buena Vista
Courtyard by Marriott-Disney Villag, 1805 Hotel Plaza Blvd., Box 22204, 32830 Ph: 407-828-8888 800-223-9930	Lake Buena Vista
Disney's All-Star Music, 1801 W Buena Vista Dr., PO Box 10,000, 32830 Ph: 407-939-5000	Lake Buena Vista
Disney's All-Star Sports, 1701 W Buena Vista Dr., PO Box 10,000, 32830 Ph: 407-939-5000	Lake Buena Vista
Disney's Beach Club, 1800 Epcot Resorts Blvd., PO Box 10,000, 32830 Ph: 407-934-8000	Lake Buena Vista
Disney's Caribbean Beach, 900 Cayman Way, PO Box 10,000, 32830 Ph: 407-934-3400	Lake Buena Vista
Disney's Contemporary Resort, 4600 N World Dr., PO Box 10,000, 32830 Ph: 407-824-1000	Lake Buena Vista
Disney's Dixie Landings, 1251 Dixie Dr., PO Box 10,000, 32830 Ph: 407-934-6000	Lake Buena Vista
Disney's Grand Floridian Resort, 4401 Grand Floridian Way, PO Box 10,000, 32830 Ph: 407-824-3000	Lake Buena Vista
Disney's Polynesian Resort, US 192 in Walt Disney World, PO Box 10,000, 32830 Ph: 407-824-2000	Lake Buena Vista
Disney's Port Orleans, 2201 Orleans Dr., PO Box 10,000, 32830 Ph: 407-934-5000	Lake Buena Vista
Disney's Wilderness Lodge, 901 W. Timberline Dr., PO Box 10,000, 32830 Ph: 407-824-3200	Lake Buena Vista
Disney's Yacht Club Resort, 1700 Epcot Resorts Blvd., PO Box 10,000, 32830 Ph: 407-934-7000	Lake Buena Vista
Doubletree Guest Suites, 2305 Hotel Plaza Blvd., 32830 Ph: 407-934-1000 800-424-2900	Lake Buena Vista
Grosvenor Resort @ Disney Village, 1850 Hotel Plaza Blvd., 32830 Ph: 407-828-4444 800-624-4109	Lake Buena Vista
Royal Plaza, 1905 Hotel Plaza Blvd., 32830 Ph: 407-828-2828 800-248-7890	Lake Buena Vista
Travelodge Walt Disney Village, 2000 Hotel Plaza Blvd., Box 22205, 32830 Ph: 407-828-2424 800-348-3765	Lake Buena Vista
Vistana Resort, 8800 Vistana Center Dr., Box 22051, 32830 Ph: 407-239-3100 800-327-9152	Lake Buena Vista
Walt Disney World Dolphin, 1500 Epcot Resorts Blvd., PO Box 10,000, 32830 Ph: 407-934-4000 800-227-1500	Lake Buena Vista
Walt Disney World Swan, 1200 Epcot Resorts Blvd., PO Box 10,000, 32830 Ph: 407-934-3000 800-248-7926	Lake Buena Vista

Resort at Longboat Key Club, 301 Gulf of Mexico Dr., 34228 Ph: 941-383-8821 800-237-8821	Longboat
Conch Key Cottages, Mile Marker 62.3, 33050 Ph: 305-289-1377	Marathon
Marriott's Marco Island Resort, 400 S. Collier Blvd., 33937 Ph: 941-394-2511 800-MARRIOTT	Marco Island
Doral Resort & Country Club, 440 NW 87th Avenue, 33178 Ph: 305-592-2000 800-22-DORAL	Miami
Punta Cana Beach Resort, E P S A-301, PO Box 524121, 33152 Ph: 809-541-271415 800-972-2139	Miami
Beacharbour Resort Hotel, 18925 Collins Ave., 33160 Ph: 305-931-8900 800-643-0807	Miami Beach
Days Inn - Oceanside, 4299 Collins Ave., 33140 Ph: 305-673-1513 800-356-3017	Miami Beach
Best Western Naples Inn, 2329 Ninth St N, 33940 Ph: 813-261-1148 800-528-1234	Naples
Cove Inn, 1191 8th St S, 33940 Ph: 813-262-7161 800-255-4365	Naples
Edgewater Beach Hotel, 1901 Gulf Shore Blvd, 33940 Ph: 813-262-6511 800-821-0196	Naples
Howard Johnson Resort, Naples, 221 Ninth St S, 33940 Ph: 813-262-6181 800-654-2000	Naples
Naples Beach Hotel & Golf Club, 851 Gulf Shore Blvd S, 33940 Ph: 813-261-2222 800-237-7600	Naples
Registry Resort, 475 Seagate Dr., 33963 Ph: 941-597-3232 800-247-9810	Naples
Ritz-Carlton, Naples, 280 Vanderbilt Beach Rd., 33963 Ph: 941-598-3300 800-241-3333	Naples
Charter Club Resort, 1000 Tenth Ave S, 33940 Ph: 813-261-5559 800-494-5559	Naples Bay
Embassy Suites International Dr. S, 8978 International Dr., 32819 Ph: 407-352-1400 800-433-7275	Orlando
Peabody Orlando, 9801 International Dr., 32819 Ph: 407-352-4000 800-42-DUCKS	Orlando
Sonesta Village Hotel, Orlando, 10000 Turkey Lake Rd., 32819 Ph: 407-352-8051 800-766-3782	Orlando
Summerfield Suites Lake Buena Vista, 8480 International Dr., 32819 Ph: 407-352-2400 800-833-4253	Orlando
PGA National Resort, 400 Avenue of the Champions, 33418 Ph: 407-627-2000 800-633-9150	Palm Beach Gardens
Palm Coast Resort, 300 Clubhouse Dr., 32037 Ph: 904-445-3000	Palm Coast
Marriott's Bay Point Resort, 4200 Marriott Dr., 32408 Ph: 805-234-3307	Panama City Beach
Club Med, The Sandpiper, 3500 S.E. Morningside Blvd., 33452 Ph: 407-335-4400	Port St. Lucie
Outdoor Resorts River Ranch, P.O. Box 30030, 33867 Ph: 813-692-1321 800-866-6777	River Ranch
Casa Ybel Resort, 2255 W. Gulf Dr., PO Box 167, 33957 Ph: 941-472-3145 800-237-8906	Sanibel Island
Gulf Breeze Cottages, 1081 Shell Basket Lane, 33957 Ph: 941-472-1626 800-388-2842	Sanibel Island
Seaside, Rt. 30A, PO Box 4730, 32459 Ph: 904-231-1320	Seaside
Ocean Gallery, 4600 Hwy. A1A S, 32084 Ph: 904-471-6663 800-940-6665	St. Augustine
St. Augustine Hostel, 32 Treasury St., 32804 Ph: 904-808-1999	St. Augustine
Don Cesar Resort & Spa, 3400 Gulf Blvd., 33706 Ph: 813-360-1881 800-247-9810	St. Pete Beach
Trade Winds on St. Petersburg Beach, 5500 Gulf Blvd., PO Box 66307, 33706 Ph: 813-367-6461 800-237-0707	St. Pete Beach
Sugarloaf Lodge, Mile Marker 17, 33050 Ph: 305-745-3741	Sugarloaf Key

Best Western - Busch Gardens, 820 E. Busch Blvd., 33612 Ph: 813-933-4011 800-288-4011	Tampa
Doubletree Guest Suites - Tampa Bay, 3050 N. Rocky Point Dr. W , 33607 Ph: 813-888-8800 800-222-8733	Tampa
Doubletree Guest Suites Tampa/Busch, 11310 N. 30th St., 33612 Ph: 813-971-7690 800-433-TREE	Tampa
Hampton Inn, 4817 W. Laurel St., 33607 Ph: 813-287-0778 800-426-7866	Tampa
Holiday Inn Tampa-Busch Gardens, 2701 E. Fowler Ave., 33612 Ph: 813-971-4710 800-HOLIDAY	Tampa
Quality Suites Hotel USF, 3001 University Center Dr., Ph: 813-971-8930 800-786-7446	Tampa
Wyndham Harbour Island Hotel, 725 Harbour Island Blvd., 33602 Ph: 813-229-5000 800-822-4200	Tampa
The Driftwood Resort, 3150 Ocean Dr., 32963 Ph: 561-231-0550	Vero Beach

Georgia

The Cottage Inn, 129 Hwy 49 N, PO Box 488, 31709 Ph: 912-924-9316 912-924-6680	Americus
Atlanta Hilton and Towers, 255 Courtland Ave. NE, 30303 Ph: 404-659-2000	Atlanta
Beverly Hills Inn, 65 Sheridan Dr., 30305 Ph: 404-233-8520 800-331-8520	Atlanta
Days Inn - Atlanta Downtown, 300 Spring St., 30308 Ph: 404-523-1144	Atlanta
Days Inn Clairmont, 2910 Clairmont Rd., 30329 Ph: 404-633-8411	Atlanta
Days Inn Northlake Stone Mountain N, 2158 Ranchwood Dr., 30345 Ph: 770-934-6000	Atlanta
Doubletree Hotel at Concourse, 7 Concourse Pkwy, 30328 Ph: 770-395-3900	Atlanta
Hawthorn Suites Hotel, 1500 Parkwood Circle, 30339 Ph: 404-952-9595	Atlanta
Holiday Inn Atlanta Central, 418 Armour Dr. NE, 30324 Ph: 404-873-4661	Atlanta
Holiday Inn Select Atlanta Perimete, 4386 Chamblee-Dunwoody Rd., 30341 Ph: 770-457-6363	Atlanta
Howard Johnson Hotel - Atlanta, 1377 Virginia Ave., 30344 Ph: 404-762-5111	Atlanta
Marriott Atlanta Northwest, 200 Interstate North Parkway, 30339 Ph: 404-952-7900	Atlanta
Occidental Grand Hotel Atlanta, 75 Fourteenth St., 30309 Ph: 404-881-9898 800-952-0702	Atlanta
Quality Inn Habersham Downtown, 330 Peachtree St., NE, 30308 Ph: 404-577-1980 800-241-4288	Atlanta
Regency Suites - Atlanta, 975 W. Peachtree St., 30309 Ph: 404-876-5003	Atlanta
Renaissance Atlanta Hotel Airport, One Hartsfield Centre Pkwy., 30354 Ph: 404-209-9999 800-HOTELS 1	Atlanta
Renaissance Waverly Hotel, 2450 Galleria Parkway, 30339 Ph: 404-952-4500 800-HOTELS-4	Atlanta
Shellmont B&B Lodge, 821 Piedmont Ave. NE, 30308 Ph: 404-872-9290	Atlanta
Summerfield Suites Hotel, 505 Pharr Rd., 30305 Ph: 404-262-7880 800-833-4353	Atlanta
Amerisuites, 1062 Claussen Rd., 30907 Ph: 706-733-4656	Augusta
Comfort Inn - Augusta, 629 Frontage Rd. NW , 30907 Ph: 706-855-6060	Augusta
Hostel in the Forest, PO Box 1496, 31521 Ph: 912-264-9738	Brunswick
Historic Columbus Hilton, 800 Front Ave., 31901 Ph: 706-324-1800 800-444-2427	Columbus
Sheraton Columbus Airport Hotel, 5351 Simons Blvd., 31904 Ph: 706-327-6868	Columbus
Dalton Days Inn, 1518 W. Walnut Ave., 30720 Ph: 706-278-0850	Dalton
Days Inn Atlanta South, 5116 Hwy. 85, 30050 Ph: 404-768-6400	Forest Park
Early Hill, 1580 Lickskillet Rd., 30642 Ph: 706-453-7876	Greensboro

Helendorf River Inn & Towers, PO Box 305, 30545 Ph: 706-878-2271   Helen
    800-445-2271

Unicoi State Park Lodge, Hwy 356, PO Box 849, 30545 Ph: 706-878-2201   Helen

Fieldstone Inn, US 76, Lake Chatuge, PO Box 670, 30546 Ph: 706-896-2262   Hiwassee
    800-545-3408

Woodbridge Inn, 411 Chambers St., 30143 Ph: 706-692-6293   Jasper

Best Western Jekyll Inn Oceanfront, 975 N. Beachview Dr., 31527   Jekyll Island
    Ph: 912-635-2531 800-736-1046

Clarion Resort Buccaneer, 85 Beachview Dr., 31527 Ph: 912-635-2261   Jekyll Island

Days Inn Oceanfront, 60 S. Beachview Dr., 31527 Ph: 912-635-3319   Jekyll Island

Holiday Inn Kingsland, 930 Highway 40E, PO Box 1869, 31548   Kingsland
    Ph: 912-729-3000

Lookout Inn, Scenic Hwy., 30750 Ph: 706-820-2000   Lookout Mtn

Pinefields Plantation, Hwy 37, Rt 2, Box 215, 31768 Ph: 912-985-2086   Moultrie

Executive Villas Hotel, 5735 Roswell Rd., 30342 Ph: 404-252-2868   Roswell

Stoval House Country Inn, Hwy 255 North, Rt 1, Box 1476, 30571   Sautee
    Ph: 706-878-3355

Days Inn - Savannah, 201 W. Bay St., 31401 Ph: 912-236-4440   Savannah

East Bay Inn, 225 East Bay St., 31401 Ph: 912-238-1225 800-500-1225   Savannah

Eliza Thompson House, 5 W. Jones St., 31401 Ph: 912-236-3620   Savannah
    800-348-9378

Foley House Inn, 14 West Hull St., 31401 Ph: 912-232-6622   Savannah

Holiday Inn Mulberry, 601 E. Bay St., 31401 Ph: 912-238-1200   Savannah
    800-HOLIDAY

Kehoe House, 123 Habersham St., 31401 Ph: 912-232-1020 800-820-1020   Savannah

Lion's Head Inn, 120 E. Gaston St., 31401 Ph: 912-232-4580 800-355-LION   Savannah

Magnolia Place Inn, 503 Whitaker St., 31401 Ph: 912-236-7674   Savannah
    800-238-7674

Olde Harbour Inn, 508 E. Factor's Walk, 31401 Ph: 912-234-4100   Savannah
    800-553-6533

Planters Inn, 29 Abercom St., 31401 Ph: 912-232-5678 800-554-1187   Savannah

Presidents' Quarters, 255 E. President St., 31401 Ph: 912-233-1600   Savannah
    800-233-1776

River Street Inn, 115 East Bat St., 31401 Ph: 912-234-6400 800-253-4229   Savannah

The Veranda, 252 Seavy St., Box 177, 30276 Ph: 706-599-3905   Senoia

Little St. Simons Island, PO Box 1078, 31522 Ph: 912-638-7472   St. Simons Island

The King and Prince Beach Resort, PO Box 798, 31522 Ph: 912-638-3631   St. Simons Island
    800-342-0212

Statesboro Inn, 106 S. Main St., 30458 Ph: 912-489-8628 800-84 MY INN   Statesboro

Susina Plantation Inn, Meridian Rd., Rt 3, Box 1010, 31792 Ph: 912-377-9644   Thomasville

Hawaii

Kapalua Bay Hotel & Villas, One Bay Dr., 96761 Ph: 808-669-5656   Kapalua, Maui

Hale Pau Hana Resort, 2480 S. Kihei Rd., 96753 Ph: 808-2715 800-367-6036   Kihei, Maui

Maui Inter-Continental Wailea, 3700 Wailea Alanui, 96753 Ph: 808-879-1922   Kihei, Maui
    800-367-2960

Poipu B&B Inn, 2720 Hoonani Rd., 96756 Ph: 808-742-1146 800-552-0095   Koloa, Kauai

Poipu Kai Resort, 2827 Poipu Rd., 96756 Ph: 808-742-7400 800-367-8020   Koloa, Kauai

Kaanapali Alii, 50 Nohea Kai Drive, 96761 Ph: 808-667-1400 800-642-MAUI   Lahaina, Maui

Napili Kai Beach Club, 5900 Honoapiilani Rd., 96761 Ph: 808-669-6271   Lahaina, Maui
    800-367-5030

Napili Sunset, 46 Hui Dr., 96761 Ph: 808-669-8083 800-447-9229   Lahaina, Maui

Whaler on Kaanapali Beach, 2418 Kaanapali Parkway, 96761   Lahaina, Maui
    Ph: 808-661-4861 800-367-7052

Manele Bay Hotel, PO Box 774, 96763 Ph: 808-565-7300 800-321-4666	Lana'i City, Lanai
Aston Kauai Beach Villas, 4330 Kauai Beach Dr., 96766 Ph: 808-245-7711 800-922-7866	Lihue, Kauai
Outrigger Kauai Beach, 4331 Kauai Beach Dr., 96766 Ph: 808-245-1955 800-688-7444	Lihue, Kauai
Embassy Suites Kauai, 5380 Honoiki Rd., 96722 Ph: 808-826-6522 800-EMBASSY	Princeville, Kauai
Princeville Hotel, PO Box 3069, 97622 Ph: 808-826-9644 800-826-4400	Princeville, Kauai
Royal Waikoloan, PO Box 5300, 96743 Ph: 808-885-6789 800-462-6262	Waikoloa, Hawaii
The Bay Club, 5525 Waikoloa Beach Dr., 96743 Ph: 808-885-7979 800-305-7979	Waikoloa, Hawaii
Grand Champions Villas, 3750 Wailea Alanui, 96753 Ph: 808-879-1595 800-367-5246	Wailea, Maui
Kokee Lodge, PO Box 819, 96796 Ph: 808-335-6061	Waimea, Kauai

Idaho

Allison Ranch, 7259 Cascade Dr., Dept K, 83704 Ph: 208-376-5270	Boise
Idaho Heritage Inn, 109 W. Idaho, 83702 Ph: 208-343-2325	Boise
Owyhee Plaza Hotel, 1109 Main St., 83702 Ph: 208-343-4611 800-233-4611	Boise
Red Lion Hotel Downtowner, 1800 Fairview Ave., 83702 Ph: 208-344-7691 800-547-8010	Boise
Red Lion Inn Riverside, 2900 Chinden Blvd., 83714 Ph: 208-343-1871	Boise
Residence Inn, 1401 Lusk Ave., 83706 Ph: 208-344-1200 800-331-3131	Boise
Stonebraker Ranch, 3190 Airport Way, Dept. K, 83705 Ph: 208-344-1881 800-635-5336	Boise
Diamond D Ranch, PO Box I K, 83227 Ph: 313-821-4975	Clayton
Idaho City Hotel, PO Box 70, 83631 Ph: 208-392-4290	Idaho City
Busterback Ranch, Star Route, Drawer K, 83340 Ph: 208-774-2271	Ketchum
Heidelberg Inn, P.O. Box 5704, 83340 Ph: 208-726-5361 800-249-7722	Ketchum
Twin Peaks Ranch, PO Box 951 K, 83467 Ph: 208-894-2290	Salmon
Schweitzer Mountain Resort, PO Box 815, 83864 Ph: 208-263-9555 800-831-8810	Sandpoint
Idaho Rocky Mountain Ranch, HC 64, Box 9934, 83278 Ph: 208-774-3544	Stanley
Redfish Lake Lodge, PO Box 9, 83278 Ph: 208-774-3536	Stanley
Best Western Tyrolean Lodge, 260 Cotton Wood, 83353 Ph: 208-726-5336 800-333-7912	Sun Valley
Clarion Inn of Sun Valley, P.O. Box 660, 83353 Ph: 208-726-5361 800-262-4833	Sun Valley
Sun Valley, 83353 Ph: 208-622-4111 800-635-8261	Sun Valley
Tamarack Lodge, 291 Walnut Drive, 83353 Ph: 208-726-3344 800-521-5379	Sun Valley

Illinois

Days Inn Lakeshore Drive, 644 N. Lake Shore Dr., 60611 Ph: 312-943-9200 800-633-1414	Chicago
Embassy Suites Hotel, 600 N. State St., Ph: 312-943-7629	Chicago
Four Seasons Hotel, 120 E. Delaware Place, 60611 Ph: 312-280-8800 800-332-3442	Chicago
Holiday Inn Mart Plaza, 350 N. Orleans St., 60654 Ph: 312-836-5000 800-HOLIDAY	Chicago

Hotel Inter-Continental, 505 N. Michigan Ave., 60611 Ph: 312-944-4100   Chicago
  800-628-2468
Hotel Nikko Chicago, 320 N. Dearborn, 60610 Ph: 312-744-1900   Chicago
  800-NIKKO-US
Hyatt Regency Chicago, 151 E. Wacker Dr., 60601 Ph: 312-565-1234   Chicago
  800-233-1234
Ohio Mouse Motel, 600 N. La Salle St., 60610 Ph: 312-943-6000   Chicago
Ritz-Carlton, Chicago, 160 E. Pearson St., 60611 Ph: 312-266-1000   Chicago
  800-621-6906
The Drake, Lake Shore Drive & Michigan Ave., 60611 Ph: 312-787-DRAKE   Chicago
  800-55-DRAKE
Hobson's Bluffdale, Hillview Rd., 62027 Ph: 217-983-2854   Eldred
DeSoto House Hotel, 230 S. Main St., 61036 Ph: 815-777-0090   Galena
Log Cabin Guest House, 11661 W. Chetlain Lane, 61036 Ph: 815-777-2845   Galena
Pere Marquette Lodge, Rt. 100, 62037 Ph: 618-786-2331   Grafton
Sweet Basil Hill Farm, 15937 W. Washington St., 60031 Ph: 708-244-3333   Gurnee
  800-228-HERB
Hotel Nauvoo, Rt. 96, PO Box 398, 62354 Ph: 217-453-2211   Nauvoo
Starved Rock Lodge, Starved Rock State Park, PO Box 471, 61373   Utica
  Ph: 815-667-4211
Wheaton Inn, 301 W. Roosevelt Rd., 60187 Ph: 708-690-2600 800-447-4667   Wheaton

Indiana

Potawatomi Inn, Pokagon State Park, 6 Lane 100A, Lake James, 46703   Angola
  Ph: 219-833-1077
Morgan's Farm, RR 2, 47102 Ph: 812-794-2536   Austin
The Columbus Inn, 445 Fifth St., 47201 Ph: 812-378-4289   Columbus
Kintner House Inn, 101 S. Capitol St., 47112 Ph: 812-738-2020   Corydon
French Lick Springs Resort, 47432 Ph: 812-936-9300 800-457-4042   French Lick
Checkerberry Inn, 62644 C.R. 37, 46526 Ph: 219-642-4445   Goshen
Seminary Place, 210 E. Seminary St., 46135 Ph: 317-653-3177 317-653-9277   Greencastle
Walden Inn, 2 Seminary Square, PO Box 490, 46135 Ph: 317-653-2761   Greencastle
Teetor House, 300 W. Main St., 47346 Ph: 317-489-4422 800-824-4319   Hagerstown
Canterbury Hotel, 123 S. Illinois, 46225 Ph: 317-634-3000 800-538-8186   Indianapolis
Comfort Inn, 5040 S. East St., 46227 Ph: 317-783-6711 800-221-2222   Indianapolis
Embassy Suites Hotel - Downtown, 100 W. Washington St., 46204   Indianapolis
  Ph: 317-236-1800 800-EMBASSY
Holiday Inn at Union Station, 123 W. Louisiana St., PO Box 2186, 46206   Indianapolis
  Ph: 317-631-2221 800-HOLIDAY
Hyatt Regency Indianapolis, 1 S. Capitol Ave., 46204 Ph: 317-632-1234   Indianapolis
  800-233-1234
Westin Hotel Indianapolis, 50 S. Capitol Ave., 46204 Ph: 317-262-8100   Indianapolis
  800-228-3000
Turkey Run Inn, RR 1, Box 444, 47859 Ph: 317-597-2211 317-597-2660   Marshall
Creekwood Inn, Rt 20-35 at I-94, 46360 Ph: 219-872-8357   Michigan City
Essenhaus Country Inn, 240 US Rt 20, 46540 Ph: 219-825-9447   Middlebury
Spring Mill Inn, PO Box 68, 47446 Ph: 812-849-4081   Mitchell
Victorian Guest House, 302 E. Market St., 46550 Ph: 219-773-4383   Nappanee
Abe Martin Lodge, PO Box 547, 47448 Ph: 812-988-4418 812-988-7316   Nashville
Brown County Inn, St Rd 46 & 135, PO Box 128, 47448 Ph: 812-988-2291   Nashville
New Harmony Inn, North St., PO Box 581, 47631 Ph: 812-682-4491   New Harmony
  800-782-8605
Larry Bird's Boston Connection, 555 S. Third St., PO Box 8386, 47808   Terre Haute
  Ph: 812-235-3333 800-262-0033
White Hill Manor, 2513 E. Center St., 46580 Ph: 219-269-6933   Warsaw

Iowa

The Abbey Hotel, 1401 Central Ave., 52722 Ph: 319-355-0291 800-438-7535	Bettendorf
Bishop House Inn, 1527 Brady St., 52803 Ph: 319-324-2454	Davenport
River Oaks Inn B&B, 1234 E. River Dr., 52803 Ph: 319-326-2629 800-352-6016	Davenport
Hancock House, 1105 Grove Terr., 52001 Ph: 319-557-8989	Dubuque
Juniper Hill Farm, 15325 Budd Rd., 52002 Ph: 319-582-4405 800-572-1449	Dubuque
Stout House, 1105 Locust St., 52001 Ph: 319-582-1894	Dubuque
Haverkamp's Linn Street Homestay, 619 N. Linn St., 52245 Ph: 319-337-4363	Iowa City
Fitzgerald's Inn, 160 N. Third St., PO Box 157, 52151 Ph: 319-538-4872	Lansing
Squiers Manor, 418 W. Pleasant, 52060 Ph: 319-652-6961	Maquoketa
English Valley B&B, 4455 135th St., 50171 Ph: 515-623-3663	Montezuma
Queen Anne B&B, 1110 Ninth St., 50201 Ph: 515-382-6444	Nevada
Hannah Marie Country Inn, Rt. 1, 51301 Ph: 712-262-1286	Spencer

Kansas

Windmill Inn, 1787 Rain Rd., 67431 Ph: 913-263-8755	Abilene
The Cottage House Hotel, 25 North Neosho, 66846 Ph: 800-727-7903	Council Groves
Plumb House B&B, 628 Exchange Rd., 66801 Ph: 316-342-6881	Emporia
The Eldridge Hotel, Seventh & Massachusetts, 66044 Ph: 800-527-0909	Lawrence
Swedish Country Inn, 112 W. Lincoln, 67456 Ph: 800-227-2985	Lindsborg
Almeda's B&B Inn, 220 S. Main, 66086 Ph: 913-845-2295	Tonganoxie
Barn B&B Inn, RR 2, Box 87, 66088 Ph: 913-945-3225	Valley Falls
Thistle Hill B&B, Rt 1, Box 93, 67672 Ph: 913-743-2644	Wakeeney
Inn at the Park, 3751 E. Douglas, 67218 Ph: 800-258-1951	Wichita
Inn at Willowbend, 3939 Comotara, 67226 Ph: 316-636-4032 800-553-5775	Wichita
Marriott, 9100 Corporate Hills Dr., 67207 Ph: 316-651-0333 800-228-9290	Wichita
Max Paul, An Inn, 3910 E. Kellogg, 67218 Ph: 316-689-8101	Wichita
Residence Inn, 411 S. Webb Rd., 67207 Ph: 316-686-7331 800-331-3131	Wichita
Wichita Suites, 5211 E. Kellogg, 67218 Ph: 316-685-2233 800-243-5953	Wichita

Kentucky

Cedar Lane Motel, Rt 1, Hwy 68, Ph: 502-474-8042	Aurora
The Old Jailer's Inn, 111 W. Stephen Foster Ave., 40004 Ph: 502-348-5551	Bardstown
Weller Haus, 319 Poplar St., 41073 Ph: 606-431-6829	Bellevue
Big Bear Resort, Rt 4, Box 143, 42025 Ph: 800-922-2327	Benton
Shawnee Bay Resort, Rt 4, Box 408, 42025 Ph: 503-354-8360	Benton
Boone Tavern Hotel, Main & Prospect Sts, CPO 2345, 40404 Ph: 606-986-9358 800-366-9358	Berea
Doe Run Inn, 500 Doe Run Hotel Rd., 40108 Ph: 502-422-2982	Brandenburg
Dupont Lodge, Cumberland Falls State Resort Park, 7351 Hwy 90, 40701 Ph: 606-528-4121 800-325-0063	Corbin
Amos Shinkle Townhouse, 215 Garrard St., 41011 Ph: 606-431-2118	Covington
Sandford House, 1026 Russell St., 41011 Ph: 606-291-9133	Covington
Palisades Resort, Rt. 1 Box 359, 42038 Ph: 503-388-7667	Eddyville
Olde Bethlehem Academy Inn, 7051 St. John Rd., 42701 Ph: 502-862-9003 800-662-5670	Elizabethtown
Hickory Hill Resort, Rt 5, Ph: 502-354-8207 800-264-8207	Fairdealing
Holiday Inn, 8050 Holiday Place, 41042 Ph: 606-371-2700	Florence
Holiday Inn Capital Plaza, 405 Wilkinson Blvd., 40601 Ph: 502-227-5100	Frankfort
Log Cabin B&B, 350 N. Broadway, 40324 Ph: 502-863-3514	Georgetown
Ramada Limited, 401 Delaplain Rd., 40324 Ph: 502-863-1166	Georgetown

Ken-Bar Inn Resort & Club, Hwy 641, PO Box 66, 42044 Ph: 502-362-8852 — Gilbertsville
Ramada Inn Resort, US 62 at Kentucky Dam, 42044 Ph: 502-362-4278 — Gilbertsville
800-628-6538
Petticoat Junction B&B, 223 High St., PO Box 36, 42740 Ph: 502-369-6804 — Glendale
800-252-0059
Kenlake Lodge, Rt 1, Box 522, 42048 Ph: 502-474-2211 800-325-0143 — Hardin
Canaan Land Farm B&B, 4355 Lexington Rd., 40330 Ph: 606-734-3984 — Harrodsburg
Shaker Village of Pleasant Hill, 3501 Lexington Rd., 40330 Ph: 606-734-5411 — Harrodsburg
800-734-5611
The Beaumont Inn, 638 Beaumont Dr., 40330 Ph: 606-734-3381 — Harrodsburg
800-352-3992
Lake Cumberland State Resort Park, 5465 State Park Rd., PO Box 380, 42629 — Jamestown
Ph: 502-343-3111 800-325-1709
Best Western Regency Lexington, 2241 Elkhorn Rd., Ph: 606-293-2202 — Lexington
800-528-1234
Campbell House Inn Suites & Golf, 1375 Harrodsburg Rd., Ph: 606-225-4281 — Lexington
Gratz Park Inn, 120 W. Second St., 40507 Ph: 606-231-1777 800-227-4362 — Lexington
Harley of Lexington, 2143 N. Broadway, 40505 Ph: 606-299-1261 — Lexington
Hyatt Regency Lexington, 400 W. Vine St., 40507 Ph: 606-253-1234 — Lexington
Marriott's Griffin Gate Resort, 1800 Newtown Pike, 40511 Ph: 606-231-5100 — Lexington
800-228-9290
Radisson Plaza Hote Lexington, 369 W. Vine St., 40507 Ph: 606-231-9000 — Lexington
Louisville Inn, 1359 S. Third St., 40208 Ph: 502-635-1574 — Louisville
The Brown, 335 W. Broadway, 40202 Ph: 502-583-1234 800-866-7666 — Louisville
The Seelbach Hotel, 500 Fourth Ave., 40202 Ph: 502-585-3200 — Louisville
800-333-3399
Gateway B&B, 326 E. Sixth St., 41071 Ph: 606-581-6447 — Newport
Glenmar Plantation, 2444 Valley Hill Rd., 40069 Ph: 606-284-7791 — Springfield
800-828-3330
Sills Inn B&B, 270 Montgomery Ave., 40383 Ph: 606-252-3601 800-526-9801 — Versailles
Otter Creek Park, 850 Otter Creek Park Rd., 40108 Ph: 502-583-3577 — Vine Grove
502-942-3641

Louisiana

Bentley, 200 Desoto St., PO Box 8276, 71301 Ph: 318-448-9600 — Alexandria
800-356-6835
Chateau Louisianne Suite Hotel, 710 N. Lobdell Ave., 70806 — Baton Rouge
Ph: 225-927-6700 800-256-6263
Loyd Hall Plantation Home, 191 Loyd Bridge Rd., 71325 Ph: 318-776-5641 — Cheneyville
Seale Guest House - A B&B Inn, Hwy 13, PO Box 568, 70535 — Eunice
Ph: 318-457-3753
Creole Rose Manor, 214 Plaquemine St., 70546 Ph: 318-824-4936 — Jennings
800-264-5521
Bois Des Chenes, 338 N. Sterling St., 70501 Ph: 318-233-7816 — Lafayette
Ti Frere's House, 1905 Verot School Rd., 70508 Ph: 318-984-9347 — Lafayette
Hardy House, 1414 Weems St., PO Box 1192, 71346 Ph: 318-776-5178 — Lecompte
Holiday Inn New Orleans I-10, 6401 Veterans Blvd, 70003 Ph: 504-885-5700 — Metairie
Breazeale House B&B, 926 Washington, 71457 Ph: 318-352-5630 — Natchitoches
Cloutier Town House B&B, 8 Ducournau Square & Front St., 71457 — Natchitoches
Ph: 318-352-5242
Bienville House, 320 Decatur St., 70130 Ph: 504-529-2345 800-535-7836 — New Orleans
Chateau Motor Hotel, 1001 Rue Chartres, 70116 Ph: 504-524-9636 — New Orleans
800-828-1822
Chimes Cottages, 1146 Constantinople St., 70115 Ph: 504-899-2621 — New Orleans

Comfort Inn Downtown/Superdome, 1315 Gravier St., 70112   New Orleans
   Ph: 504-586-0100 800-535-9141
Delta Queen, 30 Robin Street Wharf, 70130 Ph: 504-586-0631 800-543-1949   New Orleans
Fairmont Hotel, 123 Baronne St., 70140 Ph: 504-529-7111   New Orleans
Hotel Provincial, 1024 Chartres St., 70116 Ph: 504-581-4995   New Orleans
Hyatt Regency New Orleans/Superdome, Poydras & Loyola Ave., 70140   New Orleans
   Ph: 504-561-1234 800-233-1234
Jensen's B&B, 1631 7th St., 70115 Ph: 504-897-1895   New Orleans
Lafitte Guest House, 1003 Bourbon St., 70116 Ph: 504-581-2678   New Orleans
   800-331-7971
Lamothe House, 621 Esplanade Ave., 70116 Ph: 504-947-1161 800-367-5858   New Orleans
Landmark French Quarter Hotel, 920 N. Rampart St., 70116   New Orleans
   Ph: 504-524-3333 800-535-7862
Maison Dupuy, 1001 Toulouse St., 70112 Ph: 504-586-8000 800-535-9177   New Orleans
Mississippi Queen, 30 Robin Street Wharf, 70130 Ph: 504-586-0631   New Orleans
   800-543-1949
Omni Crescent Hotel, 535 Gravier St., 70140 Ph: 504-527-0006   New Orleans
   800-THE-OMNI
Omni Royal Orleans, Royal & St. Louis Sts., 70140 Ph: 504-529-5333   New Orleans
   800-THE-OMNI
Royal Sonesta Hotel, 300 Bourbon St., 70140 Ph: 504-586-0300   New Orleans
   800-SONESTA
Soniat House, 1133 Chartres St., 70116 Ph: 504-522-0570 800-544-8808   New Orleans
St. Charles Guest House B&B, 1748 Prytania St., 70130 Ph: 504-529-2952   New Orleans
Fairfield Place, 2221 Fairfield Ave., 71104 Ph: 318-222-0048   Shreveport
Remington Suite, 220 Travis St., 71101 Ph: 318-425-5000 800-444-3248   Shreveport
Green Springs B&B, 7463 Tunica Trace, 70775 Ph: 504-635-4232   St. Francisville
   800-457-4978
Maison Bleue B&B, 417 N. Main St., 70582 Ph: 318-394-1215   St. Martinville
Chretian Point Plantation, Rt 1, Box 162, 70584 Ph: 318-662-5876   Sunset
   800-880-7050
Nottoway Plantation, Mississippi River Rd., PO Box 160, 70788   White Castle
   Ph: 504-545-2730

Maine

Pleasant Bay B&B, PO Box 222, West Side Rd., 04606 Ph: 207-483-4490   Addison
Spruce Point Inn, PO Box 237, 04538 Ph: 207-633-4152   Boothbay
   Harbor
Oakland House, RR 1, Box 400, 04617 Ph: 207-359-8521 800-359-RELAX   Brooksville
Blue Harbor House, 67 Elm St., 04843 Ph: 207-236-3196 800-248-3196   Camden
High Tide Inn on the Ocean, Rt 1, 04843 Ph: 207-236-3724   Camden
Whitehall Inn, PO Box 558, 04843 Ph: 207-236-3391   Camden
Hiram Blake Camp, Harborside PO Box 59, Blake's Point, 04642   Cape Rosier
   Ph: 207-326-4951
Albonegon Inn, 04538 Ph: 207-633-2521   Capitol Island
Sugarloaf Inn, 04947 Ph: 207-237-2000 800-THE-LOAF   Carrabassett
   Valley
Castine Inn, Main St., PO Box 41, 04421 Ph: 207-326-4365   Castine
The Holiday House, PO Box 215, 04421 Ph: 207-326-4335   Castine
The Manor, PO Box 215, 04421 Ph: 207-326-4861   Castine
Quisisana, 04016 Ph: 207-925-3500 914-833-0293   Center Lovell
Westways Country Inn, Rt. 5, PO Box 175, 04016 Ph: 207-928-2663   Center Lovell
Westways on Kezar Lake, Rt 5, 04016 Ph: 207-928-2663   Center Lovell
Brannon-Bunker Inn, HCR 64 #045, Rt. 128, 04543 Ph: 207-563-5941   Damariscotta
Oxford House Inn, 105 Main St., 04037 Ph: 207-935-3442   Fryeburg

Weatherby's, 04637 Ph: 207-796-5558 207-237-2911	Grand Lake Stream
Greenville Inn, Norris St., PO Box 1194, 04441 Ph: 207-695-2206	Greenville
Le Domaine Restaurant & Inn, Rt 1, PO Box 496, 04604 Ph: 207-422-3395 800-554-8498	Hancock
Green Heron Inn, 126 Ocean Ave., PO Box 2578, 04046 Ph: 207-967-3315	Kennebunkport
Maine Stay Inn & Cottages, 34 Maine St., PO Box 500 A-FTN, 04046 Ph: 207-967-2117	Kennebunkport
Herbert Hotel, PO Box 67, 04947 Ph: 207-265-2000 800-843-4372	Kingfield
Shining Sails, Box 346, 04852 Ph: 207-596-0041 800-606-9497	Monhegan Island
Bradley Inn, Rt 130, HC 61, 361 Pemaquid Point, 04554 Ph: 207-677-2105	New Harbor
The Gosnold Arms, HC 61, PO Box 161, Northside Rd., 04554 Ph: 207-677-3727	New Harbor
Pulpit Harbor Inn, Box 704, 04853 Ph: 207-867-2219 800-867-2219	North Haven Island
Papoose Pond, Rural Route 1, Box 2480, 04267 Ph: 207-583-4470	North Waterford
Sebago Lake Lodge & Cottages, White's Bridge Rd., 04062 Ph: 207-892-2698	North Windham
Alden Camps, Inc., RR 2 Box 1140, 04963 Ph: 207-465-7703	Oakland
Bear Springs Camps, Rt. 2 Box 1900, 04963 Ph: 207-397-2341	Oakland
Sparhawk Resort, 41 Shore Rd., PO Box 936C, 03907 Ph: 207-646-5562	Ogunquit
Bald Mountain Camps, PO Box 332, 04964 Ph: 207-864-3671	Oquossoc
Holiday Inn by the Bay, 88 Spring St., 04101 Ph: 207-775-2311 800-HOLIDAY	Portland
Hotel Everett, 51A Oak St., 041 Ph: 207-773-7882	Portland
Howard Johnson, 155 Riverside St., 04103 Ph: 207-774-5861	Portland
Inn on Carleton, 46 Carleton St., 041 Ph: 207-775-1910	Portland
Keller's B&B, Island Ave., 041 Ph: 207-766-2441	Portland
Portland Regency In Old Port, 20 Milk St., 04101 Ph: 207-774-4200 800-727-3436	Portland
Mallory's B&B Inn, Hyatt Rd., PO Box 9, 04970 Ph: 207-864-2121 800-722-0397	Rangeley
Rangeley Inn, Main St., PO Box 160, 04970 Ph: 207-864-3341 800-666-3687	Rangeley
Moose River Landing, PO Box 295, 04478 Ph: 207-534-7577	Rockwood
The Birches, PO Box 81, 04478 Ph: 207-534-7305 800-825-9453	Rockwood
Homeport Inn, Rt 1, PO Box 647, 04974 Ph: 207-548-2259 800-742-5814	Searsport
Rock Gardens Inn, PO Box 178, 04530 Ph: 207-389-1339	Sebasco Estates
Buck's Harbor Inn, 04617 Ph: 207-326-8660	South Brooksville
Claremont, Claremont Rd., 04679 Ph: 207-244-5036 800-244-5036	Southwest Harbor
Lindenwood Inn, 118 Clark Point Rd., 04679 Ph: 207-244-5335	Southwest Harbor
The Craignair Inn, 533 Clark Island Rd., 04859 Ph: 207-594-7644	Spruce Head
Island View Inn, HCR 34, Box 24, Rt. 1, 04664 Ph: 207-422-3031	Sullivan Harbor
Northern Outdoors, Rt. 201, PO Box 100, 04985 Ph: 207-663-4466 800-765-7238	The Forks
Kawanhee, Lake Webb, 04938 Ph: 207-585-2000 207-778-4306 Winter	Weld
The Historic Garrison House Resort, 1099 Post Rd., 04090 Ph: 207-646-3497 800-646-3497	Wells

Lawnmeer Inn, PO Box 505, 04575 Ph: 207-633-3544 800-633-7645 — West Booth-bay Harbor

Bosebuck Mountain Camps, Rt. 16, PO Box 30, 04579 Ph: 207-243-2945 207-486-3238 Winter — Wilsons Mills

Dockside Guest Quarters, Harris Island Rd., PO Box 205, 03909 Ph: 207-363-2868 800-270-1977 — York

Maryland

Historic Inns of Annapolis, 16 Church Circle, 21401 Ph: 410-263-2641 — Annapolis
Admiral Fell Inn, 888 South Broadway, 21231 Ph: 410-522-7377 — Baltimore
Brookshire Inner Harbor Suite Hotel, 120 E. Lombard St., 21202 Ph: 410-625-1300 — Baltimore
Clarion Hotel, 612 Cathedral St., 21201 Ph: 410-727-7101 — Baltimore
Harbor Court Hotel, 550 Light St., 21202 Ph: 410-234-0550 800-824-0076 — Baltimore
Holiday Inn - Inner Harbaor, 301 W. Lombard St., 21201 Ph: 410-685-2500 800-HOLIDAY — Baltimore
Hyatt Regency Baltimore, 300 Light St., 21202 Ph: 410-528-1234 — Baltimore
Inn at Henderson Wharf, 1000 Fell St., 21231 Ph: 410-522-7777 800-522-2088 — Baltimore
Marriott Inner Harbor, 110 S. Eutaw St., 21201 Ph: 410-962-0202 — Baltimore
Omni Inner Harbor, 101 W. Fayette St., 21201 Ph: 410-752-1100 800-THE-OMNI — Baltimore
Renaissance Harborplace Hotel, 202 E. Pratt, 21202 Ph: 410-547-1200 800-HOTELS-1 — Baltimore
Sheraton Inner Harbor, 300 S. Charles St., 21201 Ph: 410-962-8300 800-325-3535 — Baltimore
Shirley-Madison Inn, 205 W. Madison St., 21201 Ph: 410-728-6550 — Baltimore
Holland House B&B, 5 Bay St., 21811 Ph: 410-641-1956 — Berlin
The Inn at Mitchell House, 8796 Maryland Parkway, 21620 Ph: 410-778-6500 — Chestertown
White Swan Tavern, 231 High St., 21620 Ph: 410-778-2300 — Chestertown
Chevy Chase B&B, 6815 Connecticut Ave., 20815 Ph: 301-656-5867 — Chevy Chase
Gross' Coate 1658, 11300 Gross Coate Rd., 21601 Ph: 410-819-0802 — Easton
Tidewater Inn, 101 E. Dover, PO Box 359, 21601 Ph: 410-822-1300 — Easton
Lewrene Farm, 9378 Downsville Pike, 21740 Ph: 301-582-1735 — Hagerstown
Kent Manor Inn, Rt. 50 & 8, Ph: 301-643-5757 — Kent Island
Deep Creek Lake, Star Rt. 1, Box 77, 21541 Ph: 301-387-5533 800-447-3034 — McHenry
Inn at Antietam, 220 E. Main St., PO Box 119, 21782 Ph: 301-432-6601 — Sharpsburg
Blue Bear B&B, 22052 Holiday Dr., 21783 Ph: 301-824-2292 — Smithsburg
River House Inn, 201 East Market St., 21863 Ph: 410-632-2722 — Snow Hill
Solomons Island Holiday Inn, 155 Holiday Dr., PO Box 1099, 20688 Ph: 410-326-6311 800-356-2009 — Solomons
Parsonage Inn, 210 N. Talbott St., 21663 Ph: 410-745-5519 800-394-5519 — St. Michaels
St. Michaels Harbour Inn & Marina, 101 North Harbor Rd., 21663 Ph: 410-745-9001 — St. Michaels
Wades Point Inn on the Bay, PO Box 7, 21663 Ph: 410-745-2500 — St. Michaels
Kent Manor Inn, 500 Kent Manor Dr., 21666 Ph: 410-643-5757 — Stevensville
Glenburn, 3515 Runnymede Rd., 21787 Ph: 301-751-1187 — Taneytown

Massachusetts

Tage Inn, 131 River Road, 01810 Ph: 508-685-6200 800-322-TAGE — Andover
Copley Plaza - A Wyndham Hotel, Copley Square, 02116 Ph: 617-267-5300 800-WYNDHAM — Boston
Eliot, 370 Commonwealth Ave., 02115 Ph: 617-267-1607 800-443-5468 — Boston
Hotel Meridien, 250 Franklin St., 02110 Ph: 617-451-1900 800-543-4300 — Boston

The Bostonian Hotel, Faneuil Hall Marketplace, 02109 Ph: 617-523-3600
  800-343-0922   Boston
High Brewster, 964 Satucket Rd., 02631 Ph: 508-896-3636 800-203-2634   Brewster
Mary Prentiss Inn, 6 Prentiss St., 02140 Ph: 617-661-2929   Cambridge
The Inn at Harvard, 1201 Massachusetts Ave., 02138 Ph: 617-491-2222   Cambridge
  800-458-5886
Lion's Head Inn, 186 Belmont Rd., West Harwich, PO Box 444, 02671   Cape Cod
  Ph: 508-432-7766 800-321-3155
Wequassett Inn, Pleasant Bay, 02633 Ph: 508-432-5400 800-225-7125   Chatham
Breakfast at Tiasquam, Middle Road, 02535 Ph: 508-645-3685   Chilmark
The Colonial Inn, 48 Monument Square, 01742 Ph: 413-369-9200   Concord
  800-370-9200
Cumworth Farm, Rt 112, 01026 Ph: 413-634-5529   Cummington
Deerfield Inn, The Street, 01342 Ph: 413-774-5587 800-926-3865   Deerfield
Breakers, 61 Chase Ave., 02639 Ph: 508-398-6905   Dennisport
Wingscorton Farm, 11 Wing Blvd., 02537 Ph: 508-888-0534   East Sandwich
Over Look Inn, 3085 County Rd., PO Box 771, 02642 Ph: 508-255-1886   Eastham
  800-356-1121
Harbor View Resort, 131 N. Water St., PO Box 7, 02539 Ph: 508-627-7000   Edgartown
  800-225-6005
Miles River Country Inn, 823 Bay Rd., PO Box 149, 01936 Ph: 508-468-7206   Hamilton
Breakwaters, 432 Sea Street Beach, Box 118, 02601 Ph: 508-775-6831   Hyannis
Captain Gosnold Village, 230 Gosnold St., 02601 Ph: 508-775-9111   Hyannis
Eastover Resort, 430 East Street, 01240 Ph: 413-637-0625 800-VACAFUN   Lenox
Kripalu Center for Yoga & Health, PO Box 793, 01240 Ph: 413-448-3400   Lenox
  800-967-3577
The Seagull Inn B&B, 106 Harbor Ave., 01945 Ph: 508-631-1893   Marblehead
Cliffside Beach Club, Jefferson Ave., PO Box 449, 02554 Ph: 508-228-0618   Nantucket
Jared Coffin House, 19 Broad St., PO Box 1580, 02554 Ph: 508-228-2400   Nantucket
Martin House Inn, 61 Centre St., PO Box 743, 02554 Ph: 508-228-0678   Nantucket
Wauwinet, PO Box 2580, 02554 Ph: 508-228-0145 800-426-8718   Nantucket
White Elephant Resort, S. Easton St., Box 359, 02554 Ph: 508-228-2500   Nantucket
  800 ISLANDS
Old Inn on the Green - Gedney Farm, 01230 Ph: 413-229-7924   New
  800-286-3139   Marlborough
Clark Currier Inn, 45 Green St., 01950 Ph: 508-465-8363   Newburyport
Gibson Cottages, PO Box 86, 02642 Ph: 508-255-0882   North
                                              Eastham
Kalmar Village, Shore Rd., PO Box 745, 02652 Ph: 508-487-0585   North Truro
  617-247-0211 Winter
Hotel Northampton, 36 King St., 01060 Ph: 413-584-3100   Northampton
Hargood House, 493 Commercial St., 02657 Ph: 508-487-9133   Provincetown
Masthead Resort, 31-41 Commercial St., PO Box 577, 02657   Provincetown
  Ph: 508-487-0523 800-395-5095
White Horse Inn, 500 Commercial St., 02657 Ph: 508-487-1790   Provincetown
Linden Tree Inn, 26 King St., 01966 Ph: 508-542-2494   Rockport
Old Farm Inn, 291 Granite St., 01966 Ph: 508-546-3237   Rockport
Seaward Inn, Marmion Way, 01966 Ph: 508-546-3471   Rockport
Hawthorne Hotel on the Common, 01970 Ph: 508-744-4080 800-SAY-STAY   Salem
The Salem Inn, 7 Summer St., 01970 Ph: 508-741-0680 800-446-2995   Salem
The Dan'l Webster Inn, 149 Main St., 02563 Ph: 508-888-3622   Sandwich
  800-444-3566
Summer House, PO Box 880, 02564 Ph: 508-257-4577   Siasconset
The House on the Hill, 968 Main St., PO Box 51, 02661 Ph: 508-432-4321   South Harwich
Merrell Tavern Inn, Main St., 01260 Ph: 413-243-1794   South Lee

The Even'tide Motel & Cottages, PO Box 41, Rt 6, 02663 Ph: 508-349-3410 — South Wellfleet, Cape Cod

Captain Farris House, 308 Old Main St., 02665 Ph: 508-760-2818 800-350-9477 — South Yarmouth

Gull Wing Suites, 822 Main St., 02664 Ph: 508-394-9300 800-541-3480 — South Yarmouth

Red Lion Inn, 01262 Ph: 413-298-5545 — Stockbridge

Colonel Ebenezer Crafts Inn, PO Box 187, 01566 Ph: 800-782-5425 — Sturbridge

Longfellow's Wayside Inn, Wayside Inn Rd., 01776 Ph: 508-443-1776 — Sudbury

Suisse Chalet Hotel, 1695 Andover Street, 01876 Ph: 508-640-0700 800-5-CHALET — Tewksbury

Causeway Harborview, Skiff Ave., Box 450, 02568 Ph: 508-693-1606 800-253-8684 — Vineyard Haven

The Lothrop Merry House, Owen Park, PO Box 1939, 02568 Ph: 508-693-1646 — Vineyard Haven

The Colony, Chequessett Neck Rd., 02667 Ph: 508-349-3761 — Wellfleet

Yarmouth Shores Cottages, 29 Lewis Bay Blvd., 02673 Ph: 508-775-1944 — West Yarmouth

Twin Maples, 106 South St., 01096 Ph: 413-268-7925 — Williamsburg

Field Farm Guest House, 554 Sloan Rd., 01267 Ph: 413-458-3135 — Williamstown

River Bend Farm, 643 Simonds Rd., 01267 Ph: 413-458-3121 — Williamstown

The Orchards, 222 Adams Rd., 01267 Ph: 413-458-9611 800-225-1517 — Williamstown

Sengekontacket Houses, c/o Woodex Properties, 968 Main St, 01890 Ph: 617-729-1230 800-621-1175 — Winchester

---

Michigan

Reynolds House at Stonefield Farm, 5259 W. Ellsworth Rd., 48103 Ph: 734-995-0301 — Ann Arbor

Lavalley's Resort & Antiques, N7017 H-03 Au Train Lake Rd., PO Box 99, 49806 Ph: 906-892-8455 — AuTrain

Greencrest Manor, 6174 Halbert Rd., 49017 Ph: 616-962-8633 — Battle Creek

The Terrace Inn, 216 Fairview, 49770 Ph: 616-347-2410 800-CLARION — Bay View

The Townsend Hotel, 100 Townsend St., 48009 Ph: 313-642-7900 800-548-4172 — Birmingham

Michigamme Lake Lodge, PO Box 97, 49814 Ph: 906-339-4400 — Champion

Keweenaw Mountain Lodge, 49918 Ph: 906-289-4403 — Cooper Harbor

Dearborn Inn, 20301 Oakwood Blvd., 48124 Ph: 313-271-2700 800-228-9290 — Dearborn

Holiday Inn - Dearborn, 22900 Michigan Ave., 48124 Ph: 313-278-4800 800-465-4329 — Dearborn

Hyatt Regency Dearborn, Fairlane Town Center, 48126 Ph: 313-593-1234 800-233-1234 — Dearborn

Quality Inn - Fairland, 21430 Michigan Ave., 48124 Ph: 313-565-0800 800-228-5151 — Dearborn

Ritz-Carlton Dearborn, Fairlane Plaza, 48126 Ph: 313-441-2000 800-241-3333 — Dearborn

The Crane House, 6051 124th Ave., 49408 Ph: 616-561-6931 — Fennville

Homestead, Wood Ridge Rd., 49636 Ph: 616-334-5100 616-334-5000 — Glen Arbor

Stuart Avenue Inn, 229 Stuart Ave., 49007 Ph: 616-385-3442 — Kalamazoo

Oak Cove Resort, 58881 46th St., 49064 Ph: 616-674-8228 708-983-8025 Winter — Lawrence

Garland Resort, Rt 1, Box 364-M, County Rd. 489, 49756 Ph: 517-786-2211 800-968-0042 — Lewiston

Grand Hotel, 49757 Ph: 906-847-3331 800-33-GRAND — Mackinac Island

Haan's 1830 Inn, Huron St., PO Box 123, 49757 Ph: 906-847-6244	Mackinac Island
Hotel Iroquois, Main St., PO Box 456, 49757 Ph: 906-847-3321 616-247-5675 Winter	Mackinac Island
Metivier Inn, Market St., PO Box 285, 49757 Ph: 906-847-6234 616-627-2055 Winter	Mackinac Island
Mission Point Resort, 1 Lakeshore Dr., PO BOx 430, 49757 Ph: 906-847-3312 800-833-7711	Mackinac Island
McCarthy's Bear Creek Inn, 15230 C. Drive North, 49068 Ph: 616-781-8383	Marshall
National House, 102 South Parkview, 49068 Ph: 616-781-7374	Marshall
The Helmer House Inn, Country Rd. 417, 49853 Ph: 906-586-3204	McMillian
San Souci, 18265 S. Lakeside Rd., 49117 Ph: 616-756-3141	New Buffalo
Bungalow B&B, Ford Dr., 49946 Ph: 906-524-7595	Pequaming
Perry Hotel, Bay & Lewis Sts, 49770 Ph: 616-347-4000 800-456-1917	Petoskey
Stafford's Bay View Inn, 613 Woodland Ave., PO Box 3, 49770 Ph: 616-347-2771 800-456-1917	Petoskey
The Montague Inn, 1581 S. Washington Ave., 48601 Ph: 517-752-3939	Saginaw
Maplewood Hotel, 428 Butler St., 49453 Ph: 616-857-2788	Saugatuck
The Park House, 888 Holland Street, 49453 Ph: 616-857-4535 800-321-4535	Saugatuck
Ojibwya Hotel, 240 W. Portage, 49783 Ph: 906-632-4100 800-654-2929	Sault Ste. Marie
Old Harbor Inn, 515 Williams St., 49090 Ph: 616-637-8480	South Haven
Snow Flake Motel, 3822 Red Arrow Hwy., 49085 Ph: 616-429-3261	St. Joseph
Blue Water Beach Resort, 1819 US 31 North, 4968 Ph: 616-938-1370	Traverse City
Cherry Knoll Farm, 2856 Hammond Road East, 49684 Ph: 616-947-9806 800-847-9806	Traverse City
Driftwood Motel, 1861 US 31 North, 4968 Ph: 616-938-1600	Traverse City
Hampton Inn, 1000 US 31 North, 49686 Ph: 616-946-8900 800-HAMPTON	Traverse City
On A Bay Motel/Resort, 1773 US 31 North, 4968 Ph: 616-938-2680	Traverse City
The Beach Condominiums, 1995 US 31 North, 4968 Ph: 616-938-2228	Traverse City
Victorian Villa Guesthouse, 601 N. Broadway St., 49094 Ph: 517-741-7383 800-34-VILLA	Union City

Minnesota

Timber Bay Lodge & Houseboats, Box 248, 55706 Ph: 218-827-3682 800-846-6821	Babbit
Kavanaugh's Resort, 2300 Kavanaugh Drive S.W., 56401 Ph: 218-829-5226 800-562-7061	Brainerd
Maplelag, Rt. 1, 56521 Ph: 218-375-4466 800-654-7711	Callaway
Fitger's Inn, 600 E. Superior St., 55802 Ph: 218-722-8826 800-726-2982	Duluth
Gunflint Lodge, HC 64, Box 750, 55604 Ph: 218-388-2294 800-328-3325	Grand Marais
Naniboujou Lodge, HC 1, Box 505, 55604 Ph: 218-387-2688	Grand Marais
Rockwood Lodge, HC 64, Box 625, 56604 Ph: 218-388-2242 800-942-2922	Grand Marais
Douglas Lodge, Itasca State Park, 56460 Ph: 218-266-3654 800-765-CAMP	Lake Itasca
Caribou Lake B&B, PO Box 156, 55612 Ph: 218-663-7489	Lutsen
Lutsen Resort, 55612 Ph: 218-663-7212 800-346-1467	Lutsen
Hotel Luxeford, 1101 LaSalle Ave., 55403 Ph: 612-332-6800 800-664-1101	Minneapolis
Hyatt Regency Hotel, 1300 Nicollet Mall, 55403 Ph: 612-370-1234 800-233-1234	Minneapolis
Minneapolis The Marquette, 71- Marquette Ve., 55402 Ph: 612-333-4545 800-HILTONS	Minneapolis
Quality Inn, 250 N River Ridge Circle, 55337 Ph: 612-890-9550	Minneapolis
Radisson Hotel Metrodome, 615 Washington Ave. E, 55414 Ph: 612-379-8888	Minneapolis
Regency Plaza Hotel, 41 N. Tenth St., 55403 Ph: 612-339-9311	Minneapolis

The Whitney, 150 Portland Ave., 55401 Ph: 612-339-9300 800-248-1879	Minneapolis
Black Pine Beach Resort, HC 83, Box 464, 56472 Ph: 218-543-4714 800-543-4714	Pequot Lakes
Best Western Kelly Inn-State Capital, 161 St. Anthony St., 55103 Ph: 612-227-8711	St. Paul
Embassy Suites St. Paul, 175 E. Tenth St., 55101 Ph: 612-224-5400 800-EMBASSY	St. Paul
Radisson Hotel St. Paul, 11 E. Kellogg Blvd., 55101 Ph: 612-292-1900	St. Paul
St. Paul Hotel, 350 Market St., 55102 Ph: 612-292-9292	St. Paul

Mississippi

Hamilton Place, 105 E. Mason Ave., 38635 Ph: 601-252-4368	Holly Springs
Redbud Inn, 121 N. Wells St., 39090 Ph: 601-289-5086	Kosciusko
Rosswood Plantation, Hwy 552, Rt 1, Box 6, 39096 Ph: 601-437-4215 800-533-5889	Lorman
The Burn, 712 N. Union St., 39120 Ph: 601-442-1344 800-654-8859	Matchez
Statehouse Hotel, Main & Jackson Sts., PO Box 2002, 39759 Ph: 601-323-2000 800-722-1903	Starkville
Anchuca, 1010 First East St., 39180 Ph: 601-636-4938 800-262-4822	Vicksburg
Belle of the Bends, 508 Klein St., 39180 Ph: 601-634-0737 800-844-2308	Vicksburg
Duff Green Mansion, 1114 First East St., 39180 Ph: 601-636-6986	Vicksburg
The Corners, 601 Klein St., 39180 Ph: 601-636-7421 800-444-7421	Vicksburg

Missouri

Still Waters Condominium Resort, HCR 1 Box 928, 65616 Ph: 417-338-2323 800-777-2320	Branson
Seven Gales Inn, 26 N. Meramec, 63105 Ph: 314-863-8400 800-243-1166	Clayton
The Elms, Regent & Elms Blvd., 64024 Ph: 816-329-4880 800-843-3567	Excelsior Springs
Captain Wohlt Inn, 123 E. Third St., 65041 Ph: 314-486-3357	Hermann
Raphael, 325 Ward Parkway, Country Club Plaza, 64112 Ph: 816-756-3800 800-821-5343	Kansas City
Ritz-Carlton, 401 Ward Parkway, 64112 Ph: 816-756-1500 800-241-3333	Kansas City
Ozark Mountain Resort Swim & Tennis, Rt 4, Box 910, 65686 Ph: 417-779-5301 800-225-2422	Kimberling City
Wilderness Lodge, Box 90, 63654 Ph: 314-637-2295 314-296-2011	Lesterville
Big Cedar Lodge, 612 Devil's Pool Rd., 65739 Ph: 417-335-2777 417-335-2340	Ridgedale
School House B&B, Third & Clark Sts., 65279 Ph: 314-698-2022 314-698-2022	Rocheport
Walnut Street Inn, 900 E. Walnut St., 65806 Ph: 417-864-6346 800-593-6346	Springfield
Adam's Mark Hotel, Fourth & Chestnut, 63102 Ph: 314-241-7400 800-444-ADAM	St. Louis
Courtyard by Marriott, 828 N. New Ballas Rd., 63146 Ph: 314-993-0515	St. Louis
Days Inn Convention Center, 1133 Washington Ave., 63102 Ph: 314-231-4070 800-329-7466	St. Louis
Doubletree Suite Hotel, 806 S. Charles St., 63101 Ph: 314-421-2500	St. Louis
Hampton Inn Downtown, 2211 Market St., 63101 Ph: 314-241-3200	St. Louis
Holiday Inn Downtown Riverfront, 4th & Pine Sts., 63102 Ph: 314-621-8200 800-925-1395	St. Louis
Holiday Inn Select Conv. Center, 9th St. & Conv. Plaza Blvd., 63101 Ph: 314-421-4000	St. Louis
Hyatt Regency St. Louis Union Sta., 1 St. Louis Sta., 63103 Ph: 314-231-1234 800-233-1234	St. Louis

Regal Riverfront Hotel, 200 S. 4th St., 63102 Ph: 314-241-9500 800-325-7353	St. Louis
Summerfield Suites Hotel, 1855 Craigshire Rd., 63146 Ph: 314-878-1555 800-833-4353	St. Louis
The Hotel Majestic, 1019 Pine St., 63101 Ph: 314-436-2355 800-678-8946	St. Louis
Washington House, 3 Lafayette St., 63090 Ph: 314-239-2417 314-239-9834	Washington

Montana

JJJ Wilderness Ranch, Box 301 K, 59410 Ph: 406-562-3653	Augusta
Flathead Lake Lodge, Box 248 K, 59911 Ph: 406-837-4391	Big Fork
Big Sky of Montana, PO Box 1, 59716 Ph: 406-995-4211 800-548-4486	Big Sky
Lone Mountain Ranch, PO Box 69 K, 59716 Ph: 406-995-4644	Big Sky
Sweet Grass Ranch, Melville Route, Box 173 K, 59011 Ph: 406-537-4477	Big Timber
Mountain Sky Guest Ranch, PO BOx 1128, 59715 Ph: 800-548-3392	Bozeman
C-B Ranch, PO Box 604 K, 59720 Ph: 406-682-4954	Cameron
Cliff Lake Lodge, PO Box 267, 59720 Ph: 406-682-4982	Cameron
G Bar M Ranch, Box AE, Dept K, 59018 Ph: 406-686-4423	Clyde Park
Diamond J Ranch, PO Box 577 K, 59729 Ph: 406-682-4867	Ennis
Izaak Walton Inn, PO Box 653, 59916 Ph: 406-888-5700	Essex
Laughing Water Ranch, Deep Creek Rd., PO Box 157 K, 59918 Ph: 406-882-4680	Fortine
Elkhorn Ranch, 33133 Gallatin Rd., Drawer K, 59730 Ph: 406-995-4291	Gallatin Gateway
Nine Quarter Circle Ranch, 5000 Taylor Fork Rd., Box K, 59730 Ph: 406-995-4276	Gallatin Gateway
Glacier Park, Ph: 406-888-5441 602-207-6000	Glacier National Park
Boulder River Ranch, Box 210 K, 59052 Ph: 406-932-6406	McLeod
Beartooth Ranch, HC 54, Box 350K, 59061 Ph: 406-328-6194 406-328-6205	Nye
Chico Hot Springs, Drawer D, 59065 Ph: 406-333-4933	Pray
Holland Lake Lodge, 1947 Holland Lake Rd., 59826 Ph: 406-754-2282 800-648-8859	Swan Valley
Sacajawea Inn, 5 North Main Street, 59752 Ph: 406-285-6934 800-821-7326	Three Forks
Blue Spruce Lodge & Guest Ranch, 410 Marten Creek Rd., Dept K, 59874 Ph: 406-827-4762	Trout Creek
Circle Bar Guest Ranch, PO Box K, 59452 Ph: 406-423-5454	Uticad
Nevada City Hotel, PO Box 338, 59755 Ph: 406-843-5377	Virginia City
Elk Canyon Ranch, Dept K, 59645 Ph: 406-547-3373	White Sulphur Springs

Nebraska

The Rogers House, 2145 B St., 68502 Ph: 402-476-6961	Lincoln
The Offutt House B&B, 140 N. 39th St., 68131 Ph: 402-553-0951	Omaha

Nevada

Hyatt Regency Lake Tahoe Resort, Country Club Dr. at Lakeshore, PO Box 3239, 89450 Ph: 702-831-1111 800-233-1234	Incline Village
Harrah's, PO Box 8, 89449 Ph: 702-588-6611 800-648-3773	Lake Tahoe
Aladdin Hotel, 3667 Las Vegas Blvd. S, 89109 Ph: 702-736-0111	Las Vegas
Downtowner Motel, 129 N 8th St, 98101 Ph: 702-384-1441 800-777-2566	Las Vegas
Las Vegas Hilton, 3000 Paradise Rd., 89109 Ph: 702-732-5755	Las Vegas
The Mirage, 3400 Las Vegas Blvd. S, 89109 Ph: 800-627-6667	Las Vegas
Treasure Island, 3300 Las Vegas Blvd. S, 89109 Ph: 800-944-7444	Las Vegas
Tropicana Resort, 3801 Las Vegas Blvd. S, 89109 Ph: 800-634-4000	Las Vegas

New Hampshire

Attitash Mountain Village, Route 302, 03812 Ph: 603-374-6500 — Bartlett
Mulburn Inn, Main St., 03574 Ph: 603-869-3389 — Bethlehem
Mountain Lake Inn, PO Box 443, 03221 Ph: 603-938-2136 800-662-6005 — Bradford
Goddard Mansion, 25 Hillstead Rd., 03743 Ph: 603-543-0603 — Claremont
Rockhouse Mountain Farm Inn, 03832 Ph: 603-447-2880 — Eaton Center
Moose Mountain Lodge, PO Box 272, 03750 Ph: 603-643-3529 — Etna
Hannah Davis House, Rt 119, 186 Depot Rd., 03447 Ph: 603-585-3344 — Fitzwilliam
Inn at Crotched Mountain, Mountain Rd., 03043 Ph: 603-588-6840 — Francestown
Blanche's B&B, Easton Valley Rd., 03580 Ph: 603-823-7061 — Franconia
Franconia Inn, Rt. 116, Easton Road, 03580 Ph: 603-823-5542 — Franconia
Horse & Hound Inn, 105 Wells Rd., 03580 Ph: 603-823-5501 — Franconia
Freedom House B&B, 1 Maple St., 03836 Ph: 603-539-4815 — Freedom
Appalachian Mountain Club, Rt. 16, PO Box 298, 03581 Ph: 603-466-2727 — Gorham
Gorham House Inn, 55 Main St., PO Box 267, 03581 Ph: 603-466-2271 — Gorham
Greenfield Inn, Rt 31, Forest Rd., 03040 Ph: 603-547-6327 — Greenfield
Inn at Elmwood Corners, 252 Winnacunnet Rd., 03842 Ph: 603-929-0443 — Hampton
Hanover Inn, East Wheelock & Main St., PO Box 151, 03755
    Ph: 603-643-4300 — Hanover
Meetinghouse Inn & Restaurant, 35 Flanders Rd., 03242 Ph: 603-428-3228 — Henniker
Carter Notch Inn, Carter Notch Rd., PO Box 269, 03846 Ph: 603-383-0630
    800-794-9434 — Jackson
Christmas Farm Inn, Rt. 16B, Box CC, 03846 Ph: 603-383-4313 800-HI
    ELVES — Jackson
Eagle Mountain Resort, Carter Notch Rd., 03846 Ph: 603-383-9111 — Jackson
Ellis River House, Rt. 16, PO Box 656, 03846 Ph: 603-383-9339
    800-233-8309 — Jackson
Inn at Jackson, PO Box H, 03846 Ph: 603-383-4321 800-289-8600 — Jackson
Nordic Village Vacation Resort, Rt. 16, 03846 Ph: 603-383-9101
    800-472-5207 — Jackson
Wentworth Resort Hotel, Box M, 03846 Ph: 603-383-9700 800-637-0013 — Jackson
Jefferson Inn, Rt 2, 03583 Ph: 603-586-7998 800-729-7908 — Jefferson
Ferry Point House, R 1, Box 335, 03246 Ph: 603-524-0087 — Laconia
Loon Mountain, Kancamagus Hwy., 03251 Ph: 603-745-8111 800-229-STAY — Lincoln
Wyman Farm, Wyman Rd., 03301 Ph: 603-783-4467 — Loudon
Cranmore Mountain Lodge, PO Box 1194, 03860 Ph: 603-356-2044
    800-356-3596 — North Conway
White Mountain Hotel & Resort, Westside Rd., 03860 Ph: 603-356-7100
    800-533-6301 — North Conway
Follansbee Inn, Rt. 114, PO Box 92, 03260 Ph: 603-927-4221 800-626-4221 — North Sutton
Anchorage, 725 Laconia Rd., 03276 Ph: 603-524-3248 — Pilton
The Angwins' Camp Driftwood, Route 1, Box 112, 03592 Ph: 603-538-6684 — Pittsburg
Sise Inn, 40 Court St., 03801 Ph: 603-433-1200 — Portsmouth
Philbrook Farm Inn & Cottages, 881 North Rd., 03581 Ph: 603-466-3831 — Shelburne
Sunset Hill House, Sunset Hill Rd., 03585 Ph: 603-823-5522 800-786-4455 — Sugar Hill
The Hilltop Inn, Main St., 03585 Ph: 603-823-5695 — Sugar Hill
Dexter's Inn & Tennis Club, PO Box 703F, 03782 Ph: 800-232-5571 — Sunapee
Waterville Valley Resort, Town Square, 03215 Ph: 603-236-8311
    800-468-2553 — Waterville Valley
Spalding Inn, Mountain View Rd., 03598 Ph: 603-837-2572 — Whitefield
Lakeshore Terrace, Box 18, 03894 Ph: 603-569-1701 — Wolfeboro

New Jersey

Cashelmara Inn, 22 Lakeside Ave., 07717 Ph: 201-776-8727 800-821-2976	Avon-by-the-Sea
Atlas Motor Inn, 1035 Beach Dr., 08204 Ph: 609-884-700	Cape May
Camelot Motel, 103 Howard St., 08204 Ph: 609-884-1500	Cape May
Captain Mey's B&B Inn, 202 Ocean St., 08204 Ph: 609-884-7793	Cape May
Carroll Villa B&B, 19 Jackson St., 08204 Ph: 609-884-9619	Cape May
Columbia House, 26 Ocean St., 08204 Ph: 609-884-2789	Cape May
Congress Hall Hotel, 251 Beach Dr., 08204 Ph: 609-884-8421	Cape May
Dormer House International, 800 Columbia Ave., 08204 Ph: 609-884-7446	Cape May
Goodman House, 118 Decatur St., 08204 Ph: 609-884-6371	Cape May
The Grand Hotel, Oceanfront at Philadelphia Ave., 08204 Ph: 609-884-5611 800-257-8550	Cape May
The Queen Victoria, 102 Ocean St., 08204 Ph: 609-884-8702	Cape May
The Virginia Hotel, 25 Jackson St., PO Box 557, 08204 Ph: 609-884-5700	Cape May
The Virginia Hotel, 25 Jackson St., PO Box 557, 08204 Ph: 609-884-5700 800-732-4236	Cape May
The Wooden Rabbit, 609 Hughes St., 08204 Ph: 609-884-7293	Cape May
Woodleigh House, 808 Washington St., 08204 Ph: 609-884-7123	Cape May
Parson's Folly, PO Box 314, 08212 Ph: 609-884-2215	Cape May Point
Somewhere in Time, 202 Ocean Ave., PO Box 134, 08212 Ph: 609-898-0962	Cape May Point
Cabbage Rose Inn, 162 Main St., 08822 Ph: 908-788-0247	Flemington
Inn at Lambertville Station, 11 Bridge St., 08530 Ph: 609-397-4400 800-524-1091	Lambertville
Acropolis Motor Inn, 3rd to 4th Sts., 08260 Ph: 609-522-5400	North Wildwood
Buccaneer Motel, 503 E. 19th Ave., 08260 Ph: 609-522-8467 215-379-4416 Winter	North Wildwood
Donaraile Motel & Apartments, 438 E. 21st Ave., 08260 Ph: 609-522-5275	North Wildwood
Montego Bay, 1800 Boardwalk, 08260 Ph: 609-523-1000 800-962-1349	North Wildwood
Surf Song, 1800 Oceam Ave., 08260 Ph: 609-523-0003 800-497-4353	North Wildwood
Crossings Motor Inn, 3420 Haven Ave., 08226 Ph: 609-398-4433 800-257-8811	Ocean City
Pebble Beach Motor Lodge, 9th St. at Wesley Ave., 08226 Ph: 609-399-3350	Ocean City
Sea Mist Hotel, 1402 Ocean Ave., 08226 Ph: 609-399-2164	Ocean City
Serendipity Bed and Brunch, 712 Ninth St., 08226 Ph: 609-399-1554	Ocean City
The Glen-Nor Hotel, 1015 Central Ave., PO Box 147, 08226 Ph: 609-399-4138 800-320-4138	Ocean City
The Parkside, 501 5th St., 08226 Ph: 609-399-1944 800-399-1944	Ocean City
The Sandaway, PO Box 115, 08226 Ph: 609-399-2779 800-367-3042	Ocean City
Top O'the Waves, 5447 Central Ave., 98226 Ph: 609-399-0477	Ocean City
Seven Springs Farm B&B, Perryville Rd., PD 3, Box 223, 08867 Ph: 908-735-7675	Pittstown
Grand Summit Hotel, 570 Springfield Ave., 07901 Ph: 908-273-3000 800-346-0773	Summit
Knoll's Resort Motel, 4111 Atlantic Ave., 08260 Ph: 609-522-8211 800-732-5665	Wildwood
The Mango Motel, 209 E. Spicer Ave., 08260 Ph: 609-522-2067	Wildwood

Admiral Resort Motel, 7200 Ocean Ave., 08260 Ph: 609-522-7704 800-759-9532	Wildwood Crest
Aqua Beach Resort, 5501 Ocean Ave., 08260 Ph: 609-522-6507 800-247-4776	Wildwood Crest
Pan American Hotel, 5901 Ocean Ave., Dept. CI, 08260 Ph: 609-522-6936	Wildwood Crest
Port Royal Hotel, 6801 Ocean Ave., 08260 Ph: 609-729-2000	Wildwood Crest
Royal Hawaiian Resort Motel, On the Beach at Orchid Rd., 08260 Ph: 609-522-3414	Wildwood Crest
The Grand Hotel, Beach & Rochester Ave., 08260 Ph: 609-729-6000 800-257-8550	Wildwood Crest
The Eden Roc Resort Motel, Atlantic & Bennett Aves., 08260 Ph: 609-522-1930	Wildwood-by-the-Sea

New Mexico

Casa del Granjero, 414 C de Baca Lane Northwest, 87114 Ph: 505-897-4144 800-701-4144	Albuquerque
Casas de Suenos, 310 Rio Grande Blvd. SW, Ph: 505-247-4560	Albuquerque
Fairfield Inn by Marriott, 1760 Menual NE, 87102 Ph: 505-889-4000 800-228-2800	Albuquerque
Holiday Inn Pyramid, 5151 San Francisco Road NE, 87109 Ph: 505-821-3333 800-461-4329	Albuquerque
Hyatt Regency Albuquerque, 330 Tijeras NW, 87102 Ph: 505-842-1234 800-233-1234	Albuquerque
La Posada de Albuquerque, 124 Second St. NW at Copper, 87102 Ph: 505-242-9090 800-777-5732	Albuquerque
Las Palomas Valley B&B, 1303 Candelaria Rd. NW, 87107 Ph: 505-345-7228	Albuquerque
Ramada Hotel Classic, 6815 Menaul NE, 87110 Ph: 505-881-0000 800-2-RAMADA	Albuquerque
St. James Hotel, Rt 1, Box 2, 87714 Ph: 505-376-2664	Cimarron
The Lodge, 1 Corona Place, PO Box 497, 88317 Ph: 505-682-2566 800-395-6343	Cloudcroft
El Rancho Hotel, 1000 E 66 Ave, 87301 Ph: 505-863-9311 800-543-6351	Gallup
Plaza Hotel, 230 Old Town Plaza, 87701 Ph: 505-435-3591 800-328-1882	Las Vegas
Plaza Travelodge Hotel, 230 On the Old Town Plaza, 87701 Ph: 505-425-3591 800-328-1882	Las Vegas
Inn of the Mountain Gods, PO Box 269, 88340 Ph: 505-257-5141 800-545-9011	Mescalero
Best Western Swiss Chalet, 1451 Mechem Dr., PO Box 759, 88345 Ph: 505-258-3333 800-477-9477	Ruidoso
Story Book Cabins, 410 Main Rd., PO Box 472, 88345 Ph: 505-257-2115 505-257-7512	Ruidoso
Chinguague Compound, Box 118, 87566 Ph: 505-852-2194	San Juan Pueblo
Canyon Road Casitas, 652 Canyon Rd., 87501 Ph: 505-988-5888 800-279-0755	Santa Fe
Inn of the Anasazi, 113 Washington Ave., 87501 Ph: 505-988-3030 800-688-8100	Santa Fe
Rancho Jacona, Route 5, PO Box 250, 87501 Ph: 505-455-7948	Santa Fe
Bear Mountain Guest Ranch, PO Box 1163, 88062 Ph: 505-538-2538 800-880-2538	Silver City
Casa Benavides, 137 Kit Carson Rd., 87571 Ph: 505-758-1772 505-758-8891	Taos
Casa de las Chimeneas, 405 Cordoba Rd., Box 5303, 87571 Ph: 505-758-4777	Taos
Casa Europa, 157 Upper Ranchitos Rd., 87571 Ph: 505-758-9798	Taos

El Monte Lodge, Kit Carson Rd., 87571 Ph: 505-758-3171   Taos
El Rincon B&B, 114 Kit Carson St., 87571 Ph: 505-758-4874   Taos
The Taos Inn, 125 Paseo de Pueblo Norte, 87571 Ph: 505-758-2233   Taos
    800-TAOS-INN
Austing Haus Hotel, Box 8, 87575 Ph: 505-776-2649 800-748-2932   Taos Ski Valley
St. Bernard Condominiums, PO Box 676, 87575 Ph: 505-776-8506   Taos Ski Valley
Taos, PO Box 90, 87525 Ph: 505-776-2291   Taos Ski Valley

New York

Mansion Hill Inn, 115 Philip St., 12202 Ph: 518-465-2038 800-477-8171   Albany
The Stewart House, 1 N. Water St., 12015 Ph: 518-945-1357   Athens
Hemlock Hall, Maple Lodge Rd., 12812 Ph: 518-352-7706   Blue Mountain Lake

The Hedges, 12812 Ph: 518-352-7325   Blue Mountain Lake

Suits Us Farm, 89 Pink St., 13740 Ph: 607-832-4470   Bovina Center
B&B on the Park, 113 Prospect Park West, 11215 Ph: 718-499-6115   Brooklyn
The Balsam House, Friends Lake Rd., 12817 Ph: 518-494-2828   Chestertown
Creekside B&B, Fork Shop Rd, RD1, Box 206, 13326 Ph: 607-547-8203   Cooperstown
Fieldstone Farm Resort, PO Box 528, 13326 Ph: 315-858-0295 800-336-4629   Cooperstown
The Inn at Cooperstown, 16 Chestnut St., 13326 Ph: 607-547-5756   Cooperstown
Greek Peak Ski Resort, 200 NYS Rt. 392, 13045 Ph: 800-955-2SKI   Cortland
Alexander Hamilton House, 49 Van Wyce St., 10520 Ph: 914-271-6737   Croton-on-Hudson

Margaret Thacher's Spruce Haven B&B, Rt. 13N, Ph: 607-844-8052   Dryden
Maidstone Park Cottages, 22 Bruce Lane, 11937 Ph: 516-324-2837   East Hampton
Point Lookout Mountain Inn, Rt 23, Box 33, 12439 Ph: 518-734-3381   East Windham
The White Inn, 52 E. Main St., 14063 Ph: 716-672-2103   Fredonia
Geneva on the Lake, 1001 Lochland Rd., PO Box 929, 14456   Geneva
    Ph: 315-789-7190
The Inn at Belhurst Castle, Lochland Rd., PO Box 609, 14456   Geneva
    Ph: 315-781-0201
Golden Acres Farm & Ranch, South Gibla Rd., 12076 Ph: 607-588-7329   Giboa
    800-847-2151
Austin Manor B&B, 210 Old Peruville Rd., Ph: 607-898-5786   Gorton
Balsam Shade Farm, Rt. 32, Ph: 518-966-5315   Greenville
Trout House Village Resort, Lake Shore Dr., 12836 Ph: 518-543-6088   Hague
    800-368-6088
Villaggio Resort, O'Hara Rd., 12436 Ph: 518-589-5000 800-843-4348   Haines Falls
Country Life B&B, 237 Cathedral Ave., 11550 Ph: 516-292-9219   Hempstead
Rocking Horse Ranch, 12528 Ph: 800-647-2624   Highland
Timberlock, 12864 Ph: 518-648-5494   Indian Lake
Hillside Inn, 518 Stewart Ave., Ph: 607-272-9507 800-427-6864   Ithaca
Spring Water Motel, Rt. 366, Ph: 607-272-3721   Ithaca
Whitetail Crossing Cottages, 21 Belvedere Dr., Ph: 607-257-3946   Ithaca
Trails End Inn, 12943 Ph: 518-576-9860   Keene Valley
Pine Grove Resort Ranch, Lower Chestertown Rd., 12446 Ph: 914-626-7345   Kerhonkson
    800-346-4626
Concord Resort Hotel, 12751 Ph: 914-794-4000 800-431-3850   Kiamesha Lake
Interlaken Inn, 15 Interlaken Ave., 12946 Ph: 518-523-3180 800-428-4369   Lake Placid
Mirror Lake Inn, 35 Mirror Lake Dr., 12946 Ph: 518-523-2544   Lake Placid
Beaverkill Valley Inn, 12753 Ph: 914-439-4844   Lew Beach
Kathleen's Country Estate B&B, 7989 Union Corners Rd., 14510   Mt. Morris
    Ph: 716-658-4627
Algonquin, 59 W. 44th St., 10036 Ph: 212-849-6800 800-548-0345   New York

Day's Inn, 440 W. 57th St., Ph: 212-581-8100 800-231-0405 — New York
Dumont Plaza, 150 E. 34th St., 10016 Ph: 212-481-7600 800-ME-SUITE — New York
Embassy Suites, 47th St. & 7th Ave., Ph: 212-719-1600 800-362-2779 — New York
Hotel Macklowe & Conference Center, 145 W. 44th St., Ph: 212-768-4400 — New York
Journey's End Hotel, 3 E. 40th St., Ph: 212-447-1500 800-668-4200 — New York
Mariott Marquis, 1535 Broadway, 10036 Ph: 212-398-1900 800-843-4898 — New York
Roger Smith Hotel, 501 Lexington Ave @ 47th, 10017 Ph: 212-755-1400 800-445-0277 — New York
Southgate Tower Suite Hotel, 371 7th Ave., Ph: 212-563-1800 800-ME-SUITE — New York
The Gorham, 136 W. 55th St., 10019 Ph: 212-245-1800 800-735-0701 — New York
Garnet Hill Lodge, 13th Lake Rd., 12856 Ph: 518-251-2821 — North River
Winter Clove Inn, 12473 Ph: 518-622-3267 — Round Top
Ram's Head, 108 Ram Island Drive, 11965 Ph: 516-749-0811 — Shelter Island Heights
Sherwood Inn, 16 W. Genesee St., 13152 Ph: 315-685-3405 — Skaneateles
The Pines Resort Hotel, Laurel Ave., 12779 Ph: 800-367-4637 — South Fallsburg
The Normandy Inn, 21 Tuttle Ave., 07762 Ph: 908-449-7172 — Spring Lake

North Carolina

Haywood Park Hotel, One Battery Park Ave., 28801 Ph: 704-252-2522 800-873-2392 — Asheville
Richmond Hill Inn, 87 Richmond Hill Dr., 28806 Ph: 704-252-7313 800-545-9238 — Asheville
Sand Villa Resort, 1400 E. Fort Macon Rd., PO Box 1090, 28512 Ph: 252-247-2636 800-334-2667 — Atlantic Beach
Bald Head Island, PO Box 3068, 28461 Ph: 919-457-5000 — Bald Head Island
Balsam Mountain Inn, Box 40, 28707 Ph: 704-456-9498 — Balsam
Pinnacle Inn Resort, PO Box 1136, 28604 Ph: 703-438-2097 — Banner Elk
River Forest Manor, 600 E. Main St., 27810 Ph: 252-943-2151 — Belhaven
Chetola Resort, N. Main St., PO Box 17, 28605 Ph: 828-295-5500 — Blowing Rock
Hounds Ears Club, PO Box 188, 28605 Ph: 828-963-4321 — Blowing Rock
Sunshine Inn, Sunset Dr., PO Box 528, 28695 Ph: 828-295-3487 — Blowing Rock
Hemlock Inn, Galbreath Creek Rd., PO Drawer EE, 28713 Ph: 828-488-2885 — Bryson City
Nantahala Village, PO Drawer J, 28713 Ph: 828-488-2826 800-438-1507 — Bryson City
Pisgah View Ranch, Rt 1, 28715 Ph: 704-667-9100 — Candler
Atlantic Towers Ocean Front Condos, 1615 S. Lake Park Blvd., 28428 Ph: 800-346-7263 — Carolina Beach
Carolina Inn, 211 Pittsboro St., PO Box 1110, 27514 Ph: 919-933-2001 — Chapel Hill
Dunhill Hotel, 237 N. Tryon St., 28202 Ph: 704-332-4141 800-252-4666 — Charlotte
Omni Charlotte, 222 E. Third St., 28202 Ph: 704-377-6664 800-OMNI-EXP — Charlotte
Radisson Hotel & Suites, 5624 Westpark Dr., 28217 Ph: 704-527-8000 — Charlotte
Still Waters, 6221 Amos Smith Rd., 28214 Ph: 704-399-6299 — Charlotte
Dillsboro Inn, 2 River Rd., PO Box 490, 28725 Ph: 704-586-3898 — Dillsboro
Sanderling Inn, 1461 Duck Road, 27949 Ph: 919-261-4111 — Duck
Arrowhead Inn, 106 Mason Rd., 27712 Ph: 919-477-8430 — Durham
Washington Duke Inn & Golf Club, 3001 Cameron Blvd., 27706 Ph: 919-490-0999 800-443-3853 — Durham
The Lords Proprietors' Inn, 300 N. Broad St., 27932 Ph: 919-482-3641 — Edenton
Woodfield Inn, Box 98, 28731 Ph: 704-693-6016 800-533-6016 — Flat Rock
Biltmore Greensboro Hotel, 111 Washington St., 27401 Ph: 336-272-3474 800-332-0303 — Greensboro
Waverly Inn, 783 N. Main St., 28792 Ph: 828-693-9193 800-537-8195 — Hendersonville

Highlands Inn, E. Main St., PO Box 1030, 28741 Ph: 704-526-9380	Highlands
Palmetto Dunes Resort, PO Box 5606, 29938 Ph: 800-845-6130	Hilton Head
	Island
Barrier Island Station, 1245 Duck Rd., 27949 Ph: 919-261-3525	Kitty Hawk
Earthshine Mountain Lodge, Rt. I, Box 30AA, 28747 Ph: 252-862-4207	Lake Toxaway
Greystone Inn, Greystone Lane, 28747 Ph: 704-966-4700 800-824-5766	Lake Toxaway
Eseeola Lodge, 175 Linville Ave., Box 99, 28646 Ph: 704-733-4311 800-742-6717	Linville
Big Lynn Lodge, Highway 226A, PO Box 459, 28749 Ph: 704-765-4257 800-654-5232	Little Switzerland
Cataloochee Ranch, Rt I, Box 500, 28751 Ph: 704-926-1401	Maggie Valley
Baird House, 41 S. Main St., PO Box 749, 28754 Ph: 704-689-5722	Mars Hill
Huntington Hall B&B, 500 Valley River Ave., 28906 Ph: 828-837-9567 800-824-6189	Murphy
Beach Colony Resort, 5308 N. Ocean Blvd., 29577 Ph: 809-449-4010	Myrtle Beach
Berkeley Center Country Inn, Box 220, 27960 Ph: 252-928-5911	Ocracoke
Holly Inn, Cherokee Rd., Box 2300, 28374 Ph: 910-295-2300 800-682-6901	Pinehurst
Pine Crest Inn, Dogwood Rd., PO Box 879, 28374 Ph: 910-295-6121	Pinehurst
Velvet Cloak Inn, 1505 Hillsborough St., 27605 Ph: 919-828-0333	Raleigh
Mid Pines - A Clarion Resort, 1010 Midland Rd., 28387 Ph: 910-692-2114 800-323-2114	Southern Pines
Pine Needles Resort, Ridge Rd., PO Box 88, 28387 Ph: 910-692-7111	Southern Pines
Mountain Brook, 208 Mountain Brook Rd., 28779 Ph: 704-586-4329	Sylva
Hallcrest Inn, 299 Halltop Circle, 28786 Ph: 828-456-6457 800-334-6457	Waynesville
Heath Lodge, 900 Dolan Rd., 28786 Ph: 828-456-3333 800-432-8499	Waynesville
The Swag, Rt I, Box 280-A Hemphill Rd., 28786 Ph: 828-926-0430	Waynesville
Dry Ridge Inn, 16 Brown St., 28787 Ph: 828-658-3899	Weaverville

North Dakota

Dakota Waters Resort, PO Box 576, 58523 Ph: 701-873-5800	Beulah
Doublewood Best Western, 1400 E. Interchange Ave., 58501 Ph: 701-528-7000	Bismarck
Radisson Inn - Bismarck, 800 S. 3rd St., 58504 Ph: 701-258-7700	Bismarck
Days Inn Devil's Lake, Hwy 20, S, 58301 Ph: 701-662-5381	Devil's Lake
Woodland Resort, Rt 1 Box 245, 58301 Ph: 701-662-5996	Devil's Lake
Red Coach Inn, 71 Museum Dr., 58601 Ph: 701-225-9510	Dickinson
Best Western Kelly Inn, 3800 Main Ave., 58103 Ph: 701-282-2143	Fargo
Radisson Hotel - Fargo, 201 5th St., N, 58102 Ph: 701-232-7363	Fargo
Ramada Plaza Suites, 1635 42nd St., SW , 58103 Ph: 701-277-9000	Fargo
C'Mon Inn, 3051 32nd Ave., S, 58201 Ph: 701-775-3320	Grand Forks
Road King Inn, Columbia Mall, 3300 30th Ave., S, 56201 Ph: 701-746-1391	Grand Forks
Andrus Resort, Ph: 701-548-8080	Little Missouri Bay
Diamond Bar Guest Ranch, Box 223, 58645 Ph: 701-873-5117	Medora
Cross Roads Range, HCR 2, Box 36A, Ph: 701-244-5225	St. John
Indian Hills Resort, 5700 Hwy 1804, Ph: 701-743-4122	West Garrison

Ohio

Cincinnatian Hotel, 6th & Wine Sts., 45202 Ph: 513-381-3000 800-942-9000	Cincinnati
Omni Netherland Plaza, 35 W. Fifth St., 45202 Ph: 513-421-9100 800-THE-OMNI	Cincinnati
Glidden House, 1901 Ford Dr., 44106 Ph: 216-231-8900	Cleveland
Ritz-Carlton, Cleveland, 1515 W. Third St., 44113 Ph: 216-623-1300 800-241-3333	Cleveland
50 Lincoln, 50 E. Lincoln St., 43215 Ph: 614-291-5056	Columbus

Crowne Plaza Columbus, 33 Nationwide Blvd., 43215 Ph: 614-461-4100 800-465-4329	Columbus
Doubletree Guest Suites Hotel, 50 S. Front St., 43215 Ph: 614-228-4600	Columbus
Embassy Suites, 2700 Corporate Exchange Dr., 43231 Ph: 614-890-8600	Columbus
Great Southern Hotel, 310 S. High St., 43215 Ph: 614-228-3800 800-328-2073	Columbus
Hyatt on Capital Square, 75 E. State St., 43215 Ph: 614-228-1234 800-233-1234	Columbus
Log House B&B, PO Box 30, 43811 Ph: 614-829-2757	Conesville
Roscoe Village Inn, 200 N. Whitewoman St., 43812 Ph: 740-622-2222 800-237-7397	Coshocton
Buxton Inn, 313 E. Broadway, 43023 Ph: 614-587-0001	Granville
Sawmill Creek Resort, 2401 Cleveland Rd. W , 44839 Ph: 419-433-3800	Huron
The Golden Lamb, 27 S. Broadway, 45036 Ph: 513-932-5065	Lebanon
Inn at Honey Run, 6920 Country Rd. 203, 44654 Ph: 216-674-0011	Millersburg
East Point Cottages, Massie Lane, Ph: 419-285-2204	Put-In Bay
Perry Holiday, 99 Concord Ave., Ph: 419-285-2107	Put-In Bay
Saunder's Resort, Catawba Ave., Ph: 419-285-3917	Put-In Bay
Breakers, Cedar Point, PO Box 5006, 44870 Ph: 419-627-2106	Sandusky
Holiday Inn Sandusky, 5513 Milan Rd., 44870 Ph: 419-626-6671 800-465-4329	Sandusky
Sandcastle Suites Hotel, Cedar Point, PO Box 5006, 44870 Ph: 419-627-2106	Sandusky
The Econo Lodge, 1904 Cleveland Rd., 44870 Ph: 419-627-8000 800-424-4777	Sandusky
JThe Inn at Brandywine Falls, 8230 Brandywine Rd., 44067 Ph: 216-467-1812 216-650-4965	Sagamore Hills
Murphin Ridge Inn, 750 Murphin Ridge Rd., 45693 Ph: 513-544-2263	West Union
The Wooster Inn, 801 E. Wayne Ave., 44691 Ph: 216-264-2341	Wooster
The Worthington Inn, 649 High St., 43085 Ph: 614-885-2600	Worthington
Worthington Inn, 649 High St., Ph: 614-885-2600	Worthington

Oklahoma

Harrison House Inn, 124 W. Harrison, 73040 Ph: 800-375-1001	Guthrie
Quartz Mountain Lodge, Route 1, 73655 Ph: 405-563-2424	Lonewolf
Montford Inn B&B, 322 W. Tonhawa, 73069 Ph: 800-321-8969	Norman
Embassy Suites, 1815 S. Meridian, 73108 Ph: 405-682-6000 800-EMBASSY	Oklahoma City
Governors Suites Hotel, 2308 S. Meridian, 73108 Ph: 405-682-5299	Oklahoma City
Holiday Inn, 1000 N. Interstate Dr., 73072 Ph: 405-364-2882 800-465-4329	Oklahoma City
Holiday Inn East, 5701 Tinker Diagonal, 73110 Ph: 405-737-4481 800-465-4329	Oklahoma City
Holiday Inn Express Airport, 801 S. Meridian, 73108 Ph: 405-942-8511 800-465-4329	Oklahoma City
Holiday Inn North, 12001 Northeast Expressway, 73131 Ph: 405-478-0400 800-465-4329	Oklahoma City
The Grandison, 18441 NW 15th St., 73106 Ph: 800-240-INNS	Oklahoma City

Oregon

Chanticleer B&B Inn, 120 Gresham St., 97520 Ph: 541-482-1919	Ashland
Inn of the Seventh Mountain, PO Box 1207, 97709 Ph: 541-382-8711	Bend
Mazama Village, PO Box 128, 97604 Ph: 541-594-2511	Crater Lake
Odell Lake Lodge, PO Box 72, 97425 Ph: 503-433-2540	Crescent Lake
Paradise Resort, 7000 Monument Dr., 97526 Ph: 541-479-4333	Grants Pass
Comfort Inn Convention Center, 431 NW Multnomah, 97232 Ph: 503-233-7933 800-228-5150	Portland

Governor Hotel, SW 10th & Adler, 97205 Ph: 503-224-3400 800-554-3456	Portland
Heathman Hotel, 1001 SW Broadway, 97205 Ph: 503-241-4100 800-551-0011	Portland
Holiday Inn Portland Downtown, 1021 NE Grand, 97232 Ph: 503-235-2100 800-343-1822	Portland
Mark Spencer Hotel, 409 SW Eleventh Ave., 97205 Ph: 503-224-3293 800-548-3934	Portland
Marriott Hotel Portland, 1401 SW Front Ave., 97201 Ph: 503-226-7600 800-228-9290	Portland
Rose Manor Inn, 4546 SE McLoughlin Blvd., 97202 Ph: 503-236-4175 800-252-8333	Portland
Shilo Inn Portland, 11707 NE Airport Way, 97220 Ph: 503-252-7500 800-222-2244	Portland
Best Western Oceanview Resort, 414 N. Prom, 97138 Ph: 503-738-3334 800-234-8439	Seaside
Boarding House B&B, 208 N. Holladay Dr., 97138 Ph: 503-738-9055	Seaside
Gilbert Inn, 341 Beach Dr., 97138 Ph: 503-738-9770	Seaside
Riverside Inn, 430 S. Holladay Dr., 97138 Ph: 503-738-8254 800-826-6151	Seaside
Ka-Nee-Ta Resort, 100 Main St., PO Box K, 97761 Ph: 541-553-1112 800-554-4SUN	Warm Springs
Fireside Motel, 1881 Hwy 101 N, PO Box 313, 97498 Ph: 503-547-3636 800-336-3573	Yachats
Oregon House, 94288 Hwy 101, 97498 Ph: 503-547-3329	Yachats

Pennsylvania

Spring House, Muddy Creek Forks, 17302 Ph: 717-927-6906	Airville
Village Inn of Bird-in-Hand, 2695 Old Philadelphia Pike, Ph: 717-293-8369	Bird-in-Hand
The Inn at Turkey Hill, 991 Central Rd., 17815 Ph: 717-387-1500	Bloomsburg
Seven Springs Mountain Resort, RD #1, 15622 Ph: 814-352-7777	Champion
Rowland Farm & Ponda-Rowland B&B, RR 1, Box 349, 18612 Ph: 717-639-3245 800-854-3286	Dallas
Historic Smithton Inn, 900 W. Main St., Ph: 717-733-6094	Ephrata
Nemacolin Woodlands Resort, Rt 40, PO Box 188, 15437 Ph: 412-329-8555 800-422-2736	Farmington
Baladerry Inn, 40 Hospital Rd., Ph: 717-337-1342	Gettysburg
Colonial Motel, 157 Carlisle St., Ph: 717-334-3126 800-336-3126	Gettysburg
Criterion Motor Lodge, 337 Carlisle St., Ph: 717-334-6268	Gettysburg
Doubleday Inn, 104 Doubleday Ave., 17325 Ph: 717-334-9119	Gettysburg
Holiday Inn Battlefield, 516 Baltimore St., 17325 Ph: 717-334-6211	Gettysburg
Homestead Guest House, 785 Baltimore St., 17325 Ph: 717-334-2037	Gettysburg
Howard Johnson Lodge, 301 Steinwehr Ave., 17325 Ph: 717-334-1188 800-654-2000	Gettysburg
Keystone Inn, 231 Hanover St., 17325 Ph: 717-337-3888	Gettysburg
Old Appleford Inn, 218 Carlisle St., Ph: 717-337-1711	Gettysburg
Quality Inn - Gettysburg Motor Lodg, 380 Steinwehr Ave., 17325 Ph: 717-334-1103 800-221-2222	Gettysburg
Mountain View Inn, 1001 Village Dr., 15601 Ph: 412-834-5300 800-537-8709	Greenburg
Settlers Inn at Bingham Park, 4 Main Ave., 18428 Ph: 717-226-2993 800-833-8527	Hawley
Woodloch Pines, RD 1, Box 280, 18428 Ph: 717-684-7121	Hawley
Hershey Lodge & Convention Center, W. Chocolate Ave & University Dr., 17033 Ph: 717-533-3311	Hershey
Hidden Valley Resort, PO Box 4420, 15502 Ph: 814-443-6454	Hidden Valley
The Bark Eater Inn, Alstead Hill Rd., 12942 Ph: 518-576-2221	Keene

Meadow Spring Farm, 201 E. Street Rd., 19348 Ph: 215-444-3903	Kennett Square
Split Rock Resort, 18624 Ph: 717-722-9111 800-255-7625	Lake Harmony
Brookdale on the Lake, The Poconos, 18438 Ph: 717-226-2101 800-233-4141	Lakeville
Eden Resort, 222 Eden Rd., 17601 Ph: 717-569-6444	Lancaster
Hilton Garden Inn, 101 Granite Run Dr., 17601 Ph: 717-560-0880	Lancaster
Holiday Inn Lancaster, 2300 Lincoln Hwy. E, 17602 Ph: 717-299-5500	Lancaster
Lincoln Haus Inn, 1687 Lincoln Hwy East, 17602 Ph: 717-392-9412	Lancaster
Willow Valley, 2416 Willow St. Pike, 17602 Ph: 717-464-2711	Lancaster
Homestead B&B, 1400 E. King St., 17602 Ph: 717-396-8928	Lewisburg
Swiss Woods Inn, 500 Blantz Rd., 17543 Ph: 717-627-3358 800-594-8018	Lititz
Great Valley House of Valley Forge, Box 110, RD 3, 19355 Ph: 215-644-6759	Malvern
Holiday Inn Pittsburgh-Monroeville, 2750 Mosside Blvd., 15146 Ph: 412-372-1022	Monroeville
Cedar Hill Farm, 305 Longenecker Rd., 17552 Ph: 717-653-4655	Mt. Joy
Embassy Suites Center City, 1776 Ben Franklin Pkwy, Ph: 215-561-1776	Philadelphia
Holiday Inn City Inn, 4100 Presidential Blvd., 19131 Ph: 800-642-8982	Philadelphia
Sheraton Society Hill, 1 Dock St., 19106 Ph: 215-238-600	Philadelphia
Harley of Pittsburgh, 699 Rodi Rd., 15235 Ph: 412-244-1600 800-321-2323	Pittsburgh
Radisson Hotel Pittsburgh, 101 Mall Blvd., 15146 Ph: 412-373-7300	Pittsburgh
Inn at Plymouth Meeting, 401 Plymouth Rd., 19462 Ph: 800-541-1980	Plymouth Meeting
Pocono Manor, 18349 Ph: 717-839-7111 800-233-8150	Pocono Manor
Inn at Reading, 1040 Park Rd., 19610 Ph: 610-372-7811 800-345-4023	Reading
Sheraton Berkshire, Rt 422 W , Paper Mill Road Exit, 19610 Ph: 610-376-3811	Reading
Mountain Springs Lake Resort, Mountain Springs Dr., PO Box 297, 18352 Ph: 717-629-0251	Reeders
Hershey Farm Motel, 240 Hartman Bridge Rd., 17572 Ph: 717-687-8635	Ronks
Shawnee Mountain, PO Box 178, 18356 Ph: 717-421-1500 X 8970 800-SHAWNEE	Shawnee-on-Delaware
Applebutter Inn, 152 Applewood Lane, 16057 Ph: 412-794-1844	Slippery Rock
The Sterling Inn, 18460 Ph: 717-676-3311 800-523-8200	South Sterling
Inn at Starlight Lake, PO Box 27, 18461 Ph: 800-248-2519	Starlight
Nethercott Inn, Main St., PO Box 26, 18462 Ph: 717-727-2211	Starrucca
Fulton Steamboat Inn, PO Box 333, 17579 Ph: 717-299-9999	Strasburg
Lenape Springs Farm, 580 W. Creek Rd., Ph: 215-793-2266	West Chester

Rhode Island

Hotel Manisses, 1 Spring St., 02807 Ph: 800-626-4773	Block Island
Island Manor Resort, Chapel St., Box 400, 02807 Ph: 401-466-5567	Block Island
New Shoreham House Inn, Water St., 02807 Ph: 401-466-2651 800-272-2601	Block Island
Surf Hotel, Dodge St., 02807 Ph: 401-466-2241 401-466-2240	Block Island
The 1661 Inn, One Spring St., 02807 Ph: 401-466-2421 401-466-2063	Block Island
The Atlantic Inn, High St., 02807 Ph: 401-466-5883	Block Island
The Bellevue House, High St., 02807 Ph: 401-466-5268 401-466-2912	Block Island
The Gothic Inn, Dodge St., 02807 Ph: 401-466-2918	Block Island
Silverthorpe Cottage, 41 Robinson St., 02882 Ph: 401-789-2392	Narragansett
Hydrangea House, 16 Bellevue Ave., 02840 Ph: 401-846-4435 800-945-4667	Newport
Ivy Lodge, 12 Clay St., 02840 Ph: 401-849-6865	Newport
Sanford-Covell Villa Marina, 72 Washington St., 02840 Ph: 401-847-0206 800-847-0206	Newport
The Meville House, 39 Clarke St., 02840 Ph: 401-847-0640	Newport
Yankee Peddler Inn, 113 Toruo St., 02840 Ph: 401-846-1323 800-999-8409	Newport

Omni Biltmore Hotel, Kennedy Plaza, 02903 Ph: 401-421-0700
   800-THE-OMNI   Providence
The Old Court, 144 Benefit St., 02903 Ph: 401-751-2002 401-351-0747   Providence
Grandview B&B, 212 Shore Rd., 02891 Ph: 401-596-6384 800-441-6384   Westerly
Shelter Harbor Inn, 10 Wagner Rd., Rt 1, 02891 Ph: 401-322-8883
   401-322-7907   Westerly

South Carolina

The Belmont Inn, 106 E. Pickens St., 29620 Ph: 803-459-9625   Abbeville
The Wilcox Inn, 100 Colleton Ave., 29801 Ph: 803-649-1377 800-368-1047   Aiken
Breeden House Inn & Carriage House, 404 E. Main St., 29514
   Ph: 803-479-3665   Bennettsville
Greenleaf Inn, 1308-10 Broad St., 29020 Ph: 803-425-1806 800-437-5874   Camden
John Rutledge House Inn, 116 Broad St., 29401 Ph: 803-723-7999
   800-476-9741   Charleston
Lodge Alley Inn, 195 East Bay St., 29401 Ph: 843-722-1611 800-845-1004   Charleston
Omni Hotel at Charleston Place, 130 Market St., 29401 Ph: 843-722-4900   Charleston
Claussen's Inn at Five Points, 2003 Greene St., 29205 Ph: 803-765-0440
   800-622-3382   Columbia
The Chestnut Cottage, 1718 Hampton St., 29201 Ph: 803-256-1718   Columbia
The Whitney, 700 Woodrow St. At Devine, 29205 Ph: 803-252-0845
   800-637-4008   Columbia
Magnolia Inn B&B, 601 E. Main St., 29536 Ph: 803-774-0679   Dillon
Fairfield Ocean Ridge, 1 King Cotton Rd., PO Box 27, 29438
   Ph: 843-869-2561   Edisto Beach
Ehrhardt Hall B&B, 400 S. Broadway, PO Box 246, 29081 Ph: 803-267-2020   Ehrhardt
Heritage Grand Hotel, 3000 Heritage Pkwy, PO Box 1087, 29715
   Ph: 803-544-8000 800-374-1234   Fort Mill
Fripp Island Resort, One Tarpon Blvd., 29920 Ph: 800-845-4100   Fripp Island
Carolinian Inn, 706 Church St., 29440 Ph: 843-546-5491 800-722-4667   Georgetown
The Shaw House, 8 Cyprus Ct., 29440 Ph: 803-546-9663   Georgetown
Embassy Suites Hotel, 670 Verdae Blvd., 29607 Ph: 803-676-9090   Greenville
Inn on the Square, 104 Court St., 29648 Ph: 803-233-4488 800-231-4109   Greenwood
Marriott's Grand Ocean Resort, 51 S. Forest Dr., PO Box 6959, 29938
   Ph: 843-785-2000 800-473-6674   Hilton Head Island
Palmetto Dunes Resort, PO Box 5606, 29938 Ph: 800-845-6130   Hilton Head Island

Hickory Knob State Resort Park, Rt 1, Box 199 B, 29835 Ph: 843-391-2450   McCormick
Beach Colony Resort, 5308 N. Ocean Blvd., 29577 Ph: 803-449-4010   Myrtle Beach
Radisson Resort at Kingston Plantation, 9800 Lake Dr., 28572
   Ph: 803-497-2444 800-333-3333   Myrtle Beach
Serendipity: An Inn, 407 71st Ave. N, 29572 Ph: 843-449-5268   Myrtle Beach
Rosemary Hall & Lookaway Hall, 804 Carolina Ave., 29841 Ph: 803-278-6222
   800-531-5578   North Augusta
Tidewater Golf Club & Plantation, 4901 Little River Neck Rd., 29582
   Ph: 843-249-1403 800-446-5363   North Myrtle Beach
Liberty Hall Inn, 621 S. Mechanic St., 29670 Ph: 803-646-6500
   800-643-7944   Pendleton
Devil's Fork State Park, 161 Kolcombe Circle, 29676 Ph: 803-944-1459   Salem
Santee State Park, Rt. 1, Box 79, 29142 Ph: 803-854-2408   Santee
Seabrook Island Resort, 1002 Landfall Way, 29455 Ph: 800-845-2475   Seabrook Island

South Dakota

Fairfield Inn by Marriott, 3000 Lefevre Dr., 57006 Ph: 605-692-3500 800-228-2800	Brookings
B&B at Skoglund Farm, Rt 1, Box 45, 57321 Ph: 605-247-3445	Canova
American Presidents Cabins, PO Box 446, 57730 Ph: 605-673-3373	Custer
Blue Bell Lodge, HC 83, Box 63, 57730 Ph: 605-255-4531	Custer
Rock Crest Lodge, 15 W. Mt. Rushmore Rd., 57730 Ph: 605-673-4323	Custer
State Game Lodge & Resort, US Hwy 16A, Custer State Park, HCR 83, Box 70, 57730 Ph: 605-255-4541	Custer
Sylvan Lake Resort, Needles Hwy, Custer State Park, HCR 83, Box 70, 57730 Ph: 605-574-2562 800-658-3530	Custer
Legion Lake Resort, Legion Lake, 57730 Ph: 605-255-4521	Custer State Park
Best Western Hickock House, 137 Charles, 57732 Ph: 605-578-1611 800-528-1234	Deadwood
Bullock Hotel & Gambling Complex, 633 Main St., 57732 Ph: 800-336-1876	Deadwood
Franklin Hotel, 700 Main St., 57732 Ph: 605-578-2241 800-688-1876	Deadwood
High Country Ranch B&B, HC 87, Box 9, 57747 Ph: 605-574-9003	Hill City
Badlands Inn, PO Box 103, 57750 Ph: 605-433-5401	Interior
Cedar Pass Lodge & Restaurant, 1 Cedar St., PO Box 5, 57750 Ph: 605-433-5460	Interior
Powder House Lodge, US 16, 57751 Ph: 605-666-4646	Keystone
Triple R Ranch, Hwy 16A, Box 124 K, 57751 Ph: 605-666-4605 800-843-1300	Keystone
Best Western Golden Hills Resort, 900 Miners Ave., 57754 Ph: 605-584-1800 800-528-1234	Lead
Nemo Guest Ranch, Box 77K, 57759 Ph: 605-578-2708	Nemo
Radisson Resort Hotel at Cedar Shore, 101 George S. Nickelson Shoreline Dr., 57365 Ph: 605-734-6376	Oacoma
Alex Johnson Hotel, 523 Sixth St., 57701 Ph: 605-342-1210 800-888-2539	Rapid City
Best Western Town and Country Inn, 2505 Mt. Rushmore Rd., 57701 Ph: 605-343-5383 800-528-1234	Rapid City
Holiday Inn - Rushmore Plaza, 505 H. 5th St., 57701 Ph: 605-348-4000 800-465-4329	Rapid City
Hotel Alex Johnson, 523 6th St., 57701 Ph: 800-888-2539	Rapid City
Quality Inn Mt. Rushmore, 2208 Mt. Rushmore Rd., 57701 Ph: 605-342-3322 605-342-9005	Rapid City
The Inn at Rapid City, 445 Mt. Rushmore, 57701 Ph: 605-348-8300 800-456-3750	Rapid City
Western Dakota Ranch Vacations, HCR 1, Dept. K, 57790 Ph: 605-279-2198	Wall

Tennessee

Chattanooga Choo-Choo Holiday Inn, 1400 Market St., 37402 Ph: 615-266-5000 800-TRACK 29	Chattanooga
Radisson Read House Hotel & Suites, M.L. King Blvd. & Broad St., PO Box 11165, 37401 Ph: 615-266-4121	Chattanooga
Hachland Hill Inn, 1601 Madison St., 37043 Ph: 615-647-4084	Clarksville
Mill Dale Farm, 140 Mill Dale Rd., 37725 Ph: 615-397-3470 800-767-3471	Dandridge
Hippensteal's Mountain View Inn, Grassy Branch Rd., PO Box 707, 37738 Ph: 615-436-5761 800-527-8110	Gatlinburg
Jonesborough B&B, 100 Woodrow Ave., PO Box 722, 37659 Ph: 615-753-9223	Jonesborough
Hyatt Regency Knoxville @ Coliseum, 500 Hill Ave. SE, 37915 Ph: 615-637-1234	Knoxville

Embassy Suites Memphis, 1022 S. Shady Grove Rd., 38120 Ph: 901-684-1777   Memphis
800-EMBASSY
French Quarter Suites Hotel, 2144 Madison Ave., 38104 Ph: 901-728-4000   Memphis
800-843-0353
Peabody, 149 Union Ave., 38103 Ph: 901-529-4000 800-PEABODY   Memphis
Comfort Suites, 2615 Elm Hill Pike, 37214 Ph: 615-883-0114   Nashville
Hancock House, 2144 Nashville Pike, Ph: 615-452-8431   Nashville
Holiday Inn - Briley Parkway, 2200 Elm Hill Pike, 37214 Ph: 615-883-9770   Nashville
800-633-4427
Opryland Hotel, 2800 Opryland Dr., 37214 Ph: 615-889-1000   Nashville
Residence Inn by Marriott, 2300 Elm Hill Pike, 37210 Ph: 615-889-8600   Nashville
800-331-3131
Shoney's Inn of Music Valley, 2420 Music Valley Dr., 37214 Ph: 615-885-4030   Nashville
Union Station Hotel, 1001 Broadway, 37203 Ph: 615-726-1001 800-331-2123   Nashville
Wilson Inn, 600 Ermac Dr., 37214 Ph: 615-889-4466   Nashville
Day Dreams Country Inn, 2720 Colonial Dr., 37863 Ph: 615-428-0370   Pigeon Forge
Fall Creek Falls Inn, Falls Creek Falls State Resort Park, Route 3, 37367   Pikeville
Ph: 615-881-5241 800-421-6683
Roan Mountain State Resort Park, Rt 1, Box 236, 37687 Ph: 615-772-3303   Roan Mountain
615-772-3314
Hale Spring Inn, Town Square, 37857 Ph: 615-272-5171 800-272-5171   Rogersville
Grey Gables B&B, Hwy 52, PO Box 5252, 37733 Ph: 615-628-5252   Rugby

Texas

Radisson Suite Hotel, 700 Ave. H East, 76011 Ph: 817-640-0440   Arlington
800-333-3333
Carton Creek, 8212 Barton Club Dr., 78735 Ph: 800-336-6158   Austin
Doubletree Hotel, 6505 I-35 North, 78752 Ph: 512-454-3737 800-222-8733   Austin
Four Seasons Hotel Austin, 98 San Jacinto Blvd., 78701 Ph: 512-478-4500   Austin
800-332-3442
Lakeway Inn, 101 Lakeway Dr., 78734 Ph: 512-261-6600 800-LAKEWAY   Austin
Stouffer Austin Hotel, 9721 Arboretum Blvd., 78759 Ph: 512-343-2626   Austin
800-HOTELS-1
The Driskill Hotel, 604 Brazos, 78701 Ph: 512-474-5911 800-252-9367   Austin
Wyndham Austin Hotel at Southpark, 4140 Governor's Row, 78744   Austin
Ph: 512-448-2222 800-433-2241
Flying L Ranch, HCR 1 Box 32 K, 78003 Ph: 512-796-3001 800-292-5134   Bandera
Mayan Dude Ranch, PO Box 577 K, 78003 Ph: 512-796-3312 512-796-3036   Bandera
Townsquare Inn, 21 South Bell, 77418 Ph: 409-864-9021   Bellville
Ye Kendall Inn, 128 W. Blanco, 78006 Ph: 210-249-2138   Boerne
Chain-O-Lakes Resort, One Country Lane, 77327 Ph: 713-592-2150   Cleveland
Best Western Sandy Shores Beach, #200 Sirfside Blvd, Corpus Christi Beach,   Corpus Christi
78403 Ph: 512-883-7456 800-528-1234
Corpus Christi Marriott Bayfront, 900 N. Shoreline, 78401 Ph: 512-887-1600   Corpus Christi
800-228-9290
Fairmont Hotel, 1717 N. Akard St., 75201 Ph: 214-720-2020 800-527-4727   Dallas
Hotel Crescent Court, 400 Crescent Court, 75201 Ph: 214-871-3200   Dallas
800-654-6541
Melrose Hotel, 3015 Oak Lawn, 75219 Ph: 214-521-5151 800-843-6664   Dallas
Stouffer Dallas Hotel, 2222 Stemmons Freeway, 75207 Ph: 214-631-2222   Dallas
The Adolphus, 1321 Commerce, 75202 Ph: 214-742-8200 800-221-9083   Dallas
The Aristocrat, 1933 Main St., 75201 Ph: 214-741-7700 800-231-4235   Dallas
The Cooper Aerobics Center, 12230 Preston Rd., 75230 Ph: 214-386-0306   Dallas
800-444-5187

The Grand Kempinski, 15201 Dallas Pkwy, 75248 Ph: 214-386-6000 — Dallas
800-426-3135

Camino Real Paso Del Norte, 101 S. El Paso St., 79901 Ph: 915-534-3000 — El Paso
800-7-CAMINO

El Paso Airport Hilton, 2027 Airway Blvd., 79925 Ph: 915-778-4241 — El Paso
800-742-7248

El Paso Marriott, 1600 Airway Blvd., 79925 Ph: 915-779-3300 800-228-9290 — El Paso

Indian Lodge, PO Box 786, 79734 Ph: 915-426-3254 — Fort Davis

Prude Ranch, Box 1431 K, 79734 Ph: 915-426-3202 800-458-6232 — Fort Davis

Radisson Plaza Hotel Fort Worth, 815 Main St., 76012 Ph: 817-870-2100 — Fort Worth

Stockyards Hotel, 109 E. Exchange, 76164 Ph: 817-625-6427 800-423-8471 — Fort Worth

Worthington Hotel, 200 Main St., 76101 Ph: 817-870-1000 800-433-5677 — Fort Worth

Hotel Galvez, 2024 Seawall Blvd., 77550 Ph: 409-765-7721 800-392-4285 — Galveston

Seascape, 10811 San Luis Pass Rd., 77554 Ph: 409-740-1245 — Galveston

The San Luis Resort, 5222 Seawall Blvd., 77551 Ph: 409-744-1500 — Galveston
800-445-0090

Tremount House, 2300 Ship's Mechanic Row, 77550 Ph: 409-763-0300 — Galveston
800-874-2300

Four Seasons Hotel Houston, 1300 Lamar St., 77010 Ph: 713-650-1300 — Houston
800-332-3442

La Colombe d'Or, 3410 Montrose Blvd., 77006 Ph: 713-524-7999 — Houston

Lancaster Hotel, 701 Texas Ave., 77002 Ph: 713-228-9500 800-231-0336 — Houston

Omni Houston Hotel, Four Riverway, 77056 Ph: 713-871-8181 — Houston
800-THE-OMNI

Ritz-Carlton, Houston, 1919 Briar Oaks Lane, 77027 Ph: 713-840-7600 — Houston
800-241-3333

Westin Galleria, 5060 W. Alabama, 77056 Ph: 713-960-8100 800-228-3000 — Houston

Westin Oaks, 5011 Westheimer, 77056 Ph: 713-960-8100 800-228-3000 — Houston

Wyndham Warwick, 5701 Main St., 77005 Ph: 713-526-1991 — Houston
800-WYNDHAM

Lacy Hills Guest Ranch, Box K, 78025 Ph: 512-367-5600 — Ingram

Four Seasons Resort & Club, 4150 N. MacArthur Blvd., 75038 — Irving
Ph: 214-717-0707

Omni Mandalay Hotel at Las Colinas, 221 E. Las Colinas Blvd., 75039 — Irving
Ph: 214-556-0800 800-THE-OMNI

Wise Manor, 312 Houston St., 75657 Ph: 903-665-2386 — Jefferson

Inn of the Hills River Resort, 1001 Junction Highway, 78028 — Kerrville
Ph: 210-895-5000 800-292-5690

South Shore Harbour Resort, 2500 South Shore Blvd., 77573 — League City
Ph: 713-334-1000 800-442-5005

Gage Hotel, PO Box 46, 79842 Ph: 915-386-4205 800-884-4243 — Marathon

Del Lago Resort, 600 Del Lago Blvd., 77356 Ph: 409-582-6100 — Montgomery
800-DEL-LAGO

Y.O. Ranch, Drawer K, 78058 Ph: 512-640-3322 512-640-3227 — Mountain Home

Island Retreat, 700 Island Retreat Ct., 78373 Ph: 512-749-6222 800-553-9833 — Port Aransas

Port Royal Ocean Resort, St Hwy 361, PO Box 336, Mustang Island, 78373 — Port Aransas
Ph: 512-749-5001 800-847-5659

Yacht Club Hotel & Restaurant, 700 Yturia St., 78578 Ph: 210-943-1301 — Port Isabell

Rancho Viejo Resort, PO Box 3918, 78520 Ph: 210-350-4000 800-531-7400 — Rancho Viejo

Inn on the Creek, Center Circle, PO Box 858, 76571 Ph: 817-947-5554 — Salado

Crockett Hotel, 320 Bonham, 78205 Ph: 210-225-6500 800-292-1050 — San Antonio

Emily Morgan Hotel, 705 E. Houston, 78205 Ph: 210-225-8486 — San Antonio
800-824-6674

Hyatt Regency San Antonio, 123 Losoya St., 78205 Ph: 210-222-1234 — San Antonio
800-233-1234

La Mansion Del Rio, 112 College St., 78205 Ph: 210-225-2581 800-292-7300   San Antonio
Plaza San Antonio, 555 S. Alamo St., 78205 Ph: 210-229-1000 800-421-1172   San Antonio
Riverwalk Inn, 329 Old Guilbeau, 78204 Ph: 210-212-8300 800-254-4440   San Antonio
San Antonio Marriott Rivercenter, 101 Bowie St., 78205 Ph: 210-223-1000   San Antonio
Sheraton Gunter Hotel, 205 E. Houston St., 78205 Ph: 210-227-3241   San Antonio
  800-222-4276
The Fairmount Hotel, 401 S. Alamo St., 78205 Ph: 210-224-8800   San Antonio
  800-642-3363
The Menger Hotel, 204 Alamo Plaza, 78205 Ph: 210-223-4361 800-345-9295   San Antonio
Bridge Point, 334 Padre Blvd., 78597 Ph: 210-761-7969 800-221-1402   South Padre
    Island
Sheraton South Padre Island Beach, 310 Padre Blvd., 78597 Ph: 210-761-6551   South Padre
  800-325-3535   Island
Lajitas on the Rio Grande, Star Route 70, Box 400, 79852 Ph: 916-424-3471   Terlingua
  800-527-4078

Utah

Recapture Lodge & Pioneer House, Box 309, 84512 Ph: 801-672-2281   Bluff
Bryce Canyon Lodge & Cabins, Route 63, Ph: 801-834-5361 801-586-7686   Bryce Canyon
The Homestead, 700 North Homestead Dr., 84032 Ph: 435-645-1102   Midway
  800-327-7220
Grist Mill Inn B&B, 64 South 300 East, PO Box 156, 84535 Ph: 801-587-2597   Monticello
  800-645-3762
Best Western Landmark Inn, 6560 N. Landmark Dr., 84060 Ph: 435-649-7300   Park City
  800-548-8824
Chamonix Lodge, 2228 Evening Star Dr., 84060 Ph: 435-649-8443   Park City
  800-443-8630
Deer Valley Resort, PO Box 1525, 84060 Ph: 435-649-1000   Park City
Edelweiss Haus, 1482 Empire Ave., PO Box 495, 84060 Ph: 435-649-9342   Park City
  800-438-3855
Inn at Prospector Square, 2200 Sidewinder Dr., PO Box 1698, 84060   Park City
  Ph: 435-649-7100 800-453-3812
Old Miners' Lodge, 615 Woodside Ave., PO Box 2639, 84060   Park City
  Ph: 435-645-8068
Stein Eriksen Lodge, P.O. Box 3177, 94060 Ph: 435-649-3700 800-453-1302   Park City
Embassy Suites Hotel, 110 W 600 South, 84101 Ph: 801-359-7800   Salt Lake City
  800-EMBASSY
Peery Hotel, 110 W. 300 South St., 84101 Ph: 801-521-4300 800-331-0073   Salt Lake City
Quality Inn City Center, 154 W Sixth St., 84116 Ph: 801-521-2930   Salt Lake City
  800-4-CHOICE
Red Lion Hotel, 255 S.W. Temple, 84101 Ph: 801-328-2000 800-547-8010   Salt Lake City
Residence Inn, 765 E 400 South, 84102 Ph: 801-532-5511 800-331-3131   Salt Lake City
Snowbird Ski & Summer Resort, 84092 Ph: 801-742-2222 800-453-3000   Snowbird
Seven Wives Inn, 217 North 100 West, 84770 Ph: 435-628-3737   St. George
  800-600-3737
Zion Park Lodge, PO Box 400, 84721 Ph: 801-772-3213 801-586-7686   Zion National
    Park

Vermont

Hill Farm Inn, RR 2, Box 2015, 05250 Ph: 802-375-2269 800-882-2545   Arlington
West Mountain Inn, River Rd., 05250 Ph: 802-375-6516   Arlington
Lilac Inn, 53 Park St., 05733 Ph: 802-247-5463   Brandon
Latchis Hotel, 50 Main Street, 05301 Ph: 802-254-6300   Brattleboro

October Country Inn, Upper Rd., PO Box 68, 05035 Ph: 802-672-3412 800-648-8421	Bridgewater Corners
Ascutney Mountain Resort, P.O. Box 699, 05037 Ph: 802-484-7711 800-243-0011	Brownsville
Radisson Hotel Burlington, 60 Battery St., 05401 Ph: 802-658-6500 800-333-3333	Burlington
Hugging Bear Inn, Main St., 05143 Ph: 802-875-2412	Chester
Inn at Long Last, Main St., PO Box 589, 05143 Ph: 802-875-2444	Chester
Mountain Top Inn, Mountain Top Rd., PO Box 410, 05737 Ph: 802-483-2311 800-445-2100	Chittenden
Silas Griffith Inn, RR 1, PO Box 66F, 05739 Ph: 802-293-5567 800-545-1509	Danby
Barrows House, Rt. 30, 05251 Ph: 802-867-4455	Dorset
The Old Cutter Inn, RR 1, PO Box 62, 05832 Ph: 802-626-5152	East Burke
Berkson Farms B&B, RR 1 Box 850, 05450 Ph: 802-933-2522	Enosberg Falls
Silver Maple Lodge, South Main St., RR 1, Box 8, 05045 Ph: 802-333-4326 800-666-1946	Fairlee
Carolyn's B&B, 15 Church St., PO Box 1087, 05843 Ph: 802-472-6338 802-472-6178	Hardwick
Inn at Long Trail, PO Box 267, 05751 Ph: 802-775-7181 800-325-2540	Killington
The Vermont Inn, Rt. 4, HC 34 - Box 37J, 05751 Ph: 800-541-775-0708	Killington
Landgrove Inn, RFD Box 215, 05148 Ph: 802-824-6673 800-669-8466	Landgrove
The Village Inn, 215 Landgrove Rd., 05148 Ph: 802-824-6673	Londonderry
Battenkill Inn, PO Box 948, Rt. 7A, 05254 Ph: 802-362-4213 800-441-1628	Manchester
The Reluctant Panther, West Rd., PO Box 678, 05254 Ph: 802-362-2568 800-822-2331	Manchester
The Equinox, Rt. 7A, 05253 Ph: 802-362-1595 800-362-4747	Manchester Village
Wilburton Inn, River Rd., 05254 Ph: 802-362-1500	Manchester Village
Black Lantern Inn, Rt. 118, 05470 Ph: 802-326-4507 800-255-8661	Montgomery Village
West River Lodge, RR 1, Box 693, 05345 Ph: 802-365-7745	Newfane
Shore Acres Inn, Box 3, RR 1, 05474 Ph: 802-372-8722	North Hero Island
Johnny Seesaw's, Rt 11, PO Box 68, 05152 Ph: 802-824-5533	Peru
Hawk North, Ltd., Rt. 100, PO Box 529, 05762 Ph: 802-746-8911 800-832-8007	Pittsfield
Hickory Ridge House, RFD 3, PO Box 1410, Hickory Ridge Rd., 05346 Ph: 802-387-5709	Putney
Harvey's Mountain View Inn, 05767 Ph: 802-767-4273	Rochester
Londonderry Inn, PO Box 301-22, 05155 Ph: 802-824-5226	South Londonderry
Kedron Valley Inn, Rt. 106, 05071 Ph: 802-457-1473	South Woodstock
Edson Hill Manor & Ten Acres Lodge, 1500 Edson Hill Rd., 05672 Ph: 802-253-7371 800-621-0284	Stowe
Logwood Inn & Chalets, 199 Edson Hill Rd., 05672 Ph: 802-253-7354 800-426-6697	Stowe
Stowehof Inn, 434 Edson Hill Rd., PO Box 1139, 05672 Ph: 802-253-9722 800-932-7136	Stowe
Timberholm Inn, 452 Cottage Club Rd., 05672 Ph: 802-253-7603 800-753-7603	Stowe
Walkabout Creek Lodge, 199 Edson Hill, 05672 Ph: 802-253-7354 800-426-6697	Stowe

Battleground, RR 1, PO Box 89, Rt. 17, 05673 Ph: 802-496-2288 800-248-2102	Waitsfield
The Lareau Farm Country Inn, Box 563, Rt. 100, 05673 Ph: 802-496-4949 800-833-0766	Waitsfield
The Mad River Inn, PO Box 75, 05673 Ph: 802-496-7900	Waitsfield
Harvey's Lake Cabins & Campground, RR 1, Box 26E, 05821 Ph: 802-633-2213	West Barnet
Indian Joe's Courts, Box 126, 05873 Ph: 802-684-3430	West Danville
Rodgers' Country Inn, RFD 3, PO Box 57, 05875 Ph: 802-525-6677	West Glover
The Colonial House, PO Box 138 R.B., 05161 Ph: 802-824-6286 800-639-5033	Weston
Misty Mountain Lodge, RR 1, Box 114, 326 Stowe Hill Rd., 05363 Ph: 802-464-3961	Wilmington
Trail's End, Smith Rd., 05363 Ph: 802-464-2727	Wilmington
Deer Brook Inn, HCR 68, Box 443, Rt. 4, 05091 Ph: 802-672-3713	Woodstock
The Woodstocker, Rt. 4, 61 River St., 05091 Ph: 802-457-3896	Woodstock

Virginia

Dulwich Manor B&B, Rt 5 Box 173A, 24521 Ph: 804-946-7207	Amherst
The River House, Rt 2, Box 135, 22620 Ph: 703-837-1476	Boyce
Nottingham Ridge, PO Box 97B, 23310 Ph: 804-331-1010 804-442-5011	Cape Charles
Boar's Head Inn, Rt. 250, PO Box 5370, 22905 Ph: 804-296-2181 800-476-1988	Charlottesville
Driftwood Motor Lodge, 7105 Maddox Blvd., PO Box 575, 23336 Ph: 804-336-6557	Chincoteague Island
Island Motor Inn, 4391 Main St., 23336 Ph: 804-336-3141	Chincoteague Island
Refuge Motor Inn, 7058 Maddox Blvd., PO Box 378, 23336 Ph: 804-336-5511	Chincoteague Island
Oak Grove Plantation, Hwy. 658, PO Box 45, 24535 Ph: 804-575-7137 703-527-6958 Winter	Cluster Springs
Fountain Hall B&B, 609 South East St., 22801 Ph: 703-825-8200 800-476-2944	Culpepper
Claytor Lake Homestead Inn, PO Box 7, 24324 Ph: 703-980-6777 800-676-LAKE	Draper
Mary's Country Inn, 218 S. Main St., Rt 2, Box 4, 22824 Ph: 703-984-8286	Edinburg
La Vista Plantation, 4420 Guinea Station Rd., 22408 Ph: 703-898-8444	Fredericksburg
Sleepy Hollow Farm B&B, 16280 Blue Ridge Turnpike, 22942 Ph: 703-832-5555	Gordonsville
Maple Hill, 11 N. Main St., 24450 Ph: 703-463-2044	Lexington
Springdale Country Inn, Rt 722, 22078 Ph: 703-338-1833 800-388-1832	Lincoln
Winridge B&B, Rt 1, Box 362, 24572 Ph: 804-384-7220	Madison Heights
Hemlock Haven Conference Center, Hungry Mother State Park, Rt 5, Box 109, 24254 Ph: 703-783-3422	Marion
Middleburg Country Inn, 209 E. Washington St., PO Box 2065, 22117 Ph: 703-687-6082	Middleburg
Fort Lewis Lodge, HCR 3, Box 21A, 24460 Ph: 703-925-2314	Millboro
"St. Moor" House, Rt 1, Box 136, 24574 Ph: 804-929-8228	Monroe
Widow Kip's Shenandoah Inn, Rt 1, Box 117, 22842 Ph: 703-477-2400	Mt. Jackson
Burger's Country Inn, Rt. 743, Postal Rt 2, Box 564, 24578 Ph: 703-291-2464	Natural Bridge
Acorn Inn, PO Box 431, 22958 Ph: 804-361-9357	Nellysford
The Holladay House, 155 W. Main St., 22960 Ph: 703-672-4893 800-358-4422	Orange
The High Street Inn, 405 High St., 23803 Ph: 804-733-0505	Petersburg

The Jefferson Hotel, Franklin & Adams Sts., 23220 Ph: 804-788-8000 — Richmond
800-424-8014
Mary Bladon House, 381 Washington Ave., S.W., 24016 Ph: 703-344-5361 — Roanoke
Manor at Taylor' Store, Rt 1, Box 533, 24184 Ph: 703-721-3951 — Smith Mountain Lake
800-248-6267
Renaissance Manor B&B, 2247 Courthouse Rd., 22554 Ph: 703-720-3785 — Stafford
Edgewood Farm B&B, RR 2, Box 303, 22973 Ph: 804-985-9405 — Stanardsville
Jordan Hollow Farm Inn, VA Rt. 626, Rt. 2, Box 375, 22851 — Stanley
Ph: 703-778-2209 703-778-2285
Frederick House, 28 N. Mew St., 24401 Ph: 703-885-4220 800-334-5575 — Staunton
Thornrose House at Gypsy Hill, 531 Thornrose Ave., 24401 — Staunton
Ph: 703-885-7026
Oceola Mill Country Inn, 24476 Ph: 703-377-6455 800-242-7352 — Steele's Tavern
Graves' Mountain Lodge, General Delivery, 22743 Ph: 703-923-4231 — Syria
Barclay Towers, 809 Atlantic Ave., 23451 Ph: 804-491-2700 800-344-4473 — Virginia Beach
Belvedere Motel, Oceanfront @ 36th St., Ph: 804-425-0612 — Virginia Beach
Cavalier Hotel, 42nd St. & Oceanfront, 23451 Ph: 804-425-8555 — Virginia Beach
800-446-8199
Days Inn Oceanfront, 3107 Atlantic Ave., 23451 Ph: 804-428-7233 — Virginia Beach
800-325-2525
Halifax Hotel, 26th St., Ph: 804-428-3044 — Virginia Beach
Holiday Inn Sunspree On the Ocean, 3900 Atlantic, 23451 Ph: 804-428-1711 — Virginia Beach
800-94-BEACH
The Friendship Inn, 1112 Pacific Ave., Ph: 804-425-0650 800-372-4900 — Virginia Beach
The Hilton Resort, Oceanfront @ 8th St., Ph: 804-428-8935 800-HILTONS — Virginia Beach
Anderson Cottage B&B, Old Germantown Rd., PO Box 176, 24484 — Warm Springs
Ph: 703-839-2975
Inn at Gristmill Square, Rt. 645, Box 359, 24484 Ph: 703-839-2231 — Warm Springs
Applewood Colonial B&B, 605 Richmond Rd., 23185 Ph: 804-229-0205 — Williamsburg
800-899-APLE
Colonial Capital B&B, 501 Richmond Rd., 23185 Ph: 804-229-9233 — Williamsburg
800-776-0570
Governers Inn, PO Box 1776, 23187 Ph: 804-229-1000 800-447-8679 — Williamsburg
War Hill Inn, 4560 Long Hill Rd., 23185 Ph: 804-565-0248 — Williamsburg
Inn at Narrow Passage, US 11 South, 22664 Ph: 703-459-8000 — Woodstock

Washington

Majestic Hotel, 419 Commercial Ave., 98221 Ph: 206-293-3355 — Anacortes
Bombay House, 8490 NE Beck Rd., 98110 Ph: 206-842-3926 — Bainbridge Island

The Inn at Semi-ah-moo, 9565 Semiahmoo Pkwy, 98230 Ph: 206-371-2000 — Blaine
800-854-2608
Hidden Valley Guest Ranch, HC 61, Box 2060K, 98922 Ph: 509-857-2344 — Cle Elum
Baker Lake Resort, PO Box 100, 98237 Ph: 360-853-8325 — Concrete
Iron Springs Ocean Beach Resort, PO Box 207, 98535 Ph: 360-276-4230 — Copalis Beach
The Captain Whidbey Inn, 2072 W. Captain Whidbey Inn Rd., 98239 — Coupeville
Ph: 206-678-4097 800-366-4097
Beach Haven Resort, Enchanted Forest Rd., Rt 1, Box 12, 98245 — Eastsound, Orcas Island
Ph: 360-376-2288
Flying L Ranch, 25 Flying L Lane, 98619 Ph: 509-364-3488 — Glenwood
Haus Rohrbach Pension, 12882 Ranger Rd., 98826 Ph: 509-548-7024 — Leavenworth
Ocean Crest Resort, Sunset Beach, 98652 Ph: 360-276-4465 800-684-8439 — Moclips
Klipsan Beach Cottages, 22617 Pacific Highway, 98640 Ph: 360-665-4888 — Ocean Park
Kalaloch Lodge, 157151 Hwy 101, 98331 Ph: 360-962-2271 — Olympic National Park

Log Cabin Resorts, 6540 E. Beach Rd., 98331 Ph: 360-928-3245	Olympic National Park
Best Western Olympia Lodge, 140 Del Guzzi Dr., 98362 Ph: 360-452-2993	Port Angeles
Domaine Madeleine, 1834 Finn Hall Rd., 98362 Ph: 206-457-4174	Port Angeles
Lake Crescent Lodge, Star Route 1, Box 11, 98362 Ph: 206-928-3211	Port Angeles
Red Lion Bayshore Inn, 221 N. Lincoln, 98362 Ph: 360-452-9215	Port Angeles
Sol Buc Hot Springs, Olympic National Park, Box 2169, 98362 Ph: 206-327-3583	Port Angeles
Anapurna Inn, 538 Adams, 98368 Ph: 360-385-2909	Port Townsend
Arcadia Country Inn, 1891 S. Jacob Miller Rd., 98368 Ph: 206-385-5245	Port Townsend
Bishop Victorian Guest Suites, 714 Washington St., 98368 Ph: 360-385-6122	Port Townsend
Diamond Point Inn, 241 Sunshine Rd., 98368 Ph: 360-797-7720	Port Townsend
Harborside Inn, 330 Benedict St., 98368 Ph: 360-385-7909 800-942-5960	Port Townsend
Lake Quinault Lodge, South Shore Rd., Box 7, 98575 Ph: 206-288-2571 800-562-6671	Quinault
Roche Harbor Resort & Marina, PO Box 4001, 98250 Ph: 360-378-2115	Roche Harbor, San Juan Island
Alexis Hotel Seattle, 1007 1st Ave., 98104 Ph: 206-624-4844 800-426-7033	Seattle
Four Seasons Olympic Hotel, 411 University St., 98101 Ph: 206-621-1700 800-223-8772	Seattle
Inn at the Market, 86 Pine St., 98101 Ph: 206-443-3600	Seattle
Quality Inn City Center, 2224 8th Ave., 98121 Ph: 206-624-6820 800-228-5151	Seattle
The Westin Hotel, 1900 Fifth Ave., 98101 Ph: 206-728-1000 800-228-3000	Seattle
Salish Lodge, 37807 SE Fall City/Snoqualmie Falls Rd., 98065 Ph: 206-888-2556 800-826-6124	Snoqualmie
Notaras Lodge, 236 E. Main St., Hwy 17, PO Box 987, 98851 Ph: 509-246-0462	Soap Lake
The Moore House, PO Box 1861, 98943 Ph: 509-674-5939	South Cle Elum
North Cascades Lodge, PO Box 275, 98852 Ph: 509-682-4711	Stehekin
Circle H Holiday Ranch, Rt 1, Box 175K, 98946 Ph: 509-964-2000	Thorp
Tokeland Hotel, 100 Tokeland Rd., PO Box 223, 98590 Ph: 206-267-7006	Tokeland
Vashon Island Ranch Hostel, 12119 SW Cove Rd., 98070 Ph: 360-463-2592	Vashon Island
Sun Mountain Lodge, PO Box 1000, 98862 Ph: 509-996-2211 800-572-0493	Winthrop

Wisconsin

Old Rittenhouse Inn, 311 Rittenhouse Ave., PO Box 584, 54818 Ph: 715-779-5111	Bayfield
Creamery Restaurant & Inn, PO Box 22, 54735 Ph: 715-664-8354	Downsville
Siebken's, 284 S. Lake St., 53020 Ph: 414-876-2600	Elkhart Lake
Chalet East Apartments, PO Box 512, Ph: 419-746-2335 813-624-3811 Winter	Kelleys Island
Sunrise Point, PO Box 431, Ph: 419-746-2543 419-433-6368	Kelleys Island
Lighthouse Cove, 53940 Ph: 800-447-5946	Lake Delton
Sandy Beach Resort, 55 Dam Rd., 53940 Ph: 608-254-8553	Lake Delton
Minocqua Shores, Island City Point, 54598 Ph: 715-356-5101	Minocqua
New Concord Inn, Hwy 41, 54598 Ph: 715-356-1800	Minocqua
Pine Hill Resort, 8544 Hower Rd., 54598 Ph: 715-356-3418	Minocqua
ust-N-Trails B&B/Farm Vacation, Rt 1, Box 274, 54656 Ph: 608-269-4522	Sparta
Sunset Resort, Old West Harbor Rd., PO Box 26, 54246 Ph: 414-847-2531	Washington Island
Wolf River Lodge, 54491 Ph: 715-882-2181 715-882-3982	White Lake

Chula Vista Resort, 5944 Christmas Mountain Rd., 53965 Ph: 608-254-8366 800-38-VISTA	Wisconsin Dells
Copa Cabana Resort Hotel & Suites, 611 Wisconsin Dells Pkwy, 53965 Ph: 608-253-1511 800-364-2672	Wisconsin Dells
Meadowbrook Resort, 1533 River Rd., 53965 Ph: 608-253-3201	Wisconsin Dells
Pine Beach Resort, 481 County A, 53965 Ph: 608-253-6361	Wisconsin Dells
Polynesian Suite Resort, Hwy 13 N, 53965 Ph: 608-254-2883 800-272-5842	Wisconsin Dells
River Inn, 1015 River Rd., 53965 Ph: 608-253-1231	Wisconsin Dells
Yogi Bear's Camp-Resort, S1915 Ishnala Rd., PO Box 510, 53965 Ph: 608-254-2568 800-GO-2-YOGI	Wisconsin Dells

West Virginia

Coolfont Resort, Rt 1, Box 710, 25411 Ph: 304-258-4500	Berkeley Springs
The Country Inn, Rt 522, 25411 Ph: 304-258-2210 800-822-6630	Berkeley Springs
Cottonwood Inn, Rt 2, Box 61S, 25414 Ph: 304-725-3371	Charles Town
Black Bear Woods Resort, Rt 1, Box 55, Canaan Valley, 26260 Ph: 304-866-4391	Davis
Blackwater Falls Lodge, PO Box 490, 26260 Ph: 304-259-5216 800-CALLWVA	Davis
Retreat at Buffalo Run, 214 Harpertown Rd., 26241 Ph: 304-636-2960	Elkins
Cliffside Inn, US 340 West, 25425 Ph: 304-535-6302	Harpers Ferry
Comfort Inn, US 340 & Union St., 25425 Ph: 304-535-6391 800-221-2222	Harpers Ferry
Hilltop House, 400 Ridge St., 25425 Ph: 304-535-2132	Harpers Ferry
The Woods Resort, Rt. 4, Mt. Lake Rd., PO Box 5, 25427 Ph: 304-754-7977 800-248-2222	Hedgesville
Hutton House B&B, Rt 215-250, 26273 Ph: 304-335-6701 800-234-6701	Huttonsville
General Lewis Inn, 301 E. Washington St., 24901 Ph: 304-645-2600 800-628-4454	Lewisburg
Maxwell B&B, Rt 12, Box 197, 26505 Ph: 304-594-3041	Morgantown
Twin Falls State Park, Rt. 97, Box 1023, 25882 Ph: 304-294-4000	Mullens
Blennerhasset Hotel, Fourth & Market Sts., PO Box 51, 26102 Ph: 304-422-3131 800-262-2536	Parkersburg
Smoke Hole Lodge, PO Box 935, 26847	Petersburg
Pipestem Resort State Park, PO Box 150, 25979 Ph: 304-466-1800	Pipestem
Prosperity Farmhouse B&B, Box 393, 25909 Ph: 304-255-4245	Prosperity
Bavarian Inn & Lodge, Rt. 1, Box 30, 25443 Ph: 304-876-2551	Shepherds- town
Thomas Shepherd Inn, 300 W. German St., PO Box 1162, 25443 Ph: 304-876-3715	Shepherds- town
Yesterdays Ltd., 808 Main St., 26003 Ph: 304-232-0864	Wheeling
James Wylie House B&B, 208 E. Main St., 24986 Ph: 304-536-9444 800-CALLWVA	White Sulphur Springs

Wyoming

Paradise Guest Ranch, PO Box 790 K, 82834 Ph: 307-684-7876	Buffalo
A. Drummond's Ranch, 399 Happy Jack Rd., 82007 Ph: 307-634-6042	Cheyenne
Bill Cody's Ranch Resort, 2604 Yellowstone Hwy, Dept K, 82414 Ph: 307-587-6271	Cody

Castle Rock Lodges Guest Ranch, 412 County Rd. 6NS, Dept K, 82414 Ph: 307-587-2076 800-356-9965	Cody
Cody's Ranch Resort, 2604 Yellowstone Hwy Box OLA, 82414 Ph: 307-587-2097	Cody
Pahaska Tepee Resort, 183-R Yellowstone Hwy., 82414 Ph: 307-527-7701 800-628-7791	Cody
Rimrock Ranch, 2828 N. Fork Rd., Dept K, 82414 Ph: 307-587-3970	Cody
Seven D Ranch, PO Box 100 K, 82414 Ph: 307-587-3997 307-587-9885 Winter	Cody
Absaroka Ranch, PO Box 929, 82513 Ph: 307-455-2275	Dubois
Bitterroot Ranch, Rt 66, Box 1042 K, 82513 Ph: 307-455-2778 800-545-0019	Dubois
CM Ranch, PO Box 217 K, 82513 Ph: 307-455-2331 307-455-2266	Dubois
Lazy L and B Ranch, Rt 66 K, 82513 Ph: 307-455-2839	Dubois
Days Inn, 1280 W. Broadway, PO Box 2986, 83001 Ph: 307-733-0033 800-DAYS-INN	Jackson
Snow King Resort, 400 E. Snow King Ave., 83001 Ph: 307-733-5200 800-522-5464	Jackson
Wildflower Inn, 83001 Ph: 307-733-4710	Jackson
Rawah Ranch, Glendevey, Colorado Route, Dept k, 82063 Ph: 303-435-5725	Jelm
Red Rock Ranch, PO Box 9 K, 83011 Ph: 307-733-6288	Kelly
Gros Ventre River Ranch, Box 151, 83012 Ph: 307-733-4138	Moose
Lost Creek Ranch, PO Box 95 K, 83012 Ph: 307-733-3435 307-856-6789 Winter	Moose
Triangle X Ranch, Star Rt Box 120 K, 83012 Ph: 307-733-2183	Moose
Colter Bay Village, Box 240, 83013 Ph: 307-543-2855	Moran
Heart 6 Ranch, PO Box 70 K, 83013 Ph: 307-543-2477 800-733-9407	Moran
Jackson Lake Lodge, Box 240, 83013 Ph: 800-628-9988	Moran
Signal Mountain Lodge, PO Box 50, 83013 Ph: 307-733-5470	Moran
H F Bar Ranch, PO Box K, 82840 Ph: 307-684-2487	Saddlestring
Spear-O-Wigwam Ranch, Box 1081 K, 82801 Ph: 307-674-4496 307-672-0002 Winter	Sheridan
R Lazy S Ranch, Box 308 K, 83025 Ph: 307-733-2655	Teton Village
Crossed Sabres Ranch, PO Box K, 82450 Ph: 307-587-3750	Wapiti
Trail Creek Ranch, PO Box 10 K, 83014 Ph: 307-733-2610	Wilson
Canyon Lodge Cabins, Reservation Dept, TW Recreational Services, Inc., 82190 Ph: 307-344-7311	Yellowstone National Park
Grant Village, Reservation Dept, TW Recreational Services, Inc., 82190 Ph: 307-344-7311	Yellowstone National Park
Lake Lodge Cabins, Reservation Dept, TW Recreational Services, Inc., 82190 Ph: 307-344-7311	Yellowstone National Park
Lake Yellowstone Hotel & Cabins, Reservation Dept, TW Recreational Services, Inc., 82190 Ph: 307-344-7311	Yellowstone National Park
Mammoth Hot Springs Hotel, Reservation Dept, TW Recreational Services, Inc., 82190 Ph: 307-344-7311	Yellowstone National Park
Old Faithful Inn, Reservation Dept, TW Recreational Services, Inc., 82190 Ph: 307-344-7311	Yellowstone National Park
Old Faithful Lodge Cabins, Reservation Dept, TW Recreational Services, Inc., 82190 Ph: 307-344-7311	Yellowstone National Park
Old Faithful Snow Lodge, Reservation Dept, TW Recreational Services, Inc., 82190 Ph: 307-344-7311	Yellowstone National Park
Roosevelt Lodge Cabins, Reservation Dept, TW Recreational Services, Inc., 82190 Ph: 307-344-7311	Yellowstone National Park

Canada

Alberta

Banff Springs, Spray Ave., PO Box 960, T0L 0C0 Ph: 403-762-2211 800-441-1414	Banff
Douglas Fir Resort, Tunnel Mountain Rd., PO Box 1228, T0L 0C0 Ph: 403-762-5591 800-661-9267	Banff
Ambassador Motor Inn, 802 Sixteenth Ave. NE, T2E 1K8 Ph: 403-276-2271 800-661-1447	Calgary
Prince Royal Inn, 618 Fifth Ave. SW, T2P 0M7 Ph: 403-263-0520 800-661-1592	Calgary
The Westin Hotel, 320 Fourth Ave. SW, T2P 2S6 Ph: 403-266-1611 800-228-3000	Calgary
Crown Plaza - Chateau Lacombe, 10111 Bellamy Hill, T5J 1N7 Ph: 403-428-6611	Edmonton
Fantasyland Hotel, 17700 87th Ave., T5T 4V4 Ph: 403-444-3000 800-661-6454	Edmonton
The Westin Hotel, 10135 100 St., T5J 0N7 Ph: 403-426-3636 800-228-3000	Edmonton
Chateau Lake Louise, 111 Lake Louise Dr., T0L 1E0 Ph: 403-522-3511 800-828-7447	Lake Louise

British Columbia

Bosman's Motor Hotel, 1060 Howe St., V6Z 1P5 Ph: 604-682-3171 800-663-7840	Vancouver

New Brunswick

Carriage House B&B, 230 University Ave., E3B 4H7 Ph: 506-452-9924	Fredericton
Lord Beaverbrook Hotel, 659 Queen St., E3B 5A6 Ph: 506-455-3371	Fredericton
Sheraton Inn Fredericton, 225 Woodstock Rd., E3B 2H8 Ph: 506-456-7000 800-325-3535	Fredericton
Chickadee Lodge, King's Landing, Ph: 506-363-2759	Prince William
Delta Brunswick, 39 King St., E2L 4W3 Ph: 506-648-1981 800-268-1133	Saint John
Parkerhouse Inn, 71 Sydney St., Ph: 506-652-5054	Saint John
Algonquin, 184 Adolphus, E0G 2X0 Ph: 506-529-8823 800-828-7447	St. Andrews by the Sea
Pansy Patch, 59 Carleton, E0G 2X0 Ph: 506-529-3834	St. Andrews by the Sea

Nova Scotia

Chateau Halifax, 1990 Barrington St., B3J 1P2 Ph: 902-425-6700 800-828-7447	Halifax
Delta Barrington, 1875 Barrington St., B3J 3L6 Ph: 902-429-7410 800-877-1133	Halifax
Keddy's Halifax Hotel, 20 St. Margaret's Bay Rd., B3N 1J4 Ph: 902-477-5611 800-561-7666	Halifax

Ontario

Chateau Laurier, 1 Rideau St., Ph: 613-232-6411 800-268-9411	Ottawa
Delta Ottawa, 361 Queen, K1R 7S9 Ph: 613-238-6000 800-268-1133	Ottawa
Minto Place Suite Hotel, 433 Laurier Ave. W, K1R 7Y1 Ph: 613-232-2200 800-267-3377	Ottawa

Delta Chelsea Inn, 33 Gerrard St. W , M5G 1Z4 Ph: 416-243-5732 800-243-5732	Toronto
Royal York Hotel, 100 Front St. W , M5J 1E3 Ph: 416-368-2511 800-828-7447	Toronto
Town Inn Suites, 620 Church St., M4Y 2G2 Ph: 416-964-3311 800-387-2755	Toronto

Province of Quebec

Hotel Novotel, 1180 Rue de la Montagne, H3G 1Z1 Ph: 514-861-6000 800-221-4542	Montreal
Westin Mont Royal, 1050 Sherbrooke St. W , H3A 2R6 Ph: 514-284-1110 800-332-3442	Montreal
Hotel Classique, 640 St. Jean St., Ph: 418-629-0227 800-463-5753	Quebec City
Hotel Du Vieux Quebec, 1190 rue Saint-Jean, G1R 1S6 Ph: 418-692-1850	Quebec City
Ramada Hotel Quebec Centre Ville, 395 rue de la Couronne, G1K 7X4 Ph: 418-647-2611	Quebec City
Chalets Montmorency et Motels, 1768 ave. Royale, G0A 3R0 Ph: 418-826-2600 800-463-2612	Saint-Ferreol-les-Neiges
Gray Rocks, PO Box 1000, J0T 2H0 Ph: 819-425-2771 800-567-6767	St. Jovite

Caribbean

Cap Juluca, Box 240, Ph: 809-497-6666 800-323-0139	Anguilla, Maunday's Bay
Malliouhana Hotel, PO Box 173, Ph: 809-497-6111 800-835-0796	Anguilla, Meads Bay
St. James Club, PO Box 63, Ph: 268-460-5000 800-274-0008	Antigua, Mamora Bay
Club Antigua, PO Box 744, Ph: 268-462-0062 800-777-1250	Antigua, St. Johns
Rex Halcyon Cove Beach, PO Box 215, Dickenson Bay, Ph: 268-462-0256 800-255-5859	Antigua, St. Johns
Bushiri Bounty Beach Resort, L. G. Smith Blvd. 35, Ph: 203-266-0100 800-462-6868	Aruba
Americana Aruba Beach Resort/Casino, 83 J.E. Irausquin Blvd, PO Box 218, Ph: 297-8-64500	Aruba, Oranjestad
Aruba Marriott Resort & Casino, L.G. Smith Blvd. 101, Ph: 297-8-69000	Aruba, Oranjestad
Costa Linda Beach Resort, 69 J.E. Irausquin Blvd., PO Box 1345, Ph: 297-8-38000	Aruba, Oranjestad
Costa Linda Beach Resort Aruba, J.E. Irausquin Blvd. 59, Ph: 297-8-38000 800-992-2015	Aruba, Oranjestad
Holiday Inn-Aruba Beach Resort, 230 J. E. Irausquin Blvd., Ph: 297-8-63600	Aruba, Oranjestad
La Cabana All Suite Resort & Casino, J.E. Irausquin Blvd. 250, Ph: 297-8-79000 800-835-7193	Aruba, Oranjestad
Sonesta Resort at Seaport Village, L. G. Smith Blvd. #9, Ph: 297-8-36000	Aruba, Oranjestad
Tamarijn Aruba Beach Resort, J.E. Irausquin Blvd. 41, Ph: 297-8-24150 800-554-2008	Aruba, Oranjestad
Wyndham Aruba Beach Resort & Casino, 77 J. E. Irausquin Blvd., PO Box 363, Ph: 297-8-64466	Aruba, Oranjestad
Hyatt Regency Aruba Resort & Casino, L. G. Smith Blvd. 85, Ph: 297-8-61234 800-233-1234	Aruba, Palm Beach

Radisson Aruba Resort & Casino, J.E. Irausquin Blvd. 81, Ph: 297-8-66555 800-333-3333	Aruba, Palm Beach
Bahamas Princess Resort & Casino, PO Box F-40207, Ph: 242-352-6721	Bahamas, Freeport
Paradise Island Fun Club, Harbour Dr., PO Box SS 6249, Ph: 242-363-2561	Bahamas, Nassau
Pirate's Cove Holiday Inn Sunspree, Casuarina Dr., PO Box SS 6214, Ph: 242-363-2100	Bahamas, Nassau
South Ocean Golf & Beach Resort, Adelaide Rd., PO Box N-8191, Ph: 242-362-4391	Bahamas, Nassau
Divi Southwinds Beach Resort, St. Lawrence Gap, Ph: 246-428-7181	Barbados, Bridgetown
Marriott - Sam Lord's Castle, Ph: 246-423-7350	Barbados, Bridgetown
Sandy Lane Hotel & Golf Club, Ph: 246-432-1311	Barbados, Bridgetown
Glitter Bay, Porters, Ph: 246-422-5555 800-283-8666	Barbados, St. James
Almond Beach Village, Ph: 246-422-4900 800-4-ALMOND	Barbados, St. Peter
Grotto Bay Beach Hotel & Tennis Clb, 11 Blue Hole Hill, Ph: 441-293-8333	Bermuda, Hamilton Parish
Elbow Beach Bermuda, 60 South Shore Rd., Ph: 441-236-3535	Bermuda, Paget Parish
Southampton Princess Hotel, 101 South Shore Rd., PO Box HM 1379, Ph: 441-238-8000	Bermuda, Southampton Parish
Captain Don's Habitat, PO Box 88, Ph: 599-7-8290 800-327-6709	Bonaire
Harbour Village, PO Box 312, Ph: 599-7-7500	Bonaire
Sand Dollar Beach Club, PO Box 262, Ph: 599-7-2288 800-328-2288	Bonaire
Sunset Beach Hotel, PO Box 333, Ph: 599-7-8291 800-354-8142	Bonaire
Divi Flamingo Beach Resort & Casino, A.J.A. Abraham Blvd., Ph: 599-5-8285 800-367-3484	Bonaire, Kralendijk
Princess Beach Resort and Casino, Martin Luther King Blvd., Ph: 599-9-614944 800-327-3286	Curacao
Flamenco Beach Resort, Playa Doradas, Puerto Plata, Ph: 809-320-5084	Dominican Republic
Hamaca Beach Hotel & Casino, Boca Chica Ave Duarte, Santo Domingo, Ph: 809-523-4611	Dominican Republic
Hotel Casino Bavaro, Bavaro Beach Resort Complex, AP N #1, Ph: 809-686-5797	Dominican Republic
Hotel Golf Bavaro, Bavaro Beach Resort Complex, AP N #1, Ph: 809-686-5797	Dominican Republic
Hotel Jardin Bavaro, Bavaro Beach Resort Complex, AP N #1, Ph: 809-686-5797	Dominican Republic
Hotel Playa Bavaro, Bavaro Beach Resort Complex, AP N #1, Ph: 809-686-5797	Dominican Republic
Jack Tar Village, PO Box 368, Playa Dorada, Ph: 809-586-3800 800-999-9182	Dominican Republic
Paradise Beach Club & Casino, Dorada Beach Complex, PO Box 337, Puerto Plata, Ph: 809-320-3663	Dominican Republic
Playa Dorada Beach Resort, PO Box 1370, Puerto Plata, Ph: 809-586-3988 800-423-6902	Dominican Republic
Punta Cana Beach Resort, PO Box 1083, Punta Cana, Ph: 809-221-2262	Dominican Republic

Holiday Inn Grand Cayman, PO Box 905, Ph: 345-947-4444 800-421-9999	Grand Cayman
Radisson Resort Grand Cayman, PO Box 30371, Seven Mile Beach, West Beach Rd., Ph: 345-949-0088 800-333-3333	Grand Cayman
Rex Grenadian, Point Salines, PO Box 893, Ph: 809-444-333 800-255-5859	Grenada, St. George's
Hotel Marissol, Bas du Fort, Ph: 590-09-84-44 800-221-4542	Guadeloupe, Gosier
Goblin Hill Villas at San San, Rt A4, PO Box 26, Port Antonio, Ph: 809-925-8108	Jamaica
Holiday Inn Montego Bay Sunspree, PO Box 480, Montego Bay, Ph: 809-953-2486	Jamaica
Plantation Inn, Rt A3, PO Box 2, Ocho Rios, Ph: 876-974-5601	Jamaica
Renaissance Jamaica Grande Resort, PO Box 100, Ocho Rios, Ph: 876-974-2201 800-228-9898	Jamaica
Round Hill Hotel & Villas, PO Box 64, Montego Bay, Ph: 809-952-5150	Jamaica
Sea Castles Resort, PO Box, 55, Montego Bay, Ph: 809-953-3250	Jamaica
Half Moon Golf Tennis & Beach Club, PO Box 80, Rose Hall, Ph: 809-953-2211	Jamaica, Montego Bay
Wyndham Rose Hall Beach Resort, PO Box 999, Rose Hall, Ph: 809-953-2650 800-996-3426	Jamaica, Montego Bay
Trelawny Beach Hotel, Famouth, Ph: 809-954-2450 800-336-1435	Jamaica, Trelawny
Diamant-Novotel, Point de la Chery, Le Diamant, Ph: 596-76-42-42	Mantinique
Golden Rock Hotel, PO Box 493, Gingerland, Ph: 869-469-3346	Nevis
Four Seasons, PO Box 565, Ph: 809-469-1111 800-332-3442	Nevis, Charlestown
Palmas del Mar, P.O. Box 2020, Humacao, 00661 Ph: 809-852-6000 800-468-3331	Puerto Rico
Caneel Bay Resort, PO Box 720, Cruz Bay, Ph: 340-776-61111 800-928-8889	St. John
Hyatt Regency, PO Box 8310, Great Cruz Bay, 00831 Ph: 340-776-7171 800-233-1234	St. John
Virgin Grand Villas, PO Box 37, 00831 Ph: 340-693-8856	St. John
Jack Tar Village, PO Box 406, Ph: 809-465-8651 800-999-9182	St. Kitts, Frigate Bay
Odyssey St. Lucia, PO Box 915, Smugglers Village, Ph: 809-452-0552 800-223-9815	St. Lucia, Castries
Wyndham Morgan Bay Resort, PO Box 2216, Ph: 809-450-2511	St. Lucia, Gros Islet
Jalousie Plantation, PO Box 251, Ph: 809-459-7666 800-392-2007	St. Lucia, Soufriere
Hotel Mont Vernon, B.P. 1174-Baie Orientale, French cul-de-sac, Ph: 590-87-6200	St. Martin
Bolongo Bay Beach Resort, 7150 Estate Bolongo, Ph: 340-775-1800 800-524-4746	St. Thomas
Marriott's Frenchman's Reef Beach, Frenchman's Bay Rd., 00801 Ph: 340-776-8500	St. Thomas
Point Pleasant Resort, 6600 Estate Smith Bay, #4, 00802 Ph: 340-775-7200 800-524-2300	St. Thomas
Renaissance Grand Beach Resort, PO Box 8267, 00801 Ph: 340-775-1510	St. Thomas
Stouffer Grand Beach Resort, Smith Bay Rd., PO Box 8267, Ph: 340-775-1510 800-233-4935	St. Thomas
Sugar Bay Plantation Resort, Estate Smith Bay, Ph: 340-777-7100 800-HOLIDAY	St. Thomas
Rhymer's Beach Hotel, PO Box 570, Gane Garden Bay, Ph: 340-495-4639 809-495-4215	Tortola

Fort Recovery, PO Box 239, Ph: 340-495-4467 800-367-8455	Tortola, Road Town
Long Bay Beach Resort, PO Box 4333, Ph: 340-495-4252 800-729-9599	Tortola, Road Town
Trinidad Hilton, Box 442, Lady Young Rd., Ph: 809-624-3211 800-445-8667	Trinidad/ Tobago, Port of Spain
Rex Turtle Beach, PO Box 201, Cortland Bay, Ph: 809-639-2851	Trinidad/ Tobago, Scarborough
Turquoise Reef Resort & Casino, Box 205, Grace Bay, Providenciales, Ph: 809-946-5555	Turks & Caicos
Biras Creek Reosrt, PO Box 54, Ph: 340-494-3555 800-223-1108	Virgin Gorda
Little Dix Bay, PO Box 70, Ph: 340-495-5555 800-928-3000	Virgin Gorda

Puerto Rico

Horned Dorset Primavera Hotel, Rincon, Ph: 787-823-4050 787-823-4030	Puerto Rico
Las Casitas Villas, 1000 El Conquistador Ave., Fajardo, Ph: 787-863-6855	Puerto Rico
Mayaguez Hilton & Casino, PO Box 3629, Mayaguez, Ph: 787-831-7575	Puerto Rico
Hyatt Dorado Beach, 00646 Ph: 787-796-1234 800-233-1234	Dorado
Caribe Hilton International, PO Box 1872, 00902 Ph: 787-721-0303 800-468-8585	San Juan
El San Juan Hotel & Casino, PO Box 2872, Avenida Isla Verde, 00902 Ph: 787-791-1000 800-468-2818	San Juan
Radisson Normandie, Box 50059, 00902 Ph: 787-729-2929 800-333-3333	San Juan
Sands Hotel & Casino Beach Resort, PO Box 6676, Loiza Station, 00914 Ph: 787-791-6100 800-443-2009	Santurce
Ponce Hilton & Casino, PO Box 7149, 00731 Ph: 787-259-7676 800-HILTONS	Ponce

Mexico

Presidente Hotel, Boulevard Kukulcan Km., 77550 Ph: 52-988-30200 800-447-6147	Cancun

. . . .

SHOPPING FOR A KID-FRIENDLY HOTEL

Most hotels allow children to stay free with their parents, and many offer special discounts, packages and amenities to traveling families. Read on for a summary of the policies and programs offered by various hotel chains.

DAYS INN, DAYS HOTEL, DAYS SUITE AND DAYS STOPS Kids Stay and Eat Free Program offers free meals to children under 12 who are accompanied by their parents, and discounts for rooms booked more than 29 days ahead. For reservations and more information, call (800) 325-2525.

FOUR SEASONS Most Four Seasons resorts have a complimentary Kids for All Seasons program, which include from fun activities and child-proof rooms to milk and cookies and a "Single Parents Weekend" package. For reservations or more information, call (800) 268-6282.

HILTON More than 80 Hiltons offer a summer-long Vacation Station, which offers welcome gifts and free use of toys and games. Some resorts offer supervised kids'programs year-round. For reservations or more information, call (310) 205-4599.

HOLIDAY INN Holiday Inn began unveiling its Kidsuites in Florida. Kidsuites are specially designed with separate or semi-separate quarters for kids in several themes, including wild west, seaside, some with bunk beds. For reservations or more information, call (800) HOL-IDAY.

HYATT More than 100 Hyatts offer welcome packets, special room rates, room-service menus and games to borrow. Sixteen resorts have supervised activities during the summer, holidays and weekends. For reservations or more information, call (800) 233-1234.

LOEWS All Loews hotels and resorts offer special menus, room rates and activities, cribs and roll-away beds are provided at no charge, child-proof kits for toddlers, gifts and information. For reservations or more information, call (800) 23-LOEWS.

MARRIOTT Fifteen Marriott resorts offer region-specific children's programs, with activities ranging from golf lessons to submarine rides. Many Marriotts also offer discounted meals. Kids under 18 stay free in their parents' rooms. For reservations or more information, call (800) 228-9290.

RADISSON Game rooms at 56 Radisson hotels, 13 offer children's programs and one has child-proof suites. For reservations or more information, call (800) 333-3333.

RITZ-CARLTON Ritz Kids offers services and activities ranging from hula lessons to kite flying. Their Boston hotel has a special children's suite. For reservations or more information, call (800) 241-3333.

WESTIN Westin's new Kids Club program provides nightlights, potty suites, and juice, gifts for the kids and children's movies. For reservations or more information, call (800) 228-3000.

Kids under 18 stay free in their parents' room at the following budget motel chains:

> Best Inns of America, (800) 237-8466
> Budgetel, (800) 428-4678
> Choice Hotels, (800) 424-4777
> Clarion, (800) 221-2222
> Comfort Inn, (800) 228-5150
> Cross Country Inns, (800) 621-1429
> Drury Inns, (800) 325-8300
> Exel Inns, (800) 356-8013
> Knight's Inn, (800) 722-7220
> La Quinta Motor Inn, (800) 531-5900
> Motel 6, (505) 891-6161
> Quality Inns, (800) 228-5151

• • • • • • • • • • • • • • • • • • • •
CONDO VACATIONS

Why not take a condo vacation as an alternative to traditional hotels and motels? A vacation condominium is a lodging which features suites rather than single rooms. Most condos have at least one separate bedroom, others may have two or three. The vast majority of condos have full kitchen facilities. Most of the conveniences of hotels are available.

Renting a condominium is like taking your home with you. The sheets are on the bed, the cable TV is ready, and the kitchen is waiting for you to prepare all the special treats your children love.

The staff at most condo resorts can recommend reliable babysitters, and offer daily maid service, giving everyone a break. Family reunions are also a natural for condominiums.

Staying at a condo can trim vacation expenses by up to fifty percent when compared with a stay in a similarly located traditional hotel with all meals taken in a restaurant.

Alabama

Compass Point, 1516 Sandpiper Lane, 36542 Ph: 205-948-6411	Gulf Shores
Seabreeze Condos, West Beach Blvd., Rt. 1, Box 1994, 36542 Ph: 205-948-6411	Gulf Shores

Arkansas

Devil's Fork Resort, Rt. 1, Box B, 72067 Ph: 501-825-6240	Higden, Greers Ferry
Resort Condominium Rentals, 6000 Central Ave., 71913 Ph: 501-525-3500	Hot Springs
Buena Vista Resort, Route 3, Box 175, 71913 Ph: 501-525-1321	Hot Springs

Arizona

Boulders Resort, 34631 N. Tom Darlington, Box 2090, 85377 Ph: 602-488-9099	Carefree
Nautical Inn Resort, 1000 McCulloch Blvd., 86403 Ph: 602-855-2141	Lake Havasu
Pointe at Tapatio Cliffs, 11111 North 7th Street, 85020 Ph: 602-997-6000	Phoenix
Pointe at Squaw Peak, 7677 North 16th Street, 85020 Ph: 602-997-6000	Phoenix
Pointe at South Mountain, 7777 South Pointe Parkway, 85044 Ph: 602-997-6000	Phoenix
The Wigwam, Litchfield Park, 85340 Ph: 602-935-3811	Phoenix
Roundhouse Resort, Buck Springs Rd., P.O. Box 1468, 85935 Ph: 602-369-4848	Pinetop
Hyatt Regency Scottsdale, 85251	Scottsdale
Scottsdale Manor, 4807 Woodmere Fairway Dr., 85251 Ph: 602-994-5282	Scottsdale
Scottsdale Camelback, 6302 E. Camelback Rd., 85251 Ph: 602-947-3300	Scottsdale
Villa Serenas, 8111 E. Broadway, 85710 Ph: 602-886-6761	Tucson

California

La Costa Hotel & Spa, Costa Del Mar Road, 92009 Ph: 619-438-9111	Carlsbad
Brockway Springs Resort, P.O. Box 276, 95719 Ph: 916-546-4201	Kings Beach
Twin Palms, 136 Cliff Drive, 92651 Ph: 714-497-4773	Laguna Beach
Snowcreek, P.O. Box 1647, 93546 Ph: 619-934-3333	Mammoth Lks.
Mammoth Mountain Inn, P.O. Box 353, 93546 Ph: 800-228-4947	Mammoth Lks.
Silverado Country Club, 1600 Atlas Peak Road, 94558 Ph: 707-257-0200	Napa
Squaw Valley Townhouses, 1604 Christy Hill Lane, Box 2008, 95730 Ph: 916-583-3451	Olympic Valley
Tavern Inn Condos, P.O. Box 2741, 95730 Ph: 916-583-1504	Olympic Valley
Woodhaven Country Club, 41-555 Woodhaven Drive East, 92260 Ph: 619-345-7642	Palm Desert

Shadow Mountain, 45750 San Luis Rey, 92260 Ph: 619-346-6123	Palm Desert
Ironwood Country Club, 49-200 Mariposa Drive, 92260 Ph: 619-346-0551	Palm Desert
Palm Valley Country Club, 76-200 Country Club Drive, 92260 Ph: 619-345-7802	Palm Desert
Palm Desert Resort, 77-622 Country Club Dr., Suite A, 92211 Ph: 619-360-6565	Palm Desert
Palm Springs Marquis, 150 South Indian Avenue, 92262 Ph: 619-322-2121	Palm Springs
Azure Sky Resort, 1661 Calle Palo Fierro, 92264 Ph: 619-325-9109	Palm Springs
Racquet Club P. Springs, 2743 North Indian Ave. Box 1747, 92262 Ph: 619-325-1281	Palm Springs
Sundance Villas, 303 Cabrillo Road, 92262 Ph: 619-325-3888	Palm Springs
Cathedral Canyon Resort, 34567 Cathedral Canyon Drive, 92264 Ph: 619-321-9000	Palm Springs
La Mancha, 444 Avenida Caballeros, Box 340, 92263 Ph: 619-323-1773	Palm Springs
Doubletree Resort, Vista Chino and Landell, 92263 Ph: 619-322-7000	Palm Springs
San Vicente Country Club, 1306 Main Street, 92065 Ph: 619-789-8678	Ramona
San Clemente Inn, 2600 Ave. Del Presidente, 92672 Ph: 714-492-6103	San Clemente
Blarney Castle, 509 Monterey Ln., 92672 Ph: 714-492-7576	San Clemente
Sea Horse Inn, 602 Avenida Victoria, 92672 Ph: 714-492-1720	San Clemente
Villa Del Mar Inn, 612 Avenida Victoria, 92672 Ph: 714-498-5080	San Clemente
Blue Sea Lodge, 707 Pacific Beach Dr., 92109 Ph: 619-483-4700	San Diego
Lakeland Village Resort, 3535 Highway 50, P.O. Box 705002, 95705 Ph: 916-541-7711	South Lake Tahoe
Bavarian Village Rentals, P.O. Box 709, 1140 Herbert, 96156 Ph: 800-822-6636	South Lake Tahoe
Tahoe Valley Condos, P.O. Box 7702, Hwy. 50, 95731 Ph: 916-541-0353	South Lake Tahoe
Christy Hill Resort, 1604 Christy Hill Ln., 95730 Ph: 916-583-3451	Squaw Valley
Prudential California, 3210 N. Lake Blvd., P.O. Box 5518, 96145 Ph: 916-583-7523	Tahoe City
O'Neal Associates, P.O. Box 802, 95730 Ph: 916-583-7368	Tahoe City
Tahoe Marina Lodge, P.O. Box 92, 95730 Ph: 916-583-2365	Tahoe City
Northstar at Tahoe, P.O. Box 129, 95734 Ph: 916-562-1010	Truckee
Redwoods Guest Cottages, P.O. Box 2085 Wawona Station, 95389 Ph: 209-375-6666	Yosemite National Park

Colorado

Inn at Aspen, 21646 W. Hwy. 82, 81611 Ph: 303-925-1500	Aspen
The Gant, 610 West End St., 81612 Ph: 970-925-5000	Aspen
Fasching Haus, 747 Galena Street, 81611 Ph: 303-925-5900	Aspen
Aspen Silverglo Condos, 940 Waters Ave., 81611 Ph: 970-925-8450	Aspen
Aspen Alps Condo Assoc., Box 1228, 81612 Ph: 303-925-7820	Aspen
The Christie Lodge, 0047 E. Beaver Creek Bl. Box 1196, 81620 Ph: 303-949-7700	Avon
Beaver Creek West, P.O. Box 5290, 81620 Ph: 303-949-4840	Avon
The Charter, 120 Offerson Rd., P.O. Box 5310, 81620 Ph: 303-949-6660	Beaver Creek
Poste Montane, 76 Avon Dale Lane, Box 36, 81620 Ph: 303-845-7500	Beaver Creek
The Inn at Beaver Creek, P.O. Box 36, 10 Elk Track, 81620 Ph: 303-845-7800	Beaver Creek
Park Plaza Lodge, P.O. Box 36, 46 Avondale Lane, 81620 Ph: 303-845-7700	Beaver Creek
Gold Point Condominiums, 169 N. Fuller Placer Road-Box 568, 80424 Ph: 303-453-1910	Breckenridge
Ski Hill Condominiums, 250 Ski Hill Road, 80424 Ph: 303-453-2262	Breckenridge
Der Steiermark Condos, 600 South Park Street, 80420 Ph: 303-453-1939	Breckenridge
Four Seasons Lodging, P.O. Box 1356, 424 S. Ridge St., 80424 Ph: 970-453-1403	Breckenridge

Blue River Condominiums, P.O. Box 1942, 80424 Ph: 303-453-2260	Breckenridge
Beaver Run, P.O. Box 2115, 80424 Ph: 303-453-6000	Breckenridge
Carbemate Pro. Management, Box 3216, 80443 Ph: 303-968-6854	Copper Mtn
Copper Mountain Resort, I-70 & US Hwy 91, Box 3001, 80433 Ph: 303-968-2882	Copper Mtn
Copper Mountain Inn, P.O. Box 3003, 80443 Ph: 303-968-6477	Copper Mtn
The Columbine Condos, Drawer C, 51, Whetstone Road, 81225 Ph: 303-349-2448	Crested Butte
Spinnaker at Lake Dillon, 317 Labonte Street, Box 2519, 80435 Ph: 303-468-8001	Dillon
Yacht Club Condos, 410 Tenderfoot Box 397, 80435 Ph: 303-468-2703	Dillon
Columbine Managment, Box 2590, 348 Lake Dillon Drive, 80435 Ph: 970-468-9137	Dillon
Snowdance Condos, Box 41 Montezuma Rte., 80435 Ph: 303-468-5178	Dillon
Purgatory-Village, 175 Beatrice St., P.O. Box 666, 81302 Ph: 303-247-9000	Durango
Ferringway, 6 Ferringway Circle, 81301 Ph: 303-247-0441	Durango
Cascade Village Resort, P.O. Box 2867, 50827 Hwy 550 N., 81301 Ph: 303-259-3500	Durango
Tamarron, P.O. Box 3131, 81302 Ph: 303-259-2000	Durango
Tenmile Creek Condos, 200 Granite St., P.O. Box 543, 80443 Ph: 303-668-3100	Frisco
Antlers Lodging Co., Box 2176, 1890, 80443 Ph: 303-668-5076	Frisco
Keystone Resort, Box 38, 80435 Ph: 303-534-7712	Keystone
Goldenwoods Condos, 81647 Ph: 303-242-5637	Mesa
Out Run Condos, 721 Gothic Road, 81224 Ph: 303-349-2800	Mt. Crested Butte
The Plaza at Woodcreek, 11 Snowmass Road, P.O. Box 5159, 81224 Ph: 303-349-6611	Mt. Crested Butte
Fairfield Pagosa, Hwy. 160, P.O. Box 4040, 81157 Ph: 303-731-4141	Pagosa Spgs.
Inn at Silver Creek, Box 4222, 80446 Ph: 303-887-2131	Silver Creek
Mountainside Silver Creek, P.O. Box 4104, 96 Mountainside Dr, 80446 Ph: 303-887-2571	Silver Creek
Paradise Condos, 221 Summit Blvd., Box 587, 80498 Ph: 303-468-5846	Silverthorne
Wildernest Lodging, P.O. Box 1069, 200 Ryan Gulch Rd., 80424 Ph: 303-468-6291	Silverthorne
The Enclave, 360 Wood Rd., P.O. Box B-2, 81615 Ph: 303-923-4310	Snowmass Vlg
Top of the Village, 855 Carriageway, P.O. Box 5629, 81615 Ph: 303-923-3673	Snowmass Vlg
Woodrun Place Condos, Box 6027, 0425 Wood Road, 81615 Ph: 303-923-5392	Snowmass Vlg
Chamonix at Woodrun, Box 6286, 0476 Wood Road, 81615 Ph: 303-923-5543	Snowmass Vlg
The Crestwood, P.O. Box 5460, 400 Wood Road, 81615 Ph: 970-923-2450	Snowmass Vlg
Snowmass Club, P.O. Drawer G-2, 81615 Ph: 303-923-5600	Snowmass Vlg
The Ranch at Steamboat, 1 Ranch Road, 80487 Ph: 303-525-2002	Steambt Spgs
Bronze Tree, 1855 Ski Time Square Drive, 80487 Ph: 303-879-8811	Steambt Spgs
Torian Plum, 1855 Ski Time Square Drive, 80487 Ph: 970-879-8811	Steambt Spgs
Trappeurs Crossing, 1855 Ski Time Square Drive, 80487 Ph: 303-879-8811	Steambt Spgs
Dulany Condominiums, P.O. Box 2995, 80477 Ph: 303-879-7900	Steambt Spgs
Kutuk, P.O. Box 2995, 80477 Ph: 303-879-6605	Steambt Spgs
LaCasa at Steamboat, P.O. Box 2995, 80477 Ph: 303-879-6036	Steambt Spgs
Pine Grove Village, P.O. Box 2995, 80477 Ph: 303-525-5502	Steambt Spgs
The Lodge At Steamboat, P.O. Box 2995, 80477 Ph: 303-525-5502	Steambt Spgs
Timber Run, P.O. Box 2995, 80477 Ph: 303-879-7000	Steambt Spgs
Waterford Townhomes, P.O. Box 2995, 80477 Ph: 303-879-7000	Steambt Spgs
Winterwood Townhomes, P.O. Box 2995, 80477 Ph: 303-879-6605	Steambt Spgs
Ptarmigan House Condos, P.O. Box 3626, 80477 Ph: 303-525-5502	Steambt Spgs

Snow Flower Condos, P.O. Box 4406, 80477 Ph: 303-879-5104   Steambt Spgs
Golden Triangle Condos, P.O. Box 774847, 80477 Ph: 303-879-2931   Steambt Spgs
Peaks at Telluride Condos, Box 2702, 136 Atop Country Club, 81435   Telluride
    Ph: 970-728-6800
Riverside of Telluride, Telluride Lodging Co., Box 276, 81435   Telluride
    Ph: 303-728-4311
Village Inn Plaza, 100 East Meadow Drive, 81657 Ph: 303-476-5622   Vail
Vail Run Resort, 1000 Lions Ridge Loop, 81657 Ph: 303-476-1500   Vail
Simba Resort, 1100 N. Frontage Rd., 81657 Ph: 970-476-0344   Vail
Holiday Inn At Vail, 13 Vail Road, 81657 Ph: 303-476-5631   Vail
Coldstream Condos, 1476 Westhaven Drive, 81657 Ph: 303-476-6106   Vail
Fallridge at Vail, 1650 E. Vail Valley Dr., 81657 Ph: 303-476-1163   Vail
The Lodge at Vail, 174 East Gore Creek Drive, 81657 Ph: 303-476-5011 Vail
Raintree Inn, 2211 N. Frontage Road W., 81657 Ph: 303-476-3890   Vail
Streamside at Vail, 2264 S. Frontage Rd., 81657 Ph: 303-476-6000   Vail
Vail International, 300 E. Lionshead Circle, Box 877, 81658 Ph: 303-476-5200   Vail
Vail Racquet Club, 4690 Vail Racquet Dr., Box l437, 81657 Ph: 303-476-4840   Vail
The Wren Condos, 500 South Frontage Road, #116, 81657 Ph: 303-476-0052   Vail
Westwind At Vail, 548 South Frontage Road, 81657 Ph: 303-476-5031   Vail
Manor Vail Lodge, 595 East Vail Valley Drive, 81657 Ph: 303-476-5651 Vail
Montaneros Condos, 641 W. Lion Head Circle, 81657 Ph: 303-476-2491   Vail
Lion Square Lodge, 660 W. Lion Head Place, 81657 Ph: 303-476-2281   Vail
Antlers At Vail, 680 West LionsHead Place, 8l657 Ph: 303-476-2471   Vail
Vail Spa, 710 West Lionshead Circle, 81657 Ph: 303-476-0882   Vail
The Willows Condos, 74 Willow Road, 81657 Ph: 970-476-2233   Vail
Mountain Haus at Vail, P.O. Box 1748, 81658 Ph: 303-476-2434   Vail
Apollo Park Lodge, P.O. Box 2157, 81658 Ph: 303-476-5881   Vail
Bighorn Condominium, P.O. Box 400, 81658 Ph: 303-476-5532   Vail
The Lodge At Lionshead, P.O. Drawer 1868,380 E. Lionshead, 81658   Vail
    Ph: 303-476-2700
Beaver Village Condos, 50 Village Drive, P.O. Box 349, 80482   Winter Park
    Ph: 970-726-8813
Iron Horse Resort Retreat, P.O. Box 1286,257 Winter Park Dr., 80482   Winter Park
    Ph: 303-726-8851
Lookout Village Condos, P.O. Box 3157, 80482 Ph: 303-726-8821   Winter Park
The Summit at Winter Park, P.O. Box 3157, 80482 Ph: 515-292-9546   Winter Park

Florida

Amelia Surf & Racquet Club, 800 Amelia Parkway S., 32034 Ph: 904-261-0511   Amelia Island
Amelia Island Plantation, Box 758, Highway A1A South, 32034   Amelia Island
    Ph: 904-261-6161
Errol Estate Club, 1355 Errol Parkway, 32712 Ph: 407-886-5000   Apopka
La Boca Casa, 365 North Ocean Blvd., 33432 Ph: 407-392-0885   Boca Raton
Bonita Beach Resort, 26395 Hickory Boulevard, 33923 Ph: 813-992-2137 Bonita Springs
Palm Island Resort, 7092 Placida Road, 33946 Ph: 813-697-4800   Cape Haze
Executive/Clearwater House, Box 7642 Heather Trail, 33518   Clearwater
    Ph: 813-797-1140
Seagull Beach Club, 4440 Ocean Beach Boulevard, 32931 Ph: 407-783-4441   Cocoa Beach
Ocean Landings Resort, 900 North Atlantic Avenue, 32931 Ph: 407-783-9430   Cocoa Beach
Sutherland Crossing, 962 Seaview Cir., P.O. Box 883, 34681 Ph: 813-786-2287   Crystal Beach
Frantony, The, 665 South A1A, 33441   Deerfield
    Ph: 305-427-3509   Beach
Inn At Deer Creek, 9 Deer Creek Road, A105, 33442   Deerfield
    Ph: 305-421-7800   Beach
Spanish River Resort, 1111 E. Atlantic Avenue, 33483 Ph: 407-243-7946   Delray Beach

Int'l Tennis Resort, 651 Egret Circle, 33444 Ph: 305-272-4126	Delray Beach
East Pass Towers, 100 Gulfshore Drive, 32541 Ph: 904-837-4191	Destin
Destin Towers Condos, 1008 Highway 98 East, 32541 Ph: 904-837-7002	Destin
SunDestin, 1040 Hwy. 98 East, 32541 Ph: 904-837-7093	Destin
Emerald Towers, 1044 Highway 98 East, 32541 Ph: 904-837-6575	Destin
Destin Beach Club, 1150 Hwy. 98 East, 32541 Ph: 904-837-3985	Destin
Waterview Towers, 150 Gulf Shore Dr., 32541 Ph: 904-837-6333	Destin
Surfside Resort, 4701 Highway 98 East, 32541 Ph: 904-837-4700	Destin
Beach House Condos, 4800 Highway 98 East, 32541 Ph: 904-837-6131	Destin
Edgewater Beach Condos, 5000 Highway 98 East, 32541 Ph: 904-837-5800	Destin
Mainsail, 5100 Hwy 98 East, 32541 Ph: 904-837-7711	Destin
Sandestin Beach Resort, Emerald Coast Parkway, 32541 Ph: 904-267-8000	Destin
Huntington by the Sea, Hwy. 98 East, 32541 Ph: 904-837-7811	Destin
Hawk's Cay Resort, Mile Marker 61, 33050 Ph: 305-743-7000	Duck Key
Sandpiper Key Condo Assoc., 1601 Beach Road, 34223 Ph: 813-475-3108	Englewood
SunBurst Condominiums, 2450 N. Beach Road, 34223 Ph: 813-474-0096	Englewood
Fantasy Island Condos, 2765 N. Beach Road, 34223 Ph: 813-475-2108	Englewood
Silver Seas, 101 N. Atlantic Blvd., 33304 Ph: 305-522-8723	Fort Lauderdale
Bahia Cabana Beach Resort, 3001 Harbor Drive, 33316 Ph: 305-524-1555	Fort Lauderdale
Inverrary House, 3363 Spanish Moss Terrace, 33319 Ph: 305-731-9278	Fort Lauderdale
Radisson Ocean Resort, 4040 Galt Ocean Drive, 33308 Ph: 305-566-7500	Fort Lauderdale
The Breakers, 909 Breakers Ave., 33304 Ph: 305-566-8800	Fort Lauderdale
Coconut Bay Resort Hotel, 919 N. Birch Rd., 33304 Ph: 305-563-4229	Fort Lauderdale
Cane Palm Beach Club, 600 Estero Blvd., 33931 Ph: 813-463-3222	Fort Myers
Pointe Estero Resort, 6640 Estero Blvd., 33931 Ph: 813-765-1155	Fort Myers Beach
Mariner's Boathouse Resort, 7630 Estero Boulevard, 33931 Ph: 813-463-8787	Fort Myers Beach
Royal Beach Club, 800 Estero Blvd., 33931 Ph: 813-463-9494	Fort Myers Beach
Seaspray Condos, 1530 U.S. Highway 98 E., 32548 Ph: 904-244-1108	Fort Walton Beach
Steamboat Landing, 161 S.E. Brooks Street, 32548 Ph: 904-244-1391	Fort Walton Beach
Pirates Bay Condos, 214 Miracle Strip Pkwy., 32548 Ph: 904-243-3154	Fort Walton Beach
Island Sands Condos, 862 Scallop Ct., 32548 Ph: 904-837-4853	Fort Walton Beach
Grenelefe Resort, 3200 State Road 546, 33884 Ph: 813-422-7511	Grenelefe
Hollywood Beach Resort, 101 N. Ocean Dr., 33019 Ph: 305-921-0990	Hollywood
Neptune Hollywood Club, 2012 N. Surf Rd., 33019 Ph: 305-922-0459	Hollywood
Hollywood Sands Resort, 2404 N. Surf Rd., 33019 Ph: 305-925-2285	Hollywood
Mission Inn Resort, Box 441, 32737 Ph: 904-324-2101	Howey-In-The- Hills
Indian River Plantation, 555 N.E. Ocean Blvd., 34996 Ph: 407-225-3700	Hutchinson Island
Sand Dollar Resort, 18500 Gulf Blvd., 34635 Ph: 813-595-8109	Indian Shores
Jupiter Bay Resort, 350 S. US Highway 1, 33477 Ph: 407-744-0210	Jupiter
Anchorage Resort, 107500 Overseas Highway, 33037 Ph: 305-451-0500	Key Largo
Moon Bay Condos, 4700 Overseas Highway, 33130 Ph: 305-451-4161	Key Largo

The Banyan Resort, 323 White Head St., 33040 Ph: 305-294-9573	Key West
Pelican Landing, 915 Eisenhower Drive, 33040 Ph: 305-296-7583	Key West
Fortune Place Resort, 1475 Astro Lake Dr., 32743 Ph: 407-348-0330	Kissimmee
Resort World Of Orlando, 2794 N. Poinciana Blvd., 34746 Ph: 305-396-8300	Kissimmee
High Point World Resort, 2951 High Point Blvd., 32741 Ph: 407-396-9600	Kissimmee
Club Sevilla, 4646 W. Irlo Bronson Memorial Hwy, 32741 Ph: 305-396-1800	Kissimmee
Lifetime of Vacations Resort, 7770 W. Irlo Bronson Memorial Hwy, 32741 Ph: 407-396-3000	Kissimmee
Orange Lake Country Club, 8505 W Space Coast Pkwy., Rt 192W , 34786 Ph: 305-239-0000	Kissimmee
Fantasy World Club Villas, 2935 Hart Blvd., 32830 Ph: 305-396-1808	Lake Buena Vista
Vistana Resort, 8800 Vistana Centre Dr, Box 22051, 32830 Ph: 407-239-3100	Lake Buena Vista
Morningstar Condos, 223 Marine Court, 33308 Ph: 305-771-5924	Lauderdale-By-The-Sea
Driftwood Beach Club, 4417 El Mar Drive, 33308 Ph: 305-776-4441	Lauderdale-By-The-Sea
Howard Johnson Resort, 4660 N. Ocean Drive, 33308 Ph: 305-776-5660	Lauderdale-By-The-Sea
Lehigh Resort Club, 225 East Joel Blvd., 33936 Ph: 813-369-2121	Lehigh
Colony Beach Resort, 1620 Gulf of Mexico Dr., 34228 Ph: 813-383-6464	Longboat Key
Four Winds Beach Resort, 2605 Gulf Of Mexico Drive, 34228 Ph: 813-383-2411	Longboat Key
Gulf Tides of Longboat Key, 3008 Gulf of Mexico Dr., Box 8059, 34228 Ph: 813-383-5595	Longboat Key
Resort at Longboat, 301 Gulf Of Mexico Drive, 34228 Ph: 941-383-8821	Longboat Key
Little Gull, 5330 Gulf of Mexico Drive, 34228 Ph: 813-383-8818	Longboat Key
Cocoplum Beach Club, 109 Cocoplum Dr., 33050 Ph: 305-743-0240	Marathon
Sombrero Resort, 19 Sombrero Blvd., 33050 Ph: 305-743-2250	Marathon
Sunrise Bay Resort, 10 Tampa Place, 33937 Ph: 813-394-5280	Marco Island
Marco Bay Resort, 1001 N. Barfield Dr., 33937 Ph: 813-394-8881	Marco Island
Beach Club Of Marco, 901 S. Collier Blvd., 33937 Ph: 813-394-8860	Marco Island
Golden Strand Resort, 17901 Collins Avenue, 33160 Ph: 305-931-7000	Miami Beach
The Inn at Ravines, 2932 Ravines Road, 32068 Ph: 904-282-2843	Middleburg
Emerald Isle, 17334 Gulf Blvd., 33708 Ph: 813-397-0441	N. Redington
Charter Club, 1000 10th Ave. S, 33940 Ph: 813-261-5559	Naples
Edgewater Beach Hotel, 1901 Gulf Shore Blvd. N., 33940 Ph: 813-262-6511	Naples
World Tennis Center, 4800 Airport Rd., 33942 Ph: 813-263-1900	Naples
Naples Bath & Tennis, 4995 Airport Rd. N., 33942 Ph: 813-261-5777	Naples
Emerald Surf, 8245 Gulf Boulevard, 32561 Ph: 904-939-3450	Navarre Beach
Beach Resort, 8459 Gulf Blvd., 32561 Ph: 904-939-2324	Navarre Beach
Islander Beach Resort, 1601 S. Atlantic Ave., 32169 Ph: 904-427-3452	New Smyrna Beach
Sea Woods, 4400 S. Atlantic Avenue, 32169 Ph: 904-423-7796	New Smyrna Beach
Bluewater Bay, 2000 Bluewater Bl., P.O. Box 247, 32578 Ph: 904-897-3613	Niceville
Redington Ambassador, 16900 Gulf Blvd., 33708 Ph: 813-391-9646	North Redington Beach
Ram Sea I, Ram Sea II, 17200 Gulf Blvd., 33708 Ph: 813-397-0441	North Redington Beach
Florida Condos, 3905 Coronation Court, 32809 Ph: 407-425-2999	Orlando
Orlando Int'al Resort, 5353 Del Verde Way, 32819 Ph: 407-351-2641	Orlando
Enclave, The, 6165 Carrier Dr., 32819 Ph: 407-351-1155	Orlando
The Villas of Grand Cypress, One North Jacaranda, 32819 Ph: 407-239-4700	Orlando
Plantation Island, 187 S. Atlantic Ave., 32074 Ph: 904-677-2331	Ormond Beach

Seascape & Sunrise Condos, 2290 Ocean Shore Boulevard, 32074 — Ormond Beach
Ph: 904-441-1058
Ocean Club of Palm Beach, 155 Ocean Ave., 33404 — Palm Beach Shores
Ph: 407-842-9966
Bay Point Yacht Club, 100 Delwood Rd., Box 314, 32407 Ph: 904-234-1618 — Panama City
Continental Condos, 15413 W. Hwy. 98, 32407 Ph: 904-234-3720 — Panama City
Panama City Resort, 16709 W. Hwy 98, 32407 Ph: 904-235-2002 — Panama City
Aquavista, 17155 W. Highway 98A, 32413 Ph: 904-234-5564 — Panama City
Seachase Condos, 17351 Front Road, 32413 Ph: 904-235-1300 — Panama City
Horizon South II Condos, 17462 W. Hwy. 98, 32407 Ph: 904-234-8329 — Panama City
Landmark Holiday Resort, 17501 U.S. Highway 98 W., 32407 — Panama City
Ph: 904-235-3100
Ramsgate Harbour, 23011 W. Hwy. 98-A Alternate, 32407 Ph: 904-235-2667 — Panama City
Moonspinner Condos, 4425 Thomas Dr., 32407 Ph: 904-234-8900 — Panama City
Largo Mar, 5715 Thomas Drive, 32407 Ph: 904-234-5750 — Panama City
Nautical Watch Condos, 6205 Thomas Dr., 32407 Ph: 904-234-6876 — Panama City
Pelican Walk, 6905 Thomas Drive, 32407 Ph: 904-234-9255 — Panama City
Moondrifter, 8815 Thomas Drive, 32407 Ph: 904-234-5564 — Panama City
Top of the Gulf, 8817 S. Thomas Dr., 32407 Ph: 904-234-6561 — Panama City
Tristan Towers, 1200 Fort Pickens Rd., 32561 Ph: 904-932-9341 — Pensacola
Shipwatch Condos, 16787 Perdido Key Dr., 32507 Ph: 904-492-0111 — Perdido Key
Vista Del Mar Condos, 13-333 Johnson Beach Road, 32507 — Perdido Key, Pensacola
Ph: 904-492-0211
Canada House Beach Club, 1704 North Ocean Boulevard, 33062 — Pompano
Ph: 305-942-8200
Inter Ocean Motel, 3240 N.E. 13th Street, 33062 Ph: 305-781-9336 — Pompano
Sea Garden, 615 N. Ocean Blvd., 33062 Ph: 305-943-6200 — Pompano
Suncoast Resort Rentals, 16401 Gulf Blvd., 33708 Ph: 800-237-6586 — Redington
San Remo, 18320 Gulf Blvd., 33708 — Redington Shores
Ph: 813-398-5591
Sanibel Siesta Condos, 1246 Fulger Street, 33957 Ph: 813-472-4117 — Sanibel Island
Sundial Beach Resort, 1451 Middle Gulf Dr., 33957 Ph: 813-472-4151 — Sanibel Island
Caribe Beach Resort, 2669 W. Gulf Dr., P.O. Box 158, 33957 — Sanibel Island
Ph: 813-472-1166
Limetree Beach Resort, 1050 Ben Franklin Dr., 34236 Ph: 813-388-2111 — Sarasota
The Meadows Golf Resort, 3101 Longmeadow, 34235 Ph: 813-378-6660 — Sarasota
Sea Club V, 6744 Sara Sea Circle, 34242 Ph: 813-349-1176 — Sarasota
Las Olas Beach Club, 1215-25 Highway A1A, 32937 Ph: 407-777-3224 — Satellite Beach
Beachside Condos, Route 2, Box 4330, 32459 Ph: 904-231-4205 — Seagrove
Hidden Beach Villas, Route 2, Box 634, 32459 Ph: 904-231-4031 — Seagrove
Beachwood Villas, Route 2, Box 640, 32459 Ph: 904-231-4031 — Seagrove
Cassine Gardens, Route 2, Box 658, Highway 30-A, 32459 Ph: 904-231-4851 — Seagrove
Ridge Resort, 4101 Sun 'n Lake Blvd., 33872 Ph: 813-385-2561 — Sebring
Sun'n Lake Estates, 4101 Sun 'n Lake Blvd., 33872 Ph: 813-385-2561 — Sebring
House Of The Sun, 6518 Midnight Pass Rd., 34242 Ph: 813-349-4141 — Siesta Key,
Ocean Village Managment, 3689 Hwy A1A South, Suite 347, 32084 — St. Augustine
Ph: 904-471-9329
St. Aug. Beach Club, 4 Ocean Trace Road, 32084 Ph: 904-471-2880 — St. Augustine
Ponce de Leon Resort, 4000 US 1 North, 32085 Ph: 904-824-2821 — St. Augustine
Sea Place Condos, 4400 A1A South, 32084 Ph: 904-471-3881 — St. Augustine
Colony Reef Club, 4670 A1A South, 32084 Ph: 800-624-5965 — St. Augustine
The Coquina, 7900 A1A South, 32086 Ph: 904-471-0055 — St. Augustine
Sand Dollar Condos, 8050 South A1A Street, 32086 Ph: 904-471-1733 — St. Augustine
Summerhouse, 8550 A1A South-Anastasia Island, 32086 Ph: 904-471-1503 — St. Augustine
Anastasia Condos, 2 Dondanville Road, 32084 Ph: 904-471-2800 — St. Augustine

Camelot, 1801 Gulf Way, Pass-A-Grille Bch, 33706 Ph: 813-360-6988	St. Petersburg
Breckenridge Resort, 5700 Gulf Blvd., 33706 Ph: 813-360-1833	St. Petersburg
Innisbrook, P.O. Drawer 1088, 34688 Ph: 813-942-2000	Tarpon Springs
Sand Pebble Resort, 12300 Gulf Blvd., 33706 Ph: 813-360-1845	Treasure Island
Lands End, 7500 Bay Shore Dr., 33706	Treasure Island
The Reef Ocean Resort, 3450 Ocean Drive, 32963 Ph: 407-231-1000	Vero Beach
Sea Oaks, 8850 North AIA, 32963 Ph: 407-231-5656	Vero Beach
Palm Beach Polo Club, 13198 Forest Hill Blvd., 33414 Ph: 407-798-7000	W. Palm Beach
Windtree Villas, 12 Windtree Ln., 32787 Ph: 407-656-1577	Winter Garden

Georgia

Sky Valley Resort, Dillard, 30537 Ph: 404-746-5301	Dillard
Loreley, 1 Bruckenstrasse, P.O. Box ll6, 30545 Ph: 404-878-2236	Helen
Calloway Gardens, US Highway 27, 31822 Ph: 404-663-2281	Pine Mountain
River Watch Inn, 1 Marina Drive, 31522 Ph: 912-638-4092	St. Simons Isl.

Hawaii

Hana Kai Maui Resort, P.O. Box 38, 96713 Ph: 808-248-8426	Hana, Maui
Pu'U Po'A, P. O. Box 1185, Ka Haku Road, 96714 Ph: 808-826-9602	Hanalei, Kauai
Hanalei Colony Resort, P. O. Box 206, 96714 Ph: 808-826-6235	Hanalei, Kauai
Pali Ke Kua, P. O. Box 899, 96714 Ph: 808-826-9066	Hanalei, Kauai
Cliffs, P.O. Box 1005, 3811 Edwards Road, 96714 Ph: 808-826-6219	Hanalei, Kauai
Hale Moi Resort, P.O. Box 1185, 96714 Ph: 808-826-9602	Hanalei, Kauai
Hanalei Bay Resort, P.O. Box 220, 96714 Ph: 808-826-6522	Hanalei, Kauai
Pat's at Punaluu Condos, 53-567 Kamehameha Highway, 96717 Ph: 808-293-8111	Hauula, Oahu
Waiakea Villas, 400 Hualani Street, 96720 Ph: 808-961-2841	Hilo, Hawaii
Aston at the Waikiki Shore, 2161 Kalia Road, 96815 Ph: 808-926-4733	Honolulu
Aston Pacific Monarch, 142 Uluniu Ave., 96815 Ph: 808-923-9805	Honolulu
Aston at the Waikiki Banyan, 201 Ohua Ave., 96815 Ph: 808-922-0555	Honolulu
Maile Court, 2058 Kuhio Ave., 96815 Ph: 800-947-2828	Honolulu
Royal Kuhio, 2240 Kuhio Ave., 96815 Ph: 808-923-2502	Honolulu
Aston Waikiki Sunset, 229 Paoakalani Ave., 96815 Ph: 808-922-0511	Honolulu
Waikiki Lanais, 2452 Tusitala St., 96815 Ph: 808-923-0994	Honolulu
Aston Waikiki Beach Tower, 2470 Kalakaua Ave., 96815 Ph: 808-926-6400	Honolulu
Aston Island Colony, 445 Seaside Ave., 96815 Ph: 808-923-2345	Honolulu
Whaler, The, 2481 Kaanapali Parkway, 96761 Ph: 808-661-3417	Kaanapali, Maui
International Colony Club, 2750 Kalapu Drive, 96761 Ph: 808-661-4070	Kaanapali, Maui
Kona Coast Resort, 78-6842 Alii Drive, 96740	Kailua-Kona, HI
Kona Reef Condos, 75-5888 Alii Dr., 96740 Ph: 808-329-4780	Kailua-Kona, HI
White Sands Village, 74-6469 Alii Dr., 96740 Ph: 808-329-6402	Kailua-Kona, HI
Kona Alii, 75-5782 Kuakini Highway, 96740 Ph: 808-329-2000	Kailua-Kona, HI
Hale Kona Kai, 75-5870 Kahakai Rd., 96740 Ph: 800-421-3696	Kailua-Kona, HI
Sea Village, 75-6002 Alii Dr., 96740 Ph: 808-329-1000	Kailua-Kona, HI
Aston Royal Sea Cliff, 75-6040 Alii Dr., 96740 Ph: 808-329-8021	Kailua-Kona, HI
Kona By The Sea, 75-6106 Alii Dr., 96740 Ph: 808-327-2300	Kailua-Kona, HI
Kona Bali Kai, 76-6246 Alii Dr., 96740 Ph: 800-272-3282	Kailua-Kona, HI
Keauhou Resort Condos, 78-7039 Kamehameha III Rd., 96740 Ph: 808-322-9122	Kailua-Kona, HI
Kona Billfisher, Alii Drive, 96740 Ph: 808-329-9393	Kailua-Kona, HI

Kona White Sands, Box 594, 96745 Ph: 808-329-9393	Kailua-Kona, HI
Puako Beach Condos, 3 Puako Beach Dr., 96743 Ph: 808-882-7711	Kamuela, HI
Elima Lani, 6803883 Lua Kula St., #1704, 96743 Ph: 808-883-8288	Kamuela, HI
Aston Shores, 69-1035, 96743 Ph: 808-885-5001	Kamuela, HI
Villas/Fairway Homes, 62-100 Mauna Kea Beach Dr., 96743 Ph: 808-880-3491	Kamuela, HI
Waikoloa Villas, Box 3066 Waikoloa Village Station, 96743 Ph: 808-883-9588	Kamuela, HI
Pono Kai, 1250 Kuhio Hwy., 96746 Ph: 808-822-9831	Kapaa, Kauai
Plantation Hale, 484 Kujia Hwy., 96746 Ph: 808-822-4941	Kapaa, Kauai
Kapaa Sands, P.O. Box 3292, 380 Papaloa Road, 96746 Ph: 808-822-4901	Kapaa, Kauai
Kapalua Bay Hotel & Villas, One Bay Dr., 96761 Ph: 800-367-8000	Kapalua, Maui
Molokai Shores, Star Route, Box 1037 Kamehameha H, 96748 Ph: 808-553-5954	Kaunakakai, Molokai
Kihei Sands, 115 North Kihei Road, 96753 Ph: 808-879-2624	Kihei, Maui
Maalaea Surf Resort, 12 South Kihei Road, 96753 Ph: 808-879-1267	Kihei, Maui
Sugar Beach Resort, 145 N. Kihei Rd., 96753 Ph: 808-879-2778	Kihei, Maui
Kealia Condominium, 191 N. Kihei Rd., 96753 Ph: 808-879-0952	Kihei, Maui
Shores of Maui, 2075 S. Kihei Rd., 96753 Ph: 808-879-9140	Kihei, Maui
Kihei Alii Kai, 2387 S. Kihei Rd., P.O. Box 985, 96753 Ph: 808-879-6770	Kihei, Maui
Royal Mauian, 2430 South Kihei Rd., 96753 Ph: 808-879-1263	Kihei, Maui
Hale Pau Hana Resort, 2480 S. Kihei Rd., 96753 Ph: 808-879-2715	Kihei, Maui
Kihei Kai Nani, 2495 South Kihei Road, 96753 Ph: 808-879-9088	Kihei, Maui
Aston at the Maui Banyan, 2575 South Kihei Road, 96753 Ph: 808-875-0004	Kihei, Maui
Haleakala Shores Condos, 2619 S. Kihei Rd., 96753 Ph: 808-879-1218	Kihei, Maui
Kamaole Sands, 2695 S. Kihei Road, 96753 Ph: 808-874-8700	Kihei, Maui
Aston Maui Hill, 2881 S. Kihei Rd., 96753 Ph: 808-879-6321	Kihei, Maui
Kihei Surfside Resort, 2936 South Kihei Road, 96753 Ph: 808-879-1488	Kihei, Maui
Mana Kai-Maui, 2960 S. Kihei Rd., 96753 Ph: 808-879-1561	Kihei, Maui
Kihei Beach Resort, 36 S. Kihei Rd., 96753 Ph: 808-879-2744	Kihei, Maui
Kihei Kai, 61 N. Kihei Rd., 96753 Ph: 808-879-2357	Kihei, Maui
Nani Kai Hale, 73 N. Kihei Rd., 96753 Ph: 808-879-9120	Kihei, Maui
Luana Kai, 940 S. Kihei Rd., 96753 Ph: 808-879-1268	Kihei, Maui
Laulea Maui Beach Club, 980 S. Kihei Rd., 96753 Ph: 808-879-5247	Kihei, Maui
Leinaala Condos, 998 S. Kihei Rd., 96753 Ph: 808-879-2235	Kihei, Maui
Mauna Lani Point, HCR 2, Box 4600, Kohala Coast, 96743 Ph: 808-885-5022	Kohala, HI
Embassy Vacation Resort, 1613 Pe'e Road, 96756 Ph: 808-742-1888	Koloa, Kauai
Makanui at Poipu Kai, 96756	Koloa, Kauai
Poipu at Makahuena, 1661 Pe'e Rd., 96756 Ph: 808-742-9555	Koloa, Kauai
Nihi Kai Villas, 1870 Hoone Rd., 96756 Ph: 808-742-1412	Koloa, Kauai
Poipu Kapili, 2221 Kapili Rd., 96756 Ph: 808-742-6449	Koloa, Kauai
Kiahuna Plantation, 2253 Poipu Rd., 96756 Ph: 808-742-6411	Koloa, Kauai
Whalers Cove, 2640 Puuholo Rd., 96756 Ph: 808-742-7272	Koloa, Kauai
Kahala at Poipu Kai, 2827 Poipu Road, 96756 Ph: 808-742-7555	Koloa, Kauai
Poipu Palms Condos, Hoone Road, 96756	Koloa, Kauai
Kuhio Shores Condos, Lawai Road, 96756 Ph: 808-742-6120	Koloa, Kauai
Prince Kuhio Resort, P.O. Box 1060, 5160 Lauai Road, 96756 Ph: 808-742-1409	Koloa, Kauai
Poipu Sands at Poipu Kai, Poipu Road, 96756	Koloa, Kauai
Poipu Kai, R.R. 1 Box 173, 96756 Ph: 808-742-6464	Koloa, Kauai
Sunset Kahili Condo Apt., R.R. 1, Box 96, 1763 Pe'e Road, 96756 Ph: 808-742-1691	Koloa, Kauai
Manualoha at Poipu Kai, RR 1, 96756 Ph: 808-742-7555	Koloa, Kauai
Poipu Crater Resort, RR 1, Box 101, 96756 Ph: 808-742-7400	Koloa, Kauai
Maui Kai, 106 Kaanapali Shores Pl., 96761 Ph: 808-667-3500	Lahaina, Maui

Aston Mahana at Kaanapali, 110 Kaanapali Shores Pl., 96761 Ph: 808-661-8751	Lahaina, Maui
Lahaina Roads, 1403 Front Street, 96761 Ph: 808-661-3166	Lahaina, Maui
Kaanapali Royal, 2560 Kekaa Drive, 96761 Ph: 808-667-7200	Lahaina, Maui
Aston Maui Kaanapali, 2805 Honoapiilani Highway, 96761 Ph: 808-661-7791	Lahaina, Maui
Napili Bay, 33 Hui Drive, 96761 Ph: 808-669-6044	Lahaina, Maui
Aston Kaanapali Shores, 3445 Honoapiilani Highway, 96761 Ph: 808-667-2211	Lahaina, Maui
Papakea Beach Resort, 3543 Honoapilani Highway, 96761 Ph: 808-669-4848	Lahaina, Maui
Paki Maui Resort, 3615 Lower Honoapiilani Hwy., 96761 Ph: 808-669-8235	Lahaina, Maui
Nohonani, 3723 Lower Honoapiilani Road, 96761 Ph: 808-669-8208	Lahaina, Maui
Kulakane, 3741 Lower Honoapiilani Rd., 96761 Ph: 808-669-6119	Lahaina, Maui
Kaleialoha Resort Condos, 3785 Lower Honoapiilani Rd., 96761 Ph: 808-669-8197	Lahaina, Maui
Hono Koa Resort, 3801 Lower Honoapiilani Rd., 96761 Ph: 808-669-0979	Lahaina, Maui
Hoyochi Nikko, 3901 Lower Honoapiilani Rd., 96761 Ph: 808-669-8343	Lahaina, Maui
Kuleana Maui, 3959 Lower Honoapiilani Road, 96761 Ph: 808-669-8080	Lahaina, Maui
Polynesian Shores, 3975 Honoapiilani Rd., 96761 Ph: 808-669-6065	Lahaina, Maui
Noelani, 4095 L. Honoapiilani, 96761 Ph: 808-669-8374	Lahaina, Maui
Sands of Kahana, 4299 Honoapiilani Rd., 96761 Ph: 808-669-0400	Lahaina, Maui
Valley Isle, 4327 Lower Honoapiilani Road, 96761 Ph: 808-669-4777	Lahaina, Maui
Royal Kahana Resort, 4365 Honoapiilani Highway, 96761 Ph: 808-669-5911	Lahaina, Maui
Hololani Resort Condo, 4401 Honoapiilani Rd., 96761 Ph: 808-669-8021	Lahaina, Maui
Kahana Village, 4531 Honoapiilani Rd., 96761 Ph: 808-669-5111	Lahaina, Maui
Lahaina Shores Resort, 475 Front Street, 96761 Ph: 808-661-4835	Lahaina, Maui
Kaanapali Alii, 50 Nohea Kai Dr., 96761 Ph: 808-667-1400	Lahaina, Maui
Honokeana Cove, 5255 Lower Honoapiilani Road, 96761 Ph: 808-669-6441	Lahaina, Maui
Napili Point, 5295 Honoapiilani Rd., 96761 Ph: 808-669-9222	Lahaina, Maui
Napili Shores Resort, 5315 Honoapiilani Rd., 96761 Ph: 808-669-8061	Lahaina, Maui
Napili Village Hotel, 5425 Honoapiilani Hwy., 96761 Ph: 808-669-6228	Lahaina, Maui
Kapalua Villas, One Bay Drive, 96761 Ph: 808-669-0244	Lahaina, Maui
Maui Luxury Vacations, P. O. Box 12046, 96761 Ph: 808-661-4640	Lahaina, Maui
Puamana, P.O. Box 515, 96761 Ph: 808-667-2551	Lahaina, Maui
Banyan Harbor, 3411 Wilcox Rd., 96766 Ph: 808-245-7333	Lihue, Kauai
Aston Kauai Beach Villas, 4330 Kauai Beach Dr., 96766 Ph: 808-245-7711	Lihue, Kauai
Kauai Hilton Beach Villas, 4331 Kauai Beach Dr., 96766 Ph: 808-245-1955	Lihue, Kauai
Kaha Lani, 4460 Nehe Rd., 96766 Ph: 808-822-9331	Lihue, Kauai
Makani A Kai, R.R. 1, Box 389, 96793 Ph: 808-244-5627	Maalaea Vlg
Ke Nani Kai, P. O. Box 126, 96770 Ph: 808-552-2761	Maunaloa,
Paniolo Hale, P.O. Box 146, 96770 Ph: 808-552-2731	Maunaloa,
Napili Kai Beach Club, 5900 Honoapiilani Road, 96761 Ph: 808-669-6271	Napili Bay, Maui
Napili Sunset, 46 Hui Drive, 96761 Ph: 808-669-8083	Napili Bay, Maui
Napili Surf Resort, 50 Napili Pt., 96761 Ph: 808-669-8002	Napili Bay, Maui
Coconut Inn, P.O. Box 10517, 181 Hui Road "F," 96761 Ph: 808-669-5712	Napili Bay, Maui
Colony One, Box 70, 96777 Ph: 808-928-8301	Pahala, Hawaii
Poipu Shores Resort, R.R. 1 Box 95, 1775 Pe'e Road, 96756 Ph: 808-742-7700	Poipu, Kauai
Mauna Kai, Country Club Drive, P.O. Box 3006, 96722 Ph: 808-826-6855	Princeville, Kauai
Sandpiper Village, P.O. Box 460, 4770 Pepelani Loop, 96722 Ph: 808-826-1176	Princeville, Kauai
Wailea Ekahi, 3300 Wailea Alanui, 96753	Wailea, Maui
Wailea Elua Village, 3600 Wailea Alanui Drive, 96753 Ph: 808-878-4726	Wailea, Maui

Destination Resorts, 3750 Wailea Alanui Dr., 96753 Ph: 808-879-1595   Wailea, Maui
Island Sands Resort, RR 1, Box 391, 96793 Ph: 808-244-0848   Wailuku, Maui

Idaho

Sun Valley Lodge, 83354   Sun Valley
Warm Springs Resort, Box 228, 119 Lloyd Drive, 83353 Ph: 208-726-8274   Sun Valley
Elkhorn Resort, Box 6009, 83354 Ph: 208-622-4511   Sun Valley
Bluff Condominium, P.O. Box 186, 83353 Ph: 208-726-0110   Sun Valley
Knob Hill Ridge, Sun Valley, 83353 Ph: 208-726-4340   Sun Valley
Villager I, Sun Valley Co, 83353 Ph: 800-635-8261   Sun Valley

Illinois

Eagle Ridge Inn, Box 777, 61036 Ph: 800-323-8421   Galena

Indiana

French Lick Springs, 47432 Ph: 812-936-9981   French Lick

Kentucky

Ken-Bar Inn Resort, Highway 641, P.O. Box 66, 42044 Ph: 502-362-8652   Gilbertsville

Louisiana

The Quarter House, 129 Chartres St., 70130 Ph: 504-523-5906   New Orleans
Windsor Court Hotel, 300 Gravier St., 70140 Ph: 504-523-6000   New Orleans

Massachusetts

Country Village At Jiminy Peak, Corey Rd., 01237 Ph: 413-738-5500   Hancock
Hyannis Harborview Resort, 213 Ocean Street, 02601 Ph: 617-775-4420   Hyannis
The Breakwaters, Box 118, 432 Sea Street, 02601 Ph: 617-775-6831   Hyannis
The Yachtsman Condos, P.O. Box 939, 500 Ocean Street, 02601   Hyannis
   Ph: 617-771-5454
Monomoy Village, 8 Federal Street, 02554 Ph: 617-228-4449   Nantucket
Tristram's Landing, Madaket, 02554 Ph: 508-228-0359   Nantucket
New Seabury Cape Cod, P.O. Box B, 02649 Ph: 617-477-9111   New Seabury
Island Country Club Inn, P.O. Box 1585, 02557 Ph: 617-693-2002   Oak Bluffs
Oak 'n Spruce Resort, P.O. Box 237, Meadow Street, 01260 Ph: 413-243-3500   South Lee
Causeway Harborview, Skiff Avenue, Box 450, 02568 Ph: 508-693-1606   Vineyard
   Haven

Maryland

Will O' Wisp, Star Route 1, Box 124, 21550 Ph: 301-387-5503   Oakland

Maine

Sugarloaf Mountain Resort, Carrabassett Valley, 04947 Ph: 207-237-2000   Carrabasst Vly
Samoset Resort, Box 78, 04856 Ph: 207-594-2511   Rockport

Michigan

Grand Traverse Resort, 6300 North US-31, 49610 Ph: 616-938-2100   Acme
Shanty Creek-Schuss Mtn., 49615   Bellaire
Pointe Royale Village, Box 1988, 65616 Ph: 417-334-0079   Branson
Crystal Mountain Resort, 12500 Crystal Mountain Dr., 49683   Thompsonville
   Ph: 616-378-2911

Minnesota

Causeway On Gull, Route 6, Box 116, 56401 Ph: 218-963-3510	Brainerd
Breezy Point International, HCR2, Box 70, 56472 Ph: 218-562-7811	Breezy Point
Ruttgers Bay Lodge, Box 400, 56444 Ph: 218-678-2885	Deerwood
Breezy Point Resort, 10560 Wayzata Boulevard, 55343 Ph: 218-562-7811	Minnetonka
Grand View Lodge, 134 Nokomis, 56468 Ph: 218-963-2234	Nissova

Missouri

Bentree Lodge, Indian Point Road, Box 967, 65616 Ph: 417-338-2218	Branson
Lake Country Resort, Hwy. Y-18, Route 3, Box 91, 65656 Ph: 417-538-2291	Galena
Kimberling Inn Resort, P.O. Box 159, Highway 13, 65686 Ph: 417-739-4311	Kimberling City
Idyllwilde Reosrt, Route 3, Box 674, 65686 Ph: 417-739-4951	Kimberling
The Lodge of Four Seasons, P.O. Box 215, Lake Road HH, 65049 Ph: 314-365-3000	Lake Ozark
Notch Estates Condos, P.O. Box 2097, 65737 Ph: 417-338-2941	Lakeview
Lake Chalet Resort, Route 2, Box 3986, 65065 Ph: 314-348-4718	Osage Beach
Marriott's Tan-Tar-A, State Road K.K., 65065 Ph: 314-348-3131	Osage Beach

Mississippi

Shoreline Oaks, 30 East Beach Blv., P.O. Box 6823, 39501 Ph: 601-868-1916	Gulfport

Montana

Bay Point Estates, 300 Bay Point Dr., 59937 Ph: 406-862-2331	Whitefish

North Carolina

Island Beach Club, 2507 West Fort Macon Rd., 28512 Ph: 919-247-3600	Atlantic Beach
Whaler Inn Beach Club, 3600 Slater Path, P.O. Box 220, 28512 Ph: 919-247-4169	Atlantic Beach
Pinnacle Inn, P.O. Box 1136, 28604 Ph: 704-387-4276	Banner Elk
Four Seasons at Beech, 608 Beech Mountain Parkway, 28604 Ph: 704-387-4211	Beech Mtn.
Hound Ears Club, Box 188, 28605 Ph: 704-963-4321	Blowing Rock
Swiss Mountain Village, Flat Top Road, Rt. 2, Box 86, 28605 Ph: 704-295-3373	Blowing Rock
Village at Green Park, Goforth Road, 28605 Ph: 704-295-9861	Blowing Rock
Chetola Resort, North Main Street, P.O. Box 205, 28605 Ph: 704-295-9301	Blowing Rock
Alpine Village, 200 Overlook Dr., 28714 Ph: 704-675-4103	Burnsville
Atlantic Towers, 1615 South Lake Park Blvd., 28428 Ph: 919-458-8313	Carolina Beach
Spinnaker Point, 400 Virginia Ave., P.O. Box 1888, 28428 Ph: 919-458-4554	Carolina Beach
Paradise Tower Resort, 901 S. Lake Park Blvd., Hwy 421, 28428 Ph: 919-458-7946	Carolina Beach
Caswell Dunes, 44 Pinehurst Drive, 28465	Caswell Beach
Southern Shore Villas, S.E. 58th Street, 28465	Caswell Beach
Barrier Island Station, State Route 1200, 27949 Ph: 919-261-3525	Duck
Belvedere Plantation, P.O. Box 400, Coastal Hwy. 17 N., 28443 Ph: 919-270-2761	Hampstead
Hatteras Cabanas, P.O. Box 387, 27943 Ph: 919-986-2241	Hatteras
Water's Edge, 427 Ocean Boulevard, West, 28462	Holden Beach
Ocean Palms, 769 Ocean Blvd. West, 28462 Ph: 919-842-7443	Holden Beach

Sun Realty of Nags Head, P.O. Box 1630, 27948 Ph: 919-441-7033	Kill Devil Hills
Heron Cove, 4517 Croatan Highway, 27949 Ph: 919-441-8070	Kitty Hawk
Sea Scape Beach Villas, P.O. Box 276, 27949 Ph: 919-261-3881	Kitty Hawk
Ocean Dunes Condos, P.O. Box 387, 27949 Ph: 919-986-2241	Kitty Hawk
Sand Castles, #1 Causeway, 28469 Ph: 910-579-3535	Ocean Isle
The Winds Golf Resort, 310 E. First Street, 28459 Ph: 919-579-6275	Ocean Isle
Foxfire Resort, P.O. Box 711, 28374 Ph: 919-295-5555	Pinehurst
Fairfield Sapphire Valley, 4000 Hwy. 64 W., 28774 Ph: 704-743-3341	Sapphire
Bald Head Island Mgmt., P.O. Drawer 10999, 704 E. Moore, 28461 Ph: 919-457-5000	Southport
Oyster Bay Plantation, 900 Shoreline, 28459 Ph: 919-579-7181	Sunset Beach
Surf, Highway 210, 28445 Ph: 919-328-2511	Surf City
Topsail Dunes, P.O. Box 2675, 28445 Ph: 919-328-0639	Surf City
Oak Island Beach Villas, 1000 Caswell Beach Road, 28465	Yaupon Beach

New Hampshire

Attitash Mountain Village, Route 302, 03812 Ph: 603-374-6501	Bartlett
Townhomes at Bretton Woods, Route 302, 03575 Ph: 603-258-1000	Bretton Woods
Nordic Village Resort, 03846 Ph: 800-472-5207	Jackson
Village of Loon Mountain, P.O. Box 508, 03251 Ph: 603-745-3401	Lincoln
Cold Spring Resort, RR 3, Box 40, 03264 Ph: 603-536-4600	Plymouth
Black Bear Lodge, Box 357, 03223 Ph: 603-236-8371	Waterville Vly
Windsor Hill Condos, Route 49, 03215 Ph: 603-236-8321	Waterville Vly
Inns of Waterville Valley, Snowbrook Road, P.O. Box 411, 03215 Ph: 603-236-8366	Waterville Valley
Cedar Lodge at Brickyard Mt., Route 3, P.O. Box 5293, 03246 Ph: 603-366-4316	Weirs Beach

New Jersey

Park Lane, 177 S. Illinois Ave., 08401 Ph: 609-344-8277	Atlantic City

New Mexico

The Springs Condos, 1230 Mechem, 88345 Ph: 505-258-5056	Ruidoso
West Winds Lodge & Condos, 208 Eagle Drive, P.O. Box 1458, 88345 Ph: 505-257-4031	Ruidoso
Quail Ridge Inn, P.O. Box 707, 87571 Ph: 505-776-2211	Taos
Sierra Del Sol, P.O. Box 84, 87525 Ph: 505-776-2981	Taos Ski Valley

Nevada

Lakeside Ski Resort, P.O. Box 5576, 987 Tahoe Blvd., 89450 Ph: 702-831-5258	Incline Village
Vacation Station, P.O. Box 7180, 89452 Ph: 702-831-3664	Incline Village
Ridge Tahoe, P.O. Box 5790, 89449 Ph: 702-588-3553	Stateline
Pine Wild, 600 Highway 50, P.O. Box 11347, 89448 Ph: 702-588-2790	Zephyr Cove

New York

Juniper Hill Villas, Route 9N, P.O. Box 449, 12814 Ph: 518-668-3286	Bolton Landing
Brookhill Residences, P.O. Box 231, Whiteface Inn Road, 12946 Ph: 518-523-2551	Lake Placid
Deer Run Resort, Route 10, P.O. Box 251, 12167 Ph: 607-652-2001	Stamford

Oregon

Beachcombers Haven Vacation, 7045 N.W. Glen, 97388 Ph: 503-764-2252 — Gleneden Beach
Ocean Terrace Condos, 4229 S.W. Beach Avenue, 97367 Ph: 503-996-3623 — Lincoln City
Sunriver Resort, P.O. Box 3609, 97707 Ph: 503-593-1221 — Sunriver

Pennsylvania

Alpine Village, 18320 — Analomink
Seven Springs Resort, R.D. #1, 15622 Ph: 814-352-7777 — Champion

Rhode Island

The Wellington Yacht Club, 543 Thames at Wellington, 02840 — Newport
Ph: 401-849-1770

South Carolina

Wild Dunes, P.O. Box 1410, 29402 Ph: 803-886-6000 — Charleston
Seabrook Conference Resort, P.O. Box 32099, 29417 Ph: 800-922-2401 — Charleston
Spinnaker & Southwind, 25 Bow Circle, P.O.Box 6899, 29938 — Hilton Head Island
Ph: 803-785-4881
Sea Pines Resort, Box 7000, 29938 Ph: 803-758-3333 — Hilton Head
Sea Pines Villas, P.O. Box 6959, 29938 Ph: 803-785-2040 — Hilton Head
Jade Tree Cove, 200 75th Avenue, 29577 Ph: 803-449-9455 — Mrytle Beach
Sands Ocean Club, 500 Shore Dr., 29577 Ph: 803-449-6461 — Myrtle Beach
Beach Colony Resort, 5308 North Ocean Boulevard, 29577 Ph: 803-449-4010 — Myrtle Beach
Ramada Ocean Forest Resort, 5523 North Ocean Blvd., 29578 — Myrtle Beach
Ph: 803-497-0044
Ocean Forest Villa Resort, 5601 North Ocean Blvd., 29577 Ph: 803-449-9661 — Myrtle Beach
Schooner Beach Club, 7100 N. Ocean Blvd., 29577 Ph: 803-449-6431 — Myrtle Beach
Sands Beach Club, 9400 Shore Drive, 29572 Ph: 803-449-1531 — Myrtle Beach
Water's Edge Resort, P.O. Box 8159, 29578 Ph: 803-651-0002 — Myrtle Beach
Condotels of America, 2703 Highway 17 South, 29582 Ph: 803-272-8400 — Myrtle Beach
Plantation Resort, 1250 U.S. Highway 17 North, 29577 Ph: 803-238-3556 — Surfside Beach
Myrtle Beach Resort, P.O. Box 14428, 5905 Frontage Rd., 29587 — Surfside Beach
Ph: 803-828-8000

Tennessee

Condo Villas of Gatlinburg, 201 Parkway, 37738 Ph: 615-436-4121 — Gatlinburg
Oak Square, 990 River Road, 37738 Ph: 615-436-7582 — Gatlinburg
Cobbly Nob, Route 3, Box 619, 37738 Ph: 615-436-5298 — Gatlinburg
Deer Ridge Mountain Resort, Route 3, Box 849, 37738 Ph: 615-436-2325 — Gatlinburg
Greenbrier Valley Resorts, US 321, Rt. 3, Box 920, 37738 Ph: 615-436-2015 — Gatlinburg
High Alpine Resort, Upper Alpine Way, Rt. 2 Box 786, 37738 — Gatlinburg
Ph: 615-436-6643
Riveredge Village Condos, 37882 Ph: 615-448-6036 — Townsend

Texas

Texas Timeshare, 18-B Schooner Cove, 78734 Ph: 512-261-6663 — Austin
Fort Brown Condo Shares, 1900 E. Elizabeth, 78520 Ph: 512-546-1574 — Brownsville
Rancho Viejo Resort, P.O. Box 3918, Hwy. 77 North 83, 78520 — Brownsville
Ph: 512-350-4000
The Gulfstream, 14810 Windward Drive, 78418 Ph: 512-949-8061 — Corpus Christi

Inverness At San Luis Pass, Route #2, Box 1270, 77541 Ph: 409-239-1433	Freeport
The Victorian Condotel, 6300 Seawall Blvd., 77551 Ph: 409-740-3555	Galveston
Horseshoe Bay Resort, Box 7766, 78654 Ph: 512-598-8561	Horseshoe Bay
Lago Vista Rentals, on Lake Travis, 78645 Ph: 512-267-0700	Lago Vista
Inverness Condominium, 13151 Walden Road, 77356 Ph: 409-582-4477	Montgomery
Walden on Lake Conroe, 14001 Walden Rd., 77356 Ph: 409-582-6441	Montgomery
Dunes Condominium, 1000 Lantana Box 1238, 78373 Ph: 512-749-5155	Port Aransas
Cline's Landing Condos, 1000 N. Station St., Box 1628, 78373 Ph: 512-749-5275	Port Aransas
The Pelican, 1107 S. 11th St. Box 1690, 78373 Ph: 512-749-6226	Port Aransas
Beachhead Resort, 1319 S. 11th St., Box 1577, 78373 Ph: 512-749-6261	Port Aransas
Sea Horse Inn, 1423 S. 11th St. Box 426, 78373 Ph: 512-749-5221	Port Aransas
Nixon Courts, 211 E. Ave. F Box 72, 78373 Ph: 512-749-5527	Port Aransas
Sunrise Courts, 302 E. Ave C Box 396, 78373 Ph: 512-749-5366	Port Aransas
Double Barr Cottages, 413 Ave. G Box 266, 78373 Ph: 512-749-5582	Port Aransas
Channelview Condos, 423 Channelview, Box 776, 78373 Ph: 512-749-6156	Port Aransas
Island Retreat Condos, 700 Island Retreat Court, Box 637, 78373 Ph: 512-749-6222	Port Aransas
Aransas Princess, 720 Beach Access Rd 1-A, 78373 Ph: 512-749-5118	Port Aransas
Mustang Island Beach Club, Park Rd. 53, 78373 Ph: 512-749-5446	Port Aransas
Sea Gull Condominium, Park Rd. 53 Box 1207, 78373 Ph: 512-749-4191	Port Aransas
Mayan Princess Condos, Park Rd. 53 Box 156, 78373 Ph: 512-749-5183	Port Aransas
Port Royal Ocean Resort, Park Rd. 53 Box 336, 78373 Ph: 512-749-5011	Port Aransas
Mustang Towers, Park Rd. 53 Box 1870, 78373 Ph: 512-749-6212	Port Aransas
Tanglewood on Texoma, Highway 120, 75076	Pottsboro
South Padre Hilton Resort, 500 Padre Blvd., P.O.Box 2081, 78597 Ph: 512-761-6511	South Padre Island

Utah

Accommodation Station, P.O. Box 44, 84719 Ph: 801-677-3333	Brian Head
The Innsbruck, 1201 Norfolk, P.O. Box 222, 84060 Ph: 801-649-9829	Park City
Silvertown Condos, 1505 Park Avenue, P.O. Box 1090, 84060 Ph: 801-649-9022	Park City
Prospector Square Hotel, 2200 Sidewinder Dr., Box 1698, 84060 Ph: 801-649-7100	Park City
Shadow Ridge Resort Hotel, 50 Shadow Ridge Street, Box 1820, 84060 Ph: 801-649-4300	Park City
Powderwood Resort, 6975 N. 2200 W., 84060 Ph: 801-649-2032	Park City
The Stein Eriksen Lodge, 7400 Lake Flat Road, Box 3779, 84060 Ph: 801-649-3700	Park City
Park Station Condos, P. O. Box 1360, 84060 Ph: 801-649-7717	Park City
Resort Center Lodging, P. O. Box 3449, 84060 Ph: 801-649-0800	Park City
Intermountain Lodging, P. O. Box 3803, 84060 Ph: 801-649-2687	Park City
Edelweiss Haus, P. O. Box 495, 1482 Empire Ave., 84060 Ph: 801-649-9342	Park City
Snowflower Condos, P. O. Box 957, 400 Silver King Dr, 84060 Ph: 801-649-6400	Park City
Silver King Hotel, P.O. Box 2818, 84060 Ph: 801-649-5500	Park City
Budget Lodging, P.O. Box 3813, 1940 Prospector Av, 84060 Ph: 801-649-2526	Park City
Coalition Lodge, P.O. Box 75, 1300 Park Avenue, 84060 Ph: 801-649-8591	Park City
Ridgepoint, P.O.Box 680128, 84068 Ph: 801-649-9598	Park City
Blue Church Lodge, P.O.Box 1720, 84060 Ph: 801-649-8009	Park City
Blooming Enterprises, P.O.Box 2340; 1647 Shortline Rd., 84060 Ph: 801-649-6583	Park City
Stag Lodge, P.O.Box 3000, 8200 Royal St. East, 84060 Ph: 801-649-7444	Park City
Acclaimed Lodging, P.O.Box 3629, 84060 Ph: 801-649-3736	Park City

Courchevel, P.O.Box 680128, 84068 Ph: 801-649-9598	Park City
Resort Village Plaza, P.O.Box 680128, 84068 Ph: 801-649-9598	Park City
Park Meadows Racquet Club, P.O.Box 680128, 84068 Ph: 801-649-9598	Park City
The Lodge At Snowbird, Snowbird Resort, Entry 3, 84092 Ph: 801-521-6040	Snowbird

Vermont

Trailside Condos, Bolton Valley, 05477 Ph: 802-434-2769	Bolton
Bolton Valley Resort, Box 300, 05477 Ph: 802-434-2131	Bolton
Eagle's Nest Inn, Lake Shore Road, P.O. Box 308, 05045 Ph: 802-333-4302	Fairlee
Killington Townhouses, R.R. 1, Box 10-A, 05751 Ph: 802-773-4488	Killington
Bromley Village Condos, Box 1130, 05255 Ph: 802-824-5458	Manchester Center
Hawk Inn Resort, Route 100, Box 64, NCR, 05056 Ph: 802-685-HAWK	Plymouth
Quechee Lakes Rentals, Box 385, Westenfeld Farm, Route 4, 05059 Ph: 802-295-1970	Quechee
The Village Smugglers Notch, Route 108, 05464 Ph: 802-644-8851	Smugglers Nch
Mountainside Resort, 930 Cottage Club Rd., Box A-9, 05672 Ph: 802-253-8610	Stowe
Stoweflake Resort, Box 369, 05672 Ph: 802-253-7355	Stowe
The Village Green, Cape Cod Rd., RR #1, Box 2975, 05672 Ph: 802-253-9705	Stowe
Mount Mansfield Townhouses, Mountain Road, 05672 Ph: 802-253-7311	Stowe
Topnotch At Stowe, P.O. Box 1260, 05672 Ph: 802-253-8585	Stowe
Golden Eagle Resort, P.O.Box 1090, Mountain Road, 05672 Ph: 802-253-4811	Stowe
Stratton Mountain Resort, Stratton Mountain, 05155 Ph: 802-197-2200	Stratton Mtn
Eagles at Sugarbush, Route 100, P.O.Box 180, 05673 Ph: 802-496-5700	Waitsfield
Sugarbush Inn, Sugarbush Access Road, 05674 Ph: 802-583-2301	Warren

Virginia

Sky Chalet, 22810 Ph: 703-856-2147	Bayse
Kingsmill Resort, 1010 Kingsmill Rd., 23185 Ph: 804-253-1703	Williamsbur
Wintergreen Resort, P.O. Box 706, 22958 Ph: 804-325-2200	Wintergreen

Virgin Islands

Secret Harbour, 6280 Estate Nazareth, 00802 Ph: 809-775-6550	Charlotte Amalie
Gentle Winds, Rivar at Gentle Winds, 1112 King, 00820 Ph: 809-778-3400	Christianste
Sugar Beach Condos, 3221 Estate Golden Rock, 00820 Ph: 809-773-5345	St. Croix
Gallows Point Resort, P.O. Box 58, 00831 Ph: 809-776-6434	St. John
McLaughlin-Anderson Villas, 100 Blackbeard's Hill, Suite 3, 00802 Ph: 809-776-0635	St. Thomas
Pineapple Villas, Box 11783, 00801 Ph: 809-775-0275	St. Thomas
Ocean Property Management, Box 8529, 00801 Ph: 809-775-2600	St. Thomas

Washington

The Resort at Port Ludlow, 60M #3 Paradise Bay Road, 98365 Ph: 206-437-2222	Port Ludlov
Alderbrook Inn Resort, E. 7101 Highway 106, 98592 Ph: 206-898-2200	Union

Wisconsin

Chanticleer Inn, 1458 East Dollar Lake Rd., 54521 Ph: 715-479-4486	Eagle Rive
Safer's Gypsy Villa, 950 Circle Dr., 54521 Ph: 715-479-8644	Eagle Rive

Heidel House, 820 Illinois Ave., P.O. Box 9, 54941 Ph: 414-294-3344 — Green Lake

Villas At Christmas Mountain, S-944 Christmas Mountain Drive, 53965 — Wisconsin
Ph: 608-253-1000 — Dells

West Virginia

Land of Canaan Resort, Route I, Box 291, 26260 Ph: 304-866-4425 — Canaan Valley

Herzwoods Condominums, P.O. Box 625, 26260 Ph: 304-866-4801 — Davis

Lakeview Resort Club, Route 6, Box 88-A, 26505 Ph: 304-594-IIII — Morgantown

The Greenbrier, White Sulphur Springs, 24986 — White Sulphur Springs

Wyoming

Jackson Hole Racquet Club, Star Rt. Box 3647, 83001 Ph: 307-733-3990 — Jackson

Teton Shadows, P.O. Box 2297, 83001 — Jackson Hole

• • • • • • • • • • • • • • • • • • • •

ALL-INCLUSIVE RESORTS—
The Hassle-Free Option

Merely a gleam in a Frenchman's eye twenty years ago, all-inclusive resorts, as pioneered by Club Med, have become a popular family travel option. A recent survey reveals that 52% of American travellers are interested in all-inclusive offers. Why? It's the cruise-ship concept on land, allowing the traveller to relax and not worry about the details. The security of knowing that one price covers everything, with none of those nasty surprises that can blast a hole in any family's travel budget. All meals, entertainment, activities and sports, as well as airfare and accommodations, are generally included in one price.

Unlimited Fun for a Limited Price

One benefit of the all-inclusive resort is that the single up-front price covers unlimited activities. You and the kids don't have to limit your adventures due to budget restrictions, a fact that automatically reduces vacation stress and whining! Bobby doesn't have to choose between a windsurfing lesson or a jet ski rental, and Marie can go horseback riding and scuba diving. Mom and Dad are free to do nothing but lounge by the pool, if that's your preference! At an all-inclusive resort, everybody can do it all. For most families, one week is about the perfect length of stay.

What to Know Before You Go

On the down side of all-inclusives, some folks get a bit weary of dining in the same restaurant night after night, though most resorts are imaginative with theme nights and special meals to vary the fare. When packing for an all-inclusive stay, it pays to know what theme nights are planned so you can pack your jeans for Western Night! Since rooms may be smaller than standard hotel rooms, you'll want to pack on the light side. And remember that you don't need to haul a lot of gear—it's all provided.

We asked around and the following resorts came up as being many families' favorites. Consider this a subjective list and go from there. For a more objective view contact Le Beach Club, a members organization that produces a newsletter and members' polls about all-inclusive resorts. They also have a vast amount of experience in the all-inclusive area and are up to date on the best prices.

Call (800) 872-8404 or (303) 442-0984, or write Le Beach Club at P.O. Box 9003, Boulder, Colorado 80301.

You may call Club Med direct at 800-CLUB-MED.

Another company which does a great deal of business with all-inclusives is Rascals in Paradise at (415) 978-9800 or (800) U-RAS-CAL.

*FRANKLIN D. RESORT
Jamaica

WINDJAMMER
(mostly inclusive)
St. Lucia

*BOSCOBEL BEACH CLUB
Jamaica

ALMOND BEACH
Barbados

THE DIAMOND RESORT
Cozamel

ST. JAMES CLUB
Antigua

BUSHIRI BEACH CLUB
Aruba

ASPEN CANYON RANCH
Colorado

CLUB MEDS
Sand Piper, Florida
St. Lucia
Eluthera, Bahamas
Puntacana, Dominican Republic
Ixtaba, Mexico

*Franklin D. Resort consistently gets top rating. Boscobel was mentioned several times as a best buy.

• •

HOME EXCHANGE INFORMATION

DISCOVER HOME EXCHANGE
—A Great Way For Family Travel

A lot of families have discovered that trading homes (yes, trading homes!) is a terrific way to travel with children and save money. The idea is that two home owners who want to visit the each other's destination swap their homes for a vacation. The result is both families having a comfortable place to stay with all the amenities of home—a kitchen, washing machine, television, books, games, toys for children, and most important, space for active kids.

Saving money is a big plus with home exchanges. A whopping amount can be saved by preparing meals less expensively (and more healthily) in a real size kitchen at the exchange home. Your family can save eating out for special occasions instead of a necessity. If a car-exchange is also involved, you save the additional car-rental costs. A strong appeal is that there's no hotel tab to pay at vacation's end. With a home exchange, whether your family vacation is for two weeks or two months, the cost is the same, because you are helping another family save on their vacation too.

Some home exchangers seek out trades with families with children because those homes usually have toys, books, and games to keep kids occupied. And if you're traveling with small children, consider the added convenience of not having to pack cribs, strollers, playpens and car seats. If your family has a pet, swapping with another member who also owns a pet will save you both kennel fees, and your pet will be a lot happier too. Some families prefer home exchanges when visiting friends of relatives abroad or in the USA to make it easier on the relatives.

Currently, home exchanges are offered widely in the United States, Canada and Europe, although there are a few home exchanges in parts of South America, Israel, and Mexico. Imagine: Potential destination homes could be a Vermont house covered in fall leaves, a comfortable cabin next to Colorado's ski slopes, an apartment flat in London, or as exotic as a villa on the Cote d'Azur. Also many parents appreciate family vacations that don't revolve around over-commercialized tourist enclaves.

In response to the growing number of home exchangers, Home Exchange Clubs have sprung up to help interested home swappers find their perfect destination home. Some clubs have over a thousand members worldwide. For a membership fee typically ranging from $30–$75, these clubs will publish your home description in a catalog of available home exchanges.

Afterwards, most of the planning of arranging the swap is up to you. Upon receiving the catalog, you can select listings that fit your travel plans and then contact the listed members. In turn, other members will see your listing and contact you. Once two home owners decide to exchange homes, they confer with each other until a suitable arrangement is agreed upon. Since this agreement can take time (contacting one another, international mail, etc.), be sure to plan well ahead of your intended travel date.

The first step is usually a letter or phone call of introduction describing your home. As mutual interest between two exchangers develops, photos are exchanged, travel plans are coordinated, and personal references are exchanged. Family travelers should especially inquire about child restrictions and whether the house is safe for the ages of their children. The next important step is to establish ground rules in a pre-traded agreement. For example, arrangements for keys, smoking restrictions, utility usage, phone calls, and, if a car exchange is involved, car usage and policy.

The number one question potential home exchangers have is "Will my home be safe?" There is no absolute assurance, but the answer is a very high percentage "YES." HomeLink USA, a home exchange club, states that in their thirty years of exchanging they have had very few instances of damage and no reports of theft, and that most problems are at the level of "housekeeping standards" at the home being visited. Most of the people into home exchanges are professionals, business executives and retirees. In general, they are in the upper income bracket and well educated. Many will have a trusted neighbor check in to make sure everything is fine. This person also provides your guests with a welcome local contact. As guests in each other's homes, both partners in an exchange enjoy that special bond of mutual respect and trust which the situation generates. Usually, home exchange companies monitor their members to safeguard the high reputation of home exchanging.

If you are concerned about insurance during the home exchange, you should discuss this with your agent. In general, most homeowner's insurance would cover damages to your home. Most auto insurance policies cover incidental drivers. Next, check with your insurance agent for any special requirements for car exchange.

Before the actual home exchange, it is a good idea to stow away personal items (financial, valuable, fragile, etc.) in a closet or room out of the way to the guest party. This is highly recommended and offers peace of mind to both parties. Then make a few "how-to-operate" notes on such things as the kitchen appliances, arrange an exchange of keys, leave a list of important telephone numbers, and consider leaving some recommendations for restaurants, shopping and sightseeing.

After setting your house up for the home exchange, it is just a matter of waiting for the big day, looking forward to a real home-away-from-home vacation, feeling like a "resident" instead of a tourist, and planning how to spend the money you've saved on your family trip.

There are some other types of home exchanges besides the direct exchange described above that might interest families as well. 1) Exchange Hospitality. This is for people with homes large enough to entertain guests. 2) Exchange or Rental. This means you would also be willing to rent your home, for a modest fee, to another member. The second type makes three-way exchanges possible.

In home exchanges, much trust is involved with families in the spirit of travel. Many people trade homes and learn the kindness of strangers who are eager to share their environment and culture they call "home". If you find yourself focusing primarily on the aspects of a home trade which could go wrong, you probably would not be comfortable with this type of arrangement. On the other hand, if you find yourself approaching the prospect of home exchange with a positive outlook and the spirit of adventure you may just swap yourself into the vacation of a lifetime!

SAMPLE LETTER

[To Send to Prospective Home Exchangers—Your First Letter]

After you've found several interesting home exchange listings, send them a letter or e-mail to show them your interest and initiate the whole home exchange process.

In your letter to potential home exchangers, be sure to:

1. Indicate general dates of exchange,
2. Describe your home fully,
3. Mention extra family amenities,
4. Describe surrounding attractions,
5. Describe your family and other members who will be vacationing with you.

Here is a sample introductory letter to send to prospective home exchangers:

"Dear _____

   We are planning a four week vacation in your area this summer and would be very interested in exchanging homes with your family. We are hoping that you will consider vacationing in San Francisco this summer. From what we read (name of home exchange directory), your home sounds perfect for our needs, and we believe that our home would suit your needs should you decide to come and explore San Francisco and the surrounding area.

   We are located right in San Francisco, one of the most beautiful cities in the world. Our home is in a stylish residential area of San Francisco called Pacific Heights, away from the bustle. Yet it is only a short distance (taxi ride or car ride) to all the sights of this great city—Golden Gate Park, Ghiradelli Square, Fisherman's Wharf, Chinatown, Alcatraz Island (by ferry), Embarcadero Center, Union Square, and Golden Gate Bridge.

   Our home is Victorian in style, with hardwood floors and carved mouldings throughout. Located in a cul-de-sac, it is surrounded by other Victorian homes. A flight of stairs from the street brings you to our three bedroom, two bathroom home. The master bedroom has a king-size bed, color television/VCR, and working marble fireplace. The other two bedrooms have twin beds and children's toys and books (suited for 9-11 yrs old). Each bathroom has a toilet, sink, and combination bath/shower. Our home also has a living room with large bay windows, a large kitchen with all modern appliances (dishwasher, sink with garbage disposal, clothes washer, dryer, gas stove, microwave, refrigerator, and freezer), a dining area attached to the kitchen, and a small grass-covered backyard that can be reached through the back staircase.

We would also be willing to exchange our car, a reliable 4-door Volvo station wagon. Our home has a garage, so parking would not be a problem.

By automobile, you can visit the nearby sights of San Francisco, or drive out over the Golden Gate Bridge to visit Marin County, relax on beautiful beaches, explore the Northern California coast, and hike through redwood forests. The East Bay also offers Berkeley sights and Oakland attractions.

My husband is an economics professor at the University of California at San Francisco, and I am a software consultant for a Marin County firm. We have one son, age 11, and one daughter, age 9. In addition, my sister, an illustrator, will be vacationing with us, for a total of three adults and two children. Over the last three years, we have exchanged homes happily and successfully with families in Boston, Massachusetts and London, England.

We have included several photocopied pictures of our family and home, and a map showing exactly where we are located. We would like to make definite exchange arrangements by May, if possible. Please write, e-mail, or call us at (415) 111-1111 in the evening.

We hope to hear from you soon. Thank you for considering us for your summer home exchange."

❦

AFTER BOTH HOMEOWNERS HAVE DECIDED TO SWAP HOMES

[The Pre-Trade Agreement Sample Letter]

After discussing the home exchange with many potential exchangers, you will eventually decide on a home exchange that is right for you! At this point, you will want to write up a pre- traded agreement, or ground rules, that both parties agree to. Here is a sample pre-traded letter and checklist with what to include in that letter.

Dear _____

   After so many letters and phone calls, I feel like we really know each other. My family and I are very much looking forward to the home exchange and vacation. We're going to do our best to make sure you have a great stay here.

   Everything seems to be coming together. I'm sure there will be a few more details to work out, and I see no problems in resolving anything that comes up.

   Meanwhile, I'd like to take this opportunity to summarize what we have agreed regarding the exchange:

[In this section, write down what you and your exchange partner have agreed to. Consider the following items]

- ❍ Exact dates that the exchange will take place.
- ❍ Total number of adults and children staying, including guests and expected visitors.
- ❍ Use of car and its maintenance.
- ❍ Arrangement of keys. Most people leave keys with friends or neighbors who can also welcome your exchange guests. Two sets are recommended.
- ❍ Phone usage. Most exchangers only pay for long distance calls or agree to use their calling card. Usually a note recording the calls made and a check or cash left at time of departure is the simplest method.
- ❍ Utility bill. Unless there is extreme cold weather or tropical climate, each home owner is responsible for the utility bill for their home.

❍ Smoking policy. Where is smoking allowed in the house, if at all?
❍ Care of pets. Your pets and theirs. Are pets allowed, and if so, where?
❍ Household repairs. Usually if repairs are necessary above an agreed cost, say $50, a telephone call to the home owner is necessary to insure payment by owners, otherwise cost is taken care of by exchange guests.
❍ Cancellation policy and back-up plan.

As with any agreement, allow for comments back and forth until both parties are comfortable with the requirements. This also develops greater trust on both sides.

BEFORE THE EXCHANGE

Preparing Your Home

This is a checklist of what to do before your exchange guests arrive.

_____ Prepare your home for your exchangers as you would for any other special guests. Clean it well and make it ready for their arrival.

_____ Leave a welcome letter for your exchange guests. With it, you can also provide additional notes for the information described below.

_____ Clear out adequate closet and storage space for your guests. Also, provide the necessary linens.

_____ Empty refrigerator. A small amount of food staples will help your guests get off to a comfortable start. A special welcome treat, like cookies or flowers, adds a nice touch.

_____ Leave "how-to" notes in the appropriate places for operating appliances and where to find house essentials, like fuse box, flashlights, batteries for the smoke detector, fire extinguishers, tool box, etc.

_____ Leave a list of important phone numbers next to the telephone. These include police, fire, and ambulance, as well as telephone numbers of friends who can be reached in an emergency or for friendly advice.

_____ Recommendations for shopping, eating or sightseeing will be greatly appreciated. Maps are very helpful as well.

_____ Leave note specifying any equipment not to be used (e.g., computer) or parts of the home that are off-limits.

_____ If applicable, leave instructions for pet or plant care.

_____ Stow away or remove from the house valuable, fragile, or personal items. This will provide peace of mind for both parties.

_____ If a car exchange is involved, make sure gas and maps are in the car.

_____ Leave keys in the agreed place or with designated friends.

AFTER THE HOME EXCHANGE

Leaving Your Host's House

In the spirit of mutual trust in home exchange, it is very important to treat the host's home as if it were your own and take extra efforts to ensure the house is left in as good, or better condition, than when you arrived. Here is a reminder checklist of things to do before you leave your exchange home:

_____ The house and linens should be clean and put in the same place and condition as when you arrived.

_____ Replace household items used up and food staples eaten.

_____ Appliances, heaters, pool equipment, etc., should be turned on or off as specified by host.

_____ If appropriate, settlement should be left for any reimbursements (e.g., long distance phone calls).

_____ A note should be left describing any problems, visitors, calls, or incidents of interest to your hosts.

_____ Keys should be left in the pre-agreed place.

_____ A 'thank you' note and small gift goes a long way in fostering the spirit of exchange and is always appreciated. (It's a small token for all the money you've saved from the exchange!)

• •

HOSTELS AT HOME & ABROAD

YOUTH HOSTELS ARE FOR FAMILIES, TOO

Youth hostels are a low-budget and unique accommodations alternative for traveling families. In addition to low-cost dormitory beds, many hostels also offer private rooms for families and couples. Your family may stay in a private room above a general store in Montana's Glacier Park for $30, or in a cabin on an old dude ranch in Colorado's Estes Park for $25. Or stay at one of several lighthouse hostels on the California coast. For a budget stay in the Big Apple, a private family room goes for $66 in New York City.

Additionally, most hostels have a community kitchen so you can save more money by preparing your own meals, and many also offer laundries and other facilities. Hostels are friendly people-oriented places, with a real international flavor where travelers from around the world gather in the common room to swap travel tales and information.

The list below contains more than 100 Hostelling International hostels across the US that offer family/private rooms with advance reservations. Because these accommodations are usually very limited, call well before your trip to get a room. The prices listed are rates for individual, usually in bunk-style rooms. Check with the hostel manager for family room rates. For more detail on these hostels, Hostelling North America, the official guide to hostels in Canada and the U.S., is free with a $35 Hostelling International membership, or when you stay at a hostel at the slightly higher, non-member price. To join, call the Hostelling International Membership Services Department at (800) 444-6111.

ALASKA

Anchorage
700 H Street
Anchorage, Alaska 99501
Phone: (907) 276-3635
Beds: 95; Overnight Rate: $15.00

Delta
P.O. Box 971
Delta Junction, Alaska 99737
Phone: (907) 895-5074
Beds: 10; Overnight Rate: $7.00

Snow River
700 H Street
c/o Alaska Council
Anchorage, Alaska 99501
Phone: (907) 276-3635
Beds: 10; Overnight Rate: $12.00

Tok
P.O. Box 532
Tok, Alaska 99780
Phone: (907) 883-3745
Beds: 10; Overnight Rate: $7.50

A R I Z O N A

Flagstaff
23 North Leroux
Flagstaff, Arizona 86001

Phone: (602) 774-2731
Beds: 52; Overnight Rate: $12.00

C A L I F O R N I A

Hilton Creek
Rural Route 1, Box 1128
Crowley Lake, California 93546
Phone: (619) 935-4989
Beds: 22; Overnight Rate: $11.00–
  13.00

Redwood National Park
14480 California Highway 101
Klamath, California 95548
Phone: (707) 482-8265
Beds: 30; Overnight Rate: $9.00–
  11.00

Hidden Villa
26870 Moody Road
Los Altos Hills, California 94022
Phone: (650) 949-8648
Beds: 33; Overnight Rate: $9.50

Los Angeles South Bay
P.O. Box 5345
San Pedro, California 90731
Phone: (310) 831-8109
Beds: 60; Overnight Rate: $11.50

Point Montara Lighthouse
P.O. Box 737
Montara, California 94037
Phone: (415) 728-7177
Beds: 45; Overnight Rate: $9.00–
  11.00

Pigeon Point Lighthouse
Pigeon Point Road, Highway 1
Pescadero, California 94060
Phone: (415) 879-0633
Beds: 52; Overnight Rate: $9.00–
  11.00

Point Reyes
P.O. Box 247
Inverness Park, California 94956
Phone: (415) 663-8811
Beds: 44 (1 private room available
  for parents with children under 5);
  Overnight Rate: $9.00–11.00

Elliott Hostel
3790 Udall Street
San Diego, California 92107
Phone: (619) 223-4778
Beds: 60; Overnight Rate: $12.00

San Diego
500 West Broadway
San Diego, California 92101
Phone: (619) 525-1531
Beds: 112; Overnight Rate: $12.00–
  14.00

San Francisco Downtown
312 Mason Street
San Francisco, California 94102
Phone: (415) 788-5604
Beds: 220; Overnight Rate: $13.00–
15.00

Los Angeles/Santa Monica
1436 Second Street
Santa Monica, California 90401
Phone: (310) 393-9913
Beds: 200; Overnight Rate: $15.00
+ tax

Sanborn Park Hostel
15808 Sanborn Road
Saratoga, California 95070
Phone: (408)741-0166
Beds: 39; Overnight Rate: $7.50

Santa Cruz Hostel at Carmelitta
P.O. Box 1241
Santa Cruz Hostel Society
Santa Cruz, California 95061
Phone: (408) 423-8304
Beds: 24; Overnight Rate: $12.00–
14.00

Marin Headlands
Building 941, Fort Barry
Sausalito, California 94965
Phone: (415) 331-2777
Beds: 66; Overnight Rate: $9.00–
11.00

**San Luis Obispo, SLO Coast
Hostel**
1292 Foothill Boulevard
San Luis Obispo, California 93405
Phone: (805) 544-4678
Beds: 8; Overnight Rate: $13.00

COLORADO

Conejos River AYH-Hostel
3591 County Road E-2
Antonito, Colorado 81120
Phone: (719) 376-2518
Beds: 10; Overnight Rate: $9.00

Fireside Inn
114 North French Street
Breckenridge, Colorado 80424
Phone: (303) 453-6456
Beds: 12; Overnight Rate: $15.00 +
tax

Denver, Melbourne Hostel
607 - 22nd Street
Denver, Colorado 80205
Phone: (303) 292-6386
Beds: 58; Overnight Rate: $10.00 +
tax

H-Bar-G Ranch Hostel
3500 H-Bar-G Road
Estes Park, Colorado 80517
Phone: (303) 586-3688
Beds: 100; Overnight Rate: $8.00 +
tax (HI members only)

Glenwood Springs Hostel
1021 Grand Avenue
Glenwood Springs, Colorado 81601
Phone: (303) 945-8545
Beds: 42; Overnight Rate: $9.50 +
tax

Grand Junction
337 Colorado Avenue
Grand Junction, Colorado 81501
Phone: (303) 242-9636
Beds: 32; Overnight Rate: $10.00

Shadowcliff
P.O. Box 658
Grand Lake, Colorado 80447
Phone: (303) 627-9220
Beds: 14; Overnight Rate: $8.00

Pitkin Hostel
P.O. Box 164
Pitkin, Colorado 81241
Phone: (303) 641-2757
Beds: 6; Overnight Rate: $10.91

Alpen Hutte
P.O. Box 919
Silverthorne, Colorado 80498
Phone: (303) 468-6336
Beds: 64; Overnight Rate: $10.00–22.00

Winter Park
P.O. Box 3323
Winter Park, Colorado 80432
Phone: (303) 726-5356
Beds: 38; Overnight Rate: $8.50–12.50

DISTRICT OF COLUMBIA

Washington, D.C.
1009 - 11th Street, NW
Washington, D.C. 20001

Phone: (202) 737-2333
Beds: 250; Overnight Rate: $16.00–18.00

FLORIDA

Ft Lauderdale, International House
3811 North Ocean Boulevard
Ft. Lauderdale, Florida 33308
Phone: (305) 568-1615
Beds: 96; Overnight Rate: $12.00 + tax

Miami Beach
1438 Washington Avenue
Miami Beach, Florida 33139

Phone: (305) 534-2988
Beds: 200; Overnight Rate: $11.00–12.00

Orlando Plantation Manor
227 North Eola Drive
Orlando, Florida 32801
Phone: (407) 843-8888
Beds: 90; Overnight Rate: $11.50 + tax

GEORGIA

Atlanta
223 Ponce de Leon
Atlanta, Georgia 30308

Phone: (404) 875-9449
Beds: 44; Overnight Rate: $12.50 + tax

HAWAII

Waikiki
2417 Prince Edward Street
Honolulu, Hawaii 96815

Phone: (808) 926-8313
Beds: 50; Overnight Rate: $13.65 + tax

IDAHO

Gooding
112 Main Street
Gooding, Idaho 83330

Phone: (208) 934-4374
Beds: 8; Overnight Rate: $10.00 + tax

Kellogg
834 West McKinley Avenue
Kellogg, Idaho 83837
Phone: (208) 783-4171
Beds: 36; Overnight Rate: $12.00

Naples
Idaho Highway 2
Naples, Idaho 83847
Phone: (208) 267-2947
Beds: 23; Overnight Rate: $10.00

ILLINOIS

Chicago Summer Hostel
3036 North Ashland Avenue
Metro Chicago Council
Chicago, Illinois 60657
Phone: (312) 327-5350
Beds: 112; Overnight Rate: $14.00–16.00

LOUISIANA

New Orleans
Marquette House
2253 Carondelet Street
New Orleans, Louisiana 70130
Phone: (504) 523-3014
Beds: 162; Overnight Rate: $11.27 + tax

MAINE

Wadsworth Blanchard Farm Home Hostel
Rural Route 2, P.O. Box 5992
Hiram, Maine 04041
Phone: (207) 625-7509
Beds: 8; Overnight Rate: $10.00

MARYLAND

Harper's Ferry Lodge
19123 Sandy Hook Road
Knoxville, Maryland 21758
Phone: (301) 834-7652
Beds: 36; Overnight Rate: $10.00–12.00

MASSACHUSETTS

Boston
12 Hemenway Street
Boston, Massachusetts 02115
Phone: (617) 536-9455
Beds: 196; Overnight Rate: $15.00–17.00

Friendly Crossways
P.O. Box 2266
Littleton, Massachusetts 01460
Phone: (508) 456-3649
Beds: 50; Overnight Rate: $10.00–15.00

Back Bay Summer Hostel
1020 Commonwealth Avenue
Boston, Massachusetts 02115
Phone: (617) 731-8096
Beds: 63; Overnight Rate: $15.00–17.00

Monroe & Isabel Smith Hostel
P.O. Box 2602
Northfield, Massachusetts 01360
Phone: (413) 498-5311
Beds: 13; Overnight Rate: $13.00

Mid Cape
75 Goody Hallet Drive
Eastham, Massachusetts 02642
Phone: (508) 255-2785
Beds: 50; Overnight Rate: $12.00

Portland Summer Hostel
c/o HI-AYH Eastern New England
Council
1020 Commonwealth Avenue
Boston, Massachusetts 02215
Phone: (207) 784-3281
Beds: 48; Overnight Rate: $14.00

M I C H I G A N
Country Grandma's Home Hostel
22330 Bell Road
New Boston, Michigan 48164

Phone: (313) 753-4901
Beds: 6; Overnight Rate: $9.00–
11.00

M I N N E S O T A
Caecilian Hall
2004 Randolph Avenue
Caecilian Hall
Saint Paul, Minnesota 55105
Phone: (612) 690-6604
Beds: 103; Overnight Rate: $14.00

Mississippi Headwaters
HCO5 Box 5A
Lake Itasca State Park
Lake Itasca, Minnesota 56460
Phone: (218) 266-3415
Beds: 34; Overnight Rate: $12–14

M O N T A N A
Brownie's
P.O. Box 229
1020 Highway 49 East
Glacier Park, Montana 59434

Phone: (406) 226-4426
Beds: 31; Overnight Rate: $10.00 +
tax; private room $15.00

N E B R A S K A
Cornerstone
640 North 16th Street
Lincoln, Nebraska 68508

Phone: (402) 476-0355
Beds: 8; Overnight Rate: $8.00

N E W   H A M P S H I R E
Peterborough
52 Summer Street
Peterborough, New Hampshire
03458

Phone: (603) 924-9832
Beds: 26; Overnight Rate: $10.00–
12.00

N E W   M E X I C O
The Carter House
101 North Cooper Street
Silver City, New Mexico 88061
Phone: (505) 388-5485
Beds: 22; Overnight Rate: $12.00

Taos
P.O. Box 3271
Taos, New Mexico 87571
Phone: (505) 776-8298
Beds: 76; Overnight Rate: $8.50–
12.50

Riverbend Hot Springs
100 Austin Avenue
Truth or Consequence, NM 87901
Phone: (505) 894-8183
Beds: 14; Overnight Rate: $11.00

Rio Grande Gorge
P.O. Box B4
Pilar, New Mexico 87531
Phone: (505) 758-0090
Beds: 17; Overnight Rate: $9.50–11.50

NEW YORK

New York
891 Amsterdam Avenue
New York, New York 10025
Phone: (212) 932-2300
Beds: 480; Overnight Rate: $20.00

Downing International Hostel
535 Oak Street
HI-AYH Syracuse Council
Syracuse, New York 13203
Phone: (315) 472-5788
Beds: 31; Overnight Rate: $9.00

Rose Ridge Home Hostel
5041 Galen Road
Wolcott, New York 14590
Phone: (315) 594-2750
Beds: 3; Overnight Rate: $6.00

NORTH CAROLINA

Pembroke House
P.O. Box 5025
Baptist Student Union P.S.U.

Pembroke, North Carolina 28372
Phone: (919) 521-8777
Beds: 8; Overnight Rate: $6.00

OHIO

Columbus
95 East 12th Avenue
Columbus, Ohio 43201
Phone: (614) 294-7157
Beds: 22; Overnight Rate: $10.00

Malabar Farm
3954 Bromfield Road
Lucas, Ohio 44843
Phone: (419) 892-2055
Beds: 26; Overnight Rate: $10.00

Stanford House
6093 Stanford Road
Peninsula, Ohio 44264
Phone: (216) 467-8711
Beds: 30; Overnight Rate: $11.00–13.00

OREGON

The Ashland Hostel
150 North Main Street
Ashland, Oregon 97520
Phone: (503) 482-9217
Beds: 45; Overnight Rate: $11–13

Sea Star
375 Second Street
Bandon, Oregon 97411
Phone: (503) 347-9632
Beds: 38; Overnight Rate: $12.00

Bend Alpine Hostel
19 Southwest Century Drive
Bend, Oregon 97702
Phone: (503) 389-3813
Beds: 40; Overnight Rate: $14.00

Fordson Home Hostel
250 Robinson Road
Ave Junction, Oregon 97523
Phone: (503) 592-3203
Beds: 5; Overnight Rate: $8.00

Lost Valley Hostel
81868 Lost Valley Lane
Dexter, Oregon 97431
Phone: (503) 937-3351
Beds: 12; Overnight Rate: $9.00

Portland
3031 SE Hawthorne Boulevard SE
Portland, Oregon 97214
Phone: (503) 236-3380
Beds: 47; Overnight Rate: $12.00–13.00

Seaside
930 North Holladay
Seaside, Oregon 97138
Phone: (503) 738-7911
Beds: 30; Overnight Rate: $12.00

P E N N S Y L V A N I A

Evansburg State Park
837 Mayhall Road
Collegeville, Pennsylvania 19426
Phone: (215) 489-4326
Beds: 12; Overnight Rate: $10.00–12.00

Marsh Creek State Park
P.O. Box 376
Lyndell, Pennsylvania 19354
Phone: (215) 458-5881
Beds: 12; Overnight Rate: $10.00–12.00

Geigertown
P.O. Box 49-B
Geigertown, Pennsylvania 19523
Phone: (215) 286-9537
Beds: 48; Overnight Rate: $8.50

Poconos
Rural Route 2, P.O. Box 1026
Cresco, Pennsylvania 18326
Phone: (717) 676-9076
Beds: 40; Overnight Rate: $10.00–12.00

Tyler State Park
P.O. Box 94
Newtown, Pennsylvania 18940
Phone: (215) 968-0927
Beds: 25; Overnight Rate: $10.00–12.00

Ohiopyle
P.O. Box 99
Ohiopyle, Pennsylvania 15470
Phone: (412) 329-4476
Beds: 25; Overnight Rate: $9.00–11.00

Chamounix Mansion Philadelphia
Chamounix Drive
West Fairmount Park
Philadelphia, Pennsylvania 19131
Phone: (215) 878-3676
Beds: 48; Overnight Rate: $10.00–12.00

Weisel
7347 Richlandtown Road
Quakertown, Pennsylvania 18951
Phone: (215) 536-8749
Beds: 24; Overnight Rate: $8.00

Living Waters Hostel
Rural District 1, P.O. Box 206
Schellsburg, Pennsylvania 15559
Phone: (814) 733-4607
Beds: 24; Overnight Rate: $10.00

Crystal Laker
Rural Route 1, P.O. Box 308
Hughesville, Pennsylvania 17737
Phone: (717) 584-2698
Beds: 12; Overnight Rate: $8.00

SOUTH DAKOTA

Pleasant Valley
Rural Route 1, P.O. Box 256
Gary, South Dakota 57237

Phone: (605) 272-5614
Beds: 18; Overnight Rate: $12.00

TENNESSEE

Great Smokey Mountains
3248 Manis Road
Sevierville, Tennessee 37862

Phone: (615) 429-8563
Beds: 18; Overnight Rate: $13.25

TEXAS

Austin
2200 South Lakeshore Boulevard
Austin, Texas 78741
Phone: (512) 444-2294
Beds: 40; Overnight Rate: $12.00

Houston International Hostel
5302 Crawford
Houston, Texas 77004
Phone: (713) 523-1009
Beds: 30; Overnight Rate: $11.39

El Paso
311 East Franklin Avenue
El Paso, Texas 79901
Phone: (915) 532-3661
Beds: 40; Overnight Rate: $12.00–
14.00

San Antonio International Hostel
P.O. Box 8059
San Antonio, Texas 78208
Phone: (512) 223-9426
Beds: 38; Overnight Rate: $12.85–
14.85

VERMONT

Capitol Home Hostel
Rural District 1, P.O. Box 2750
Montpelier, Vermont 05602
Phone: (802) 223-2104
Beds: 2; Overnight Rate: $10.00–
12.00

Greenwood Lodge
P.O. Box 246
Bennington, Vermont 05201
Phone: (802) 442-2547
Beds: 40; Overnight Rate: $13.00 +
tax

Sleepers River Home Hostels
Main Street
P.O. BOX 42
St. Johnsbury, Vermont 05819
Phone: (802) 748-1575
Beds: 6; Overnight Rate: $12.00–
14.00

Vagabond
Route 30, P.O. Box 224
East Jamaica, Vermont 05343
Phone: (802) 874-4096
Beds: 20; Overnight Rate: $12.00 +
tax

Greenmont Farms
P.O. Box 148
West Balton Road

Underhill Center, Vermont 05490
Phone: (802) 899-2375
Beds: 20; Overnight Rate: $10.00

VIRGINIA

Bear's Den Lodge
Rural Route 1, P.O. Box 288
Bluemont, Virginia 22012
Phone: (703) 554-8708
Beds: 20; Overnight Rate: $10.00–12.00

Sangraal-By-The-Sea
P.O. Box 187
Urbanna, Virginia 23175
Phone: (804) 776-6500
Beds: 20; Overnight Rate: $15.00 + tax

WASHINGTON

Birch Bay
7467 Gemini Street
Blaine, Washington 98230
Phone: (206) 371-2180
Beds: 45; Overnight Rate: $9.00–11.00

Fort Columbia
Fort Columbia State Park
P.O. Box 224
Chinook, Washington 98614
Phone: (360) 777-8755
Beds: 21; Overnight Rate: $9.00–11.00

Fort Flagler
Fort Flagler State Park
Nordland, Washington 98358
Phone: (206) 385-1288
Beds: 15; Overnight Rate: $9.00–11.00

Port Townsend
Fort Worden State Park
Port Townsend, Washington 98368
Phone: (360) 385-0655
Beds: 30; Overnight Rate: $9.00–11.00

Seattle
84 Union Street
Seattle, Washington 98101
Phone: (206) 622-5443
Beds: 139; Overnight Rate: $15.00–17.00 + tax

Spokane
930 South Lincoln
Spokane, Washington 99204
Phone: (509) 838-5968
Beds: 22; Overnight Rate: $10.00

Vashon Island Ranch Hostel
12119 SW Cove Road
Vashon Island, Washington 98070
Phone: (206) 463-2592
Beds: 36; Overnight Rate: $9.00

WISCONSIN

Laona, Wisconsin
P.O. Box 325
Laona, Wisconsin 54541

Phone: (715) 674-2615
Beds: 12; Overnight Rate: $9.00 + tax

Wellspring Hostel
P.O. Box 72
Newburg, Wisconsin 53060

Phone: (414) 675-6755
Beds: 25; Overnight Rate: $12.00

WYOMING

Thermopolispo
P.O. Box 671
Hot Springs State Park
Thermopolis, Wyoming 82443

Phone: (307) 864-2251
Beds: 20; Overnight Rate: $10.00

BOOKS FROM LANIER

The Complete Guide to Bed & Breakfasts, Inns & Guesthouses – 19th Edition
With over 10,000 listings, this is the one annual source preferred by experienced travelers who love the warmth and intimacy of this style of accommodation.Over 2 million copies in print. Rated #1 guide by innkeepers nationwide.

Elegant Small Hotels—A Connoisseur's Guide – 16th Edition
A tradition in the capital cities of Europe, these exquisite hotels can be found today throughout the United States. Each of the 220 great American hotels described in this guide is unique.Over 50,000 copies in print.

Elegant Hotels of the Pacific Rim A Connoisseur's Guide – 1st Edition
This is a guide to the finest lodging in the Pacific area from California to Bangkok. Each of the 200 hotels described in highly rated.

All-Suite Hotel Guide – 10th Edition
This guide is an indispensable aid for the business traveler, listing over 1,400 all-suite hotels in the United States and around the world.

Golf Courses—The Complete Guide – 5th Edition
A definitive directory and travel guide for the nation's 20 million avid golf players. This comprehensive guide includes over 14,000 golf courses in the United States that are open to the public.

Golf Resorts—The Complete Guide – 7th Edition
This is a complete update to over 1,000 golf resorts and is certain to be a hit with the millions of devotees of the game.

Golf Resorts International – 3rd Edition
This wish book and travel guide for the wandering golfer reviews the creme de la creme of golf resorts all over the world.

Condo Vacations—The Complete Guide – 7th Edition
An extensive revision and updating of the first ever national guide to condominium vacations, just as this form of vacation is growing ever more popular.

The Back Almanac
The best new thinking on an age old problem. 25 chapters packed with easy to read information about back problems.

Cinnamon Mornings
This gracefully illustrated cookbook brings to your home outstanding regional cuisine from more than 150 of America's finest bed and breakfasts.

Bed & Breakfast—Australia's Best
A compendium of the best B&Bs "Down Under" reflecting the spirit and atmosphere of their regions.

Sweets & Treats
This delightful cookbook features over 100 of the most requested, cherished, and best-loved sweets and treats recipes from the chefs of America's finest Bed & Breakfast Inns and Guesthouses.

LANIER GUIDES
ORDER FORM

QTY	TITLE	EACH	TOTAL
	Golf Courses—The Complete Guide	$19.95	
	Golf Resorts—The Complete Guide	$14.95	
	Golf Resorts International	$19.95	
	Condo Vacations—The Complete Guide	$14.95	
	Elegant Small Hotels	$19.95	
	Elegant Hotels of the Pacific Rim	$14.95	
	All-Suite Hotel Guide	$14.95	
	The Complete Guide to Bed & Breakfasts, Inns & Guesthouses	$16.95	
	Family Travel—The Complete Guide	$19.95	
	Cinnamon Mornings	$17.95	
	The Back Almanac	$14.95	
	Sweets & Treats	$14.95	
	Bed & Breakast—Australia's Best	$14.95	
	Sub-Total	$	
	Shipping U.S.A.	$3.00 each	
	Shipping Int'l.	$5.00 each	
	TOTAL ENCLOSED	$	

Send your order to:

LANIER PUBLISHING,   P.O. Drawer D,   Petaluma, CA 94953

Order Books online by going to http://www.TravelGuideS.com/store

- -

Allow 3 to 4 weeks for delivery

Please send my order to:

NAME ———————————————————————

ADDRESS ————————————————————

CITY ———————————— STATE ——— ZIP ———